CHAR

DICKENS

My Life

C000262215

EDITED BY DERWIN HOPE

© Derwin Hope 2019
All rights reserved. No part of this publication may be
reproduced in any form or by any means without the written
permission of the publishers.

Published by Clink Street Publishing 2020
Copyright © 2020

First edition.

The author asserts the moral right under the Copyright, Designs and Patents Act 1988 to be identified as the author of this work.

All rights reserved. No part of this publication may be reproduced, stored in a retrieval system or transmitted, in any form or by any means without the prior consent of the author, nor be otherwise circulated in any form of binding or cover other than that with which it is published and without a similar condition being imposed on the subsequent purchaser.

ISBN: 978-1-913340-86-5 (paperback)
ISBN: 978-1-913340-87-2 (ebook)

Clink
Street

London | New York

Contents

Charles Dickens: My Life

Introduction

I have always been fascinated by the story of people's lives. My career path took me into the law, joining Middle Temple as my Inn of Court (I discovered later that Dickens had done the same) and qualifying as a Barrister. Many years later I became a Judge, so almost every day of my working life I was dealing with people's life stories – usually those that had taken a wrong turn. In what little spare-time I had I read biographies; the reality of people's lives became all-encompassing.

I came to Dickens comparatively late in life, and it was not until my appointment as a Judge in Portsmouth, the city of his birth, that my interest became centred upon him. I read modern biographies about him, and then turned the clock back to read the 3 volumes of "The Life of Charles Dickens" produced shortly after his death by his great friend and adviser, John Forster. I visited the humble house of his birth, now kept as a museum by the city, and as I stood in the bedroom where he was born, the question went through my mind: "How did he get from here to the life of fame he went on to lead, and how much of this did he explain in his own words?"

I began my research, focussing only on things that Dickens himself had said about his life. He had written to Forster in the 1840's about his experiences in the blacking factory when he was a child, but the memories of it had been so powerful and painful that he and Forster had kept it secret and it was only revealed by Forster (in Volume I, Chapter II of The Life) after Dickens had died. I found also that Dickens had written sporadically in his later journalism about happier periods and events in his younger life, and I now also had available to me the extraordinary collection of approximately 15,000 letters he had written that had been produced by Oxford University Press and published in 12 volumes as "The Pilgrim Edition." I was aware that Dickens had burnt all the letters he had received and had urged all those to whom he had written to do the same. Fortunately, they had not complied with his wishes.

CHAPTER I

My Early Life

Friday the 7th of February 1812 and I was born at Portsmouth, an English seaport town, principally remarkable for mud, Jews, and sailors. Thereafter in my life a Friday has always been a special day for me; whatever projects I may have determined on otherwise, I have never begun a book or begun anything of importance to me, save it has been on a Friday. I arrived in this world in a small, first floor bedroom of a rented terraced house at Mile End, Landport, but a short distance from Portsmouth Dockyard. At the time this provided home for my father and mother and my sister, Fanny, who had been born some 18 months before. Three weeks after my birth, we all attended at the nearby church of St. Mary's, Kingston, where I was christened Charles John Huffam Dickens – Charles from my mother's father, John from my father and Huffam the surname of my godfather, Christopher Huffam, a good friend of my father.

If truth be told, I remember now very little about the home of my birth and indeed, when I returned to Portsmouth on a reading tour much later in life, I had difficulty in fixing its location. I had been told it was a little house with a small front garden and I know that we all lived there with a servant. I confess however that I did not feel any strong sentimental attachment to the place, but that was my beginning.

I also have very little recollection of my grandparents, save for my father's mother who died when I was 12 years old. She was a housekeeper in the family of Lord Crewe, and I particularly remember she loved to have children around her and to beguile them with stories from the pages of history as well as fairy tales and reminiscences of her own. I can fully understand the joy this must have given her as it is reflected in the way my own life has unfolded. Before she died she gave me a large, old silver watch, a treasured possession that belonged to her husband, a grandfather I never knew.

My father, John Dickens, was brought up by my grandmother within the Crewe household, at Crewe Hall in Cheshire and at their London home, 18 Grosvenor Street. He had an elder brother, William, who, through hard work and sound business sense, came to be the keeper of a London coffee house in Oxford Street; but sadly, my father had a tendency not to exhibit these qualities and it is painful for me to recall that my grandmother was constantly inveighing against his idleness, general incapacity, and his apparent inability to live within his means. I know she proposed to leave him nothing in her Will, saying that he had already received from her many sums on differing occasions. It was a trait of his that I was to come to know only too well. His requirement that he be treated as a gentleman and the need to dress and entertain according to such fashion added only to his financial straits, but throughout his life he remained constantly of the belief that when penury struck, something would turn up – and it usually did, often in the form of my good self. I have heard him liken himself to a cork which, when submerged, bobs up to the surface again, none the worse for the dip; he regarded optimism as the finest of all arts.

Through the good auspices of Lord Crewe, he was fortunate to get a job at Somerset House in the Strand, London, as a clerk to the Navy Treasurer's Office. This not only provided him with a job and income but, just as important as he saw it, status – a *"responsible situation under Government"* as he called it. It also brought him into contact with another newcomer to the office, Thomas Barrow, who introduced him to his sister, Elizabeth.

In due course, my father was moved to the Naval Pay Office and then transferred to Portsmouth, a town renowned for its hard-living sailor folk who would oft times resort to fighting, even during the course of being paid. Despite these circumstances that befell him, all reports I have heard from his workplace describe him as the jolliest of men, a fellow of infinite humour, chatty, lively and agreeable – a true bobbing cork. He was also still drawn to Elizabeth Barrow in London and in June 1809, they married at the Church of St. Mary-le-Strand opposite Somerset House before travelling back to Portsmouth and their new home in the terrace at Landport.

My mother was 23 years of age when I was born. It is said that I inherited from her bright hazel eyes and a curiosity that knows no bounds. I am aware that on entering a room, she would, almost unconsciously, take an inventory of all its contents and if anything happened to strike her as out of place or ridiculous, she would later describe it in the quaintest manner. She had an uncanny power of imitating others and highlighting the ludicrous, but was also able to bring tears to the eyes of her listeners if narrating some sad event. I discovered later, however, that her father Charles Barrow had systematically falsified the accounts and thereby embezzled almost £6,000 from the Naval Pay Office whilst he worked as Chief Conductor of Moneys (a position superior to my father), and had absconded out of the jurisdiction and eventually to the Isle of Man when his disreputable activities had been uncovered. Her mother, Mary Barrow, took to living in Liverpool with another daughter and this worthy grandmother never cared twopence about us – until that is I grew famous, and then sent me "an affectionate request for five pounds or so". I cannot but say that, long before, I had become utterly indifferent to the fact of her existence.

I only lived for five months in the Landport terrace before we moved to 16 Hawke Street in Portsea, closer to the Dockyard. We stayed there for some 18 months before moving to accommodation at 39 Wish Street (now Kings Road) in the new area of Southsea. There we were joined by Mary Allen, my mother's sister whose husband, Thomas Allen, had drowned at sea off Rio de Janeiro shortly before her arrival with us. For reasons that I cannot now remember, she came to be known as 'Aunt Fanny' in our family.

My youngest childhood recollections surround Christmas time, with a richly decorated Christmas tree in the centre of the room and looking upward into the dreamy brightness of its branches and top. I can also clearly remember the celebrations that brought in the New Year of 1814. I still have a vivid remembrance of the sensation of being carried downstairs in a woman's arms and holding tight to her in the terror of seeing the steep perspective below. Once down, I remember timidly peeping into a room and seeing a very long row of ladies and gentlemen sitting against a wall, all drinking at once out of little glass cups with handles, like custard cups. It was very like my first idea of the good people in Heaven, as derived from a picture in a prayer book I had, with their heads a little thrown back and all drinking at once. Toys came to play a large part in my life. One was a tumbler with his hands in his pockets, who wouldn't lie down, but whenever he was put upon the floor, persisted in rolling his fat body about, until he rolled himself still, and brought those lobster eyes of his to bear upon me – when I affected to laugh very much, but in my heart of hearts was extremely doubtful of him. Close beside him was an infernal snuff-box, out of which there sprang a demoniacal counsellor in a black gown, with an obnoxious head of hair, and a red cloth mouth, wide open, who was not to be endured on any terms, but could not be put away either; for he used suddenly, in a highly magnified state, to fly out of mammoth snuff-boxes in dreams, when least expected. A mask, too, that gave me nightmares – but happier times were had with a great black horse with rounded red spots all over him that I could even climb upon by myself.

I recall as well from these times being carried in someone's arms to witness soldiers drilling on a nearby parade ground, a place I later found again as an adult. I can also remember a small front garden at our house and trotting about with my sister Fanny with something to eat, whilst being overseen by a nurse through a low kitchen window almost level with the gravel walk. And I do have an impression on my mind which I cannot distinguish from actual remembrance, of the touch of my nurse's forefinger as she used to hold it out to me, and of it being roughened by needlework, like a pocket nutmeg-grater.

Perhaps that nurse was there to assist my mother because on the 28th March 1814 a brother, Alfred Allen (named in remembrance of Thomas Allen), was born. This new arrival and competitor for my mother's affections, however, turned out to be a sickly child who only lived for some six months and died from what was said to be water on the brain. My tumbled emotions left me wondering if I had in some way been responsible for what had happened and a strange intangible feeling of guilt still lingers with me.

In early 1815, my father was recalled to Somerset House and I remember the snow falling as we left for London. We went into lodgings above a greengrocer's shop run by Mr. John Dodd at 10 Norfolk Street (now 22 Cleveland Street) on the corner of Tottenham Street, and I became introduced to the ways of London at the tender age of three. Open fields gave way to streets and I felt imprisoned, yet strangely fascinated by the myriad activities of the city. A year later, on the 26th

April 1816, my sister Laetitia was born, so my father had another mouth to feed and I know now that he began to run seriously into debt at this time, failing to pay our landlord the rent that was owed.

After two years in London, it was a relief to me that my father received another posting, this time to Sheerness at the mouth of the River Medway. I enjoyed this enormously, particularly because he had rented a small house next door to the local theatre and in the evenings we took great delight in sitting listening to performances taking place on the stage next door, as well as joining in with gusto in the singing of "Britannia Rules the Waves", "God Save the King" and the like. This lasted some four months before my father was moved upstream to Chatham, the main port standing alongside the cathedral town of Rochester. I didn't know it then but was later to discover that Chatham in that muddy river had come to be known as "the wickedest place in the world".

At the start, I was protected from this by the location of our new accommodation. It was on the brow of a hill with a most airy and pleasant aspect looking out over fields to the harbour and dockyard below. It was a newly constructed house (Number 2) in a row called "Ordnance Terrace" and comprised a narrow hallway (illuminated by a fan light over the door) leading, I remember, to a dining room and small living room, whilst upstairs was a parlour room and my parents' bedroom on the first floor, with a further staircase up to two attic rooms, one for the servants and one for the children. There was a kitchen, cellar and small living area in the basement. As my parents, Aunt Fanny and we three children had now been joined by two nurses (Mary Weller and the older Jane Bonney), we were somewhat crowded in that compacted terraced house, but I do remember it being comfortable as well as noisy and my attic window allowed me to look out to the world outside and wonder what part I would play in it.

We lived at Ordnance Terrace for some four years from the spring of 1817. Looking back on it now, I was between the ages of five and nine years and in a childhood paradise of my own. The field in front of the house where I used to play with my sister and my nurse came to be filled with golden sheaves of corn, which gave me a wonderful feeling of peace and abundance. I met George Stroughill (nicknamed "Struggles") from next door at Number 1 who had, I remember, a marvellous magic lantern for us to play with, and Lucy, his sister, whose golden hair flowed in the wind as she ran. Also in the terrace (at Number 5) lived a dear old lady Mrs. Newnham and next door to her a retired "half-pay" captain who smoked cigars, drank ale and raised marigolds, but seemed to be always quarrelling with the parish authorities. He also took to breeding silk-worms, which he would frequently bring, in little paper boxes, to show the old lady, generally dropping a worm or two at every visit. I later found out that Mrs. Newnham's kindness and generosity extended to leaving us some money and possessions when she died. My memories of living at Ordnance Terrace have nothing but happiness to fill them, but life can be a cruel handmaiden and when I returned some years later to relive some of this happiness, I found that the field opposite that was part of my life had been taken for the London to Chatham railway line.

It was gone. The two beautiful hawthorn-trees, the hedge, the turf and all those buttercups and daisies, had given place to the stoniest of jolting roads whilst, beyond the station, an ugly dark monster of a tunnel kept its jaws open, as if it had swallowed them and was ravenous for more destruction. The locomotive engine that had brought me back spat ashes and hot water over the now-blighted ground. I looked in again over the low wall, at the scene of departed glories. Could it be that, after all this and much more, my playing-field was now a station, and locomotive number 97 expectorating boiling water and red-hot cinders on it, the whole belonging by Act of Parliament to the South Eastern Railway? It could be and was and my heart is heavy with the remembrance of those happy times and the desolation now caused to it.

The hill that Ordnance Terrace stood upon led to a fortification called "Fort Pitt", one of the many military constructions that abounded in the area. There was a system called the "Chatham Lines" that I explored when curiosity struck. Holes in innocent grass knolls would lead to labyrinths of underground passages, rooms and dark vaults that would seep with an odour that lives with me still. Chatham itself was filled with sailors and soldiers, many suffering ghastly mutilations from the bloody wars with the French tyrant. It was a squalid and lawless place where brothels and drinking quarters of the lowest repute held sway, but it had a vigour to it that I could not help but find enthralling. In the dockyard where my father worked, I would never tire of watching the rope-makers, the anchor-smiths (nine of them at once, like the "muses in a ring") and the block-makers at their work. "The Yard" resounded with the noise of hammers beating upon the iron, and the slips or great sheds where the mighty Men-of-War were built loomed business-like when contemplated from the opposite side of the river – all resounding to the stupendous uproar of twelve hundred men to each ship being worked upon. And yet for all that and the five thousand souls working there, the Yard made no display, but kept itself snug under hill-sides of corn fields, hop-gardens and orchards; its great chimneys smoking with a quiet – almost a lazy – air, like giants smoking tobacco; and the great shears moored off it, looking meekly and inoffensively out of proportion, like giraffes of the machinery erection. The streets of the town itself were always lively and animated, filled with shops and stalls of every kind; I would particularly seek out the old clothes shops whose wares on display would spell out to me stories about their past occupants. And then a drunk would stagger past, filled to overflow and affording a source of innocent fun as the boy population followed him down the street.

Rochester, although close by, was of a different ilk. It set itself with an air of perceived respectability that spread around the cathedral, guildhall and castle like a dusty old cloak. The narrow high street and the streets around seem to cling to the past, afraid to let it go. Countless pilgrims had worn away the steps to the cathedral before evaporating into the decaying alleyways, leaving only mystery and silence behind them. As a child, I found it an eerie sort of place, one that was naturally at odds with my youthful high spirits. But it must be acknowledged that there are few things in this beautiful country of England more picturesque to the eye and agreeable to the fancy than an old cathedral town. Seen in the distance, rising from among corn-fields, pastures, orchards, gardens, woods, the river, the bridge, the roofs of ancient houses, and haply the ruins of a castle or abbey, the venerable cathedral spires, opposed for many hundred years to the winter wind and summer sun, tower, like a solemn historical presence above the city, conveying to the rudest mind associations of interest with the dusky past. On a nearer approach this interest is heightened, within the cathedral building, by long perspectives of pillars and arches; by the earthy smell, preaching more eloquently than deans and chapters of the common doom; by the praying figures of knights and ladies on the tombs, with little headless generations of sons and daughters kneeling around them; by the stained glass windows, softening and mellowing the light; by the oaken carvings of the stalls where the shorn monks told their beads; by the battered effigies of archbishops and bishops, found built up in the walls, when all the world has been unconscious, for centuries, of their blunt stone noses; by the mouldering chapter-room; by the crypt, with its barred loopholes, letting in long gleams of slanting light from the cloisters where the dead lie, and where the ivy, bred among the broken arches, twines about their graves; by the sound of the bells, high up in the massive tower; by the universal gravity, mystery, decay and silence.

My father subscribed to the publication "The History of Rochester", whilst living in the area, but at the time I did not feel the need for such stimulation. My real delight came from "the splash and flop" of the tide and the enthralling sights of the river. My greatest excitement was to venture out into the Medway with my father on the old navy pay yacht "The Chatham" and travel the length of the river to Sheerness and back. The river was filled with vessels of every variety; ships, barges, schooners and yachts, prison and hospital ships, and boats of all sizes. The dockyard was this hive of noisy activity, together with the smell of clean timber shavings and turpentine that pervaded everywhere; the sea birds would go squawking overhead, free to travel as they please but happy to cling to the magic and mystery of the sea and marshes. Impressions I find indelibly cast in my mind are of the sun, away at sea, just breaking through the heavy mist and showing us the ships, like their own shadows; of convicts guarded by soldiers and with great numbers on their backs as if they were street doors, returning every night after labour in the dockyard to ship-hulks moored in the river and roofed like Noah's Arks set across the marshes; and of other ships sailing away into the golden air bound for ports unknown on the other side of the horizon.

This was my real education. My mother first taught me the alphabet and how to read and write, including a small amount of Latin, but when I was six I was sent to a dame school in Rome Lane with my sister

Fanny. It was over a dyer's shop and run by an old lady who seemed to delight in ruling the world with hard knuckles and the birch. Even now I can never see a row of large, black, fat staring Roman capitals without her hideous vision appearing before me. At this establishment, being instilled with the first principles of education for ninepence a week, I also encountered a puffy pug-dog, with a personal animosity towards me. The bark of that baleful pug and a certain radiating way he had of snapping at my undefended legs, the ghastly grinning of his moist black muzzle and white teeth, and the insolence of his crisp tail curled like a pastoral crook, all live and flourish. From an otherwise unaccountable association of him with a fiddle, I concluded that he was of french extraction, and his name *Fidèle*. He belonged to some female, chiefly inhabiting a back-parlour, whose life appeared to me to have been consumed in sniffing, and in wearing a brown beaver bonnet. For her, he would sit up and balance cake upon his nose, and not eat it until twenty had been counted. To the best of my belief I was once called in to witness this performance; when, unable even in his milder moments to endure my presence, he instantly made at me, cake and all.

Why a something in mourning, called 'Miss Frost', should still connect itself with my preparatory school, I am unable to say. I retain no impression of the beauty of Miss Frost – if she were beautiful; or of the mental fascinations of Miss Frost – if she were accomplished; yet her name and her black dress hold an enduring place in my remembrance. An equally impersonal boy, whose name has long since shaped itself unalterably into 'Master Mawls', is not to be dislodged from my brain. Retaining no vindictive feelings towards Mawls – no feeling whatever, indeed – I infer that neither he nor I can have loved Miss Frost. My first impression of death and burial is associated with this formless pair. We all three nestled awfully in a corner one wintry day, when the wind was blowing shrill, with Miss Frost's pinafore over our heads; and Miss Frost told us in a whisper about somebody being "screwed down". It is the only distinct recollection I preserve of these impalpable creatures, except a suspicion that the manners of Master Mawls were susceptible of much improvement. Generally speaking, I may observe that whenever I see a child intently occupied with its nose, to the exclusion of all other subjects of interest, my mind reverts, in a flash, to Master Mawls.

Yet, despite these experiences, I managed with my own diligence to unlock the wonders of words and the power of communication that they could bring and, by the age of eight, I began dreaming my first dreams of authorship. I liked the feel of books with their deliciously smooth covers of bright red or green. My first favourites were picture books of "Little Red Riding Hood" (she was my first love; I felt that if I could have married her, I should have known perfect bliss) and "Jack the Giant Killer", followed by tales of scimitars and slippers and turbans and dwarfs and giants and genii and fairies, Bluebeards and beanstalks and riches and caverns and forests – all tumbling out of the pages and into my inquisitive mind. This was the reality of my world, a wondrous fantasy but real to me nonetheless. And for the little reader of story-books, by the firelight, the most testing time of all came about twilight, in the dead winter time, when the shadows closed in and gathered like mustering swarms of ghosts. When they stood lowering, in corners of rooms, and frowning out from behind half-opened doors; when they had full possession of unoccupied apartments. When they danced upon the floors, and walls, and ceilings of inhabited chambers, while the fire was low, and withdrawing like ebbing waters when it sprang into a blaze. When they frantically mocked the shapes of household objects, making the nurse an ogress, the rocking-horse a monster, the wondering child half-scared and half-amused, a stranger to itself, and made the very tongs upon the hearth a straddling giant with his arms a-kimbo, evidently smelling the blood of Englishmen, and wanting to grind people's bones to make his bread.

I also had, I remember, a nurse who used to tell me the most ghoulish of ghostly tales, tales of "Captain Murderer" whose speciality appeared to be the chopping up of a succession of brides into pies in the bloodiest of fashion – or tales of members of her family transformed into hideous zoological phenomenon. This young female bard had a fiendish enjoyment of my terrors and used to begin, as a sort of introductory overture, by clawing the air with both hands and suffering a long low hollow groan, before proceeding onward. I used to plead against it, maintaining that I was hardly strong enough and old enough to hear these tales, but she never spared me one word of them in her remorseless ghoulish pleasure, terrifying me to the utmost confines of my reason.

She reappears in my memory as the daughter of a shipwright, a sallow woman with a fishy eye, an aquiline nose and wearing a green gown; her name was Mercy, though she had none on me.

Pictures from the books that I read at this time have stayed with me throughout my life – of a bull pulling the bell rope to sound the death knell of poor Cock Robin; a shaft of light transfixing Cain as he murdered his brother; a Russian peasant standing alone in the vast expanse of snow surrounding him. I recollect, in short, everything I read as a very small boy as perfectly as I forget everything I read now. I can still recite verses that I discovered when I was seven and that have never left me since that time.

I also discovered when I was seven that I was to have a new sister. What I did not know then was the severity of the family's finances. My father, ever the optimist, bobbed along but at times he had fits of anger and when they came they were frightening to behold. These "passion bursts" as he called them were, I suppose, his way of releasing the tension that built up inside him but, like his asthma, he seemed to believe there was nothing he could do about it and that it was his cross to bear. I later found that, in the summer of 1819 and three weeks before the birth of a new sister, christened Harriet, he had cause to borrow the substantial sum of £200 from a businessman and lender, James Milbourne, that saddled him with an annual repayment of £26 for the rest of his life. The Deed of Loan had to be countersigned and he managed to persuade Thomas Barrow to affix his signature to it – an inscription that he was to sorely regret, for my father, despite an increase in salary, failed to keep up with the necessary repayments and the hapless man was eventually forced to repay the loan for him. This Deed and its consequences came to hang like a damnable leaden cloud over our family affairs and thereafter caused my father to be excluded from the Thomas Barrow household, due to him failing to ever settle it with them.

In 1819, and again in 1820, I was taken up to town to behold the splendour of the Christmas Pantomime and the humour of the master Clown, Joseph Grimaldi. Even now I have betaken myself not infrequently to that jocund world of pantomime, where there is no affliction or calamity that leaves the least impression; where a man may tumble into the broken ice, or dive into the kitchen fire, and only be the droller for the accident; where everyone is so superior to the accidents of life, though encountering them at every turn, that I suspect this to be the secret (though many persons may not present it to themselves) of the general enjoyment which an audience of vulnerable spectators, liable to pain and sorrow, find in this class of entertainment. Many years later I was tasked to edit Grimaldi's Memoirs for Richard Bentley, the publisher of "Bentley's Miscellany".

In March 1820, my father witnessed a calamitous fire in Chatham that started in a bakehouse in the High Street, but eventually involved the destruction of fifty-three houses and thirteen warehouses. A great many families were rendered homeless and he sent a report of the events, both to the local Kentish Gazette and also to "The Times" newspaper. Imagine our pride and delight when we saw it published in both and the importance we felt when he joined the committee that arranged the assistance needed for those devastated by the disaster. And then just over four months later, another addition to our family – my brother, Frederick, was born in August.

My memories of Chatham from this time are punctuated by clear visions of particular experiences – of a kite that once plucked at my own hand like an airy friend; of stealthily conducting a man with a wooden leg into the coal cellar and whilst getting him over the coals to hide him behind a partition, seeing his wooden leg bore itself in amongst the small coals and stick fast; of being cuffed around the ear for informing a lady visitor to the house that a certain ornamental object on the table, which was covered with marble paper, wasn't marble at all; of attending wonderful performances at the Theatre Royal, Rochester, that sweet, dingy, shabby little country theatre at the foot of Star Hill, with the intoxicating odour within of sawdust, orange peel and lamp oil; of performing myself in song and entertainment on the dining table of the Tribe family at the Mitre Inn, High Street, Chatham, sometimes with my sister Fanny, who was learning to play the piano; of being lifted up by my mother and sitting on a wall in Chatham to wave my hat at the Prince Regent as he drove by; of watching a line of convicts bound together with manacles from an iron chain heading for Rochester jail in the shadow of the Medway gibbet.

I remember too that in my very young days I was taken to so many lyings-in that I wonder I escaped becoming a professional martyr to them in after-life. I suppose I had a very sympathetic nurse, with a large circle of married acquaintances. At one little greengrocer's shop, down certain steps from the street, I remember to have waited on a lady who had four children (I am afraid to write five, though I fully believe it was five) at a birth. This meritorious woman held quite a reception in her room on the morning when I was introduced there, and a later sight of the house brought vividly to my mind how the four (five) deceased young people lay, side by side, on a clean cloth on a chest of drawers; reminding me by a homely association, which I suspect their complexion to have assisted, of pigs' feet as they are usually displayed at a neat tripe-shop. A subscription was entered into among the company, which became extremely alarming to my consciousness of having pocket-money on my person. I was earnestly exhorted to contribute, but resolutely declined; therein disgusting the company, who gave me to understand that I must dismiss all expectations of going to Heaven.

I also remember well the first funeral I attended. It was a fair representative funeral after its kind, being that of the husband of a married servant, once my nurse. She married for money, Sally Flanders, but after a year or two of matrimony, became the relict of Flanders, a small master builder; and either she or Flanders had done me the honour to express a desire that I should 'follow'. Consent being given by the heads of houses, I was jobbed up into what was pronounced at home 'decent mourning', and was admonished that if, when the funeral was in action, I put my hands in my pockets, or took my eyes out of my pocket-handkerchief, I was personally lost, and my family disgraced. On that eventful day, having tried to get myself into a disastrous frame of mind, and having formed a very poor opinion of myself because I couldn't cry, I repaired to Sally's. Sally was an excellent creature, and had been a good wife to old Flanders, but the moment I saw her I knew that she was not in her own real natural state. She formed a sort of coat of arms, grouped with a smelling-bottle, a handkerchief, an orange, a bottle of vinegar, Flanders's sister, her own sister, Flanders's brother's wife, and two neighbouring gossips – all in mourning, and all ready to hold her whenever she fainted. At sight of poor little me she became much agitated (agitating me much more), and having exclaimed "Oh, here's dear Master Charles!" became hysterical, and swooned as if I had been the death of her. An affecting scene followed, during which I was handed about and poked at her by various people, as if I were the bottle of salts. Reviving a little, she embraced me, said, "You knew him well, dear Master Charles, and he knew you!" and fainted again: which, as the rest of the coat of arms soothingly said, "done her credit".

When we got out into the streets, and I constantly disarranged the procession by tumbling on the people behind me because my cloak was so long, I felt that we were all making game. I was truly sorry for Flanders, but I knew that it was no reason why we should be trying (the women with their heads in hoods like coal-scuttles with the black side outward) to keep in step with a man in a scarf, carrying a thing like a mourning spy-glass, which he was going to open presently and sweep the horizon with. Then, when we returned to Sally's, it was all of a piece. The impossibility of getting on without plum-cake; the ceremonious apparition of a pair of decanters containing port and sherry and cork; Sally's sister at the tea-table, clinking the best crockery and shaking her head mournfully every time she looked down into the teapot as if it were the tomb; the coat of arms again, and Sally as before; lastly, the words of consolation administered to Sally when it was considered right that she should "come round nicely", which were, that the deceased had had "as com-for-ta-ble a fu-ne-ral as comfortable could be!"

My most abiding memory of all in these times, however, is walking with my father up the hill of Falstaff's robbery on the outskirts of Rochester towards Gravesend that led to a house called "Gad's Hill Place". My father often remarked that if I were to be very persevering and work hard, I might some day come to live in this house when I became a man. It seemed to me then that this wonderful mansion, as I saw it, was so far beyond our existence at Ordnance Terrace that this was an impossible dream, and yet as I secretly returned time and again to admire the house from a distance, this very queer small boy, with the first faint shadows of authorship of books in his head, just began to feel that it might not be such an impossible dream after all.

Early 1821 brought some changes. I was sent to a school on the corner of Rhode Street and Best Street in Chatham and run by 23-

year old William Giles, a dissenter and son of a Baptist minister. He had been banned from residence at Oxford University because of his nonconformity, but had previously taught at a school in that city before moving to Chatham and had gained a high reputation. Cultivated reading, good handwriting and elocution, as well as the proper use of grammar, were all instilled into an eager 9-year old by this noble teacher. It was at this school that I wrote my first little story called "Misnar the Sultan of India" and also faced my first examination. I had to learn and recite verses to the assembled throng from the "Humorist's Miscellany", and report that I was successful in receiving a double encore from my audience.

Soon after I began at my new school, however, I was dismayed to learn that we were to leave Ordnance Terrace, and my fields of play, that had turned from summer gold to Christmas white, were extinguished from me. We moved to the area in Chatham close to the dockyard (and my new school) known as "The Brook" which housed, in the main, dockyard officialdom. The house we took at 18 St. Mary's Place was plain looking, with a whitewashed plaster front, attached to the Baptist chapel – "Providence Chapel" – where William Giles's father and others breathing fire and brimstone held ministry. On summer evenings, when every flower and tree and bird might have better addressed my soft young heart, I would instead be caught in the palm of a female hand by the crown, violently scrubbed from the neck to the roots of the hair as purification for this temple next door, and then carried off highly charged with spontaneous electricity, to have my head steamed like a potato in the unventilated breath of a thunderous preacher and his congregation. I came to hate with an unwholesome hatred those two hours and often felt the fatal sleep stealing over me, so I have no curiosity these days to hear powerful preachers. Those who strew the Eternal Path with the greatest amount of brimstone, and who most ruthlessly tread down the flowers and leaves by the wayside now generate in me an unwholesome hatred for this most dismal and oppressive charade.

18 St. Mary's Place, however, was where my voyage of discoveries really began. In the room next to my own, and where nobody else in our house ever troubled, I found that my father had set out his collection of books on shelves and from that blessed little room, Robinson Crusoe,

Don Quixote, Arabian Nights and Tales of the Genii, Roderick Random, Peregrine Pickle, Humphrey Clinker, Gulliver's Travels, Pilgrim's Progress, Sinbad the Sailor, Tom Jones (the child's Tom Jones, a harmless creature) and the Vicar of Wakefield all came tumbling out – a glorious host to keep me company. They kept alive my fancy and my hope of something beyond that place. In all these golden fables, there was never gold enough for me. I always wanted more. When I think of it, the picture always rises in my mind of a summer evening, the boys at play in the churchyard, and I sitting on my bed, reading as if for life.

As I chose not to participate in boyish games any more, a puny, weak youngster began to emerge and I was not a very robust child at all. I began to have spasmodic attacks, particularly on my left side, and this torment – perhaps from an inflamed left kidney – I took into later life with me. I also began to have bad dreams. They were frightful, though my more mature understanding has never made out why. I vividly recall an interminable sort of rope-making, with long minute filaments for strands which, when spun home together close to my eyes, occasioned screaming. Immense areas of shapeless things would slowly come close to my eyes and then recede to an immeasurable distance. Few people know what secrecy there is in the young under terror, but I was one who knew, and fear came to be a regular associate with me. On one occasion, just after dark, I came upon a figure chalked upon a door in a little back lane near a country church. It smoked a pipe and had a big hat with each of its ears sticking out in a horizontal line under the brim. The mouth stretched from ear to ear below a pair of staring goggle eyes; its hands appeared at its side like two bunches of carrots, five in each cluster, ready to grip at a passerby. I fled in horror, running to the sanctity of my home and room, looking behind me all the while to see if it was following with others risen from their graves. It is a memory that is still vaguely alarming to me to recall, as I have often done lying awake with my own private thoughts.

In March 1822, shortly after my 10th birthday, came another addition to our family, another brother christened Alfred Lamert. However, it was not long before we were witnessing the hand of death reaching out to our family again, for my little sister, Harriet, was struck down with smallpox and died. Then, in June, my father got the recall to London, to work once again at Somerset House and we had the task of packing up our household possessions, some for shipment nailed up in packing cases as big as houses, whilst disposing of others. Before the leaving, I managed to persuade my father to allow me to stay a while further with my schoolteacher, William Giles. This was agreed and, as I stood in the road at their departure looking wistfully at them, a mist cleared from my mother's eyes and she beckoned me to climb up so that she might put her arm around my neck and give me a kiss. Having done so, I had barely time to get down again before the coach started, and I could hardly see the family for the handkerchiefs they waved as they set off to Camden Town and a new house at 16 Bayham Street.

Three months later, and it was then time for me to leave Chatham. On the night before departure, William Giles, my good master, came flitting into my room among the packing cases and gave me Goldsmith's "Bee" as a keepsake. The next morning we headed for Simpson's coach office in Chatham, where I noticed an oval window with a picture showing one of their coaches in the act of passing a milestone on the London road with great velocity, completely full inside and out, all the passengers dressed in the first style of fashion and enjoying themselves tremendously. Then a commodore coach, melodiously called "Simpson's Blue-Eyed Maid", drawn by four horses and driven by Old Chumley, pulled up and having embraced the Giles family and thanking them for their exceeding kindness to me, I climbed aboard. By the time the clock struck for the nine-thirty departure, I was still alone therein but now packed around with damp straw, like game to be forwarded to the Crosskeys, Wood Street, Cheapside, London. The smell of that lingers with me to this day, and as the coach moved off, I waved final goodbyes and left Chatham behind me. Turning out onto the London road, I pondered on how my fate differed from those so happily depicted on the office wall. I consumed my sandwiches in solitude and dreariness. It rained hard all the way and I did not believe that life could ever be so magical again. And now I was on my way to London, that Great City that I had sampled but briefly in the past. What, I wondered, would that place now hold in store for me? All beyond was so unknown and great that, in a moment and with a strong heave and a sob, I broke into tears.

CHAPTER II

Growing Up in London

Bayham Street I found was located in one of the poorest parts of the suburbs; Camden Town was as quiet and dismal as any neighbourhood about London. Its crazily built houses – the largest, eight-roomed – were rarely shaken by any conveyance heavier than the spring van that came to carry off the goods of a 'sold-up' tenant. The whole neighbourhood felt itself liable, at any time, to that common casualty of life. A man used to come regularly, delivering the summonses for rates and taxes as if they were circulars. We never paid anything until the last extremity, and Heaven knows how we paid it then. The streets were positively hilly with the inequalities made in them by the man with the pickaxe who cut off the company's supply of water to defaulters. It seemed as if nobody had any money except old Mrs. Frowze, who lived with her mother at 14 Little Twig Street, and who was rumoured to be immensely rich; though I didn't see why, unless it was that she never went out of doors, and never wore a cap, and never brushed her hair, which was immensely dirty.

Number 16 was in a terrace surrounded by many houses. It was a mean, small tenement on two storeys, with a wretched little back garden abutting onto a squalid court. A washerwoman lived next door, a Bow Street officer over the way, but it had no boys near with whom I might hope to become familiar. At the top of the street were some alms houses and I used to go to this spot to look from it over the dust-heaps and dock-leaves and fields to the cupola of St. Paul's looming through the smoke. I was put into a scantily furnished little back garret at the top of the house, which only served to make me acutely aware of all that I had lost in losing Chatham. Shoehorned into this building were my father and mother, five children, an orphaned servant girl we had brought from the workhouse in Chatham, and George Lamert. George was the son of Aunt Fanny's new husband, Doctor Matthew Lamert (who was later to stand for Dr. Slammer in Pickwick) but, upon their marriage, the couple had moved away to Cork in Ireland; we then heard the terrible news that Aunt Fanny had died there in September 1822. George had lately completed his education at Sandhurst and was now lodging with us whilst waiting in hopes of a commission.

I knew my father to be as kind-hearted and generous a man as ever lived in the world; but, in the ease of his temper and the straitness of his means, he appeared at this time to have utterly lost the idea of educating me at all and to have utterly put from him the notion that I had any claim upon him, in that regard, whatever. And so I degenerated into cleaning his boots of a morning and my own, and making myself useful in the work of the little house and looking after my younger brothers and sisters and going on such poor errands as arose out of our poor way of living. I longed to have been sent to school, any school, to have been taught something, anywhere, but it was not to be. In April 1823 my sister, Fanny, had the singular good fortune to be elected as a pupil at the Royal Academy of Music which made my loss the harder to bear. My simple consolation was a little painted theatre that George Lamert made for me and for which I wrote some small sketches of my own in the feeble notion that it might allow me some form of escape from the miserable reality that now surrounded me.

One of the earliest and most memorable things that happened to me after our arrival was that I got lost one day in the city of London. I was taken out by somebody (I cannot remember now who this was) as an immense treat, to be shown the outside of St. Giles's Church. We set off after breakfast and saw the outside of the church with sentiments of satisfaction, much enhanced by a flag flying from the steeple. I infer that we then went down through Seven Dials – a place of profound attraction to me, full of wickedness, want and beggary – to Northumberland House in the Strand to view the celebrated lion over the gateway. At all events, I know that in the act of looking up with mingled awe and admiration at that famous animal I lost that somebody.

A child's unreasoning terror of being lost comes as freshly on me now as it did then. I verily believe that if I had found myself astray at the North Pole instead of in the narrow, crowded, inconvenient street over which the lion in those days presided, I could not have been more horrified, but this first fright expended itself in a little crying and tearing up and down; and then I walked, with a feeling of dismal dignity upon me, into a court, and sat down on a step to consider how to get through life. To the best of my belief, the idea of asking my way home never came into my head. It is possible that I may, for the time, have preferred the dismal dignity of being lost; but I have a serious conviction that in the wide scope of my arrangement for the future, I had no eyes for the nearest and most obvious course. I had one and fourpence in my pocket, the remains of half-a-crown presented on my birthday by my god-father, Christopher Huffam, a man who knew his duty and did it.

I made up my little mind to seek my fortune, and came out of the court to pursue my plans. These were, first to go (as a species of investment) and see the Giants in Guildhall – which I thought meant somehow Gold or Golden Hall – out of whom I felt it not improbable that some prosperous adventure would arise; failing that contingency, to try about the City for any opening of a Whittington nature; baffled in that too, to go into the army as a drummer.

I remember how immensely broad the streets seemed now that I was alone, how high the houses and how grand and mysterious everything. When I came to Temple Bar, it took me half an hour to stare at it, and I left it unfinished even then. I had read about heads being exposed on the top of it, and it seemed a wicked old place, albeit a noble monument of architecture and a paragon of utility. When at last I got away from it, behold I came, the next minute, on the figures at St Dunstan's! Who could see those obliging monsters strike upon the bells and go? Between the quarters there was the toyshop to look at and even when that enchanted spot was escaped from, after an hour and more, then St. Paul's arose, and how was I to get beyond its dome, or to take my eyes from its cross of gold?

I felt now very lonely and began to roam about the City seeking my fortune, wandering about like a child in a dream, inspired by a mighty faith in the marvelousness of everything, but producing no result according to the Whittington precedent. There was a dinner preparing at the Mansion House, and when I peeped in at a grated kitchen window, and saw the men cooks at work in their white caps, my heart began to beat with hope that the Lord Mayor, or the Lady Mayoress, or one of the young Princesses, their daughters, would look out of an upper apartment and direct me to be taken in. But, nothing of the kind occurred. It was not until I had been peeping in some time that one of the cooks called to me (the window was open): "Cut away, you sir!" which frightened me so, on account of his black whiskers, that I instantly obeyed. No British merchant seemed at all disposed to take me into his house. The only exception was a chimney-sweep; he looked at me as if he thought me suitable to his business, but I ran away from him.

I suffered very much, all day, from boys; they chased me down turnings, brought me to bay in doorways, and treated me quite savagely, though I am sure I gave them no offence. Then I must have strayed, as I recall my course, into Goodman's Fields, and to a theatre in that neighbourhood. Of its external appearance I only remember the loyal initials "G.R." untidily painted in yellow ochre on the front – and I waited, with a pretty large crowd, for the opening of the gallery doors. The greater part of the sailors and others composing the crowd were of the lowest description, and their conversation was not improving; but I understood little or nothing of what was bad in it then, and it had no depraving influence on me. I have wondered since, how long it would take, by means of such association, to corrupt a child nurtured as I had been, and innocent as I was. When the doors opened, with a clattering of bolts, and some screaming from women in the crowd, I went on with the current like a straw. My sixpence was rapidly swallowed up in the money-taker's pigeon-hole, and I got into the freer staircase above and ran on (as everybody else did) to get a good place. When I came to the back of the gallery, there were very few people in it, and the seats looked so horribly steep, and so like a diving arrangement to send me, head foremost, into the pit, that I held by one of them in a terrible fright. However, there was a good-natured baker with a young woman, who gave me his hand, and we all three scrambled over the seats together down into the corner of the first row. The baker was very fond of the young woman, and kissed her a good deal in the course of the evening.

I was no sooner comfortably settled, than a weight fell upon my mind. It was a benefit night, the benefit of the comic actor, a little fat man with a very large face and, as I thought then, the smallest and most diverting hat that ever was seen. The comedian, for the gratification of his friends and patrons, had undertaken to sing a comic song on a donkey's back, and afterwards to give away the donkey so distinguished, by lottery. In this lottery, every person admitted to the pit and gallery had a chance. On paying my sixpence, I had received the number forty-seven and I now thought, in a perspiration of terror, what should I ever do if that number was to come up the prize, and I was to win the donkey! At last the time came when the fiddlers struck up the comic song, and the dreaded animal came clattering in with the comic actor on his back. As the donkey persisted in turning his tail to the audience, the comedian got off him, turned about, and with his face that way, sang the song three times, amid thunders of applause. All this time, I was fearfully agitated; and when two pale people, a good deal splashed with the mud of the streets, were invited out of the pit to superintend the drawing of the lottery, and were received with a round of laughter from everybody else, I could have begged and prayed them to have mercy on me, and not draw number forty-seven.

But I was soon put out of my pain now, for a gentleman behind me, in a flannel jacket and a yellow neck-kerchief, answered to the winning number, and went down to take possession of the prize. The gentleman appeared to know the donkey from the moment of his entrance, and although was thrown by him on first mounting – to the great delight of the audience, including myself – rode him off with great skill afterwards, and soon returned to his seat quite calm. Calmed myself by the immense relief I had sustained, I enjoyed the rest of the performance very much indeed.

It was late when I got out into the streets, and there was no moon and no stars, and the rain fell heavily. When I emerged from the dispersing crowd, I felt unspeakably forlorn; and now, for the first time, my little bed and the dear familiar faces came before me, and touched my heart. By daylight, I had never thought of the grief at home. I had never thought of my mother, but now I ran about, until I found a watchman in his box. It is amazing to me, now, that he should have been sober; but I am inclined to think he was too feeble to get drunk. This venerable man took me to the nearest watch-house – a warm and drowsy sort of place embellished with great-coats and rattles hanging up. When a paralytic messenger had been sent to make inquiries about me, I fell asleep by the fire, and awoke no more until my eyes opened on my father's face. They used to say I was an odd child, and I suppose I was; maybe I took some of that into later life – but this is literally and exactly how I went astray at that time.

I do have some pleasant memories in these times of visits to my godfather, Christopher Huffam. He lived at 12 Church Row, Limehouse in a substantial, handsome sort of way and was always kind to me. He was in the business of sail-making and ships' chandlery, and the sights and smells of the River Thames rekindled my link with Chatham. He would have guests whom, I know, I greatly entertained with comic singing, one of my favourite songs being "The Cat's Meat Man":

In Gray's Inn, not long ago, an old maid lived a life of woe;

She was fifty-three, with a face like tan – and she fell in love with a cat's meat man.

Oh! Much she loved this cat's meat man, he was a good-lookin' cat's meat man,

Her roses and lilies were turned to tan – when she fell in love with this cat's meat man.

Every morning when he went by, whether the weather was wet or dry,

Right opposite her door he'd stand – and cry "cat's meat", did this cat's meat man.

One morn she kept him at the door, talking half an hour or more;

For you know it was her plan – to have a good look at the cat's meat man.

"If I had the money" says the cat's meat man, "I'd open a pie-shop" says the cat's meat man,

"And I'd marry you tomorrow". She admired his plan – and lent a five-pound note to the cat's meat man.

He pocketed the money and went away; she waited for him all next day,

But he never came, and then she began – to think she had been cheated by the cat's meat man.

She went to seek this cat's meat man, but she could not find the cat's meat man;

Some friends then gave her to understand – he'd got a wife and seven children, this cat's meat man!

So home she went, with sighs and tears, as her hopes were all transformed to fears;

And her hungry cat began to mew – as much as to say: "When's the cat's meat due?"

But she couldn't help thinking of the cat's meat man, the handsome, swindling cat's meat man;

So you see, in one day's short span – she lost her heart, a five-pound note... and the cat's meat man!

However, such visits were but a short interlude in the otherwise unremitting gloom. Visits to my uncle, Thomas Barrow – who was now suffering from the effects of an accident to his left leg and which he later had to have amputated – only brought to the surface debate over this mysterious "Deed". He lodged at this time at 10 Gerrard Street, Soho in the upper part of a house belonging to a bookseller, Mr. Manson, who had recently died. My one consolation in these visits lay in the fact that Mrs. Manson, his widow, kindly lent me books for amusement. In one comic tale from George Colman's "Broad Grins" entitled the "Elder Brother", I found a description of Covent Garden that was so bewitching that I vowed I would go and see for myself. One day, not long thereafter, I stole down to the market on my own to compare it with the book. As I wandered around, the intoxicating vigour of the place was as captivating as any theatre I had ever seen. I remember snuffing up the flavour of the faded cabbage-leaves as if it were the very breath of comic fiction and on that day began my lifelong addiction to the greater comedy and tragedy of the living theatre that is London.

My father's resources were so low and all his expedients so thoroughly exhausted that my mother sought to expound that she "must do something". Christopher Huffam was said to have an Indian connection and it was known that people in the East Indies always sent their children here to be educated. So, she would set up a school; we would all grow rich by it. Perhaps, I thought, even I might go to school myself. A house was found at 4 Gower Street North, to where we moved just after Christmas 1823, and affixed a large brass plate to the door announcing "MRS. DICKENS'S ESTABLISHMENT" in bold lettering. For my part, I left, at a great many other doors, a great many circulars calling attention to the merits of the establishment.

And yet, nobody ever came to the place. The whole idea collapsed in a heap of ruin that served only to enhance our plight. The large brass plate was taken off the door and carried away by the man who had no expectation of ever being paid for it. The pawn shop with its three golden balls of doom now became a furtive port of call, sucking up our belongings for miserly sums in return – though, through it all, I was determined never to pawn my Goldsmith's "Bee" and extinguish my constant reminder of happy school days in Chatham. Almost everything, by degrees, was sold or pawned. My father's books went first. I carried them, one after another, to a bookstall in the Hampstead Road – one part of which, near our house, was almost all bookstalls and bird-shops then – and sold them for whatever they would bring. The keeper of this bookstall, who lived in a little house behind it, used to get tipsy every night, and to be violently scolded by his wife every morning. More than once, when I went there early, I had audience of him in a turn-up bedstead, with a cut in his forehead or a black eye, bearing witness to his excesses over-night (I am afraid he was quarrelsome in his drink), and he with a shaking hand, endeavouring to find the needful shillings in one or other of the pockets of his clothes, which lay upon the floor, while his wife, with a baby in her arms and her shoes down at heel, never left off berating him. Sometimes he had lost his money, and then he would ask me to call again; but his wife had always got some – had taken his, I dare say, while he was drunk – and secretly completed the bargain on the stairs, as we went down together.

And at the pawnbroker's shop, too, I began to be very well known. The principal gentleman who officiated behind the counter, took a good deal of notice of me and often got me, I recollect, to decline a Latin noun or adjective, or to conjugate a Latin verb, in his ear, while he transacted my business. Things went from bad to worse with the butcher and the baker and very often we had not too much for dinner. Other creditors came banging at the door at all hours, some being quite ferocious; and the Poor Rate due to be paid by my father remained unpaid until I learnt he had been issued with a Summons. We simply retreated to two parlours of the Gower Street house, as most of our furniture – including my own little bed – disappeared. A sale was held at the premises and my little bed was so superciliously looked upon by a power unknown to me, but hazily called "the trade", that a brass coal-scuttle, a roasting jack, and a birdcage were obliged to be put in to make a lot of it, and then it went for a song; or so I heard mentioned, and I wondered what song, and I thought what a dismal song it must have been to sing. Our furniture was carried away in a van, all that was left being my parents' bed, a few chairs and the kitchen-table. We were there left, encamped night and day with the young servant girl from the Chatham workhouse, huddled up and praying that something would turn up.

In these circumstances, I believed I was experiencing the deepest ocean of despair, for I can speak in truth now that there is no more miserable thing than to feel ashamed of home. But, for me, this was just the prelude for what was about to unfold and the ghost that grew within me at this time still haunts me to this day with the infliction of its pain and humiliation.

Just two days after my twelfth birthday, in an evil hour for me, I was sent out to work, to begin my business life. George Lamert had acquired proprietary rights to a particular boot blacking recipe from the claimed inventor, a Mr. Jonathan Warren (uncle of Mr. Robert Warren, who ran a more famous blacking warehouse at Number 30, Strand), and George was now operating this Warren's blacking warehouse at Hungerford Stairs; the warehouse was the last place on the left-hand side of the way, and competitively described as "30, Hungerford Stairs". It was a crazy, tumbledown old house, abutting onto the river, and literally overrun with rats. Its wainscoted rooms and its rotten floors and staircase, with the old grey rats swarming down in the cellars, and the sound of their squeaking and scuffling coming up the stairs at all times, and the dirt and decay of the place, rise up visibly before me as if I were there again. George Lamert had proposed that I should go there, to be as useful as I could be, at a salary, I think, of six or maybe seven shillings a week, and this offer was accepted all too willingly by my father and mother. My hours were to be 8am to 8pm, with a one-hour break for lunch and half an hour for tea, six days a week.

It is wonderful to me how I could have been so easily cast away at such an age. It is wonderful to me that, even after the descent into the poor little drudge I had been since we came to London, no-one had compassion enough on me – a child of singular abilities, quick, eager, delicate and soon hurt, bodily or mentally – to suggest that something might have been spared to place me at any common school. My father and mother, however, were quite satisfied; they could hardly have been more so if I had been 20 years of age, distinguished at a grammar school, and going to Cambridge.

And so I walked there to begin. There was a counting-house on the first floor, looking over the coal barges and the river, with a recess in it, in which I was to sit and work. My work was to cover the pots of paste blacking: first with a piece of oil paper and then with a piece of blue paper: to tie them around with a string, and then to clip the paper close and neat all round, until it looked as smart as a pot of ointment from an apothecary's shop. When a certain number of grosses of pots had attained this pitch of perfection, I was to paste on each a printed label, and then go on again with more pots. Two or three other boys were kept at similar duty downstairs on similar wages. One of them came up, in a ragged apron and a paper cap, on the first Monday morning to show me the trick of using the string and tying the knot. His name was Bob Fagin, and I took the liberty of using his name, long afterwards, in Oliver Twist.

George Lamert had promised me some schooling during the lunch hour each day, but within a short time, I vanished out of the recess in the counting-house and kept company on my small work table with the other small work tables, grosses of pots, paper, string, scissors and paste pots downstairs, with all thoughts of schooling now being totally abandoned. It was not long before Bob Fagin and I, and another boy whose name was Paul Green, but who was currently believed to have been christened Poll (a belief which I transferred, long afterwards again, to Mr. Sweedlepipe in Martin Chuzzlewit), worked generally side by side. Bob Fagin was an orphan, and lived with his brother-in-law, a waterman. Poll Green's father had the additional distinction of being a fireman, and was employed at Drury Lane Theatre, where another relation of Poll's, I think his little sister, did imps in the pantomimes.

No words can express the secret agony of my soul as I sunk into this companionship; compared these everyday associates with those of my happier childhood; and felt my early hopes of growing up to be a learned and distinguished man crushed in my breast. The deep remembrance of the sense I had of being utterly neglected and helpless; of the shame I felt in my position; of the misery it was to my young heart to believe that, day by day, what I had learned, and thought, and delighted in, and raised my fancy and my emulation up by, was passing away from me, never to be brought back any more, cannot be written. My whole nature was so penetrated with the grief and humiliation of such considerations, that even now I often forget in my dreams that I am a man and wander desolately back to that time of my life.

But I have not yet revealed to you the full horror of my position, for on the 20th February 1824, only eleven days after I began in the blacking warehouse, my father was arrested as an insolvent debtor and taken to the sponging house run by the bailiff. I ran around frantically seeking assistance, but none was forthcoming and, in that event, he was taken off to the Marshalsea Prison. As he was led away for incarceration, I shall never forget that he remarked that the sun was now set upon him for ever, and I really believed at the time that these words had broken my heart. The key of the house at Gower Street North was soon sent back to the landlord, who was very glad to get it; my mother and the others from there went to live in the Marshalsea whilst I (small Cain that I was, except that I had never done harm to anybody) was handed over as a lodger to a reduced old lady, Mrs. Roylance (long known to our family) at 37 Little College Street, Camden Town, who took children in to board, and had once done so at Brighton; and who, with a few alterations and embellishments, unconsciously began to sit for Mrs. Pipchin in Dombey and Son.

This old lady had a little brother and sister under her care then, somebody's natural children who were very irregularly paid for, and also a widow's little son. The two boys and I slept in the same room. My own exclusive breakfast, of a penny cottage loaf and a pennyworth of milk, I provided for myself. I kept another small loaf, and a quarter of a pound of cheese, on a particular shelf of a particular cupboard, to make my supper on when I came back at night. I was out at the blacking warehouse all day, and had to support myself upon that money all the week, with no advice, no counsel, no encouragement, no consolation, no support, from anyone that I can call to mind.

I know I do not exaggerate, unconsciously and unintentionally, the scantiness of my resources and the difficulties of my life. I was so young and childish and so little qualified – how could I be otherwise? – to undertake the whole charge of my existence, that, in going to Hungerford Stairs of a morning, with some cold hotch-potch in a basin tied up in a handkerchief, I could not resist the stale pastry put out at half-price on trays at the confectioners' doors in Tottenham Court Road, and I often spent on that the money I should have kept for my dinner. Then I went without my dinner, or bought a roll or a slice of pudding. If a shilling or so were given to me by anyone, I spent it on a dinner or a tea. We had half an hour for tea. When I had money enough, I used to go to a coffee-shop and have half a pint of coffee and a slice of bread and butter. When I had no money, I took a turn in Covent Garden Market and stared at the pineapples. The coffee-shops to which I most resorted were, one in Maiden Lane, one in a court (non-existent now) close to Hungerford Market; and one in St Martin's Lane, of which I only recollect that it stood near the church, and that in the door there was an oval glass plate, with 'Coffee-Room' painted on it, addressed towards the street. If I ever find myself in a very different kind of coffee-room now, but where there is such an inscription on glass, and read it backwards on the wrong side 'mooR-eeffoC' (as I often used to do then, in a dismal reverie), a shock even now goes through my blood.

I worked from morning to night, with common men and boys, a shabby child. I tried, but ineffectually, not to anticipate my money, and to make it last the week through by putting it away in a drawer I had in the counting-house, wrapped into six little parcels, each parcel containing the same amount, and labelled with a different day. I know that I have lounged about the streets, insufficiently and unsatisfactorily fed and I know that, but for the mercy of God, I might easily have been, for any care that was taken of me, a little robber or a little vagabond.

But I held some station at the blacking warehouse. I never said how it was that I came to be there, or gave the least indication of being sorry that I was there. That I suffered in secret, and that I suffered exquisitely, no-one ever knew but I. I felt keenly, moreover, being cut off from my parents and my younger brothers and sisters and, when my day's work was done, going home to such a miserable blank. On my first visit to the Marshalsea, which was the Sunday after my father had been taken there, I went with my sister Fanny. She was at the academy in

Tenterden Street, Hanover Square, and I was there at 9 o'clock in the morning to fetch her. We walked over Westminster Bridge to the prison, just off Borough High Street, and entered a narrow alley that led to the turnkey's lodge and main entrance at the bottom end. My father was waiting for us in the lodge and we went up to his room (on the top storey but one) and cried very much. I see the fire we sat before, now; with two bricks inside the rusted grate, one on each side, to prevent its burning too many coals.

We were able to stay at the Marshalsea until 10 o'clock in the evening, when a bell tolled, warning visitors of the imminent locking of the gates. Fanny and I walked back together to her place in Tenterden Street and then I walked on alone to my lodgings in Camden Town, thinking all the while of what my father had told me: to take warning by the Marshalsea, and to observe that if a man had twenty pounds a year and spent nineteen pounds nineteen shillings and sixpence, he would be happy; but that a shilling spent the other way would make him wretched.

Each Sunday, Fanny and I passed in the prison. As I trudged back to my lodgings, each time the feeling grew in me that this might, in some small way, be corrected. One Sunday night, I remonstrated with my father on his head, so pathetically and with so many tears, that his kind nature gave way. It was the first remonstrance I had ever made about my lot, and perhaps I opened up a little more than I intended, but a back attic was found for me at the house of an Insolvent Court agent, who lived in Lant Street in the Borough, and where I had Bob Sawyer in Pickwick lodged many years afterwards. I was now able to breakfast "at home" each day in the Marshalsea before heading off to the blacking warehouse; and supper there when I returned. The landlord of my little lodging, Archibald Russell, was a fat, good natured, kind old gentleman. He was lame and had a quiet old wife and a very innocent grown-up son, who was lame too. They were all exceedingly kind to me and I was later happy to record them for posterity as the Garland family in the Old Curiosity Shop. One night I was taken with one of my old attacks of spasm disorder and the whole three of them were about my bed until morning.

I had a similar illness one day in the warehouse. Bob Fagin was very good to me on this occasion. I suffered such excruciating pain that time that they made me a temporary bed of straw in my old recess, and I rolled about on the floor, and Bob filled empty blacking bottles with hot water and applied relays of them to my side, half the day. Bob did not like the idea of my going home alone, and took me under his protection. I was too proud to let him know about the prison, and after making several efforts to get rid of him, to all of which Bob Fagin in his goodness was deaf, shook hands with him on the steps of a house near Southwark Bridge on the Surrey side, making believe that I lived there. As a finishing piece of reality in case of his looking back, I knocked at the door, I recollect, and asked, when the woman opened it, if that was Mr. Robert Fagin's house.

I forget at what hour the gates at the Marshalsea were opened in the morning, admitting of my going in; but I know that I was often up at six o'clock, and that my favourite lounging-place in the interval was old London Bridge, where I was wont to sit in one of the stone recesses, watching the people going by, or to look over the balustrades at the sun shining in the water, and lighting up the golden flame on the top of the Monument. The Chatham workhouse girl met me here sometimes. She also now had lodgings in the neighbourhood so that she might be early on the scene of her duties in the Marshalsea and I used to tell her some astonishing fictions respecting the wharves and the Tower; of which I can say no more than that I hope I believed them myself. I later took her sharp little worldly and also kindly ways as my first impression of "The Marchioness" in the Old Curiosity Shop. In the evenings I used to go back to the prison for supper, and to walk up and down the parade with my father, before going back to my lodging for the night.

I also became in the habit of wandering about, particularly to begin with in the Adelphi area between Waterloo and Hungerford Bridges, as I found it a mysterious place with dark arches. I can see myself now emerging one fine evening from one of these very arches at a little public-house ("The Fox-under-the-Hill") close to the river and with an open space before it, where some coal-heavers were dancing; to look at whom I sat down upon a bench. But, living as I was, I began to realize that I had to become more emboldened to survive. I was such a little fellow, with my poor white hat, little jacket and corduroy trousers, that frequently, when I went into the bar of a strange public house for a glass of ale or porter to wash down the saveloy and loaf I had eaten in the street, they didn't like to give it to me. I remember, one evening when I went into a public house ("The Red Lion") in Parliament Street at the corner of the short street leading into Cannon Row, and said to the landlord behind the bar: "What is your very best, the VERY best ale, a glass? "Two pence" says he. "Then" says I, "just draw me a glass of that, if you please, with a good head to it." The landlord looked at me, in return, over the bar, from head to foot, with a strange smile on his face; and instead of drawing the beer, looked round the screen and said something to his wife, who came out from behind it with her work in her hand, and joined him in surveying me. And there we stood, the landlord in his shirtsleeves, leaning against the bar window frame; his wife, looking over the little half-door; and I, in some confusion, looking up at them from outside the partition. They asked me a good-many questions, as what my name was, how old I was, where I lived, how I was employed, etc., to all of which, that I might commit nobody, I invented appropriate answers. They served me with some ale, though I suspect it was not the strongest on the premises, and the landlord's wife, opening the little half-door and bending down, gave me a kiss that was half-admiring and half-compassionate, but all womanly and good, I am sure.

In the meanwhile, all my father's attempts to avoid going through the courts had failed and, as a result, certain needful ceremonies had to be undertaken to obtain the benefit of the Insolvent Debtors' Act. In one of these, I had to play my part. One condition of the statute was that the wearing apparel and personal matters retained were not to exceed £20, so it was necessary, as a matter of form, that the clothes I wore should be seen by the official appraiser. I had a half-holiday to enable me to call upon him, at his own time, at a house somewhere beyond the Obelisk. I recollect him coming out to look at me with his mouth full, and a strong smell of beer upon him, and saying good naturedly that "that would do" and "it was alright". Certainly, the hardest creditor would not have been disposed (even if he had been legally entitled) to avail himself of my poor white hat, little jacket or corduroy trousers. But I had the fat old silver watch in my pocket which had been given to me by my grandmother before the blacking days, and I had entertained my doubts as I went along whether that valuable possession might not bring me over the £20. So I was greatly relieved that he did not seek it out, and made him a bow of acknowledgement as I went out.

My father's case came before the Insolvent Court in Portugal Street, Lincoln's Inn Fields – a stinking place full of people with unwashed skins and grizzly beards and with more old suits of clothes in it at one time than will be offered for sale in all Houndsditch in a twelve month. The place reeked with steams of beer and spirits that perpetually ascended to the ceiling, there to be condensed by the heat and to roll down the walls like rain. My father's debts, both from Chatham and London, were solemnly reviewed by a panel of judges, and I learnt that the considerable legacy of £450 from my grandmother had accrued not long before and had enabled sums to be paid into court during his imprisonment. Nevertheless, substantial further sums were ordered to be paid over the next two and a half years and an overseer appointed to ensure that the orders of the court were carried out.

Release brought a measure of relief but no escape from reality. The family, all except Fanny, went to stay with Mrs. Roylance at 37 Little College Street for a while before occupying a very small house in the poverty-stricken area of Somers Town, at 29 Johnson Street. Fanny, meanwhile, was doing well at the Royal Academy of Music, and I remember attending at a prize giving at Tenterden Street where she received one of the prizes given to the pupils – but such attendance put my emotions into turmoil for, although I was happy for her, I could not bear to think of myself beyond the reach of all such honourable emulation and success. The tears ran down my face; I felt as if my heart were rent. I never had suffered so much before, but there was no envy in this. I prayed, when I went to bed that night, to be lifted out of the humiliation and neglect in which I was.

And yet there seemed no end. I continued to work at the blacking warehouse which came to be removed from Hungerford Stairs to Chandos Street, Covent Garden. Next to the shop at the corner of Bedford Street were two rather old-fashioned houses and shops adjoining one another; they were thrown into one for the blacking business. Bob Fagin and I worked, for the light's sake, near the second window as you came from Bedford Street, and we were so brisk at it, that the people used to stop and look in. Sometimes there would be quite a little crowd there. I even saw my father with Charles Dilke, a fellow clerk from Somerset House, come in at the door one day when we were very busy; Dilke gave me half a crown and I gave him a very grateful bow as they left, but I wondered how my father could bear it.

Then, one day, my father and George Lamert quarreled; quarreled by letter, for I took the letter from my father to him which caused the explosion, and quarreled very fiercely. It was about me. It may have had some backward reference, in part for anything I know, to my employment at the window. All I am certain of is that, soon after I gave him the letter, he told me he was very much insulted about me; and that it was impossible to keep me. After that, I cried very much, partly because it was so sudden, and partly because in his anger he was violent about my father, though gentle to me. With a relief so strange that it was like oppression, I went home.

My mother set herself to accommodate the quarrel and did so next day. She brought home a request for me to return next morning, and a high character of me, which I am very sure I deserved. But my father said I should go back no more, and should go to school. I know how all these things have worked together to make me what I am: but I never afterwards forgot, I never shall forget, I never can forget, that my mother was warm for my being sent back. Thereafter, the matter was never raised again in our family, but the indelible stain of it will live with me forever.

Until old Hungerford Market was pulled down, until old Hungerford Stairs were destroyed, and the very nature of the ground changed, I never had the courage to go back to the place where my servitude began. I never saw it. I could not endure to go near it. For many years, when I came near to Robert Warren's in the Strand, I crossed over to the opposite side of the way to avoid a certain smell of the cement they put upon the blacking-corks, which reminded me of what I was once. And it was a very long time before I liked to go up Chandos Street. My old way home by the Borough made me cry for a great many years thereafter, well into my manhood. In my walks at night I have walked there often since then, and by degrees I have come to write this, but it does not seem a tithe of what I might have written, or of what I meant to write.

I was greatly relieved that my father's will prevailed and a school sought for me. There was a school in Mornington Place at the corner of Granby Street and Hampstead Road, not far from Johnson Street, kept by Mr. Jones, a Welshman, to which my father dispatched me to ask for a card of terms. The boys were at dinner, and Mr. Jones carving for them, when I acquitted myself of this commission. He came out and gave me what I wanted; and hoped I should become a pupil. I did. At seven o'clock one morning, very soon afterwards, I went as a day scholar to Mr. Jones's establishment, with its board over the door graced with the words: WELLINGTON HOUSE ACADEMY.

It seemed to me so long since I had been among such boys, or among any companions of my own age, except Bob Fagin and Poll Green, that I felt as strange as ever I had done in my life. I was so conscious of having passed through scenes of which they could have no knowledge, and of having acquired experiences foreign to my age, appearance, and conditions as one of them, that I half believed it was an imposture to come there as an ordinary schoolboy. I had become, in the blacking warehouse time, so unused to the sports and games of boys, that I knew I was awkward and inexperienced in the commonest things belonging to them. My mind ran upon what they would think if they knew of my familiar acquaintance with the Marshalsea. What would they say, those who made so light of money, if they could know how I had scraped my halfpence together for the purchase of my daily saveloy and beer or my slices of pudding? But within a short space of time I began to feel my uneasiness softening away.

The school itself was considered at the time a very superior sort of school, but soon I found it was most shamefully mismanaged and the boys made but very little academic progress. The Chief and proprietor, Mr. Jones, turned out to be a most ignorant fellow and a mere tyrant, whose chief employment was to scourge the boys (numbering something in the order of two hundred) on their palms with a bloated mahogany ruler or viciously drawing a pair of pantaloons tight with one of his large hands and caning the wearer with the other.

The ushers appeared to know more than the masters. I recall one of our ushers – I believe called Taylor – who was considered to know everything. He was a bony, gentle-faced, clerical-looking young man who dressed in rusty black, and we all liked him. He had a good knowledge of boys, and would have made it a much better school if he had had more power. He acted as writing master, mathematical master, made out the bills, mended the pens and did all sorts of things. He divided the little boys with deaf Mandeville, the Latin master, and always called at parents' houses to inquire after sick boys, because he had gentlemanly manners. He was rather musical, and on some remote quarter-day had bought an old trombone; but a bit of it was lost, and it made the most extraordinary sounds when he sometimes tried to play it of an evening!

Mandeville, on the other hand, was different. He was a colourless, doubled-up, near-sighted man with a crutch, who was always cold. He would disclose ends of flannel under all his garments and was almost always applying a ball of pocket-handkerchief to some part of his face, with a screwing action round and round. He was a very good scholar and would take great pains where he saw intelligence and a desire to learn – otherwise not. He had the intriguing habit of stuffing his ears with small onions and fell asleep one sultry afternoon before a class of boys; he did not wake even when the footsteps of the Chief fell heavily on the floor. In the midst of a dead silence, the Chief aroused him and said: "Mr. Mandeville, are you ill sir?" He blushingly replied: "Sir, rather so", to which the Chief retorted with severity: "Mr. Mandeville, this is no place to be ill in" (which was very very true) and walked back solemn as the ghost in Hamlet – until catching a boy's wonderous eye, he caned that boy for inattention, and so happily expressed his feelings towards the Latin master through the medium of a substitute.

There was also a fat little dancing-master called Shiers, who used to come in a gig and taught the more advanced among us hornpipes (as an accomplishment of great social demand in after-life); I tried to learn the piano, but my teacher told the Chief that I had no aptitude for music and that it was robbing my parents to continue giving me lessons. There was a brisk little French master who used to come in the sunniest weather with a handleless umbrella, and to whom the Chief was always polite, because (as we believed) if the Chief offended him, he would instantly address the Chief in French and forever confound him before the boys with his inability to understand or reply. A serving man named Phil also attended, who mended whatever was broken and made whatever was wanted. He had a sovereign contempt for learning and was morose, even to the Chief, and never smiled except at breaking-up when, in acknowledgement of the toast: "Success to Phil! Hurray!" he would slowly carve a grin out of his wooden face, where it would remain until we were all gone. Nevertheless, one time when we had scarlet fever in the school, Phil nursed all the sick boys of his own accord, and was like a mother to them.

At the school I can also clearly remember red-polls, linnets and canaries being kept by boys in desks, drawers, hat boxes and other stranger refuges – but above all, white mice were the favourite stock. It can truly be said that the boys trained the mice much better than the masters trained the boys. I recall, in particular, one white mouse who lived in the cover of a Latin dictionary, ran up ladders, drew Roman chariots, shouldered muskets, turned wheels, and even made a very creditable appearance on the stage as the Dog of Montargis, who might have achieved greater things but for having had the misfortune to mistake his way in a triumphal procession to the Capitol, when he fell into a deep inkstand, was dyed black and drowned.

I took to writing small tales and there was a sort of club for lending and circulating them. I read a penny weekly called "The Terrific Register" which was full of tales of murder and mayhem and frightened the very wits out of my head, but which, considering that there was an illustration to every number in which there was always a pool of blood and at least one body, was cheap. I would occasionally put together a periodical myself with a friend called Bowden (we occupied adjoining desks) which we entitled "Our Newspaper", to be lent out to other boys on payment of marbles or pieces of slate pencil. I also helped invent, for the use of my friends, a sort of gibberish "lingo", produced by the addition of a few letters of the same sound to every word which, with practice, made us quite unintelligible to bystanders.

What pleased me particularly was that the school was very strong in theatricals. We mounted small theatres and got up very gorgeous scenery to illustrate the plays, with a young Master Beverley, the scene painter, assisting us. I was always a leader at these plays, which were occasionally presented with much solemnity before an audience of boys, and in the presence of the ushers. I remember one called "The

Miller and his Men" which we got up in particularly spectacular form. Master Beverley constructed the mill for us in such a way that it could tumble to pieces with the assistance of crackers. At one representation, the fireworks in the last scene, ending with the destruction of the mill, were so very real that it caused the police to interfere and knock violently at the doors!

In all, I was at this school for just over two years, distinguishing myself like a brick, but despite the pervading nature of Mr. Jones, I had enough guile myself to keep out of his way when the need arose. I felt like a spring, inexorably uncoiling itself, to bounce along in high spirits without coming in for any of Mr. Jones's scourging propensity. It is said that I was probably connected with every mischievous prank in the school – an exaggeration, of course, but one that I am happy to go along with.

Then my circumstances changed and I had to leave the school because my father could not meet the arrangements as set out by the Insolvent Court. Fanny also, in due course, had to leave the Royal Academy of Music because, despite her successes there, my father was not able to stave off their demands for fees. He had by now retired from the Naval Pay Office on a pension and had taken to journalism, working for a while for "The British Press" as a parliamentary reporter and contributing articles of marine interest, but it was still not enough. From time to time I would go to the newspaper's office myself with reports of incidents that I hoped they would print at a penny a line, but the newspaper went out of business in October 1826 and our financial circumstances were once again dire. We were ousted from our house in Johnson Street and went into lodgings nearby for a while at 17, The Polygon in Clarendon Square before, some months later, we were able to return to Johnson Street. There was also another child on the way, my brother Augustus. I realized now that any further schooling for me was a forlorn hope and that it was time for me to begin in the world. I was just three months past my fifteenth birthday.

CHAPTER III

Law, Journalism and Sketches by Boz

The world I turned to was the law. My mother had a great-aunt, Mrs. Charlton who, with her husband Charles, ran a boarding house at 16 Berners Street – and it was there that I was introduced to one of her lodgers, Mr. Edward Blackmore. He was a young attorney from Alresford, who was then in practice in Gray's Inn under the title: "Ellis and Blackmore". The practice agreed to take me on, but I found it was housed in a poor old dismal set of three rooms at 5 Holborn Court; the chambers themselves being so dirty that I could take off the distinctest impressions of my figure on any article of furniture by merely lounging on it for a few moments. It used to be a private amusement of mine to print myself off all over the rooms; it was the first large circulation I ever had! At other times I have accidentally shaken a window curtain while in animated conversation and struggling insects which were certainly red, but were certainly not ladybirds, have dropped on the back of my hand.

It was in May 1827 that I started my business life there, as a junior clerk on the modest salary of thirteen shillings and sixpence, part of my task being to keep an account book of petty disbursements (which included my salary) in the office. I also copied documents and ran errands to the various courts of law, public offices and other lawyers' offices – all dressed in my new uniform of a dark blue frock-coat, trousers to match, black neckerchief and leather straps over the boots. When I went out I wore a military-looking cap which had a strap under the chin; the first time out a big blackguard fellow knocked my cap off as I was crossing over Chancery Lane from the Lincoln's Inn gateway. He said "Halloa, sojer!" which I could not stand, so I at once struck him and he then hit me in the eye. Although still a little fellow, I had learnt by now to stand up for myself, and they were somewhat surprised in the office when I returned from my first errand exhibiting such a black eye!

I walked everywhere and got to know all the London streets and the positioning of shops in every part of the West End and it was said in the office that I came to know it all from Bow to Brentford. A fellow clerk named Potter shared my taste for theatricals; we took every opportunity of going to performances, and were not infrequently being engaged in parts at the theatres. I enjoyed entertaining the office with low-character mimicry and I remember in particular one dirty old snuff-taking laundress who frequented Holborn Court, whose repulsive mannerisms I found were a special mimic's delight. I gleaned many characters that I encountered during my time in the office that I was later able to incorporate into Pickwick and Nickleby, including Mr. Perker and Newman Noggs.

At the end of the year, the practice moved to rooms on the second floor at 1 Raymond Buildings, where we junior clerks used to amuse ourselves by dropping cherry stones onto the hats of pedestrians below, but I became bored and dreamed of better things. I met Thomas Mitton, who had been at school with my brothers and who was now working in another law office, one belonging to Mr. Charles Malloy at 8 New Square, Lincoln's Inn, and in November 1828 I moved there in the hope of improving on the overall drudgery I felt at Ellis and Blackmore. Indeed, Gray's Inn itself I had found to be a stronghold of melancholy, one of the most depressing institutions in brick and mortar known to the children of men, with its dreary arid Square comprising a Sahara Desert of the Law. My mood, however, did not change in the alternative surrounds of Lincoln's Inn and, whilst my friendship and association with Tom Mitton remained steadfast thereafter, I vowed to move on to other things.

I had seen, from my father's work in the press gallery of the House of Commons, the benefits of shorthand writing and I set about becoming proficient in it. I bought Mr. Thomas Gurney's half-guinea book and plunged into a sea of perplexity that brought me, in a few weeks, to the confines of distraction. It was almost heart-breaking, but I persevered and worked my way steadily through; it was about equal in difficulty to the mastering of six languages. My father had now moved to reporting in the Commons for the "Morning Herald" and I took a sudden determination to qualify myself thoroughly as a newspaper parliamentary reporter - at that time a calling pursued by many clever men who were young at the Bar. I also later became an assiduous attendant in the British Museum Reading Room acquiring a ticket the day after my 18th birthday and joining also a library housed at 24 Fetter Lane, run by a Mr. Haine. These days of study I can now reveal as decidedly the most useful to myself that I ever passed. I later put into the beliefs of David Copperfield the golden rules that came to guide me:

"Whatever I have tried to do in life, I have tried with all my heart to do well. What I have devoted myself to, I have devoted myself to completely. Never to put one hand to anything on which I could throw my whole self, and never to affect depreciation of my work, whatever it was."

I never could have done what I have done, without the habits of punctuality, order, and diligence, without the determination to concentrate myself on one object at a time, no matter how quickly its successor should come upon its heels, which I then formed. Heaven knows I write this in no spirit of self-laudation. The man who reviews his own life, as I do mine, in going on here, from page to page, has need to have been a good man indeed, if he would be spared the sharp consciousness of many talents neglected, many opportunities wasted, many erratic and perverted feelings constantly at war within his breast, and defeating him. I do not hold one natural gift, I dare say, that I have not abused, but from this time on I was determined to follow this course.

I endeavoured to find myself a place as a parliamentary reporter but I could find no opening in the gallery. Instead, in the spring of 1829, now aged 17 years, I began my new life, enrolled as a reporter for an office in Doctors Commons, that area in the City near St. Paul's Cathedral set aside for the business and jurisdiction of naval and church matters. The Proctors of the firms were very self-important looking personages, who went about their business as if nothing else in the world mattered outside the intricacies of their profession. I was hired to take down transcripts of the proceedings in the various courts that seemed to abound but which all used to sit in turns in the main hall. This was an old quaint-looking columned room with black carved wainscoting, not unlike a chapel, with its farther end fenced off from the rest. Inside this area was a raised semi-circular platform and, within its curve, a pulpit-like desk. Doctors, sometimes in red gowns and grey wigs, surrounded the platform; whilst others, Proctors in black gowns with white fur collars, sat at a green table, like a billiard table without the cushions and pockets. And above them all in the pulpit-like desk, surveying proceedings like an owl, was the Presiding Judge. I used the shorthand that I had learnt to try and ensure I captured all that was said in the court, later setting it out in longhand for my employers. But it was a difficult task, particularly as the Judges were prone to babble exceeding fast in a language known only to themselves. Their lives seemed to revolve around obsolete old monsters of Acts of Parliament giving them ancient monopoly in suits about people's wills and people's marriages and disputes among ships and boats which monkish attorneys sought to manipulate to the full before them. Nevertheless, I stuck to my business, despite having to resign myself to coffee, which I seem, on looking back, to have taken by the gallon, and indeed it was not long before I became employed on my own account. I rented a reporter's box in the main hall and shared the costs of a transcribing room nearby at 5 Bell Yard with a Proctor, Mr. Charles Fenton, for whom I also reported cases. I was proud to have my own business card printed with *"Mr. Charles Dickens, Shorthand Writer"* thereon, together with the address to which I and my parents had lately moved, once again to 10 Norfolk Street (22, Cleveland Street) over the greengrocer's shop.

I passed nearly two years at Doctors Commons before the drudgery there finally overwhelmed me. During that time I had continued to make evening visits to the theatre, and spurred on by the comic talents of Charles Mathews – a particular favourite of mine with his brilliant impersonations of a host of characters – I engaged in some further attempts in the direction of the stage myself, for the weary uncertainty of the work at Doctors Commons had in fact made me think of the theatre as a possible career in quite a business-like way. I came to go (with very few exceptions) to some theatre every night, really studying the bills first and going to where there was the best acting: and always to see Charles Mathews wherever he played. I practiced immensely and prescribed to myself a system for learning parts, learning a great number. When I knew many of Mathews's *"At Homes"* from sitting in the pit to hear them, I wrote to George Bartley, who was stage-manager at Covent Garden, and told him how young I was, and exactly what I thought I could do; and that I believed I had a strong perception of character and oddity, and a natural power of reproducing in my own person what I observed in others. I recollect I wrote the letter from the little office I had at 5 Bell Yard, where the answer came also. There must have been something in my letter that struck the authorities, for Bartley wrote to me almost immediately to say that they were busy getting up a play, but that they would communicate again with me in a fortnight. Punctual to the time another letter came, with an appointment to do anything of Mathews's I pleased before him and Charles Kemble, on a certain day at the theatre. My sister Fanny was in the secret, and was to go with me to play the songs. But I was laid up when the day came, with a terrible bad cold and inflammation of the face; the beginning, by the bye, of an annoyance in one ear to which I am subject to this day. I wrote to say so, and added that I would resume my application next season.

I also did occasional part-time work in the House of Commons gallery for the weekly publication "Mirror of Parliament", which only served to whet my appetite for a full-time placement there. Eventually, the opening came and I was taken on in parliamentary service by a new radical London evening journal called "The True Sun", causing me to leave off any thoughts in the direction of the professional theatre at that time. I was nineteen years old when, with a great splash, I at last entered the gallery full-time alongside my father, witnessing, as I did, the final monumental struggles over what was to become the Great Reform Act of 1832.

I had also by now met – through a friend, Henry Kolle, a bank clerk – a pocket Venus of a girl called Maria Beadnell, and fallen hopelessly in love. She was some fifteen months older than me, the youngest of three daughters of banker George Beadnell living at 2 Lombard Street, and her flirtish charms provided her with many admirers. But no matter, I was smitten. I was swallowed up in an abyss of love in an instant. It was the maddest romance that ever got into any boy's head and stayed there, but it fairly lifted me up into that newspaper life and floated me away over a hundred men's heads. It fired my determination to overcome all the difficulties, and the desperate intensity of my nature was such that it excluded every other idea from my mind for four years at a time of life when four years are equal to four times four. The thoughts of this came to pervade every chink and crevice in my mind. I held volumes of *Imaginary Conversations* with her mother on the subject of our union, and I wrote letters more in number than Horace Walpole's, to that discreet woman (who would persist in calling me "Mr. Dickin"), soliciting her daughter's hand in marriage. I never had the remotest intention of sending any of those letters; but to write them, and after a few days tear them up, was a sublime occupation.

Despite my new job at The True Sun, it was still an unsettling time at home. In November 1831, my father had again been declared insolvent but he obviously managed to come to some arrangement with his creditors and the Insolvent Court that allowed him to escape the clutches of the Marshalsea. He was now working for the Mirror of Parliament, as well as at the Morning Herald, and continued to do so though we moved from house to house at this time, no doubt in an effort to escape persistent creditors. I took lodgings of my own on occasions, one being in Cecil Street off the Strand and another at 15 Buckingham Street, Adelphi run by Mrs. Rogers, who later sat for Mrs. Crupp in David Copperfield. I was writing where I could – some of my work entering Maria and her sister Anne Beadnell's albums – as well as making attempts at cartoon drawing. In December 1832, I worked as a polling clerk at the Lambeth Election for the Reformer, Charles Tennyson M.P., uncle of the poet, and sought extra employment where I could for my talents as a shorthand writer.

Then, in January 1833, our family moved to 18 Bentinck Street, Cavendish Square, above Burr's upholstery and cabinet maker's shop, and it was there that I came into the dignity of twenty-one. Maria Beadnell was at the party, but I was by now only too aware of difficulties in her behaviour towards me. Behind a door, in the crumby part of the night when wine glasses were to be found in unexpected spots, I spoke to Her – spoke out to Her. She was all angelic gentleness, but she called me "Boy" which, as I remembered at the moment, scorched my brain. She went away soon afterwards, and when the hollow throng dispersed, I issued forth with a dissipated scorner and "sought oblivion". It was found, with a dreadful headache in it, but it did not last, for, in the shaming light of next-day's noon, I raised my heavy head in bed, looking back to the birthdays behind me, and tracking the circle by which I had got round, after all, to the bitter powder and the wretchedness again.

I used Henry Kolle to deliver messages to Maria, but my over-spilling emotions for her came to be met with real indifference and, no doubt urged on by her family and friends, including a duplicitous tormentor named Marianne Leigh, she eventually rejected me. I remember well that long after I came of age – I say long; well! it seemed long then – I wrote to her for the last time of all, with a dawn upon me of some sensible idea that we were changing into man and woman, saying would she forget our little differences and separations and let us begin again? She answered me very coldly and reproachfully – and so I went my way. But nobody can ever know with what a sad heart I resigned her, or after what struggles and what conflict. My entire devotion to her, and the wasted tenderness of those hard years which I have ever since half loved, half dreaded to recall, made so deep an impression on me that I refer to it a habit of suppression which now belongs to me, which I know is no part of my original nature, but which makes me chary of showing my affections, even to my children, except when they were very young.

I loved that girl with the most extraordinary earnestness. I have always believed since, and always shall to the last, that there never was such a faithful and devoted poor fellow as I. Even when we were falling off each other, I would come from the House of Commons many a night at two or three o'clock in the morning, walk up an odd little court at the back of the Mansion House and come out by the corner of Lombard Street, just to wander past the place where she was sleeping. Whatever of fancy, romance, energy, passion, aspiration and position belong to me, I never have separated and never shall separate from the hard-hearted little woman whom it is nothing to say I would have died for with the greatest alacrity. I later used the memory of Maria as the basis for Dora in David Copperfield; but no one can imagine in the most distant degree what pain that recollection gave me in Copperfield.

My persistence with my writing at last paid off and my first published piece saw the light. I wrote a little story entitled "A Sunday Out of Town", which was a tale about a Mr. Minns and his cousin Octavius Budden (a person I took from Marianne Leigh's loud and red-faced father, a corn chandler in Clapton), that I enjoyed very much and thought I might try the old "Monthly Magazine" with it. I will never forget dropping this paper stealthily one evening at twilight, with fear and trembling, into a dark letterbox in a dark office up a dark court (Johnson Court) in Fleet Street. I waited with trepidation for the next monthly issue, December 1833, to appear and as soon as it did, I purchased a copy of the magazine from a young man at a shop in the Strand. My hands trembled as I opened the pages and there, suddenly, lo, it appeared in all the glory of print, the name now transmogrified to "A Dinner at Poplar Walk". I walked down to Westminster Hall and had to turn into it for half an hour, because my eyes were so dimmed with joy and pride that they could not bear the street and were not fit to be seen there. I was an author at twenty-one.

But I still had to earn a living. And I had to fight within me the rejection by Maria Beadnell. The discipline of severe newspaper work proved to be a wholesome training and I was determined that I would never end up in the Marshalsea. I assisted on the Mirror of Parliament and had been especially pleased to be asked for on one occasion by the Chief Secretary for Ireland, Edward Smith-Stanley (later 14th Earl of Derby) to transcribe one of his lengthy speeches, as he had found my reporting to be of the highest order. In the months of 1834, I wrote a further eight stories for the Monthly Magazine; comic tales for which I was not paid, but which I was convinced would lead me on to greater things. I considered a further series of sketches and even a proposed novel, and in August 1834 began to use the name "Boz", borrowed from my brother, Augustus, as a secret way of identifying my authorship. I had been the one who had dubbed him "Moses" as a nickname in honour of Moses Primrose in "The Vicar of Wakefield"; which being facetiously pronounced through the nose, became "Boses", and being shortened, became "Boz". So Boz was a very familiar household word to me, long before I was an author and came to adopt it.

It was my wish of all things, however, to become one of the new parliamentary reporters of the "Morning Chronicle", the esteemed London daily newspaper recently purchased by a group led by the Liberal, Sir John Easthope, reorganized to espouse the Reformist and Whig cause and setting its sights on rivalling and beating The Times. I had met Thomas Beard when he worked with my father at the Morning Herald and he was now working for the Morning Chronicle, from their offices at 332 Strand opposite Somerset House, and after much persuading, finally in August 1834, at the age of twenty-two, I proudly became one of their reporters. I came under the direction of their pioneering editor, John Black, and am pleased to report that he soon became my first hearty out-and-out appreciator. He was a Scotsman with the broadest of accents and of heart as ever I knew, and I flung myself wholeheartedly and with relish into the services of his newspaper. I was employed at a salary of five guineas a week (the "Fleet-Street minimum") as one of their twelve parliamentary reporters, but John Black was good enough to ensure that not only did I work in Parliament but that I did not get stifled by tedious office work, and was instrumental in sending me out and about to all parts of the nation and opened to me a wide and varied range of experiences.

I saw the last of the old coaching days and of the old inns that were a part of them, and there never was anybody connected with newspapers who, in the same space of time, had so much express and post-chaise experience as I. And what gentlemen they were to serve, in such things, at the old Morning Chronicle! Great or small, it did not matter. I have had to charge for half-a-dozen breakdowns in half-a-dozen times as many miles. I have had to charge for the damage of a greatcoat from the drippings of a blazing wax candle, in writing through the smallest hours of the night in a swift-flying carriage and pair. I have had to charge for all sorts of breakages fifty times on a journey without question, such being the ordinary results of the pace which we went at. I have charged for broken hats, broken luggage, broken chaises, broken harness – everything but a broken head, which is the only thing they would have grumbled to pay for.

Returning home at speed from exciting political meetings in the country to the waiting press in London, I do verily believe I have been upset in almost every description of vehicle known in this country. I have been, in my time, belated on miry by-roads, towards the small hours, forty or fifty miles from London in a wheel-less carriage with exhausted horses and drunken post boys, and have got back in time for publication, beating The Times in the process; I have worn my knees by writing on them having squeezed into the back row of the old gallery of the old House of Commons (before it burnt to the ground in October

1834) and have worn my feet by standing to write in a preposterous pen in the old House of Lords, where we used to huddle together like so many sheep – kept in waiting until the woolsack might want re-stuffing. There were some eighty or ninety reporters in the gallery and I was proud to rise to the highest rank, not merely for accuracy in reporting, but for the quickness in transcribing. The experience became so embedded within me that later, whenever sitting in a hall or elsewhere hearing a dull speech (the phenomenon does occur), I sometimes beguile the tedium of the moment by mentally following the speaker in the old, old way; and sometimes, if you can believe me, I even find my hand going on the tablecloth, taking an imaginary note of it all.

As well as the stories for the Monthly Magazine, I also now began writing sketches for the Morning Chronicle. Then my father was once again arrested for debt – at the behest of Shaw and Maxwell, wine merchants of 16 Woburn Place, on this occasion – and taken to Sloman's Detention House at 4 Cursitor Street, in the vicinity of Chancery Lane. I went and bailed him out, though I had to borrow money from my friends Beard and Mitton to do so and felt able to incorporate events at Sloman's into a story for the Monthly Magazine entitled "A Passage in the Life of Mr. Watkins Tottle".

The "Evening Chronicle" then arose as an evening off-shoot to the Morning Chronicle, and was placed under the guidance of Mr. George Hogarth, a friend and advisor to Sir Walter Scott and fellow countryman of John Black. Mr. Hogarth asked me, as a favour to himself, to write an original sketch for the first number of the enterprise. I begged to ask whether it was probable if I commenced a regular series of articles under some attractive title for the Evening Chronicle, its conductors would think I had any claim to some additional remuneration for so doing. The request was thought fair; I began the sketches, "Scenes of London", and my salary was raised from five to seven guineas a week. At the end of the year, with my father once again "taking to the winds" to avoid creditors and causing the break-up of the Bentick Street establishment, I rented three unfurnished back rooms (together with a cellar and lumber room) on my own account in the 3rd floor chambers at 13 Furnival's Inn for £35 per year and into that somewhat melancholy stronghold I now moved with my brother, Frederick.

My life was brightened by the kindness of George Hogarth, who not only published my "Sketches by Boz" in the Evening Chronicle but also invited me to his family home at 18 York Place, just off the Fulham Road. He had been the music and drama critic of the Morning Chronicle before taking over the editorship of the Evening Chronicle; musical evenings at his home with his large family were a delight and I became a frequent visitor. I became well acquainted with his three daughters: Catherine, aged nineteen, who was usually known as "Kate"; Mary, fourteen; and Georgina, seven, and I remember on one occasion going to the house and taking with me a sailor's uniform. I saw that the family were sitting quietly in their drawing room so I put on the outfit with the hat pulled well down over my face and jumped in at the window. I then danced a hornpipe, whistling the tune to the startled audience before jumping out again. I hid around the corner, discarded the uniform and a few minutes later walked gravely in at the door and shook hands all round as if I had just arrived. I was not able to look long at their puzzled faces before the laughter took over.

For my twenty-third birthday, I held a party at my Furnival's Inn chambers. It was a jolly affair and I know that Kate, in particular, enjoyed herself very much. I had by now become very attached to the Hogarth girls, and they to me. In due course Mary gave me a silver inkwell that I treasured, and Georgina was to give me unswerving companionship throughout my whole life. Just three months after my birthday, I announced my engagement to Kate amid much celebration and took additional lodgings at 11 Selwood Terrace near the Hogarth's home for the convenience of being nearby. At the same time, I was delighted with the enthusiastic reception my Sketches under the authorship of "Boz" were receiving in the Evening Chronicle, and began contemplating seriously how I might fulfil my desire to have a novel published. I know it was my powers of observation and the ability to transcribe this to writing that received most praise, and I was anxious to extend this as far as I could before the public. I was, however, working long hours as a parliamentary reporter, writing far into the night in order to meet deadlines, and the torture from the old spasms in my side reappeared. I was relieved by medication that I obtained from Francis Beard (Thomas's brother), who was studying to become a doctor.

In June 1835, I was approached by Vincent Dowling, the editor of the magazine "Bell's Life in London", a weekly publication that exceeded all others in popularity. He wanted me to write my sketches instead for his magazine and notably was prepared to offer me more money than the Evening Chronicle; he further proposed that I appear on the front page of his publication. It was an offer I could not refuse given my financial circumstances, and George Hogarth came to understand this, but I did use the pseudonym of "Tibbs" (taken from a character in my sketch "The Boarding House") rather than "Boz".

Then I was invited to an evening (one of many) at the house of the author, Harrison Ainsworth, at Kensal Lodge, Harrow Road near Willesden, where he introduced me to many persons, including John Forster (who was to become a special lifelong friend), the artists Daniel Maclise and George Cruikshank, and a young publisher named John Macrone. Macrone and I walked together back to Furnival's Inn at the end of that first evening (I found he also lived there then) and he told me he had the desire to reprint my sketches and stories in volume form, to be coupled with picture cuts provided by George Cruikshank. Macrone said he was prepared to offer me a conditional payment of £100 for the privilege of my copyright and, as a result, I began in excited earnest the task of collecting together and editing my writings from all the published sources for collective reprint in this form. I had by now written so many that, with some new additions for increased remuneration, I was later able to fill two volumes. I wrote a preface and, on the 7th February 1836, my twenty-fourth birthday, the first editions of the first volume appeared under the title: "Sketches by Boz, Illustrative of Everyday Life and Everyday People". I sent Forster a copy to emphasize my desire to cultivate the friendship that had already arisen between us. The general reviews of the Sketches were excellent and the hearty praise I received quashed any nervousness I had had in venturing alone before the public. They were greatly talked about and I was enthusiastically launched on a high tide into my next voyage.

CHAPTER IV

The Pickwick Papers

On the 10th February, only three days after publication of the first volume of Sketches by Boz, William Hall called on me at my chambers in Furnival's Inn. I instantly recognized him as the young man from the shop in the Strand where I had purchased my copy of the December 1833 edition of the Monthly Magazine containing my first published story. I told him of the coincidence, which we both hailed as a good omen, and so fell to business. I found that he had lately joined with Edward Chapman as partners in a publishing venture based at 186 Strand, under the title "Chapman and Hall"; he told me that they had produced a little book called "The Squib Annual of Poetry, Politics and Personalities" to show up the cartoons of the well-known artist Robert Seymour to their best effect and had met with success, and now wished to run a monthly publication of a similar kind to sell for a shilling a time.

The idea propounded to me was that this monthly should be a vehicle for certain plates to be executed by Mr. Seymour; and there was a notion, either on the part of that admirable humorous artist, or of my visitor, that a "Nimrod Club", the members of which were to be Cockney sportsmen who would go out shooting, fishing and so forth, and getting themselves into difficulties through their want of dexterity, would be the best means of introducing these. I objected, on consideration that, although born and partly bred in the country, I was no great sportsman, except in regard to all kinds of locomotion; that the idea was not novel and had already been much used; that it would be infinitely better for the plates to arise naturally out of the text; and that I would like to take my own way, with a freer range of English scenes and people, and was afraid I should ultimately do so in any case, whatever course I might prescribe to myself at starting.

After deliberations, my views were deferred to and this course was agreed. I was to produce sufficient material to form twenty-four printed pages (approximately twelve thousand words) each month and receive in return £14 for each production. I told Kate what had been agreed and that although the work would be no joke, the emolument was too tempting to resist. We were planning to marry in early April and had already begun buying furniture for our home together. As soon as matters were agreed with Chapman and Hall, I moved to some better, sunnier and larger rooms facing south, at 15 Furnival's Inn, at £50 a year, and there on the 18th February 1836, with "The first ray of light which illumines the gloom", I started on my first novel. I had mused on the central character and about his name and had been amused by the name of a coach proprietor in Bath that I had come to know called Moses Pickwick. I elected to use this surname for my purposes and began to write the first number. I connected Mr. Pickwick (now christened Samuel by me) with a club because of the original suggestion, and put in the sporting Mr. Winkle expressly for the use of Mr. Seymour, who had been contracted to provide four drawings for each chapter. Mr. Seymour made his drawing of the club and his portrait of its founder from the first proof sheets I delivered to Chapman and Hall. I later learnt that his first sketch of Pickwick was of a long, thin man but, upon the intervention of Chapman, he changed it. Chapman described to him a friend at Richmond, a fat old beau who would wear, in spite of the ladies' protests, drab tights and black gaiters. His name was John Foster and he became the figure by which all came to see as Mr. Pickwick.

I had agreed I would provide the first part by the beginning of March and the second by the end of the same month, so there was much to do; the ability to use my own free range of imagination, however, was a delight to me and I became imbued with the feeling of joy and freedom that it brought. The first instalment I produced and delivered and immediately set about the next. When it became clear that the deadline would be met for this, Chapman and Hall arranged for a notice to be posted in The Times which, on the 26th March 1836, announced that on the 31st would be published the first shilling number of "The Posthumous Papers of the Pickwick Club, edited by Boz".

And so it came about that the first monthly instalment was published. There were twenty-four pages of print, and Seymour provided four drawings. It was bound with covers of light green, priced at one shilling, and had the full title: "The Posthumous Papers of the Pickwick Club, containing a faithful record of the Perambulations, Perils,

Travels, Adventures and Sporting Transactions of the Corresponding Members", and stated to be "Edited by Boz". I understand that, in hopeful anticipation, some 400 were printed for distribution by Chapman and Hall.

Meanwhile, as Kate was a minor, I had arranged for another notice through Doctors Commons to be placed in The Times and a few days later it announced: "On the 2nd April, Mr. Charles Dickens married Catherine, the eldest daughter of Mr. George Hogarth". It was a quiet affair at St. Luke's Church in Sydney Street, Chelsea (the newly erected church to serve the parish in which the Hogarths lived) and was attended by our two families, together with Thomas Beard, my best man, John Macrone and Henry Burnett, my sister Fanny's intended. We had a wedding breakfast at the Hogarth house and then Kate and I set off on honeymoon to a small cottage owned by Mrs. Nash in the quiet little village of Chalk on the road between Gravesend and Rochester. The letting of this cottage was kindly arranged for me by Mrs. Newnham, our neighbour from the time at Ordnance Terrace. We stayed at Chalk for just under a fortnight before returning to Furnival's Inn – now transformed by female attention and some great bargains I had acquired – where I set to work again in earnest on Pickwick. Mary, Kate's sister, stayed with us for a month on our return.

On the 18th April I had my one and only meeting with the artist, Mr. Seymour. At my invitation this troubled man came to Furnival's Inn with Hall to discuss the drawings for the next issue. I made some suggestions as to how he might alter one of his illustrations for the "Stroller's Tale" in that number and he seemed content as he left to do the further touches that were required. Those he did, working late into the following night. I then received the terrible news that the next day he used his own gun upon himself in the summerhouse of his garden. He was a talented, though melancholy, man but I always held his work in high regard and was deeply saddened to hear of his death. However, it provided us with a real dilemma. A visit to his workroom revealed only three engravings for his drawings and these we were able to use for the second instalment, but I was already well into the third and illustrations were urgently required. I recalled Robert William Buss, with whom I had been acquainted in the past, and he was approached.

He agreed to take on the task and did so for the third instalment but he was inexperienced in the art of etching that was required for the printing process and a further replacement was sought. In the meanwhile, I had agreed with Chapman and Hall that the proposal should become one of thirty-two pages from me for £18, with only two illustrations per month.

For the fourth instalment others, including William Makepeace Thackeray and John Leech had applied as illustrator, but I approached another known to me, Hablot Knight Browne. He was a shy person, slightly younger than myself, and not yet sure of the path he was to follow, but he had been an engraver's apprentice and I was impressed with his talents, particularly his abilities at caricature drawing. I explained my purpose to him and how I would guide him and felt he would be steadfast in the enterprise I was now engaged upon. Chapman and Hall readily agreed to my choice and Browne was employed. I suggested to him that he might adopt a name to accord with my use of "Boz", and "Phiz" was agreed and under this guise he was to illustrate for me. He proved to be an inspirational choice.

The success of the Sketches and the beginnings of Pickwick had spurred me on to further ventures. My sister Fanny's connections with music inspired me to write a comic operetta called "The Village Coquettes" in conjunction with John Hullah (one of her friends from the Royal Academy of Music) and based on one of my own stories written for the purpose. I turned another of my stories – "The Great Winglebury Duel" – into a stage farce entitled "The Strange Gentleman". Both of these were performed before the year's end for Mr. Braham's enterprise at the new St. James's Theatre; at the conclusion of the first-night performance of "The Village Coquettes" the audience screamed so loudly for "Boz" that I eventually had to take the unusual step of going up on stage to take their acknowledgement. I also wrote a Treaty entitled "Sunday under Three Heads" against the Sunday Observance Bill (sponsored by Sir Andrew Agnew MP) as a protest towards the restrictions being proposed by rich people against the amusements and recreations of the poor on Sundays, although I had it published by Chapman and Hall under the name of "Timothy Sparkes". Illustrations for it were done by Hablot Knight Browne, and it was this that had caused me to consider him for the illustrating role in Pickwick.

In May, Macrone got my agreement to produce, when I was able, an historical novel under the title "Gabriel Vardon, the Locksmith of London" for the payment of £200, only to be paid however on delivery of the entire manuscript. In August, by which time the true identity of "Boz" had been revealed, another publisher, Thomas Tegg, agreed to pay me £100 if I would write a children's Christmas book to be entitled "Solomon Bell, the Raree Showman" or something similar. By now I had introduced Sam Weller into Pickwick and the prospects of a lengthy and successful run with this project seemed firmly based, though where or how it was to end was as little known to myself at this time as to any of my readers, my plan simply being to amuse the reader for as long as I was able.

Then, through George Hogarth, I was approached by a further publisher, Mr. Richard Bentley – a short, pink-faced Jewish man with huge whiskers, of 8 New Burlington Street – and on the 22nd August 1836, on the eve of the issue of the sixth number of Pickwick, signed an agreement with him to produce two novels for £500 each; followed by a further agreement in November to undertake the editorship of a monthly magazine that he proposed to start the following January and to which I was to supply every month an original article of my own writing. I signed with alacrity, perhaps not giving sufficient consideration to the terms and conditions that Bentley in particular had put forward, such was my youthful and inexperienced eagerness to proceed. That summer, Kate and I took a country cottage belonging to Mrs. Denman at Petersham, a beautiful place near Richmond with extensive garden grounds enabling much athletic competition, particularly with Maclise and Beard. I was also able to continued writing "Pickwick", before returning to town to finalize the second volume of Sketches to be published by Macrone, and to continue with my reporting for the Morning Chronicle.

By November I decided that I should leave the Morning Chronicle to concentrate upon my own affairs and prospects that were opening up before me. I was greatly honoured when my colleagues presented me with a silver goblet on my departure, but I had come to hate the falseness of talk and the bombastic eloquence of Parliament, that Great Dustheap of Westminster, and was pleased to visit it no more. The body of the House and the side galleries would be full of Members, some with their legs on the back of the opposite seat, some with theirs stretched out to the utmost length on the floor; some going out, others coming in – all talking, laughing, lounging, coughing, oh-ing, questioning or groaning – and presenting a conglomeration of noise and confusion; to be met with in no other place in existence, not even excepting Smithfield on market day or a cock-pit in its glory. It may be from some imperfect development of my organ of veneration, but I do not remember having ever fainted away, or having even been moved to tears of joyful pride, at the sight of either our own or any other legislative body. I have borne the House of Commons like a man, and have yielded to no weakness, but slumber, in the House of Lords. I have seen elections for borough and county, and have never been impelled (no matter which party won) to damage my hat by throwing it up into the air in triumph, or to crack my voice by shouting forth any reference to our glorious constitution, to the noble purity of our independent voters, or the unimpeachable integrity of our independent masters. Having withstood such strong attacks upon my fortitude, it is possible that I may be of a cold and insensible temperament, amounting to iciness in such matters, but I had had enough of it. Furthermore, I had been writing late in the night and into the early hours of the morning around my parliamentary duties and had experienced severe headaches and a form of rheumatism in the face sufficient to cause me concern. Nevertheless, I was pleased I had left the reputation behind me of being the best and most rapid reporter ever known, and that I could do anything in that way under any sort of circumstance – and often did; I dare say it enabled me to become the best short-hand writer in the world.

The beginning of 1837 saw me commence work as editor of Mr. Bentley's magazine – originally titled "The Wits' Miscellany", but now thankfully re-titled "Bentley's Miscellany" – together with an altered requirement upon me to produce a new serial story for each monthly edition. At the same time was born, in Furnival's Inn, our first child, Charles Culliford Boz Dickens. "Culliford" was a name from my mother's family; the inclusion of the name "Boz" was not initially intended but my father, somewhat inebriated beside the font, called out the name and the cleric included it and it remained thereafter. For our part, however, we usually called him "Charley".

Following Charley's birth on the 6th January, I was concerned over Kate who fell into severe depression. She reached a very low and alarming state and I was obliged to be constantly with her, being the only person who could prevail upon her to take ordinary nourishment. I remember, too, that I had a heavy cold and violent headaches at this time, and was taking about as much medicine as would be given to an ordinary sized horse to confine him to his stall for a week. We also had my mother and Kate's mother staying with us during this chaotic period, but through it all a wondrous ray of sunshine shone, with the visits to Furnival's Inn of Kate's sister, Mary. She came again and again to keep home for me and brought with her such an intoxicating air of joy and happiness that she became the grace and life of our home.

As 1837 progressed, I became more troubled about Kate's health. She did not appear to improve and, despite my busy schedule, I decided that we should have a change of scenery from London for a while. I knew she had been happy at Mrs. Nash's cottage in Chalk so she and I, together with baby Charley and her sister, Mary, left for another stay in the Kent countryside. There I continued my work, travelling to London when necessary, including supervising rehearsals at the St. James's Theatre for a new comic burletta I had written entitled "Is She His Wife?" I also contemplated a move from the accommodation that had by now become too cramped for us at Furnival's Inn.

I searched and found a house to rent at £80 per annum in Bloomsbury, at 48 Doughty Street. It was in an elegant private road with gates at either end that were supervised by porters resplendent in dark red uniforms with buttons sporting the arms of the Doughty family and topped off with gold laced hats. I arranged that we move during the weekend of our first wedding anniversary of the 2nd April, and a reinvigorated Kate appeared delighted. My brother, Fred, came to live with us and Mary Hogarth agreed to stay as often as possible. I regarded it as a first-class family mansion – but involving awful responsibilities, as I had to borrow money from Bentley to furnish it out and keep a cook, a housemaid and a nurse in employ. But I had a first-floor study overlooking our small rear garden and there I continued to write in more pleasing surroundings.

On 8th April, Chapman and Hall organized a grand celebration dinner at "The George and Vulture" Tavern in George Yard, Lombard

Street to honour the success of Pickwick. It was the most convivial of evenings, full of fun and hilarity. I was delighted to be elected a member of the Garrick Club and then on the 3rd May, at the Literary Fund Dinner, I made my first public speech, where I was toasted with long-continued cheering. It was indeed an exhilarating time.

That exhilaration, however, lasted just three more days. On the evening of the 6th May, Kate, Mary and I went to see a performance of "Is She His Wife?" and eventually returned to Doughty Street at about 1 a.m. Mary said "goodnight" and made her way upstairs to the back room we had set aside for her. She appeared to be in perfect health and in her usual delighted spirits. I heard her go into her room and close the door but almost immediately there was a strange choking cry and the sound of her falling to the floor. I rushed up with Kate to find her collapsed, still in her evening clothes. We got her to bed and called a doctor and her mother, whilst one of us stayed with her throughout. Her mother became hysterical and had to be forcibly removed from the room. The doctor believed she had suffered a heart failure and that her heart had been diseased for a length of time. We continued to nurse her, praying for a recovery through the morning and early afternoon; no danger apprehended until she sank beneath the attack and at about 3 o'clock, as I nursed her on that dreadful Sunday afternoon, she died in my arms – died in such a calm and gentle sleep that, although I had held her in my arms for some time before, when she was certainly living (for she swallowed a little brandy from my hand), I continued to support her lifeless form long after her soul had fled to Heaven.

The sense of grief and loss was the most intense I have ever experienced. She was just 17 years of age but in the brief time that I had known her she had transformed my life into one of intense happiness. The very last words she whispered were of me and now she was gone. Young, beautiful and good, God in his mercy numbered her with his angels. She had not a fault and her passing left an aching chasm in my heart. I took a lock from her hair and kept it, and a ring from her finger that I put on mine so that I might have something from her with me for evermore. And then that one, appalling, never to be forgotten, knock of the undertaker upon the door and the sight of the coffin going up to her room is an experience I shall never ever forget. She lay in the coffin in the bedroom for six days before we buried her in the new cemetery at Kensal Green and, as that happened, I could feel within me an overwhelming desire to be buried in the same grave with her.

After she died, I dreamed of Mary every night for the better part of a year, sometimes as a spirit, sometimes as a living creature, and I never laid down at night without a hope of her vision coming back to me in one shape or another. And then it did. I was in Yorkshire at the time, and finding her presence there, in a strange scene and a strange bed, I could not help mentioning the circumstance in a note I wrote home to Kate thereafter. From that moment, however, I have not dreamed of her again, save once, though the undiminished love of her remains so much in my thoughts.

During this anguish, Kate had a miscarriage, and in the midst of her own affliction, had to soothe the sufferings of her bereaved mother who, having seen her child expire, then remained in a state of total insensibility for a week afterwards and had to be kept by force from the room where poor Mary lay in her coffin. I experienced the same violent pain in my side that I had had in the blacking factory and felt totally unable to write. I took Kate away to Collins's Farm in Hampstead for a fortnight of retreat from our immediate surroundings and to allow the first anguishes of grief to pass. Forster, in his kindness, came to visit us and confirmed to me that, in him, I had indeed found a true friend. In the second week, I did decide to return to Doughty Street on a daily basis and also began to regularly visit the Chapel of the Foundling Hospital in Coram Street nearby to seek solace in prayer, but I cannot erase the memory of Mary and I can still recall everything we said and did in those times we spent together.

And then a literary bombshell struck. I heard from the binder of Pickwick that Macrone intended publishing a new issue of my Sketches in monthly parts of nearly the same size and in just the same form as Pickwick. This was clearly an intention by Macrone to foist old work upon the public in new dress without my sanction and for added profit to himself, all at the expense of my new-found reputation with the success of Pickwick. I took the view that it was calculated to injure me most seriously and immediately wrote to Forster, begging him to see Macrone and to state in the strongest and most emphatic manner my feelings on the point and request Macrone to desist from such a notion.

Forster reported back to me that he had seen Macrone and found him inaccessible to all arguments of persuasion. He had, as a result, broached the subject of repurchase of the copyright, unsold print and the 28 copper plates produced for Cruikshank's illustrations from Macrone, who then stated he wished in total £2,250 if he was to take such a course. Forster strongly counselled me to keep quiet for a time and let matters be, but the worry and the vexation was too great with all the work I had in hand and the very next day I agreed to go along with Macrone's avariciousness to rid myself of the intolerable suspense that hung over me. Chapman and Hall too had met with Macrone, but after a long discussion he peremptorily refused to take one farthing less than this stated sum. Hall, whose judgment may be relied upon in such matters, told me he could not dispute the justice of the calculation and I eventually was forced to agree to Chapman and Hall's considered proposal that we should purchase the copyright, plates and unsold print between us for such sum and Chapman and Hall then publish the Sketches in monthly parts to repay the expenditure, whilst I wrote an address explaining that we had been driven into that mode of publication or the copyright would have been lost.

The sensitive handling of publication of the "Sketches" ensured the continuing and ever-increasing success of Pickwick. Advertisements were introduced into the front of the issues that began as references to other books but expanded into all manner of items – clothing, grooming oils and potions of all kinds – so much so that the popularity of the text drew more pages of advertisements than the text itself. Word spread about the various perambulations of the members of the Pickwick Club and soon all from the highest in the land to very poorest were enjoying my stories. Judges on the Bench and boys in the street, gravity and folly, the young and the old, those who were entering life and those who were quitting it, found it to be irresistible. It was of particular delight to me when, close to the conclusion of Pickwick, Mr. William Giles, my former tutor in Chatham, sent me a silver snuff box engraved with delicate inscription to "The Inimitable Boz".

I saw Pickwick hats, coats, cigars and the like appearing on sale everywhere; china figurines, Sam Weller corduroys and Wellerism jest books, tradesmen of all description recommending their goods by using the names therefrom. Performances and adaptations were pirated for the stage and plagiarism abounded everywhere. So great became the craze for the Pickwick issues that they came to secure far more attention than was given even to the ordinary politics of the day. Chapman and Hall were constantly increasing the numbers printed, thereby allowing them to provide me with added remuneration (I eventually received a total of £2,000 for the completed work), and shops were besieged when the new monthly issues arrived. By the time I concluded Pickwick with the issue of the twentieth part in November 1837, Chapman and Hall were publishing in excess of 40,000 copies of each issue, thereby outstripping all the most famous books of the century, and making the names of "Boz" and "Charles Dickens" known throughout the land and beyond the seas. It was said that there did not appear to be a place where English was spoken to which "The Inimitable Boz" had not penetrated. And yet I knew in my mind, as we celebrated its triumphant conclusion at a wonderful banquet at the Prince of Wales Tavern in Leicester Square, that Pickwick was just the beginning of what I intended to do.

CHAPTER V

Oliver Twist and Nicholas Nickleby

As editor of "Bentley's Miscellany", I had circulated a prospectus for contributors and became inundated with articles from people believing they had literary talent, nearly all of it the most appalling nonsense I ever had the ill-fortune to peruse. Eventually however, through extreme diligence and long hours, the show of names became excellent, but Bentley had also required me to furnish an original article of my own writing for every monthly number, with illustrations by George Cruikshank.

For this I turned back to Chatham and began a series of comic sketches from that place, disguised under the name of "Mudfog". But my secret thoughts also constantly drove me back to my childhood and the private hell I had endured through feelings of being helplessly trapped in a world of poverty. I had witnessed in Parliament the passing of the Poor Law Amendment Act in 1834 which established "The New Poor Law", comprising the abolition of outdoor relief for the destitute and substituting instead a system that required all who now wished to receive benefits to enter into a workhouse. I had had many debates and quarrels with John Black at the Morning Chronicle over this; to my mind, such a system was oppressive in the extreme. Furthermore, the way it operated decimated families and sought to reinforce the view that poverty was a crime and that those who partook in such activity should be imprisoned in institutions – institutions moreover that should be made, by their administration, as uninviting as possible in order to discourage all but the most desperate to enter therein.

I now vowed that I would take on and bring to a wider audience the iniquities of such a system, for I was determined that in my life I would pursue cruelty and oppression so long as I had the energy of thought and the power of giving it utterance. It is also in my nature that I never can write with effect, especially in a serious way, until I have got my steam up – until I have become so excited with my subject that I cannot leave off – and this is how I now became. My own circumstance at home, with the birth of Charley, turned my thoughts to viewing such a system through the eyes of a child – and so was born, in the workhouse, Oliver Twist.

I took a great fancy to Oliver, hoped he would deserve it, and resolved to run with him from the second edition of the Miscellany. I felt I had now hit on a capital notion for my own contribution, as well as one which would bring Cruikshank out, and Bentley agreed, so the requirement on me was altered to the production of this as a serial story for each monthly edition. I was so pleased that I signed a further agreement with Bentley, extending my period of editorship of the Miscellany to five years, and furthermore suggesting to him that I might write the "Gabriel Varden" story for him – although under an altered title – as I no longer trusted Macrone.

However, the moment this further agreement had been put in place, Bentley then took it upon himself to make alterations to the contents of the Miscellany without my authorization which, in my opinion, very greatly injured it. I became highly irritated by his actions and determined to make a stand upon my editorial rights. I then had to deal with the devastation caused by the death of Mary Hogarth, and in doing so felt the greatest comfort in being able to turn to friends for assistance, none more so than Forster. He had helped me deal with Macrone and I now asked for his assistance in coping with Bentley. He agreed readily and asked for details of the documents I had signed. When I looked at them carefully I was very much surprised at my doing business in this way, for in most matters of labour and application I am punctuality itself but, in the bad terms that I now saw, I feared that in my desire to avoid present vexations, I had laid up a bitter store for myself for the future. I sent Forster the documents and felt the need to be away for a short period of time to turn matters over in my mind.

I hit on the notion of foreign travel, something I had not engaged in before, and took Kate and Browne to Calais, where we stayed at the Hotel Rignolle. On the afternoon of our first day we went in an open barouche to some gardens, where people danced and were footing it most heartily – especially the women who, in their short petticoats and light caps, looked uncommonly agreeable. A gentleman in elegant attire accompanied us from the hotel and acted as curator; he even waltzed with a very smart lady just to show us, condescendingly, how it ought to be done, and waltzed elegantly too. Imagine our surprise when we rang for slippers after we came back to the hotel and found out that this gentleman was "the Boots"!

That evening I wrote to Bentley, pointing out to him that he had often told me that it was his anxious desire to treat me "with the utmost liberality" and I hoped he would be good to his word. I arranged for further travel by post-coach to Ghent, Brussels, Antwerp and a hundred other places that I cannot recollect now, and could not spell if I did. It proved to be a most agreeable interlude, but it also gave me time to think how others now appeared to have taken advantage of my considerable business inexperience.

Upon my return home, I set down to work in earnest again as I was so terribly behindhand, and spoke again with Forster, towards whom I now felt this special affinity. He was living in some style at 58 Lincoln's Inn Fields and worked as sub-editor at "The Examiner" newspaper. I decided to send him copies of the Miscellany – not as a matter of business, or with any view of notices thereof, but because (as I told him) I should really be greatly disappointed if I now wrote anything in the future which he had not had an early opportunity of reading and commenting upon. I realized this may have looked like vanity, but I did not mean it so; I valued his opinion and assessment in the highest degree and was delighted when he agreed upon this course.

In my next number of Oliver, I felt I must have a Magistrate, and casting about for one whose harshness and insolence would render him a fit subject to be shown up, I alighted upon Mr. Laing of Hatton Garden celebrity. I knew of his character perfectly well beforehand but I had never seen him and felt the necessity to do so in order to describe his appearance in the forthcoming narrative. So I wrote to Thomas Haines, a well-respected police reporter, asking him if I could, under his auspices, be smuggled into the Hatton Garden office for a few moments one morning. This was duly arranged and thereafter I was able to reliably incorporate 'Mr. Fang' into the life of Oliver Twist. Not long after publication, upon a fresh outbreak of intolerable temper, the Home Secretary found it an easy (and popular) step to remove Mr. Laing from the Bench.

I wrote again to Bentley, proposing that Oliver Twist should now be regarded as one of the novels set down in our agreements, as a fair and reasonable way forward in a difficult situation. Bentley, however, visited me at Doughty Street, threatening legal action and in little mood to compromise. He flatly rejected considering Oliver Twist as a novel under these terms and I became substantially irritated at his attitude. I told him that if he persisted in such a stance I would not write any novel for him at all, but before he left I said I would propose to refer the matter to the arbitration of Mr. Serjeant Talfourd as a means of resolution. He was a Serjeant-at-Law and Member of Parliament who, a few months earlier, had introduced the Copyright Bill into Parliament; I had met him shortly before my meeting with Bentley and had been highly impressed, as well as discovering that he was a hearty out-and-out supporter of Mr. Pickwick. Bentley, however, as a colourable proceeding to my mind and to gain time, told me he would merely wish a friend of mine to meet a friend of his to discuss matters. In the circumstances I felt I should concede to this, and asked Thomas Beard to undertake this task for me.

Beard agreed and went to Burlington Street, but I was very much surprised to hear from him that the disinterested, unprejudiced, private friend that Bentley had selected with so much care was none other than his own solicitor! I regarded this as an act of bad faith by Bentley and a gross breach of a distinct undertaking between us for this meeting. I declined to have any further direct dealings with him, and told him that any further correspondence should be through a third party.

The strain of these dealings did nothing for my well-being, so I took the family to the delightful Kentish seaside village of Broadstairs, where we rented 12, High Street, a short walk from the sea. I had an attack of illness soon after we arrived, but the sea air brought about a speedier recovery than might otherwise have been the case and I remember walking alone upon the sands at low-water to Ramsgate and sitting there at high tide until flayed with the cold, watching stout gentlemen looking at nothing through powerful telescopes for hours, until at last seeing a cloud of smoke and fancying a steamer behind it, they would go home comfortable and happy.

The Brigand of Burlington Street, however, continued to make his avaricious demands and I became determined not to give way. I declined to write further on Oliver, nor to contribute in any way to the Miscellany, due to his serious interference with my office as editor and his manner, that I regarded as being in direct violation of our agreement and a gross insult to me. The non-appearance of the next monthly edition of Oliver eventually forced Bentley to reconsider his stance and, with the assistance of Forster and solicitors, a form of compromise was concluded at the end of September – which allowed me to continue on as editor without interference and to resume Oliver in the Miscellany, with the production of a new novel postponed until November of the following year. Forster and I were aware that Chapman and Hall would also be wanting a serial story to follow on from Pickwick and Forster doubted the wisdom of all this workload upon me, but I felt I could do no more in the circumstances than to accept the arrangement for the time being and press on with my writing that had been so sorely interrupted by events.

Before beginning again with Oliver, I re-read all the parts and now felt I could do great things with Nancy. I sought to work out the idea of her, together with another female (Rose Maylie) in contrast, and felt reinvigorated. I wrote the next chapter in a single day and went to Brighton with Kate for a week of sea-air, engaging there with Defoe's "Political History of the Devil" to assist in bringing out the true character of Fagin. Oliver became part of my life again.

As my relations with Bentley now appeared to be on a more satisfactory footing, I agreed to edit for him the life of Grimaldi, the celebrated clown. A manuscript had been prepared by a Mr. Egerton Wilks from Grimaldi's autobiographical notes, but when I saw the mass of material that Wilks had raked together, my most charitable description of it was "twaddle". I worked manfully upon it at Doughty Street, assisted by my father, who dictated to me some modifications and additions, but apart from this my only contribution was the preface. Nevertheless, by the end of the first week of publication, seventeen hundred "Grimaldi's" had already been sold and the demand was increasing daily!

Into 1838, I continued on apace with Oliver, but all the while was also turning over in my mind the new work I had to begin for Chapman and Hall, the first instalment of which was due to be delivered to them by the 15th March. What had taken my interest for a considerable period was a law case, reported in The Times in 1832, against a Mr. Shaw of Bowes

Academy in Yorkshire for gross neglect and starvation leading to blindness of boys entrusted to his care. There had been subsequent commentary in The Times that revealed how barbaric cruelties were being committed on many children in particular in Yorkshire, at so-called "Cheap Schools" within that county, and I resolved to go in secret to see for myself.

I took Browne with me on my pilgrimage, having consulted with Tom Mitton's partner, Smithson (he had a Yorkshire connection), who agreed to construct a pious fraud for me. He gave me some letters of introduction, making out that they were from a widowed mother who had a little boy and I was their friend. She did not know what to do with her boy and thought of sending him to a Yorkshire school – so, as her friend was travelling that way, could he be informed of a school in the neighbourhood that would be suitable? I took these letters with me as we travelled, in very severe winter weather, via Grantham, to Greta Bridge in Yorkshire.

We only needed a couple of days to confirm the realities of the situation. We met, at Grantham, a mistress of a Yorkshire school returning from a holiday-stay in London who was a very queer old body, and who showed us a long letter she was carrying to one of the boys from his father, containing a severe lecture (enforced and aided by many texts from scripture) on the boy refusing to eat boiled meat. She was very communicative, the more so as she drank a great deal of brandy and water, although towards the evening became insensible, in which state we left her.

From Greta Bridge, we travelled on by post-chaise the four miles to Barnard Castle, where I questioned every likely person I encountered in order to elicit information on these Cheap Schools and incidents of local school life. I came to believe that there were approximately twenty such schools located in this area alone, and while at Barnard Castle I met a local solicitor, Mr. Barnes, who, upon receipt of one of Smithson's letters, provided me with some introductions to these local schools. On leaving his office, I went back across to "The Kings Head" where we were staying and gazed out onto the market place from the coffee-room window therein, noticing in the process a clockmaker's shop with the name "Master Humphrey" upon it. Shortly thereafter, I saw Mr. Barnes (who was a well-fed man of business and a rough Yorkshire man) now hurriedly walking across to me and, after much hesitation and confusion, told me – with a degree of feeling one would not have given him credit for – that these schools were, in reality, sad places for mothers to send orphaned boys. I was fully intrigued when he went on to tell me that it really would be a better thing to let them run errands, hold horses or fling themselves in any way upon the mercy of the world than to consign such boys to such dens.

The next day, Browne and I travelled to the nearby village of Bowes, where no less than four of these Cheap Schools were located. We came there upon the academy of Mr. William Shaw, who was described to me in the locality variously as a saint, a devil, or someone who was merely "a bit merry with the stick". I knew, however, that he continued to advertise in The Times and also employed a London agent; a particular feature of his advertisement I noted was that his curriculum featured: "No vacations except by parents' desire" – a clear indication to me that he was seeking out boys who were unwanted by parents or guardians. Mr. Shaw himself was not particularly forthcoming or friendly during my visit, no doubt because by now my identity had been revealed to him and he feared exposure, but I did glean some information from a school usher about conditions. My concerns were reinforced when it was later confirmed in a local newspaper that several boys at his school did go blind from gross neglect.

During the afternoon of the same day, with snow lying deep on the ground, Browne and I made our way to Bowes churchyard. There was revealed to me the final confirmatory evidence that was required. We counted in all some thirty-four tombs of school children between the ages of 10 and 18 years that had perished at the hands of these Cheap Schools in that district alone, and in less time than I had been in this world. And then I found one gravestone in the snow that pierced my heart as I brushed aside the covering blanket. It read:

"Here lie the remains of GEORGE ASHTON TAYLOR, son of John Taylor of Trowbridge, Wiltshire, who died suddenly at Mr. William Shaw's Academy of this place, April 13th 1822, aged 19 years. Young reader, thou must die, but after this the judgement".

As I stood in silence and horror before that gravestone, I can reveal to you now that the ghost of that young boy put Smike into my head at that very spot.

I was now in no doubt at all that this class of school long afforded a notable example of the monstrous neglect of education in England. Any person who had proved his unfitness for any other occupation in life was free, without examination or qualification, to open a school anywhere – and although school masters, as a race, were the blockheads and imposters that might naturally be expected to arise from such a state of things and to flourish in it, these Yorkshire school masters were the lowest and most rotten round in the whole ladder. Ignorant, sordid, brutal men to whom few considerate persons would have entrusted the board and lodging of a horse or a dog, they formed the worthy corner-stone of a structure which, for absurdity and a magnificent high-handed laissez-aller neglect, has rarely been exceeded in the world.

Returning to London, I was now anxious to begin forthwith on my new work for Chapman and Hall. I had selected the name "Nicholas Nickleby" for the central character, and devised for my purpose the full title of: "The Life and Adventures of Nicholas Nickleby, Containing a Faithful Account of the Fortunes, Misfortunes, Uprisings, Downfallings and Complete Career of the Nickleby Family. Edited by Boz". On the night before my twenty-sixth birthday, I set to work and within a further two days the first chapter of Nickleby was done. However, I was now troubled in my head by the distraction that I had agreed with Bentley to produce and finish a new novel (now under the revised title of "Barnaby Rudge") by November of this year in order to mollify his avaricious demands, and I realized that Forster had, of course, been right all along to express disquiet over such an undertaking. I felt it now hanging over me like a hideous nightmare, ready to engulf me at any moment.

Accordingly, I wrote again to Bentley:

"I have recently been thinking a great deal about Barnaby Rudge. Grimaldi has occupied so much of the short interval that I had between the completion of Pickwick and the commencement of the new work, that I see it will be wholly impossible for me to produce it by the time I had hoped with justice to myself or profit to you.

What I wish you to consider is this: Would it not be far more to your interest, as well as within the scope of my ability, if Barnaby Rudge began in the Miscellany immediately on the conclusion of Oliver Twist, and were continued there for the same time and then published in three volumes?"

The Burlington Street Brigand acted like Fagin himself at this request, and it took me a further six months of wrangling and hostilities, with the assistance of Forster and Mitton, together with another refusal by me to produce a monthly part of Oliver, before he finally gave way and Barnaby was now placed on the footing desired, to begin in the Miscellany when Oliver closed.

It was during this period of time that I had become greatly interested in mesmerism – the use of induced trances to effect healing. In early January I had taken George Cruikshank to University College Hospital in Gower Street and there met Dr. John Elliotson, the Professor of Medicine, who showed us some of his patients and the benefits he was able to obtain by the use of mesmerism. I was so intrigued that not long after I made further visits, on these occasions taking Ainsworth and then Macready (the fine actor, to whom I had been introduced by Forster) with me. Having witnessed the most extraordinary powers Dr. Elliotson was able to demonstrate, I became – against all my preconceived opinions and impressions – a firm believer in this practice of mesmerism. John Elliotson became one of my most intimate and valued friends and taught me how I might develop and use these powers myself. I also took him as a family doctor, for I saw him as a good, as well as a clever man, and knew through witnessing his skill, patience and humanity that if my own life, or that of any member of my family were in peril, I would trust it to him implicitly.

On the 6th March, our second child, Mary, was born – though we came to know her as "Mamie". Three days later I finished and thereafter delivered the first full part of Nickleby to Chapman and Hall (Browne – "Phiz" – doing the illustrations) and introduced readers to Nicholas, his family, Newman Nogs, Snawley, Mr. Wackford Squeers and Dotheboys Hall "at the delightful village of Dotheboys, near Greta Bridge in Yorkshire." I had been away from town when the first number of Pickwick had come out and I decided to do the same with Nickleby, as superstition got the better of me. I took Kate to The Star and Garter Hotel in Richmond for a change of scenery, and there awaited publication at the beginning of April. It was due on Saturday the 1st, and the evening before I sent the peremptory summons to Forster: "Meet me at the Shakespeare (the club we frequented at the Piazza Coffee-House in Covent Garden) on Saturday night at eight; order your horse at midnight, and ride back with me."

Forster duly arrived at the club and, as St. Paul's sounded the smallest hour into the night, we set off on horseback. The night was not one of the pleasantest but when we arrived at Chapman and Hall's office, I received the news that lightened every part of the road – Nickleby had sold almost 50,000 copies on that day alone! We rode at speed to Richmond and The Star and Garter, drenched to the skin but happy, to celebrate later that day my second wedding anniversary, as well as Forster's birthday. Apart from the time when Kate and I were living out of England, we celebrated our wedding anniversary at the same time and place for twenty successive years.

CHAPTER VI

Oliver Twist, Nicholas Nickleby, Bentley and My Father

After Mamie's birth and delivering the first number of Nickleby to Chapman and Hall, I had to straightway turn my thoughts again to Oliver. It was no easy task and to Forster I described myself as "sitting patiently at home waiting for Oliver Twist, who has not yet arrived". I dwelt on Nancy and how I could make a contrast to her. My mind, in my moments of contemplation, was still filled with Mary Hogarth, the beautiful 17-year old who could not have been in greater contrast to Nancy, the prostitute and member of Fagin's gang. I was driven to make Rose Maylie in Mary's image, although when Rose hovered on the brink of death, I could not bring myself to allow her to die. Instead, I caused that fate to befall Nancy, but in totally differing circumstances.

Once I had located the direction for Oliver again however, it took a great hold on me. I worked long hours after dinner and late into the nights at Doughty Street, endeavouring to get well ahead of the monthly parts and hoping, perhaps, to complete it before October, although its close in the Miscellany was not due until the following March. In June, I took the family to Twickenham Park (at 4, Ailsa Park Villas), a quiet country retreat close to the River Thames, which gave Kate and I a beneficial change of scenery, as well as allowing me to entertain friends in the most pleasant of surroundings. We did however, venture into town on the 28th June to witness the Coronation Procession of the new Queen and I contributed an article to Forster's Examiner about the roisterous beer drinking at the Fair in Hyde Park in honour of the occasion. Social invitations grew in number. I was elected to the Athenaeum Club, and in August Talfourd introduced me to Lady Holland at the sumptuous Holland House in Kensington, attending at one of the many large social gatherings she held there.

But all the while I pressed onward with Oliver, and by the beginning of October, Nancy was no more. I showed what I had done to Kate, which caused her to be in an unspeakable state, but also made me feel it augured well for the closing part of the narrative. I resolved to send Sikes to the Devil, but I did not yet know how to dispose of Fagin, who was such an out and outer to me that I still did not know what to make of him. I eventually decided but then, before I wrote the last chapter, I invited Forster and Talfourd around to Doughty Street for dinner. They came and, after a delicious lamb chop meal, we sat and talked of what should be the fate of those remaining. I remember, in particular, Talfourd pleading as earnestly in mitigation of judgement for Charley Bates as ever at the Bar for any client he most respected. He won me over, and later that evening I wrote the final part about him, as well as concluding with a few more words about Rose Maylie, Mr. Brownlow and the tomb of "Agnes", before I was done. The tide of Oliver behind me was running a great career of popularity and success and I was content within myself that I had created a marvellous tale. Those within it had become as real persons to me and I wished to linger longer with them, but I knew I must refrain from doing so and move on.

I had, of course, all the while been continuing with Nickleby, sometimes working exceedingly close to Chapman and Hall's deadlines, but I was determined to manage them and so it proved. After I had closed Oliver, I went with Browne north again to work up some possible further studies for the Nickleby story, but this time we headed for Manchester for I wished to see for myself the conditions in the cotton mills, as it was my belief that child labour was being exploited in such places and wished to strike the heaviest blow in my power for these unfortunate creatures if such was the case.

We reached Manchester on the 5th November and had now been joined by Forster. We spent three days searching for information and during that time saw the worst cotton mill and the best; there was no great difference between them, and what I saw disgusted and astonished me beyond all measure. I had not yet determined however when to strike the blow over this, before we met the Quaker calico merchants, the brothers William and Daniel Grant. I found them the kindest of men, whose faces would light up with beaming looks of affection of a childlike quality, and whose inclination to philanthropy in and from their factory was, to my mind, worthy of high praise. I was pleased to later add them to the Nickleby story as the brothers Cheeryble.

I had to cut short my visit to Manchester as I wished to review speedily some of Cruikshank's illustrations before they became part of the Oliver Twist volumes, and so for the first time in my life, I rode the railway on my journey back to London. It was smooth and exhilarating, with the speed and noise of the rails providing an intoxicating backdrop to the mixture of progress at the expense of destruction that was to characterize so much of the new Victorian era that we were all entering.

My work on Nickleby, meanwhile, had stirred up a hornets' nest in Yorkshire and a number of school masters there, William Shaw amongst them, threatened me with all manner of mayhem, including libel action. I stood my ground, however, knowing that I had to put an end to their hideous practices and exploitation of children, and was confident my readers would publicly back me. The success of the first number of Nickleby had continued unabated, and in the end all their posturing came to naught. Depend upon it that the rascalities of those Yorkshire school masters could not easily be exaggerated; and that I kept down the strong truth and threw as much comicality over it as I could, rather than disgust and weary the reader with its fouler aspects. Shaw ended his advertising in The Times a couple of years later, and within a short time thereafter they all began dropping away to the extent that, before the generation was through, there was not a single such school remaining. What a thing it is to have Power! Power in the pen that can indeed turn that simplest of devices into the mightiest of weapons.

Although I had now finished writing Oliver well ahead of the publication date in the Miscellany, the shadow of Barnaby Rudge began almost immediately to appear over me. Without hardly a pause for breath, Bentley began advertising that Barnaby would be appearing "forthwith" in the Miscellany and I spent many hours discussing this matter with Forster. My frustrations caused me to tell him that I was minded to throw up the agreement with Bentley altogether; this was no idle threat for it was no fiction to say that at present I could not write this tale. Forster, however, with his usual powers of persuasion, restrained me from a precipitous rejection of the agreement and counselled that I write to Bentley stating that I must have a postponement of a kind very common in all literary agreements. I was not easily persuaded of this for I felt strongly that morally, before God and man, I held myself released from such hard bargains as these after I had done so much for those who drove them. My constant impulse was to break, at whatever cost, the net that had been wound about me as it so chafed me, so exasperated and irritated my mind that I could think of little else.

But I did not yet yield to that and, on the 22nd January 1839, sent a letter to Bentley declaring that I must have a postponement of six months from the conclusion of Oliver in the Miscellany and during that time wash my hands of any fresh accumulation of labour on Barnaby Rudge; meanwhile I resolved to proceed as cheerfully as I could with the other editorial duties which already pressed upon me. Bentley realized I was serious in my declaration, but the publishing Fagin sought to place his own conditions upon the six-month postponement. He required that I extend my contract to edit the Miscellany for another six months and to engage in no other writing, except Nickleby, until Barnaby Rudge was ready. I regarded this as offensive impertinence on his part, told him so, and felt I could no longer edit the Miscellany for him in the circumstances. On the 28th January I resigned from the post forthwith, having persuaded Harrison Ainsworth to take over the position of editor. Meanwhile, Bentley ran off to his solicitors and I was forced into protracted negotiations, again involving Forster and my solicitors, over the agreement for Barnaby Rudge and for the copyright of Oliver Twist.

Throughout all of these distractions, Nickleby was demanding my attention, with the Chapman and Hall deadlines of the 15th of each month arriving with unyielding regularity. My own benevolence was also being tested in extremis. My family, and particularly my father, were constantly looking to me as a source of funds, and I also learnt that my father had taken to contacting Chapman and Hall and badgering them for gifts of money, much to my severe embarrassment. Creditors constantly beat a path to his door at 30, King Street, Holborn (where he now lived) and the full extent of what I later found there almost floored me. I resolved that I must do something and that a little cottage in the country was the best place for him and my mother, well away from creditors and their existing life in London.

Accordingly, at the beginning of March, I travelled to Devonshire, this most beautiful of English counties (and the original home of the Nickleby family) and set up in the New London Inn in Exeter. The next morning, directly after breakfast and by some strange impulse, I set out walking along the Plymouth road. Exactly a mile beyond the city, in the village of Alphington, I came upon two white cottages joined together and built of brick with thatched roofs, one of which – Mile End Cottage, a jewel of a place – was to rent. Upon inspection I found it clean beyond all description, with the paint and paper throughout being new and fresh and cheerful looking, and the neighbourhood the most beautiful I had seen – the views to Exeter and the Cathedral towers rising up into the sky in the most picturesque manner possible – whilst in the cottage next door lived the landlady, Mrs. Pannell, the finest old countrywoman conceivable. The rent was agreed at £20 A YEAR (!) and when the agreement was signed, the old lady instantly put it away in a disused tea caddy! I furnished the cottage out in every detail for the convenience of my parents and, when they moved there, agreed to provide my father with a quarterly stipend of seven pounds ten shillings so that they might live in retirement, hopefully away from the attention of the creditors. The discovery of the cottage I seriously regarded as a blessing and I was sure they would be happy there, as I felt I could be if I were older and my course of activity run.

I greatly missed Kate and the children whilst I was away and had to keep Mamie's birthday after a lonely fashion in Exeter. I returned to Doughty Street, happy to see them all again, and drove on with Nickleby, almost to the point where I felt I should "bust the boiler". I had to postpone engagements and stick rigorously to the work, save for an annual gathering at home (a family dinner with uncles, aunts, brothers, sisters, cousins) that I could on this occasion have most joyfully dispensed with.

And then I had to engage again with Ainsworth over Bentley and the Miscellany. I had heard of an accusation by Bentley that Forster had counselled me to break my agreement with him, which was false and undeserved; Forster had expressly said to me during my frustrations that he was bound to see the old agreement performed. In the end matters resolved themselves, but not without a great deal of additional anguish to myself and disruption to Nickleby. It served to reinforce what I had heard, that booksellers (as a class) are not remarkable for anything but dishonesty.

All of these matters put me in need of a break from Doughty Street as I was so unsettled and could hardly work. I searched and found a place, Elm Cottage at Petersham, that I took from the beginning of May until the end of August, which proved to be a real delight. It had an extensive garden and grounds, admitting to much athletic competition, particularly when friends arrived, though Forster in general modestly retired from such accomplishments. I took to swimming feats in the River Thames from Petersham to Richmond Bridge before breakfast, I myself rising at 6 a.m. and plunging head foremost into the water to the astonishment and admiration of all beholders. I now felt able, too, to get on with Nickleby like a house on fire and also sat for Daniel Maclise, who painted what came to be known as "The Nickleby Portrait".

I was greatly encouraged by the glowing reviews I was now receiving about Nickleby, so I put an idea to Forster that he might approach Chapman and Hall (to whom I was well disposed) in confidence and on my behalf that, if they were prepared to behave with liberality towards me, I would be happy to engage in a new project with them, and at the same time to remind them that when Barnaby Rudge was published I would be clear of all engagements. I had in mind a new work on an entirely new plan which, instead of only being published in monthly parts at a shilling each, would be published in both weekly parts at three pence and monthly parts at a shilling – my object being to baffle the imitators and make it as novel as possible. My initial plan was to comprehend a great variety of fictional tales and I also proposed that I should be a proprietor and a sharer in the profits as well as binding myself to write a certain portion of each number. I stated that I would be willing to commence this on the 31st March 1840.

My ideas met with a favourable response from Chapman and Hall and I began to contemplate the form and name for such a venture. My mind went back to my visit to Yorkshire and my sighting of the clockmaker's shop run by Master Humphrey in Barnard Castle. I came to imagine a collection of manuscripts being found in the case of one of Master Humphrey's old clocks and he and his friends gathering weekly to read them one at a time, the publication of such tales being under the title "Master Humphrey's Clock". Details and financial terms were then satisfactorily concluded with Chapman and Hall and I signed an agreement to this effect. Shortly thereafter, Chapman and Hall and I agreed terms with Messrs. Lea and Blanchard in America to treat with them for the transmission of the proposed "Master Humphrey's Clock" publication at such times as would enable them to publish it in America at a similar time as publication in England.

At the end of August I returned to Doughty Street, but I knew immediately that I had to get away again from the distractions of London in order to finish Nickleby. It was very difficult indeed to wind up so many people in parts and make each part tell by itself, but I hoped to get out with flying colours notwithstanding. So I and the family went again to Broadstairs and took 40, Albion Street (two doors down from the Albion Hotel run by Mr. James Ballard) with the most beautiful view of the sea from its bay-windows. Once we had settled in, I sent up to town for our cook, but until she arrived the landlady of our house recommended a woman to act, who came in one morning but then got drunk – remarkably drunk – by the night and was removed by constables, whereupon she lay down in front of the house and addressed the multitude for hours! Nevertheless we enjoyed the place amazingly and, in a study overlooking the sea, I concentrated upon the winding-up of Nickleby.

I worked hard at it as it was pretty stiff work and windings-up do wind slowly if great pains are taken with the process, but I did so and discussed carefully with Forster what I had done before committing to publication. Chapman and Hall came down with Browne's sketches and also spoke about some form of "Nicklebein Fete" upon completion. I was eventually well pleased at the conclusion, which I managed on the 21st September, but once again had the greatest difficulty in parting company with those that I had come to know so well.

A wonderful Nickleby dinner of celebration was held in London at The Albion, Aldersgate Street, on the 5th October, with the new Maclise portrait on display, but thereafter I knew I had to turn myself forthwith, tooth and nail, to Barnaby Rudge. Meanwhile Kate was expecting our third child and this, together with my continued success, caused me to consider terminating the lease at Doughty Street for more favourable premises. On the 29th October, a second daughter, Kate – whom we invariably called Katey – was born and I was pleased to add the name of Macready to her name in honour of my good friend, who had shortly before asked me to be godfather to his son. I also dedicate Nickleby to him in celebration of the great friendship that had now grown between us.

At the beginning of November, I engaged in house-hunting and, after much searching, confirmed with Tom Mitton that I wished to take over the tenancy of No.1 Devonshire Terrace, York Gate, near Regent's Park, a house of great promise, undeniable situation and excessive splendor – though, as I found out, needing considerable expenditure to bring it up to such a state as I wanted. It had a garden of substantial size, all shut out from the New (Marylebone) Road by a high brick wall, and I became in a state of ecstatic restlessness until we finally agreed the move for the beginning of December. 1839. I paid £800 for the residue of the lease to March 1851, together with a requirement to pay rent of £160 per annum. I negotiated suitable arrangements with our Doughty Street landlord, Mr. Banks on behalf of his father, for the hand-over, including the taking of the fixtures and some of the furnishings off my hands; I told him, however, that the drains had been a serious annoyance to us and that, although we had had the plumbers in the house half a dozen times, we had not been able to make them last our time and they would need attention.

Once the lease of Devonshire Terrace had been agreed, I had appointments with carpenters, bricklayers, upholsterers, painters and joiners, causing me to go to and fro to the house by day and night to supervise matters. I also decided to enrol with the Honourable Society of Middle Temple Lawyers in anticipation of one day following it through to Call and practising as a Barrister if my fame as an author did not last. I needed two securities for entry, one being Edward Chapman (my publisher) and the other my good friend Talfourd, Serjeant-at-Law and himself a member of Middle Temple. I paid the deposit of £100 to the Middle Temple and agreed to pay their annual dues thereafter. I also informed my securities that the responsibility they incurred by signing my bond at the Middle Temple Treasurer's office was a very slight one, extending very little beyond my good behaviour, and honourable intentions to pay for all the wine-glasses, tumblers, and other dinner furniture that I may break or damage whilst I ate my beef and mutton and drank my ale and wine at the Inn!

The move to Devonshire Terrace took up a good deal of my time, but I had again begun to put pen to paper over thoughts of Barnaby Rudge;

I never at this time committed thoughts to paper until I was obliged to write, being better able to keep them in regular order on different shelves of my brain, readily ticketed and labelled, to be brought out when I wanted them. But then, on this occasion, the process became sorely distracted when I happened to see an advertisement in the Morning Herald, placed by none other than Bentley, announcing that "Mr. Dickens's new work, Barnaby Rudge in three volumes, is preparing for publication". I immediately wrote to my solicitors, Smithson and Mitton, to contact his solicitors, informing them that their client should be told this was not the case and that, because of his attitude towards me, I would decline to produce it for him altogether. I stood my ground as solicitor's letters flew, for I now saw it as war to the knife with the Burlington Street Brigand.

CHAPTER VII

The Old Curiosity Shop and a Hanging at Newgate

The truth however, as I was now discovering, was that by the close of Nickleby, after Pickwick, Oliver Twist and all the exertions with Bentley and the Miscellany, I had been left unwell and exhausted, utterly lost in misery and unable to contemplate taking on any new long-term venture. I was then distracted by the Royal Wedding and fell hopelessly in love with the Queen. Disputes erupted with two of my neighbours about the smoking of my stable chimney, which my groom, Topping, by his stupidity, only succeeded in aggravating. Christmas time came with the house full of relations from the country, and on the 14th January 1840, I was summoned to Marylebone Workhouse and obliged to sit as a juryman at an Inquest on the body of a newly-born child alleged to have been murdered by its mother, Eliza Burgess. She was a 25-year old domestic servant and the baby had been discovered dead at her employer's house in Edgware Road. The coroner in these proceedings, Mr. Thomas Wakley, was however a humane man and, with his help, I was eventually able to persuade my fellow jurymen to charge the mother only with the concealment of birth, upon our finding that the child had been "found dead" rather than murdered. At this, the poor desolate creature dropped upon her knees before us with protestations that we were right – protestations among the most affecting that I have ever heard in my life – and she was carried away insensible. Whether it was the sight of the poor dead baby that I had seen stretched out on a clean white cloth on the box in which the mother had first put it (and which was now situate in the midst of a perfect panorama of coffins of all sizes), or its mother, or my fellow jurymen, or a combination, I cannot say, but that night I had a most violent attack of sickness and indigestion, which not only prevented me from sleeping but even from lying down. I sat up through the dreary watches with Kate, reliving those harrowing proceedings, and subsequently caused some extra care to be taken of the mother in prison, and counsel to be retained for her defence when she was tried at the Old Bailey for concealment. Although found guilty on this charge, the jury gave a strong recommendation for mercy and her resulting sentence was lenient. Her history and subsequent conduct proved that this was right, and I was gratified that I had played a part in sparing her life and providing her with a second chance.

I set about to rectify my out-of-sorts by a perfected regimen of diet and exercise, including on horseback for lengthy rides. Lengthy walks too (including in the streets at night) were a way I constantly used to relieve the pressures I felt upon me. I was also in the habit of making, particularly with Forster, a circuit of nearly all the London prisons, never knowing what surprises I should meet in such places. I once encountered a man called Wainewright and, much later, used his circumstance to produce a short story entitled "Hunted Down".

At the end of February, Forster took me to Bath to meet the old poet and essayist, Walter Savage Landor. We passed three happy days there, and it was during this time that, in continued thinking about material for Master Humphrey's Clock, I came up with the idea of a child who lives with her grandfather in an old curiosity shop that he runs; and in my mind I christened this young girl "Little Nell". I also saw a character in Bath called Prior, a frightful little dwarf who let donkeys out on hire and who appeared to beat his animals and wife in equal measure. I later used the memory of him in the tale as the basis for Quilp.

My original intention was to have Master Humphrey meet this young child as he was out walking, and thereby produce a couple of stories for Master Humphrey's Clock. These I began to set down in March ready for publication, and I was sure they would be effective. However, I had to first prepare an opening story in time for the initial publication date and so, to set the scene for Master Humphrey from his clock-side in the chimney corner, I introduced "The Giant Chronicles", the first being "Magog's Story". When all was ready, I left town on the eve of publication (as was now my established custom), on this occasion travelling with Kate to Birmingham. Chapman and Hall had organized a print run of sixty thousand for this first issue of Master Humphrey's Clock, and I waited with apprehension and anticipation for news of sales. Forster soon joined me in Birmingham with the news. Not only had there been sale of the whole of the sixty thousand copies, but orders were already in hand for ten thousand more! I had always had a quiet confidence in the Clock, but I never expected this to be the first reaction.

The next publication date was soon upon me and the second chronicle which I published was "A Confession found in a prison in the time of Charles the Second"; I also now introduced "The Old Curiosity Shop" to my readers and the little child that Master Humphrey had found wandering. However, by the third issue I came to realize that orders were diminishing because my public found there was no continuous tale and this is what their anticipation demanded. I had not by this stage written more than two chapters concerning Little Nell, introducing in the process Dick Swiveller, but I found the more I thought about her and her associates, the more capability for more extended treatment pressed itself upon me. So I now resolved to throw everything else aside and devote myself in the Clock to this one story alone, and it was not long before I discovered that Little Nell was following me everywhere.

At the end of May I suddenly had the notion that I should like to be in Broadstairs once again, the sea air invigorating for both body and mind, and Albion Street on the sea front the most delightful of places. I made a habit of rising at seven in the morning and commencing work at half-past eight, writing well into the afternoon until exhaustion set in. I fell into a pattern of completing one lengthy chapter before a shorter, which seemed to cause the tale to flow in agreeable fashion, and I had much pleasure with the characters, particularly Dick Swiveller. At the end of the month, Forster and Maclise joined me and we passed two agreeable days in slow return to London, through Chatham, Rochester and Cobham, revisiting well-remembered scenes of my childhood. I was particularly taken by the little graveyard close to Rochester Cathedral, to which I felt such a profound bonding that there arose an instant belief in me that there could be no finer place in all the world to go into dust and ashes than this.

Back in London, I was mightily relieved to find I had now finally freed myself from Bentley's leech-like grip, though at some considerable cost. For the sum of £2,250 (which I had to borrow from Chapman and Hall), I got back my copyright in Oliver Twist, together with unsold numbers, and relieved myself of the contract to write Barnaby Rudge for him. I wrote to Chapman and Hall setting out the means of repayment of the monies loaned and the turning over of Barnaby Rudge to them, the first two chapters of which I had already written and now put into their hands.

Not many days later, I was dining with Maclise and my brother-in-law Henry Burnett, when the subject turned to the fate of Francois Courvoisier. He was a 23-year old Swiss valet who had been tried and convicted of the murder of his employer, Lord William Russell, by cutting his throat with a carving knife as he lay in his bed in the early hours of the morning and then stealing silver plate, money and jewellery from the bedside. I had read of Courvoisier's trial at the Old Bailey whilst in Broadstairs, but had been so outraged by the conduct of his counsel, Mr. Phillips, that I had written two lengthy letters to the Morning Chronicle on the subject. A correspondent from the Middle Temple had sought to justify counsel's conduct, but I did not have my opinion altered. I recognize the right of any counsel to take a brief from any man, however great his crime and, keeping within due bounds, to do his best to save him; but I deny his right to defeat the ends of truth and justice by wantonly scattering aspersions upon innocent people, which may fasten a serious imputation upon them for the remainder of their lives – as those so profusely showered by Mr. Phillips would have done in this instance, in the not impossible case of Courvoisier having been acquitted. In doing so, I maintain he far outsteps his duty, and renders his office, not a public protection, but a public nuisance.

Following the trial, Courvoisier was now due to hang by Newgate Prison in the early morning of the 6th July, and we resolved forthwith to go and survey the scene for ourselves. Upon arrival at Newgate, we found hordes of people already milling about, many clearly the worse for wear for drink. I was drawn along and something inside me said that just for once I should like to watch a scene like this and see the end of the drama, so we set about trying to find an upper room to let from where we could watch events unfold. After some considerable searching, I found such a place and Maclise, Burnett and I mounted the stairs and posted ourselves by the open window. I saw Thackeray, who was also there at the scene, and as we watched the scaffold being constructed, the crowd swelled and grew noisier with nothing but ribaldry, debauchery, levity, drunkenness and flaunting vice in fifty other shapes to behold – so much so that I came to believe that I should have deemed it impossible that I could have felt any large assemblage of my fellow creatures to be so odious. And then came the hanging. At 8 o'clock the nearby church bell of St.Sepulcre's tolled out the hour and the mob, estimated now to be 40,000 strong, roared in anticipation of their spectacle. Shouts went up to those at the front wearing hats to remove them immediately, and not many moments later the door to Newgate Prison swung open and Courvoisier stepped out. I saw him lift his shackled hands as if in final prayer, before the noose was placed around his neck. The deed was then done, accompanied by the greatest cheering imaginable, before his corpse was cut down and taken back within the prison confines on a wooden bier.

As we made our way from that tumultuous scene, with the sated crowds dispersing in all directions through thoroughfares large and small, I confess that my mind was in turmoil at what I had just witnessed. Fascination had given way to loathing, and my instant reaction was to turn against the concept of capital punishment as a public sanction, even for the most heinous of crimes. Years later I came to revise this view, concluding that the ultimate sanction was still needed, but that it should be executed within the confines of the prison and far away from the baying, vulgar mob.

Back in my study at Devonshire Terrace, I felt more bound to the Clock and Little Nell than I had ever been yet – Nickleby was nothing to it, nor Pickwick, nor Oliver – for Nell demanded my constant attention and obliged me to exert all the self-denial I possessed. At the end of July, after signing the formal agreement with Chapman and Hall over Barnaby Rudge, I went with Kate to Devonshire to visit my parents in Alphington; on the surface my father and mother seemed perfectly contented and happy, but I sensed all was not well and soon came to believe that my father was still living beyond his means, even forging my signature as a way of paying his bills, or purportedly guaranteeing them. I subsequently confirmed that this outrage was indeed true and as a result had cause, through my solicitors, to issue notices in all the leading London newspapers that I would not be responsible for any debts so incurred. I further had them demand directly of my father that he should leave England and live on the continent (I suggested Calais, Boulogne or Antwerp) to a fixed stipend, but to this directive he turned deaf ears and continued to reside at Alphington as before.

On Sunday the 16th August, a distressing scene occurred with Forster at Devonshire Terrace when he, Macready and Maclise dined with us. After dinner, Forster got into one of his headlong streams of talk with some sharp observations – which caused me great anger, such that I told him I would be glad if he were to leave the house. Kate went out in tears and it was left to Macready to pacify the situation. He observed that for an angry instant Forster and I were about to destroy a friendship valuable to both of us, and eventually passions were calmed. I admitted I had spoken in passion and would not have said what I said if I could have reflected, but I also made it clear that I could not answer for my temper under Forster's provocations and should do the same again. Forster eventually acknowledged the stupidity of his conduct, but it was a painful process.

In early September I took myself, family and work to Broadstairs again, the sea and sea bathing stimulated my mind and night walks along the cliffs helping to fill my "mental museum". I was always pleased to have friends visit, one of whom on this occasion was the Scot, Angus Fletcher. He sketched here, getting beggars and idiots to sit to him on the sands and pier, dressing them in fragments of his own attire and rewarding them with shillings for their pains. He would also read poems to the public, on one occasion performing with a pocket-handkerchief on his head to imitate a veil. One day, seeing me go to one of the bathing machines on the beach (presided over by the pretty and obliging chatterbox, Miss Collins), he plucked up and said he'd have another. He had the next one. Determined that he should not escape, I waded under the hood of his bath and seeing him standing with only his coat off, urged him to make haste. In about five minutes more he fell heavily into the water and, feeling the cold, set up a scream which pierced the air – you never heard anything so horrible! And then he splashed like a fleet of porpoises, roaring most horribly and howling like a wolf all the time, and dancing a maniac dance which defies description. Such a devil – such a bald, howling, fearful devil in buff I never beheld. And then he emerged naked from the sea, right amongst the people on the beach!

I pressed on with Little Nell and The Old Curiosity Shop, keeping to my regular weekly discipline; moreover, by now, Forster had suggested that Nell might die. Before such a notion I had not thought of killing her and now I hardly knew what to do. Forster asked me to consider whether it did not necessarily belong even to my own conception and I began to see the reality of what he was saying. But then I began suffering night and day with insupportable torture from some complaint in the face and, despite taking fomentations of various kinds, experienced little or no relief and was desperately beaten in consequence.

On returning home to Devonshire Terrace, I received news that the expenses of producing the Clock were substantially in excess of what had been anticipated, and so profits that I had expected had not fully materialized. But all the time Little Nell was driving me onward. She took over my life, but I now knew she must die. As the weather closed in and the winter chills began, this child pursued me as I walked the streets and back slums of London at night; then all day she engulfed me as I sat at my desk cloaked in misery. I became exhausted by my daily labours and would go to bed utterly dispirited and done up – and yet all night I was pursued by the child, leaving me in the morning unrefreshed and miserable. And time and again the memory of Mary Hogarth came flooding back to me. I knew it was breaking my heart over this story of Little Nell, and I could not bear to finish it; I was slowly murdering her and growing wretched over it, and yet in my wrung-out heart I knew it must be. It cast the most horrible shadow upon me and it was as much as I could do to keep it moving at all.

It took me seven full days of the most agonizing torture to kill Little Nell, and when at last I did, I felt myself nearly dead with the work and grief-stricken at the loss of my child. And, for me, Dear Mary died again too. The pain and swelling in my face returned and a heavy cold struck me; nevertheless, I felt the need to read the course of Nell's death to Forster and share my grief with him. This I did and the obvious deep affection he held for her was a great comfort to me. Thereafter I pushed onward to finish the story, eventually working until 4 o'clock in the early hours of the morning of the 17th January 1841 to do so. Even then I was just three weeks away from the publication of it when my pen finally came to rest.

The public response to Nell was exceedingly gratifying to me. I had been inundated with imploring letters recommending poor Little Nell to mercy and begging me in the fullest terms not to have her die. Clock numbers went beyond one hundred thousand in sales. Word also came to me that passengers sailing to New York had been besieged by crowds in that land demanding to know "Is Little Nell dead?" People wept openly at the news of her demise. At the close of the tale, I made a few minor amendments to the overall text to enable publication in volume form, but it made me very melancholy to think that all these people were now lost to me forever, and felt again as if I could never become attached to any new set of characters. But I had immediately to press onward with my new task.

CHAPTER VIII

Barnaby Rudge and a Bonnie Welcome in Scotland

My task was now to finally tackle Barnaby Rudge and have it run on in the Clock in weekly parts directly after the closing of The Old Curiosity Shop. I felt considerable difficulty in settling down into the new track I had to pursue – and then, for a while, domestic problems intervened. Kate was soon to give birth again and again fell into deep melancholy; she was taken very unwell at four o'clock in the morning of the 23rd January and for two days I slept not a wink, exhaustion again overwhelming me. Thereafter, however, I turned to the opening parts of Barnaby that I had already set down and also made up and wrote the needful insertions for the second number – so that I came back to the mill a little, but it was really hard going. Meanwhile, on the 8th February – and after Kate had had a very hard trial indeed – our second son was born, whom we eventually christened Walter Landor Dickens, after my great friend in Bath and someone who had shown such an affection for Little Nell.

Towards the end of the month, and getting out of harm's way, I rode the box of a Brighton coach to that place, to be for a week shut up alone as a Spartan and working with the energy of fourteen dragons on Barnaby – which proved effective. The story took well with a great stride at this point; I felt that Grip, as young Barnaby's pet raven, would be strong and that I could build greatly upon the Varden household. But upon my return to Devonshire Terrace, I found that my pet raven Grip had been ailing for some days and, not long after, he died. Whilst I was yet uncomfortable for his loss, solicitor Charles Smithson discovered an older but more gifted bird in a village public house in Yorkshire, which he prevailed upon the landlord to part with for a consideration and sent up to me. This raven could say anything and, because his infancy and youth had been passed at this country public house, I was told that the sight of a drunken man would call forth his utmost powers. He also had the art of swallowing door-keys and reproducing them at pleasure, which filled all beholders with mingled sensations of horror and satisfaction, and a kind of awful delight. I had this older and larger Grip installed forthwith in the stable, and had the remains of his honoured predecessor stuffed and placed in a glass case as ornament in my study.

Through the spring and early summer of 1841, I worked hard at Barnaby, continuing to be pleased to have the helpful and constant assistance of Forster when I needed him. I told him again, as with the Old Curiosity Shop, that when he read the first proof, if there was anything there that he objected to, he should knock it out ruthlessly. I wanted him to erase anything that seemed too strong, for I found it difficult to judge what told too much and what did not. To assist me, I continued to walk mile upon mile of the most wretched and distressful streets of London, searching for pictures I wanted to build upon and filling my mind with images of the most vivid kind. I had also witnessed recent Chartist insurrection and drew upon the memory of the odious mob at Corvoisier's execution to help fashion my concentration upon the "No Popery" rioters led by Lord George Gordon.

In the spring, word came to me that I was to be offered a public dinner in Edinburgh as part of their wish to entertain me in Scotland. I was deeply moved that this should be so, and Kate too – who was mad to see her place of birth at 8, Hart Street in that city – was joyful that her native land had alighted on this course for me. Lord Francis Jeffrey, Judge of the Court of Session and co-founder and previous editor of the Edinburgh Review, had called upon me at Devonshire Terrace on the 6th April and told me of this proposed honour, and a few days later he invited me to dine with him and thereafter took me to the home of Lord Denman, Lord Chief Justice of England, and introduced me to him. An intimate friendship quickly grew with Jeffrey and he would often come to Devonshire Terrace and sit an hour or so or take a long walk with me in Regent's Park. I set aside three weeks in June for the visit to Scotland and was able to continue on with Barnaby in higher spirits than before and on the highest crag of expectation.

Shortly after, I had the most hearty letter from Washington Irvine from his home in America. As a small boy I used to devour his stories, and so wrote and told him that his kindness and heartfelt appreciation of my work heightened the desire in me that had already been kindled to visit America before long. I also became aware that he had lent his powerful aid to the International Copyright question – a matter of immense importance to me, and likewise to the Americans if they desired ever to have a literature of their own.

In early June, as the time for our visit to Scotland approached, I made added effort at Barnaby to be ahead of the printer and in due course finished four chapters in six days, before setting off with Kate and our servant Tom for Scotland. We travelled by rail to York and stayed with the Smithsons at Easthope Hall near Malton before continuing by posting carriage to Edinburgh. We arrived at the Royal Hotel on the evening of Tuesday 22nd June, and found ourselves very well off in point of rooms that Fletcher had helped organize for us. As soon as my arrival became known however, the hotel was perfectly besieged and the next day I was forced to take refuge in a sequestered apartment at the end of a long passage, where I was able to find a small amount of quiet privacy. Later that morning I went to the Parliament House and felt I was introduced to everybody in Edinburgh. There was much talk of the forthcoming Friday evening when, it was said, 300 guests would be at the dinner. I was greatly moved at all of this, the first public recognition and encouragement I had ever received.

The dinner in the Waterloo Rooms was the most brilliant affair you could conceive; the completest success possible from first to last. The room was crammed, and I heard that more than 70 applicants for tickets were of necessity refused. There were also nearly 200 ladies present in the gallery. The place was so contrived that the cross table was raised enormously, much above the heads of people sitting below; and the effect on me on first coming in with the tumultuous cheering was rather tremendous. I felt quite self-possessed however, and notwithstanding the "enthoosemoosy" which was very startling, I was as cool as a cucumber. I remember feeling, as I sat at the high table, how very remarkable it was to see such a number of grey-headed men gathered about my brown flowing locks! People spoke famously and I think (ahem!) that I spoke rather well. It was an evening that beat all nature and it took me until morning to come down to earth and be a man again.

We stayed in Edinburgh a further eight days, during which time I was granted the Freedom of the City and continued to be most wonderfully received everywhere. I recall on one occasion deciding on the spur to visit a theatre, whereupon the moment I did so the whole audience, upon recognition, rose spontaneously with tumultuous shouts of delight and the orchestra, in cavalier air, struck up with "Charlie Is My Darling"!

One of the many people I met in Edinburgh was Lord Murray. He had succeeded Jeffrey as Lord Advocate in 1835 and then, in 1839, had become a Judge of the Court of Session. I found him a delightful and charming man and he provided me with a map and itinerary of the Highlands and letters of introduction. So, on the morning of the 4th July, Kate, Tom and I left Edinburgh for our tour, heading for the Highlands and taking Fletcher as our additional guide. I had by now christened him "kindheart" on account of his manner that overlaid all his eccentricities and absurdities and with him we had many comic adventures and witnessed rain as it never does rain anywhere but here – the sky appearing on occasions to be a vast waterspout itself that never left off emptying – but through it all the scenery conveyed a glory that is impossible to properly furnish through description. I don't bore you with accounts of Ben this and that, and Lochs of all sorts of names, but this is a wonderful region. The way the mists stalk about and the clouds lay down upon the hills; the deep glens, the high rocks, the rushing waterfalls, and the roaring rivers down in deep gulfs below, are all stupendous. These tremendous wilds of Scotland are fearful in their grandeur – the more so when set against such amazing solitude.

On my return to London, I wrote a letter of sincerest thanks to Lord Murray for all his assistance, but then received the news that the Clock was not now, following the death of Little Nell, selling as well as had been hoped. Sales were now thirty thousand. Nevertheless, I pressed on, writing a further six chapters of Barnaby in twelve days, and decided to retire once again to Broadstairs with the family for the summer and to continue writing in those most pleasing surroundings. But I now knew that I had to look beyond Barnaby and to a different style of life. I had seen how Sir Walter Scott had become a shadow of his former self, with broken powers and mental weakness through overwork, and took it as a warning for myself. I discussed the situation with Forster and we decided to raise the issue with Chapman and Hall. There was firmly placed in my mind the need to discontinue the Clock at the close of Barnaby and thereafter for me to have a one year's break from writing.

With Forster also present, the matter was discussed with Chapman and Hall. I thought Chapman very manly and sensible, Hall morally and physically feeble, though perfectly well intentioned. Forster made my situation very clear to them and they came to agree as to the principle. I was happy to leave Forster to work out the detail of the arrangement we had come to and a fortnight later, on the 7th September, the agreement he drafted was signed by all parties. This provided that the Clock was to cease with the close of Barnaby Rudge and a new work in twenty monthly numbers, similar to those of Pickwick and Nickleby, was to arise, but not for me to begin again until after an interval of twelve months, and with publication thereafter commencing in November 1842. During that publication, it was agreed that I was to receive £200 monthly, with further arrangements for the distribution of profits of each number, whilst during the twelve months' interval before the parts began, I was to be paid £150 each month, to be secured against my existing works and offset against subsequent profits.

I now felt enabled to continue on with Barnaby in greater heart – and soon had the storming of Newgate in full cry and a clear vision of the way through to the end. I was always sure I could make a good thing of Barnaby and now felt it coming out strong to the last word. Suddenly the pressures of the printer did not seem so great, although I now became taken night and day with another vision.

For some time, particularly from the commencement of the Clock and its simultaneous publication in America, I had this increasingly serious notion in my mind of visiting America. It began merely as an idea for gathering material for the Clock, but then, as well as receiving the very hearty letter from Washington Irving, I began to receive yearnings for me to visit America pouring in from every part of the States. Washington Irving wrote again, saying that if I came it would be such a triumph from one end of the States to another. So, upon my return from Scotland, it began to take shape in my mind as a thing that somehow or other, at no very distant date, it must be managed somehow. And now the conclusion of the agreement for a year's pause in my writing from the ending of Barnaby gave me the opportunity, which to miss, I felt, would be a sad thing. When I mentioned the subject to Kate however, she cried dismally and stressed the difficulties with the children; I could not persuade her to go and leave the children at home or let me go alone.

I told Forster, on the 19th September, that I had made up my mind to go, and to start soon after Christmas. I also told Macready of my decision, and asked his advice as to the children. I told him that Kate was averse to taking them, and that at the same time she found it difficult to contemplate a subject which was so new to her and so startling, in any reasonable light. When I have once made up my mind to anything, I can normally keep it as much at ease as though the thing were done, but in this case I was sorely tossed and tumbled on a moral ocean. Macready, who had himself been to America, advised me not to take the children. Kate wept whenever the matter of America was spoken about and I asked Macready if he could write to Kate about the situation and he agreed to do so; he also agreed that he would help care for and attend to the children whilst we were away. I kept Forster informed, and told him that the instant I had wrung a reluctant consent from Kate, I would take our joint passage in the mail-packet for next January.

Macready's letter to Kate calmed her fears and anxieties and, whilst I knew it would be a very severe trial for both of us to leave the children behind, she began talking of our American adventure. Whilst I had it in mind to go for five or six months, I did not tell Kate this at this time, but merely booked the tickets to leave from Liverpool on the 4th January 1842. I enlisted the help of my brother Fred, as well as the Macreadys, to undertake the care of the children whilst we were away and arranged for Anne Brown, our maid (who gave me great confidence as a moral cork-jacket) to come as companion for Kate on the journey. Kate, feeling now more cheerful, wrote to Maclise asking him if he would make a drawing of the children so that we could have it with us in America, and he readily agreed.

We finally left Broadstairs at the beginning of October and stopped off for three nights in the Rochester area, where Forster was pleased to join us. However, it was whilst in Rochester that I experienced the severest of pains; I had noticed for a while some pain in my rectum and had put it down merely to the long hours I was sitting to complete Barnaby. Whilst in Rochester it grew far worse and, on returning to London, I visited the specialist surgeon, Frederick Salmon, and learnt I had suffered a tear in the wall of my rectum. I was obliged to submit to a cruel operation, where the diseased and frayed tissue had to be cut away and the tear stitched – all in an agonizing operation without anaesthetic. Macready called at Devonshire Terrace that evening and when I told him about it, he could scarcely bear it himself. Kate wrote letters at my dictation, but I had to soldier on with Barnaby, writing several hours a day whilst lying down on the sofa, which was extremely awkward and very irksome.

At last Barnaby was complete, and I arranged to travel with Kate to Windsor for rest and a little change of air. It was now three weeks since the painful operation and, although I had recovered with a rapidity whereat the doctors were astounded, I had only just begun to feel my legs at all steady under my diminished weight. I booked into the White Hart Hotel for a fortnight from the 6th November and once there began to feel immeasurably better, particularly now being able to walk about the Windsor Parks. For a while Forster and Kate's sister Georgina, now aged 15, joined us there and I was delighted that Georgina agreed to live with the children and help look after them whilst we were away in America. Master Humphrey's Clock was finally laid to rest, with notice therein of my intention to lay down my pen for a year. And now, at last, I could turn my attention to the necessary preparations for America.

I found a suitable house to rent at 25 Osnaburgh Street – not far from Macready's home at 5 Clarence Terrace – for Fred and Georgina to have to look after the children whilst we were away and let Devonshire Terrace for the time I planned to be away. I studied as many guide and travel books of America as I could muster and hung my study with highly coloured maps to familiarize myself with each State. I heard talk of the threat of war in America over the much-disputed Canadian boundary, particularly after a ship called the "Caroline" had been attacked whilst anchored on the American side of the Niagara River and a number of her crew killed – but it did not deter me from going. An American journalist (John D. Sherwood) visited me at home and I was pleased to be interviewed by him about my impending visit. Macready was busying himself with his new management duties at Drury Lane, but in December I saw and dined with as many friends as possible, as well as spending an additional amount of time with the children and making Christmas and New Year as special a time as I could for them to remember. But I was now living in a perpetual state of weighing anchor.

CHAPTER IX

Voyage to America

On the 2nd January 1842, Kate and I, together with Anne Brown, bid our farewells and set off for Liverpool. Forster, my sister Fanny, and brother Alfred also came, as did Fletcher. Upon arrival at the dock the next day and going on board, I shall never forget the one-fourth serious and three-fourth's comical astonishment with which I opened the door of, and put my head into, a "State Room" on board the Cunard steam packet "Britannia", bound for Halifax and Boston and carrying Her Majesty's mails. That this state room had been specially engaged for "Charles Dickens Esquire and Lady" was rendered sufficiently clear, even to my scared intellect, by a very small manuscript announcing the fact, which was pinned on a very flat quilt, covering a very thin mattress, spread like a surgical plaster on a most inaccessible shelf. Any one of the beds with pillows, sheet and blankets complete, was like a muffin beaten flat and might be sent from one place to another through the Post Office, with only a double stamp. Neither of the portmanteaus could by any mechanical contrivance be got in than a giraffe could be persuaded or forced into a flower pot. However, in less than two minutes after coming upon it for the first time, we all by common consent agreed that this state room was the pleasantest and most facetious and capital contrivance possible; and that to have one inch larger would have been quite a disagreeable and deplorable state of things, though I do verily believe that, deducting the two berths, one above the other, nothing smaller for sleeping in was ever made, except coffins. But it was contiguous to the lady's cabin where Anne would be, and that was really a comfortable room, the only good one in the ship. So I hoped to be able to sit there very often, as the stewardess thought there was only one other lady on board besides Kate. There were more, but I nevertheless established myself from the first in the ladies' cabin, where the women were all unusually pretty.

We bid our farewells and our visitors returned to shore. Kate's face, which had been swollen, was better and she was now in glorious spirits. After much cheering and waving, to-ing and fro-ing, and all hands very busy stowing away meat and greens and an enormous cow for milk, we awaited and awaited the last boat with the latest mailbags. And then a speck in the mist at last! The boat we wait for! The captain, Captain Hewett, appeared on the paddle box with his speaking trumpet; the officers took their stations and all hands were on the alert. The boat came alongside, the bags dragged in anyhow and flung down for the moment anywhere; three cheers sounded and as the first one rang in our ears, the vessel throbbed like a strong giant that had just received the breath of life, the two great wheels turning fiercely round for the first time, and the noble ship, with wind and tide astern, began breaking proudly through the lashed and foaming water.

Although every plank and timber creaked as if the ship were made of wickerwork, and crackled like an enormous fire of the driest possible twigs, the passage out was relatively calm – until the third day when, on that morning, I was awakened out of my sleep by a dismal shriek from Kate, who demanded to know whether there was any danger. I roused myself and looked out of bed. The water-jug was plunging and leaping like a lively dolphin; all the small articles were afloat, except my shoes which were stranded on a carpet-bag, high and dry like a couple of coal-barges. Suddenly I saw them spring into the air and beheld the looking-glass, which was nailed to the wall, sticking fast upon the ceiling. At the same time the door entirely disappeared and a new one opened in the floor. Then I began to comprehend that our state room was standing on its head; and before it was possible to make any arrangement at all compatible with this novel state of things, the ship righted. Before I could say "Thank Heaven!" she wronged again. Before I could say "she is wrong", she seemed to have started forward and to be a creature actually running of its own accord, with broken knees and failing legs, through every variety of hole and pitfall, and stumbling instantly. Before I could so much as wonder, she took a high leap into the air. Before she had well done that, she took a deep dive into the water. Before she gained the surface, she threw a summerset. The instant she was on her legs, she rushed backwards. And so she went on, staggering, heaving, wrestling, leaping, diving, jumping, pitching, throbbing, rolling and rocking: and going through all these movements, sometimes in turns and sometimes together, until I felt disposed to roar for mercy.

For two or three hours we gave the ship up as a lost thing and, with many thoughts of the children and those others dearest to us, waited quietly for the worst. I never expected to see the day again and resigned myself to God as well as I could. During this time I say nothing of what may be called the "domestic noises" of the ship, such as the breaking of glass and crockery, the tumbling down of stewards, the gambols overhead of loose casks and truant dozens of bottled porter, and the very remarkable and far from exhilarating sounds raised in their various state rooms by the seventy passengers, who were too ill to get up to breakfast. I say nothing of them: for although I lay listening to this concert for a further three or four days, I don't think I heard it for more than a quarter of a minute, at the expiration of which term I lay down again, excessively seasick. Not seasick, be it understood in the ordinary acceptation of the term; I wish I had been, but in a form which I have never seen or heard described, though I have no doubt it is very common. I lay there all day long, quite coolly and contentedly, with no sense of weariness, with no desire to get up, or get better, or take the air; with no curiosity, or care or regret of any sort of degree, saving that I think I can remember, in this universal indifference, having a kind of lazy joy – of fiendish delight, if anything so lethargic can be dignified with the title – in the fact of my wife being too ill to talk to me.

The storm and gale continued unabated for days on end. A steward fell down the cabin-stairs with a round of beef and injured his foot severely. Another steward fell down after him, and cut his eye open. The baker was taken ill; so was the pastry-cook, and a new man, sick to death, was required to take his place. This man was dragged out of bed and propped up in a little house upon deck, between two casks, and ordered (the captain standing over him) to make and roll out pie-crust, which he protested, with tears in his eyes, it was death to him in his bilious state to look at. The ship's cook became drunk (having got at some salt-water-damaged whisky) and the captain ordered the boatswain to play upon him with the hose of the fire engine until he roared for mercy – which he didn't get, for he was sentenced to look out, for four hours at a stretch for four nights running, without a great coat, and to have his grog stopped. Four dozen plates were broken at dinner, a passenger got drunk before dinner was over, while another was blinded with lobster sauce spilt over him by a steward, and a further passenger fell on deck and fainted.

Once – only once during this time – did I find myself on deck. I don't know how I got there, or what possessed me to go there, but there I was; and completely dressed too, with a huge pea-coat on, and a pair of boots such as no weak man in his senses could have ever got into. I found myself standing, when a gleam of consciousness came upon me, holding on to something, I don't know what. I think it was the boatswain: or it may have been the pump: or possibly the cow. I can't say how long I had been there; whether a day or a minute. I recollect trying to think about something (about anything in the whole wide world, I was not particular) without the smallest effect, my stomach, with its contents, appearing to be in my forehead. I could not make out which was the sea and which the sky, for the horizon seemed drunk and was flying wildly about in all directions. Even in that incapable state I recognized a person standing before me but then, after another interval of total unconsciousness, I found he had gone, and recognized another figure in its place. It seemed to wave and fluctuate before me as though I saw it reflected in an unsteady looking-glass, but I knew it for the captain; and such was the cheerful influence of his face, that I tried to smile: yes, even then I tried to smile. I saw by his gestures that he addressed me; but it was a long time before I could make out that he remonstrated against my standing up to my knees in water – as I was; of course I don't know why. I tried to thank him, but couldn't. I could only point to my boots – or whatever I supposed my boots to be – and say in a plaintive voice: "cork soles", at the same time endeavouring, I am told, to sit down in the pool. Finding that I was quite insensible, and for the time a maniac, he humanely conducted me below.

I heard also that Lord Mulgrave, who was on board laid a wager with twenty-five other men one night, whose berths, like his, were in the fore-cabin (which could only be got at by crossing the deck), that he would reach his cabin first. Watches were set by the captain's and they sallied forth, wrapped up in coats and storm caps. But the sea broke over the ship so violently that they were five and twenty minutes holding on by the handrail at the starboard paddle box, drenched to the skin by every wave and not daring to go on or come back lest they should be washed overboard.

I myself never went into the saloon (a place not nearly so large as on the Ramsgate boats) since the first day – the noise, the smell and the closeness being quite intolerable. In the ladies' cabin, the ladies turned to being in such ecstasies of fear and utmost terror that I scarcely knew what to do with them. It certainly did seem difficult to comprehend the possibility of anything afloat being more disturbed, without toppling over and going down. What the agitation of a steam-vessel is, on a bad winter's night in the wild Atlantic, it is impossible for the most vivid imagination to conceive. To say she is flung down on her side in the waves, with her masts dipping into them, and that, springing up again, she rolls over on the other side, until a heavy sea strikes her with the noise of a hundred guns, and hurls her back – that she stops, and staggers, and shivers, as though stunned, and then, with a violent throbbing at her heart, darts onward like a monster goaded into madness, to be beaten down, and battered, and crushed, and leaped on by the angry sea – that thunder, lightning, hail and rain, and wind, are all in fierce contention for the mastery – that every plank has its groan, every nail its shriek, and every drop of water in the great ocean its howling voice – is nothing. To say that all is grand, and all appalling and horrible in the last degree, is nothing. Only a dream can call it up again, in all its fury, rage, and passion.

Then one day I literally "tumbled up" on deck at noon and my eyes met a scene of utter dreariness and desolation. Ocean and sky were all of one dull, heavy, uniform, lead colour. There was no extent of prospect even over the dreary waste that lay around us, for the sea ran high and the horizon encompassed us like a large black hoop. Viewed from the air or some tall bluff on shore, it would have been imposing and stupendous, no doubt; but seen from the wet and rolling decks, it only impressed one giddily and painfully. The lifeboat had been crushed by one blow of the sea like a walnut shell; and there it hung, dangling in the air, a mere faggot of crazy boards. The planking of the paddle boxes had been torn sheer away. The wheels were exposed and bare and they whirled and dashed their spray about the decks at random. Chimney, white with crusted salt; topmasts stuck; storm sails set; rigging all knotted, tangled, wet and drooping: a gloomier picture it would be hard to look upon.

The weather continued obstinately and almost unprecedently bad. And then, on the fifteenth night, after some comparative smoothness, we were running (as we thought) into Halifax harbour under little wind and a bright moon, having given the ship in charge to the pilot, when suddenly the ship struck upon a bank of mud. A rush upon deck followed. The crew were kicking off their shoes and throwing off their jackets preparatory to swimming ashore; the pilot was beside himself; the passengers dismayed; and everything in the most intolerable confusion and hurry. Breakers were roaring ahead; the land within a couple of hundred yards; and the vessel driving upon the surf, although her paddles were worked backwards, and everything done to stay her course. It was not the custom of steamers, it seemed, to have an anchor ready and an accident occurred in seeking to get ours over the side. For half an hour we were throwing up rockets, burning blue lights and firing signals of distress, all of which remained unanswered; but by passengers and guns, and water casks and other heavy matters being all huddled together aft to lighten her in the head, she was eventually got off and we then dropped anchor in a strange, outlandish-looking nook which nobody on board (including the pilot) could recognize, although there was land all about us and so close that we could plainly see the waving branches of the trees. The sudden and unexpected stoppage of the engine created a strange, dead stillness in the silence of midnight. Enquiries revealed we were in a place called "The Eastern Passage", which was about the last place in the world in which we had any business or reason to be, but a sudden fog and an error on the pilot's part were the cause.

And then in the morning, I found us gliding down a smooth, broad stream, at the rate of eleven miles an hour, our colours flying gaily, our crew rigged out in their smartest clothes, our officers in uniform again and the sun shining, as on a brilliant April day in England – before we then, soon after, tied up alongside the wharf at Halifax.

CHAPTER X

My Welcome in America

The Britannia was to stay tied up in Halifax for seven hours to deliver and exchange the mails, but no sooner had we docked than I was suddenly confronted by a breathless man who had been shouting my name as he tore along, and who then introduced himself as the Speaker of the Nova Scotia House of Assembly. It happened to be the day of the opening of their Legislative Council and General Assembly and I, the Inimitable, was suddenly dragged first up to the Governor's house (Lord Falkland being the Governor) and then here and there in a tumultuous showing, being welcomed by all manner of civic dignitaries and crowds cheering in the streets, before being shown to a great elbow-chair by the Speaker's throne and sitting down in the middle of the floor of their House of Commons, the observed of all observers, listening with exemplary gravity to the queerest speaking possible, and breaking, in spite of myself, into a smile as I thought of this commencement to the thousand and one stories in reserve for home.

My stay in Halifax was all too brief, before we left for Boston in the Britannia. During the three-day journey, a number of the passengers met together, with Lord Mulgrave in the chair and I as secretary and treasurer, to record our highest appreciation of Captain Hewett's nautical skill and his indefatigable attention to the management and safe conduct of the ship during our more than ordinary tempestuous passage. We opened a subscription for the purchase of some form of engraved silver plate to be presented to him as a consequence. £50 was collected and I later presented him with an engraved silver goblet (with a second to follow) at the Tremont Theatre in Boston as a token of our lasting gratitude to him for his ability, courage and skill, to which we owed our safety and preservation under circumstances of unusual peril.

As we came alongside in Boston, the town poured itself out upon the wharf and journalists and editors fought their way on board to speak to me, leaping on board at the peril of their lives long before we had moored to the wharf and tearing violently up to me and shaking hands like madmen. One then ran off, two miles at least, to the hotel, the Tremont House, and ordered rooms and dinner for us, before we followed in a carriage through streets filled with ribbons and feathers and cheering crowds. We found we were placed in Room 29 of this most excellent hotel, which had more galleries, colonnades, piazzas and passages than I can remember or anyone unaware would believe. Lord Mulgrave, who was going back to his regiment in Montreal after the weekend, had agreed to live with us in the meanwhile and he, Kate and I sat down in a spacious and handsome room to a very handsome dinner. I promised him that, when I reached Montreal on my travels (as I proposed to do), I would play at his regimental theatre with his fellow officers for the benefit of a charity.

I found the City of Boston an exciting and beautiful place, with every thoroughfare looking exactly like a scene in a pantomime. I did much visiting of establishments, met many fine people and found the tone of society in Boston to be one of perfect politeness, courtesy and good breeding. But how can I give you the faintest notion of my reception here; of the crowds that poured in and out of the hotel the whole day, and who lined the streets when I went out? And it was not just Boston; the cry of greeting now ran through the whole country! I had deputations from the Far West, who came from more than two thousand miles distance: from the lakes, the rivers, the backwoods, the log houses, the cities, factories, villages and towns. Authorities from nearly all the States wrote to me. I heard from the universities, Congress, the Senate, and bodies, public and private, of every sort and kind – so much so that I had to hire a secretary, George Putnam, to help me cope for the rest of my stay in America. Henry Dexter, a sculptor even spent time with me at Tremont House whilst I ate my breakfast and, as I read my letters and dictated answers to Putnam, he was measuring bits of my face with callipers and studying my head from all different angles. Kate thought the bust he produced was a most beautiful likeness of me.

In Boston we were escorted everywhere, and were constantly out two or three times in the evenings, dining and socializing until midnight, every moment of my time being fully occupied and engaged. I met with many who became firm friends thereafter, two in particular being Cornelius Felton, Professor of Greek Literature at Harvard University and Henry Wadsworth Longfellow, Professor of Modern Languages at the same establishment. At a splendid dinner in the drawing-rooms of Papanti's Hall and given by the "Young Men of Boston" (one of whom was James Fields, later partner in the publishing firm of Ticknor and Fields), I received a most hearty welcome from two hundred guests such as no man ever had, flocking about me like a host of brothers and making this place feel like home. I told them, in a speech, of my philosophy in life – an earnest and true desire to contribute, as far as in me lies, to the common stock of healthful cheerfulness and enjoyment and that it was my belief that virtue showed quite as well in rags and patches as she does in purple and fine linen. I also thanked them for taking to their hearts Oliver, Smike and Nell, but before I sat down I made it clear that there was one topic on which I was desirous to lay particular stress here in America, namely the need for International Copyright as a matter of justice, though I also stressed that, whilst not incompatible, I would rather have the affectionate regard of my fellow men, than I would have heaps and mines of gold.

I settled in Boston on a course of visits to establishments and institutions as I should take in my future travels in America. One such visit was a one-day excursion by railroad to nearby Lowell to witness its factory system. This manufacturing town had been in existence for barely twenty-one years, and nothing in the whole town looked old to me – except the mud, which at some points was almost knee deep. The mills all worked by water power and I visited many and was able to compare with those in England, where I had visited many in Manchester and elsewhere in the same manner. I was heartily impressed with what I saw from the demeanour of the workers – particularly the large number of females, many of whom were only just then verging upon womanhood and who laboured in these mills, upon an average, twelve hours a day. I can solemnly declare that from all the crowd I saw in the different factories that day, I cannot recall or separate one young face that gave me a painful impression; not one young girl whom, assuming it to be a matter of necessity that she should gain her daily bread by the labour of her hands, I would have removed from those works if I had the power. I learnt that there was no manufacturing population in Lowell, so to speak, for these girls (often the daughters of small farmers) came from other States, remained a few years in the mills, and then went home for good.

Leaving Boston on the afternoon of Saturday the 5th February, we proceeded by another railroad to Worcester, one of the prettiest villages in New England, where we had arranged to remain under the hospitable roof of the Governor of the State until Monday morning. On the Monday morning we went on, still by railroad, to Springfield and then along the Connecticut River by small steamboat for two and a half hours to Hartford. It certainly was not called "a small steamboat" without reason; I omitted to ask the question, but I think it must have been of about half a pony power. The cabin was fitted with common sash windows like an ordinary dwelling house, with bright red curtains hung on slack strings across the lower panes so that it looked like a parlour of a Lilliputian public house which had got afloat in a flood or some other water accident and was drifting, nobody knew where. But even in this chamber there was a rocking-chair; it would be impossible to get on anywhere in America without a rocking-chair! We all kept to the middle of the deck lest the boat should unexpectedly tip over; the machinery by some surprising process of condensation, worked between it and the keel, the whole forming a warm sandwich about three feet thick. The Connecticut River was full of floating blocks of ice and the depth where we went (to avoid the ice and current) no more than a few inches, but it is a fine stream and the banks in summertime are, I have no doubt, beautiful: at all events I was told so by a young lady in the cabin; and she should be a judge of beauty, if the possession of a quality included the appreciation of it, for a more beautiful creature I never looked upon.

We tarried in Hartford four days and, though Kate's face was now horribly bad, we nevertheless held a formal assembly or "levee" (as they rather oddly call it) every day for two hours and received at each from two hundred to three hundred people. The town I found beautifully situated in a basin of green hills, but for me too much of the old Puritan spirit existed in these parts. Nevertheless, I shall always entertain a very pleasant and grateful recollection of Hartford. It is a lovely place, and I developed many friends there whom I can never remember with indifference. Before leaving I raised once again the issue of International

Copyright – in a speech at the City Hotel on the 7th February, my 30th birthday. My friends were paralysed with wonder at such audacious daring, but I emphasized again that I did not do so in a sordid sense for my own personal enrichment and that of my children, and pointed out that if there had existed any law in this respect, Sir Walter Scott might not have sunk beneath the mighty pressure of his brain, but lived to add new creatures of his fancy to those that he had produced. I wish you could have seen the faces that I saw, down both sides of the table, when I began to talk about Scott, and wish you could have heard how I gave it out. My blood so boiled as I thought of the monstrous injustice, and felt as if I were twelve feet high when I thrust it down their throats. But I came to believe that there was no country on the face of the earth where there was less freedom of opinion on the need for International Copyright, and my raising it caused an outcry.

We left Hartford on Friday 11th February, and travelled by railroad towards New Haven. On the way the train stopped expressly at a place called Wallingford to gratify the curiosity of the whole town, which had turned out to see me. We arrived in New Haven at about eight o'clock and put up for the night at the best inn, the Tontine Hotel. Once again the excitement was immense and the hotel appeared to be besieged by the whole population of the town. The moment we had had tea we were forced to open another levee for the students and professors of Yale College and the townspeople. I suppose we shook hands, before going to bed, with considerably more than five hundred people – and I stood, as a matter of course, the whole time. We were inexpressibly worn out and yet, when at last we got to bed and were going to fall asleep, the choristers of the college turned out in a body, with a great many voices and a regular band, under the window and serenaded us!

After a night's rest we rose early, and in good time went down to the wharf and on board the packet steamer for New York. Before the boat left there was another levee, this one actually on the deck, and then "Three times Three for Dickens!" as we moved off. This was the first American steamboat of any size that I had seen, and when I descended into the cabin it looked, in my unaccustomed eyes, about as long as the Burlington Arcade. I was then delighted to find on board Professor Fenton, who was going on to "The Boz Ball" that I knew by now was being organized for me in New York. Like most men of his class whom I saw in America, he was a most delightful fellow – unaffected, hearty, genial, jolly; quite an Englishman of the best sort. We drank all the porter on board, ate all the cold pork and cheese and were very merry indeed – and, after the larder and stock of bottled beer was all exhausted, I lay down and fell asleep.

When I awoke, we were now in a narrow channel, with sloping banks on either side besprinkled with pleasant villas, and made refreshing to the sight by turf and trees. We emerged into a noble bay, whose waters sparkled in the now cloudless sunshine like nature's eyes turned up to Heaven, and so arrived in New York. The wharves were, once again, thronged with crowds, as well as coachmen and drays. People rushed up to shake hands with me or to screw small dabs of fur out of the back of the costly great coat I had bought in Regent Street! I had to be helped along by Professor Fenton, whilst the captain safely piloted Kate through the dense crowds to our transport for the Carlton House Hotel. Once there, we found a very splendid suite of rooms prepared for us, but just as we sat down for dinner, David Colden (the secretary of the Boz Ball Committee) made his appearance and when he had gone and we were taking our wine, Washington Irvine came in alone, with open arms, and to my delight stopped until ten o'clock that night.

I found this metropolis of America by no means so clean a city as Boston, though many of its streets had the same characteristics, except that the houses were not so freshly coloured and the knobs and plates upon the street doors not quite so bright and twinkling. There were many by-streets, almost as neutral in clean colours and positive in dirty ones as by-streets in London; and one quarter, commonly called the Five Points, which, in respect of filth and wretchedness, may be safely backed against Seven Dials or any other part of famed St. Giles. The great promenade and thoroughfare, as most people know, is Broadway, a wide and bustling street which housed our hotel and which, from the Battery Gardens to its opposite termination in a country road, may be four miles long. And was there ever such a sunny street as this Broadway! No stint of omnibuses here, with plenty of hackney cabs and coaches too; and Heaven save the ladies, how they dress! You see more colours in ten minutes here than elsewhere in as many days. And what various parasols! What rainbow silks and satins! What pinking of their stockings and pinching of their shoes, and fluttering of ribbons and silk tassels, and display of such cloaks with gaudy hoods and linings! The young gentlemen are fond of turning down their shirt collars and cultivating their whiskers, especially under the chin; but they cannot approach the ladies in their dress or bearing.

Then, walking by Broadway, I came across a dismal-fronted pile of bastard Egyptian, like an enchanter's palace in a melodrama – a famous prison called "The Tombs". I entered out of curiosity and a man with keys appeared to show me around. I found the prisoners had little exercise in their routine and seldom walked in the yard. There was a male and a female side, and then I found a young boy of ten or twelve years locked in a cell and inquired of his circumstance. I was told that he was the son of a man I had seen in a cell not many minutes before who had murdered his wife and was awaiting trial and would probably be hanged, and that this boy was a witness against his father and was detained here for safe keeping until the trial. I was also shown into the prison yard, in which my guide paused now, and which had been the scene of terrible performances. Into this narrow, grave-like place, men are brought out to die. The wretched creature stands beneath the gibbet on the ground, the rope about his neck; and when the sign is given, a weight at its other end comes running down and swings him up into the air – a corpse. The law requires that there be present at this dismal spectacle, the judge, the jury and citizens to the amount of twenty-five, but from the community it is hidden.

I went out into the cheerful streets again, but arranged a visit into the Five Points, where it was needful to take an escort (two heads of police) for poverty, wretchedness and vice were rife enough there. We came upon the place: these narrow ways, diverting to the right and left, and reeling everywhere with dirt and filth. Such lives as are led bear the same fruits here as elsewhere; the coarse and bloated faces at the doors have counterparts at home and all the wide world over. The squalid street led to a kind of square of leprous houses, some of which were attainable only by crazy wooden stairs without. Beyond one tottering flight of steps that creaked beneath the tread, lay a miserable room lit by one dim candle, and destitute of all comfort, save that which might be hidden in a wretched bed. And within the room was revealed a man, sitting with head in hands, suffering the fever. Leaving him and exploring this wolfish den of pitch-dark stairs and trembling boards, where neither ray of light nor breath of air appeared to come, scores of sleeping negroes were revealed. From every corner, as you glanced about in these dark retreats, some figure crawled half-awakened, as if the judgement hour were near at hand and every obscene grave were giving up its dead. Where dogs would howl to lie, women and men, and boys, shirked off to sleep, forcing the dislodged rats to move away in quest of better lodgings.

I visited many institutions during my time in New York – the City Watch House (that forms part of "The Tombs"), where common offenders against the police discipline of the town are thrust into holes of such indecent and disgusting filth and offensive stench as would bring disgrace upon the most despotic empire in the world; a Lunatic Asylum on Long Island or Rhode Island (I forget which) where everything had a lounging, listless madhouse air which was very painful to behold – and turned my feelings into deep disgust and measureless contempt at the notion that, as one side or other in party politics fluctuated and varied, and their despicable weathercocks were blown this way and that, the miserable strife in this sad refuge of afflicted and degraded humanity continued; nearby, an Alms House (the Workhouse of New York) lodging, I believe when I was there, nearly a thousand poor in badly lighted and badly ventilated conditions; the prisons at Sing Sing and Auburn; the Refuge for the Destitute, an admirable establishment whose object was to reclaim youthful offenders (male and female, black and white) without distinction. I also found excellent hospitals and schools, literary institutions and libraries, an admirable fire department and charities of every sort and kind.

The hospitality I received was remarkable and, at times, quite overwhelming. This was particularly so at an extraordinary festival (quite unparalleled) and named "The Boz Ball", held at the Park Theatre on the evening of Monday the 14th February. We were waited upon by David Colden and General George Morris, the former habited in full ball costume, the latter in the full-dress uniform of Heaven knows what regiment of militia. The General took Kate, Colden gave his arm to me, and we proceeded downstairs to a carriage at the door of the hotel, which took us to the stage door of the theatre – greatly to the disappointment of an enormous crowd who were besetting the main door and making a most tremendous hullaballoo. The scene upon our entrance was very striking. There were three thousand people present in full dress; from the roof to the floor, the theatre was decorated magnificently; and the light, glitter, glare, show, noise and cheering when I entered baffles my descriptive powers. We were walked in through the centre dress-box, the front whereof had been taken out for the occasion; then to the back of the stage where the mayor and other dignitaries received us; and we were then paraded all around the enormous ball-room – twice – for the gratification of the many-headed. That done, we began to dance – Heaven knows how we did it, for there was no room. We continued dancing until about half past midnight when, being no longer able to stand and I with a violent sore throat, we slipped away quietly and came back to our hotel. It was, however, the most splendid, gorgeous, brilliant affair anyone could possibly conceive.

But at the hotel I was obliged to have a doctor and was not myself by any means. I was confined to bed for the next two days with an inflammatory affection of the throat and so had to cancel engagements, as well as missing a further ball for me, held two days later on the 16th, again at the Park Theatre. However, by the 18th I was able to attend at a dinner presided over (with some difficulty in public speaking) by Washington Irving, when nearly eight hundred of the most distinguished citizens of New York were present, and where I expressed my sincere and full gratitude to them and to Washington Irving – as well as claiming once again that (through the establishment of International Copyright) justice should be done on the question of literary interest.

CHAPTER XI

Travelling South

I now began to feel of my time in America that everything was public and nothing private, and that I might be guilty of giving myself up as a spectacle. I found that I could do nothing that I wanted to do, go nowhere where I wanted to go, and see nothing that I wanted to see. The newspapers spoke of "Boz Mania". When I turned into a street I was followed by a multitude. If I stayed at home the house became, with callers, like a fair. I'd go to a party in the evening and be so enclosed and hemmed about by people – stand where I will – that I was exhausted for want of air. I dined out and had to talk about everything to everybody. When I went to church for quiet, there was a violent rush to the neighbourhood of the pew I sat in, and the clergyman preached at me. I could not arrive at any railway station without the crowds surrounding my car, letting down all the windows, thrusting in their heads, staring at me and comparing notes respecting my appearance, with as much coolness as if I were a marble image. If I drank a glass of water, I felt as if a hundred people were looking down my throat when I opened my mouth to swallow. My image was everywhere, and yet I never knew less of myself in all my life, or had less time for those interviews with myself whereby I earn my bread. I had no rest or peace and was in a perpetual worry. In truth, I had become sick to death of the life I had been leading in America – worn out in mind and body – and quite weary and distressed. So, I decided to decline all future invitations of a public nature; and meant to be resolute from this time forth.

And how my thoughts did at this time turn to England and my dear children – Oh for news of home! And how I yearned for home, three thousand miles away! Before I left New York, I made arrangements for securing our passage on the "George Washington", a 600-ton packet sail-ship which was advertised to sail from New York to Liverpool on the 7th June; that being the month in which I had determined, if prevented by no accident in the course of my wider travels, to leave America.

I planned to go south into the regions of slavery, to Charleston – before going into the west, through the wilds of Kentucky and Tennessee, across the Alleghany Mountains, and so on until we should strike the Lakes and could get to Canada. But it was represented to me that this was a track only known to travelling merchants; that the roads were bad, the country a tremendous waste, the inns log-houses, and the journey one that would play the very devil with Kate. I was staggered, but not deterred. If I found it possible to be done in the time, I meant to do it.

I sent George Putnam on ahead to Philadelphia, but then Kate fell ill with a bad ulcerated sore throat and the doctor forbad her to get up. I determined to remain in New York until she could come on with me, for I feared that if I left her alone in sickness at such a great distance from home, she would feel distressed after I had gone. I so much enjoyed the quiet I had in those days, owing to its having been generally supposed that I had left New York, that I was more anxious than ever to travel peaceably.

Kate improved, and on the evening of the 5th March we eventually left for Philadelphia. We made the journey by railroad and two ferries, which occupied us between five and six hours. It was a fine evening as we travelled along in the train, and watching the bright sunset from a little window near the door by which we sat, my attention was attracted to a remarkable appearance issuing from the gentlemen's car immediately in front of us, which I supposed for some time was occasioned by a number of industrious persons inside, ripping open feather beds, and giving the feathers to the winds. At length, it occurred to me that they were only spitting, which was indeed the case; for I had discovered that this spitting was universal. In the courts of law, the Judge had his spittoon (or "spit-box" as they called it here) on the Bench; the counsel had theirs, the witness had his, the prisoner his, and the crier his. The jury were accommodated at the rate of three men to a spit-box; and the spectators in the gallery were provided for, as so many men, in the course of nature, expectorated without cessation. There were spit-boxes in every steamboat, bar-room, public dining room, house or office, and place of general resort, no matter where I might be. In the hospitals, the students were requested by placards to use the boxes provided for them and not to spit on the stairs. I twice saw gentlemen at evening parties in New York turn aside when they were not engaged in conversation and spit upon the drawing-room carpet. And in every bar-room and hotel passage the stone floor looked as if it were paved with open oysters – from the quantity of this kind of deposit which tessellated it all over. It was the most sickening, beastly, and abominable custom that ever civilization saw.

We arrived in Philadelphia quite late and then, through misunderstood circumstances, the following morning I was again forced to stand for some two hours in a private room in the hotel, greeting one Philadelphian after another as five hundred people presented themselves. Philadelphia itself I found to be a handsome city, but distractingly regular. After walking about for an hour or two, I felt I would have given the world for a crooked street; but it is most beautifully provided with fresh water, which is showered and jerked about, and turned on and poured off everywhere. There are various public institutions, among them a most excellent hospital – a Quaker establishment but not sectarian in the great benefits it confers; a quiet, quaint old library named after Franklin; a handsome Exchange and Post Office; whilst on the outskirts stands a great new prison called "The Eastern Penitentiary", conducted on a plan peculiar to the State of Pennsylvania or, I believe, anywhere in the world. The system here operated and known as the "Separate System" is rigid, strict and with hopelessly solitary confinement. I believe it, and in its effects, to be cruel and wrong.

Prisons are intended to be, and should be, places of punishment but of a proper kind. The inspectors, immediately on my arrival in Philadelphia, invited me to pass the day in the Eastern Penitentiary and to dine with them when I had finished my inspection, that they might hear my opinion of the system. Accordingly, I passed a whole day in going from cell to cell and conversing with the prisoners. Every facility was given to me; and no constraint whatever imposed on any person's free speech. I never shall be able to dismiss from my mind the impressions of that day. I saw men who had been there five years and more, one man shut up in the same cell by himself for nearly twelve years; some whose term was nearly over, and some whose term had only just begun. Women were there too, under the same variety of circumstances. Every prisoner who came into the jail, came at night, was put into a bath, and dressed in prison garb; and then a black hood drawn over their face and head as they are led to the solitary cell, from which they never stir again until the whole period of confinement has expired. I looked at some of them with the same awe as I should have looked at those who had been buried alive and then dug up again, in the meantime being dead to everything but torturing anxieties and horrible despair.

I believe that very few men are capable of estimating the immense amount of torture and agony which this dreadful punishment, prolonged for years, inflicts upon the sufferers; and in guessing at it myself and in reasoning from what I have seen written upon their faces, and what to my certain knowledge they feel within, I am only the more convinced that there is a depth of terrible endurance in it which none but the sufferers themselves can fathom, and which no man has a right to inflict upon his fellow creature. I hold this slow and daily tampering with the mysteries of the brain to be immeasurably worse than any torture of the body; and because its ghastly signs and tokens are not so palpable to the eye and sense of touch as scars upon the flesh; because its wounds are not upon the surface, and it extorts few cries that human ears can hear; therefore, I the more denounce it, as a secret punishment which slumbering humanity is not roused up to stay.

I dined in the jail with the inspectors, and told them after dinner how much the sight had affected me, and what an awful punishment it was. After leaving I began debating with myself whether, if I had the power, I would allow it to be tried in certain cases, where the terms of imprisonment were short; and now I solemnly declare that I could not walk a happy man beneath the open sky or lie me down upon my bed at night, with the consciousness that one human creature, for any length of time, lay suffering this unknown punishment in his silent cell, and I the cause, or I consenting to it, in the least degree.

We left Philadelphia at six o'clock on a very cold morning and turned our faces towards Washington, travelling by steamboat on James River and then by railcar, before stopping to dine in Baltimore. Being now in Maryland, we were waited on for the first time by slaves. The sensation of exacting any service from human creatures who are bought and sold, and being, for the time, a party as it were to their condition, is not an enviable one. The institution exists, perhaps, in its least repulsive and most instigated form in such a town as this; but it is slavery, and though I was, with respect to it, an innocent man, its presence filled me with a sense of shame and self-reproach.

After the dinner, we went down to the railroad again and travelled on to Washington. Washington has no trade or commerce of its own, having little or no population beyond the President and his establishment, the members who reside there during the session, and the Government clerks and officers employed in the various departments. The House of Representatives has an elegant chamber to look at, but a singularly bad one for all purposes of hearing; the Senate, which is smaller, is free of this objection and is exceedingly well adapted to the uses for which it is designed. During my stay I visited both Houses nearly every day and found the parliamentary forms modelled on those of the old country – but there are more quarrels than with us, and more threatenings than gentlemen are accustomed to exchange in any civilized society, although farmyard imitations have not, as yet, been imported from our Parliament. The feature on oratory which appears to be the most practiced, and most relished, is the constant repetition of the same idea or shadow of an idea, in fresh words; and the inquiry out of doors is not "What did he say?" but "How long did he speak?"

Both Houses are handsomely carpeted; but the state to which these carpets are reduced by the universal disregard of the spittoon with which every member is accommodated, and the extraordinary improvements on the pattern which are squirted and dabbled upon it in every direction, do not admit of being described. I will merely observe that I strongly recommend all strangers not to look at the floor; and if they happen to drop anything, though it be their purse, not to pick it up with an ungloved hand on any account. It is strange enough too, to see an honourable gentleman leaning back in his tilted chair with his legs on the desk before him, shaping a convenient "plug" of tobacco with his penknife and, when it is quite ready for use, shooting the old one from his mouth, as from a pop-gun, and clapping the new one in its place. I was surprised to observe that even steady old chewers of great experience are not always good marksmen, which has rather inclined me to doubt that general proficiency with the rifle, of which we have heard so much in England. Several gentlemen called upon me who, in the course of conversation, frequently missed the spittoon at five paces; and one (but he was certainly short-sighted) mistook the closed sash for the open window at three.

The President's mansion is more like an English clubhouse, both within and without, than any other kind of establishment with which I can compare it. On the morning after my arrival I was carried thither by an official gentleman, who was so kind as to charge himself with my presentation to the President, President Tyler. We entered a large hall, and having twice or thrice rung a bell, which nobody answered, walked without further ceremony through the rooms on the ground floor as divers other gentlemen (mostly with their hats on and their hands in their pockets) were doing very leisurely. We went upstairs into another chamber where were certain visitors waiting for audiences. At the sight of my conductor and I, a black in plain clothes and yellow slippers (who was gliding noiselessly about and whispering messages in the ears of the more impatient) made a sign of recognition and glided off. We had not waited many minutes before the black messenger returned and conducted us into another room of smaller dimensions where, at a business-like table covered with papers, sat the President himself.

The expression of his face was mild and pleasant, and his manner was remarkably unaffected, gentlemanly, and agreeable. I thought that in his whole carriage and demeanour he became his station singularly well, but I came to see that he looked somewhat worn and anxious – as well he might be, being, as I heard, at war with everybody. He expressed great surprise at my being so young. I did not return the compliment as he looked too worn and tired to justify it. We talked briefly before I left, but went once more to his house before leaving Washington. I went with Kate and found a crowd of people, including Washington Irving who had recently been appointed Minister at the Court of Spain and was there in his new character for the first and last time before going abroad. I also attended a private dinner held in my honour at Boulangers on the 14th March with George M. Kleim, U.S. Marshall for East Pennsylvania, in the chair, and with one of the honoured guests being John Quincy Adams, previous President and now Member of the House of Representatives, who had taken strongly against slavery. It was a most pleasant evening.

From Washington, I had at first intended going south to Charleston. But when I came to consider the length of time which this journey would occupy, the dismal swamp of the country, and the premature intense heat of the season – and weighed, moreover, in my own mind the pain of living in the constant contemplation of slavery and the odious sight of it, I determined instead to travel south only to Richmond in Virginia, my object being to see some tobacco plantations, before then turning and shaping our course for the Far West. We took our way to Richmond, first by steamer to Potomac Creek, then jolting stage-coach to Fredericksburg, before taking to the railroad to Richmond. On the rail journey, I witnessed, in the black car (for they don't let them sit with the whites), a mother and family that had just been sold and were being conveyed away, whilst the man (the husband and father) was left behind, retained to work on his owner's plantation. The children cried the whole way and the mother was misery's picture. Americans will ask you what you think of slavery; and will expiate on it as if it were one of the greatest blessings of mankind; and telling you its damned nonsense that you hear in England. I have been asked if I believed in the Bible. Yes, I said, but if any man could prove to me it sanctioned slavery, I would place no further credence in it.

Richmond itself was so hot that we could scarcely breathe. I visited a tobacco manufactory, where the workmen were all slaves and saw the whole process of picking, rolling, pressing, drying, packing in casks and branding, the slaves all labouring quietly until after two o'clock in the day, when they were allowed to sing. On the following day I visited a plantation or farm of about twelve hundred acres on the opposite bank of the river. The planter's house was an airy rustic dwelling; the quarter where the slaves lived comprised very crazy, wretched cabins near to which groups of half-naked children basked in the sun or wallowed on the dusty ground. There were two bridges across the river: one belonging to the railroad and the other, a very crazy affair, was the private property of some old lady in the neighbourhood who levied tolls upon the townspeople. Crossing this bridge on my way back, I saw a notice painted on the gate, cautioning all persons to drive slowly: under a penalty, if the offender were a white man, of five dollars; if a negro, fifteen stripes. My heart is lightened, as if a great load has been taken from it, when I think that we in England are turning our backs on this accursed and detested system of slavery. I really don't think I could have born it any longer.

CHAPTER XII

West to the Prairie, then North East to The Lakes

We were unable to take the route I intended from Richmond, so returned to Washington and from there to Baltimore, where we stayed in Barnham's Hotel, the most comfortable of all the hotels of which I had any experience in the United States. Washington Irving came here from New York to pass another day or two with me before I went westward and these days were made among the most memorable of my life by his delightful fancy and genial humour. From Baltimore we went by railroad to York, where we dined, before taking the stage-coach on the twenty-five mile journey to Harrisburg. This stage-coach was like nothing so much as the body of one of the swings you see at a fair, set upon four wheels and roofed and covered at the sides with painted canvas. And there were twelve inside! I, thank my lucky stars, was on the box. The luggage was on the roof; among it, a good-sized dining table and a big rocking-chair. There were four horses to this land-ark, but we did not perform the journey until after half past six o'clock at night – and, before doing so, took up an intoxicated gentleman, who sat for ten miles between me and the coachman; and another intoxicated gentleman who got up behind, but in the course of a mile or two fell off without hurting himself, and was seen in the distant perspective reeling back to the grog-shop where we had found him!

At Harrisburg we stayed the night and then took the canal-boat for Pittsburgh. At night the ladies' section of the cabin was separated off by a red curtain, leaving some thirty men in my section. Temporary narrow shelves for sleeping on were erected, one on top of another in the low cabin, with the atmosphere of the place, as you may suppose, by no means fresh. And you never can conceive what the hawking and spitting was like the whole night through. But I made no complaints and showed no disgust. I cracked jokes with everyone near me until we fell asleep – and then, upon waking at half-past five, I ran up on deck bare-necked and, fishing the dirty water out of the canal with a tin ladle chained to the boat, scrabbled my face with the half-frozen water, before jumping from the boat to the towing-path and walking five or six miles before breakfast, keeping up with the horses all the time. In a word, they were quite astonished to find a sedentary Englishman roughing it so well, and taking so much exercise; and questioned me very much on that head. The greater part of the men here will sit and shiver round the stove all day, rather than put one foot before the other; and as to having a window open, that is not to be thought of.

After two days we reached the foot of the Allegheny Mountains. There the canal stopped and the passengers conveyed across by land-carriage on a railroad, assisted by stationary engines, taking rather more than five hours to perform this strange part of the journey (lifting us to an inn upon the mountain, where we dined, and then progressing down the other side, with some queer precipices close to the rails) – before being taken on to Pittsburgh by another canal boat, the counterpart of the first, which awaited us on the other side of the mountains.

Pittsburgh is like Birmingham in England; at least its townspeople say so. It certainly had a great quantity of smoke hanging about it, and was famous for its iron works. We lodged at a most excellent hotel where, on one of the nights, Kate sat down, laughing, for me to try my hand on her at magnetism. I had been holding forth upon the subject rather luminously, and asserting that I thought I could exercise the influence, but had never tried. In six minutes I magnetized her into hysterics, and then into the magnetic sleep. I tried again the next night, and she fell into the slumber in little more than two minutes; I could wake her with perfect ease, but I confess (not being prepared for anything so sudden and complete), I was on the first occasion rather alarmed.

We tarried three days before going on, by way of a high-pressure (and very tremulous) steamboat called "The Messenger" that, for another three days, skimmed us down the Ohio River to Cincinnati. The inhabitants of Cincinnati are proud of their city as one of the most interesting in America – and with good reason, for beautiful and thriving as it is now and containing as it does a population of fifty thousand souls, but two and fifty years have passed away since the ground on which it stands (bought at that time for a few dollars) was a wild wood, and its citizens were but a handful of dwellers in scattered log huts upon the river's shore.

We left Cincinnati on the steamboat for Louisville and, on this journey, I met Pitchlynn, a chief of the Choctaw tribe of Indians. He was a remarkably handsome man with a very bright, keen, dark and piercing eye. He had chiefly been at Washington on some negotiations pending between his tribe and the Government, which were not settled yet (he said in a melancholy way), and he feared never would be: for what could a few poor Indians do against such well-skilled men of business as the whites? He had no love for Washington; tired of towns and cities very soon, and longed for the forest and prairie. He told me there were but twenty thousand of the Choctaws left and their number was decreasing every day. Several times he told me that, unless they tried to assimilate themselves to their conquerors, they must be swept away before the strides of civilized society. He took his leave of me, as stately and complete a gentleman of nature's making as ever I beheld. He sent me a lithographed portrait of himself soon afterwards; very like, though scarcely handsome enough, and which I have carefully preserved in memory of our brief acquaintance.

Our stop in Louisville was at the splendid Galt House Hotel, where we were as handsomely lodged as though we had been in Paris. Then on we went, by another steamboat, to a place called Cairo, a detestable morass at the junction of the Rivers Ohio and Mississippi. On ground so flat and low and marshy, that in certain seasons of the year it is inundated to the house-tops, lies this breeding-place of fever, ague and death; vaunted in England as a mine of Golden Hope, and speculated in, on the faith of monstrous representations, to many people's ruin. A dismal swamp on which the half-built houses rot away: cleared here and there for the space of a few yards; and teeming, then, with rank unwholesome vegetation, in whose baleful shade the wretched wander who are tempted hither, to droop and die and lay their bones; a hotbed of disease, an ugly sepulchre, a grave uncheered by any gleam of promise; a place without one single quality, in earth or air or water, to commend it – such is this dismal Cairo.

We continued along the Mississippi towards St. Louis, the river now an enormous ditch, sometimes two or three miles wide, running liquid mud at six miles an hour, with its strong and frothy current choked and obstructed everywhere by huge logs and whole forest trees. At St. Louis they would, once again, not let me alone about slavery. A certain Judge went so far about it that I fell upon him (to the indescribable horror of the man who brought him) and told him a piece of my mind. I said that I was very averse to speaking on the subject here, and always forbore if possible, but when he pitied our national ignorance of the truths of slavery, I must remind him that we went upon indisputable records, obtained after many years of careful investigation, and at all sorts of self-sacrifice; and that I believed we were much more competent to judge of its atrocity and horror than he who had been brought up in the midst of it. I told him that men who spoke of it as a blessing, as a matter of course, as a state of things to be desired, were out of the pale of reason; and that for them to speak of ignorance or prejudice was an absurdity, too ridiculous to be combated.

As I had a great desire to see a prairie, a day was fixed before my departure for an expedition to the Looking Glass Prairie, which was within thirty miles of the town. We were fourteen in all, all young men, and moved off in the early morning into an area where, on either side of the track (if it deserves the name) was the thick "bush" and everywhere stagnant, slimy, rotten, filthy water. We were attended always by the music of the frogs and pigs, until nearly noon, when we halted at a place called Belleville, a small collection of wooden homes huddled together in the very heart of the bush and swamp. It also had a criminal court, which was sitting and trying some criminals for horse stealing, and where the horses belonging to the Bar, the Judge and the witnesses were tied to temporary racks set up roughly in the road – by which is to be understood a forest path, nearly knee deep in mud and slime.

For the rest of the day we travelled through the same desolate kind of waste, through a village called Lebanon, until we saw the prairie at sunset. I had heard and read so much about this – but the effect on me was one of disappointment. It was lonely and wild, but was oppressive in its barren monotony. You stood upon the prairie, and saw the unbroken horizon all around you; you were on a great plain, which was like a sea without water and, although I am exceedingly fond of wild and lonely scenery, I felt little of that sense of freedom and exhilaration which a Scottish heath inspires, or even our English Downs awaken. But we dined upon this plain, the meal delicious and the entertainers the soul of kindness and good humour. I have often recalled that cheerful party to my pleasant recollection since, and shall not easily forget, in junketings nearer home with friends of older date, my boon companions on the prairie.

We stayed in Lebanon that night at the Mermaid House, a little inn we had halted at in the afternoon, and the next morning set off and returned, through some ancient Indian burial places, to St. Louis. That evening we attended another very crowded levee, before turning our faces homeward. We took a steamboat back to Louisville, and then the mail boat back to Cincinnati, arriving at one o'clock in the morning. Resting one day in Cincinnati, we resumed our journey, now by mail stagecoach (with Kate, Anne and Putnam inside and I on the box) through the interior of the State of Ohio to Columbus and thence to "strike the lakes" (as the phrase is) at a small town called Sandusky. To Columbus the distance was a hundred and twenty miles, the road macadamized and, for an American road, very good. We travelled all night, and reached Columbus at seven in the morning. We breakfasted, went to bed until dinner time, but then at night held a levee for half an hour, the people pouring in as they always did, before next morning resuming our journey.

The stagecoach from Columbus to Sandusky only ran thrice a week, and not on this day, so I bargained for an "exclusive extra" with four horses, for which I paid $40, the horses changing, as they would as if it were the regular stage. To ensure our getting on properly, the proprietors sent an agent on the box; and, with no other company but him and a hamper full of eatables and drinkables, we went on our way. It is impossible, however, to convey an adequate idea of the kind of road over which we now travelled; I can only say that it was, at the best, but a track through the wild forest, and among the swamps, bogs, and morass of the withered bush. A great portion of it was what is called a "corduroy road": which is made by throwing round logs or whole trees into a swamp, and leaving them to settle there. Good Heaven! If you only felt one of the least of the jolts with which the coach fell from log to log! It was like nothing but going up a steep flight of stairs in an omnibus. Still, the day was beautiful, the air delicious, and we were alone: with no tobacco spittle, or eternal prosy conversation about dollars and politics (the only two subjects the Americans ever seemed to converse about) to bore us. We really enjoyed it, made a joke of being knocked about, and were quite merry.

We went on, through an awful three-hour lightening-storm, until ten o'clock at night, when we reached Lower Sandusky. The inn at which we halted was a rough log-house, the people all abed, and we had to knock them up. We had the queerest sleeping room, with two doors, one opposite the other; both opening directly on the wild black country, and neither having any lock or bolt. The effect of these opposite doors was that one was always blowing the other open, an ingenuity in the art of building which I don't remember to have met with before. You should have seen me, in my shirt, blockading them with portmanteaus, and desperately trying to make the room tidy! But the blockading was really needful, for in my dressing case I had about £250 in gold; and for this amount there were not a few men in the West who would murder their fathers.

After breakfasting we started again, and reached Sandusky at six o'clock in the evening, where we put up at a comfortable little hotel ("The Steamboat") on the brink of Lake Erie. We lay there that night and had no choice but to wait the next day until a steamboat, bound for Buffalo, appeared. The town itself, which was sluggish and uninteresting enough, was something like the back of our English watering place out of the season. Moreover, the demeanour of the people in these country parts was invariably morose, sullen, clownish and repulsive; I should think there is not, on the face of the earth, a people so entirely destitute of humour, vivacity, or the capacity of enjoyment. It is most remarkable. I am quite serious when I say that I had not heard a hearty laugh these six weeks, except my own; nor had I seen a merry face on any shoulders but a black man's. People lounging listlessly about; idling in bar-rooms; smoking; spitting; and lolling on the pavement in rocking-chairs, outside the shop doors - these are the only recollections I have of the place. When a steamboat came in sight and touched the wharf, we hurried on board with all speed, and soon left Sandusky far behind us.

CHAPTER XIII

Niagara, Canada, and back to New York

The steamboat "Constitution" was a large vessel of some five hundred tons, and handsomely fitted up, though with high pressure engines, which always conveyed that kind of feeling to me, which I should be likely to experience, I think, if I had lodgings on the first floor of a powder mill. Furthermore, it is all very fine talking about Lake Erie, but it won't do for persons who are liable to sea-sickness. We were all sick. It was almost as bad in that respect as the Atlantic, the waves being very short and horribly constant. We came at midnight to Cleveland, where we lay all night and until nine o'clock next morning. There was a gentleman on board to whom I, as I unintentionally learned through the thin partition which divided our state room from the cabin in which he and his wife conversed together, was unwittingly the occasion of very great uneasiness. I appeared to run in his mind perpetually and to dissatisfy him very much. I heard him say "Boz is on board still, my dear" and then, after a considerable pause, he added complainingly "Boz keeps himself very close", which was true enough, for I was not very well and was lying down, with a book. Then, after a long interval, he broke out again with "I suppose that Boz will be writing a book by and by and putting all our names in it!", at which imaginary consequences of being on board a boat with Boz, he groaned and became silent.

At six in the morning, people poured on board in crowds to see me, and a party of gentlemen actually planted themselves before our little cabin, stared in at the door and windows whilst I was washing and Kate lying in bed. Thereafter, we were able to travel to Erie and on to Buffalo, where we took the two-hour journey by railroad to Niagara. Upon alighting, and for the first time, I heard the mighty rush of water and felt the ground tremble underneath my feet. After going to the inn (the Clifton House), I dragged Kate down a deep and slippery path leading to the ferry boat; bullied Anne for not coming fast enough; perspired at every pore; and felt, it is impossible to say how, as the sound grew louder and louder in my ears – and yet nothing could be seen for the mist. I left Kate and Anne on a crag and was soon at the bottom, climbing with two English officers (who were crossing and had joined me) over some broken rocks, deafened by the noise, half-blinded by the spray, and wet to the skin. We were at the foot of the American Falls. I saw the water tearing madly down from some immense height, but could get no idea of shape, or situation, or anything but vague immensity.

Then, when we were seated in the little ferry boat and were crossing the swollen river immediately before both cataracts, I began to feel what it was: but was stunned and unable to comprehend the vastness of the scene. It was not until I came on Table Rock and looked – great Heavens, on what a fall of bright green water! – that it came on me in its full might and majesty.

I went back to the inn, changed my clothes, and hurried to the Horseshoe Fall. I went down alone into the very basin, and it would be hard for a man to stand nearer to God than he does here. There was a bright rainbow at my feet, and from that I looked up to – great Heaven WHAT a fall of water! The broad, deep, mighty stream seemed to die in the act of falling, and from its unfathomable grave arose that tremendous ghost of spray and mist which is never laid and has been haunting this place with the same dread solemnity – perhaps from the creation of the world. When I felt how near to my Creator I was standing, the first effect and the enduring one – instant and lasting – of the tremendous spectacle was peace; peace of mind, tranquility, calm recollections of the dead, great thoughts of eternal rest and happiness: nothing of gloom or terror. Niagara was at once stamped on my heart, an image of beauty; to remain there, changeless and indelible.

Ten memorable days we passed on that enchanted ground. What would I have given if the dear girl, whose ashes lie in Kensal Green, had lived to come so far along with us – but she has been here many times, I doubt not, since her sweet face faded from my earthly sight. When the sun is on the Falls they shine and glow like molten gold. When the day is gloomy, the water falls like snow – or sometimes it seems to crumble away like the face of a great chalk cliff – or sometimes again, to roll along the front of the rock like white smoke. But at all seasons, gay or gloomy, dark or light, by sun or moon, from the bottom of both falls, there is always rising up a solemn ghostly cloud, which hides the boiling cauldron from human sight, and makes it, in its mystery, a hundred times more grand than if you could see all the secrets that lie hidden in its tremendous depth. I found it the most wonderful and beautiful place in the world.

At the culmination of our stay, we took the steamboat onto Lake Ontario and thence to Toronto. The steamboat, now laden with flour, then took us eastwards along the lake, calling at Port Hope, Cobourg and Kingston, before taking us down the St. Lawrence River towards Montreal. The beauty of this noble stream at almost any part, but especially in the commencement of this journey when it winds its way among the thousand islands, can hardly be imagined. In the afternoon, we shot down some rapids where the river boiled and bubbled strangely and where the force and headlong violence of the current were tremendous. At seven o'clock in the evening we reached Dickenson's Landing, from where we proceeded by stagecoach to Montreal.

The town of Montreal was full of life and bustle. We stayed here (at Rasco's Hotel, St. Paul Street) in all for just over a fortnight, but included a steamboat trip taken at night to Quebec, this Gibraltar of America, where Wolfe and his brave companions climbed to glory. The vessel in which we returned from Quebec to Montreal was crowded with emigrants who had newly arrived from England and Ireland and were on their way to the backwoods and new settlements of Canada.

In Montreal, I had agreed with Lord Mulgrave to engage in some private theatricals with the officers of his regiment, which turned out splendidly. You should have seen me in that very dark and dusty theatre (the Queen's), with my coat off, the Stage Manager and Universal Director, for ten days urging impracticable ladies and impossible gentlemen on, to the very confines of insanity, shouting and driving about, to an extent which would justify any philanthropic stranger in clapping me into a straight-waistcoat without further enquiry; endeavouring to goad Putnam into some dim and faint understanding of a prompter's duties; and struggling in such a vortex of noise, dirt, bustle, confusion and inextricable entanglement as you would grow giddy in contemplating! This kind of voluntary hard labour used to be my great delight and I felt the furore had come strong on me again; I began to be once more of opinion that nature intended me for the lessee of a National Theatre and that pen, ink and paper had spoiled a manager!

A private performance took place on the 25th May, with an audience of between five and six hundred strong. We had the band of the 23rd Royal Welsh Fusiliers (one of the finest in the service) in the orchestra, the theatre was lighted with gas, the scenery excellent and the properties all brought from private houses. The military portion of the audience were all in full uniform; it was really a splendid scene. We performed "A Roland for an Oliver", "Past Two O'Clock in the Morning" (an interlude in one scene by Charles Matthews) and "Deaf as a Post" (a farce in one act), the last including Kate in the parts! She played devilish well – indeed all the ladies were capital and we had no wait or hitch for an instant. Three days later we repeated in public, concluding on this occasion with "High Life Below Stairs", with real actresses substituted for the ladies, all for the Theatre Manager's benefit. It went with a roar all through.

As to the extraordinary kindness and attention we experienced in all parts of Canada, no words can express. I verily believe that all the carriages, horses, boats, yachts, boat crews and servants in the colony (whether belonging to Government or private individuals) were, or have been, at our disposal. But now I began to get fevered with anxiety for home. Oh! How I looked forward across that rolling water to Home, and its small tenantry. How I busied myself into thinking how my books look; and where the tables are; and in what position the chairs stand relative to the other furniture; and whether we shall be able to surprise our loved ones. I set my heart on rushing into Forster's study and into Maclise's painting room, and into Macready's managerial ditto, without a moment's warning. How I pictured every little trait and circumstance of our arrival to myself, down to the very colour of the bow on the cook's cap! I left all these things – God only knows what a love I have for them – as coolly and calmly as any animated cucumber; but I knew that when I came upon them again I should have lost all power of self-restraint, and should as certainly make a fool of myself as ever Grimaldi did in his way, or George the Third in his.

We left Montreal for New York again on the 30th May, taking a floating palace of a steamboat along Lake Champlain to the town of Burlington and then on to Whitehall, where we took the stagecoach for Albany. At Albany, at seven in the evening, we went on board a great

North River steamboat, which was so crowded with passengers that the upper deck was like the box lobby of a theatre between pieces and the lower one like Tottenham Court Road on a Saturday night. But we slept soundly notwithstanding, and soon after five o'clock next morning reached New York and the Carlton House Hotel.

We had yet five days to spare before embarking for England, and I had a great desire to see the "Shaker Village", which is peopled by a religious sect from whom it takes its name. We went up the North River again as far as the town of Hudson, and there hired an extra to carry us to another place called Lebanon thirty miles distant. The Shaker Village was some two miles off and in the morning, as we rode along, we passed a party of Shakers who were at work upon the road, wore the broadest of all broad-brimmed hats and were, in all visible respects, such very wooden men that I felt about as much sympathy for them and as much interest in them as if they had been so many figureheads of ships. These people are called "Shakers" from their peculiar form of adoration, which consists of a dance performed by the men and women of all ages, who arrange themselves for the purpose in opposite parties, the men first divesting themselves of their hats and coats, which they gravely hang against the wall before they begin, and tying on a ribbon around their shirt sleeves, as though they were going to be bled. They accompany themselves with a droning, humming noise, and dance until they are quite exhausted, alternatively advancing and retiring in a preposterous sort of trot. The effect is said to be unspeakably absurd: and if I may judge from a print of this ceremony which I have in my possession, and which I am informed by those who have visited their chapel is perfectly accurate, it must be infinitely grotesque.

That the chapel was closed to the public for the space of one year, I found from a grim old Shaker with eyes as hard and dull and cold as the great round metal buttons on his coat and waistcoat; a sort of calm goblin. He produced a newspaper wherein the body of elders, whereof he was a member, had advertised but a few days before that the closure was in consequence of certain unseemly interruptions which their worship had received from strangers. The sect was presently governed by a woman, and her rule understood to be absolute, though she had the assistance of elders. She lived, it was said, in strict seclusion in certain rooms above the chapel, and never shown to profane eyes. If she at all resembled a lady I witnessed (something alive in russet, which the elder said was a woman, and which I supposed was a woman, though I should not have suspected it) who presided over the local Shaker store, it would be a great charity to keep her as close as possible, and I cannot too strongly express my perfect concurrence in this benevolent proceeding.

I left the grim Shaker Village with a hearty dislike of the old Shakers, and a hearty pity for the young ones. I so abhor and from my soul detest that bad spirit which would strip life of its healthful graces, rob youth of its innocent pleasures, pluck from maturity and age their pleasant ornaments, and make existence but a narrow path towards the grave. And if there must be people vowed to crush the harmless fancies and the love of innocent delights and gaieties, which are a part of human nature – as much a part of it as any other love or hope that is our common portion – let them, for me, stand openly revealed among the ribald and licentious; they are not on the immortal road, and we will despise them, and avoid them readily.

We returned to Lebanon and then to Hudson, where we took the steamboat once again down the North River towards New York. We stopped on the way for two nights at West Point, a beautiful place and where stands the Military School of America. We saw the beauty and freshness of this calm retreat in the very dawn and greenness of summer – being the beginning of June – and it was exquisite indeed. Leaving it on the 6th, and returning to New York to embark for England on the succeeding day, I was glad to think that among the last memorable beauties which glided past us and softened in the bright perspective, were those whose pictures, traced by no common hand, were fresh in most men's minds and not easy to grow old or fade beneath the dust of time: the Kaatskill Mountains, Sleepy Hollow and the Tappan Zee. Then, returning to the Carlton House Hotel for the last time, we dined exquisitely that evening with many friends.

CHAPTER XIV

My Thoughts on America

Before leaving these shores, my final thoughts were of the American people as they seemed to me. They were friendly, earnest, hospitable, kind, frank, very often accomplished, far less prejudiced than you would suppose, warm-hearted, fervent and enthusiastic. They are chivalrous in their universal politeness to women, courteous, obliging, interested and, when they conceive a perfect affection for a man (as I may venture to say of myself), entirely devoted to him. I received thousands of people of all ranks; in every town where we stayed, though it may be only for a day, we would hold a regular levee or drawing room, where I would shake hands with hundreds of people each time, and who passed on from me to Kate, to be shaken again by her. Two hours of this, and the people coming in by the hundreds – all fresh and piping hot and full of questions – would take us to a point where we were literally exhausted and hardly able to stand. But I was never once asked an offensive or impolite question – except by Englishmen, who, when they have been 'located' here for some years, are worse than the devil in his blackest painting.

The American State itself is a parent to its people: has a parental care and watches over all poor children, women labouring of child, sick persons and captives. The common men render you assistance in the streets, and would revolt from the offer of a piece of money. The desire to oblige is universal, and I have never once travelled in a public conveyance without making some generous acquaintance whom I have been sorry to part from, and who has in many cases come on miles to see us again. The country is vast; there are thousands of millions of acres of land as yet unsettled and uncleared and, on every rood of which, vegetable decomposition is annually taking place. Where there are so many great rivers, and such opposite varieties of climate, there cannot fail to be a great amount of sickness at certain seasons, but I may venture to say, after conversing with many members of the medical profession in America, that I am not singular in the opinion that much of the disease which does prevail might be avoided if a few common precautions were observed. Greater means of personal cleanliness are indispensable to this end; the custom of hastily swallowing large quantities of animal food, three times a day, and rushing back to sedentary pursuits after each meal, must be changed; the gentler sex must go more wisely clad and take more healthful exercise; and in the latter clause, the males must be included also. Above all, in public institutions and throughout the whole of every town and city, the system of ventilation, drainage and removal of impurities requires to be thoroughly revised. The local legislature in America may study Mr. Chadwick's excellent Report upon the Sanitary Conditions of our Labouring Classes with immense advantage.

I am forced, however, to say that I don't like the country and would not live here on any consideration. It is not the Republic I came to see. It is not the Republic of my imagination. I infinitely prefer a liberal Monarchy – even with its sickening accompaniments of Court Circulars and Foreign Kings – to such a Government as in this country. Being a lover of freedom, in every respect but that of national education, America disappoints me. The exhausted treasury; the paralyzed government; the unworthy representatives of a free people; the desperate contests between the North and South; the iron curb and brazen muzzle fastened upon every man who speaks his mind – even in the Republican Hall, to which Republican men are sent by Republican people to speak Republican Truths. And I abhor the odious entrenched attitude for the continuation of slavery. It goes fully against the grain with me, and I think it impossible, utterly impossible, for any Englishman now to live here and be happy. A further great blemish in the popular mind of America, and the prolific parent of an innumerable brood of evils, is Universal Distrust. Yet the American citizen plumes himself upon this spirit of national vanity, even when he is sufficiently dispassionate to perceive the ruin it works; and will often adduce it in spite of its own reason as an instance of the great sagacity and acuteness of the American people and their superior shrewdness and independence. England, even England, bad and faulty as the old land is, and miserable as millions of her people are, rises in the comparison. Strike down the established church, and I would take her to my heart for better or worse; and reject this new love without a pang or moment's hesitation. The American Nation is a body without a head; and the arms and legs are occupied in quarrelling with the trunk and each other, and exchanging bruises at random. There are stabbings and shootings. Coarse and brutal threatenings are exchanged between Senators under the very Senate's roof, and the most pitiful, mean, malicious, creeping, crawling, sneaking party spirit intrudes into all transactions of life.

Another prominent feature of American life is the love of "smart" dealing, which gilds over many a swindle and gross breach of trust; many a defalcation, public and private, and enables many a knave to hold his head up with the best, who well deserves a halter; though it has not been without a retributive operation, for this smartness has done more in a few years to impair the public credit and to cripple the public resources than dull honesty, however rash, could have effected in a century. The merits of a broken speculation or a bankruptcy or of a successful scoundrel, are not gauged by its or his observance of the golden rule "Do as you would be done by", but are considered with reference to their "smartness". I recollect, on both occasions of our passing that ill-fated Cairo on the Mississippi, remarking on the bad effects such gross deceits must have, when they explode, in generating a want of confidence abroad, and discouraging foreign investment: but I was given to understand that this was a very smart scheme by which a deal of money had been made: and that its smartest feature was that they forget these things abroad in a very short time, and speculate again as freely as ever. There is, in America, a national love of "doing" a man in any bargain or matter of business that prevails to an extent which no stranger can possibly estimate.

But the foul growth of America has a more tangled root than this, and it strikes its fibres deep into its licentious press. Schools may be erected, pupils taught, and masters reared by scores upon scores of thousands; colleges may thrive, churches may be crammed, temperance may be diffused, and advancing knowledge in all other forms walk through the land with giant strides: but while the newspaper press of America is in, or near, its present abject state, high moral improvement in the country is hopeless. Year by year, the tone of public feeling must sink lower down; year by year the Congress and Senate must become of less account before all decent men; and year by year, the memory of the Great Fathers of the Revolution must be outraged more and more in the bad life of their degenerate child. And I do fear that the heaviest blow ever dealt at liberty will be dealt by this country, in the failure of its example to the earth. Among the herd of journals which are published in the States, there are some of character and credit. But the name of these is few and of the others legion; and the influence of the good is powerless to counteract the moral poison of the bad. It is sometimes contended – I will not say strangely, for it is natural to seek excuses for such a disgrace – that their influence is not so great as a visitor would suppose. I must be pardoned for saying that there is no warrant for this plea, and that every fact and circumstance tends directly to the opposite conclusion.

There is but one other head upon which I wish to offer a remark. I have never in my life been so shocked and disgusted or made so sick and sore at heart as I have been by the treatment I have received in America in reference to the International Copyright question. I went to America with no express intention of starting this question in any way; and, certainly, with no belief that any such remark upon it as a person in my position would be expected to make would be resented strongly by any section of the American people. I spoke upon it twice publicly, which caused great indignation to some editors, who attacked me right and left for doing so. And the notion that I, a man alone by himself in America, should venture to suggest to the Americans that there was one point on which they were neither just to their own countrymen nor to us, actually struck the boldest dumb, not daring to raise their voice and complain of the atrocious state of the law. But I felt a deep injustice was being perpetrated upon foreign authors by American publications feeling free to reproduce works without any form of permission or recompense. Is it not a horrible thing that scoundrel-booksellers should grow rich from publishing books by the scores of thousands, the authors of which do not reap one farthing from their issue? And that every vile, blackguard and detestable newspaper – so filthy and so bestial that no honest man would admit one into his house for a water-closet doormat – should be able to publish those same writings, side by side, cheek by jowl, with the coarsest and most obscene companions with which they must become connected in course of time in people's minds? I, the greatest loser by the existing law alive, said in perfect good humour and disinterestedness (for God knows that I have little hope of its ever being changed in my time) that I hoped the day would come when writers would be justly treated; and straightway there fell on me scores of American newspapers; imputing motives to me, the very suggestion of which turns my blood to gall; and attacking me in such terms of vagabond scurrility as they would denounce no murderer with. I vow to Heaven that the scorn and indignation I have felt under this unmanly and ungenerous treatment has been to me an amount of agony such as I have never experienced since my birth. But it has had the one good effect of making me iron upon the theme; and iron I will be by word of mouth and in writing, as long as I can articulate a syllable or hold a pen.

CHAPTER XV

Homeward Bound

My heart overflowed with joy as we prepared to sail for England, desperate to be reunited with children and old friends alike. I never had so much interest before, and very likely shall never have so much interest again, in the state of the wind as on that long looked-for morning of departure – Tuesday the 7th June 1842. Some nautical authority had told me a day or two previous: "Anything with West in it will do"; so when I darted out of bed at daylight and, throwing up the window, was saluted by a lively breeze from the North-West which had sprung up in the night, it came upon me so freshly, rustling with so many happy associations, that I conceived upon the spot a special regard for all airs blowing from that quarter of the compass. After a hearty breakfast with friends at a house just out of New York, we hurried to the quay and there, with our guests, took a steamboat out to the "George Washington". She had already left the crowded dock and was now full sixteen miles away. A gallant sight she was when we, fast gaining on her in the steamboat, saw her in the distance riding at anchor: her tall masts pointing up in graceful lines against the sky, and every rope and spar expressed on delicate and threadlike outline. Gallant too the toasts that rang out when we were all aboard; whereupon the guests, after final goodbyes, soon left, the anchor came up (to the sturdy chorus of "Cheerily men, Oh Cheerily!") and our ship followed proudly in the towing steamboat's wake. But bravest and most gallant of all was the moment when, with the tow-rope being cast adrift off Sandy Hook, she spread her great white wings and soared away on her free and solitary course for England.

We were only fifteen passengers in all in the after-cabin (the area where we were located on board), the greater part being from Canada, where some of us had known each other. The first night was rough and squally, and so were the next two days, but they flew by quickly and we were soon as cheerful and snug a party – with an honest, manly-hearted captain, Captain Ambrose Burrow Jr, at our head – as ever came to the resolution of being mutually agreeable, on land or water. We had an abundance of amusements, with dinner not the least among them, its duration being seldom less than two and a half hours and the subject of never-failing entertainment. A select association of four, entitled "The United Vagabonds", was formed at the lower end of the table below the mast, to whose distinguished presidency modesty forbids me to make any further allusion, which, being a very hilarious and jovial institution, was (prejudice apart) in high favour with the rest of the community, and particularly with a black steward, who lived for three weeks in a broad grin at the marvellous humour of these incorporated worthies.

We had chess for those who played it, whist, cribbage, books, blackgammon, and shovelboard. In all weathers, fair or foul, calm or windy, we were everyone on deck, walking up and down in pairs, lying in the boats, leaning over the side, or chatting in a lazy group together. We had no lack of music, for I played the accordion (a steward had lent me one on the passage out, and I had now bought my own in America), another the violin and another (who usually began at 6 a.m.) the key-bugle: the combined effect of which instruments, when they all played different tunes in different parts of the ship, at the same time and within hearing of each other, as they sometimes did (everybody being intensely satisfied with his own performance), was sublimely hideous. At other times, for hours, together we could watch the dolphins and porpoises as they rolled and leaped and dived around the vessel; then on other days we had a dead calm or very light winds, during which the crew amused themselves with fishing.

When we were five or six days out, there began to be much talk of icebergs, of which wandering islands an unusual number had been seen by the vessels that had come into New York a day or two before we left, and of whose dangerous neighbourhood we were warned by the sudden coldness of the weather and the sinking of the mercury in the barometer. But the wind obliged us to hold a southward course and we saw none of them, the weather soon growing bright and warm again.

We carried in the steerage nearly a hundred passengers: a little world of poverty: and as I came to know individuals among them by sight, from looking down upon the deck where they took the air in the daytime, and cooked their food, and very often ate it too, I became curious to know their histories, and with what expectations they had gone out to America and on what errands they were going home. Some had sold their clothes to raise the passage money, and had hardly rags to cover them; others had no food, and lived upon the charity of the rest. And one man, it was discovered nearly at the end of the voyage, had had no sustenance whatever but the bones and scraps of fat he took from the plates of our after-cabin dinner when they were put out to be washed.

The whole system of shipping and conveying these unfortunate persons is one that stands in need of thorough revision. It should be the duty of any Government, be it monarchy or republic, to interpose and put an end to the system by which a firm of traders in emigrants purchase of the owners the whole tween-decks of a ship, and send on board as many wretched people as they can lay hold of, on any terms they can get, without the smallest reference to the conveniences of the steerage, the number of berths, the slightest separation of the sexes, or anything but their own immediate profit. Nor is even this the worst of the vicious system: for certain crimping agents of these houses, who have a percentage on all the passengers they inveigle, are constantly travelling about those districts where poverty and discontent are rife, and tempting the credulous into more misery, by holding out monstrous inducements to emigration which can never be realized. Many go out to America expecting to find its streets paved with gold; instead they find them paved with very hard and very real stones. Enterprise being dull, labourers are not wanted; even if jobs of work are to be got, payment is not. And now they come back even poorer than they went.

At length and at last, the promised wind came up in right good earnest, and away we went before it, slashing through the water nobly with every stitch of canvas set. There was a grandeur in the motion of this splendid ship as, overshadowed by her mass of sails, she rode at a furious pace upon the waves, which filled one with an indescribable sense of pride and exultation. As she plunged into a foaming valley, how I loved to see the green waves, bordered deep with white, come rushing on astern, to buoy her upward at their pleasure, and curl about her as she stooped again, but always own her for their haughty mistress still! On, on we flew, with changing lights upon the water, being now in the blessed region of fleecy skies; a bright sun lighting us by day, and a bright moon by night; the vane pointing directly homeward, alike the truthful index to the favouring wind and to our cheerful hearts; until at sunrise, one fair Monday morning – the 27th of June, I shall not easily forget the day – there lay before us old Cape Clear, God Bless it, showing in the mist of early morning like a cloud: the brightest and most welcome cloud to us that ever hid the face of Heaven's fallen sister – Home.

The wind was very light on this morning, but it was still in the right quarter and so, by slow degrees, we left Cape Clear behind, and sailed along within sight of the coast of Ireland. And how merry we all were, and how loyal to the "George Washington", and how full of mutual congratulations, and how venturesome in predicting the exact hour at which we should arrive at Liverpool! We drank the captain's health heartily that day at dinner and two or three of our most sanguine spirits rejected the idea of going to bed at all that night as something it was not worthwhile to do, so near the shore, but went nevertheless and slept soundly. And being so near to our journey's end, it was like a pleasant dream from which one feared to wake.

The friendly breeze freshened again next day and, with every inch of canvas crowded on, we dashed gaily past an English ship going homeward under shortened sail and left her far behind. Towards evening the weather turned hazy, with a drizzling rain; and soon became so thick that we sailed, as it were, in a cloud. Still we swept onward like a phantom ship, and many an eager eye glanced up to where the look-out on the mast kept watch for Holyhead. At length his long-expected cry was heard, and at the same moment there shone out from the haze and mist ahead, a gleaming light which presently was gone, and soon returned, and soon was gone again. There we all stood, watching this revolving light upon the rock at Holyhead. Then it was time to fire a gun for a pilot; and almost before its smoke had cleared away, a little boat with a light at her mast-head came swiftly bearing down upon us through the darkness. And presently, our sails being backed, she ran alongside; and the hoarse pilot, wrapped and muffled in pea-coats and shawls to the very bridge of his weather-ploughed-up nose, stood bodily amongst us on the deck. And I think if that pilot had wanted to borrow fifty pounds for an infinite period on no security, we should have engaged to lend it to him, among us, before every scrap of news in the paper he brought with him had become the common property of all on board.

We turned in pretty late that night and turned out pretty early next morning. By six o'clock that morning we clustered on the deck, prepared to go ashore; and looked upon the spires, and roofs, and smoke of Liverpool. By eight we all sat down in one of its hotels, to eat and drink together for the last time. And by nine we had shaken hands all round, and broken up our social company for ever.

The country, by the railroad to London, seemed, as we rattled through it, like a luxuriant garden. The beauty of the fields (so small they looked!), the hedge rows, and the trees; the pretty cottages, the beds of flowers, the old churchyards, the antique houses, and every well-known object; the exquisite delights of that one journey, crowding in the short compass of a summer's day, the joy of many years, with the winding up of Home and all that makes it dear, no tongue can tell or pen of mine describe.

Upon arriving in London, we took a hackney-coach and with all possible speed headed to 25 Osnaburgh Street. It was now dark in the late evening of the 29th June and as we drove up, and before the coach could stop, I jumped out, to see the children hurrying to the gate – and the intense hugging and kissing began. We found our darlings quite well (thank God), and most rejoiced to see us. Charley, however, told his mother he was "too glad" and fell, soon afterwards, into very alarming convulsions. We were obliged, besides having our regular apothecary Doctor Pickthorn, to call up Doctor Elliotson in the middle of the night, who said that the sudden joy had perfectly turned his brain and quite overthrown his system; and that he had never seen such a case before. Charley was in a dangerous state, but happily the disorder took a favourable turn in a few hours, and he very soon recovered. He had apparently confided to a confidential friend of his (a washerwoman) that he was afraid that when we did come home, he should "shake very much".

These events with Charley kept me up the whole night and caused me to be too much exhausted to attend to other matters, but the next day we all – including Kate's sister Georgina – moved back into Devonshire Terrace. When we sat down in our own dear home again, I never in my life felt so keenly over it. After we had fully expended ourselves on the children, I hurried away to see Macready, who had had charge of them in our absence. He was sitting in a dark room by an open window, and had no idea who it was, until I laid my hand upon his sleeve and spoke. Such a scene as we had then! I held him in my arms in a transport of joy. I then bustled off to see Forster. I found that he was not at home in Lincoln's Inn Fields, but was dining out. Thereupon I drove up to the house where he was and, admonishing the servant there not to say who it was, told him to carry in the message to Forster that a gentleman wanted to speak to him. Guessing directly who it was, Forster came flying out of the house, got in the carriage, pulled up the window and began to cry. Our pleasure at meeting again was unbounded. We drove off together and had gone a couple of miles in our joy, before he suddenly remembered that he had left his hat behind him!

CHAPTER XVI

American Notes and a Visit to Cornwall

Upon my return, I resolved that a dinner must be held to bring friends together once again and not long thereafter (on the 9th July) twenty-seven of us gathered for a splendid evening in Greenwich to celebrate my return – full of toasts, speeches and songs. We were all very jovial indeed, and George Cruikshank in particular was perfectly wild at the reunion. After singing all manner of maniac songs, he wound up the entertainment by coming home (six miles) in a little open phaeton of mine, on his head – to the mingled delight and indignation of the Metropolitan Police!

But I now also wasted no time in circulating friends and acquaintances alike over the matter of International Copyright law. The wholesale piracy of British works by the American press had caused me, whilst in America, not only to speak out about it in public, but also to join with a whole body of American authors and Senator Henry Clay in presenting petitions to Congress whilst I was in Washington, earnestly praying for the enactment of an International Copyright Law. For myself, I had resolved that I would never from this time enter into any negotiation with any person for the transmission, across the Atlantic, of early proofs of anything I may write; and that I would forego all profit derivable from such a source. Furthermore, I now knew that the persons who exerted themselves to mislead the American public on this question, to put down its discussion and to suppress and distort the truth in reference to it in every possible way, were those who had a strong interest in the existing system of piracy and plunder; inasmuch as, so long as it continued, they could gain a very comfortable living out of the brains of other men, while they would find it very difficult to earn bread by the exercise of their own. These were, in the main, editors and proprietors of newspapers who were almost exclusively devoted to the republication of popular English works. They were, for the most part, men of very low attainments and of more than indifferent reputation; and I had frequently seen them, in the same sheet in which they boasted of the rapid sale of many thousand copies of an English reprint, coarsely and insolently attacking the author of that very book and heaping scurrility and slander upon his head. I never knew what it was to feel disgust and contempt until I travelled in America and witnessed the activities of such men.

My mind turned again to Broadstairs, a place far removed from the sights and noises of the busy world, and filled with the delicious repose of the broad ocean. I was pleased in due course to hear that we were able to secure the same house as last year, 37 Albion Street. I began contemplating a new venture and wrote to Lady Holland about the possibility of establishing a new evening paper for the Liberal side. I knew it would be impossible for me to do this unless I could receive direct pecuniary assistance from members of the late Whig Government or from the Reform Club and, knowing how strongly she sympathized with such views, I asked her if she would assist by making known my thoughts to such people and ascertain the sentiments of these leading members of the party. She kindly did so, but the response came back that such a venture could not rely upon Liberal financial support, and so I pursued it no further. I was pleased, however, during the process to dine with Lady Holland at Holland House.

Within a fortnight of returning home, I began the enormous task of shaping American sketches in my head and soon was working like a dray-horse upon my "American Notes" for publication. I was pleased to have the letters I had written to Forster on my travels to assist me and soon had an introductory chapter done. In it I set out what I saw was honest and true about America, but neither Forster nor Macready liked it and eventually I reluctantly agreed to omit it from the book.

Whilst I had been in America, Lord Ashley had moved the Mines and Collieries Bill in the House of Commons – an Act to prohibit the employment of women and girls in mines and collieries; to regulate the employment of boys; and make provisions for the safety of persons working therein. On the 25th July I wrote a lengthy letter to the editor of the Morning Chronicle setting out my public support for this legislation, as the Bill was to be committed in the House of Lords that very evening and I was fearful that the Colliery Lords would so distort and maim it that Members of the Commons would be sorely puzzled to know it again when it returned to them – Lord Londonderry in particular being the most vocal against it. References had been made to "little trappers" – children as young as six years old, sitting alone in the dark of the mines for twelve hours or more a day, to open and shut the numerous doors or "traps" for the coal wagons to pass through. And, quoth Lord Londonderry: "If I were not this great peer, I would be that jolly little trapper!" Oh, for the cindery days of trapper infancy! Jolly, jolly trappers indeed!

The Morning Chronicle published my letter in full. In it I also drew attention to the many women being employed in mines in Scotland, particularly those under the ownership of Sir John Hope of Hopetoun House, and praised the sub-commissioners whose investigations had revealed the true extent of the abuses being perpetrated. Despite the many amendments made in the Lords, when the Bill returned to the Commons it thankfully passed in substance on the 1st August, and in doing so barred all females and all boys under the age of 10 from working underground; prohibited parish apprentices being bound beyond 18 years of age; and enforced safety regulations with the appointment of teams of inspectors.

Pressing on with my American Notes, I became busily engaged upon it, but the subjects at the beginning of the book were of that kind that I could not dash at them and now and then fretted me in consequence. Then, after further thought, I resolved that the book would simply be a record of the impressions I received from day to day during my hasty travels, and sometimes (but not always) of the conclusions to which they led me; a description of the country I passed through; of the institutions I visited; of the kind of people among whom I journeyed; and of the manners and customs that came within my observation.

I could, however, scarcely be supposed to be ignorant of the hazards I ran in writing of America at all. I knew perfectly well that there was, in that country, a numerous class of well-interested persons prone to be dissatisfied with all accounts of the Republic which were not couched in terms of exalted and extravagant praise; persons so tenderly and delicately constituted that they cannot bear the truth in any form. And I did not need the gift of prophecy to discern afar off that those who would be aptest to detect malice, ill-will, and all uncharitableness in my Notes, and to show, beyond any doubt, that they are perfectly inconsistent with that grateful and enduring recollection which I profess to entertain of the welcome I found awaiting me beyond the Atlantic, would be certain native journalists, veracious and gentlemanly, who were at great pains to prove to me, on all occasions during my stay there, that the aforesaid welcome I received was utterly worthless.

But, in asserting (as I invariably did on all public occasions) my liberty and freedom of speech while I was among the Americans, and in maintaining it at home, I believe I best show my sense of the high worth of that welcome, and of the honourable singleness of purpose with which it was extended to me. From first to last I saw, in the friends who crowded around me in America, old readers (over-grateful and over-partial perhaps) to whom I had happily been the means of furnishing pleasure and entertainment; not a vulgar herd who would flatter and cajole a stranger into turning with closed eyes from all the blemishes of the nation, and into chaunting its praises with the discrimination of a street ballad singer.

Therefore I took the plain course of saying what I thought and noting what I saw; and as it is not my custom to exalt what in my judgement are foibles and abuses at home, so I had no intention of softening down or glossing over those that I had observed abroad. I may be asked: "If you have been in any respect disappointed in America, and are assured beforehand that the expression of your disappointment will give offence to any class, why do you write at all?" My answer is, that I went there expecting greater things than I found, and resolved as far as in me lay to do justice to the country, at the expense of any (in my view) mistaken or prejudiced statements that might have been made to its disparagement. Coming home with a corrected and sobered judgement, I considered myself no less bound to do justice to what, according to my best means of judgement, I found to be the truth.

At the beginning of August we travelled to Broadstairs where, for the next two months I was able to continue on with, and virtually complete the American Notes. But, at the end of August I had the distraction of hearing of a scandalous letter, blatantly forged with my name, that had been sent to the American press, who printed it in prominent form and were only too willing to believe that it was the genuine article from me, and to deem me a fool and a liar as a result. It had been widely distributed in letter-form all over the States; and the felon who invented it was no doubt a "smart man" of course. To the many concerned people who wrote to me from America, I made it clear that I had not contradicted these forgeries (as false as our felons swing for) nor did I intend to do so. I had not been many weeks in America (no stranger can be) before I was amazed and repelled beyond expression by these human instruments of public degradation. No deed of their doing would surprise me and no falsehood of their telling would move me into communication with them for an instant; nothing but honesty or common sense would startle me from such a quarter. But it did exasperate me very much (I can be rather a fierce turn at times) and caused me such pain as, for a week or two, I walked about with a vague desire to take somebody by the throat and shake him, such an act being more than should, perhaps, have become awakened in any honourable man.

At the beginning of October we returned to London where, at midnight on the 4th October, I finished my American Notes, and Chapman and Hall were then able to publish them in two volumes beginning on the 19th. Meanwhile, I was very pleasantly surprised by an unexpected visit to Devonshire Terrace from Harvard Professor, Henry Wordsworth Longfellow, whom I had been pleased to invite to stay with me whenever he visited our shores. He was on his way home from the continent of Europe and we spent a delightful fortnight together, during which time I was able to show him some of the best and the worst aspects of life in England. We toured the pleasant parts of London, Rochester and Bath, but I also ensured I showed him the "rookeries" of London, with people crammed seven or eight to a room, in conditions of the most appalling filth and squalor – with open ditches used as sewers running into cess lakes, vermin and starvation rife, as well as dead lying unburied in houses and in overflowing burial grounds. Edwin Chadwick's Report had had a most profound effect on me and I was determined to bring it and the conditions described therein to the attention of all so that something was done about it. And, unlike some in America, I saw it as my duty to speak out with the utmost vigour whenever I saw anything anywhere that was abhorrent to me. Longfellow read my American Notes and I gave him further copies to take back to other friends I had made in America. At the end of his time, Forster and I travelled with him, first to Bath to enjoy the hospitality of Landor, and then to Bristol to see him off on the "Great Western" on the 21st October.

Following publication of the Notes in America, I received an immense number of letters and innumerable newspapers from across the Atlantic. Whilst on shipboard coming home, I had solemnly determined with myself that I would never read any American criticism of these Notes and I was resolute on that course. If such arrived and there was anything to pay, it went back to the Post Office; if nothing, they went unopened into the fire. I never once departed from my resolution in the least degree and felt the wisdom of it in my continuing good spirits and good humour.

I knew now that I had to give my attention to a new work (in twenty monthly numbers) that I had promised Chapman and Hall the year before. Publication was due to begin under the agreement in November, but I was not yet ready to start as I had no clear idea of the theme I wished to adopt. I reviewed a notion I had of visiting as desolate and dreary a portion of sea coast that England might have to offer for inspiration, and settled on seeking out such in Cornwall. I also wished to visit a tin mine in that county, to view for myself the conditions experienced by the workers in such places, and in doing so to give added support to Lord Ashley and his campaigning. I wrote to Dr. Southward Smith, one of the four Infant Labour Commissioners who had reported upon conditions in the mines, telling him of my proposed visit to the St. Michael's Mount area of Cornwall and asking for his assistance. He replied that the coast about Land's End was incompatibly more dreary than St. Michael's Mount, but that the place above all for dreariness was Tintagel (King Alfred's) Castle near Camelford where, he said, you see nothing but bleak-looking rocks and an everlastingly boisterous sea – both in much the same state as when King Arthur reigned. He also told me that a Cornish tin mine was quite different from a coal mine and, whilst it was much less disagreeable to the senses and they did not employ women, it was far more fatal in its effects upon the men and boys used there.

Forster, Maclise and Clarkson Stanfield ("Stanny") were happy to go with me to Cornwall; I regarded Stanny as a fine painter, and the natural historian of England's speciality, the sea. We left London on the 27th October and travelled by train to Exeter, where we stayed at the New London Inn. From there I visited Alphington again and found to my dismay that my father and mother were making plans to move from the cottage. However we did not linger long in Exeter, and continued on by train to Plymouth. There we hired an open carriage from an innkeeper patriotic in all Pickwickian matters and went on with post horses into Cornwall, passing the Eddistone Lighthouse on the way. Sometimes we travelled all night; sometimes all day; sometimes both. I kept the joint stock purse; ordered all the dinners and drinks; paid all the turnpikes; conducted facetious conversations with the post-boys; and regulated the pace at which we travelled. Stanny (an old sailor) consulted an enormous map on all disputed points of wayfaring: and referred moreover to a pocket compass and other scientific instruments. The luggage was in Forster's department; and Maclise, having nothing particular to do, sang songs. Heavens! I never laughed in my life as I did on this journey. I was choking and gasping and bursting the buckle off the back of my stock, all the way. And Stanny got into such apoplectic entanglements that we were often obliged to beat him on the back with portmanteaus before we could recover him.

We had headed for St. Michael's Mount, ascending there to the cradle of the highest tower, and then on, through Liskeard, Bodmin and Truro, before travelling to Land's End, where we witnessed a most wonderful sunset from the top of the rock projecting farthest into the sea. We thence travelled to St. Just, where a great annual Miner's Feast was being held at the inn where we planned to stay. We presented ourselves at night amongst the wild crowd that were dancing before it by torchlight, but we had had a breakdown in the dark on a stony morass some miles away – a bleak desert moor, where monstrous masses of rude stones were cast about, as though they were the burial place of giants – and I had the honour of leading in one of the unharnessed post-horses. The inn was full – and twenty times full – and only the post-horse could be received; we were left to debate how to pass the night and part of the next day to the time when the jovial blacksmith and the jovial wheelwright might be in a condition to go out onto the morass and mend the coach. After much searching, we found lodgings with a local chair-maker whilst the fair continued, hundreds parading in the streets, bands playing, and all accompanied by much drinking of beer and 'moonshine'. Eventually, the next day, the coach was fixed and we were able to carry on our way.

We travelled to Tintagel on the northern coast, where no parts of mountain or sea consecrated to the legends of Arthur were left unexplored. At nearby St. Nighton's Kieve, Maclise made a sketch of a waterfall which he later used as the setting for his painting of Georgina Hogarth as "A Girl at a Waterfall". I subsequently acquired this from him by means of a pious fraud to his advantage, insisting he charge the full price of 100 guineas and making out, through Beard, that Beard had a rich old enthusiast country friend in Sussex who wished to acquire the painting and could afford to pay well, to avoid Maclise giving it to me for less than its true worth. During our travels, both Maclise and Stanny had indeed made sketches in the most romantic of our halting places, so much so that you would have sworn we had the Spirit of Beauty with us, as well as the Spirit of Fun. We arrived back in Exeter on the 3rd of November, changed in the New London Inn and immediately went on to Taunton by train to stay the night at the Castle Hotel, before carrying on to London the following day.

CHAPTER XVII

Martin Chuzzlewit begun, and the Pegasus disaster

Back in Devonshire Terrace, my mind became truly focused on my task ahead, the tremendous process of plotting and contriving a new book. In the agonies of this I was accustomed to walk up and down the house smiting my forehead dejectedly; and to be so horribly cross and surly, causing the boldest to fly at my approach. The name of the character I was to work to had first to be set in my mind, and I had had the name "Martin" in my thoughts for some considerable time, but without an appropriate adjunct; I was greatly frustrated that I could not alight on the full name that would make me content. I tried Sweezleden, Sweezleback and Sweezlewag; then Chuzzletoe, Chuzzleboy, Chubblewig and Chuzzlewig, before finally alighting, after much hesitation and debate, upon "Chuzzlewit". My main object in the story was to exhibit, in a variety of aspects, the commonest of all vices: to show how selfishness propagates itself and to what a grim giant it may grow from small beginnings. I decided eventually to commence the tale not at a lighthouse or mine in Cornwall, but at a Wiltshire village forge on a windy autumn evening.

And so I began on the new venture. It was again hard going at first and it took me a while to hit upon the main track, but by the beginning of December I had the first chapter done and introduced the world not only to the Chuzzlewit family, but also to Seth Pecksniff the architect and his assistant, Tom Pinch. Before sending the copy to the printers, I went, with the ink hardly dry on the last slip, to read the manuscript to Forster, who had been kept in his rooms for some days by illness. He heartily approved of the tale so begun, and I told him that the notion of taking Pecksniff for a type of character was really the origin of the book, the design being to show, more or less by every person introduced, the number and variety of humours and vices that have their root in this folly of selfishness. I sent the copy off to the printers in good heart, and when it was finally published at the beginning of January 1843, I received many pleasing responses to the characters therein.

On Twelfth Night, and in honour of Charley's sixth birthday, we held a splendid party at Devonshire Terrace, attended by friends and a large number of children. For this occasion I provided a magic lantern and divers other engines of that nature. But the best of it was that Forster and I purchased between us the entire stock in trade of a conjurer from Hambley's Toy Warehouse in High Holborn, the practice and display thereof being entrusted to me. You should have seen me conjuring the company's watches into impossible tea caddies, and causing pieces of money to fly, and burning pocket handkerchiefs without hurting them! In those tricks which required a confederate, I was assisted (by reason of his imperturbable good humour) by Stanny, who always did his part exactly the wrong way – to the unspeakable delight of all beholders!

But I had also been hammering away at home for hours and days on end seeking out the next number of Chuzzlewit, stopping only for afternoon breaks with a walk out; I recall one afternoon when, for two hours, I ploughed through snow half a foot deep round about the wilds of Willesden before settling down again. Then I noticed that my mother was in London and found I had to contact Tom Mitton once more to enable him to settle further debts my father had incurred whilst in Devon. I was then obliged to travel to Alphington after receiving further letters from him and, much to my distress, he declined to stay in Devon any longer. I therefore asked Mitton to make an offer of £70 for a little house nearer London – money I could sorely afford at this time – and in due course, he and my mother were lodged at Manor House, Lewisham, an old wooden house facing the foot of Lewisham Hill. The thought of my father beset me night and day, and I really did not know what was to be done with him. It was now quite clear to me that the more I did for him, the more outrageous and audacious he became. I was amazed and confounded by his ingratitude, and nothing made me so wretched or unfit for what I had to do than he, and other members of my family, looking upon me as a something to be plucked and torn to pieces for their advantage. They appeared to have no idea of, and no case for, my existence in any other light and were such a drag-chain on my life that they utterly dispirited and weighed me down, my soul being sickened at the thought of them.

The beginning of February saw the publication of the second number of Chuzzlewit, and I began to feel additionally distressed at the way it was now beginning to be received. I was in no doubt that the story was encompassing my best work to date, but sales were very disappointing; whilst there were forty and fifty thousand purchasers for Pickwick and Nickleby, and sixty and seventy thousand for the early numbers of Master Humphrey's Clock, only just over twenty thousand appeared for Chuzzlewit. Such was my state that, by the 11th February, I had ground to a halt; I couldn't write a line, not a word, though I really tried hard. In a kind of despair, I started off with my pair of petticoats, Kate and Georgina (Maclise had, by now, sketched a portrait of us together), to Richmond, and upon arrival at the Star and Garter we dined there. Oh, what a lovely day it was in those parts! I can trace in many respects a strong resemblance between Georgy's mental features and Mary's – so strange a one at times that when she, and Kate and I were sitting together, I seemed to think that what had happened was a melancholy dream from which I was just awakening. The perfect like of what Mary was will never be again, but so much of her spirit shines out in Georgy that the old time comes back again at some seasons, and I can hardly separate it from the present.

I felt also at this time that I needed to talk my whole circumstance over with Forster, and furthermore to get away from all the distractions of home. I rented a lonely farm house at Cobley's Farm in Finchley, where thereafter Forster often joined me. We talked much and walked time and again and at length in the green lanes, into the season when the rains continued but the midsummer months began to come on. I told him of my plans to send the younger Martin Chuzzlewit to America and to introduce a character that I foresaw had enormous comic possibilities. I had witnessed the nurse, hired by Charley's godmother, Miss Coutts, to look after her companion and secretary Miss Meredith, carrying out some remarkable peculiarities in the sick room, one common habit being to rub her nose along the top of the tall fender. I was pleased to incorporate her into the Chuzzlewit story and develop her as Mrs. Gamp. I meant to make a mark with her.

Sales rose somewhat to about twenty-three thousand but then, on the 27th June, my publishers – and William Hall in particular – sought to hit me with a sledge-hammer blow. Hall told me that they were proposing to invoke a penal clause in the agreement I had signed in September

1841, shortly before my visit to America. This clause, inserted only to satisfy the lawyers, spoke of a provision against the improbable event of profits proving inadequate to sustain the repayment of advances made during the one-year period before I took to writing again, and to be ascertained against the proceeds of the first five numbers of my new work. By this clause, the publishers were given the power, if they so wished, to appropriate fifty pounds a month out of the two hundred pounds payable for authorship in the expenses of each number. On the eve of the seventh number of Chuzzlewit being published, in which Mrs. Gamp was making her first appearance, Hall dropped the inconsiderate hint to me that it might now be desirable to put this clause into force.

I was so irritated by this insult from the younger partner of the firm that had enriched itself by Pickwick and Nickleby; so rubbed in the tenderest part of my eyelids with bay-salt that my head burnt with a wrong kind of fire. I doubted if I could write further; nevertheless I was at pains to try. I became resolved and bent on paying the money down to Chapman and Hall and that when that was done, Mr. Hall should have a piece of my mind. I also recalled that it was more than a year and a half since my printers, Bradbury and Evans, had written to me asking to give them a hearing in case I should ever think of altering my business plans, so I asked Forster to approach them now to see if this could be of advantage to me.

Forster made the communication I desired, but told me that it had taken the printers too much by surprise to enable them to form a clear judgement respecting it; and that they had replied by suggestions which were in effect a confession of a want of confidence in themselves. They had enlarged upon great results that would follow a re-issue of my writings in a cheap form, which they strongly urged; and they offered to invest to any desired amount in the establishment of a magazine or other periodical to be edited by me.

I thought over these proposals but did not think the time a good one just now for a new magazine or periodical. And I was so afraid of Bradbury and Evans's desire to force on the cheap issue of my books prematurely, sure that if it took place yet awhile it would damage me and damage the property, enormously.

I expressed my views to Forster, who agreed with them and prevailed upon me to suspend any such proceedings until my return in October from my annual visit to Broadstairs. Meanwhile, within my wider family, I continued to constantly feel beset with annoyances – whilst my own domestic expenses were increasing at an alarming rate. And I was besieged by petitioners with begging letters, some of whom would lie about their circumstances – whilst all the while the vitriol from certain sections of the American press continued unabated. Above all I felt angry and frustrated at being hemmed in and entrapped in my existence. I was putting everything I could into my writing and yet it was, once again, others who were reaping the benefit. And I was constantly being called upon to attend and make speeches at a whole host of other public dinners and functions, to say nothing of balls to attend and meetings to chair. I became quite weary and worn out by it all.

Then, in July, there was a pleasant interlude, when Kate, Georgy and I went to Yorkshire to stay with the Smithsons at their home, Easthorpe Hall, paying a long-promised visit to what I regarded as the most remarkable place of its size in England and the most beautiful. Whilst there I did nothing but ride over all manner of country – including paying visits to Mulgrave and Castle Howard – as well as strolling amongst ancient ruins, eating, drinking and sleeping. Well refreshed, I returned to London later that month to set to work again, in earnest and for long hours, upon Chuzzlewit – buoyed up by a letter from Sydney Smith, who told me he had found Chuzzlewit excellent, that "nothing could be better!", and it being "full of wit, humour and power of description". From such an authority this was worth having.

Before leaving for Broadstairs, I consented to act as Chairman of a Committee for the assistance of the children of the actor Edward Elton, children whose condition was as melancholy and destitute beyond all painting. Elton was a struggling man through his whole existence – always very poor, and never extravagant. His wife had died mad some three years before, leaving him a widower with seven children, six daughters and a son. He took an engagement at the Theatre Royal, Edinburgh, but whilst returning home to Hull by sea aboard the "Pegasus", the vessel struck a rock near Holy Island and he was drowned. The children were expecting his knock at the door and, in anticipation of his return, had decked his room with flowers, when a friend arrived instead with the terrible news of his death. It was the saddest case imaginable. I wrote to all I could think of to assist in their plight and the Committee pursued their philanthropic mission with the utmost vigour and determination. Many theatrical performances were organized, with proceeds going for the children's benefit, and whilst at Broadstairs I wrote many letters of thanks to those who had contributed so nobly. In all, with all contributions, £2,380 was collected, at a time when I satisfactorily ascertained that the weekly expenses of the Elton Family were £3, not more.

At Broadstairs I continued on further with Chuzzlewit, aware by now that the American chapters in particular had raised further ire in that land, and that from a letter I received, did I believe firmly that Martin had made them all stark raving mad across the water. I consulted with Forster as to what I should do, but was determined upon my course, and instructed Browne as to the illustrations needed. Macready had ended his Drury Lane management and was now preparing to go to America, so I organized a farewell dinner for him at the Star and Garter in Richmond, but where I begged him not to mention my name in America. I had an initial notion of going to Liverpool and on board the steamer to bid him a final farewell, but then felt great doubts as to the propriety of this, as it would be crowded with Americans at this season of the year, and I strongly believed that my accompanying him on board would be, after the last Chuzzlewit, fatal to his success in America and certain to bring down upon him every species of insult and outrage. I then determined within myself to remain in the hotel in Liverpool, and charge the landlord to keep my being there a secret, but after being counselled further by friends, I instantly renounced the delight of even going to Liverpool at all to be amongst the last to say farewell to him. I further felt obliged to urge him never to claim me for his friend, or champion me in America, and to maintain silence even when hearing any monstrous assertions to my disparagement.

At the beginning of October I travelled to Manchester to preside at the opening of its great Athenaeum and to be assisted in this task by Mr. Cobden and Mr. Disraeli. The meeting, held in the great Free Trade Hall, was a very brilliant success. Men of all parties were present and a thousand tickets were sold, most of them admitting two – though many three – persons, all to raise funds for the Athenaeum. I was later given the testimonial of a Life Membership, and it was grand for me to know that, whilst Manchester's factories echoed with the clanking of stupendous engines and the whirl and rattle of machinery, the mind was not forgotten in the din and the uproar. In my speech, I chose to emphasize the matter that had always been nearest to my heart – the liberal Universal Education of the people, including particularly the education of the very poor. I protested most vigorously at those who sought to say that "a little learning is a dangerous thing" and that therefore it should not be attempted; my preference has always been for the very least of the little over none at all.

In fact, shortly before going to Manchester, I had travelled from Broadstairs to visit a very different place, the Ragged School located in Field Lane, Saffron Hill – the place where Fagin had kept his den. I found the school housed in three rooms on the first floor of a dilapidated house, in which every plank and timber and brick and lath and piece of plaster shook as you walked. Stanny, who had come with me, did not stay long as he found the smell and the dread of typhus fever too overwhelming. But I stayed. There were seventy pupils, two rooms devoted to the boys and one to the girls. I have very seldom seen, in all the strange and dreadful things I have seen in London and elsewhere, anything so shocking as the dire neglect of soul and body exhibited in these children – and there are countless examples of such doomed childhood all over London.

I sent Miss Coutts a full account of my visit to Saffron Hill as I had seen her name for £200 in the clergy education subscription list, but I took pains to show her that religious mysteries and difficult creeds would not do for such pupils. I told her, too, that it was of immense importance that the pupils should be washed and housed properly. She wrote back to know what the rent of some large airy premises would be and the expense of erecting a regular bathing or purifying place; touching which points I had been in correspondence with the Committee of Council of Education, set up by the Government to provide grant assistance, as I believed, for situations such as these. But my pleas there fell on deaf ears. Is it any wonder that, in such circumstances, Ignorance is the hand-maiden of Crime, Disease and Misery?

CHAPTER XVIII

A Christmas Carol, and Martin Chuzzlewit concluded

On my trip to Manchester I had been thinking over how I might supplement my income and had become greatly taken by a little scheme to publish an additional book, written especially for the Christmas season. Upon my return I plunged headlong into this whilst, at the same time, continuing to give lengthy thoughts to my future wellbeing. I had had this idea of foreign travel and foreign living in my head for some months and at the beginning of November wrote to Forster telling him that at the close of Chuzzlewit (which had taken so much out of me) I proposed drawing from Chapman and Hall my share of the subscription for the volume edition and telling them also that it would not be likely that I should do anything for a year thereafter; and that, in the meantime, I would make no arrangement whatever with anybody, leaving business matters resting in status quo; the same to be told to Bradbury and Evans. I proposed to let Devonshire Terrace if I could and, if not, leave it to be let. I explained that I intended to take all the family, and two servants – three at most – to some place which I knew beforehand to be CHEAP and in a delightful climate, in Normandy or Brittany perhaps (to which I would go over first), and there rent some house for six or eight months. During that time I thought of travelling; through France and Italy, crossing the Alps, walking through Switzerland, taking Kate perhaps to Rome and Venice (but not elsewhere) – in short, seeing everything that was to be seen.

The next day I wrote again to Forster, emphasizing how resolute I was upon this, and that I was convinced that my expenses abroad would not be more than half my expenses here in England. I also felt the influence of change and nature upon me would be enormous. I told him that I thought Chuzzlewit in a hundred points immeasurably the best of my stories, and that I felt my power now more than I ever did; that I had a greater confidence in myself than I ever had – but also that I knew that others did not agree. I reflected on how coldly Chuzzlewit went on for months, until it forced itself up in people's opinion – but without forcing itself up in sales. It had warned me that if I could leave matters for a time, I had better do so, and must do so. I felt it was impossible to go on for ever working the brain to the extent I had been, all the while remembering poor Scott in his miserable decay. I walked about the back-streets of London, fifteen and twenty miles, many a night when all sober persons had gone to bed, turning my plans over and over in my mind, for I knew Forster would look upon my scheme with dislike, and at the same time saw very little pleasure in it myself, but I came to look upon it as a matter of policy and duty in my circumstance.

Meanwhile I was now working upon both Chuzzlewit and the Christmas tale. It continued to be hard going, and at times I was in agonies over Chuzzlewit, so much so that, on some days, I worked from morning to night only upon my little Christmas book. I was driven on both by my financial straits – for the first time I had found, to my horror, that I had overdrawn my account at Coutts Bank – and the knowledge that Kate was expecting another child (our fifth) in the early New Year. I calculated, and was expecting, that the Christmas tale would bring me a profit of at least a thousand pounds, which would be of the greatest assistance in the circumstance, and so I powdered away into the early hours, weeping, laughing and weeping again over the ways of Ebenezer Scrooge, the Cratchit family and the ghosts that would appear and disappear. But I continued taking the long night walks, and grappling with the ghosts that were, all too vividly, coming to haunt me in my own life.

As the twelfth part of Chuzzlewit fell to be published, so I finished writing my Christmas tale, which I now entitled "A Christmas Carol". I felt relieved and broke out like a madman when it was done, holding with a strong sense of the immense effect I could produce with this entire little book. With Forster's encouragement, I agreed to put aside my differences with Chapman and Hall for the time being, and have them publish it on a commission-only basis. I hoped it would sell well, and set about arranging for stylish production in proper form, bound with red cloth and gilt designs and with woodcuts and colour etchings for the illustrations. I fixed the price at five shillings for the volume and, on the first print run, six thousand copies were made for publication on the 19th December. By Christmas Eve all were sold and, by the 3rd of January, two thousand of the three printed for the second and third editions were already taken by the trade. Letters poured in daily from readers telling me how the Carol had come to be read aloud in their homes, and was to be kept on a little shelf by itself, and did them no end of good. Then, on the 15th January 1844, our son Francis Jeffrey Dickens, was born, named in honour of my good friend and founder of the Edinburgh Review.

By now, however, fraudsters were hard at work pirating the Carol, and I vowed to pursue those that I could for all I was able in the English law. I did not have the least doubt that if these vagabonds and gang of robbers could be stopped, they must be. Talfourd took up my cause and obtained an Injunction; in the ensuing Breach of Copyright action in the Court of Chancery, the six offending publishers and printers were beaten flat, without Talfourd even being called upon. But then, true to form, they declared themselves either without funds or bankrupts, and I was left saddled with legal costs of £700 for my Action, with no recompense whatever to show for it, save for some worthless affidavits. This I regard as the villainy of the law which, after declaring me robbed, obliged me to bring a further Action, against men from whom it demands no security, for the expenses to which I had been put. When, a couple of years later after this experience, I suffered a similar act of piracy again and was again advised to go to law, I declined, informing Forster that it was better to suffer a great wrong than to have recourse to the much greater wrong of the law. I could not easily forget the expense and anxiety and horrible injustice of the Carol case wherein, in asserting the plainest right on earth, I was really treated as if I were the robber instead of the robbed.

Meanwhile, on the evening of the 10th February, I received the Carol accounts from Chapman and Hall – which caused me such a night that I really believed I should never get up again, until I had passed through all the horrors of a fever. The first six thousand copies showed a profit of £230, and the last four thousand (now printed) to yield only as much again – and I had set my heart and soul on a Thousand clear! What a wonderful thing it is, that such a great success should occasion me such intolerable anxiety and disappointment! My year's bills, unpaid, were so terrific and I now knew that all the energy and determination

I could possibly exert would be required to clear me before I went abroad, which I was now determined to do if the next June came and found me alive. I was so utterly knocked down by these accounts – I did not have the least doubt that Chapman and Hall had run the expenses up purposely, to bring me back and disgust me with charges – that by morning I was quite bold to let the house for a season and be off to some seaside place as soon as a tenant offered. I was not afraid if I reduced my expenses; but if I did not, I felt I should be ruined past all mortal hope of redemption. And then, my father made further demands. I really now thought I should begin to give in one of these days; for anything like the damnable shadow which this father of mine cast upon my face, there never was – except in a nightmare.

My private agonies were not shared by the public bodies who continued the more to have me address them. On the 26th February I took the chair in Liverpool at the meeting of the Mechanics' Institution, and again spoke on that subject dear to me – Educational Reform – and two days later spoke likewise to the Polytechnic Institute in Birmingham, both speeches being exceedingly well received by large gatherings. During the course of the proceedings in Liverpool, a most wonderful 18-year old girl, by the name of Miss Christiana Weller (no less), performed upon the pianoforte with such dexterity and charm that I was captivated, and the last remnant of my heart went out and into that instrument. I even feared that this spiritual creature might be destined to an early death of the kind suffered by Mary Hogarth, but my feelings for her were shaken to their very foundations when, a short time later, I heard from Thomas (T.J.) Thompson, a friend and Smithson's brother-in-law, who told me in a letter that he was proposing to marry her. I never in my life was so surprised, or had the whole current of my life stopped for the instant, as when I read what his letter said.

But, now that the excitement of the visits to Liverpool and Birmingham were all over, I felt perfectly exhausted, dead, worn-out and spiritless. Then I heard of the death of Smithson and was much grieved by it. He was just thirty-nine years of age, and I little thought when we had parted at Easthorpe that I should never see him again. I went to Yorkshire for his funeral, and he was buried immediately outside his own garden wall, but it appeared that he died without a will, and had even dropped a certain life insurance for £3,000 which, in a man of his business, was extremely strange. It all added to the great distress of the family circumstances.

The actions of Messrs. Chapman and Hall – and particularly those of Hall – had now placed a firm intention in my mind not to open fresh publishing relations with them after the close of Chuzzlewit. My father's debts, two quarters' income tax and other demands coming all at once had driven me into a most uncomfortable corner. With the assistance of Forster, I began negotiating with others for more favourable arrangements and, after many and grave deliberations and discussions, they settled themselves at last into the form of agreements with Bradbury and Evans that I executed on the 1st June 1844. Upon them advancing me the sum of £2,800 (enabling me to pay Chapman and Hall their balance of £1,500, before I left for the Continent) I assigned to Bradbury and Evans half the copyright of Oliver Twist and a quarter of the Carol, as well as a quarter share in whatever I might write during the next ensuing seven years, to which the agreements were strictly limited. There were the usual protecting clauses, together with the lodging of a life assurance policy in the sum of £2,000, but no interest was to be paid, and no obligation was imposed on me as to what works I should write, if any, or the form of them; the only further stipulation being that, in the event of a periodical being undertaken, where I might be only partially editor or author, my proprietorship of copyright and profits would be two-thirds instead of three-fourths. I gave no more than a general understanding that a successor to the Carol would be ready for the Christmas of 1844, and I was careful to give no promise in regard to any other book; nor, moreover, had I decided what form I should give to my experiences of Italy – where I had by now determined to go – or even if I should publish such at all.

As I made preparations for Italy, a tenant, Mrs. Sophia Onslow, came up for Devonshire Terrace unexpectedly, who proposed to take our house for the whole term of our intended absence abroad, on condition that she had possession of it straightway. Accordingly, at the beginning of June, we all moved to 9, Osnaburgh Terrace before our departure. There I was able to finish Chuzzlewit in the rather different and cramped surroundings, and had to rearrange my proposed farewell dinner party. I eventually decided to make Genoa my base in Italy (Byron had had a villa at Albaro, close to Genoa) and both Kate and I took lessons in Italian. I learnt that Angus Fletcher, my "kindheart" guide from Scotland, was now living in Genoa and I sent a request out to him to see if he could locate a suitable house for us all. I also cast about for a means of transport, found a good old shabby devil of a carriage at a good price, and was also fortunate in finding a courier, Louis Roche, a native of Avignon, to direct our travelling to Italy.

There was much packing up to be done, and a farewell dinner held at the Trafalgar Tavern in Greenwich, presided over by Lord Normanby, and attended by over forty guests, which also took the form of a celebration for my completion of Chuzzlewit. It was a most convivial evening with many speeches, and I can recall Forster sitting next to the great painter JMW Turner, who had come with Stanny and had enveloped his throat, that sultry summer day, in a huge red belcher handkerchief, which nothing would induce him to remove! He was not otherwise demonstrative, but enjoying himself in a quiet silent way, less perhaps for him at the speeches than at the changing lights on the river.

The last Chapter of Chuzzlewit was released to the public on the last day of June and two days later, after a parting dinner at Forster's in Lincoln's Inn Fields, we set off for Italy in the carriage, leaving my personal affairs in England in the capable hands of Forster and Tom Mitton.

CHAPTER XIX

Living in Italy, The Chimes, and Travelling

The travelling party comprised myself and Kate, together with the children Charley, Mamie, Katey, Walter and Francis, as well as Georgy, Anne Brown, Charlotte (the nurse), two further domestic servants and Louis Roche – all packed into and around the carriage, together with Timber, a small white shaggy dog that had been given to me in America. We crossed from Dover to Boulogne and then on to Paris, all the while my spirits rising at the novelty of new circumstances that came swimming before me; I felt I had a new head on, side by side with the old one.

I found Paris a place so perfectly and wonderfully expressive of its own character – a secret character no less than that which was on the surface – that it made an immense impression upon me in the two days that we tarried there. I walked about the streets – in and out, up and down, backwards and forwards – and almost every house, and every person I passed, seemed to be another leaf in an enormous book that stood wide open here. My eyes ached and my head grew giddy at novelty, novelty, novelty; nothing but strange and striking things came swarming before me. It seemed then the most extraordinary place in the world.

We headed southwards, through Lyons, Avignon and Aix, thence onward for the boat at Marseilles. The children did not cry even in their worst troubles, the carriage glided lightly over abominable roads, and the courier Roche proving himself to be a perfect gem. We caught the boat from Marseilles to Genoa, the quiet beauty of the sea and sky unspeakable, and arrived in Genoa on the 16th July. By evening we had taken up residence at a villa properly called the "Villa di Bella Vista", although I came to call it in the locality the "Villa di Bagnerello", that being the name of an amiable but drunken butcher into whose hands it had fallen and who, being universally known (in consequence of being carried home from some wine shop or other every night), was a famous address which even the dullest errand boy recognized immediately. It was a large dwelling found for us by Angus Fletcher, close to Byron's house in Albaro, on a hill in the suburbs of Genoa and overlooking the bay. I had initially wanted to take Byron's house, but it had fallen into neglect and become the refuge of a third-rate wine shop; instead Fletcher had come up with this "Pink Jail" of a place, a lonely, rusty, stagnant old staggerer of a domain, at a rent absurdly above its value. But the situation was one of the most splendid imaginable – and Oh! the colours! The Mediterranean lay before me now, as deeply and intensely blue as can be imagined. Such lofty emotions rose within me when I saw the sun set upon such impenetrable blue. By Heaven, it was majestic! The sea had such an absorbing, silent, deep, profound effect upon me that it looked as if a draught of it – only so much as you could scoop up on the beach in the hollow of your hand – would wash out everything else and make a great blue blank of your intellect.

We were fortunate in being deliciously cool by comparison to the heat in Genoa itself, being high up in Albaro and having the sea breeze. There was always some shade in the vineyards too, and underneath the rocks on the sea shore, so if I chose to saunter I could do it easily, even in the hot time of the day. I was now happy however to be lazy, and do little but eat and drink and read. I never knew what it was to be lazy before; I should think a dormouse was in very much the same condition before he went under the wool in his cage or a tortoise before he buried himself. I could sit down in a church, or stand at the end of a narrow vigo, zig-zagging uphill like a dirty snake, and not feel the least desire for any further entertainment. I'd lie down on the rocks in the evening, staring the blue waters out of countenance, or stroll up the narrow lanes and watch the lizards running up and down the walls.

Then my stationery, inkstand and other tools of trade (together with my talisman of a pair of bronze fighting frogs) arrived from London and I arranged them, with my pens spread out in the usual form, in the best bedroom, so as to be able to write. I found that, after the most agreeable bathing in the early morning, I could set to work and, when the sun was off the corner window at the side of the house by a very little after twelve, I could then throw the blinds open and look up from my paper at the sea, the mountains, the washed-out villas, the vineyards and other scenes of such cheerful and peaceful view – and all as quiet as quiet could be. I began reworking the parts of Oliver Twist into a single volume for publication by Bradbury and Evans and to think each morning, with as much business-like air as I could muster, of a new Christmas book.

I also began hunting for better lodgings for the winter (there were no fire-places in the Pink Jail), and in due course found such a place – the "Palazzo Peschiere" – on a height within the walls of Genoa. It had very splendid rooms and a Great Hall, some fifty feet in height and with three large windows at the end overlooking the whole of Genoa and affording one of the most fascinating and delightful prospects in the world. Every inch of its walls was painted with frescoes, three hundred years old, and reported to the Fine Arts Commission as amongst the finest in Italy, causing anyone – even of the coldest spirit – to gaze in wonderment at the splendour of it all. These paintings were designed by Michael Angelo and were as fresh as if the colours had been laid on the previous day, making it within like being in an enchanted palace in an Eastern story. Outside featured fish ponds (hence the name) in beautiful and delicious gardens, filled with statutes, vases, seven fountains, marble basins, terraces, walks of orange trees and lemon trees, with fragrances abounding. It provided the most splendid and charming habitation, in all respects. I arranged to move into these magnificent surroundings from the 1st October.

The day of our move came with great guns blowing, the lightening incessant and the rain driving down in a dense cloud. But fortunately the worst of the storm was over when we reached the Peschiere, and as we passed into it along the stately old terraces, flanked on either side with the antique sculptured figures, all the seven fountains were playing in the gardens, and the sun was shining brightly on the groves of camellias and orange trees. We were somewhat above the old part of the city and could look down upon it; and once installed could, in particular, hear the chimes of the bells from the churches below that comprised our orchestra.

It was now that I began to think of my new Christmas book in earnest. I had the theme that I was determined upon – the poor and who was to blame for the lot they had to suffer – but not a title or the machinery to work it with. And then I had a return of rheumatism in my back, which also knotted around my waist like a girdle of pain. That night I lay awake nearly all night under this infliction and, when I finally fell asleep, I dreamed this dream full of animation and passion. In an indistinct place, which was quite sublime in its indistinctness, I was visited by a Spirit. I could not make out the face, nor do I recollect that I desired to do so, but I think I recognized the voice and assuredly knew it was poor Mary's spirit. I was not at all afraid, but in a great delight, so that I wept very much and, stretching out my arms to it, called it 'Dear'. I awoke with the tears running down my face, and myself in exactly the condition of the dream. It was just dawn, and calling up Kate, repeated it three or four times over, that I might not unconsciously make it plainer or stronger afterwards.

One morning soon after, sitting down resolute for work but frustrated at the blockage of it – seeming as if I had plucked myself out of my proper soil when I had left Devonshire Terrace and could take root no more until I returned to it – suddenly such a peal of chimes arose from the city below as I instantly found maddening. Born on the wind and coming into my room in one fell sound, the clang and clash of all the steeples in Genoa poured into my ears, again and again, in a tuneless grating, discordant, jerking, hideous vibration that made my ideas spin round and round till they lost themselves in a whirl of vexation and giddiness. This performance, I later found, was achieved by boys up in the steeples, who took hold of the clapper, or a little rope attached to it, and tried to dingle louder than every other boy similarly employed. Once the cacophony had abated, I steadied my thoughts upon Shakespeare and Falstaff – "We have heard THE CHIMES at midnight, Master Shallow" – and suddenly I was off on my task.

Once begun, I became in regular, ferocious excitement with my story, that I now named: "The Chimes". I would get up at seven, have a cold bath before breakfast, and blaze away, wrathful and red-hot, until three o'clock or so. It took great possession of me every moment of the day; and dragged me to where it will. For the next month I wore myself to death at the work. None of my usual reliefs were at hand; and, although I took long walks, I craved for the London streets and missed my long night-walks there before beginning anything. Put me down on Waterloo Bridge at eight o'clock in the evening, with leave to roam about as long as I like, and I come home panting to go on. But it was a great thing now to have my title, and see my way how to work the bells. Once taken and not able to divest myself of the story, I suffered very much with my sleep in consequence, and was so shaken by such work in the trying climate that I became as nervous as a man dying of drink and as haggard as a murderer. My cheeks, which were beginning to fill out, sunk again; my eyes grew immensely large; my hair very lank; the head inside the hair hot and giddy; and my face white in a foreign land.

Even though the weather was bad, I took long walks to clear my head, and liked more and more my notion of making, in this little book, a great blow for the poor. As I worked my tale of the old London ticket-porter Toby ('Trotty') Veck, I believed I had written a tremendous book, one that would knock the Carol out of the field. I was in no doubt however that it would make an uproar on account of its content. I sent Forster the quarter parts as they arose, to read and pass on to Bradbury and Evans, keeping a copy in shorthand in case of accidents. The music of the tale drove me on and at last, on the afternoon of the 3rd November, I was finished – and had what women call "a real good cry".

I was restless to return to London to see the last proofs and the woodcuts, but more especially I wished to lay my tale before friends in advance of publication. I particularly wanted Thomas Carlyle to see it before the rest of the world, and so wrote to Forster asking him to get up a little circle, including Carlyle, one evening when I came to town. Meanwhile, with the help of Roche, I began planning the route we would take – Roche measuring bits of maps with a carving fork, and going up mountains on a teaspoon! I proposed to first visit Parma, Modena, Bologna, Venice, Verona, Brescia and then to Milan where, being within a reasonable journey from Genoa, Kate and Georgy could come to meet me, before Roche and I headed north towards England. There I proposed to put up at Cuttris's (the Piazza Hotel and Coffee House in Covent Garden) to be close to Forster, and asking only for a good bedroom and a cold shower-bath. Forster had initially tried to persuade me not to travel, dwelling on the fatigue and cost of such a visit, but I wrote to him enthusiastically telling him that I intended to come.

On the 6th November, soon after five o'clock in the evening, I bade a tearful farewell to disconsolate Kate, Georgy and the others and set off with Roche on my travels. Later I faithfully recorded, in "Pictures from Italy", my impressions of the places I visited, but one place shone above all others: Venice. Nothing in the world that ever you have heard of Venice is equal to the magnificent and stupendous reality of Venice. I stayed at the wondrous Hotel (Royal) Danieli and explored the city by gondola and on foot; the three days passed there went by me like a dream. I hardly think it possible to exaggerate its beauties, its sources of interest, its uncommon novelty and freshness; the gorgeous and wonderful reality is beyond the fancy of the wildest dreamer. I am liable to disappointment in such things from over-expectation, but Venice is above, beyond, out of all reach of coming near, the imagination of man. All that I had heard of it, read of it in truth or fiction, fancied of it, was left thousands of miles behind. It is a thing you would shed tears to see, and is a bit of my brain from this time. But to tell what Venice is, I feel to be an impossibility. Venice is truly the wonder and new sensation of this world.

In Milan I met up with Kate and Georgy; they had travelled the eighty miles from Genoa to pass a couple of days with me in Prospero's old dukedom before my departure with Roche to London. We spent two pleasant days together before, at five o'clock the following morning, Roche and I left and Milan soon lay behind us; and before the golden statute on the summit of the cathedral spire was lost in the blue sky, the Alps, stupendously confused in lofty peaks and ridges, clouds and snow, were towering in our path. Still we continued to advance towards them until nightfall; and, all day long, the mountain tops presented strangely shifting shapes, as the road displayed them in different points of view. The beautiful day was just declining, when we came upon Lago Maggiore, with its lovely islands. For however fanciful and fantastic the Isola Bella may be, and it is, it still is beautiful; anything springing out of that blue water, with that scenery around it, must be.

It was ten o'clock at night when we got to Domo d'Ossola, at the foot of the Pass of the Simplon. But as the moon was shining brightly, and there was not a cloud in the starlit sky, it was no time for going to bed, or going anywhere but on. So, we got a little carriage, after some delay, and began the ascent. The snow lay thick, and the air was piercing cold, but the serenity of the night, and the grandeur of the road, with its impenetrable shadows, and deep glooms, and its sudden turns into the shining of the moon and its incessant roar of falling water, rendered the journey more and more sublime at every step. The stupendous track, after crossing a torrent by a bridge, struck in between two massive perpendicular walls of rock that quite shut out the moonlight, and only left a few stars shining in the narrow strip of sky above. Then, even this was lost in the thick darkness of a cavern in the rock, through which the way was pierced, the terrible cataract thundering and roaring close below it, and its foam and spray hanging in a mist about the entrance. Emerging from this cave, and coming again into the moonlight, and across a dizzy bridge, it crept and twisted upward, through the Gorge of Gondo, savage and grand beyond description, with smooth-fronted precipices, rising up on either hand, and almost meeting overhead. Thus we went, climbing our rugged way higher and higher all night, without a moment's weariness, lost in the contemplation of the black rocks, the tremendous heights and depths, the fields of smooth snow lying, in the clefts and hollows, and the fierce torrents thundering headlong down the deep abyss.

Towards daybreak, we came among the snow, where a keen wind was blowing fiercely. Having, with some trouble, awakened the inmates of a wooden house in this solitude – round which the wind was howling dismally, catching up the snow in wreaths and hurling it away – we got some breakfast in a room built of rough timbers but well warmed by a stove, and well contrived for keeping out the bitter storms. A sledge being then made ready, and four horses harnessed to it, we went, ploughing through the snow, still upward, but now in the cold light of morning, and with the great white desert on which we travelled, plain and clear. We came well upon the summit and had before us the rude cross of wood, denoting its greatest altitude above the sea, when the light of the rising sun struck, all at once, upon the waste of snow and turned it a deep red. The lonely grandeur of the scene was then at its height.

We sledged through the snow on the summit for two hours with the weather perfectly fair and bright, and there was neither difficulty nor danger – except the danger that there always must be, in such a place, of a horse stumbling on the brink of an immeasurable precipice.

The cold was piercing; the north wind high and boisterous; and when it came diving in our faces, bringing a sharp shower of little points of snow and piercing it into our very blood, it really was what it is often said to be, "cutting" – with a very sharp edge too. There were houses of refuge here – bleak, solitary places for travellers overtaken by the snow to hurry to, as an escape from death; and one great house called the Hospital or Hospice, founded by Napoleon but now kept by monks, where wayfarers could get supper and bed for nothing. We saw some wayfarers coming out and pursuing their journey. If all monks devoted themselves to such uses, I should have little fault to find with them.

Taking to wheels again, we descended rapidly into Switzerland. The cold in Switzerland was again something quite indescribable. We rested in Fribourg, and I found my eyes tingling as one may suppose cymbals to tingle when they have been lustily played. After three hours sleep, we pressed on and got to Strasbourg; there my impatience grew further, to such an extent that I urged Roche to press on with me to Paris with all speed. He obliged and, after a further fifty-hour journey in a French coach, we arrived there. I had planned to see Macready, who was due to be acting in the English theatre in the city after his tour of America, and went around to his hotel, personally examining the attendants as to his whereabouts, but he was not there and they did not know where he was. So, as I hoped I would soon see him in London – where I now longed to be – I elected to press on.

We set off for Boulogne, there catching the steamer for England. Arriving at the hotel in Covent Garden, I paused just long enough to ready myself before hurrying around to Lincoln's Inn Fields to greet Forster on that wintry Saturday night, the 30th November. My joy at seeing him once again and grasping his hand was unconfined. We talked of many things and plans, and I was also able to meet up with Macready, whereupon the next night I read to him the whole of The Chimes. If you had seen Macready, undisguisedly sobbing and crying on the sofa as I read, you too would have felt, as I did, what a thing it is to have power.

The following day I was at Bradbury and Evans's premises all day, finalizing The Chimes for publication, and was delighted at the result. That night, on my instruction, Forster organized the famous "tea-party" in his house, punctually at half-past six, where a select group of friends (Carlyle, Stanny, Laman Blanchard, Fox, Jerrold, Harness, Dyce, Forster himself, and Maclise – who captured the moment in sketch) all gathered around the Inimitable to hear The Chimes read aloud. Shrieks of laughter and floods of tears flowed from the assembled few, the evening proving to be one of immense gladness and gratitude for me – and set within me a train of thought that I might do such readings more often and to a wider audience. I gave a further reading after dinner at Forster's three days later and made arrangements for Gilbert A'Beckett and Mark Lemon to produce The Chimes on stage at the Adelphi Theatre in the Strand – the same place incidentally where, as a young boy, I had seen Charles Matthews perform his comic sketches.

I pressed as much into that week in London as I could manage. For me it was a most memorable week, and when Forster subsequently wrote to me in the belief that I had so tempestuous a journey from Italy for such brief enjoyment in London, I was able to reply in truth that I would not have missed it for any stated consideration.

CHAPTER XX

Further Travelling, and Pictures from Italy

Leaving London with Roche, we headed back to Paris, where I met once again with Macready. He and I passed some memorable days in each other's company, including visiting theatres, but with mixed results. At the Odeon, Madame St. George – once Napoleon's mistress – played 'Christine' in an Alexander Dumas play, and I never in my life beheld such a sight. She was now of an immense size, from dropsy I suppose, and with little weak legs which she could not stand upon. Her age, withal, somewhere about 80 or 90 and every stage conventionality she ever picked up (and she had them all) had got the dropsy too, and was swollen and bloated hideously. The other actors never looked at one another, but delivered all their dialogues to the pit, in a manner so egregiously unnatural and preposterous that I couldn't make up my mind whether to take it as a joke or an outrage. But then at the Italian Opera, where Grisi was singing in 'Il Pirato', the passion and fire of a scene between her, Mario and Fornasari was as good and great as it is possible for anything operatic to be. I also witnessed Macready himself rehearsing in his production of Othello with his customary ingenuity and brilliance.

Roche and I left Paris on the night of the 13th December and after three days and three nights of travelling over horrible roads, we finally arrived in Marseilles, fifteen hours late. There was then confusion between the two rival packets for Genoa, and I unwillingly detained one of them for more than an hour, before the matter was sorted and I managed at last to get to the steamer just as she was moving out of harbour. As I went up the side I heard an angry voice exclaim: "I'm blarmed if it ain't Dickens!" and found it was one of a group of five Americans on board. Their chief man or leader, however, revealed himself to be one I had met in New York and at once introduced his colleagues all round with the remark: "Personally our countrymen and you can fix it friendly, sir, I do expectuate" and so it proved on our stormy passage to Genoa. I was pleased to be back at Palazzo Peschiere once again in time for Christmas and New Year with the family, but I did miss England.

Upon my return, I was truly distressed to hear, and then see, the severe troubles of Madame Augusta De la Rue, wife of the Swiss banker Emile, whom I had met before going to London. She would exhibit a form of convulsion to her face and, on speaking to her in depth, I discovered the poor woman was filled with anxieties and strange visions. I spoke with her husband, and then engaged her with mesmeric powers, noting what she said during the trances, and showing this to him. This proved beneficial to her as her anxieties reduced and her sleep increased, but Kate much disapproved of my actions and made her feelings quite clear. Nevertheless, I pressed on with it, keeping in extensive contact through her husband on my subsequent travels.

In the New Year of 1845, on the 20th January, I set off with Roche again, now southward, to explore further parts of Italy. Kate on this occasion came with me and I also arranged for Georgy to join us later in Naples. We travelled along the beautiful coast road to La Spezia, Carrara, and then on to Pisa where, like all good travellers, we studied and then climbed the leaning Tower. But if Pisa is the seventh wonder of the world in right of its Tower, it may be at least the second or third in right of its beggars. They waylay the visitor at every turn, escort him to every door he enters at, and lie in wait for him, with strong reinforcements, at every door by which they know he must come out. The grating of the portal on its hinges is the signal for a general shout, and the moment he appears he is hemmed in, and fallen on, by heaps of rags and personal distortions. The beggars seem to embody all the trade and enterprise of Pisa; nothing else is stirring but warm air.

We travelled on further south, turning inland on a somewhat wild journey, through the beautiful old city of Sienna and on towards Rome. As we approached Rome, we began, in perfect fever, to strain our eyes and when the Eternal City appeared at length in the distance, it looked like – I'm half afraid to write the word – like LONDON!! There it lay, under a thick cloud, with innumerable towers, and steeples, and roofs of houses, rising up into the sky, and high above them all, one Dome. I swear, that keenly as I felt the seeming absurdity of the comparison, it was so like London at that distance, that if you could have shown it me, in a glass, I should have taken it for nothing else.

We stayed in Rome for a week, exploring the delightful intricacies of the city and engaging in its carnival, before continuing on southward. The weather now was bad in the main, and grew worse as we travelled – rain, snow, wind, darkness, hail and cold were all encountered – broken only by the sun coming up across the sea at Terracina, before we reached Naples. The famous bay I found immeasurably inferior to that of Genoa and to the city I took the greatest dislike, with the condition of the common people abject and shocking. There is nothing on earth that I have seen so dirty as Naples – excepting Fondi that we passed through shortly before. There are miles of miserable streets and wretched occupants, and I witnessed a pauper burial-place which was shocking to behold. It was a great paved yard with 365 pits in it, every one covered by a square stone which was fastened down. One of these pits is opened every night in the year, the bodies of the pauper dead collected in the city, brought out in a cart and flung in, uncoffined. Some lime is then cast down into the pit, whereupon it is sealed up to allow the lime and the earth to do its work, until a year is past and its turn comes around again. The cart itself has a red lamp attached, and at about ten o'clock every night you see it glaring through the streets of Naples, stopping at the doors of hospitals and prisons and such places to increase its freight, before rattling off again.

Georgy joined us and we undertook a three-day excursion to Paestrum to see the magnificent temples, followed by visits to Herculaneum and Pompeii, all of which had greater interest and wonderment than it is possible to imagine. We then made our way to Vesuvius. We began our ascent at four o'clock in the afternoon of Friday 21st February, a small party of six (myself, Kate, Georgy, a fat Englishman, Roche and another) together with an armed soldier for a guard, six saddled-horses, and twenty two guides; the latter rendered necessary by the severity of the weather, which had been greater than known for twenty years and had covered the precipitous part of the mountain with deep snow, the surface of which was now glazed with one smooth sheet of ice from the top of the cone to the bottom. By starting at this hour I intended to catch the sunset about half way up, and night at the top, where the fire was raging. It was an inexpressibly lovely night without a cloud; and when the day was quite gone, the moon (within a few hours of the full) came proudly up, showing the sea, and the bay, and the whole country, in such majesty as no words can express.

We rode to the beginning of the snow and then dismounted. The others were put into litters (just chairs with poles) whilst I was accommodated with a tough stick, and we began to plough our way up. The ascent now was very nearly perpendicular and we were all tumbling at every step, but I knew there was little chance of another clear night before I left this, and gave the word to get up somehow or other. By prodigious exertions, we passed the region of snow and came into that of fire – desolate and awful. There it was like walking one's way through a dry waterfall, with every mass of stone burnt and charred into enormous cinders, and smoke and sulphur bursting out of every chink and crevice, so that it was difficult to breathe. High before us, bursting out of a hill at the top of the mountain and shaped like an 'A', the fire was pouring out, reddening the night with flames, blackening it with smoke, and spotting it with red-hot stones and cinders that fell down in showers. At every step everybody fell, now into a hot chink, now into a bed of ashes, now over a mass of cindered iron; and the confusion in the darkness (for the smoke obscured the moon in this part), and the quarrelling and shouting and roaring of the guides; and the waiting every now and then for somebody who was not to be found, and was supposed to have tumbled into some pit or other, made such a scene of it as I can give you no idea at all.

My ladies were now on foot, but we dragged them on as well as we could (they were thorough game and didn't make the least complaint) until we got to the foot of the topmost hill. Here we all stopped; but the head guide – an English gentleman by the name of Le Gross – and I, together with Roche, resolved (like jackasses) to climb that hill to the brink and look down into the crater itself. You may form some notion of what was going on inside it, when I tell you it was a hundred feet higher than it was six weeks before. I remember the sensation of struggling up it, choked with the fire and smoke, and feeling at every step as if the crust of ground between one's feet and the gulf of fire would crumble in and swallow one up, but we did it. We looked down into the flaming bowels of the mountain, the noise and fire and smoke and sulphur making me feel as if I were dead drunk, and with red-hot ashes falling in showers and the trembling crust of ground below my feet contributing to the appearance of flaming Hell itself.

We came back again, burnt from head to foot. Roche had been tearing his hair like a madman, and crying that we should all three be killed, but we swallowed a little wine, and a great deal more sulphur, before we began to descend. It was like a tremendous dream, sliding down the ashes to the edge of the smooth solid sheet of ice, whereupon the guides made a chain, holding by each other's hands, and beat a narrow track with their sticks. It was impossible to stand, and the only way to prevent oneself from going sheer down the precipice every time one fell, was to drive one's stick into one of the holes the guides had made and hold on by that. At one point Le Gross, being on one side of Georgy and I on the other, suddenly staggered away from the narrow path on the smooth ice, gave us a jerk, let go and plunged headforemost down the ice into the black night, five hundred feet below! Almost at the same instant, a man far behind, carrying a light basket on his head with some of our spare clothes in it, missed his footing and rolled down in another place (he was not found when we left the mountain at midnight); and after him, rolling over and over like a black bundle, went a boy, shrieking until the breath was tumbled out of him. We eventually made our way down; I was rather stiff thereafter, but quite unhurt, though my clothes burnt to pieces and my ladies the wonder of Naples.

Taking a more inland route, through Capua, past the monastery of Monte Cassino and the walled town of Valmontone, we arrived back in Rome on Sunday 2nd March for the ceremonies of Holy Week; although one day we walked out to Albano (14 miles distant) going by the ancient Appian Way, long since overgrown, climbing over an unbroken succession of mounds and heaps and hills of ruin, ruin enough to build a spacious city. The Holy Week is supposed to offer great attractions to all visitors; but, saving for the sights of Easter Sunday, I would counsel those who go to Rome for its own interest, to avoid it at that time. The ceremonies, in general, are of the most tedious and wearisome kind; the heat and crowd at every one of them, painfully oppressive; the noise, hubbub, and confusion, quite distracting. And then I heard, on Good Friday evening, that a man who, some nine months before, had robbed and then beaten to death (with her own staff) a Bavarian countess travelling as a pilgrim to Rome, was to be executed the next morning. It was very unusual to execute in Lent, but this crime being a very bad one, it was deemed advisable to make an example of him at that time, when great numbers of pilgrims were coming towards Rome from all parts, for the Holy Week. I saw the bills up at the churches, calling on the people to pray for the criminal's soul.

The place of execution was near the church of San Giovanni Decollato and I determined to go. I was on the spot by half-past seven, but there were not many people lingering about at that time, and these were being kept at a considerable distance from the scaffold – a guillotine being set up – by parties of the Pope's dragoons. Two or three hundred foot-soldiers were under arms, but the time for the execution (a quarter to nine in the forenoon) passed and nothing happened. All the bells of all the churches rang as usual and eleven o'clock had passed, when suddenly there was a noise of trumpets. "Attention!" was among the foot-soldiers instantly. They were marched up to the scaffold and formed around it. The dragoons galloped to their nearer stations and a long straggling stream of men and boys, who had accompanied the procession from the prison, came pouring into the open space. Some monks were then seen approaching from a nearby church, and above their heads, coming on slowly and gloomily, the effigy of Christ upon the Cross, canopied with black. The criminal appeared and within a short space of time he was beheaded. There was a great deal of blood but nobody cared, or was at all affected. There was no manifestation of disgust, or pity or indignation, or sorrow. My empty pockets were tried, several times, in the crowd immediately below the scaffold, as the corpse was being put into its coffin. It was an ugly, filthy, careless, sickening spectacle, meaning nothing but butchery beyond the momentary interest, to the one wretched actor. Yes! Such a sight has one meaning and one warning; let me not forget it. But the body was carted away in due time and the scaffold taken down, and all the hideous apparatus removed. The executioner, an outlaw ex officio who dare not, for his life, cross the Bridge of St. Angelo but to do his work, retreated to his lair, and the show was over.

We left Rome on the 25th March and travelled through Tuscan roads lined with wayside crosses and religious memorials, to the Falls of

Terni, Perugia and Arezzo before, on a fair clear morning, we looked from the summit of a hill upon Florence, lying before us in a sun-lighted valley, bright with the winding River Arno and shut in by swelling hills; its domes and towers and palaces rising from the rich country in a glittering heap, and shining in the sun like gold.

The streets of beautiful Florence, I found, were magnificently stern and somber; prodigious palaces, constructed for defence, with small distrustful windows heavily barred, and walls of great thickness formed of huge masses of rough stone, frowned, in their old sulky state, on every street. In the midst of the city – in the Piazza of the Grand Duke, adorned with beautiful statutes and the Fountain of Neptune – rose the Palazzo Vecchio, with its enormous overhanging battlements, and the Great Tower that watched over the whole town. Among the four old bridges that spanned the river, the Ponte Vecchio – that bridge covered with the shops of jewellers and goldsmiths – was a most enchanting feature in the scene. The Cathedral with its great Dome, the beautiful Italian Gothic Tower the Campanile, and the Baptistery with its wrought bronze doors; the Stone of Dante; the chapel of the Medici; the church of Santa Croce where Michael Angelo lies buried; innumerable churches; all arrested our lingering steps in strolling through the city.

It was now early spring as we finally headed back to Genoa and the Palazzo Peschiere, arriving there on the 9th April. I corresponded with Forster about the letters I had written to him with my Italian experiences, these pictures from Italy, and he thought them worth the looking at, as did D'Orsay, who remarked that they reminded him vividly of the real aspect of the scenes. Bradbury and Evans sent me an account of The Chimes; I was greatly pleased at the profit it had shown and the contrast with Chapman and Hall over the Carol and felt Bradbury and Evans were the men for me to work with.

I now fell into an idleness so complete that I could not rouse myself sufficiently to travel anywhere. Two men were hanged in the city, but I did not attend. The weather all the time was now without a flaw, but then my mind became set once more on London and I became impatient to be back in our dear old home again, discoursing with friends and renewing happy old walks. I put designs in place to leave Genoa on the 9th June and, on the day of departure with the carriage packed, we set off northward for the Great St. Gothard Pass and Switzerland. We came over the Pass, which had been open only eight days, with the road cut through the snow and the carriage winding along a narrow path between two massive snow walls, twenty feet high or more. Vast plains of snow ranged up the mountain-sides above the road, itself seven thousand feet above the sea; and tremendous waterfalls, hewing out arches for themselves in vast drifts, went thundering down from precipices into deep chasms. The pass itself, the mere pass over the top, was not so fine, I thought, as the Simplon; and there was no plain upon the summit, for the moment it was reached the descent began. But being much higher, the ascent and descent ranged over a much greater space of country; and on both sides there were places of terrible grandeur, unsurpassable, I should imagine, in the world.

The whole descent between Andermatt (where we slept) and Altdorf (William Tell's town, where we passed through), is the highest sublimation of all you can imagine in the way of Swiss scenery. Oh God! what a beautiful country it is! But the coming down from this pass, with the carriage and four horses and only one postilion, I now look upon as the most dangerous thing a carriage and horses could do. We had two great logs for drags, and snapped them both like matches. The road was like a geometrical staircase, with horrible depths beneath it; and at every turn it was a toss-up, or seemed to be, whether the leading horses should go round or over. The lives of the whole party could depend upon a strap in the harness; and if we broke our rotten harness once, we broke it at least a dozen times. The difficulty of keeping the horses together in the continual and steep circle was immense. They slipped and slid, and got their legs over the traces, and were dragged up against the rocks; carriage, horses, harness, all a confused heap. The brave Roche and I and the postilion were constantly at work, in extricating the whole concern from a tangle, like a skein of thread. We broke two thick iron chains, and crushed the box of a wheel as it was; and the carriage had to be repaired once we eventually got to Lucerne, before continuing on to Zurich.

I had written on ahead to Forster hoping that he and Maclise would come and meet me at Brussels, so we pressed on through Zurich and down the Rhine to Frankfurt, before heading for Brussels. There, I was overjoyed at greeting again not only Forster (who now looked thinner but quite well after his illness, although he would roar out sometimes without any notice in consequence of rheumatic twinges in one of his knees) and Maclise, but also Douglas Jerrold, clever author and gentlest and most affectionate of men, who had been in the party for the reading of The Chimes and was now in the most brilliant spirits – I doubt if he was ever more humorous in his life. Together we spent the most delightful week in Flanders, before returning to England at the close of June.

CHAPTER XXI

Theatricals, The Cricket on the Hearth, and the Daily News

Back at Devonshire Terrace, I had wished to paint and enliven the place with brightest Genoese Italian green, making it cheerful and gay, but Kate stood firm in objection and I was eventually forced to give up the idea. I caught a strong cold which knocked my spirits further and after my initial excitement of return, felt as if I found nothing new in London. Once the form of my "Pictures from Italy" had been settled for publication, I turned my mind to other thoughts. I revisited places of my childhood and had, once again, a notion of committing my life to paper, but eventually decided against it. I did have, however, a strong desire in me to establish a periodical and turned it over very much in my mind, whilst discussing it with Forster and Bradbury and Evans. I inclined to a weekly, and for a title turned to natural history and the cricket, that cheerful creature that chirrups on the hearth. Forster, however, countenanced against such a scheme, and particularly a weekly one, but I kept the notion of "The Cricket on the Hearth" within me and in due course resolved that it would instead be a delicate and beautiful fancy for a Christmas book, following on from the success of The Chimes.

My thoughts turned to my love of the stage and my mind went back to the time when I was performing in Montreal, where I was as much astonished at the reality and ease, to myself, of what I had done there as if I had been another man. I discussed these theatrical notions with Forster, and he agreed that we might proceed with it. We selected a play for our purpose: "Every Man in his Humour" by Ben Johnson, with myself to direct and also to play the cowardly but boastful Captain Bobadil, with Forster as Master Kitely. We engaged a little theatre, "The Royalty" in Dean Street, Soho, run by Fanny Kelly – which the Duke of Devonshire's munificence had enabled her to build – and began rehearsals with the players we had gathered under my direction.

In August the family, once again, rested in Broadstairs and I joined them at the Albion Hotel during breaks in rehearsals, delighted at being able to walk twenty miles a day at such an invigorating place. The play, together with an accompanying farce ("Two o'clock in the Morning", which I had twice played in Canada), was eventually performed on the 21st September with a success that out-ran our wildest amateur expectations; it turned our little enterprise into one of the small sensations of the day. The audience comprised over six hundred ladies and gentlemen, Lords and Ladies, all in elegant evening dress, The Times describing them as "the most select that could have been found in the English metropolis." Indeed, the applause of the theatre found so loud an echo in the press, that for the time nothing else was talked about in private circles; and shortly after we had to yield (we did not find it difficult) to pressure of demand – not least from Prince Albert himself, who was now President of Southwood Smith's Sanatorium Committee and wished a performance in aid of the Sanatorium. I arranged for a further performance, still of a private nature, but experienced so many problems with the arrangements and over-demand for tickets meant that the performance nearly did not take place; but I managed to hire a larger theatre (the St. James's) and the performance eventually went ahead there on the 15th November, to great effect. I always had a misgiving in my inmost heart that I was born to be the manager of a theatre, and now, from this experience, I was quite sure of it!

Meanwhile, on the 28th October at Devonshire Terrace, Kate gave birth to another boy, again suffering very much, but recovered wonderfully well, and after a couple of days was going on quite brilliantly. I was partial to girls and had set my heart upon one – but never mind me. We named our new son Alfred D'Orsay Tennyson Dickens after his two godfathers.

All this while I knew I must turn my mind to my new Christmas story, but I confess that, in seeking to do so, I found myself in such bad writing cue as in all my life I never experienced; sick, bothered and depressed over it to the point of distraction. The principal cause for this distraction was my new discussions with Bradbury and Evans, following their approach to me. They had perfectly amazed me with another new notion – with capital of £50,000 down, and ready! This involved the proposal for a new daily newspaper that was now taking root and proceeding apace, but when I mentioned it to Forster in confidence, he expressed the strongest reservations, particularly at the suggestion of the proposal that I act as editor. Bradbury and Evans had combined with Joseph Paxton at Chatsworth – Bradbury, being a native of Bakewell close to Chatsworth, had become on friendly terms with Paxton – and Paxton had himself engaged with a great number of railway promoters and seemed to have command of every railway and railway influence in England and abroad, except the Great Western. In their lucrative desires, those promoters not only sought to invest in the railway business – in London there was nothing to talk about but railroad shares and all the world raving mad about railroad speculations – but also to seek to establish a new progressive and independent newspaper to take on the established publications, in a new spirit for the age.

I was then formally offered the post of editor, at the handsome sum of £2,000 per annum. I visited Chatsworth and discussed the proposal with Paxton himself. I found he was in it, heart and purse, and he made me so excited about the prospect that I agreed to it. An office was provided for me in a back room on the second floor at 90, Fleet Street and there I began attending each day to set the project in motion. The newspaper was given the title of the "Daily News", and I now felt able to speak enthusiastically about its prospects. I began hiring staff, including W.H. Wills (recommended by Forster) as my sub-editor and secretary; a number from Punch Magazine (also published by Bradbury and Evans); Kate's father, George Hogarth; my father to manage the reporting staff; and Lady Blessington to provide social commentary. But I soon began to feel entwined in a maze of distractions, which nothing could have enabled me to anticipate or prevent; everything else I had to do became interfered with and cast aside, and my health suffered as a consequence. I felt I had never in my life had so many insuperable obstacles crowded into the way of my pursuits – and all the while the time for my new Christmas book drew in on me.

I had my title for it, "The Cricket on the Hearth" and felt I must press on with it. But in doing so I became as giddy as if I were drunk, and could hardly see. I was not able to take my usual walks, which further put me out of sorts, and Forster's appeals to me to give up on the Daily News weighed with me heavily – but I was determined to go on with it. I drafted the prospectus for the newspaper and worked ferociously upon my Christmas story – a fairy tale of the home life of John and Dot

Peerybingle, when a stranger comes into their midst – and managed to complete it in time for publication on the 20th December. I also made it possible, by prior release of proofs to those concerned, for a production to be adapted and staged at the English Opera House Lyceum Theatre, opening on the same date. I was delighted when, despite the critics, the story found great success with the public and in printed form sold almost twice as many copies as The Chimes. Furthermore, most of the theatres in London came to have a production of it upon their stage thereafter.

I was now able to give more undivided attention to the Daily News. The main topic of the day, apart from railway mania, was the debate over free trade and the repeal of the Corn Laws, and we planned to have the appearance of the first number of the Daily News on the day following Peel's speech on the subject. Matters built up to fever pitch; my office was moved to the Whitefriars printing works of Bradbury and Evans and, after a dummy run, everything looked well for our start – although I could not sleep and if I fell into a doze, I dreamt of first numbers till my head swam. Then, on the night planned for the launch, our printer failed us. I fought hard for the next night, and at six o'clock in the morning of Wednesday 21st January 1846 I was able to write a short, exhausted note to Forster telling him that I was now going home, that we had been at press three-quarters of an hour, and were out before The Times. First day sales were above 10,000 across the counter, despite Peel postponing his speech until the 27th January, when we reported it in excellent and express fashion.

As well as my editorial work, I had begun, in that first issue, the serialization of my letters descriptive of my Italian travel, and also received shares in the newspaper company in recognition of my work in its launch. But it was not many days into my role as editor that I realized Forster had been right all along and that I should never have taken on this task at all. On the 30th January I expressed my deep misgivings to Bradbury and Evans, and wrote to Forster that I wanted to have a long talk with him. We met at Devonshire Terrace over dinner the next night and I told him that I had been revolving plans in my mind that morning for quitting the paper and going abroad again, this time to write a new book in shilling numbers. I asked him to go with me to Rochester for my birthday and to talk things over.

To Rochester we went on that weekend, having our quarters for two days at the Bull Inn, a place now well-known through the adventures of Mr. Pickwick. Forster and Jerrold came, as well as Kate and Georgy, and on the Saturday we went over the old Castle, Watts Charity and Chatham fortifications whilst Sunday we passed in Cobham and Cobham Park – all places known to me from my childhood. I expressed my belief to Forster and the others that those with railway connections had too strong a hold on the newspaper so as to stifle the independence I desired, and that Bradbury in particular was seeking to interfere too much in my role as editor. The editorial work itself was very laborious indeed, and the group was in full agreement that if long continuance with the paper was not likely, the earliest possible departure from it was desirable. Soon after, I wrote a note to Forster stating that I had resigned my editorial functions, as I really was tired to death and quite worn out. Forster himself was persuaded, very reluctantly, to assume supreme control, with Charles Dilke operating as his manager, and he did so for the greater part of that year, but I know he came to find the task wearisome, anxious and laborious and he too was pleased to step aside when the time came.

I was now joyful to be free once again and to be able to consider my next venture. I returned to my usual propensity at such time, wondering about at night in the deserted streets of London seeking rest but finding none, turning over and over in my mind what I should do. Thoughts of a new story began to be rife within me; I wanted to write this new story in monthly parts, though I found I could not shut out the newspaper sufficiently in England to write well here. I constantly talked of going back to Genoa for another year and wished to Heaven I could pluck myself up by the roots again – let the house, pack up, buy another carriage and set off again.

Then Miss Coutts spoke to me about fallen women. Knowing of her great interest in charitable works, I had accompanied her to Limehouse to see the Pauper School there – presenting her with a lively and most encouraging picture of the good she could do by supporting such an establishment adjacent to the church (St. Stephen's) she had built in Rochester Row, Westminster – when she also told me that, from the windows of her house at 1, Stratton Street, Piccadilly, she had seen many fallen women at night apparently engaged in prostitution and crime, that had caused her heart to bleed at the sight. This had so troubled her in her bed that she expressed the wish to help them, providing some form of refuge or asylum. When she spoke thus to me, I felt this to be an excellent proposal and also, to my mind, could be a way of allowing them thereafter to be sent for marriage in distant parts of the world, with the greatest hope for their future families, and also providing the greatest service to the existing male population in such places. She was not sure about emigration leading to marriage, but I was certain that this would be the possible consequence of a sincere, true, practical repentance and an altered life, so I gave her my full and enthusiastic support for such a scheme and provided her, in a letter of the 26th May and before I left London again, with much detail as to how it should operate, including putting it in the power of governors of prisons to recommend girls for such a scheme.

Kate, who was never very well in Genoa, could not be got to contemplate the Peschiere again, though I beset her in all kinds of ways to do so. I had, however, been much taken by my sights of the Swiss mountains on my travels and felt a passion to visit them again; so also wishing to come as near to Madame De la Rue as I could, I resolved to pitch my tent somewhere on the Lake of Geneva – say at Lausanne – whence I could run over to Genoa immediately if required. After further thoughts, I became resolved to write my new story in Lausanne and forget everything else if I could; and in living in Switzerland for the summer, and possibly in Italy or France for the winter, I knew I should be saving money as I wrote.

So I set my plans in motion. I again let Devonshire Terrace, this time for twelve months to Sir James Duke, M.P. and sold my shares in the Daily News; I arranged for things to be settled there, including the termination of Lady Blessington's engagement with the paper, as she desired. I oversaw the printing of the full volume edition of "Pictures from Italy", attended celebratory dinners, had many outings with friends, and hired Roche to be my courier once again. At last all was ready and, at the end of May, after a final family dinner with Forster, we all left London heading for Switzerland, Forster insisting on travelling with us to Ramsgate to bid us a final farewell.

CHAPTER XXII

Switzerland, Dombey and Son, and The Battle of Life

We parted from Forster at Ramsgate and crossed to Ostend. In beautiful but hot weather with hardly a cloud in the sky, we travelled on, taking a steamboat ride along the Rhine to Strasburg, a train to Basle, and thence, in three coaches, to Lausanne, where we arrived at the Hotel Gibbon (commanding a fine view of the lake) on the evening of Thursday the 11th June. The next day I, at once, began house-hunting and found a delightful and quite a "doll's house" of a place (such as you might put it all into the great Sala of the Peschiere) called "Rosemont", beautifully situated on the hill that rose from the lake towards Ouchy and within ten minutes' walk of the hotel. The landlady and her husband now lived in a smaller house, like a porter's lodge, just within the gate and proposed to rent the main house out furnished (though scantily) for £10 a month for half a year, with reduction to £8 for the second half, if I should stay so long. I took it on these terms, moved in the family, and established my little study upstairs which looked out – from two French windows opening into a balcony – onto the lake and upon the mountains around, the peacefulness and grandeur of this wonderful scenery being indescribable. And there were roses enough to smother the whole establishment of the Daily News in!

I took my customary evening walks and began planning my new novel with detailed care. I conceived the title and theme: "Dealings with the Firm of Dombey and Son, Wholesaler, Retail and for Exportation" and began writing, planning to deal with the emotion of pride on this occasion. My aim was to get four monthly numbers of Dombey, together with a Christmas book, done in Lausanne by the end of November, before running over to Forster in England, leaving Roche to move the caravan to Paris (where I then planned to go) in the meanwhile. But you can hardly imagine what extraordinary difficulty I found, in getting on fast; it was almost an impossibility. I suppose this was partly the effect of two years' ease, and partly of the absence of streets and numbers of figures. I can't express how much I wanted these. It seems as if they supply something to my brain which I cannot bear, when busy, to lose. For a week or a fortnight

I can write prodigiously in a retired place (as at Broadstairs), and a day in London then sets me up again and starts me. But the toil and labour of writing day after day, without that magic lantern I find IMMENSE!

During this time I was fortunate to meet some charming English residents, wonderfully friendly and hospitable – indeed I do not think I could have fallen on better society – amongst them being William Haldimand, a former Member of Parliament who, with his sister Mrs. Jane Marcet (the well-known authoress), had long made Lausanne his home. He had a very fine place just below Rosemont and was an accomplished man, having founded and endowed many hospitals and institutions in Lausanne, including the Blind Institution. Through his kindness I met William de Cerjat and his wife Maria (she drew well and made a sketch of Rosemont for us), George and Elizabeth Goff (she being the sister of Maria de Cerjat) and The Honourable Richard and Lavinia Watson, whose home in England was the splendid Rockingham Castle in Northamptonshire. It was a small circle certainly, but quite large enough. Everybody was very well informed; and we were all as social and friendly as people can be – and very merry.

As well as Dombey, the new Christmas story began unfolding in my mind on my dark evening walks. It started as an odd shadowy undefined idea connected with a great battle-field; shapeless visions of the repose and peace pervading in it after-time, with the corn and grass growing over the slain, and people singing at the plough. The visions came to be so perpetually floating before me, that I felt I could turn them to something good when I saw them more plainly. I worked hard and laboriously upon the story alongside Dombey, but wondering now if I had taken on too much in beginning two stories together, and becoming sick, giddy and capriciously despondent. I had bad nights, was full of disquietude and anxiety, and was constantly haunted by the idea that I was wasting the marrow of the larger book and ought to be at rest. I felt myself in serious danger, and yet continued hammering away morning noon and night. I then lodged for a week at the Hotel de l'Ecu in Geneva, where I became a great deal better in the changed scene and felt quite myself again. I also took to making expeditions as a way of relief from constant writing.

One such expedition was to Chamonix. We went by way of the mountain pass called the Col de Balme, not often crossed by ladies, where your imagination may picture Kate and Georgy on mules for ten hours at a stretch, riding up and down the most frightful precipices. A guide, a thorough-bred mountaineer, walked all the way leading a lady's mule, and all the rest struggled on as they pleased. Roche (the Brave) rode a very small mule up the road exactly like the broken stairs of Rochester Castle, with a brandy bottle slung over his shoulder, a small pie in his hat, a roast fowl looking out of his pocket and a mountain staff of six feet long carried cross-wise on the saddle before him! We climbed up and up and up for five hours and more, and looked – from a mere unguarded ledge of the path on the side of the precipice – into such awful valleys, until at last you were firm in the belief that you had got above everything in the world, and that there was nothing earthly overhead. But just as you arrived at this conclusion, a different, free and wonderful air came blowing on your face. We crossed a ridge of snow, and lying before us (wholly unseen until then), towering up into the distant sky, was the vast range of Mont Blanc, with attendant mountains diminished by its majestic side into mere dwarfs tapering up into innumerable rude Gothic pinnacles; deserts of ice and snow; forests of firs on mountain sides of no account at all in the enormous scene; villages down in the hollow that you could shut out with a finger; waterfalls, avalanches, pyramids and towers of ice, torrents, bridges; mountain upon mountain until the very sky was blocked away, and you must look up, overhead, to see it. Good God, what a country Switzerland is, and what a concentration of it is to be beheld from that one spot! We spent two days at Chamonix before returning, by the Pass of the Tête Noire, which is of a different character, but astonishingly fine too. The valley of Chamonix and all the wonders of that most wonderful place, are above and beyond one's wildest expectations.

Another expedition was to the Great St. Bernard. Although the St. Bernard Convent is the highest inhabited spot but one in the world, this ascent on mules was extremely gradual and uncommonly easy, really presenting no difficulties at all, until the last league, when the ascent, lying through a place called the Valley of Desolation, was very awful and tremendous, with the road rendered toilsome by scattered rocks and melting snow. The Convent itself was a most extraordinary place, full of great vaulted passages, divided from each other with iron gratings; and presenting a series of the most astonishing little dormitories, where the windows were so small (on account of the cold and snow) that it was as much as one could do to get one's head out of them. Here we slept: supping, thirty strong, in a rambling room with a great wood-fire in it set apart for that purpose; with a grim monk in a high black sugar-loaf hat with a great knob at the top of it, carving the dishes. At five o'clock in the morning the chapel bell rang in the dismallest way for matins: and I, lying in bed close to the chapel, and being awakened by the solemn organ and the chanting, thought for a moment I had died in the night and passed into the unknown world! The place was in a great hollow on the top of a range of dreadful mountains, fenced in by riven rocks of every shape and colour: and in the midst, a black lake, with phantom clouds perpetually stalking over it. Peaks, and points, and plains of eternal ice and snow bounded the view, and shut out the world on every side: the lake reflecting nothing: and no human figure in the scene. Beside the Convent, in a little outhouse with a grated iron door which you could unbolt for yourself, were the bodies of people found in the snow, who had never been claimed and were withering away – not laid down or stretched out, but standing up, in corners and against walls; some erect and horribly human, with distinct expressions on their faces; some sunk down on their knees; some dropping over on one side; some tumbled down altogether, and presenting a heap of skulls and fibrous dust. There is no other decay in that atmosphere; and there they remain during the short days and the long nights, the only human company out of doors, withering away by grains, and holding ghastly possession of the mountain where they died. This Convent was the most distinct and individual place I had ever seen, even in this transcendent country, but the St. Bernard Holy Fathers and the Convent in themselves are, I am sorry to say, a piece of as sheer humbug as we ever learnt to believe in, in our young days. Trashy French sentiment and the dogs (of which, by the bye, there were only three remaining) have done it all. They are a lazy set of fellows; rich; and driving a good trade in inn-keeping, the Convent being a common tavern in everything but the sign. No charge is made for their hospitality to be sure; but you are shown to a box in the chapel, where everybody puts in more than could, with any show of face, be charged for the entertainment, and from this the establishment derives a right good income.

I continued to work hard on my Christmas book – thinking as I did that it would be all the better, for a change, to have no fairies or spirits in it, but to make it a simple domestic tale – and eventually produced "The Battle of Life: A Love Story", which I dedicated to my English friends in Switzerland. I had also continued on apace with Dombey and in due course read to those friends not only the Christmas story, but also the first number of Dombey. It had me thinking that in these days of lecturing and readings, a great deal of money might possibly be made (if it were not infra dig) by having readings of my own books. I thought it would take immensely and put the idea to Forster, though he sought to oppose it strongly.

I spent time again in Geneva, lodging once more for a week in the Hotel de l'Ecu, and could not help rambling in my mind among all sorts of old days and once familiar faces as I had now made up my mind never to grow old myself (within, at all events) and never to believe anyone else had done so, except on the strongest evidence. I cast my mind back to my childhood and told Forster that Mrs. Pipchin's establishment that I had written into Dombey, was from life and that I was there. I didn't suppose I was eight years old, but I remembered it all as well, and certainly understood it as well, as I did when writing it into Dombey and felt strongly that we should be devilish sharp in what we do to children. Thinking of that passage in my small life, and Forster telling me soon after that Charles Dilke had told him of seeing me at the blacking factory in Chandos Street when I was a young boy, I was stunned that this should now return to me, and for a while did not know how to deal with it; I wondered then if I should leave Forster my life in manuscript when I died.

We finally departed Lausanne on the 16th November, with deep regrets at leaving our little society behind, and after a five-day carriage journey (where we were up at five every morning and on the road before seven), arrived in Paris and took up lodgings at 48, Rue de Courcelles Faubourg Saint-Honoré in a modest and curious house. I pressed on with Dombey, which I was pleased to hear was now selling passed thirty thousand already, the first number of Dombey having outstripped the first of Chuzzlewit by more than ten thousand copies. Brilliant! I was very thankful.

I took long walks in the streets of Paris – a city as bright, and as wicked, and as wanton as ever, though wonderfully attractive – and though I lost myself fifty times and longed once again for the familiar thoroughfares and alleyways of London, I was refreshed by all the novelty of the sights. But then I became deeply grieved when I had word from my father that my sister Fanny was seriously taken with consumption and it caused me to become most hopelessly out of sorts with my writing. I now couldn't begin in this strange place; took a violent dislike to my study, and came down into the dining-room; couldn't find a corner that would answer my purpose; fell into a black contemplation of the waning month; sat six hours at a stretch and wrote as many lines. I tried to settle to my desk, and went about and about it, and dodged at it, like a bird with a lump of sugar. Moreover, the cold was now intense; the water in the bedroom-jugs froze into solid masses from top to bottom, bursting the jugs with reports like small cannon and rolling out on the tables and wash-stands, hard as granite. And then, as if being dragged by an invisible force, I went into the City Morgue. I never wanted to go there, but repeatedly felt myself being pulled there, to see the dead bodies that had come into the net across the river and been hauled therefrom, to be exposed for public inspection and possible identification. One day, however, I was so shocked at what I saw that I did not have the courage to go back again.

I made plans with Roche to set off for London together (I had no use for him there, but he would have died if I had not taken him with me), left the family in Paris and, once in London, put up in the Piazza Coffee House Hotel in Covent Garden. I was there eight days, and saw poor Fanny and her son Harry, upon whom I had based little Paul Dombey. I also sought to go over the proofs of Dombey for the next number, settle the form for cheap editions of my writings to begin in 1847, and meanwhile attend to the staging of "The Battle of Life" at the Lyceum. The Christmas book was published on the 19th December, and by the end of the day twenty-three thousand copies were already gone! The play was staged on the 21st, with every place in the house taken, and I heard it went with great effect. I was told there was immense enthusiasm at the close, with great uproar and shouting for me.

CHAPTER XXIII

Dombey, Fallen Women, Theatricals and Public Meetings

The weather continued bitterly cold as I journeyed back to Paris and began the fifth number of Dombey. I toiled away and eventually, on the 14th January 1847, slaughtered the young and innocent Paul Dombey. As I had no hope of getting to sleep afterwards, I immediately took to the night streets and walked about Paris until the light of dawn broke through. Forster visited the next day and we then crammed into the space of the following fortnight every description of impossible and inconsistent occupation in the way of sight-seeing: prisons, palaces, theatres, hospitals, the Morgue and the Lazare, as well as the Louvre, Versailles, St. Cloud and all the places made memorable by the first revolution – whirling out of one and into another with breathless speed. We attended many theatrical performances together, met with Victor Hugo, his wife and daughter, at his address at 6 Place Royale, and also dined with Alexandre Dumas, whilst paying our respects to many others in French society.

Forster returned to London on the 2nd February, taking Charley, now aged 10, with him, to place him at King's College School, Wimbledon, whilst I turned back once again to Dombey. I was finding it very difficult indeed to fall into the new vein of the story after young Paul's death, when I was horrified to then suddenly discover that the current number I had supplied to Bradbury and Evans was two pages short. As time for publication was now so pressing, there was no means of rectifying this accident otherwise than by going to London again to write them there. I did so, crossing from Boulogne in a gale and frightful sea, running nearly as bad as the Atlantic, and leaving me horribly bilious and queer for some considerable time. After rectifying the mistake, I returned to Paris, but then received the devastating news that Charley – on the very day I went away – had contracted scarlet fever at King's College. I immediately returned to London with Kate, who was now pregnant again, and we lodged for a time at the Victoria Hotel in Euston Square as Devonshire Terrace remained let. Charley was now staying under the care of his grandmother, Mrs. Hogarth, at their new address in Albany Street, and after a short while I found and secured a temporary house nearby for us at 1, Chester Place and sent Roche to Paris to bring Georgy and the remaining children back so that we could all be together again. Because of her pregnancy, Kate was not able to visit Charley, and I and the others when they arrived had to wait for almost a further month for the contagion to pass before we could then see him again.

I then heard that William Hall had died suddenly in his office at 186 Strand on the 7th March. I went to his funeral, though they seemed to have had a delicacy in asking anyone not of the family, so I communicated with Chapman and told him that I wished to pay a last mark of respect if it did not interfere with their arrangements. They agreed and I attended. Then I had to deal with my brother Fred, who had now been transported to madness with love for Anna Weller, younger sister of Christiana. His subsequent engagement to her, I regarded as one of the greatest mistakes ever made, and I wrote and told him so in the most explicit terms.

I continued to support enthusiastically Miss Coutts in her desire to open a home for the salvation of fallen women. I introduced her to George Chesterton, Governor of the Middlesex House of Correction, Coldbath Fields, Clerkenwell, whom I had known for a considerable period of time. I sought his assistance in seeking out suitable premises for the "Home" – the name I proposed to give it – and one was found in Shepherd's Bush, between Acton Road and New Road. Miss Coutts agreed it was suitable and took a lease on the premises at sixty guineas per year. I then engaged busily upon preparation for its opening, including searching prisons and other institutions for those that we might help and setting up a beneficial routine for the women to follow. Miss Coutts subsequently adopted the name for the premises that it once had possessed – "Urania Cottage" – and I prepared for the opening with eager anticipation.

Despite all these other matters that took my attention, I had to press on with Dombey. After some hard labour, I was pleased to introduce the Honourable Mrs 'Cleopatra' Skewton, mother of Edith Dombey who, although now aged 70 years of age, dressed as if she was 27, and used all of the cosmetic arts to present herself as Cleopatra, the subject she modelled in a fashionable sketch in her youth. I conversed with Browne over Dombey illustrations, and was pleased to have many friends who wrote kindly to me over the story, none more so than Francis Jeffrey. Then, on the 18th April, Kate gave birth to another boy, suffering terribly and to my alarm in the process. We named him Sydney Smith Haldimand Dickens after two further great admirers, although I came to call him "Ocean Spectre" from the look he exhibited in his large wondering eyes. Shortly after his birth, I drove down to Chertsey Cottage for a spell of hunting, but one of the horses I drove took it into his head to make a sudden attack upon me in the stable, tore my coat sleeve and shirt sleeve off, and very nearly took the great muscle of my arm with it. I began to feel very unwell for a number of days, and decided to take some sea air for recovery; I took lodgings in Brighton for a short while (at 148 King's Road) and there felt able to continue on with the next number of Dombey.

Upon my return, I dined with friends at the Trafalgar in Greenwich and it was there that I heard about the circumstances of the author and journalist Leigh Hunt. He had been introduced to me by Forster (who had a great admiration for him) some time before, but had now fallen on hard times and had been refused assistance by the Government. We had a meeting at Forster's home and considered assisting him financially through the idea of reviving our old amateur theatrical company for this special purpose, and even of taking it bodily to Manchester and Liverpool. I wrote to my contacts in those places and meanwhile searched for a large London theatre that we might use before the close of the season, the aim being, if possible, to perform "Every Man in his Humour" and a farce on the 14th July and "The Merry Wives of Windsor" together with a farce five days later, followed by performances in Manchester on the 26th and Liverpool on the 28th July. I was delighted to be able to secure agreement from the actors, my splendid strollers, to appear for this noble cause.

Eventually the politicians relented under pressure and granted Leigh Hunt a civil-list pension, so it was decided not to now proceed with the London performances, but I knew of another writer, John Poole, and was aware that he, too, was in financial difficulties. So it was decided to now produce two performances of "Every Man in his Humour" in Manchester and one in Liverpool, together with accompanying farces (including Poole's own "Turning the Tables") for the joint benefit of both Hunt and Poole. Whilst preparing for these performances, I transported the family once again to Broadstairs (to 38 Albion Street on this occasion) at the end of June, but I, of course, had to be continually going back and forth to town to deal with business, including rehearsals at Miss Kelly's Theatre and writing a hundred letters a day about these plays and their performances.

On Sunday 25th July our party of twenty-four (including eight ladies) travelled from Euston to Manchester, with great excitement, for our performances. In Manchester both houses were crammed full with people in full dress and the theatre rang with enthusiasm, laughter and tremendous applause – indeed I never heard or saw such laughing in a theatre. The people were drooping over the fronts of boxes like fruit and the carpenters and the people behind, who were attending to the machinery of the scenes (of which there was a good deal) had the most ridiculous tears rolling down their faces all the time. It was impossible to keep a grave face and, at times, all but impossible to go on. We followed with a wonderful supper afterwards, with much champagne, and I danced as a madman into the early hours. Then on to the Adelphi Hotel in Liverpool. By now I was quite hoarse and had a mustard poultice on my throat and ate a bushel of anchovies (the oldest and best theatrical recipe) to keep my voice going; whilst Mrs Leech in our party gave birth to a daughter! Again we found the theatre was large and crammed to the roof with people in full dress, who again took everything in a manner that I had never seen equalled. And you can imagine nothing like the reception they gave me in both places, standing up as one person and shouting incessantly for a good ten minutes. Nothing could have been more complete; it amply repaid all the trouble, and was perfectly splendid. We were able to raise substantial funds for both beneficiaries.

But all the while Dombey was never far from my mind and I pressed on with it at Broadstairs. I then heard that Sir James Duke had now vacated Devonshire Terrace, so arranged to return at the end of September. The accounts for the first half-year of Dombey came through and were much in excess of what had been expected from the new publishing arrangements; I considered the profits for myself to be brilliant and was excited also at the prospect of the issue of cheap editions of all my novels. Meanwhile I began turning over the possibility in my mind of a new Christmas book under the title of "The Haunted Man" but, although I did not wish to disappoint my readers, as well as being very loath to lose the money, I felt that to continue on with Dombey without distraction was of far greater importance.

At the end of September we all returned to Devonshire Terrace. By now the Shepherd's Bush Home was very nearly ready for the furniture and I sought Miss Coutts's authority to proceed with the fittings in all respects – which I did do so, despite finding myself over my eyebrows in paper and correspondence. I drafted a letter in the form of an appeal that might be read and then given to women in prison, setting out what might be made of their life and the opportunity offered by the Home if they would be resolved to change. I visited again Mr. Chesterton's prison and found there two women who had been recently discharged but had elected to remain in the prison – prison clothed and fed – until we were enabled to take them, thereby giving of the best proof of the sincerity of their desire to come to us.

By the end of October, two House Matrons (Mrs. Holdsworth and Mrs. Fisher) had been installed at Shepherd's Bush and women were beginning to reside at the Home. I also arranged for the Reverend Edward Illingworth (Chaplain at Coldbath Fields) to be the visiting Minister and I made regular visits – including chairing weekly Committee meetings – to assist in the detail of management. I helped to keep the Case Book on each of the residents, as well as keeping Miss Coutts fully apprised of events.

Towards the end of 1847 I was invited north to chair a meeting of the Leeds Mechanics' Institute, to be held on the 1st December in the Albion Street Music Hall, and also to attend at the opening of the Glasgow Athenaeum that was to take place on the 28th December. On my way to Leeds with Kate, I was delighted to stay with the Watsons at Rockingham Castle and to read to them the latest number of Dombey. In both Leeds and also later in Glasgow there were immense assemblages where I was most wonderfully received and the responses to my addresses gave me enormous satisfaction.

I was delighted to receive a generous letter of praise from Thackeray about Dombey, and wrote telling him so, but I then developed such a cold that I was not even able to see the paper to write further. Dombey, however, would admit of no postponement and was one over which I had no power of arrangement; the doctors confirmed that my daily morning cold shower bath should do wonders for my general health and so I continued with it, though it was startling when encrusted with ice. My general health did improve gradually, but when I got to the point of dense stupidity and could hardly write a thing all day, I took to the sea air of Brighton once again, and on the 24th March 1848 was finally able to draw Dombey to its conclusion.

By now sales of the Dombey numbers were running far stronger than Chuzzlewit, being in the order of thirty-five thousand copies per issue and quite prodigious, and on the evening of the 11th April I held a "Dombey Dinner" at Devonshire Terrace, with thirteen special friends to celebrate, in the happiest style, the completion of the story. I always had had great faith in Dombey, and now held a strong belief that it would be remembered and read years hence. I later discovered that it had inspired the whole of my works to be translated into Russian, that my name enjoyed a wide celebrity in Russia, and that from the banks of the Neva to the remotest parts of Siberia I was read with avidity.

CHAPTER XXIV

Further Theatricals, Fanny, and The Haunted Man

I felt I needed a change for a short while from constant writing, and turned back to my enthusiasm for the stage, together with my desire to raise funds for impoverished writers and artists. I set about contacting my amateur players once more and decided upon suitable plays and farces to alternate with "Every Man in his Humour". Eventually the choice was again made of Shakespeare's "The Merry Wives of Windsor", together with a number of farces, and rehearsals began in earnest at Miss Kelly's theatre, where the company were all nearly worked to death.

We held our first performances at the Haymarket Theatre on the 15th May, with The Merry Wives of Windsor and Animal Magnetism, and then, two days later, with Everyman and his Humour and Love, Law and Physick, with crowded and brilliant houses, that also included an attendance on the 17th by the Queen and Prince Albert. We played at Manchester, Liverpool and Birmingham; I visited Stratford with Georgy and some of the Company on the 7th June, and then the following month we all headed north to perform in Edinburgh and Glasgow, each place again rewarding us with crowded and brilliant houses. I felt a joy and a vitality coursing through my veins at these splendid strollings, and the knowledge that aid and assistance was being rendered to other men of letters by our performances was particularly rewarding. The Queen also commanded a complimentary benefit to Macready at Drury Lane on the 10th July and I assisted in making these arrangements, but caused Macready to be all aghast at me because I would not put on court dress and receive the Queen. I had never been to court, or presented myself before her, either in my public capacity or as a private gentleman, and felt it would not be becoming or agreeable to me to claim her recognition on such an occasion.

Throughout the whole of this period, my thoughts were never far from my sister Fanny and her illness. I suggested that she and her family move from Manchester to the London area to allow her to have the best treatment for her consumption, and I assisted them in moving to Hanley Road, Hornsey. I spoke to the Queen's physician, Sir James Clark, telling him of her condition; he told me, however, that she could not possibly live many weeks. I spoke also to Dr. Hastings, whom I knew, and who had been so extraordinarily successful in affections of the mucus membrane and done such wonderful things. I had perfect faith in him, and he promised very readily to go and see Fanny immediately to help relieve her cough and do all he could to assist. He had succeeded to Sir James Clark over and over again to my certain and absolute knowledge, and had done wonders where Clark really did nothing, but I feared that Fanny was now dying, and not by very slow degrees. This was confirmed to me by Dr. Hastings after visiting her, as he said immediately on coming out that Sir James Clark was quite right and that it would be monstrous in himself if he held out the least hope – that the disease must be fatal and was too far gone to admit any chance of recovery. Although he made no appointment to see her again, I arranged for him to do so as I thought it so important to her hope and peace that she should not think that he too had given her up. But she became aware of her hopeless state, to which she resigned herself with extraordinary sweetness and consistency.

I visited her as often as I could, and she shed tears frequently as she talked to me, including telling me of her wish to be buried in Highgate cemetery. I was deeply moved and greatly impressed by her overall calmness and courage, and the surety she had that we would meet again in a better world. She said she was quite calm and happy, relied upon the mediation of Christ, and had no terror at all. She told me she could not help thinking sometimes, as her husband was young and her children infants, that it would be very long in the course of nature before they could be reunited – but she knew also that this was a mere human fancy, and could have no reality after she died. Such an affecting exhibition of strength and tenderness, in all that early decay, was quite indescribable and I need not tell you how it moved me. God knows how small the world looks to one who comes out of such a sick-room on a bright sunny day.

It was with a heavy heart that I left to join Kate (who was expecting another child, and not very well), Georgy and the children at Broadstairs, although I made visits to London throughout August to see Fanny at

Hornsey, the Home at Shepherd's Bush and Miss Coutts in Stratton Street, as well as visiting Macready before he went to America. Apart from my London visits, I passed the remainder of August reading and in quiet contemplation of a possible Christmas book, but returned to Devonshire Terrace at the beginning of September due to Fanny's deteriorating condition. During August, when I had visited her, no words can express the terrible aspect of suffering and suffocation I had found, the appalling noise in her throat and the agonized look around she gave – before she would sink into a kind of lethargy, with sleep seemingly quite gone. She was, by now, very weak, but did speak to me of how the smell of fallen leaves in the woods that we had walked as young children together had come to her, with such strength of reality that she believed they were now strewn on the floor at her bedside. She died on the 2nd September, just 38 years of age, and was buried six days later in unconcecrated ground (as was her wish) in Highgate cemetery – an occasion that filled me with such deep and intensive feelings of sadness, that was only added to by the sight of Henry, the little deformed boy she had left, half unconscious of his bereavement.

Immediately after Fanny's death I received a most unwelcomed letter from my brother Fred, informing me that not only was he in debt, but that he proposed to press ahead with marriage to Miss Anna Weller. I told him that I could say nothing of it that would be gratifying to him; that I could not help him further at this time with the heavy claims upon me, and that to fling any sum of money into the unfathomable sea of such a marriage with debt upon its breast, was not something I could possibly enter on now. Despite my strong protestations, Fred decided to go ahead with the wedding, which eventually took place on the 30th December; before this I agreed to provide him with £83 towards his debts, but declined to attend the wedding.

Speaking with Fanny before she died had, once again, brought my childhood back upon me – reinforced by receiving, in the month following her death, a kindly letter from William Giles (my first schoolmaster in Chatham, but who was now living in Chester); upon reading his handwriting, indeed I half believed I was a very small boy again and wondered, once more, if I should commit my life to writing. I eventually wrote to Forster about my time in the blacking shop and my father's incarceration in the Marshalsea, but that is as far as I could manage, such was the pain of it, and I put the rest aside but with thoughts again that I might leave Forster my life in manuscript when I died.

Meanwhile a much more pressing concern was my new Christmas book. I had first had thoughts of it in the summer of 1846 in Lausanne, and then again in the autumn of 1847, but only now was it fully maturing in my mind. I planned it with care and with thoughts of Fanny's memory coming back to me all the while – in music, in the wind, and in the dead stillness of the night as the years revolved around me. I took as the central character a professor of chemistry, Redlaw, who had been granted the ability to eliminate painful memories from people, but who came to understand the importance that these memories have in bringing people together in love and understanding. I finished the book, which I entitled "The Haunted Man and the Ghost's Bargain", late into the night of the last day of November, crying my eyes out over it for three days – not painfully but pleasantly, as I hoped my readers would. I dedicated it to my daughters Mamie and Katey, dispatched it to Bradbury and Evans, and arranged for Stone, Leech and Stanny to do the illustrations. On the 18th December, after dinner at Devonshire Terrace, I read the little book to friends, including Forster, Stanny, Miss Coutts and the Watsons (who came especially from Rockingham Castle) before publication took place the following day, as well as arranging for Mark Lemon to give performances of it at the Adelphi Theatre. Once published, the book was a wonderful success, the initial subscription being twenty thousand copies all sold, and the stage play ran to the 7th February 1849.

CHAPTER XXV

I begin David Copperfield

I had been circulating in my mind for some time thoughts of a new book, and had discussed it with Forster on a number of occasions. He had made the suggestion that I might, on this occasion, use the first person as a basis for the narrative and this appealed to me. Then, at the beginning of 1849, I went on a short walking tour with Lemon and Leech (Forster being too unwell to join us) in an effort to settle my mind. We decided upon East Anglia as I had been drawn to that location by the recent news that, on the 28th November, at Stanfield Hall, Wymondham (9 miles from Norwich), the dastardly James Rush – a tenant farmer on that estate – had entered in disguise at the mansion and shot dead the owner Isaac Jermy (the Recorder of Norwich), together with his son, and seriously wounded his wife and a servant. Many had visited the scene and I had an interest to do likewise.

Norwich was a disappointment, all save the place of execution – the gallows being set up on a bridge under the walls and over the dry moat of the castle – which we found fit for that gigantic scoundrel Rush's exit. We rode out to Stanfield Hall, to find it had nothing attractive about it, unless the term might be applied to a murderous look that seemed to invite such a crime as had been perpetuate.

From there we made our way to Yarmouth, staying at the Royal Hotel, and then walked the coast to Lowestoft and back, a journey of some twenty-three miles. On the way I saw a signpost to a place near Lowestoft called Blundeston, a name that caught my attention for its sound, and which I later took, adapted to Blunderstone, and used as the birthplace for my new companion.

On the 16th January, our eighth child, a boy we christened Henry Fielding Dickens, was born. Kate's confinement was almost as bad a one as its predecessor, but chloroform did wonders, and she knew nothing of it. Foreseeing the possibility of such a repetition of last time, I had made myself thoroughly acquainted of the facts of chloroform and had insisted on the attendance of a gentleman from Bartholomew's

Hospital, who administered it in the operations there, and had given it four or five thousand times. I had also promised Kate that she should have it. The doctors were dead against it, but I stood my ground, and (thank God) triumphantly. It spared her all pain and saved the child all mutilation. The shock to Kate's nervous system was reduced to nothing; and she was, to all intents and purposes, well the next day – and ditto Number 8!

I continued to visit the Home in Shepherd's Bush and helped in the arrangements for the emigration of our first girls. Three of them (Jane Westway, Martha Goldsmith and Julia Mosley) all sailed for Adelaide, South Australia on the S.S. Calcutta, followed by a further two (Emma Lea and Rubina Walker) aboard the S.S. Posthumous. But at the Home itself I began brooding very gloomily over our prospects – the main cause being Miss Cunliffe, the new assistant matron, who violently mistook her office and its functions, and I did not descry any prospect of our keeping the young women in the house when she had sole charge of them. I was sure that her idea of hectoring and driving them was the most ignorant and the most fatal that could be possibly entertained, and so it proved. She was found to have made enquiries into the past history of one or more of the girls – something I was resolved should not happen – and she was dismissed.

On the 29th January, all the sadness over Fanny returned to me again when Henry, her 9-year old crippled son (and upon whom I had based Tiny Tim as well as little Paul Dombey) died. He was buried in Fanny's grave at Highgate cemetery. Shortly after, I went with Forster to visit Landor in Bath to celebrate his 74th birthday but, on my return, received a letter from my mother in Lewisham telling me that my father was now exceedingly unwell. I set out immediately to visit him; he was in bed and seemed low and weak, though I did not, on the whole, find him so ill as I had expected. Nevertheless, seeing him in such a condition only added to the turmoil of my emotions at this time; I walked perpetually trying to resolve the new book in my mind and, once again, felt the need for sea air and the tranquility that it brought.

So, in the middle of February, I took Kate, Georgy and the children to Brighton, and soon thereafter we were joined by John Leech and his wife. However, within a week, our landlord and his daughter both went raving mad and had to be taken away – with an atmosphere of the Mrs Gamps (strait-waistcoats, struggling friends and servants) surrounding the whole procedure – so we were obliged to move out and stay at the Bedford Hotel instead. All the while my mind was running, like a high sea, on a name for my new companion, but I was not yet satisfied I had alighted on the right one. Deepest despondency in commencing was, as usual, besetting me. Having started with "Mr. Thomas Mag the Younger of Blundelstone House", I went through a number of different names until I alighted on the one I was satisfied with: "David Copperfield" – whose initials, Forster then pointed out to me, happened to be the exact reverse of my own. I was much startled by this and protested that it was just in keeping with the fates and chances that were always befalling me.

Back at home in Devonshire Terrace at the end of February, I began writing to my usual order, always at my desk by nine o'clock and remaining in my study until at least two. I would then walk for at least three hours each day, organizing my mind and taking in things into my mental museum. It was important to me to maintain a strong sense of order and business-like regularity, with a firm belief in punctuality; and with such discipline I drove myself onwards. But, despite my resolution, I was finding it no easy task to construct the opening of Copperfield. I finally resolved to write around the notion of: "The Personal History, Adventures, Experience, and Observation of David Copperfield the Younger, of Blunderstone Rookery, which he never meant to be published on any account" and endeavoured to press on. I worked steadily through the next month, the characters coming slowly upon me at first, but I sent each chapter to Forster and then to the printer as soon as I had it ready and, when I had the proofs returned, I sent a copy to Browne for him to consider his drawings. The Murdstones entered David's life and I, like David, was suffering – but I was firmly set on my purpose and, with the arrival of Peggoty and the willin' Mr. Barkis, I began to know my way forward, beginning even now to wallow in my new book very comfortably and (I hoped) successfully.

On the 23rd May, I enjoyed a day out to the Epsom Derby, with Lemon and Leech in the carriage, together with a very neat little collation in a hamper from Fortnum and Mason; and then in June I revisited the countryside of my youth around Cobham and Rochester with Leech, the reason being that I intended David to walk through there on his way to Dover. On returning to London, I began to incorporate some of the memories of my early childhood into the life that David was now experiencing. I had discussed this with Forster and sought to introduce a great part of the manuscript that I had drafted and shown him into the fourth number of Copperfield. I really thought I was able to do it ingeniously, with a very complicated interweaving of truth and fiction. As I was doing this, however, there was another of those fates and chances that befell me; I slipped and got an awkward fall on my weak (left) side, where there is an inflamed kidney sometimes, and caused me pain. It reawakened my old injury that I had first suffered in the blacking factory warehouse all those years before. As a result I was obliged, on this occasion, to be cupped and lost a good deal of blood, as well as being blistered, and felt very unwell. I went for a week to the Albion Hotel in Broadstairs with Kate and Georgy for some sea bathing to aid my recovery, and there was able to finish the fourth number.

In July I considered making a visit to the Isle of Wight, and first lodged in a house in Shanklin before, on the 16th July, was able to write to Kate that I had taken a most delightful and beautiful house called "Winterbourne" at Bonchurch, which belonged to the very jovial Reverend James White, someone I had met at Macready's three years earlier. The house was close to that of White's and had recently been converted from a barn; it stood one hundred and fifty feet above the Channel, but with large grounds containing a stream that extended down to the sea shore. It was cool, airy, and with private bathing – everything delicious and I thought it was the prettiest place I ever saw in my life, at home or abroad. I also found a waterfall in the grounds, which I arranged with a carpenter to convert into a perpetual shower-bath with a high fall. I told Kate that Anne could now begin to dismantle Devonshire Terrace and I arranged the family move to Bonchurch until the end of September. Once settled there, Winterbourne and its surroundings put me in the highest of spirits. I set up my study in an upper floor room overlooking the sea and, after work, engaged in the greatest degree of fun with the family – along with the Leeches, who came to stay at "Hill Cottage" above Winterbourne, and other visitors I was happy to invite. Although I had a wretched cough that I could not seem to shake off, I found the variety of walks in the area extraordinary and came to delight in particular in the long walks that could be taken across the Downs. From the top of the highest Downs, I found there were views which are only to be equalled on the Genoese shore of the Mediterranean, and we were able to take dinners at Blackgang and picnics of tremendous success on Shanklin Down.

I worked intensively on Copperfield through July, August and into September, and determined to mount daily to the top of the Downs if I was able, though there were often times when I was obliged to return to London on business. The result of all of this, however, was that I became mentally and physically exhausted. I came to have an almost continual feeling of sickness, accompanied with great prostration of strength, so that my legs trembled under me, and my arms quivered when I wanted to take hold of any object. I fell into an extraordinary disposition to sleep (except at night, when my rest, in the event of having any, was broken by incessant dreams) and if I had anything to do requiring thought and attention, this overpowered me to such a degree that I could only do it in snatches, lying down on beds in the fitful intervals. At times, too, I came to have extreme depression of mind and a disposition to shed tears from morning to night. I became incapable of reading and my bilious system was so utterly overthrown that a ball of boiling fat appeared to be always behind the top of the bridge of my nose, simmering between my haggard eyes. I came to feel it was the results of the climate of Bonchurch and the generally depressing influence of the Undercliffe that had the effect of reducing and overpowering my vitality. I now found that, of all the places I had ever been in, I had never been in one so difficult to exist in pleasantly as Bonchurch and became quite convinced that I should die there in a year. It was not hot, it was not close, I didn't know what it was, but the prostration of it was awful.

I felt in somewhat better spirits when I finished the next number of Copperfield – and danced quadrilles at a party at the White's house to celebrate – but I made my plans to leave at the end of September, and to go again to the Kent coast. Then Leech suffered a serious accident whilst bathing in a sea that had been running very high; he was knocked over by a bad blow from a great wave to his forehead and suffered blood congestion of the brain. He had twenty of his namesakes placed on his temple to draw the blood, but continued in excessive pain and had ice to his head continuously, being also bled in the arm besides. Thomas Beard (who was visiting) and I assisted by sitting up with him all night, but he became much worse and again had to be very heavily bled. He became in such an alarming state of restlessness, which nothing could relieve, that I proposed to Mrs. Leech to try magnetism. She agreed, and after a very fatiguing bout where his restlessness had become most distressing and it was quite impossible to get him to maintain any one position for five minutes – he was more like a ship in distress, in a sea of bedclothes, than anything else – I began the magnetism.

I eventually succeeded in calming him and talked to the astounded little Mrs. Leech across him when he was asleep, as if he had been a truss of hay or a woolpack. At the end of the sleep he expressed himself much refreshed and took some breakfast in good spirits. The doctor, who earlier had been despondent and uneasy to me about him, came again and pronounced him greatly better and was much pleased with the improvement. To prevent talk about it, we agreed not to tell the doctor of the magnetism, though I understand he was favourable to it.

My plans were all unsettled by Leech's illness as, of course, I did not like to leave whilst I could be of any service to him and his good little wife and would not think of going away unless he were, to all intents and purposes, quite well. I was required to magnetise him further during the next few days, and he steadily improved, to the great surprise of the doctor. I observed similar effects in Leech as those I had witnessed in Madame De la Rue – whom I had magnetised every day for six months as her disorder was in a most horrible form – but Leech improved so readily that I soon was able to leave. I made the arrangements for Kate, Georgy, Mamie, Katey and I to go to the Albion Hotel in Broadstairs, where I proposed to write the next number of Copperfield before going back to town, whilst organizing the other children to go straight home from Bonchurch.

CHAPTER XXVI

Copperfield, a Villain in America, and Fallen Women

Once at Broadstairs, I was delighted to receive a good report of himself from Leech and a kind letter from his wife, but found myself unexpectedly mowed down by a fit of laziness – so I went over to Canterbury alone and refreshed myself with a day's rain there. Then I began writing again with – as Mr. Micawber would say – "a sickly mask of mirth" but, as I was now rather behind time, I was hammering away all day until I did not know whether it was my head that was oppressing my shoulders, or a pumpkin stuffed with lead. I forwarded, as usual, preliminary despatches and advices to Forster and also raised with him the idea that had been floating around in my mind for a while of a weekly periodical to be produced, as earlier envisaged in my agreement with Bradbury and Evans. I had looked over the accounts relating to the publication of the cheap editions of my works by Chapman and Hall and had wished the profit larger, but realized that the times had not been such as to justify any sanguine expectations in that regard. Copperfield sales were now running at about twenty-five thousand for each monthly part and, as time progressed, I became more and more favourably disposed towards also starting this periodical. I spoke to no one about it other than Forster, showering him with my ideas. He, once again, expressed grave doubts about such a scheme, but I became in a state of such enthusiasm about it that I did not lay much stress upon his cautioning and began searching in my mind for a name for this new publication.

Upon finishing the next number of Copperfield, we all returned to Devonshire Terrace to join with the rest of the family again. I immediately paid visits to Miss Coutts and the Home in Shepherd's Bush, where I had a long talk with Mrs. Morson, the matron, and found all was now going on very well. I planned to go again for some hours to make up the book there on the young women and also perhaps make a little change to the mark system upon which the Home was run, which I calculated would improve their business habits. I also agreed to speak at a dinner, to be given on the 21st November by the Newsvendors' Benevolent and Provident Institution, and made plans to now send Charley to Eton, which Miss Coutts (as his godmother) had kindly agreed to support financially.

I then had to deal with news from America of an execrable rascal named Thomas Powell, who was to publish a book there entitled "The Living Authors of England", which contained a section of villainous and unblushing falsehood about me. It was, once again, striking proof of the justice of the estimation in which I held the American press and I considered that such an unmitigated villain should be denounced, with me setting forth his history in the plainest possible terms, as I knew his falsehood would go all over the States instantly. I wrote to persons who had contacted me, including those from America, setting out clearly that this man was a forger and a thief. Powell threatened thereafter to sue me for libel but, of course, never did so as I had set out the truth.

At the beginning of November, I made the Committee at the Shepherd's Bush Home acquainted with the contents of a letter to Miss Coutts from the Bishop of Adelaide, that caused an impression of heavy disappointment and great vexation. He told us that both ships containing the five girls from the Home had now arrived, but that all the girls appeared to have returned to their old courses and were totally unfit to be recommended as household servants. They had quit the ships when asked not to, before the Bishop could get to see them and get them places, leaving the worst character behind them and doing no credit to the Home. They were all said to be beyond control and the committee of ladies set up to help them upon their arrival had dissolved themselves.

At the same Committee meeting at the Home, we also found that one of the resident girls, Isabella Gordon, was endeavouring to make a party in the house against Mrs. Morson and Mrs. Macartney (the new assistant matron), was disturbing the general peace again (as she had done before) and intended coming to us with complaints. We investigated them with the utmost care, confronted her with Mrs. Morson, and were convinced that her whole story was utterly false and malicious. We ordered her to her room while we considered the subject, and she danced upstairs before Mrs. Morson, holding her skirts like a lady at a ball. After further deliberation, we had her down again some time afterwards and, to her utter bewilderment and amazement and that of the whole house, dismissed her. We were also obliged to give severe warnings to two other girls, Hannah Myers and a girl by the name of Sesina, about their conduct.

Then, the following morning, Mrs. Morson came to Devonshire Terrace in a fly to tell me that little Sesina had been very insolent last night, and had been ordered to her own room; and that this morning she positively refused to get up, or to return any answer whatever, to any of the remonstrances that were made to her. In consequence of her behaviour they had kept the gardener in the house all night – a precaution at which I could not help laughing, when I thought of its object being a little dumpy atom of a girl whose head may be somewhere on a level with Mrs. Macartney's waist. I directed Mrs Morson to tell Sesina she was to dress herself, and leave the place directly; and that when I came, in half an hour, if I found her there at all, I should send for a policeman and give her into custody for being there without our consent and making a disturbance. I understand that, on receipt of this message, she parleyed a little and, after making a slight pretence of being ill, threw her nightcap to one end of the room and her nightgown to the other and proceeded, very leisurely, to dress herself. On coming down stairs, she objected that she couldn't go away in the rain, at which she was told she better sit in the long room then until I came. Declining this offer, she walked off. I met her in the Lane, taking her departure. Before she went she told Mrs. Morson that "she know'd Miss Coutts's address, and would write her a good long letter, telling her what treatment was had there." I passed her afterwards, walking in a jaunty way up Notting Hill, and refreshing herself with an occasional contemplation of the shop windows. All the rest in the Home were very quiet, and Hannah Myers very much subdued. My belief was that Sesina would join Isabella Gordon somewhere very shortly. I think she would corrupt a nunnery in a fortnight.

CHAPTER XXVII

A Double Hanging, Letters to "The Times",
and more of Copperfield

During this time, the trial had proceeded at the Old Bailey of Frederick Manning and his Swiss-born wife Maria, for the joint and violent murder of Patrick O'Connor, who had been at one time Mrs. Manning's lover. The case aroused great public attention and when they were both found guilty they were sentenced to be hanged together outside Horsemonger Lane Jail on the 13th November, the first time in almost 150 years a husband and wife had been due to be executed together. I gave in about the Mannings and decided not to go; the doleful weather, the beastly nature of the scene, the having no excuse for going (after seeing Courvoisier), and the constantly-recurring desire to avoid another such horrible and odious impression, decided me to cry off – but then, as the day approached, I changed my mind.

A group of five of us, including myself, Forster and Leech, took the whole of the roof and back kitchen of a house overlooking the jail for the extremely moderate sum of ten guineas (two guineas each) and from there witnessed, at intervals all through the night, and continuously from daybreak until after the spectacle was over, the crowd that gathered to behold it. I believe a sight so inconceivably awful as the wickedness and levity of the immense crowd collected at that execution that morning could be imagined by no man, and could be presented in no heathen land under the sun. The horrors of the gibbet and the crime that brought the wretched murderers to it, faded in my mind before the atrocious bearing, looks and language of the assembled spectators. When I came upon the scene at midnight, the shrillness of the cries and the howls that were raised from time to time, denoting that they came from a concourse of boys and girls already assembled in the best places, made my blood run cold. As the night went on, screeching, and laughing and yelling in strong chorus of parodies on negro melodies, with substitutions of "Mrs. Manning" for "Susannah," and the like, were added to those. When the day dawned, thieves, low prostitutes, ruffians and vagabonds of every kind, flocked on to the ground, with every variety of offensive and foul behaviour. Fightings, faintings, whistlings, imitations of Punch, brutal jokes, tumultuous demonstrations of indecent delight when swooning women were dragged out of the crowd by the police with their dresses disordered, gave a new zest to the general entertainment. When the sun rose brightly – as it did – it gilded thousands upon thousands of upturned faces, so inexpressibly odious in their brutal mirth or callousness, that a man had cause to feel ashamed of the shape he wore, and to shrink from himself, as fashioned in the image of the devil. When the two miserable creatures who attracted this ghastly sight about them appeared and were turned quivering into the air, Manning's form became a limp, loose suite of clothes as if the man had gone out of them; that of his wife however remained in fine shape, so elaborately corseted and artfully dressed in black satin, that it was quite unchanged in its trim appearance as it slowly swung from side to side. There was no more emotion, no more pity, no more thought that two immortal souls had gone to judgement, no more restraint in any of the previous obscenities, than if the name of Christ had never been heard in this world, and there was no belief among men but that they perished like the beasts.

Later that day I wrote to The Times and spoke of this, adding:

"I have seen, habitually, some of the worst sources of general contamination and corruption in this country, and I think there are not many phases of London life that could surprise me. I am solemnly convinced that nothing that ingenuity could devise to be done in this city, in the same compass of time, could work such ruin as one public execution, and I stand astounded and appalled by the wickedness it exhibits. I do not believe that any community can prosper where such a scene of horror and demoralization as was enacted this morning outside Horsemonger Lane Jail is presented at the very doors of good citizens, and is passed by, unknown or forgotten. And when, in our prayers and thanksgivings for the season, we are humbly expressing before God our desire to remove the moral evils of the land, I would ask your readers to consider whether it is not a time to think of this one, and to root it out."

I also asked that the Government might be induced to give its support to a measure making the infliction of capital punishment a private solemnity within the prison walls, and for the Home Secretary (Sir George Grey) to originate such a legislative change himself.

Following my letter, a correspondent, using the name "Milo", wrote to the newspaper asking if I would explain myself more clearly, and whilst I had had no intention originally of writing again, I did so on the 17th November, setting out in detail my positions in reference to the demoralizing nature of public executions. In principle I was opposed to capital punishment and should be glad to abolish it if I knew what to do with the savages of civilization but, as I did not, I am sorry to confess that I did now believe capital punishment to be necessary in these extreme cases; simply because it appeared impossible otherwise to rid society of certain members of whom it must be rid, or there was no living on this earth. But I believed a public execution to be a savage horror far behind the time, affording an indecent and fearful gratification to the worst of people, and that it should only be carried out in very solemn manner within the walls of a prison.

I now had to press on, with very hard work indeed, at Copperfield. I completed the eighth number, but had also to deal with a roaring sea of correspondence, brought upon me by my two letters in The Times. So I was happy to leave town for a few days and go, at their invitation, to stay with the Watsons at Rockingham Castle. Everything undertaken there eventuated in most magnificent hospitality, and on this occasion I was also enamoured to meet Mrs. Watson's cousin, the delightful Miss Mary Boyle, authoress and renowned amateur actress. As a result, we got up in the Great Hall, some scenes from the School for Scandal; also the scene with the lunatic on the wall from Nicholas Nickleby; some conjuring; and then finished off with country-dances of a most frantic description, and danced all night. Getting the words, and making the preparations occupied the whole day; and it was three o'clock in the morning before I got to bed. It was an excellent entertainment, and we were all uncommonly merry. On returning home I was plunged into the deepest gloom for my love of Mary Boyle, and was a blight and mildew upon my house. I felt to be in such an incapable state with my mind wandering, that I sat and composed a poem, a parody of Gray's Elegy, which I sent to her.

Then I became a slave of the lamp called Copperfield once more, which occupied me for about ten days onward every month. In every one of my books published in twenty numbers, there was about three times the amount of matter comprised in an ordinary novel, so I was hard at work when, one day, I received a letter from a near neighbour, Mrs. Jane Seymour Hill (who lived at 6 York Gate, Regent's Park) – a letter that I was most exceedingly and unfeignedly sorry to receive. She was a manicurist and chiropodist of dwarf-like stature and I was bound to admit that, in relation to the character of Miss Moucher (that I had just introduced into the December number of Copperfield), I had yielded to several little recollections of her general manner, matters which, she said, had caused her great distress, sleepless nights and being tearful in her daily work. I immediately wrote to her a letter of apology, assuring her that the original of a great portion of that character was well known to me and to several friends of mine and was wholly removed from her and a very different person; indeed I never represented in my work an individual, but always a combination of individuals in one. I also stressed to her that I should be most truly pained if she were to remain under the impression that she had any cause of complaint against me or that I had done her any injury, however innocently. I was so sincere in this that I assured her that I would alter the whole design of the character and remove it, in its progress, from the possibility of that bad construction at which she hinted. I was quite serious in this, determining to make it into a very good character and obliging the reader to hold it in a pleasant remembrance – and duly kept to my word as I progressed onward. I was in no doubt that I was wrong in being tempted to such use of power – as I told Forster when sending him the letter I had received from Mrs. Hill. Then, three days later, I received a letter from a Mr. Rogers, a solicitor on behalf of Mrs. Hill, threatening a suit for libel. I assured him also of my serious intent for alteration of the character, but begged him to understand that the alteration I offered could only be made in the natural progress and current of the story, and that even if the next number were not already in the press, it would be impossible to be made there. I heard no more of this matter thereafter.

CHAPTER XXVIII

Household Words, Copperfield, and more Fallen Women

For the New Year of 1850, Mamie and Katey took much pains to teach me the polka so that I might dance it with them at our usual celebrations for Charley's birthday and Twelfth Night. After the celebration party (where a splendid cake was, as usual, provided by Miss Coutts), Charley soon left like a man to go to Eton – amongst a prodigious wailing from his brothers and sisters – and I continued on with Copperfield, being assisted by people who had written to me setting out words from the Suffolk and Norfolk dialect, that caused me much amusement. I also turned my attention to the ideas I had had of a new weekly journal, to be produced in association with Bradbury and Evans. I did not yet have a fixed title for this proposed miscellany, but agreed that bills and advertisements could now begin to be issued, stating that it was forthcoming and would be conducted by me. Having fully discussed the matter with Bradbury and Evans, we offered the job of sub-editor to W.H.Wills, upon terms of £8 a week and one eighth share in all profits, as well as of any other works that we might publish in connection with it. I was delighted when he accepted our offer.

Forster had now come around to this idea of a periodical and assisted me as confidential adviser, in due course reading proofs of my articles, encouraging his friends to write for us, and writing himself on occasion, as well as agreeing to render all possible assistance for an eighth share. It was agreed that Bradbury and Evans should have a quarter share in the proprietorship (with them having charge of all matters concerning printing, distribution and accounting) whilst I had a half share of the profits, £500 a year as editor, with complete editorial control, and separate payment for any serialized works written by me that appeared therein.

I now continued to put forward many names to Forster for the periodical and then, at the beginning of February, alighted upon a line adapted from Shakespeare's Henry V: "Familiar in their mouths, as household words". I considered "Household Words" a very pretty name and this was decided upon as the title. We searched and found premises at 16 Wellington Street North (on the corner of Exeter Street, and near the Strand), took these as our office, and began readying for production. R.H. Horne, and then later others, were taken on to assist; Forster, working as editor at "The Examiner", was not far away at 5 Wellington Street South.

One of the persons I wished to have write for the first number of Household Words was Mrs. Elizabeth Gaskell. She was a Unitarian (a creed that both Forster and I embraced), and had written "Mary Barton", a book published in October 1848 that revealed the desperate poverty of the millworkers in Manchester. It was a book that most profoundly affected and impressed me, and I had twice had her to dine at Devonshire Terrace thereafter. I asked her if she would also write a short tale, or any number of tales, for our projected pages. She agreed, to my true delight and gratification, and the first of a large number of her contributions (this one entitled "Lizzy Leigh") began in our first volume of Household Words.

This first volume was published on Saturday 30th March and sold nearly 100,000 copies; thereafter it was published weekly each Saturday with continuing success. We also proposed to include, on a monthly basis, the "Household Narrative of Current Events", and I put George Hogarth in place as compiler of this section.

I had been working away so hard at Household Words, that I decided to go to Brighton for a fortnight to pursue Copperfield in peace. The weather in Brighton was bright and beautiful and I sat glowering over Copperfield all day – though God forbid I should represent there being any hardship in that. I was working at it like a steam engine, to the time where, half dead, I did not know where my head was, feeling as if it was swimming on a wild sea, out in the Pacific at least. But I completed the number and returned to London, plunging once again into the business of Household Words, the Home at Shepherd's Bush, and the many other demands on my time.

At the Home itself, difficulties constantly arose that called for the promptest measures, and at times had to be dealt with by my ferocity. One night, Mrs. Morson being out and Mrs. Macartney at home, the very bad and false subject, Jemima Hiscock, forced open the door of the little beer cellar with knives, and drank until she was dead drunk; when she used the most horrible language and made a very repulsive exhibition of herself. She induced Mary Joynes to drink beer with her; and that young lady was also drunk, but stupidly and drowsily. Mrs. Morson, with the gardener's assistance, wisely abstaining from calling in the police, got them both to bed, locked them up, and came to me in the morning. Being obliged to write all day, I told her to go back straight and immediately discharge Jemima Hiscock – to put her in her own clothes, however bad – and on no account to give her any money. As to Mary Joynes, to keep her in disgrace until I could get out there that afternoon and enquire further into the matter.

I had no doubt myself that these girls had had spirits from outside. I was perfectly sure that no woman of Jemima Hiscock's habits could get so madly intoxicated with weak beer, though I was inclined to think, from the difference in the states of the two, that she had had spirits and Mary Joynes had not. A woman had been seen looking over the palings where others had broken out and, from certain circumstances and artifices recently observed in Jemima, I was strongly impressed with the belief that she was in communication with people outside; and also that she wanted to lay hands upon the linen on the first convenient opportunity after it was washed and ironed, and had no doubt of her having a design to make off after robbing the Home. She had made the most pious pretences of any in the place and written the most hypocritical letters; I'm afraid that Mr. Illingworth, the clergyman to whom she wrote, made grave mistakes, in attaching undue importance to this prostitution of religion. He believed her when she made pretence of seeing somebody she alleged she knew in church on Sunday, and then wishing to stay away from the Home with that person. I thought it (knowing Jemima's antecedents) a piece of unmitigated falsehood.

I went out to Shepherd's Bush wondering what on earth was to be done with Mary Joynes. I had most strongly suggested to Miss Coutts that nothing ought to induce us ever to retain a woman we had seen reason to discharge, and that in every case in which we had shown vacillation the end had been failure; and God knows how they infected the rest. I had not the least doubt that spirits were handed over the wall and, upon making further enquiries, utterly discredited Mary

Joynes's story about her case. I became more indignant with her than I had ever been with any of them, and she was also discharged. I then recommended to Miss Coutts that a very big dog in a barrel be placed at that point of the garden where spirits and other items were being handed over, so that Mrs. Mason would then always know of a stranger appearing on the other side.

CHAPTER XXIX

Paris, Household Words, and Copperfield continued

Having again broken my head with hard labour upon Copperfield and Household Words, I felt the need for a change of scenery and accordingly, at the end of May, wrote to Maclise, proposing that we go to Paris together for a fortnight. He agreed, and so we set off for Paris by railroad, I now coughing abominably all the way to Dover, but the boat passage across was wonderfully fine, my cough got better in the sea air, and we drank brandy and water on deck. We were in Paris at a quarter before 9 on the morning of the 23rd June, and took a very nice apartment at the Hotel Windsor in the Rue de Rivoli. But I found the heat there absolutely frightful and could do nothing but drink and go to sleep in the daytime. Maclise and I dined well; dinners were proposed for me with all the notables of Paris present, but I could not stand it; I really had undergone so much fatigue from work that I was resolved only to please myself on this occasion. I visited friends and acquaintances, and on one day, with Maclise, looked in at the Morgue. In there was a body horribly mutilated with a musket-ball in the head and afterwards drowned, which made Maclise so sick that, to my infinite disconcernment, he sat down on a doorstep in the street for about ten minutes, resting his cheek (like Juliet) on his hand, before taking to the swimming bath on the Seine. He later came back to the hotel looking much cleaner, but continuing a little heavy in his mood and rather disposed to be cross.

Through all of this I had much ado to get to work, the heat still being so intense that often I could do nothing but lie on the bare floor all day or write only in a shirt and pair of white trousers, sitting for four hours and being as faint with the heat as if I had been at some tremendous gymnastics. I managed little of Copperfield, but did produce an article for Household Words that I sent to Wills to discuss when I got home. My continued anxiety over Household Words however, made me feel as if I had been away a year, and so, on the 29th June, Maclise and I set off, going via Rouen and Dieppe, for London. Then, the day after my return, I was very sorry to see the announcement in the morning newspapers of the death of Sir Robert Peel following a riding accident. There were great expressions of national sorrow for he was a man of mark and great importance to the country at this time, and could ill be spared from among the great dust-heap of imbeciles and dandies that there was no machinery for sifting down in Westminster. I was in a very despondent state of mind about his death.

Turning to Household Words, I wrote to Mrs. Gaskell, urging her in earnest to write me another story. I was also pleased that Harriet Martineau was contributing to the publication. Moreover, I felt particularly encouraged that everyone was cheering Copperfield on, for I liked it very much myself and when at work on it had felt an energy of the fieriest description. I now did so once again, which obliged me to avoid all public meetings and almost all other interruptions of my attention, except long country walks and fresh air. I also made plans to stay at Broadstairs again.

On this occasion, I took a good bold house called "Fort House", something I had wanted to do for ten years. It stood on the top of a cliff, sea winds blowing through it, the gulls occasionally falling down the chimneys by mistake, and was a tremendous fortification that used, in the ferocious old days, to keep the pirates out. I decided to take it from early in August until the end of October, and meanwhile take steps to purchase a house in London as my lease on Devonshire Terrace was due to expire in March 1851. But I did not now want to come back to London until I had finished Copperfield. For some time passed I had carefully planned out the story to the end and was making my purposes out with great care. I was glad that there seemed a bright unanimity about it from my readers, and I remained very much interested and pleased with it myself.

Household Words was also pleasing me. Although expensive to produce, and so demanding a large circulation, it had taken a great and steady stand and went on thoroughly well. Furthermore, I had no doubt that it already yielded a good round profit. Then, for a short while, Wills became ill and I sat in the office at Wellington Street North, up to my neck in a quagmire of material of an intensely dreary and commonplace description that had been submitted. In particular I was waylaid by a parcel, in dimensions like a spare bed, containing "doubtful articles" on which decision was necessary to the peace of mind of the writers – and extremely dreary they were, all with a drone of imitation of myself in them, which pervaded the whole parcel.

The Home at Shepherd's Bush also continued to take up a good deal of my time. Whenever I could, I attended the weekly management meetings, kept the books and finances in order for Miss Coutts, and oversaw the marks system for the orderly running of the place, as well as dealing firmly with any disputes that arose. I sought to increase the ways we found girls to help, and wrote to Magistrates, as well as attending at Ragged Schools, to seek out suitable girls who might be helped. One such school was the Westminster Ragged School, situated in the area of narrow streets and courts behind Westminster Abbey, well-known as "The Devil's Acre". It was an awful place, in a maze of filth and squalor, so dense and deserted by all decency that my apparition in those streets in whose heart this school lay, brought out the people in a crowd.

Before going to Broadstairs, I received an invitation from Sir Edward Bulwer Lytton to attend at Knebworth, his most splendid baronial seat near Stevenage in Hertfordshire. Regrettably I was not able to attend, but Forster reported to me that Bulwer wished to have a performance at Knebworth by our amateur players of "Every Man in his Humour" for the benefit of his friends, neighbours and tenants, with perhaps some parts being given to local gentlemen. Forster also told me that Bulwer had been writing a play himself, a comedy set in the time of George the First, the news of which stirred my blood like a trumpet.

On the 16th August, Kate was delivered of another child, a girl that we named Dora, after my Dora in Copperfield. As soon as I had the relief and happiness of knowing that the birth was over and Kate was feeling well, I decided to take the rest of the children down to Broadstairs with Georgy, leaving Kate to fully recover in London for a week or so, although I thought of her all day and thanked God most heartily for her safe delivery. When we arrived in Broadstairs, Fort House, though excellent, was in mighty confusion and we spent some time getting it to rights, whereupon it became quite orderly, full of sweet air, sea views and comfort. We felt quite incomplete however without Kate, with a great blank everywhere, and I was not immediately successful in getting to work again on Copperfield, which made me feel rather low and penitent. But the next day I arranged to write in the drawing room and pressed on, working for nine hours at a stretch that day, and the same for the following two days. I was coming to the point where I was about to describe Dora's death, but was pleased to see my children playing happily in the garden – none more so than Ocean Spectre, who was in great glory, although nearly blown off his legs by a fresh wind, hair all over his face, hat nowhere in particular, and lugging a seat, about equal in weight, I should think, to six legs of mutton!

CHAPTER XXX

Copperfield Concluded

I settled down again and killed Copperfield Dora, before returning to London to see Kate and little Dora. I also had a good deal before me at the Household Words office and spent time there. Kate was now in a noble condition, ditto little Dora, and Household Words taking its ground vigorously, so I was pleased to invite friends to visit Broadstairs for good company. Kate wished to stay a little further in London, so I returned to Broadstairs, where Frank Stone and Charles Knight arrived on short visits. I played cricket with them and the children all the morning, plunged into the sea (over and above my early shower bath) before lunch, then over to Margate to pick up Stanny – who did not appear – before playing with the children in the garden again. Also, in the afternoon, I read the latest Copperfield number to Stone and Georgy and threw them into a dreadful state. Stone left and we were by ourselves again, but it had been a most lovely time, basking in the sun and in idleness, after some very hard work.

The next few days I was in a kind of prostrated condition as to any power of thinking about anything since finishing my last Copperfield. Consequently, what I proposed to do for Household Words was still a sheet of blank paper, though I supposed (like Mr. Micawber) that something would turn up. Stanny eventually arrived and I spent time with him, before returning again to London to dispatch all needful business at Household Words office. I also saw four girls, attendant at the Field Lane Ragged School, and wrote to Miss Coutts about them; I thought we might try them at the Home, as they represented a class, fairly, that I believed was worth the experiment. Miss Coutts agreed to give these girls a chance at the Home, and they were taken in.

I returned again to Broadstairs, on this occasion with Forster joining me there in a tip-top state of amiability, though I think I never heard him half so loud! Kate again chose to stay in London and whilst I invited Maclise to come also, he did not arrive. I made another visit to London and, happily on this occasion, brought Kate back with me to join the children, who were all in great force and much excited to see her again. She looked greatly fatter, rosier, and better, and I felt obliged to now remain in Broadstairs without going to town until I had got through the next Copperfield.

So, I got tremendously to work again with Copperfield, until it completely knocked me over and utterly defeated me in a paroxysm that caused me to cease again for a while. I began thinking and planning for Bulwer's theatricals, as well as those at Rockingham that had now been proposed, and went again to London, to the Household Words office. I also went to Shepherd's Bush, where I found the Ragged School girls already improving and decidedly much changed for the better in their appearance. I was searching for another house for myself in London when my brother Frederick contacted me again, requesting that I now guarantee a loan for him, as his debts had risen to £600. I declined his invitation.

Back in Broadstairs, there were some things in my next number of Copperfield that I thought better than any that had gone before and I pressed on towards its conclusion. I also continued to plan the amateur theatricals proposed for both Knebworth and Rockingham – but then found there were some serious problems with this and I became much out of sorts. The beginning of October found me looking very hard at a blank quire of paper again and trying to persuade myself that I was going to begin Numbers 19 and 20 of Copperfield in earnest; but then happily it was not long before I was able to report a stunning day's work prior to going for a lengthy walk with Stone – where he addressed me for two hours on the theatrical subject of his choice! But by the 21st October, I was able to report to Forster:

"I am within three pages of the shore; and am strangely divided, as usual in such cases, between sorrow and joy. Oh, my dear Forster, if I were to say half of what Copperfield makes me feel tonight, how strangely, even to you, I should be turned inside-out! I seem to be sending some part of myself into the Shadowy World."

Two days later I had finished, and was in such a state that I did not know whether to laugh or cry. Again, I did not find it easy to get sufficiently away from the story in the first sensations of having finished it, or to refer to it with composure, when a crowd of the creatures of my brain were going from me for ever. I wrote a preface for the completed book that reflected my feelings and dedicated the book to the Watsons, dearest friends from Rockingham and Switzerland (I had lodged David there at the commencement of Number 19), sending them the sheets of the conclusion of the story, as it had occurred to me that they might like to see the end of it before the rest of the world did.

When the rest of the world finally read it, the suspicion arose that underneath the fiction lay something of my life, but only I knew the reality when working my childish experiences and many young struggles into it. And now that I had concluded, I knew without doubt that, in David Copperfield, I had created for all time my favourite child.

CHAPTER XXXI

Death of my Father and of Dora, Performance for The Queen,
and Tavistock House

Once I had concluded Copperfield, I was now able to turn my attention to the performances at Knebworth and Rockingham. I went to Knebworth to supervise the preparations, the banqueting hall converted splendidly into a theatre, and the three performances went off in a whirl of triumph. On the final night Bulmer announced that he intended to write a play that our players might perform in due course, in order to raise money for a Guild of Literature and Art and provide new homes on his estate for literary persons.

I now had to turn my attention to the Christmas Number that I planned for Household Words and wrote "A Christmas Tree" based on my childhood recollections, which was published with success on the 21st December. Then, after celebrating the New Year of 1851 at Devonshire Terrace with country dancing of the wildest description and the most appalling duration, I turned my attention to our further performances at Rockingham. Though Rockingham was to be done, comparatively, as a mere Christmas game, the same care was necessary to make the lesser means tell their utmost worth; I would not go into such a thing – or anything – halfway and wished to make performances something utterly astounding and bewildering to all beholders.

We had a joyful evening performing at Rockingham on the 15th January, followed by dancing. Dearest Mary Boyle was enchanting, but I could not delay my departure as I had been invited to dine with the Prime Minister, Lord John Russell, at his town house the following day. There was no man in England that I respected more in his public capacity, or from whom I had received more remarkable proof of his honour and love of literature. I regarded him as having the soul of a giant, a statesman of whom opponents and friends alike could feel sure that he would rise to the level of every occasion, however exalted. I was later pleased and honoured to dedicate "A Tale of Two Cities" to him.

Bulmer produced and sent me his new comedy, which I suggested could be entitled "Not So Bad As We Seem"; this he adopted and we began consideration of the arrangements for its production. After my great exertions at Knebworth and Rockingham however, I now felt feeble and liable to sudden outbursts of causeless rage and demonical gloom. What a thing it is that we can't be always instantly merry and happy, without looking out at the back windows of life. I had now been married fourteen years and had nine children, but I did not remember that I ever, on any occasion, dreamed of myself as being invested with these responsibilities, or surrounded by these relations; my dreams were usually of twenty years before. London, I now sincerely believed, was a vile place; I had never taken kindly to it since I had lived abroad. Whenever I came back from the country and saw that great heavy canopy lowering over the housetops, I wondered what on earth I did there, except on obligation. I thought of Rockingham, after coming away, as if I belonged to it and had left a bit of my heart behind – which it was so very odd to find wanting, twenty times a day. I had concerns over our poor little Dora who had become very ill – with something like congestion of the brain – and although she recovered, was nevertheless not considered to be entirely out of danger. Meanwhile, I had to hunt for a replacement house, as the termination of my tenancy at Devonshire Terrace drew ever closer.

I took steps to produce Bulwer's new play and wrote to the Duke of Devonshire asking whether we might use Devonshire House for it to be played for the first time. Bulwer and I also wished that this first representation be before Her Majesty and the Court, so that it would have great weight with those who would form the staple of our after-audiences, and to thereafter perform at other venues, allowing me to hope that we might be endowed for our purpose, before the year was out, with three or four thousand pounds of profitable account. The Duke replied enthusiastically in agreement and, with this news, I now began in earnest recruiting players. I remembered Augustus Egg had told me that Wilkie Collins would be glad to play any part in it, and I considered him a very desirable recruit. I knew his father well and told Egg that I should be very glad to know Wilkie.

I planned a reading of the play, but was disturbed as Kate became very unwell. She had been suffering for some time, at intervals for three or four years, with a nervous condition that produced fullness in the head, attended with giddiness and dimness of sight, but now also had violent headaches. After speaking with Dr. Southwood Smith, I became anxious to place her under the care of Dr. James Wilson at Malvern, to put her under a rigorous discipline of exercise, air and cold water in order to relieve her symptoms and, as I believed it advisable for her to remain there some time, I took Knotsford Lodge in Great Malvern for her without the children for the purpose. I proposed however to be backwards and forwards to London, as not only had I the business of Household Words, but Bulwer's play now sat heavily on my shoulders.

Then, suddenly on the morning of the 25th March, as I was in the Household Words office, news was brought to me of the alarming illness of my father and the necessity of his instantly undergoing a terrible operation. He and my mother had been residing during his illness with the eminent surgeon Robert Davey at the house where he practiced (34 Keppel Street, Russell Square) and Mr. Davey came to my office that morning to say that he thought it impossible that my father could now live many hours. He was in that state of active disease of the bladder (which he had mentioned to nobody) that mortification and delirium, terminating in speedy death, seemed unavoidable. I rushed to the address and Robert Wade, recently appointed Senior Surgeon to Westminster General Dispensary, was called in and who instantly performed, without chloroform, the most terrible operation known in surgery, as the only chance of saving him.

My father bore it with astonishing fortitude, and I saw him directly afterwards – his room a slaughter-house of blood, but he was wonderfully cheerful and strong-hearted. The danger was then that the wounds would slough and he would fall into a low fever, but I hoped that the strength of his constitution might save him. I went about to get what was necessary for him, engaging me all day and absorbing my whole attention. I was so shaken that I could scarcely write to let others know the circumstances – and all this went to my side directly, feeling as if I had been struck there by a leaden bludgeon. Father slept well that night, and the following morning they sent word that he was as well as anyone in such a state, so cut and slashed, could be, but he was very weak and low. It rained incessantly, putting the streets into a most miserable state, and making the whole scene a picture of dreariness.

I saw Father again before returning to Great Malvern, and he appeared to be doing quite well. I made another visit to him, but it was clear to me that he was now very dangerously ill; he did not know me, or anyone, and was quietly declining. On the evening of the 30th March they sent for me while I was at Malvern, and I travelled to London, arriving at Keppel Street at a quarter past eleven. My mother was present, as were other family members and friends. I stayed with him for hours, standing or sitting by his bedside and holding his hand, but he slipped away, oh so quietly, and died in the morning at five and twenty minutes before six; he was in his 66th year. At this point I embraced my mother, and we both wept bitterly together. Although I hardly knew what to do, I told her she must rely on me for the future. The whole scene was such a sad sight, but later that day I went to Highgate Cemetery to get the ground for him, and he was buried there on the 5th April, I ensuring that his gravestone bore tribute to his "zealous, useful, cheerful spirit". His worldly effects were valued at under £40 and I immediately paid off all that he owed. My mother went to stay with my sister Laetitia for six months, and then I helped arrange for her to take lodgings at 33 Ampthill Square, Mornington Place, off the Hampstead Road.

I was so worried and worn by events and the arrangements over my father's death that I could not take my natural rest. I was up three whole nights and for two of these was out and walking about, sometimes feeling as if I could have given up and let the whole battle ride on over me. But that did not last long, for God knows I had plenty to cheer me in the long run, and within a few days I was back to it. I had to return to Malvern to be with Kate and wrote to Mr. James Ballard at the Albion Hotel in Broadstairs asking if he could discover from the owner of Fort House on what terms I could have that place from the middle of May until the end of October. I planned to let Devonshire Terrace at that time, and to use two back rooms at 16 Wellington Street so that I could occasionally make my tent comfortable at the Household Words office.

Visits to London continued, and on the 14th April, I presided at the sixth annual dinner of the General Theatrical Fund at the London Tavern. Forster there proposed my health and remarked that he had never heard me to greater advantage – but then at the end of the evening, as I rose out of the chair, he passed me the devastating news he had received during that evening, that our poor little Dora had died in a moment. I had been nursing her before I went out; she was quite gay then and I had not detected anything amiss, but on returning to Devonshire Terrace with Lemon (who had also been at the dinner) I confirmed the awful event for myself and knew then I had to break the news to Kate by way of a letter to Malvern. In the letter, I sought to make out that the poor little pet was hopelessly ill, to try and make the shock as gradual as I could, while Lemon sat up with me all night.

I did not like to leave home in the circumstances and Forster, with his usual affection for us, agreed to take the letter to Kate and to then bring her home. He did so, and she grieved bitterly. I had hoped to keep my composure, but when some beautiful flowers were sent to us and I was about to take them upstairs and place them on the little dead baby, I confess I gave way completely. On the 17th April I took the little pet to Highgate and, for the moment, put her into the catacombs. Kate was as well as I could have hoped for in the circumstances; I was anxious to try and direct her attention away from these events and to our removal from Devonshire Terrace, and to keep it so engaged.

On account of these happenings I now sought to delay the presentation of Bulwer's play by asking if the Queen would postpone the day. She most graciously agreed to a new date of the 16th May, and I became up to the throat in work at Devonshire House; I felt I could have no peace until the night of the 16th May was over. Kate was still very low, and a number of houses I had looked at had fallen through; we had soon to move from Devonshire Terrace, so I spoke with Frank Stone, who lived at Tavistock House on the east side of Tavistock Square, about the possibility of taking over the lease of his house, and arranged for Kate and I to look it over. We did so on the afternoon of the 21st April, but found it to be in the dirtiest of all possible condition, so much so that I was hesitant of taking it.

The performance at Devonshire House on the 16th May was an immense success. The Queen's party took up 17 places, the acting highly praised, and a great deal of money was raised for the Guild. We performed the play again at Devonshire House on the 27th May, now together with my farce "Mr. Nightingale's Diary" where Lemon and I played the main characters. This too proved to be an immense success and thereafter the Duke provided the whole cast with a splendid celebration, comprising a magnificent ball and supper. Kate and the children were now at Broadstairs, so I camped out at the Wellington Street office.

On finishing at Devonshire House I was quite full of melancholy of having turned a leaf in my life; it was so sad to see the curtain dropped on what had been so bright and interesting and triumphant, that something of the shadow of the great curtain which falls on everything seemed for a little while to be upon my spirits. I have an indescribable dread of leave-takings; and the taking leave of such a gracious scene made me most miserable. I hoped we might perform the play again (we did so on the 18th June at the Hanover Rooms), but meanwhile I joined the family at Fort House in Broadstairs, this airy nest perched by itself on the top of the cliff, with the freshness of the sea, the associations of the place with the finishing of Copperfield there, and the walks to restore my customary great vigour. I was, furthermore, pleased to be away from the invaders from all nations that came for the Hyde Park Exhibition and terrified me by their letters of introduction. I went twice to the exhibition, but found too much in it. So many things bewildered me; I have a natural horror of sights, and the fusion of so many sights in one did not decrease it. The whole building was later taken down and erected in expanded form as the terrific puffery of the Crystal Palace at Sydenham, which appeared to me, in respect of puffery and pretence, to be the most gigantic humbug ever mounted on a long-suffering people's shoulders.

I wrote "Our Watering Place" for Household Words, as well as welcoming guests to Fort House. I also began making enquiries as to the best times of playing Bulmer's comedy at towns around the country on behalf of the Guild, with more than a dozen places responding favourably over the next fifteen months, causing a substantial amount of money to be raised over this period by our amateur players for this noble cause.

My mind turned again to Stone's Tavistock House, and having a great idea of buying it for five and forty years (Stone only having a three-year tenancy), but because of its condition, I wanted a surveyor's opinion as to its substantial repair. After negotiations, I agreed to give

£1,500 for the house and fixtures in its present state, and for the longer term that I proposed. I knew however, after having the house carefully examined, that it required considerable improvement, so allowed Stone and his family to use Devonshire Terrace for a while, in order that I might do these improvements before moving in.

Kate, however, was still far from well, so I remained at Broadstairs, particularly working on Household Words articles and making enquiries about emigrant ships for Miss Coutts, taking only occasional visits to London. By the beginning of September, Tavistock House became available, but it put me into a state of mind sometimes described in the newspapers as "bordering on distraction" over the work being done, until calmed somewhat by the assistance of Henry Austin, husband of my sister Laetitia. But then I became distracted beyond belief over thoughts of a new book, walking by the sea every day dwelling on this, and the house in Tavistock Square (which would never leave me), endeavouring to think of both sets of distraction to some practical end – a situation that left me extremely weak and all but exhausted, particularly as I thought of the effect of the works to the house was having on my pocket. I was wild to begin a new book, but could not do so until I was settled. I sought to move into Tavistock House almost before the workmen had finished, but then had to delay until the beginning of November. At last the workmen fled, order was re-established and we were able to move in. I settled into my study, and was most pleased at the admirable manner in which book-backs had been produced for the room to fulfil my whim, with titles including "Hansard's Guide to Refreshing Sleep", "History of a Short Chancery Suit" (21 volumes), "Paxton's Bloomers", and "Catalogue of Statutes of the Duke of Wellington"!

CHAPTER XXXII

Bleak House, and Guild Theatricals

I now turned my thoughts in earnest to my new book. The story I proposed was to be about the Court of Chancery, and I eventually settled upon the title: "Bleak House and the East Wind; How they both got into Chancery and Never Got Out". I had really got my steam up once again, this time over these wicked courts of equity which, with all their means of evasion and postponement, had given scoundrels confidence in cheating. If justice had been cheap, sure and speedy, few such things would have been, but it had become, through the vile dealing of these courts and the vermin they had called into existence, a positive precept of experience that a man had better endure a great wrong than go, or suffer himself to be taken, into Chancery with the dream of setting it right. I was strong that I would have no part in engendering in the mind of any human creature a hopeful confidence in that den of iniquity – and so I began to write my story, like a prisoner myself, in my rear sanctum at Tavistock House.

I stocked my cellar with some good port to assist with the New Year celebrations to usher in 1852, and at these we pretty nearly danced down the floor of the Tavistock House school room. Forster and Lemon came for our Twelfth Night celebrations, but I now had a most deplorable bilious cold, and thereafter it became so bad that I could hardly hold up my head. I tried bed, occupation, medicine, compressing – every sort of remedy, but became thoroughly imbecile and could hardly see out of my eyes. For the first time in I don't know how many years, I was floored, robbed of my appetite and felt the dull knobs of two rusty pokers in my head instead of eyes. But I had to continue on with Bleak House, something I found dreadfully difficult in the dull days of winter – as well as prepare for the new theatrical performances for the Guild. There was nothing in the country but earnestness and enthusiasm for the Guild, and although the managers of country theatres tried to stop us performing, because we didn't pay them, I flatter myself that I was a match for those gentry, and that they had vague suspicions of it. The sales of tickets at Manchester were quite unprecedented, and at

Liverpool the enthusiasm so great that the local secretary wrote, asking me if we could undertake a second performance. I immediately sent a circular around to all the company and they agreed.

At Manchester it was the most prodigious scene from the stage that I ever saw. There were at least 3,000 people in the audience and (I believe) £600 taken in money. I stepped forward to the front when we were called after the comedy, and made them a little speech. Then, as to the farce, they cannot have heard half of it, for they laughed to that amazing extent! There was a call after the farce too – and, in short, I never saw such people. My health was drunk three times and I was embraced in a state of enthusiastic delight all round; the earnest admiration and love of the people towards me was something quite bewildering – or would have been if I were not steady in such matters.

We moved on to Liverpool, staying at the Adelphi Hotel, and played two nights running to a hall crowded to the roof on each occasion, more like the opera at Genoa or Milan than anything else I can compare it to. We had such prodigious success, the people rising up when the performances were over with a perfect fury of delight, that I was sure we should bank for the Guild a thousand pounds from this short trip alone. I left from Liverpool so blinded by excitement, gas, and waving hats and handkerchiefs that, when I got home, I could scarcely see to write to Bulwer telling him of the triumph we had had. I was so happy in all this that I could have cried on the shortest notice any time, and believe that the whole body would have gone to the North Pole with me if I had shown them good reason. I do not speak for myself alone in this, but for all our people, as they had been absolutely stunned by the tremendous earnestness in these great places.

I returned to Tavistock House to work on Bleak House, continuing my habit of long walks to arrange my mind, and when the first number of Bleak House was published on the 28th February, I was greatly pleased that it proved to be such a very great success, with sales in excess of thirty thousand. There was much favourable comment, which now caused me to blaze away merrily, and was especially pleased to receive a kind note from George Hogarth and to find he thought so highly of it

On the 13th March Kate confined with a brilliant boy of unheard-of dimensions, and was wonderfully well. We settled on Edward Bulwer

Lytton Dickens for a name (he later also became known as "Plorn"), but whilst Kate was now in a most blooming state, I had to shut myself up in Bleak House again. Sitting to write I felt for a while an inability to grind sparks out of this dull blade, and held discussions with Forster over the character Skimpole that I planned to introduce, one that I had based upon Leigh Hunt. I went over every part carefully and sought to make it much less like Hunt; changed the proposed name from Leonard to Harold, and recognized that I had no right to give Hunt pain. I was so bent upon not doing so that I asked Forster to look at all the proofs once more and indicate any particular place in which he felt it had a particular likeness, which I would then alter. He indicated a considerable number of alterations and I adopted them, but he still seemed to feel that a radical wrong remained. I pressed on with the next number for I knew I had soon further engagements due with the Guild theatrical players. Despite the difficulties over Hunt, I had no difficulty (between ourselves) in making Mr. Lawrence Boythorn in the story a most exact portrait of Walter Savage Landor, and was delighted with the way Bleak House had taken – with all the prestige of Copperfield (which was very great) and rising its first circulation above all my recent books.

Performances for the Guild took place in Shrewsbury and Birmingham with great success, before I became hard at work again on Bleak House. I remained more than ever bent on success for the Guild, and resolved to come up smiling and at it again – planning two more trips, one in July and another in September, before closing our theatrical campaign. I was later able to combine these two tours into one lengthy one between the 22nd August and the 3rd September, when we were invited to play at Derby, Nottingham, Birmingham, Newcastle, Sunderland, Sheffield, Manchester, and Liverpool; we had to decline other invitations (including one from Cork in Ireland) as being too difficult to manage.

But I was restless and felt as if I had been thinking my brain into a sort of cabbage net, worrying myself into the belief that I could not write without a change. Accordingly, I found a pleasant and commodious family residence fronting the sea at 10 Camden Crescent in Dover, which I took for twelve weeks from the third week in July. Before going, I dined on Sunday the 11th July with the Honourable Richard Watson, after he had been newly elected as Member of Parliament for

Peterborough. He was in unusually good spirits and full of plans for future enjoyment at Rockingham. He said he was going abroad the next day to Homburg to join his wife (who had not been well) and go on with her and the children to Lausanne for a month, where we had all passed so many happy days together.

But no sooner had I settled into our house in Dover, than I got the devastating news from Homburg that he was dead. I was never so amazed and shocked. He was as true a friend as I ever had, a thoroughly good man, of a most amiable and affectionate nature, and as simple-hearted as a child. My respect for him was equal to my love for him; I really held him in my heart and could not bear to think that he was now dead. When I thought of his bright house, and his fine simple honest heart, both so open to me, the blank and loss were like a dream.

Although I knew I had to press on with Bleak House, I had to now overcome what I call "my wandering days" before I fell to work. I seemed to be always looking at such times for something I had not found in life, but might possibly come to a few thousands of years hence, in some other part of some other system – God knows. And to let you into a secret, I was not quite sure that I ever did like, or ever would like, anything quite so well as Copperfield; but I did foresee some very good things looming in the distance in Bleak House, and wept as I beheld them for the months ahead. I had made Chesney Wold in the image of Rockingham, and came to take many bits of the descriptions (chiefly about trees and shadows) from observations I had made at Rockingham; and Mrs. Watson and the four children – the eldest 11years old, and she herself in the family way, expecting to be confined sometime hence with another child – were now never far from my thoughts. I wrote to her expressing just how much we really loved Watson and how much we felt for her and the children at this time of such sorrow. Watson was buried in his own church at Rockingham and I was at least glad to think that she could associate her home with his grave.

As well as Bleak House, I assisted with articles for Household Words, the running of the Home at Shepherd's Bush, and also a new project for Miss Coutts in Westminster, where she sought the improvement in sanitation for 150 houses in that location. I had always been convinced that sanitation reform must proceed all other social reforms, and was pleased to enlist for her the assistance of Henry Austin and Doctor Southwood Smith in the carrying out of this scheme for the avoidance of cholera.

I now had to turn my attention to the final Guild trip and, after conducting rehearsals in town, I left (with legs useless and feet swollen) on the morning of Sunday 22nd August with the company for the fortnight of engagements. The comedy I had greatly improved by compression and it went like wildfire, the farces were riotously received, and everywhere we were received with prodigious enthusiasm and cheering. I returned to Tavistock House happy but half dead, before going back to the breezes of Dover.

I had long learnt the lesson that when I had a book to write I must give it the first place in my life, and an undivided mind – and I knew I must now, after the interval of the previous fortnight, undertake this with Bleak House. Most writers of fiction write partly from their imagination and partly from their experience; I had recourse to both sources in this regard, and had become content to set the pains and cares it required against the pleasures of society (otherwise than in a sparing degree), putting my fictitious companions in an upper place. I wrote a very short preface to the Cheap Edition of the Christmas books now proposed by Bradbury and Evans and then set about in earnest on Bleak House again. Wilkie Collins joined us at Dover, and after a fortnight of the very hardest work to make up for the time lost in the theatrical excursion, I was able to read to him, Kate and Georgy the chapters from the next number (Number 8) with full dramatic presentation, making them laugh and cry with equal fervour and equal sincerity.

It was while I was hard at work in Dover that the announcement came of the death of the Duke of Wellington at Walmer Castle. I had been walking at Walmer that very afternoon and little thought that the great old man was dying or dead. I considered it a grievous thing – a relapse into semi-barbarous practices – concerning the way the whole public seemed to have now gone mad over the Duke's funeral. But to say anything about it at this time, or to hope to leaven with any grain of sense such a mass of wrong-doing, I considered would be utterly useless; I may as well have been whistling to the sea. But I resolved to try and present the sense of the case afterwards in Household Words, and duly wrote the article "Trading in Death" for publication.

CHAPTER XXXIII

Boulogne, and Bleak House concluded

To relieve myself of the fervent situation in England, I resolved to cross the Channel and go to Boulogne for ten days or a fortnight. We had a very bad passage over, and I felt as if I had exchanged my eyes for two brass bullets, but we put up in the Hotel des Bains and found Boulogne not a bad place by any means. I liked the novelty, and was able to go to work straight away, proposing to remain while I wrote the next number of Bleak House.

I grew to greatly enjoy Boulogne. It was genteel, quaint, picturesque, and with a walk all around the Haute Ville on the ramparts that was charming. The boatmen and fishing-people I found quite a race apart, with some of their villages being as good as the fishing villages in the Mediterranean. The country walks around were delightful; everything was cheap and good, the whole place the best mixture of town and country (with sea air into the bargain) as I ever saw; and I wrote and told Forster that I never saw a better instance of our countrymen than in this place.

I sent Bradbury and Evans the first slips of the next number (Number 9) for Bleak House, and also wrote to Wills about Household Words and Guild business. I began thinking of the Household Words Christmas Number, but not very successfully, as I was constantly occupied with Bleak House and wished to complete the number. I did so, and we then returned home again to Tavistock House for the winter.

I now gave great attention to our plan to have an extra Christmas Number for Household Words and, proposing to give it some suitable name, deciding upon "A Round of Stories by the Christmas Fire". It was to consist entirely of short stories supposed to be told by a family sitting round the fire, though I did not care about their referring to Christmas at all, nor did I design to connect them together otherwise than by their names in relation to a family member. I wrote two myself: "The Child's Story" and "The Poor Relation's Story", while arranging for eight other people to also contribute in a similar way; as well as busily projecting a great variety of other subjects for Household Words for future inclusion.

I continued on with Bleak House, made visits to Shepherd's Bush and also continued to assist Miss Coutts with her plans for proper sanitation in Westminster. Charley, now sixteen years of age and in a somewhat unsettled state, expressed a wish to leave Eton at the end of the year and I had to speak with him about what he should do for the future. Initially he proposed to go into the army, but I cautioned him to reflect upon this and, once he had done so, he became more interested in a mercantile career. I did not doubt that he had chosen well, and arranged for him to go to Germany – to the home of Professor Müller in Leipzig - to improve his language skills.

In the midst of this I became more vexed than ever about the proposed state funeral for the Duke of Wellington. I thought it altogether wrong as regards the memory of the Duke, and at least equally wrong in the court estimate it implied of the people. The frippery and nonsense of the Herald's College and the absurdities of the Lord Chamberlain's Office highly irritated me and, when combined with a vulgar public holiday, meant that a good deal of business for the thieves and the public houses would, I was convinced, be its chief result. I declined the invitation from the Dean and Chapter to attend the funeral itself in St. Paul's, but later accepted the kind behest of the Duke of Devonshire for my family and friends to watch the procession from Devonshire House. The Military part of the show was very fine. If it had been an ordinary funeral of a great commander, it might have been impressive, but for forms of ugliness, horrible combinations of colour, hideous motion, and general failure, there never was such a work achieved as the Car – the tasteless and tawdry Car, decorated with "Trophies and Heraldic Achievements" and drawn by twelve horses as it nodded and shook its way through the streets of London.

The circulation of Bleak House was proving extremely gratifying to me. It was half as large again as Copperfield, and I had now come to the point (at Number 11) that I had been patiently working up to in the writing. I had high hopes for increased success and, feeling in better spirits, took a day's outing to Brighton with Leech, where we walked the Downs. Then I shut myself up again on Bleak House at Tavistock House, but was now driven mad by dogs that had taken it into their heads to assemble every morning in the piece of ground opposite and bark for five hours without intermission – positively rendering it impossible for me to work, and making what was really so ridiculous quite serious to me. I took steps to see if a gunman could be hired to discharge a few charges of small shot and be the death of some of them.

Household Words with its Christmas Extra Number was published, but I was suddenly laid by the heels two days before Christmas in consequence of Wills going blind without any notice (fortunately only a temporary condition due to mere inflammation) and so was obliged to be in the Wellington Street office all day and on Christmas Eve in a heap of confusion, as you may faintly imagine when such a mill is stopped in full whirl. I went carefully through the next number (for New Year's Day) and found it an awful one for the amount of correction required. I did eventually, however, make everything right and the edition was rescued.

The New Year of 1853 was seen in with much enthusiastic dancing in the schoolroom at Tavistock House, with the floor now reinforced with pillars to prevent it falling into the kitchen. I had told Henry Austin during the restorations that whatever we did we wanted to dance there freely and in peace, and only go into the kitchen by way of the staircase! Bleak House and Household Words continued to occupy a great deal of my time, as well as continuing to assist Miss Coutts on her sanitary schemes and the running of the Home in Shepherd's Bush. Then I had to deal with highly critical open letters about me in "The Leader" magazine by Mr. Lewes, someone I knew well, claiming that the spontaneous combustion I had incorporated into Bleak House to account for Krook's death was not only a scientific error, but was, according to Mr. Lewes, "absolutely impossible according to all known laws of combustion and to the constitution of the human body". Before writing that chapter, I had looked up all the more famous cases on the subject – as anyone could have divined in reading the description I had given – and I also now consulted Dr. Elliotson, who gave me the loan of his remarkable and learned lecture on the subject, which made me not a little pleased to find myself fortified by such high authority. Two of the additional cases he mentioned were new to me, but his explanation I found so beautifully clear that I resolved, with his permission, to refer to it several times before I came to the last number of Bleak House, and also in the preface to the volume edition. I considered that, on good authority, there were about 30 cases on record, supported by the medical opinions and experiences of distinguished medical professors, showing how people, particularly those addicted to heavy drinking, caused an astonishing change to take place in the body when it arrived at that pass, the body then being, in the main, destroyed to the point where gas was released and a combustion take place. The question was a question of evidence, and it was inconceivable to me how people could reject such evidence, supported by so much familiar knowledge, and such reasonable analogy. But I suppose the long and the short of it was that they didn't know, and did not want to know, anything about the matter. I wrote a lengthy letter to Lewes, telling him that his assumptions that I knew nothing at all about the question and had no kind of sense of my responsibility were inaccurate; and assured him that, when I thought of the incident, I had looked into a number of books with great care, expressly to learn what the truth was, and that I had examined the subject as a Judge might have done, placing the evidence impartially before myself as the Jury, before writing as I did.

What with Bleak House and Household Words and the Shepherd's Bush Home, together with invitations to feasts and festivals, I really felt as if my head would split like a fired shell if I remained in London. Accordingly, I made arrangements to go to Brighton for a fortnight at the beginning of March to continue with Bleak House, and took lodgings at 1, Junction Parade. It was wonderfully propitious for walking, but it then began pouring with rain and, in the night, I was seized with rheumatism in my back and horrid nervous choking. Nevertheless, I was able to take to authorship again and pressed on in earnest. The next number (Number 14) was due to be published on the 1st April and I had much to do, being put in better spirits by the accounts that Bradbury and Evans sent me for the first six numbers showing a noble and glorious balance in excess of £3,200 in my favour, greatly exceeding that of Copperfield. I had it in mind to rent a house in Boulogne for the summer and invited Bradbury and Evans to join me there, and also began to give thought to our agreement as it was presently set to terminate at the conclusion of Bleak House.

I put plans in place to retreat from London to Boulogne in early June for some months, to work in peace and quiet, something I knew was an absolute impossibility in London at that time of year, when all the nations of the earth brought letters of introduction to me, and England was filled with all manner of social endurances. I had been working long hours on Bleak House, commencing shortly after 5 o'clock in the morning, and wishing to take great care in finishing the story – but then fell ill again, this time with my old afflicted kidney, once the torment of my childhood, again causing me problems with violent inflammation in the side, and acute pain. It necessitated six days in bed for the first time in my life. I found myself shaving a man every morning – a stranger to me – with big gaunt eyes and hollow cheeks, whose appearance I found rather irksome and oppressive. Happily, he at last retired from the looking-glass and was replaced by the familiar personage whom I had lathered and scraped for the previous twenty years, but it was an unnerving experience and I grew extremely weak during it. As I recovered, Dr. Elliston recommended I wear a broad flannel belt around my waist, which I found gave me quite an extraordinary protection and comfort, and I have never had that illness since.

Once in Boulogne, we stayed again at the Hotel des Bains before taking, on the 13th June, a large house on the high ground near the Calais road – Villa des Moulineaux, in the Rue de Beauepaire. It was an odd French place with the strangest little rooms and halls but, to my delight, no end of cold water. It had a coach-house with stabling for half a dozen horses, and stood in the midst of a large garden made in terraces up the hillside, like an Italian garden, with five summer houses, a waterfall, and a wood at the top. There was a conservatory opening onto a great bank of roses, paths and gates on one side to the ramparts, with the sea on the other. It was the best place I had ever lived in abroad, except the Palazzo Peschiere, and was owned by a capital proprietor, Monsieur Ferdinand Beaucourt-Mutuel, who lived on the hill behind, just outside the top of the garden. He was a jolly, portly fellow, with a fine open face, who proved to be endlessly obliging.

Once settled, I took up Bleak House again, now with great ease, and sent to Bradbury and Evans the next number, feeling thankful at having been able to have done it, and a great relief at having it available for publication at the end of the month. I had picked up in the most extraordinary manner, now being brown, well, robust, vigorous, and growing a moustache! I was also able to review fully the numbers for Household Words that Wills sent to me, and told Wills that I would be delighted to see him here at any time. I invited other friends to visit, as I planned to stay in Boulogne until the middle of October, though visiting London from time to time in the meanwhile when required to do so, and felt myself the Sparkler of Albion once more.

I pressed on with Bleak House, continuing to correspond with Browne over the sketches and plates that were needed for the illustrations. He was now making ready with four subjects for the concluding double number and I wished him to so contrive his arrangements to come and pay us a visit as I had it in contemplation that, on the 22nd August at the Villa, I would arrange the best French dinner that could be done in these regions to celebrate the conclusion of the twenty numbers. Bradbury and Evans and Lemon already stood pledged to come over, and many more did so, including Leech and his wife, Wilkie Collins, Wills and his wife, and Forster. Thomas Beard proposed to visit too and I gave him some clear advice upon his entry, telling him that, whilst he must be passed through the customs house on his arrival, he would have no need to say anything whatever if he was forearmed with a card with the words: "Restant chez M. Charles Dickens, Villa des Moulineaux, Boulogne" written legibly upon it. If he was then waylaid with the inquiry: "Est-ce que Monsieur ait quelque chose a declarer?" he must blandly smile and reply: "Rien". I warned Beard of this, for I did not wish him to imitate Forster on his visit who, not understanding this enquiry, said after a moment's reflection and with the sweetness of some choice wind instrument: "Bonjour!" and was immediately seized and detained!!

I finished Bleak House, and on the 22nd August at the Villa I held a banquet of celebration, the table splendidly decorated with flowers and a nosegay placed by each napkin, before food (as Collins remarked) "to make a classical epicure's mouth water" was served. I read the final double number of the story on the 25th to those at the Villa, before it was published on the 31st. The story had taken extraordinarily – especially during the previous five or six months when its purpose had been gradually working itself out – and I liked the conclusion very much and thought it very pretty indeed. It had retained its immense circulation from the first, and continued beating dear old Copperfield by a round ten thousand and more, but I was now in the first drowsy lassitude of having finished and, retaining my rather formidable and fierce moustache, hoped to now spend time lying in the sunshine. But I also began looking up my Italian again preparatory to an autumn trip that I now proposed. Wilkie Collins and Augustus Egg agreed to accompany me and I advertised in The Times for a travelling servant. From the responses, I chose Edward Kaub, a German national, to accompany us.

CHAPTER XXXIV

Travelling Again, Readings, and Hard Times

At the beginning of October I returned to London on a short visit to finalize matters, and on the 10th October bade farewell to the family and, with Wilkie, Egg and Kaub, headed for Lausanne, arriving on the evening of the 16th. I met with old acquaintances Halimand and Cerjat and paid a visit to Chamonix, before then heading, via the Simplon Pass, for Genoa. There I showed Wilkie and Egg the Peschiere (which had now been converted into a girl's college) and met with further old acquaintances. We left Genoa on the 1st November, taking a steam ship to Naples, but finding we had no berths or sleeping accommodation of any kind despite having paid heavy first-class fares! The scene on board beggared description, with no mattresses, no blankets, nothing – a tropical rain fell and, in a moment, drowned the whole ship. Arriving in Naples on the 4th November, we climbed Vesuvius (the mountain being very peaceable on this occasion) and visited Herculaneum and Pompeii, before travelling northwards to Rome. After exploring the city, we left on the 18th and headed for Venice and then Paris, where I had arranged to meet Charley on his way back from Germany for Christmas. We met him and pressed on homeward, arriving back at Tavistock House late on the night of the 11th December and found all well and happy.

Once home, I had to fall on the Christmas Number for Household Words tooth and nail, as well as preparing for three readings I had promised to do at the Birmingham and Midland Institute, the last being for the working people, which I believed would be by far the most interesting evening. I wanted the people involved to appeal to the working man's sense and spirit; to give him his rightful share in the management of the Institute; and to associate him therein with his employer, to the enduring advantage and improvement of both.

These readings in Birmingham proved to be a great success. I began with the Carol on the first night, the 27th December, and, although I felt The Cricket on the Hearth was not nearly so well adapted for reading, the Committee had requested it and so I complied two days later. More than 2,500 working people came to the final night on the 30th December, and a more delicately observant audience it is impossible to imagine. I again read the Carol; during the reading they lost nothing, misinterpreted nothing, followed everything closely, laughed and cried with most delightful earnestness, and animated me to the extent that I felt as if we were all bodily going up into the clouds together. It was an enormous place for the purpose, but I had considered all that carefully and, I believed, made the most distant person hear as well as if I had been reading in my own room. At the end a working-man gave three cheers, with three times three for me, and I escaped not only the least hoarseness or sense of fatigue from the three nights of almost three hours each in that enormous hall (which required great effort), but felt as if I could have gone on for three weeks. £340 was raised for the Institute from nearly 6,000 people in all that attended over the three nights.

I came home to manage preparations in the schoolroom at Tavistock House for a presentation by the children – mine and Lemon's – of "Tom Thumb" on the Twelfth Night of 1854. These plays by the children had proved extremely popular, "William Tell" having been performed the previous year and "Guy Fawkes" the year before that. The children derived considerable notions of punctuality and attention from the parental drilling, and both Lemon and I joined in with them, this year I to enact the Ghost and Lemon (as great a child as himself) the queen of the Giants. Forster and Thackeray were amongst the audience on this occasion – Thackeray at one point even rolling off his seat, such was his uncontrolled laughter!

I now began thinking over what to do with Charley. His inclinations were all good, but I felt he had less fixed purpose and energy than I supposed possible in my son. He did not appear aspiring or imaginative in his own behalf and, with all the tenderer and better qualities which he had inherited from Kate, he had also inherited an indescribable lassitude of character – a very serious thing in a man – which seemed to me to express the want of a strong, compelling hand always beside him. When I told him that when I was a year older than he, I was in the gallery of the House of Commons; and that when I was his age I was teaching myself the very difficult art of shorthand, and walking miles every day to practice it all day long in the courts of law at Doctors Commons, he seemed to think I must have been one of the most unaccountable of youths. He told me he was quite resolved and determined in his wish to devote himself to mercantile pursuits and it occurred to me that, in the short remainder of his holidays, the best thing I could do for him would be to send him down to the Household Words office for some three hours every day, to help with the great deal of correspondence arriving there and for Wills to find occupation for him that would require his attention. Thereafter I was disposed to think it best to send him back to the professor's house to study German and arithmetic, but only until the midsummer, when he might then go into some place of business in France for a little while, to furbish up his French. I later heard from Wills, who gave me the best account of Charley at the office, finding him very quick and extremely attentive, "knocking off" writing from dictation with great vigour, copying with all possible exactness, making extracts from manuscripts cleverly, and being as willing and punctual as it was possible to be. Charley was proud of being so employed, and I think it did him great good.

I began discussing with Forster what should now be done for Household Words. There was such a fixed idea on the part of my printers and co-partners that a story by me, continuing from week to week, would make some unheard-of effect upon its circulation, that I agreed to write one. I sent Forster some prospective titles (14 of them) and eventually settled on "Hard Times" there from; which was the one title contained in the short lists of favourites each of us drew up. I was to be paid £1,000 for the twenty weekly instalments, and so I fell to work again. It was also in our contemplation that Mrs. Gaskell might herself produce a story to then follow on in weekly instalments from mine. Forster had seen the beginnings of a story she was writing and believed it was by far the best material she had yet worked with, and urged her to continue with it. She did so, and it came to be called "North and South".

At the same time, I was now receiving – after my experiences in Birmingham – requests from all parts of England to read for a fee and, if I did, I might take as many hundred pounds as I chose. I discussed this also with Forster, who felt that to become publicly a reader would alter without improving my position publicly as a writer, and that it was a change to be justified only when the higher calling should have failed of the old success. Accordingly, with some reluctance, I decided to put this idea aside for a while, and meanwhile sent every kind of refusal and evasion to those requesting readings by me of my work.

I became strongly at work on Hard Times and asked Lemon for assistance, if he could note down and send me any slang terms among tumblers and circus people that he could call to mind as I wanted them for the story. I also felt the need however to mix work with a regimen of fresh air, and took Lemon for a few days down to the countryside and sea – at Dover and Ramsgate – as I felt repeatedly in need of a stroll and a breeze to assist me with my writing and I found Lemon an excellent walking companion. Having originally intended to be as lazy as I could be all through the summer, here I now was with my armour on again and up to my eyes in the story, soon having done sufficient to announce in Household Words that the first portion of my new work would be published there on the 29th March.

In the meanwhile, the newspapers had now been full of accounts of possible war with Russia for their refusal to evacuate the Principalities around the Danube; indeed, England declared war on the 28th March, following on from France the previous day. Income Tax was doubled to pay for it, everything became very dear, and I suspected the war would be a little less popular in a year's time when the cost of it was practically understood.

At the beginning of April, Hard Times began its serialization in Household Words and had the immediate effect of doubling its circulation, despite my apprehensions as to the probable effects of the war on the sale of books and magazines. After a strong reminder, Bradbury and Evans paid me the first instalment of £500 for the story, which caused me relief as I had overdrawn my account at Coutts. I continued, being about a month ahead of the publication dates, greatly anxious to keep ahead, and pressed on – as well as going very carefully over the whole numbers of Household Words, before becoming satisfied that, from the materials on hand, we were quite safe for a good few numbers.

As was my custom, I wished to leave London for the summer months, and proposed to spend time again in Boulogne. I took the Villa du Camp de Droit, situated on the top of the same hill, above the Molyneaux, where we had stayed the year before; it was also owned by Beaucourt. Kate, Georgy and I headed for Boulogne on the 17th June, followed by the children (together with two of the Lemon children) three days later.

The Villa du Camp de Droit proved to be a delightful place, with not only larger rooms than the old house, but more of them – though the oddities were almost as great – and the situation on top of the hill, instead of three parts down it, was most beautiful. Not a mile off was now a military camp and I went over to reconnoitre the enemy. I found a very curious and picturesque scene. The 4,000 soldiers now there were building mud huts thatched with straw for the 60,000 who were to come. There were about 100,000 trusses of straw piled up ready for use and the 4,000 men (lazier than any men I ever saw) were constantly wheeling little barrows of earth about – containing twelve tablespoon-fulls each, as nearly as I could estimate. It looked like the opening of some capital French play!

I pressed on with Hard Times, to the point of being stunned with the work, three parts mad and the fourth delirious with perpetual rushing at it, but now hoped to have it finished by the middle of July. On the 11th July Napoleon III arrived to review the troops, with a great expenditure of tricolour floating thereabouts, though no stir made its way to our inaccessible retreat – our positioning now feeling like being up in a balloon.

I continued to send the manuscripts of Hard Times to Forster for proof reading and also wrote to Thomas Carlyle, telling him that I now planned to publish Hard Times in August in one volume in a compact cheap form and wished to put in the first page that it was inscribed to him. No man knew Carlyle's books better than I, and I knew Hard Times contained nothing in which he did not think with me. I was delighted when he agreed to this dedication upon my completion of the story.

CHAPTER XXXV

Household Words, War in Crimea, and Past Re-awakenings

I found myself so "used up" after Hard Times and scarcely knew why. Perhaps it was because I had intended to do nothing in that way for a year, when the idea had then laid hold of me by the throat in a very violent manner; and because the compression and close condensation necessary for that disjointed form of publication had given me perpetual trouble. But I really was – tired! – which was a result so very incomprehensible to me that I could not forget it. I read the continuation of Mrs. Gaskell's manuscript and again showed how it should be split into weekly parts for Household Words, and also very materially improved if she would make some curtailment that I indicated in the printed proof.

I was happy now to invite others to visit the Villa, and one who arranged to do so was Wills, who proposed to come with his wife from the end of August for a fortnight. Meanwhile, I discussed with him my concerns over North and South, becoming alarmed by the quantity of it that was now arriving from Mrs. Gaskell. To my mind it was not objectionable for a beginning, but would become so in the progress of a not compactly written and artfully devised story – and I wrote again to Mrs. Gaskell with my recommendations. It was perfectly plain to me that if we put in more, every week, of North and South than we did of Hard Times, it would ruin Household Words, and I therefore instructed Wills that it must at all hazards be kept down. I was extremely irritated that Bradbury and Evans appeared to have encouraged her in this course and became unspeakably vexed by all the needless trouble and bewilderment it caused. As the tale progressed in the journal it became wearisome to me in the last degree and I was not surprised to hear that the sale of Household Words was now dropping.

In the middle of October we returned, in stormy passage, to London. I drafted an article for Household Words on "Our French Watering Place" (that also contained a faithful portrait of our landlord), but the war continued, the book trade suffered, taxes increased and the Emperor of Russia was holding out, not yet beaten. I was full of mixed feelings about the war – admiration for our valiant men, burning desires to cut the Emperor of Russia's throat, but something like despair to see how the old cannon smoke and blood-mist obscured the wrongs and sufferings of the people at home. Letters in The Times over the sanitary conditions in London (where nine separate water companies operated, charging high rates for inconsistent supply of often impure water) showed to me the Metropolitan Sewers Commissions living in a world of balderdash, really talking more rotten filth, and letting their engineers write more and sit on all manner of dregs, than all the sewers of London themselves contained. Children in particular would never be saved from the dreadful and unnatural mortality now prevailing among them until they had cheap pure water in unlimited quantity. It was more than ever necessary to keep the need for social reforms before them at this time, for I could clearly see that the war would be made an administrative excuse for all sorts of shortcomings and that nothing would be done before the cholera came again.

I, meanwhile, turned my thoughts to the readings I had agreed to perform – the first of these being the Carol on the 19th December at Reading, where I had undertaken the Presidency of their Literary Institute after the death of Talfourd; following which I had agreed to go on to Sherborne to do the like for the Literary Institute there, which was one of the few remaining pleasures of Macready's life. I proposed to come home for Christmas Day, before going to Bradford in Yorkshire to read once more – this time to a little fireside party of four thousand! – and coming home again, to get up a new little version of The Children in the Wood (which I had not yet written) for the children to act on Charley's birthday.

By the beginning of December I had been so much disappointed in the nature of the contributions as yet received for this year's Christmas Number, and was concerned as it required to be upon the steam engine of printing by the 8th. It needed my utmost care and assistance to produce, and I contributed the story of "The Seven Poor Travellers" who lodged at Watts's Charity in Rochester, whilst other contributions came from Sala, Proctor, Collins and Elizabeth Lynn. I also arranged for complete sets of the Cheap Edition of my books to be sent to the troops in the Crimea, through Mr. Albert Smith of Egyptian Hall

Entertainments, as it had been reported that there was a great want in the troops for such books. I saw a report in The Times shortly thereafter that Mr. Smith had sent upwards of 22,000 volumes of books to the Crimea and also to the military hospital established on the Asian shore of the Bosphorus at Scutari on the outskirts of Constantinople. But I was greatly concerned, as tales of incompetence in the administration of the war began to be commonplace.

Applications for me to read at various venues up and down the country were now beginning to hail and blow upon me with such force that I spent many hours doing nothing but incessantly answering such correspondents – all of whom I felt were tearing at me like so many zoological creatures before dinner! They came in such enormous numbers that I could no more comply with their entreaties than I could divide myself into fifty men. The Household Words Christmas Edition, containing my Poor Travellers story, sold exceedingly well, particularly considering the times, and just a few days into January I learnt that 80,000 had been sold. It had moved me not a little in the writing and I believe it touched a vast number of people in the reading.

But the war in Crimea overshadowed everything. My concerns and anger towards our administrators grew as I read regular reports in The Times about conditions for our brave troops and how our administrators, representatives of the wickedest and most enormous vice of our time, were operating. These addled heads would take the average of cold in the Crimea during twelve months, as a reason for clothing a soldier in nankeen on a night when he would be frozen to death in fur. The Times reported that our expedition to the Crimea was now "in a state of entire disorganization", contrasting it with the French who had been effectively organized. The British Army sent out was originally 53,000 strong, but by the beginning of 1855 only 14,000 fighting men could be mustered, and of these only 2,000 were said to be in good health. I had a dreadful belief that our army would be really (virtually) no more in another 6 weeks – and yet, for all this, it was an undisputed fact to me that Russia must be stopped and that the future peace of the world rendered the war imperative upon us.

Reports of the conditions at the hospital in Scutari were shocking. Miss Florence Nightingale and her team of ladies went to try and assist, but 20,000 men were now reported to be in the hospital after the bloody battles at Balaclava and Inkerman, though it was found that only six shirts had then been washed, as the facilities for the drying of clothes were grossly inadequate. Immediately she heard of this, Miss Coutts spoke to me about it and together we set about seeking some form of solution. I found that Mr. Tracey at Tothill Fields Correction House had a hot closet that was worn out and a new man erecting a new successor to it. He was William Jeakes of 51 Great Russell Street, Bloomsbury, a man ingenious in his trade. I spoke to him, and although he never had made such a thing to be carried away and put together, he was positively sure he could. He thought it should be 6 feet square and 7 feet high, made of iron with an outside covering of wood. In answer to my enquiry whether it would be necessary to send a man out with it, he said he would number all the pieces and component parts "so that anyone who could put a gun-carriage together, could put this machine together with perfect ease". I found it would be an expensive thing to be made in this way – he estimated about £150 – but said he could get it ready in three weeks. Miss Coutts did not hesitate in ordering one for the hospital.

For my birthday on the 7th February I arranged for a little dinner with friends at Wates Hotel in Gravesend. On the day I walked from Gravesend to Rochester between walls of snow varying from three to six feet high, through which a road had been hewn out by men, and saw in the process that Gad's Hill Place was to be sold. In remembrance of my poor father and what he used to say to me, I had always in passing looked to see if it was to be sold or let. It had never been to me like any other house, being literally "a dream of my childhood", and I found that had not changed at all. I asked Wills if he would investigate matters for me. And then, two days later on the night of the 9th February, four and twenty years suddenly vanished before me like a dream.

As I was reading by my fire at Tavistock House, a handful of letters was laid down on my table. I constantly received hundreds of letters, in great varieties of writing all perfectly strange to me, and had no particular interest in the faces of such general epistles. I looked these over and, recognizing the writing of no private friend, let them lie there and went back to my book. But I then found my mind curiously disturbed, and wandering away through so many years to such early times of my life, that I was quite perplexed to account for it. There was nothing in what I had been reading or immediately thinking about to awaken such a train of thought, and at last it came into my head that it must have been suggested by something in the look of one of those letters. So, I turned them over again – and suddenly the remembrance of the hand of Maria Beadnell came upon me with an influence I cannot express. I opened the letter with the touch of my young friend David Copperfield when he was in love, and found something so busy and pleasant in the letter from her – so true and cheerful and frank and affectionate – that I read on with perfect delight until I came to her mention of her two little girls. In the unsettled state of my thoughts, the existence of these dear children appeared such a prodigious phenomenon, that I was inclined to suspect myself of being out of my mind, until it occurred to me that perhaps I had nine children of my own! Then the three or four and twenty years began to rearrange themselves in a long procession between me and the changeless past, and I could not help considering what strange stuff all our little stories were made of.

I wrote back to her – now Mrs. Winter – at length, telling her that she could not more tenderly remember our old days than I did, and that I forgot nothing of those times; they were just as still and plain and clear as if I had never been in a crowd since and had never seen or heard my own name out of my own house. I particularly recalled how I had met her one day with two others and her mother on Cornhill; also told her that hundreds of times I had passed the church in the City near where she used to live and invariably now associated it with her poor sister Anne who, I had been told, was buried there after she had died in 1836, just three years after her marriage to Henry Kolle; and that I had seen Marianne Leigh many years before in Broadstairs and recently read in The Times that she had just married. I expressed my wish to see Maria again and would be charmed to have a long talk with her after all this length of time. I told her I was to go to Paris the following day, but would be back within a fortnight, when a private dinner might also be arranged at Tavistock House for her and her husband, allowing us to set in, without any restraint, for a tremendous gossip.

I heard again from Maria whilst in Paris, and wrote back telling her in detail how I had got the heartache again when I read her commission and how old fancies had been stirred within me once again by the receipt of it. I felt now that I had never been so good a man since, as I was when she made me wretchedly happy and should never be half so good a fellow any more. I told her that, in David Copperfield, I had presented a faithful reflection of the passion I had had for her and that she may have seen in little bits of "Dora" touches of her old self sometimes, and a grace here and there that might be revived in her little girls, years hence, for the bewilderment of some other young lover – though he could never be as terribly in earnest as I and David Copperfield were.

I received communication from Wills, who had kindly and promptly taken trouble over Gad's Hill Place. It was clear to me that the merits of the little freehold resolved themselves into the view and the spot and, if I had more money, these considerations might – with me – over-top all others. But as it was, I considered the matter now quite disposed of – finally settled in the negative – and to be thought no more about. I decided not to go down and look at it, as I felt I could add nothing to his report.

On returning to Tavistock House, I received a further letter from Maria. I replied at length, remembering the times we shared together and not believing her when she said she was now "toothless, fat, old and ugly". I told her that she was always the same in my remembrance and that I would very much like to see her. I also wrote to Forster, telling him of the circumstance of Maria's reappearance and the reawakening of the feelings that I had had four and twenty years before. He believed I was over-rating the strength of such feelings from that time; I assured him that he was wrong, and that the prospect of seeing the mere cause of it all now had loosened my hold upon myself. Without for a moment sincerely believing that it would have been better if we had never got separated, I could not see the occasion of so much emotion as I should see anyone else. I could never open Copperfield as I opened any other book and could not see the face even now, or hear the voice, without wandering away over the ashes of all that youth and hope in the wildest manner.

On the evening of the 7th March we dined together, Maria and her husband with Catherine and I, at Tavistock House. Whilst always tall, she had now grown to be very broad too, extremely fat and short of breath. She had a bad cold which could be overlooked, but not the fact that she had become diffuse and silly. She had been spoiled and artless long ago, but was determined to be spoiled and artless now, which for me was a fatal blow. I later incorporated her new character into Flora Finching in Little Dorritt, the novel I was already beginning to formulate both in my mind and in my Book of Memoranda that I had now begun to keep for fear I might someday lose my memory. She wrote to me again after our meeting; I replied, telling her that I could not positively be sure to be at home if she called again as I was very busy, but promised to write a letter to her little Ella in response to the one she had written me, which I duly did.

By now I was sure that a career in the law was one I no longer wished to pursue. I had suffered much boredom in the Honourable Society of the Middle Temple and accordingly, on the 17th March, petitioned the Benchers to withdraw myself from the student list and have my deposit money returned. In due course they agreed and returned my £100.

Meanwhile the debate over the Crimea continued to rage with reports, particularly in The Times, showing what we had been doing to our valiant soldiers and what miserable humbugs those put in charge were – involving themselves in meshes of aristocratic red tape to the unspeakable confusion, loss and sorrow of the situation in the process. During this time I dined in the presence of an old General, General Sir Charles Pasley, who went perfectly mad about The Times at the dinner – with exudations that were partly foam and partly turbot with white sauce taking place from his mouth while he denied all the statements in the newspaper. I was sick and sour to think of all such things at this age of the world and proposed to set out my thoughts in articles for Household Words, in a fine little bit of satire very like the Arabian Nights, with new versions of the best known stories entitled "The Thousand and One Humbugs" – as well as supporting Miss Coutts in the sending of the drying machine to the hospital at Scutari. I had heard John Macdonald, The Times reporter from Scutari, being examined by a Committee of Enquiry on the Army before Sebastopol, where Lord Stratford had angrily denied that there was anything amiss in the Hospitals or anything wanted there and said that the "Sick and Wounded Fund" that had been established by The Times in October

1854 had best be given to him so that he might use it towards the building of a Christian Church in Constantinople!

One of the foremost persons in attacking the administration was Sir Austen Layard, who had ascended Vesuvius with Collins, Egg and I when we had visited Naples in November 1853. He went to the Crimea in September 1854 and witnessed the landings, together with the subsequent battles at Alma, Balaclava and Inkerman and, from what he had seen, he had returned to England at the end of the year to begin his assault on the Government, particularly in the House of Commons. I had thought a good deal on the duty owed to him of helping him as much as I could in Household Words and elsewhere, and I also sought to enlist as many journals to his cause as I was able. He told me in the strictest confidence of his proposed resolutions in the House of Commons and I was happy to go over them with him, for there was nothing to me at this time that was at once so galling and so alarming as the alienation of the people from their own public affairs. I had no difficulty in understanding it; the people had had so little to do with the game through all the years of Parliamentary reform that they had sullenly laid down their cards and taken to looking on. Meanwhile, all our English tuft-hunting, toad eating and other manifestations of accursed gentility – to say nothing of Palmerston, his Cabinet and the Lord knows who's defiances of the proven truth before Members of Parliament – were expressing themselves every day. An Administrative Reform Society was formed in the City and I put myself down for £20 as a subscription to it, for I am a Reformer heart and soul, but I had my doubts as to whether it would be able to reach out to the millions so affected by the situation.

CHAPTER XXXVI

"Nobody's Fault", The Lighthouse, and Little Dorritt

I was now in the first stages of a new book, which consisted of going round and round the idea of "Nobody's Fault", as you would see a bird in his cage go about and about his sugar before he touches it. The necessity was coming upon me now – as at most such times – of wishing to wander about in my own wild way, to think. I could no more resist this upon a Sunday or any day of the week than a man could dispense with food, or a horse help himself from being driven. I became in a state of restlessness impossible to describe – impossible to imagine – with wearing and tearing only to be experienced. I held my inventive capacity on the stern condition that it must master my whole life, often have complete possession of me, make its own demands upon me and, sometimes for months together, put everything else away from me. Such is the restlessness and waywardness of an author's mind, and if I had not known long ago that my place could never be held unless it were at any moment ready to devote myself to it entirely, I should have dropped out of it very soon. "It is only half an hour" – "it is only an evening" – people would say to me over and over again, but they did not know that it is impossible to command one's self sometimes to any stipulated and set disposal of five minutes – or that the mere consciousness of an engagement will sometimes worry a whole day. But these are the penalties for writing books. It is my firm belief that whoever is devoted to an art must be content to deliver himself wholly up to it, and to find his recompense in it. All this I explained to Maria Winter, who had written to me again, and felt unable to see her again.

I worked at my ideas for "The Thousand and One Humbugs" for Household Words and attended the Committee of the Literary Fund on the 16th April, where I took the chair to press for reform of the organization. I also went carefully over the house at Shepherd's Bush and wrote out a specification of work to be done there, obtained estimates for the painting and repairing that was needed, and sent them to Miss Coutts. I was then delighted to hear from her that she had received a communication from Miss Nightingale at Scutari Hospital thanking her for the drying machine that had been sent out. I now regarded the thing as done successfully, but I was afraid there would be sad use for it as I had heard there were forewarnings already of pestilence out there. The closet, however, I really believed, would be invaluable, and a subsequent note I received from Dr. Southwood Smith in Constantinople confirmed my belief, for he had been to Scutari, found the closet in operation, working well and giving great satisfaction. Lord Paulet, in command and with the military hospitals under his charge, also wrote to Miss Coutts saying that the machine had been assembled, given a week's trial, and that it "answers admirably", whilst another report to her described it as being "first rate". It seemed to me to be about the only solitary "administrative" thing connected to the war that had been a success.

Layard meanwhile continued to be attacked in the House of Commons, where a mistake he had made in a speech at Liverpool was seized upon. I dined with him the next day and besought him for Heaven's sake to be careful. Some may think me impetuous, because I sometimes speak of things I have long thought about, with a suddenness that brings me only to the conclusion I have come at, and does not show the road by which I have arrived there, but I will assert a principle in my own way and will not be bound by any conditions of others. On the evening of the 13th May I presided at the Newsvendors' Benevolent Institution Annual General Meeting and was pleased to have the opportunity of speaking my mind on the inefficient state of Parliament and the aristocratic influence that continued to pervade in the place, as well as firmly portraying those that had baited Layard as "howling Dervishes".

I now began preparations at Tavistock House for production of a play by Wilkie Collins entitled "The Lighthouse". Stanny designed a back-drop for the interior of the lighthouse and also painted a front-drop of the lighthouse in a storm. He entered into the project with the greatest delight, full of his nautical and theatrical ardour. My condition of restlessness, however, did not improve; all the symptoms remained very bad, but the only new feature now was that I was actually at work and in the middle of the first number of my new book, working under this capital name of "Nobody's Fault". I also began to realize that we would have to present The Lighthouse on three nights, as it was impossible otherwise to dispose of the list of invitees I had drawn up, and so settled on the 16th, 18th and 19th June.

We had a special meeting for the Literary Fund at Bulwer's house at 1, Park Lane on the afternoon of the 16th June, where I presented the report for reform and moved that it be adopted, which was seconded by Forster. However, there were doubts expressed at the meeting about the proposed changes to the constitution and moves made to reject the report. Bulwer supported my proposals, but in the end the report was rejected. I then had to hurry back to Tavistock House, for our first performance of Wilkie's play. At the performance tears flowed and some members of the audience I observed crying vigorously, but after half-an-hour break for refreshment we were much cheered on in the farce I had written, "Mr. Nightingale's Diary". After the performance on the 18th, we had a joyous supper, where Lord Campbell told those present that he would have much rather written Pickwick than be Chief Justice of England and a peer of Parliament! On the final night we had such a brilliant success from first to last! And in the farce, Lemon and I did every conceivable absurdity, and the audience never left off laughing. Then some five and twenty of us danced the maddest Scotch Reels, with all the steps conscientiously executed, until 5 o'clock in the morning!

I spoke at the Drury Lane Theatre, at a meeting held there by the Administrative Reform Association. By now I was feeling a little vicious against Palmerston for his comments in the House of Commons about the Association, claiming that our meetings were "private theatricals", and made my feelings clear in my speech. We also, having been approached on behalf of the Bournemouth Sanitorium for Consumption and Diseases of the Chest, gave a charity performance of The Lighthouse at Camden House in Kensington on the 10th July, the evening giving universal satisfaction and a worthwhile contribution to the workings of the Sanitorium. Then, on the 16th July, I took the family to Folkestone, to stay at 3, Albion Villas. It was a very pleasant little house on the cliff overlooking the sea, though it rained with the greatest vigour in honour of our arrival. I invited my sister Laetitia and her husband Henry Austin to come as I had revived my interest in Gad's Hill once again, and had a delicacy in entertaining the idea of Henry going himself to the place to look it over. He agreed to do so, and reported back, clearly taking a great deal of trouble over the matter, and from what he said I decided to offer £1,500 for the place.

But above all I had to cool down from theatricals and speechmaking, and all other things, to my new book. Lighthouses faded into the past and I became hard at work again, looking at the sea as I wrote, and climbing all the hills and cliffs around when I had done for the day. I soon established my daily routine of an early salt water swim, before being by myself in my room from nine to two, and then going out to walk afterwards until five. My dinner time, bed time, and whole time I managed according to the system that experience had shown me to make my work easiest and happiest; I cannot comfortably do what I want to do, unless I am systematic in my own way. I got into the second number of what I was still calling Nobody's Fault, but became dissatisfied and had half a mind to begin again and work in what I had done afterwards. It occurred to me that, by making the fellow-travellers at once known to each other, I missed an effect. It struck me that it would be a new thing to show people coming together, in a chance way, as fellow-travellers and, being in the same place, ignorant of one another, as happens in life; and to connect them afterwards, and to make the waiting for that connection a part of the interest. I put an enormous outlay into the Father of the Marshalsea chapter, in the way of getting a great lot of matter into a small space, and although I was not quite resolved, I had a great idea of overwhelming that family with wealth. Their condition would be very curious, but I now felt and hoped that I could make Amy Dorrit very strong in the story.

I was now trying to settle to the next number (Number 3), turning myself into a hideous state of mind in which I walked down stairs once in every five minutes, looked out of the window every two, and did nothing else, when William Giles, my old schoolmaster, wrote to me again – amongst hundreds of other letters – asking me if I would carry out a reading in Chester, but I had to decline him too, as I did not wish to be distracted or to take on more than I had already agreed. My new story was now everywhere about me – heaving in the sea, flying with the clouds, blowing in the wind – and I could settle to nothing, and wondered (in my old way) at my own incomprehensibility. I was so steeped in my story, rising and falling by turns into enthusiasm and depression that I barely noticed that Sebastopol had now been taken. But I stuck at it day after day and by the end of September had almost finished the number – in which I relieved my indignant soul with the "Circumlocution Office", which contained the whole science of Government. I really was serious in thinking that representative Government had become altogether a failure with us without an educated and advanced people to support it, that the English gentilities and subserviences (teaching people to "keep in their stations") rendered the people unfit for it, and that the whole thing had broken down since that great seventeenth-century time, and had no hope for it. I had no present political faith or hope – not a grain.

As I began drafting Number 4, I decided to alter the title from "Nobody's Fault" to "Little Dorrit", a name that had a pleasanter sound in my ears and which was equally applicable to the same story. I also turned my thoughts to the Household Words Christmas Number and drafted a prospectus for contributors to follow. On this occasion I conceived of a traveller, who found himself the only person staying at an inn on Christmas Day and was at his wits' end what to do with himself; the rather as he was of a timid and reserved character, and, being shut up in his solitary sitting room, did not well know how to come out of it and speak to anybody. The general idea was that he overcame this feeling – found out the stories of the different people belonging to the inn, or some curious experience that each had had – and wrote down what he had discovered. In due course I wrote "The Guest", "The Bill" and then "The Boots"; Collins wrote "The Ostler"; and others "The Landlord", "The Barmaid" and "The Poor Pensioner" – all being produced for the extra Christmas Number under the collective title of "The Holly-Tree Inn".

I wished to move to Paris for a while, and found accommodation at 49, Avenue des Champs-Elysees, the six front apartments all looking upon the main street, the view delightfully cheerful, and wonderful life perpetually flowing up and down; I thought the situation itself almost the finest in Paris. The servants arrived safely to get the place into good order and I directed Catherine, together with Mamie, Katey, Harry and Plorn to join us there forthwith, and was now able to continue on with Little Dorrit in higher spirits, making visits to England only when the need arose.

CHAPTER XXXVII

Readings, Gad's Hill Place, Paris, and Little Dorrit

I spent time in England in December, for in the middle of the month I had agreed to a reading at Peterborough as a mark of affectionate respect to Watson, and wrote to Mrs. Watson at Rockingham making arrangements for her to come to the performance with me. I had also promised to the Mayor of Sheffield to do my best to read there at this time, but I heard from them that the Sheffield Mechanics' Institute was in such serious difficulties that it was unclear to me whether they would continue as an organization.

I further considered the situation about Gad's Hill Place. I had now proposed offering £1,700, but the owner, Mrs. Eliza Lynn Linton was pressing for £1,800. I thought this a little too much considering the improvements to be made, and so did Henry Austin. I finally offered £1,750 (calculating that it would require an expenditure of about £300 more before it would yield £100 a year let) and awaited Mrs. Linton's reply.

Upon going back to Little Dorrit, I found she was not working very well for me, but I had been delighted to hear from Bradbury and Evans the news of sales following publication of the first number, a stimulating report of brilliant triumph, with sales of 32,000 and further reprinting being required! It was a noble start indeed, and I hoped that the strength of Numbers 2 and 3 would clinch the blow. It had beaten even Bleak House out of the field, a most tremendous start, and I was overjoyed at it.

I then travelled to Rockingham and found it inexpressibly sad. The Boyle family, including Mary, were also there, but the weight upon my own spirits, imposed there by the sight of the place, necessarily fell to some extent on everybody else – everybody knowing that I had not been there since poor Watson's death – and it really was a mournful evening. At a quarter past ten, I left those long low downstairs rooms and retired to the old bedroom, monstrously depressed; I was obliged to read and smoke before my fire till past midnight, before I could become myself again. In the morning, however, we got on much better, and we were much more like our old selves but, before we started off, I went quietly into the church to see poor Watson's grave. Mrs. Watson's two eldest boys went with us to Peterborough and the reading, conducted in the Corn Exchange to more than 700 people, was a wonderful success, with as fine an audience as could possibly be – and I think I never did the Carol so well.

A few days later I agreed to read at Sheffield, in the lecture hall of the Sheffield Mechanics' Institute. By now I had had my copy of the Carol pasted onto large paper with a red morocco cover, and during the performance used my large paper knife to divide the leaves if they proved any obstinacy in turning. I used powerful lighting (a row of gas lights) concentrated upon my face and the reading went, once again, with enormous effect. They took the line: "and to Tiny Tim who did not die" with a most prodigious shout, the whole assembly rising spontaneously with a universal feeling of joy that seemed to pervade everywhere, coupled with a tremendous burst of cheering. At the conclusion, the Mayor presented me with a very handsome service of table cutlery, a pair of razors and a pair of fish carvers, all inscribed, as a substantial manifestation of their gratitude. They were beautiful specimens of Sheffield workmanship.

On Christmas Eve, I took the train back to Paris. The passage across the Channel was rough and wet, but I was brought triumphantly through it by 15 drops of my laudanum, when almost everyone was very ill. Straight after Christmas, despite feeling very tired indeed, I set busily to work again, finishing Little Dorrit Number 4, as well as drawing up a new article for Household Words – but I now began to feel in a fit of depression once more, thinking I had over-worked and so floored myself. The troops returned from the Crimea and were greeted in Paris by the Emperor, before they marched in style from the Place de la Bastille to the Place Vendome, and in the night there were illuminations, with the whole of Paris, bye streets and lanes and all sorts of out of the way places, most brilliantly lit up.

On New Year's Day 1856, I was much cheered by the news that 35,000 copies of Little Dorrit Number 2 had been sold within two days of issue. Furthermore, I had received a proposal of a French translation of all my books, a pleasant thing to have happen in one's lifetime. A volume was planned to appear about once a month, so that it would take a year and a half or two years to complete and I calculated that I should receive between £300 and £400 from this alone, which would pay my rent for the whole year, and travelling charges to boot. Little Dorrit was also being produced in Germany, by Tauchnitz who had taught German to Charley in Leipzig.

I felt the need to return to London for a few days once every month or so, my next visit being planned for the beginning of February, before which I tried to force myself to write the next number of Little Dorrit, sitting down and holding myself prisoner in the process. It was then excessively pleasant to get a letter from Collins telling me that he had almost finished his book "After Dark" and would therefore be able to join me in travelling back from London to Paris in jovial manner following my next visit. This opened a prospective of theatrical and other lounging evenings in Paris together, as well as having him write for Household Words and dining at my favourite restaurant, the Trois Frères. I arranged to meet up with him in London, while meanwhile deciding to engage with Beaucourt in Boulogne again and take his Villa Moulineaux for June.

I stayed in London between the 4th and 11th February conducting much business; the weather was however as vile as could be and the streets hideous to behold, with an ugliness quite astonishing. But I got the news from Bradbury and Evans that the first number of Little Dorrit had now gone to 40,000 and others were fast following. I spent a day with Wills going to Gad's Hill, where I found the Rector, the Reverend Joseph Hindle, living in the place and had done so for some twenty-six years. I asked him how and when it would suit his convenience to come out if I purchased the place; he said he had an ardent desire to stay until Lady Day the following year. The place was old-fashioned, plain, and comfortable, on the summit of Gad's Hill, with a noble prospect at the side and behind, looking down into the Valley of the Medway; the country, even against every disadvantage of the season, being beautiful. Lord Darnley's Park of Cobham – a beautiful place, with a noble walk through a wood – was close by, and Rochester within a mile or two. It was only an hour and a quarter from London by the North Kent railway line (from Charing Cross to Higham Station) and to crown all, the sign of the Sir John Falstaff Inn was over the way. Henry Austin had surveyed the house for me, and had been greatly struck by it. There was a very pretty garden, and a shrubbery on the other side of the high road, at which the house looked, and I could not help but recall how I used to look at it as a wonderful mansion (though God knows it is not) when I was that very odd little child. I estimated that the changes absolutely necessary would take a thousand pounds and bore such a long, long train that I had never been rich, and believed I never would be, but I eventually agreed a price of £1,790 with Mrs. Linton, which was something more than I had hoped to pay.

Wilkie meanwhile had a touch of his "old complaint", and rather than coming on to Paris with me, had to consult his doctor instead. I turned back to Little Dorrit, again aware that I could not do my best without an entire devotion to it. When I had been thus engaged all day, I found I could not properly relieve my mind or prepare myself for the morrow, unless I was perfectly free from promises and engagements, and could wander about in my own queer way. The weather in Paris had by now improved, and taking advantage of such a happy change, for my exercise and meditation I took it into my head to walk around the walls of Paris. I found it a very odd walk and felt it would make a good description. One day I turned to the right when I got outside the Barrière de l'Étoile and walked around the wall until I came to the river, and then entered again beyond the site of the Bastille; the following day I turned to the left on getting outside the Barriere.

So I settled myself into Little Dorrit again, but in the usual wretchedness of such settlement – which is unsettlement. Prowling about the rooms, sitting down, getting up, stirring the fire, looking out of the window, tearing my hair, sitting down to write, writing nothing, writing something and tearing it up, going out, coming in, a monster to my family – but by the beginning of March I had finished the greater part of the next number (Number 6) and sent it to Bradbury and Evans. I was still however struggling with the last chapter of that number, but by now Wilkie had arrived and on the 3rd March, in my distressed condition, not having been able to write one word that day or to fashion forth the dimmest shade of the faintest ghost of an idea, I petitioned him that I was desirous of being taken out, and was not at all particular where. After a spirited evening with him, I was able, within the next three days, to complete the number, and so become in that state of weary excitement that was a part of me at such periods.

CHAPTER XXXVIII

Forster's Surprise, Little Dorrit, and Unsettled Domesticity

Upon my next arrival in London, I delivered the remaining part of Number 6 of Little Dorrit to Bradbury and Evans, spent some time surveying the ruins of the Covent Garden Theatre that had burnt down four days before, and then went to the Household Words office. But I developed an excessively violent cold, unspeakably vile and oppressive, and for a number of days had to spend half of each day in bed to be able to get myself up for the other half. Whilst in this state, I then had, on the morning of the 11th March, news from Forster himself that caused me to lay down flat, as if an engine and tender had fallen upon me. He told me the most prodigious, overwhelming, crushing, astounding, blinding, deafening, pulverizing, scarifying secret imaginable by the united efforts of the whole British population, and of which he was the hero – namely that he was to be married!!! The lady concerned was Eliza Colburn, an agreeable and rather pretty 37-year old widow of the publisher Henry Colburn, who had died the year before and had left her almost as many thousand pounds as she was years of age. I never was so flattened by such news in all my life! Forster also pronounced to me that "Collins is a decidedly clever fellow", and I hoped Forster was a better fellow in health too.

I returned to Paris and felt I could now charge at Little Dorrit Number 7 with new spirits, for I had finally resolved to make Dorrit rich which, I felt, should be a very fine point in the story. Wilkie dined with us every day, and I began talking over with him a mighty original notion that I had for another play at Tavistock House – this time based upon arctic voyages that had taken my interest. I proposed opening it on the next Twelfth Night – for a four-night theatrical season at that great establishment! – and Wilkie was much enthused by the idea. Macready came to Paris for a short while, but his situation of living now a lonely life set me thinking of my life. I had always felt that I must, please God, die in harness, but I never felt it more strongly than in looking at, and thinking of, him. How strange it is to be never at rest, and never satisfied, and ever trying after something that is never reached, and be always laden with plot and plan and care and worry; how clear it is that it must be, and that one is driven by an irresistible might until the journey is worked out! For me, it is much better to go on and fret, than to stop and fret. As to repose – for some men there's no such thing in this life, and this was so often in my head in these days. I was now 44 and that looked a good deal on paper, but I believed I was very young-looking still and knew that I was a very active vigorous fellow, who never knew in his own experience what the word "fatigue" meant. I wrote every word of my books with my own hand (no dictation) and did not write them very quickly either. I wrote with great care and pains, being passionately fond of my art, and thinking it worth any trouble, and persevered and worked hard. I was a great walker besides, and plunged into cold water every day, even in the dead of winter. When I was last in Switzerland, I found that I could climb as fast as the Swiss guides, and few strangers thought I looked like one who passed so many hours alone in his study. And then my thoughts would turn to old days – the old days! Should I ever, I wondered, get the frame of mind back as it used to be then? Something of it perhaps – but never quite as it used to be. And now I was all too aware that I found the skeleton in my domestic closet was becoming a pretty big one.

Wilkie departed to see his doctor in London, and I decided upon long country walks to get into train for work again, though I did find the evenings sufficiently dull as I missed Wilkie's company very much. I finished Little Dorrit Number 7, and did an article for Household Words, but then found I could not work in the midst of my unsettled domesticity. The first blank page of Little Dorrit Number 8 eyed me on the desk with a pressing curiosity, but got nothing out of me all day. The Hogarth family were living at Tavistock House and not due to leave until Saturday 3rd May, but I could not in the meantime bear the contemplation of their imbecility any more. I planned to quit Paris by train on the morning of Tuesday 29th April, but then remain at Dover, in the Royal Ship Hotel on Custom House Quay, where I hoped to work in the mornings and then take some walks thereafter on the high cliffs by the sea, until going to town early on the Saturday to meet with Wilkie.

Despite Little Dorrit Number 6 being published on the 30th April, I did nothing at Dover except for Household Words business, still feeling unable to yet begin Little Dorrit Number 8. But I took twenty-mile walks in the fresh air – including over the Downs towards Canterbury in a gale wind one day, and to Deal and back on another – and perhaps in the long run did better than if I had been at work. Then when I got to see Tavistock House again I became up to my eyes in dust! John Thompson, my servant, and I wallowed in it for four hours, getting books and papers put away, and making things neat and comfortable about us again.

Each day I breakfasted at half-past eight with Charley, and met him again at dinner when he did not dine in the City or had no engagement. He looked very well and appeared to be progressing in high spirits at Barings Bank where he now worked. By the 9th May I had resolved to go furiously to work again, and became incessantly at work at my desk every day, not only on Little Dorrit but also Household Words – and conducting other business, including selecting those from the Home at Shepherd's Bush to be sent abroad (after looking at the cases and consulting with the matron, Mrs. Marchmont), and going on several excursions into Kent now that I had agreed to purchase my little Kentish freehold.

On the 7th June we all travelled to Boulogne, where I hoped to write in a garden of peace, and swarm up and down all the hills in the locality. Upon arrival at the Villa des Moulineaux, I found the place beautiful, with a burst of roses, and Beaucourt had thinned the trees, grubbing up about half of them that had been there when we were here before, greatly improving the garden – and, upon my life, expressly making at least twenty distinct smoking spots for me within it! The story for Little Dorrit now lay before me, strong and clear, and I did not expect for another month to see land from its running sea, but I knew it would not be easily told – nothing of that sort is to be easily done that I know of. I became hard at work at it again, sitting late, before lying down among the roses in the garden and reading until after tea, whereupon I would begin my usual walking until night. Household Words continued to need my guidance, with Wills constantly sending me material to review before publication. One morning I had to take four hours of close attention away from Little Dorrit to hack and hew a story for the magazine that caused me to be perfectly addled by its horrible want of continuity after all. I made a dreadful spectacle of the proofs, making them look, after my labours, like an inky fishing net.

All the while Little Dorrit kept me busy, and it would not have been easy to increase upon the pains I took with her. I was now beginning Number 10 with, in my mind, the prospect of soon bringing riches to the Dorrit family – but I also began to get a floating idea in my mind that after Little Dorrit was finished, Wilkie and I might do something in Household Words together. I had talked with him so much within the previous 3 or 4 years about fiction writing, and saw him so ready to catch at what I had tried to prove right, and to avoid what I thought wrong, and altogether to go at it in the spirit I had fired within him, that this notion took some shape within me. He had written "The Diary of Anne Rodway" for Household Words, a mystery story in two parts that I considered very specially good, and I told Wills to pay him £20 in a handsome note, stating that I had told him to do so, as I had seen such great pains in Wilkie's story and so much merit, that I wished to remove it from ordinary calculations, and hoped to encourage him further.

Wilkie arrived in Boulogne and we took to working on the new play together. But then, towards the end of August, I heard news from enquiries made among the doctors in the town by Edward Pigott (a friend of Wilkie's) that there was an epidemic of a malignant sore throat (diphtheria) and that it had undoubtedly been very bad. It had apparently been considered at its worst about the end of June, when 20 children had died of it in a day, and whilst there were at present no cases, and there had been none reported for two or three weeks – and never been a single case in the Haute Ville – I was most concerned. On the 24th August I received a letter of the strongest possible warning from a friend, Dr. Olliffe in Paris, that was so pressing of the necessity of removing the children out of the reach of this dangerous epidemic that I decided to send Catherine and the younger children back to London immediately.

Everyone began dispersing, and I arranged to leave with Wilkie and Pigott on the 3rd September. Once we arrived off the boat in England we decided to take to walking, at least in part, towards London. As I did so, I began to contemplate the advantages of Gad's Hill, for a railroad had recently opened in June that year (1856) from Rochester to Maidstone, which connected Gad's Hill at once with the whole sea coast – and which was certainly an addition to the place, and an enhancement of its value. I knew also that, by and bye, we were to have the London, Chatham and Dover Railway too, and that would bring Gad's Hill within an hour of Canterbury and an hour and a half to Dover, as well as being able to take me to and from London with ease. And there was no area (marshes avoided) that was healthier in my mind, and none more beautiful in my eyes.

CHAPTER XXXIX

Wilkie Collins, and The Frozen Deep

Once back at Tavistock House, and after a plunge of 24 hours duration among the wrecks of my dismantled study, I happily fished up all the fragments of that noble ship and pieced them together, with the neat result that it was afloat again, and looking none the worse! Wilkie continued to work on the play for Twelfth Night, and his ideas seemed to me to supply and include everything the play wanted, and it became very strong. We went very well together on it, and the leading role of Richard Wardour that I proposed to play, gave me capital things to do with him that I believed would greatly strengthen and suspend the interest through the second act before the culmination in the third. The strength of the situation was prodigious – and I felt that if we didn't bring the house down with it, I was a Tory!

I had been thinking a good deal about Wilkie, and by Forster's description of him as "a decidedly clever fellow". I had found him very suggestive and exceedingly quick to take my notions, as well as being industrious and reliable, and told Wills that it struck me that the best thing we could just now do for Household Words was to add him to the staff (which now included Henry Morley) and offer him five guineas a week for such a role, initially for the next twelve months. The getting of his name before the public was important to a man in his position, fighting to get on; however, as we did not normally publicize the names of contributors to the magazine, some little compensation for his name not being constantly announced was needed, and I considered that might be afforded to him by a certain engagement. I proposed to give him permission to collect his writings from Household Words and to publish them under his own name, believing this would have him handsomely and generously considered in all respects. I also proposed that any long story of his of up to six months for the magazine would be advertised, as a rider to all our advertisements, before it was begun, and to state that it was to be by him. I believed it would do him, in the long run, a world of good, and was also certain that by Wills, Wilkie and I meeting and dining together (and sometimes calling in Morley to boot) we would knock out much new fire for the magazine. I was delighted when Wilkie agreed to join our staff on this basis in early October.

I came home to such an immense arrear of demands on my attention that I was falling behind-hand with that reserve of Little Dorrit which had kept me easy during its progress, and which I knew would be a serious thing to lose. I was now writing Number 12, and for a full week was hard at it as it was the number due to be published at the end of October. But I was not in a quick vein and made but tardy way. I could not therefore let a day go, for if I did there was no saying when I might work round again and come right; and so I stuck resolutely to it for a further week, declining all invitations.

At the end of September I set out the memorandum to contributors for this year's Christmas Number for Household Words. In it I proposed the scheme of an English trading-ship, "The Golden Mary", with passengers aboard bound for Australia, getting foul of an iceberg and becoming a wreck. I saw the crew and passengers, not very many in number, and the captain a cool man with his wits about him, having one of the boats hoisted out and some stores got over the side into her before The Golden Mary went down. All hands, with a few exceptions, were then got into this open boat, and getting clear of the wreck, they put their trust in God. At sea in the open boat for many days and nights, the people began to be horribly dispirited, but the captain, remembering that the narration of stories had been attended with great success on former occasions of similar disasters, by preventing the shipwrecked persons minds from dwelling on the horrors of their condition, proposed that such as could tell anything to the rest should do so – and thus the stories were to be introduced.

On the evening of the 2nd October, immense excitement was occasioned by Wilkie arriving at Tavistock House in a breathless state with the first two acts of the play completed. He called it: "The Frozen Deep", and upon reading I found it very serious and very curious, but nevertheless extremely clever and interesting. Although I was obliged to make a very short visit to Birmingham, I immediately set preparations in train for the production at Tavistock House. I had found that the proposed rake of the stage in the school room was too much and so wrote to instruct my carpenter, Henry Rudkin, to alter the measurements to the details I now set out. On my return I found the school room had become in the hands of carpenters; and men from underground habitations in theatres, who looked as if they lived entirely upon smoke and gas, beset me at unheard of hours, with the sounds in the house growing to be like Chatham Dockyard or the building of Noah's Ark. I begun considering that we should perform the play on four nights and not just the once on Charley's birthday – I later decided upon a performance on the night before Twelfth Night for only our trades-people and the servant's relations, followed by 4 further performances for selected audiences on Twelfth Night, the 8th, 12th and 14th January – and took to growing a beard for the part of Richard Wardour.

I engaged Francesco Berger to compose the overture and incidental music that was needed and began rehearsals in earnest. There was so much to do – the clink of hammers constantly giving awful note of preparation – and in the evening hours my elder children went through fearful drill under their rugged parent. But it not only united us in a pleasant amusement, it was a wonderful discipline to my young people in patience, punctuality, perseverance and order; but, best of all, in that kind of humility which is got from the earned knowledge that whatever the right hand finds to do, must be done with the heart in it, and in a desperate earnest. I have always held the firm belief that nothing satisfactory can be done by halves or without trying hard to do it.

Because I had so much to do with my managerial responsibilities, and also with the need to press on with Little Dorrit, I decided that this Christmas I could read nowhere, and turned down all invitations to do so. I took a 20-mile walk and managed to get up all of Richard Wardour's words in the play – to the great terrors of Finchley, Neasden, Willesden, and the adjacent country! – and then it came into my head how Wilkie could get his division of the Christmas Number for Household Words very originally and naturally. I put these suggestions to him; we went down to Gad's Hill and walked through Cobham Woods to talk it over and he then went at it cheerfully. I was now writing hard on the Christmas Number myself, and though I was concerned that the half-year's balance of Household Words had been very indifferent indeed, I was pleased with the way the Christmas story was now going. I intended to get it out very early this year, to get it all over England, Ireland and Scotland a good fortnight before Christmas Day.

Matters for the play at Tavistock House continued apace, with the stage grown to be thirty feet long, four stage-carpenters entirely boarding on the premises, and a carpenter's shop erected in the back-garden. Size was always boiling over on all the lower fires, to be replaced by a labourer who, all day long, heated this glutinous substance in a great crucible, causing us to eat it, drink it, breathe it and smell it incessantly. A gas-fitter's shop was all over the basement; a dressmaker's shop housed at the top of the house; and a tailor's shop occupied my dressing room. Stanny was perpetually elevated on planks, splashing himself with paint from head to foot, whilst a legion of prowling nondescripts were forever slinking in and out of the house. Amidst this wrack, I sought to calmly glide away on the Dorrit stream, forgetting the uproar for a stretch of hours and thereafter refreshing myself with a 10 or 12-mile walk, before pitching myself head-foremost into foaming rehearsals and placidly emerging for Household Words editorial purposes – before again floating upon the Dorrit waters.

With news that we were to perform to a limited audience of about ninety persons on each of the four nights, the run upon the seats passed belief. By now the last performance on the 14th January was the one that had an awfully judicial character about it, ranging from the Lord Chief Justice, Lord Campbell, to the youngest of the Puisne Judges, and I was greatly pleased that Lord Lyndhurst, the previous Lord Chancellor, also desired to come. The places filled to capacity and I had a large reserved list of friends whom we were unable to ask for want of room.

For the days of the performances, I gave detailed written instructions to Thompson as to how he must keep all the inner hall doors closed once all the gas lights had been lit, keeping them closed all night, and never be on any account opened while the street door was open – as well as setting out exactly how our guests must be treated. The performance on the 5th January went to great effect, and the one on Twelfth Night splendidly. I was in perfect order thereafter – calm, and perfectly happy with the success – and taking in enormous draughts of gin punch! Not so Macready, who was perfectly raging on the night he came, because Forster had taken him away after the performance and positively shouldered him out of the Green Room Supper, on which he had set his heart!

On the play days, Mark Lemon and I dined at 3, off steak and stout, at the Cock Tavern in Fleet Street and I invited Wilkie to join us. I substituted "Uncle John" as the farce (to replace "Animal Magnetism") for the three final performances and visions of another play in another year already rose before my mind's eye. On the 8th January everything went to perfection and the effect on the audiences of this and the other nights was the same, and I certainly had never seen people so strongly affected by theatrical means; our audiences were excellent, with a wonderful power of crying. Thackeray, who was present on the final night, was heard to say that if I were to go upon the stage, I would make £20,000 a year, and it was also said that I was considered as great an actor as a writer. But I believed that nothing so complete would ever be done again. Upon the night of its conclusion, we danced the insanest of reels and country dances at Tavistock House until 6 o'clock the following morning, in consequence of having nothing else to do!

My one special regret in all this was that Mrs. Watson had not been able to attend from Rockingham, although she sent me a kind note, which I received in the depressed agonies of workmen battering and smashing down my theatre. The house was now again a mere chaos of scaffolding, ladders, beams, canvas, paint pots, sawdust, artificial snow, gas pipes and ghastliness. I had taken such pains with it for ten weeks in all my leisure hours that I felt, now, shipwrecked – as if I had never been without a play on my hands before – but it had been the talk of all London from the beginning of the New Year. The reviews that appeared were full of praise for myself, the company and the effects of the performance. My part as Richard Wardour (which required me to die on stage at the close) was described as "most touching and beautiful" and that I had all the technical knowledge and resources of a professional actor, but adding: "the dry bones of acting were kindled by that soul of vitality which can only be put into them by the man of genius and the interpreter of affections." As to the play itself, when I had now made it as good as my care could make it, I derived a strange feeling out of it, like writing a book in company – giving me a satisfaction of a most singular kind, which had no exact parallel in my life. It was something that I suppose belongs to the life of a labourer in art alone; I had expended an incredible amount of pains and ingenuity upon it, but the result had been the most remarkable, even to me.

CHAPTER XL

Works at Gad's Hill, and Little Dorrit Concluded

With dove-eyed peace enthroned again in my study – though fire-eyed radicalism still beat in my breast – I felt as calm as Pecksniff, save for my knitted brows now turning into cordage over Little Dorrit. As I pressed on with the story, communicating with Browne over the illustrations, I then heard of the wildest legends circulating about town – to the effect that the Queen proposed to ask to have The Frozen Deep performed at Windsor. I spoke to Wilkie about it, who said he would like it very much if offered, thinking it would express to theatres that they were not doing their duty, and that their noble art was sliding away from them. I resolved, of course, to stipulate for as complete mastery and inaccessibility on the stage as if we were at home – and would put a cheerful and dutiful face on the matter if it came about. Wilkie was a great consideration and so, knowing his feeling, I became ready with my reply if I had occasion to give one, but I heard nothing of it otherwise, so slunk about holding my breath and carried on – including, in my walks, striding over the frosty country with my seven-league boots on.

On the 12th February I went with Wills down to Gad's Hill to consider the works I required to be done. Mr. Hindle gave me the name of a builder in the neighbourhood of whom he had heard the best account (though he had never had occasion to employ him himself) and I passed this name on to Henry Austin. I asked Henry to write to him, seeking to know if he would be disposed to attend us at the house on the day following Lady Day with a view to the immediate preparation of an estimate and, if agreed upon, to the immediate execution of the works. I now wished to raise the roof 6 feet (the roof itself seeming to be in want of great repair), as well as carrying out painting and papering and a full examination of the drains – my purpose being to arrange for everything being done at once, out of hand, and got rid of. I hoped the work could be started on the 26th March, and considered that the whole business ought to be disposed of in 6 weeks if done without pause or postponement, any taste of circumlocution being inadmissible.

By now I was working on Number 17 of Little Dorrit, and though finding it a little heavy going with long days of work, I knew I must stick to it, whilst nevertheless exploring a visit to Brighton or other trip-possibilities with Wilkie. I made another visit to Gad's Hill and if there was a pretty little place in England, accessible at all times by railway or steamboat, I now believed that this house was it, and I began to invite friends to visit there once I had taken possession. On the 7th March I went with Wilkie to Brighton for three days and taking with me "The Dead Secret" in manuscript that Wilkie had just completed and presented to me for inclusion in Household Words. It was such a pleasure to be with him, and the news that he would come with me for a walk on the Downs lifted me out of my depression consequent upon the exacting and exhausting work I was undertaking on Little Dorrit. The day after arriving we went for a burst on the Downs, but we were so rained upon, hailed upon, snowed upon and blown, that my face became like a cullender from the hail and ice and my hat a solid cake of ice, half an inch thick!

At the beginning of April I received a letter from Hans Christian Anderson telling me he was now considering coming to London in June – he had been "coming" for about 3 years! – and I wrote to him hoping that my answer would at once decide him to now make this summer visit to us. I planned to finish Little Dorrit by the end of April and was keeping to my long-held resolution, kept for twenty years, not to know of any critical attack on myself whilst I was writing. But then I was ludicrously foiled one night whilst out, by stumbling, before I could pick myself up, on a short extract in the Globe from Blackwood's Magazine, informing me that Little Dorrit was "twaddle". I was sufficiently put out by it to be angry with myself for being such a fool to take notice of this, but then pleased with myself for having so long been constant to a good resolution.

By the beginning of May I still had not yet finished Little Dorrit, and so continued to turn down engagements – including a request by Paxton that I attend a dinner at Coventry – as it was an absolute necessity now that urged me on to write to finish the book. But I did agree that Paxton might announce at the dinner, if he thought it worthwhile, that, as a little mark of my interest in and regard for him, I would read my Carol on any day he might appoint within a fortnight before or a fortnight after Christmas Day next, and to do it for the pleasure or benefit (or both) of any public society in Coventry that he chose to name.

On the morning of the 6th May, before going to Gad's Hill, I went out of curiosity to the Borough, to see if I could find any ruins of the Marshalsea Prison, for I did not know whether any portions were yet standing. I found the outer front courtyard now metamorphosed into a butter shop, and then almost gave up every brick of the jail for lost. Wandering, however, down a certain "Angel Court, leading to Bermondsey" I came to "Marshalsea Place": the houses in which I recognized, not only as the great block of the former prison, but as preserving the rooms that arose in my mind's eye when I became Little Dorrit's biographer. There was a room there – still standing to my amazement – that I even thought of taking! I found a very small boy there (carrying the largest baby I ever saw) who, seeing me standing on the Marshalsea pavement looking about, told me how it all used to be. God knows how he had learnt it, for he was a quarter of a century too young to know anything about it of himself, but he offered a supernaturally intelligent explanation of the locality in its old uses, and was very nearly correct. I pointed to the room where Little Dorrit was born, and where her father lived so long, and asked him: what was the name of the lodger who tenanted that apartment at present? He said: "Tom Pythick". I asked him who was Tom Pythick? and he said "Joe Pythick's uncle"! Three days later I finally finished Little Dorrit.

Catherine's birthday was on the 19th May, and I gave a promise that she should make her first appearance at Gad's Hill on that occasion, and I asked some of her friends to come down there for two or three days to join the small and noble army I had invited to inaugurate the house. On the afternoon of the 19th I organized for a train to bring down the main group of this compact body of attackers of cold meat "on the premises" for the first time, taking the journey from London Bridge Station to Higham (one station beyond Gravesend, and a mile from Gad's Hill) where I was on the spot to receive them. I now planned to take to Gad's Hill for the summer from the 1st June, and was happy to invite others to stay during that period. Hans Christian Anderson, I believed, was now to stay for a fortnight in England and would stay for some of that time with us. Workmen were still lingering in the yard and I felt the need to squeeze them out by bodily pressure or they would never go. After we had all collected together at Gad's Hill – I now feeling like an honest Robin Hood among the green trees – I then found we had a very serious business respecting the water supply. By merely raising the family supply for the next day, the well was pumped dry. Very little water got into the cisterns, and the next morning it was dry again. It was pretty clear to me that the thing had to be looked at in the face, and at once bore, deepen, dig or do something beastly or other to secure the necessary water in abundance. Accordingly, I immediately wrote to Henry Austin, imploring for his presence and counsel.

Further workmen arrived and began first digging and then boring for water – at the rate of £2 per day for wages. The men seemed to like it very much, and to be perfectly comfortable, but the matter became prolonged and I watched the process with the resignation of despair as week followed week, with the garden dug over. They then finished, and the garden was just beginning to recover and look pretty, when the whole of the drain from the wash-house became stopped up through a considerable part of the pipe. I was obliged to have other men in from Strood, only to find that the garden had to be dug up again! I feebly acceded to these suggestions, although I had some idea of running away from the place altogether instead. Soon after this I then saw them forcing long sticks through the choked pipes, which I entirely foresaw would come out in the eye of a man who was lying on his stomach looking in at the other end of the pipe, causing him to be blinded and having a claim on me to be supported for life!

CHAPTER XLI

Death of Jerrold, and Benefit Performances for the Jerrold Fund

Whilst I was organizing the works at Gad's Hill, I learnt that Douglas Jerrold had died on the 8th June. I knew nothing about it, except that he had been ill, but believed he was better, until, going up to town with Catherine and Georgy on the morning of the 9th, I heard a man in the carriage, unfolding his newspaper, say to another "Douglas Jerrold is dead". I had been with him ten days before, but this I now discovered had turned out to be the last day he was out. Jerrold was complaining much when we met, said he had been sick three days, and attributed it to the inhaling of white paint from his study window. I did not think much of it at that moment, as we were very social; but while we walked through Leicester Square he suddenly fell into a white, hot, sick perspiration, and had to lean against the railings. He was then able to walk on to Covent Garden, and before we had gone fifty yards, he was very much better. On our way we were joined by William Russell (The Times reporter from the Crimea) and Jerrold became better still, walking between us unassisted and, after I got him a hard biscuit and a little weak cold brandy, both of which he consumed, he said the sickness was overcome at last and that he was quite a new man. Russell was giving a dinner at Greenwich and Jerrold said it would do him good to have a few quiet hours in the air, and that he would go with us, which he did do.

You can imagine how shocked we all were on hearing the news. Jerrold was one of the gentlest and most affectionate of men. I had first met him in about 1835 and had had many happy hours afterwards passed in his society. He worked as a journalist and was also a dramatist and wit, as well as being one of the founders of Punch magazine, and I particularly remember him meeting me in Brussels with Forster and Maclise when I came home from Italy in 1845, and being in the most brilliant and humorous of spirits. Later there had been an estrangement between us over the subject of capital punishment (though not involving any angry words) and a good-many months passed without my once seeing him in the street, when it fell out that we dined, each with his own separate party, in the strangers' room of a club. Our chairs were almost back to back and I took mine after he was seated and at dinner. I said not a word (I am sorry to remember) and did not look that way. Before we had sat so long however, he openly wheeled his chair round, stretched out both his hands in a most encouraging manner, and said aloud, with a bright and loving face that I can still see as I write this – "For God's sake, let us be friends again! Life's not long enough for this!" He had an unrestrained openness of heart that quite captivated me, and it quite saddened me to think on his passing of our short estrangement when put against his generosity.

In remembrance of him, I immediately went to the office of Bradbury and Evans at Whitefriars to urge the necessity of exertion on behalf of his widow and daughter. I suggested a plan for certain benefit nights at the theatre, and got hold of Arthur Smith as the best man in the business I knew for arranging such occasions. He agreed to be the Honorary Secretary and opened an office at the Gallery of Illustration for the purpose, and a Committee was put together comprising myself and seventeen others (soon to be joined by more), all of whom held Jerrold as a friend and in the dearest remembrance. It was my confident hope that we should raise close to £2,000 by this means.

On the 11th June Hans Christian Anderson arrived at Gad's Hill for what I believed would be a stay for a week or so. On the 15th June I attended as a pall-bearer (one of 10, including Bradbury, Forster, Lemon, Paxton and Thackeray) at West Norwood Cemetery when Jerrold was buried. Apart from members of his family, literary friends and others of distinction, a vast concourse of people – estimated at about six thousand – also attended, and the Committee then announced the programme of planned evening occasions in memory of him:

June 27th	St. Martin's Hall	Concert
June 30th	"	My reading of the Carol
July 7th	"	Russell's lecture on the Crimean War
July 11th	Gallery of Illustration	The Frozen Deep

July 15th	Theatre Royal, Haymarket	Comedy: "The Housekeeper" & Drama: "The Prisoner of War" – both by Jerrold
July 22nd	St. Martin's Hall	Thackeray's Lecture on "Week-Day Preachers"
July 29th	Theatre Royal, Adelphi	Dramas: "The Rent Day" and "Black-Eyed Susan" – both by Jerrold

Tickets for these occasions went on sale from the 23rd June at the Committee's office at the Gallery of Illustration.

I was aware of the Queen's interest in The Frozen Deep, and now felt I should try for her. I proposed that the Queen should come to the Gallery of Illustration – which was in effect but a great drawing room in the previous home of John Nash – on the 4th July, a week before the proposed subscription date, and should have the room entirely at her own disposal, and should invite her own company. This, with the good sense that seemed to accompany her good nature on all occasions, she resolved within a few hours to do.

I immediately set about organizing the participants for these occasions, together with Albert Smith and his brother Arthur. For The Frozen Deep, Mrs. Wills's lameness made a new Nurse Esther the first thing wanted and, through Wilkie, I was able to engage Frances Dickinson for the part. In all there were 30 people in the cast, and I set down a schedule of rehearsal times at the Gallery of Illustration before the private performance for the Queen and her guests.

I then had a letter from John Deane in Manchester. He had worked with Paxton on the Great Exhibition in London, and he asked me if I could perform The Frozen Deep in Manchester and whether I had thought of doing so. I had not, but was prepared to consider it if a sum of money of any importance could be gained by it. I became immersed in the business of organization and the labour of making the arrangements for gathering up money for the Jerrold Fund into something enormous, although I began to hear of unpleasant comments being made about the money-affairs of Jerrold and his family. I pressed on, determined to have the fund raise £2,000, attending the musical concert at St. Martin's Hall,

Long Acre on the 27th June and reading the Carol there to a packed audience three days later. At the end of my reading the whole audience of two thousand and odd people rose to their feet like one and cheered and waved their hats and handkerchiefs. I never saw such an audience in my life; their enthusiasm was something awful and was, I must confess, a very extraordinary thing. Then I had to prepare for the private Royal Performance at the Gallery of Illustration. There were only to be twenty-five people present in addition to the Queen's party, and I sought to arrange a welcoming party for the Queen and her guests for their stated arrival at 9 o'clock. I could not receive her myself as I had to be half dressed in North Polar costume and busy at this time, so I contacted Committee members (including Paxton and Maclise) and arranged for it.

We acted "The Frozen Deep" and then Lemon and I performed the farce "Two O'Clock In The Morning". It all went off splendidly and the Queen was so pleased at the conclusion that she sent round begging me to go and see her and accept her thanks. I replied that I was now in my farce dress, and must beg to be excused. Whereupon she sent again, saying that the dress "could not be so ridiculous as that", and repeated the request. I sent my duty in reply, but again hoped her Majesty would have the kindness to excuse my presenting myself in a costume and appearance that were not my own.

The Frozen Deep was now making such a noise in London that I verily believed we could have filled St. Paul's if we had played there. I had by now agreed to an additional performance at the Gallery of Illustration for the 18th July and, by the time of our Royal performance on the 4th, both of the public performances for the 11th and the 18th had been sold out. On the 11th July we played "The Frozen Deep" with the farce "Uncle John" and the review in The Times contained high praise indeed, not only for myself (I was described as "a great actor who might teach professionals much that they will never learn") but also others, including Mamie, Georgy, Lemon and Egg. I was also greatly pleased that Wilkie was much praised as an original and theatrically effective dramatist. The public clamour was now so great for further occasions that I agreed to repeat my reading of the Carol at St. Martin's Hall on the 24th, and to repeat The Frozen Deep at the Gallery of Illustration for the last time on the 25th – later changed to the 8th August.

On the 15th July Anderson finally left Gad's Hill, much to the relief of Georgy and the children. I took him over to Maidstone and booked him for Folkestone. At our parting he said almost nothing, tears choking his voice, but he did tell me he was going to Paris, to go thence to Dresden before home to Copenhagen. Upon my return to Gad's Hill however, I could not resist putting up a card in his room stating: "Hans Anderson slept in this room for five weeks – which seemed to the family AGES!"

My son Walter sailed for India on the 20th July to join with the army. On the 22nd I attended Thackeray's lecture at St. Martin's Hall, and two days later (as additionally requested) read again the Carol to a vast assembly. Then, on the 29th, I attended at the performance of Jerrold's plays, but as our sum of £2,000 was not yet made up, I agreed to the further production of The Frozen Deep on the 8th August in London and meanwhile arranged to go to Manchester to read the Carol there on the 31st. In Manchester the audience crowded every part of the great room at the Free Trade Hall, and in the interval, a delegation of leading men of the city requested me to bring my amateur company here to perform The Frozen Deep. As a result of this request, I returned to London and, after negotiations, was able to arrange to act it in the Free Trade Hall on Friday and Saturday nights, the 21st and 22nd August; this was subsequently extended to a third night on the 24th, due to overwhelming demand. The number of people to be moved, the number of skilled workmen to be employed, and the quantity of material to be carried about, made up such a cost, that it was not worthwhile to play once only, in any place I knew of. But by playing further, these performances became sheer profit. But the Free Trade Hall was an immense place, with seating for 4,000 people and, having seen it, I knew for certain that we should have to replace my amateur girls with professional actresses.

The last Frozen Deep in London (together with the farce "Uncle John") took place at the Gallery of Illustration on the 8th August. It was again an enormous success, with a greater house than ever, and we might have played the piece for twelve months to come, but the agitation and exertion of playing Richard Wardour was now so great to me that I found it difficult to rally my spirits in the short time I was to get before performing again in Manchester. After the performance

I was in bed all day with exhaustion and considered being helped out of the farce Uncle John in Manchester. I approached Frank Stone (who now lived in Russell House, adjacent to me in Tavistock Square) to play my part in it if he was half up to the job. He agreed to do so, and I began preparing him, but I was then urged in the strongest manner by Arthur Smith and other business men, both in Manchester and London, to remain in the farce for Manchester. I had been named in the bills that had already been published and any change was feared. It was well known in Manchester that I had done the part in London and there was a danger that it might be thought disrespectful in me to give it up, as well as doing so at the last minute after an immense let. And so, having no desire but for the success of our object, and a becoming recognition on my part of the kind Manchester public's cordiality, I gave way, thinking it best in the circumstances to go on. I did so against the grain and against every inclination, and knowing also that my people at home would be miserable too when they knew I was going to do it, but despite my exhaustion, I was determined that the Jerrold Fund should raise the £2,000 clear before the close of our exertions.

I booked hotel accommodation for our Manchester expedition and left Arthur Smith to book, altogether separately, the accommodation for the professional ladies we were to engage. I spoke to Alfred Wigan, a friend and retiring actor-manager of the Olympic Theatre in Wych Street, Drury Lane (where they were about to put on a performance of "The Lighthouse") and he introduced me to the Ternan family of actresses – Mrs. Francis ("Fanny") Ternan, and her three daughters: Francis (also known as "Fanny"), Maria, and Ellen (known as "Nelly"). They had been encouraged in the past with their acting careers by Macready, and I found that Maria had been to see "The Frozen Deep" at a performance at the Gallery of Illustration and had been deeply moved by it. Mrs. Ternan readily agreed to help with our production in Manchester, and I began rehearsing with them immediately. I also resolved that they should play in our farce "Uncle John", with Nelly playing the part opposite me of Eliza Comfort, a young girl that I, as Uncle John had educated and with whom, in the process, had fallen madly and hilariously in love. Mrs.Ternan I cast as her mother Mrs. Comfort, and Maria in the role of an onlooker Mrs. Hawk.

On the opening day for the Manchester bookings, Arthur Smith reported an onslaught upon him for tickets, which was very cheering – though I hoped he would yet get torn to pieces! I was still spending time at Gad's Hill, where the workmen continued looking to fix the water supply, when suddenly, on the morning of the 15th August, they got at a famous spring in the stable yard, which caused the bright clear water to rush in 10 feet deep! They now talked of supplying "a ton a minute for yourself and your family, Sir, for hevermore"!! I immediately contacted Henry Austin with the news and stood the workmen a bottle of gin, whereupon they all got rather drunk. I asked Henry if he could attend and endeavour to decide on the mechanical forces to be used for raising the water; meanwhile, the aggravation of knowing that the water was at the bottom of the well – and of paying for an accursed water-cart that came jogging backwards and forwards – and of looking at the dry bath, morning after morning, gradually changed me from a honey-pot into a mad bull. Henry came, and the newly driven-out workmen re-appeared like mice and began digging again!

The whole party – including Catherine, Georgy, Mamie and Katey – left Euston Station by railroad for Manchester on the morning of the 20th August, in the highest of spirits. During the journey the train was halted and delayed and some complained of hunger, so I organized a game of "conundrums" whereby food was passed by means of umbrellas and walking sticks from carriage window to carriage window in the heartiest and jovial of fashion. On arriving in Manchester, I plunged into further rehearsals and the three performances, each to capacity houses, were the most triumphant success imaginable. Wilkie stated that I had surpassed myself and had "electrified the audience" in The Frozen Deep, while Berger (the musician) considered it surpassed anything he had seen, even on the professional stage. The farce "Uncle John" allowed a joyous conclusion of hilarity. Nelly, with her golden hair, was adorable and I was taken up in a transport of delight.

CHAPTER XLII

Restlessness, and a "Lazy Tour"

I travelled with the company back from Manchester the following day, exhausted, but filled with my restlessness once again, and now also in an amazing misery, which I observed with as much curiosity as if I were another man. The work for the Jerrold Fund was over, and more than £2,000 in store for his widow and daughter, so I wrote to The Times on behalf of members of the Committee, making the result known to the public, but I also began arranging to go on a journey with Wilkie of some 10 or 12 days. I wanted something for Household Words, but also wanted to escape from myself. Ever since the close of the Manchester proceedings, I had found that thoughts of Nelly Ternan, that fair-haired girl, were constantly in my mind and had discovered that the Ternan family were next to perform in the theatre at Doncaster during race week at the beginning of September. So, on the 3rd September, I wrote to the master of the Angel Hotel, Doncaster seeking to book a sitting room and two bedrooms for the whole of race week. A positive reply, even in the sum of twelve guineas for the week, took me out of my dark corner and into the sun again.

Talking with Wilkie, we decided upon a foray first upon the Fells of Cumberland, I having discovered in the books some promising moors and bleak places thereabouts, but I then needed to turn the expedition to Doncaster without arousing suspicion, and so for the moment kept my counsel with everyone including Wilkie, even though I had already booked the rooms there. I did however write to Forster, in response to a kind and hearty letter from him, where I set out the true situation I lived under at home, and what had long been pent up in my mind:

"Poor Catherine and I are not made for each other, and there is no help for it. It is not only that she makes me uneasy and unhappy, but that I make her so too – and much more so. She is exactly what you know, in the way of being amiable and complying; but we are strangely ill-assorted for the bond there is between us. God knows she would have been a thousand times happier if she had married another kind of man, and that her avoidance of this destiny would have been at least as equally good for us both. I am often cut to the heart by thinking what a pity it is, for her own sake, that I ever fell in her way; and if I were sick or disabled tomorrow, I know how sorry she would be, and how deeply grieved myself, to think how we had lost each other. But exactly the same incompatibility would arise, the moment I was well again; and nothing on earth could make her understand me, or suit us to each other. Her temperament will not go with mine. It mattered not so much when we had only ourselves to consider, but reasons have been growing since which make it all but hopeless that we should ever try to struggle on. What is now befalling me I have seen steadily coming, ever since the days you remember when Mary was born; and I know too well that you cannot, and no one can, help me. Why I have even written I hardly know; but it is a miserable sort of comfort that you should be clearly aware how matters stand. The mere mention of the fact, without complaint or blame of any sort, is a relief to my present state of spirits – and I can get this only from you, because I can speak of it to no one else."

Forster replied, and in the main he understood, but I did not find him perhaps so tolerant as he might have been of the wayward and unsettled feeling which is part (I suppose) of the tenure on which one holds an imaginative life, and which I had (as he ought to have known well) often only kept down by riding over it like a dragoon. But I told him:

"I make no maudlin complaint. I agree with you as to the very possible incidents, even not less bearable than mine, that might and must often occur to the married condition when it is entered into very young. I am always deeply sensible of the wonderful exercise I have of life and its highest sensations, and have said to myself for years, and have honestly and truly felt, this is the drawback to such a career, and is not to be complained of. I say it and feel it now as strongly as ever I did; and as I told you in my last, I do not with that view put all this forward. But the years have not made it easier to bear for either of us; and, for her sake as well as mine, the wish will force itself upon me that something might be done. I know too well it is impossible. There is the fact, and that is all one can say. Nor are you to suppose that I disguise from myself what might be urged on the other side. I claim no immunity from blame. There is plenty of fault on my side, I dare say, in the way of a thousand uncertainties, caprices, and difficulties of disposition; but only one thing will alter all that, and that is, the end which alters everything."

As I sat in Gad's Hill contemplating my situation, I thought of reviving the old idea of some readings from my books to pay for the place. I was very strongly tempted and put the idea once again to Forster, though I knew he had strongly opposed it in the past. I was then very glad to get the accounts from Bradbury and Evans, and thought they came out very well indeed, particularly in relation to Little Dorrit, but I knew that Forster had a strong impression that my copyrights were not being turned to anything like the account that the time demanded; and he set particular store by the fact that there was no good edition of them for the better class of readers who buy them for well-furnished bookshelves. I did not at first take his view of the matter when he propounded it to me, but I gradually came to the conclusion that he was right, and not only was there money to be made, but that good was to be done, to the place and station (so to speak) of my writings. I raised this now with Bradbury and Evans and also the question in what form, and at what price, and how as to periods and regular intervals, such an edition could be best devised. They were warm to the idea and, together with the co-operation of Chapman and Hall, the "Library Edition" of all my works was eventually published.

I began to feel rather inventive again and set off in good spirits from Euston Station with Wilkie on the morning of the 7th September, by North Western train heading straight for Carlisle. The Cumberland Fells seemed a promising start to what we now dubbed "The Lazy Tour of Two Idle Apprentices", with Wilkie as Mr. Thomas Idle and I as Mr. Francis Goodchild, Wilkie having bedecked himself out in a brand new shooting-jacket for the occasion for the large sum of two guineas, and reporting it a noble success, though I didn't think so! We had a delightful journey to Carlisle, with the Express exhibiting the greatest power in nature and art combined, issuing steam as from a huge brazen tea-urn and boring through the harvest countryside with a smell like a large washing day.

We considered Carlisle something of a humbug and, scenting the pleasant early morning air the next day, rode south straight for Carrock Fell, a gloomy old mountain 1,500 feet high, that I had secretly resolved to climb. We put up in a little inn where the master volunteered to take us up. It began to rain as we set off, and the sides of Carrock looked fearfully steep, the top hidden in mist, with the rain falling faster as we began our ascent, Wilkie bringing up the rear and gradually getting further back. On we went and on the edge of the mist the landlord stopped and told me he hoped it would not get any thicker, as it was 20 years since he last ascended Carrock and if the mist increased the party could be lost. I was not in the least impressed by this and marched on towards the top, where at last, a dreary little cairn of stones appeared at the summit. The landlord walked all round it as if he were about to perform an incantation, before dropping a stone on the top of the heap. I sat down by the cairn and Wilkie arrived, drenched and panting. He stood with his back to the wind, ascertaining distinctly that this was the top at last, looked around him with all the little curiosity that was left in him, and got in return a magnificent view of....nothing!!

Before attempting to descend, I pulled out a neat pocket-compass and we began down, Wilkie once again bringing up the rear. A canopy of mist began to develop much thicker than a London fog when, upon drawing my compass tenderly from my pocket and seeking to consult it again, the glass fell into the turf, followed immediately by the needle, the compass broken and the exploring party lost! In dead silence, I restored the useless compass to my pocket without saying a word and trusted to the chapter of chances.

After a quarter of an hour we came upon the brink of a ravine, at the bottom of which flowed a muddy little stream. Following consultation, we decided the running stream was a sure guide to follow from the mountain to the valley and descended to its rugged and stony banks. Wilkie again had difficulty proceeding at the same pace; and as we leapt, splashed and tumbled, his foot slipped on a wet stone, his ankle giving a twist outwards, and with a hot, rending, tearing pain, he fell, crippled in an instant and lay writhing with pain. I bandaged his ankle with a pocket handkerchief, the great ligament of his foot and leg swollen I don't know how big and, assisted by the landlord, raised him to his legs and offered him a shoulder to lean on. He managed to hobble along though in great pain. We walked for three-quarters of an hour from his accident, before the mist suddenly brightened and the landlord recognized where we were. We were then all able to travel back to the inn with the assistance of a dog-cart that the landlord obtained, with Wilkie still in the greatest pain and I grateful that a worse accident had not befallen him in the wilds of Carrock. He really, however, was so crippled that I doubted him getting to Doncaster, though I continued saying nothing about it as yet. I was, however, determined to go.

CHAPTER XLIII

To Doncaster, and Seized by Lunacy

After some days, Wilkie felt able to travel to Carlisle and then to Lancaster. We began writing the story of our "Lazy Tour", not only of the events that had befallen us, but also now at my instigation bringing the story – through a fictional tale later completed by Wilkie – round to my planned visit to Doncaster. Although Doncaster was not a hundred miles off from Lancaster, a study of the complicated lists of trains meant we had an overnight stop in Leeds before arriving, which we did on Monday the 14th September, the first day of race week. We took up the rooms I had reserved at the Angel Hotel looking down into the main street, which was full of horse jockeys, bettors, drunkards and other blackguards – and remained so from morning to night, and all night. Going out amongst them, I felt as if I was in a lunatic asylum. On the Monday evening there were more lunatics out than ever; I made for the Theatre Royal on my own, while Wilkie remained at the hotel. At the theatre I was recognized, but found that it was the next night that Maria and Nelly were to perform there. I told Wilkie of this circumstance and he decided to try and come to the theatre with me that following evening; he hated horses, and it was noise and turmoil all day long outside.

On Tuesday Wilkie and I breakfasted at half-past eight, following which we fell to work for Household Words. The Mayor called on me to do the honours of the town, but when he propounded an invitation to a public dinner I graciously rejected such a suggestion. I then went out to – hem! look for subjects. I wandered about finding no one I knew and then left town, but found all had gone "t'races"! I returned to the hotel and that evening, gathering up Wilkie, we made our way in a carriage to the Theatre Royal. As we entered the boxes, each of us – and I especially – at once became objects of the most marked attention and conversation. We delighted in the performances of Maria and Nelly and at the close met with them, and I invited them to join us the following day in our carriage to the great St. Leger. I was overjoyed when they assented.

The next day we collected the Ternans at a quarter past one, and I instantly fell into a dreadful state and became seized by lunacy on seeing Nelly dressed in a pair of little lilac gloves and a winning little bonnet which, in conjunction with her golden hair, made quite a glory in the sunlight round her pretty head, and made me think of nothing in the world but she and me! Filled with this lunacy, we drove to the course where I bought a race-card and a wonderful, paralyzing coincidence befell me. I facetiously wrote down three names for the winners of the three chief races (never in my life having heard or thought of any of the horses, except the winner of the Derby, who proved to be nowhere) and if you can believe it without your hair standing on end, those three races were won, one after another, by those three horses!!! But it was noticeable that all around nobody had won, for there was nothing but grinding of teeth and blaspheming of ill luck, and the losses were enormous.

We bid farewell to the ladies and returned to our hotel, where I could not refrain from repeating to Wilkie, with an appearance of being lunatically seized, rhapsodies of delight over the appearance of Nelly. I saw nothing more of her before the weekend, when she then agreed to come with me into the country on the Sunday morning. I arranged an open carriage for the trip, met her and we went alone to the ruins of Roche Abbey near Maltby, some nine miles distant from Doncaster, and walked the area enhanced by Capability Brown. She told me she was due to stay in Doncaster with her mother and sisters until the end of the month, but after that meeting and speaking with her, I decided it best to leave Doncaster on my parting with Wilkie the following day, and return to Gad's Hill, so letting Nelly and I go our own wild way, and no harm come of it.

CHAPTER XLIV

Home Separation, "The Princess whom I Adore", and More Readings

I returned to Gad's Hill to find six men perpetually going up and down the well in the stable yard – I felt somebody would be killed – in the course of fitting a pump; which was quite like a railway terminus, it was so much iron and so big. I feared that by the time it was finished the cost of this water would be something absolutely frightful, but there was no going on without it, and I comforted myself (as well as I could) with the reflection that the spring might have lain much deeper, or might not have been at all. When the first glassful was later drunk at the surface, I calculated that it had cost me £200!

I continued to work on the Lazy Tour, confirming with Wills that it would be published in Household Words in five weekly parts during October. I received Wilkie's copy, which I corrected and introduced into Part 3, and was now at work on Part 4. I told Wills that I had no doubt of Wilkie being devoted to Household Words and doing great service; looked to complete the "Lazy Tour"; and then turn my mind to the Christmas Number of Household Words, with a working title of "The Perils of Certain English Prisoners". I wanted to do a good deal to it myself; Forster had tried to urge me to put a curb on matters and "not rush at hills", but I was the wrong man to say this to. I had now no relief but in action. I had become incapable of rest. I was quite confident I should rust, break and die, if I spared myself; much better to die doing. I knew that what I was in that way, nature made me first, and my way of life had of late, alas! confirmed. I had to accept the drawback – since it was one – with the powers I had, and knew I must hold upon the tenure prescribed to me. I asked Anne Brown (now Cornelius) to arrange for changes to be made in the dressing-room and bathroom at Tavistock House, and for the recess to Catherine's room closed in with a door.

At the beginning of October, Nelly, together with her mother and Maria, had returned to their small home at Park Cottage, St. Paul's Place, Islington (where Nelly slept in the basement), while sister Fanny alone continued to work, going out on tour. I sought to see Nelly when I was able, and on one occasion, whilst out walking with her on Hampstead Heath, we happened to meet Charley, also walking on the Heath. Nelly, I found, was without any commission in the theatre at that time, and so I wrote to John Buckstone, who was now managing the Haymarket Theatre, asking if he could assist her with some parts. He replied that he would be happy to engage her in a one-act farce entitled "My Son, Diana" that was soon to open at the Haymarket and I sent him my cordial thanks for obliging me very readily. I also told him:

> "I need hardly tell you that my interest in the young lady does not cease with the effecting of this arrangement, and that I shall always regard your taking care of her and remembering her, as an act of personal friendship to me. On the termination of her present engagement, I hope you will tell me, before you tell her, what you see for her 'looming in the future'."

I sent him a cheque for £50 and invited him for Sunday dinner at Gad's Hill.

I needed to work at the Household Words office and was residing at Tavistock House when, one night, on returning home after a hard day, I was very much put out by Catherine. On going to bed and lying there, I thought: "After all, it would be better to be up and doing something, than lying here." So, I performed my celebrated feat of getting out of bed at two in the morning, and walking to Gad's Hill – over 30 miles – through the dead night to breakfast. I had seldom seen anything so striking in the way in which the wonders of an equinoctial dawn presented themselves during that walk; I had never before happened to see night so completely at odds with morning – and which was which.

I pressed on with the Christmas Number, the whole number being one story, of which I did the greater part, with Wilkie providing one chapter (Chapter 2). I had planned it with great care in the hope of commemorating some of the foremost qualities of the English character that had been shown in India, without laying the scene there, or making any vulgar association with real events or calamities. I believed it was rather a remarkable production and would make a great noise. I could clearly see it would be dramatized everywhere, although I did not want it done upon the stage at all, because I never did want to see any composition there which was not intended for it. Nevertheless, it was adapted in the New Year of 1858 for three separate dramatized versions – at the Britannia, Strand and Victoria Theatres.

But my inner state of mind left me – as my art always found me and always left me – the most restless of created beings, and I had now an additional cause upon me that would not leave me. I wrote of it to my dear friend Mrs. Watson in the following terms:

"I am the modern embodiment of the old enchanters, whose familiars tore them to pieces. I weary for rest, and have no satisfaction but in fatigue. Realities and idealities are always comparing themselves together before me, and I don't like the realities except when they are unattainable – then, I like them of all things. I wish I had been born in the days of ogres and dragon-guarded castles. I wish an ogre with seven heads (and no particular evidence of brains in the whole lot of them) had taken the Princess whom I adore – you have no idea how intensely I love her! – to this stronghold on the top of a high series of mountains, and there tied her up by the hair. Nothing would suit me half so well this day, as climbing after her, sword in hand, and either winning her or be killed. – There's a state of mind for you, in 1857."

I read the Carol twice in December, once on the 15th at Coventry for Paxton, where the audience gathered up subscriptions sufficient to present me with a locally made Gold Repeater Watch; and again, on the 22nd, for the Chatham and Rochester Mechanics' Institute. I had also bound myself to read at Bristol on the 19th January and, in March, at Edinburgh; all other requests I turned down

Into 1858 at Tavistock House, an unusually violent rush of letters, imposing all sorts of other people's botherations on me, caused me yet further frustration and tearing at myself – my usual occupation now, at most times. Wild and misty ideas of a story (with a possible title of "One of These Days") were floating about somewhere (I didn't know where); I was looking after them, but nothing came of it, and I was met with further frustration from Catherine. In my life I was at such a crisis, worse than ever.

The 3rd March was Nelly's 19th birthday. She had been acting both at the Haymarket Theatre and also at the Lyceum, where two days later, I attended, as her sister Maria, who had also been acting there, was given a benefit performance on that evening. I had ordered a bracelet as a present for Nelly, but it was wrongly addressed and delivered to Catherine at Tavistock House, which caused much upset, so I took Catherine to meet the Ternan family at their little rented cottage in Islington.

In my state of energetic restlessness, I came back to the reading idea that I had had some time before, for whenever I read the Carol an effect was produced which seemed to belong to nothing else – and the number of people who wanted to come could not by any means be got in. I now had in my mind a project that, after reading for the benefit of the Great Ormond Street Children's Hospital on the 15th April (which I had agreed readily to do), I should announce by advertisement that I had resolved upon a course of readings both in town and country, and that those in London would take place at St. Martin's Hall on certain evenings – four or six Thursdays through May and into June – and then, in August, September, and October, in the Eastern Counties, the West of England, Lancashire, Yorkshire and Scotland, where I would read 35 to 40 times.

Because of Forster's previous strong objections to such an idea, I decided to consult with my publisher, and wrote privately and in the strictest confidence to Evans setting out this proposal. I felt a very large sum of money could be cleared, but told him the question I wanted his opinion on was: "Assuming these hopes to be well-grounded, would such a use of the personal (I may almost say affectionate) relations which subsist between me and the public, and make my standing with them very peculiar, at all affect my position with them as a writer?" Evans's reply encouraged me to continue, and I had The Chimes and The Haunted Man bound in similar way to the Cricket and the Carol for readings. Forster, however, continued to maintain his objections; persons represented to me that returns would be enormous, but Forster seemed to me to be extraordinarily irrational about it. I had a misgiving sometimes that his money must have gone into his head.

Meanwhile I confided to Wilkie:

"The Doncaster unhappiness remains so strong upon me that I can't write, and (waking) can't rest one minute. I have never known a moment's peace or content since the last night of the Frozen Deep. I do suppose that there never was a man so seized and rendered by one spirit. In this condition, though nothing can alter or soften it, I have a turning notion that the mere physical effort and change of the readings would be good, as another means of bearing it. – I suppose it is the penalty I pay for having written all these red-backed books upon my shelves –?"

I travelled with Wills to Edinburgh to read the Carol for the Philosophical Institution in the Music Hall on the 26th March. It was a tremendous success; but the crowd too enormous, and the excitement too great, to have the opportunity of asking any one's advice as to readings for my own benefit. But I told Forster, on returning to London, that my determination was now all but taken, and that I must do something or I should wear my heart away. I could see no better thing to do that was half so hopeful in itself, or half so well suited to my restless state.

I then, very opportunely, heard from Wills, whose account of the impression that my reading had given in Edinburgh even exceeded my hopes. Arthur Smith, who I proposed as my readings' manager, sent me a suggested list of readings and I had demurred to his idea of returning to several large places, but felt bound to send him Wills's unconscious confirmation of his opinion, and he was extremely glad to receive it. It had become so impossible to comply with the reading petitions that I had been continuously receiving, and when I did carry out a reading it attracted such very large audiences, that I had by now all but decided to read on for my own profit.

The reading at St. Martin's Hall for the hospital on the 15th April was a tremendous success; a profit of £165 was raised on that evening alone, and I was extremely pleased to help such a worthwhile charity. Arthur Smith was now hard at work organizing, for my benefit, three further readings at St. Martin's Hall, which were advertised for the evenings of the 29th April, the 6th and 24th May. For the 29th April, whereas they usually made some 250 stalls at St. Martin's Hall, Arthur Smith made 560, and they all went. 70 more were crammed in than were ever got into the hall before, but there was such further great demand, that all stalls applicants had to go over to another night, hundreds having to be turned away. As I stepped onto the platform, with a bud in my button-hole and gloves in hand, such a roar of cheering went up, that was again and again renewed, that it was said the sound of it might have been heard at Charing Cross! Once they had settled, I made a few opening remarks, which were again met with loud cheering, before I went on to read The Cricket on the Hearth to them.

The evening proved to be a complete success and all apprehensions were swept away. Likewise, with The Chimes on the 6th May, and then the Carol on the 24th. But at home I was beset with the many, many perplexities of thought that I had been involving with myself, particularly over my silence to Miss Coutts, and so I now wrote to her a lengthy letter on the subject of my situation. I also spoke with my son Charley, who subsequently sent me a letter saying that he loved me dearly but, in the event of a separation, he felt it his duty to stay with his mother.

CHAPTER XLV

The Separation

I now became aware that Catherine had sought out Miss Coutts to intervene with me on her behalf, but I made it clear to Miss Coutts that nothing on earth – no consideration, human or divine – could move me from the resolution I had taken. Forster had, in the meanwhile, been assisting me in settling the terms of the separation, whilst Mark Lemon had been assisting Catherine; but I then heard of wicked lies being perpetrated by Catherine's mother and her younger sister, Helen, concerning the separation and coupling it with the name of Nelly Ternan. As a result, on the 25th May, I wrote an open letter, addressed from Tavistock House to Arthur Smith, telling him that he had not only my full permission to show this, but begged him to do so to anyone who wished to do me right, or to anyone who may have been misled into doing me wrong:

"Mrs. Dickens and I have lived unhappily together for many years. Hardly anyone who has known us intimately can fail to have known that we are, in all respects of character and temperament, wonderfully unsuited to each other. I suppose that no two people, not vicious in themselves, ever were joined together, who had a greater difficulty in understanding one another, or who had less in common. An attached woman servant (more friend to both of us than a servant), who lived with us sixteen years, and is now married, and who was, and still is, in Mrs. Dickens's confidence and in mine, who had the closest familiar experience of this unhappiness, in London, in the country, in France, in Italy, wherever we have been, year after year, month after month, week after week, day after day, will bear testimony to this.

Nothing has, on many occasions, stood between us and a separation but Mrs. Dickens's sister, Georgina Hogarth. From the age of fifteen, she has devoted herself to our home and our children. She has been their playmate, nurse, instructress, friend, protectress, adviser and companion. In the manly consideration towards Mrs. Dickens which I owe towards my wife, I will merely remark of her that the peculiarity of her character has thrown all the children on someone else. I do not know – I cannot by any stretch of fancy imagine – what would have become of them but for this aunt, who has grown up with them, to whom they are devoted, and who has sacrificed the best part of her youth and life to them.

She has remonstrated, reasoned, suffered and toiled, again and again to prevent a separation between Mrs. Dickens and me. Mrs. Dickens has often expressed to her her sense of her affectionate care and devotion in her home – never more strongly than within the last twelve months.

For some years past Mrs. Dickens has been in the habit of representing to me that it would be better for her to go away and live apart; that her always increasing estrangement made a mental disorder under which she sometimes labours – more, that she felt herself unfit for the life she had to lead as my wife and that she would be better far away. I have uniformly replied that we must bear our misfortune, and fight the fight out to the end; that the children were the first consideration, and that I feared they must bind us together "in appearance."

At length, within these three weeks, it was suggested to me by Forster that even for their sakes, it would surely be better to reconstruct and rearrange their unhappy home. I empowered him to treat with Mrs. Dickens, as a friend of both of us for one and twenty years. Mrs. Dickens wished to add on her part, Mark Lemon, and did so. On Saturday last Lemon wrote to Forster that Mrs. Dickens "gratefully and thankfully accepted" the terms I proposed to her.

Of the pecuniary part of them, I will only say that I believe they are as generous as if Mrs. Dickens were a lady of distinction, and I a man of fortune. The remaining parts of them are easily described – my eldest boy to live with Mrs. Dickens and take care of her; my eldest girl to keep my house; both girls and all my children but the eldest one, to live with me, in the continued companionship of their aunt Georgina, for whom they have all the tenderest affection that I have ever seen among young people, and who has a higher claim (as

I have often declared for many years) upon my affection, respect and gratitude than anybody in the world.

I hope that no one who may become acquainted with what I write here, can possibly be so cruel and unjust, as to put any misconstruction on our separation, so far. My elder children all understand it perfectly, and all accept it as inevitable. There is not a shadow of doubt of concealment among us – my eldest son and I are one, as to it all.

Two wicked persons who should have spoken very differently of me, in consideration of earned respect and gratitude, have (as I am told, and indeed to my personal knowledge) coupled with this separation the name of a young lady for whom I have the greatest attachment and regard. I will not repeat her name – I honour it too much. Upon my soul and honour, there is not on this earth a more virtuous and spotless creature than this young lady. I know her to be innocent and pure, and as good as my own dear daughters. Further, I am sure quite that Mrs. Dickens, having received this assurance from me, must now believe it, in the respect I know her to have for me, and in the perfect confidence I know her, in her better moments to repose in my truthfulness.

On this head, again, there is not a shadow of doubt or concealment between my children and me. All is open and plain among us, as though we were brothers and sisters. They are perfectly certain that I would not deceive them, and the confidence among us is without a fear.

C.D."

I sent Nelly a small gift but, in the meanwhile, Forster had been acting strenuously with my solicitor, Frederic Ouvry, to affect the settlement. Lemon had written that Catherine had accepted the proposal of "£400 a year and a brougham" and had named Messrs. Smith, Wright and Shepherd of 15, Golden Square as her lawyers. However, I then heard that the Hogarth family were now also focusing their attention and wrath upon Georgy and helping to spread malicious rumours that she was my mistress, and even with child by me. My fury at hearing these disgusting and horrible slanders knew no bounds, and I refused to sign any deed of settlement with Catherine until members of the Hogarth family responsible for this state of affairs did themselves sign a statement of repudiation. I instructed Ouvry to take the matter up and to write to Mr. Smith at Golden Square accordingly. He did so, and a statement of repudiation was signed by Mrs. Hogarth and her daughter Helen, but nothing would ever now reconcile me to those two signatories.

With my agreement and that of the solicitors on both sides (as well as Forster), it was finally agreed that the settlement for Catherine should be £600 a year and a place to live with Charley – that place being later agreed as 70, Gloucester Crescent, Regent's Park. Mr. Smith had the Deed of Settlement drawn up by Counsel and sent to Catherine in Brighton, where she was staying for the time with her mother, for signature. She signed it, and in due course, on the 10th June, I did likewise. During these negotiations I had heard from Albert Smith that Mrs. Hogarth had actually repeated the smashing slanders to him in a concert room, but I had wanted Ouvry to expressly detach Catherine immediately from these wrong-doings. I did not in the least suspect her of them, and wished her to know that.

Nevertheless, I continued to hear such thronging multitudes of wonderful and inexplicable lies about myself and the reason for the separation; I knew myself, however, that this separation was the natural end of a course of years. It would have been a poor thing to have been driven mad myself, or to drive Catherine mad; and one or both of the two results must have happened, if we had gone on living together. I was sure we only wanted to forgive and forget, and live at peace; that it was an unhappy day for both, when two such contrasted people came together – but that we quietly accepted all that, and did not blame the day, and only sought to make the best of it.

I expected, of course, the misconstruction of knaves and fools, and that indeed persisted, particularly in America. I arranged to see Forster to discuss the situation, and also consulted with Ouvry, but it was perfectly clear to me that Forster's American idea of asking some distinguished person there to deny rumours on my behalf was altogether untenable. In my mind it was not feasible that I should write to any distinguished man in America, asking him to do for me what I had not done for myself here. It was absurd – and it was just because no public step could possibly be taken for my good, anywhere, until I had taken one here myself, that I felt I must move, somehow.

After consideration, I felt I must now publish a Personal Statement in the newspapers and in Household Words setting an end to the rumours. Forster and Ouvry advised strongly against such publication, and I offered to suppress it if, upon reference to the opinion of the distinguished editor of The Times (John Delane), that opinion should prove to be in agreement with theirs. But it was not, and accordingly I decided to take my course. I drafted the statement and, in advance of publication, sent Wills with it to Brighton. Catherine raised no objection, but wished to send it to her solicitor, Smith, who attempted to have its publication postponed. But neither I nor The Times was for postponement, and on the 7th June it was published in that newspaper, followed, on Saturday 12th June, by being prominent on the front page of Household Words. I had written it in the clearest terms.

PERSONAL

Three and twenty years have passed since I entered on my present relations with the Public. They began when I was so young, that I find them to have existed for nearly a quarter of a century.

Through all that time I have tried to be as faithful to the Public, as they have been to me. It was my duty never to trifle with them, or deceive them, or presume upon their favour, or do anything with it but work hard to justify it. I have always endeavoured to discharge that duty.

My conspicuous position has often made me the subject of fabulous stories and unaccountable statements. Occasionally, such things have chafed me, or even wounded me; but I have always accepted them as the shadows inseparable from the light of my notoriety and success. I have never obtruded any such personal uneasiness of mine, upon the generous aggregate of my audience.

For the first time in my life, and I believe for the last, I now deviate from the principle I have so long observed, by presenting myself in my own Journal in my own private character, and entreating all my brethren (as they deem that they have reason to think well of me, and to know that I am a man who has ever been unaffectedly true to our common calling), to lend their aid to the dissemination of my present words.

Some domestic trouble of mine, of long-standing, on which I will make no further remark than that it claims to be respected, as being of a sacredly private nature, has lately been brought to an arrangement, which involves no anger or ill-will of any kind, and the whole origin, progress, and surrounding circumstances of which have been, throughout, within the knowledge of my children. It is amicably composed, and its details have now but to be forgotten by those concerned in it.

By some means, arising out of wickedness, or out of folly, or out of inconceivable wild chance, or out of all three, this trouble has been made the occasion of misrepresentations, most grossly false, most monstrous, and most cruel – involving, not only me, but innocent persons dear to my heart, and innocent persons of whom I have no knowledge, if, indeed, they have any existence – and so widely spread, that I doubt if one reader in a thousand will peruse these lines, by whom some touch of the breath of these slanders will not have passed, like an unwholesome air.

Those who know me and my nature, need no assurance under my hand that such calumnies are as irreconcilable with me, as they are, in their frantic incoherence, with one another. But, there is a great multitude who know me through my writings, and who do not know me otherwise; and I cannot bear that one of them should be left in doubt, or hazard of doubt, through my poorly shrinking from taking the unusual means to which I now resort, of circulating the Truth.

I most solemnly declare, then – and this I do, both in my own name and in my wife's name – that all the lately whispered rumours touching the trouble at which I have glanced, are abominably false. And that whosoever repeats one of them after this denial, will lie as wilfully and as foully as it is possible for any false witness to lie, before Heaven and earth.

CHARLES DICKENS.

CHAPTER XLVI

The Reading Tour

While the terms of the settlement were being arranged, I had sought as best as I could, leaving the misery and unhappiness at home, to proceed onward with my life, feeling heartedly that I should wear and toss my storm away. But derogatory reports kept persisting, and I had to authorize Thackeray to contradict the rumours that had arisen from a comment he had made outside the Garrick Club that I had separated from Catherine on account of an intrigue with an actress; and as Lemon and Bradbury and Evans had deliberately failed to print my Personal Statement in the Punch magazine, I felt unable to forgive them for this. Arthur Smith had arranged additional readings at St. Martin's Hall on the 13th May (the Carol) and the 27th May (The Chimes) due to overwhelming demand for tickets, and was now beginning to assemble a reading tour for me to various towns in England, Ireland and Scotland.

On the 10th June at St. Martin's Hall I decided to read from something other than my Christmas books, choosing "The Life and Death of Little Dombey". It produced amazing scenes of weeping and cheering, but it frightened Arthur Smith, and the people cried so on going out, that he thought "it wouldn't do" to put it up again!

I continued to read each Thursday (as well as other days) in London, at St. Martin's Hall, but spent much time at Gad's Hill, in the midst of blessed woods and fields, seeking to forget things and to calm down before I went on my reading tour. The woods and fields did me a world of good and I felt quite myself again, but I had to make it clear to the children how matters had to proceed in the future. I positively forbade the children ever to utter one word to their grandmother, or to Helen Hogarth (what a little serpent that daughter of poor honest good Hogarth was); and in the light of the attitude exhibited by Lemon and Bradbury and Evans, I positively forbade the children ever to see Lemon, or ever be taken to Mr. Evans's house.

As I prepared for my reading tour, I had a great many offers of hospitality from those in places I was to visit, but, to them all, whilst thanking them very heartily for their great courtesy, I told each one that I had been obliged to resolve that I would deny myself all such pleasures during my tour. I knew that it would be so very fatiguing that I was quite sure I could intermingle no social enjoyments with its occupations, and I had therefore (putting a virtuous constraint upon myself with a very bad grace), doggedly made up my mind to confine myself to inns. Even when I was to be in Scotland among many old friends, I resolved to stick to this heroic resolution. Meanwhile, Nelly had left to join her company (Charles Kean's Princess's Theatre Company), who were performing in Manchester for a six-week summer season.

I set off from London for my first reading at Clifton on the 2nd August, and then on to Exeter. Arthur Smith had booked me into the best hotels and noble nights resulted, with numbers having to be turned away. Arthur was like something between a Home Secretary and a furniture-dealer in Rathbone Place, either always corresponding in the genteelest manner, or dragging rout-seats about with the greatest violence and without his coat! Even he, though, could not squeeze more than £75 into the room at Exeter and, despite a prodigious cram, we had to turn away no end of people.

The next night in Plymouth was not so bright; we had a fair house but not at all a great one. They didn't quite understand beforehand what it was, I think, and expected a man to be sitting down in some corner, droning away like a mild bagpipe. The room (at St. George's Hall) was very handsome, but it was at Stonehouse on the top of a windy and muddy hill leading (literally) to nowhere and some distance from Plymouth. I read two days there, the next day on two occasions. All the notables came in the morning (3 p.m.) to Little Dombey, for which we let 130 stalls (which local admiration of local greatness considered very large) and at night, when I read "Mrs. Gamp" and "The Boots at the Holly-Tree Inn", the company was enormous and there was a very great scene, with a shout all through. The local magnate was heard to say: "Now they know what it is, Mr. Dickens might stay a month and always have a cram"!

I read again at Clifton, where a torrent of five hundred shillings bore Arthur Smith away, pounded him against the wall, flowed on to the seats over his body, scratched him and damaged his best dress suit – all to his unspeakable joy! We took nearly £400 during the week.

I was then able to return to London to attend to business at the Household Words office, and for two days of peace and quiet at Gad's Hill, where Charley visited, before I set off again. The first week had been an immense success and, while I missed the thoughtfulness of my quiet room and my own desk and looked forward to resuming it, I found it a great sensation to have a large audience in one's hand. But perhaps it was best for me not to have my own room just now as I sought to wear and toss my storm away – or as much of it as would ever calm down while the water rolled – in this restless manner.

On the 10th August I set off for Worcester, then Wolverhampton, Shrewsbury and Chester, before returning to Gad's Hill. There I took to an exceedingly bad cold when I was playing among my children; I mustard-poulticed and barley-watered myself tremendously and hoped to stagger through at Liverpool, my next venue. I travelled up on the 18th August to stay in the Adelphi Hotel, and read at the Philharmonic Hall. An audience of 2,300 people greeted me there on the first night and, besides the tickets sold, more than £200 was taken at the doors. They turned away hundreds, sold all the books, rolled on the ground of my room knee-deep in cheques, and made a perfect pantomime of the whole thing. I read three nights, the Carol on the 18th, Little Dombey on the 19th, and The Poor Traveller, Boots at the Holly-Tree Inn, and Mrs. Gamp on the 20th. We were reduced sometimes to a ludicrous state of distress by the quantity of silver we had to carry about, Arthur always being accompanied by an immense black leather-bag full. I did a fourth reading at 3 p.m. on Saturday the 21st, and, in all, the audiences in Liverpool amounted to about 6,300 people.

I was now to travel to Ireland for the first time in my life, with many readings planned for Dublin, Belfast, Cork and Limerick. Arriving in Dublin, I was surprised to find it very much larger than I had supposed; and its by-parts, though bad enough, were certainly very much cleaner than the old town of Edinburgh. I walked about it in all directions for six or eight hours until tired, and then toured in a jaunting-car.

While in Dublin I received another letter from Miss Coutts, once again referring to the separation. She had seen Catherine and some of the children in her drawing room and spoke of this, but I made it clear in my reply that my resolve to part from Catherine had not changed and that I would not enter on the wretched subject upon false pretences. I told Miss Coutts that since I had spoken to her before, I had found that Catherine had caused me unspeakable agony of mind, and that the little play acted in her drawing room with the children was not the truth – and the less the children played it, the better for themselves, because they too knew it was not the truth. I had to put before her what I knew to be true, and what nothing would induce me to affect to doubt – that Catherine did not, and never did, care for the children, and the children did not, and never did, care for her. And as to her "simplicity" in speaking of me and my doings, in conjunction with the wickedest people – whom I had loaded with benefits in the past – I wanted now to communicate with her no more, wanted to forgive her and forget her, and speak of it no more. I also resolved in my mind that the support Miss Coutts was giving to Catherine now caused me to estrange myself from her and the Home at Shepherd's Bush, while I turned my life into another direction.

We had good houses for the first two nights in the Dublin Rotunda, that is to say a great rush for shillings and good half-crowns, though the stalls were comparatively few. The audience were highly excitable on the 24th, but the next night certainly did not comprehend, internally and intellectually, The Chimes as a London audience did. For Little Domby however, we had an immense stall let, more than 200, with people fighting in the agent's shop to take more. In consequence there was excessive crowding in the place with difficulty of shaking people into their seats and, although as a result I had some little difficulty to work them up, the effect became unmistakable and profound. The crying was universal, and they were extraordinarily affected.

On the 27th August we travelled on to Belfast, the whole railway ride from Dublin to Belfast being through a very picturesque and various country, all particularly neat and orderly, and the houses (outside at all events) all brightly whitewashed and remarkably clean, with charming gardens, prettily kept with bright flowers. We had three tremendous houses and the same scenes were repeated as in Dublin; we turned away half the town, and I found the audience on the last night more competent to appreciate the points of the narrative than elsewhere, and the personal affection for me something overwhelming. Indeed, every night since I had been in Ireland, the ladies beguiled Thompson out of the bouquet I had in my coat, and when in Belfast reading Little Dombey and had showered the leaves from my red geranium, the ladies I am told mounted the platform after I was gone and picked them all up as keepsakes!

People greeted me everywhere with respect and affection and wished to shake my hand in the street. I walked about Belfast and found it a fine place, surrounded by lofty hills; the streets were very wide and the place appeared very prosperous. I took a walk by the sea to Carrickfergus, some ten miles to the North, which was greatly memorable, as well as engaging in a sixteen-mile ride. Before leaving Belfast, Arthur and I each ordered a trim, sparkling, slap-up Irish jaunting car to be made up for us. It was the oddest carriage in the world, and you were always falling off, but it was gay and bright in the highest degree – wonderfully Neapolitan, and I flattered myself that I should astonish the Kentish people with mine!

At Cork, in the Athenaeum, we again proposed the three readings; once again, they were an immense success. Upwards of 1,000 stalls were let for these readings, and a great many people were turned away too, particularly on the last night. From Cork we travelled north to Limerick, where I read twice in the Theatre Royal. Limerick was the oddest place, and Arthur said that when he opened the doors on the first night, there was a rush of – three ducks! We only took £40 that night, although they seemed to think that amazing. And in the month of August my success had been something wonderful; I had made the profit of a thousand guineas – this after not only paying our expenses back to London, but also halfway to Huddersfield, which was our next reading engagement. I was greatly pleased.

CHAPTER XLVII

The Violated Letter, and continuation of the Reading Tour

We travelled, with a pretty hard journey, back to London, and I went to Gad's Hill for a rest of forty-eight hours. The work of the readings had been very hard – sometimes almost overpowering – but I felt none the worse for it, quite fresh and as strong and well as if I had been doing nothing. But upon arrival at Gad's Hill I was exceedingly pained to find a communication from Ouvry, informing me that the letter I had written for Arthur Smith on the 25th May as a private and personal communication, had now been violated. Arthur had given a copy of it to the London correspondent of the New York Tribune, who had then published it in full on the 16th August, to be followed by it being reprinted in all manner of English and American newspapers thereafter. This was in violation of my intention that it should remain as a private correspondence and was never meant to appear in print, as I supposed to have been quite manifest from its own nature and terms. The letter had been painfully necessary at the time as a private repudiation of monstrous scandals, and I now wished Ouvry to inform Catherine's solicitor that I was no consenting party to this publication; that it could not possibly be more offensive to anyone in the world than it was to me; and that it shocked and distressed me very much.

I spent a few hours in town on Tuesday 7th September in the Household Words office before travelling to Yorkshire the following day for a series of eleven readings at a variety of locations in that county. I began at Huddersfield, then Wakefield, but I was still dwelling on the violated letter and was exquisitely distressed, utterly desolate and lost, and could not bear it. It was no comfort for me to know that any man who wanted to sell anything in print, had but to anatomize my finest nerves, and he was sure to do it; and it was no comfort for me to know (as of course the dissectors did) that when I spoke in my own person it was not for myself but for the innocent and good, on whom I had unwittingly brought the foulest lies.

We travelled on to York, where a lady, whose face I had never seen, stopped me in the street as I walked about, and said to me: "Mr. Dickens, will you let me touch the hand that has filled my house with many friends." The sky brightened before me once more, and that evening I read the Carol in the Festival Concert Room to a large and most magnificent audience – and we might have filled the place for a week!

We journeyed on to Harrogate, Scarborough and then Hull, where the people were not generally considered excitable, even on their own showing, but towards me they were so enthusiastic that we were obliged to promise to go back there again for two further readings. Arthur had his shirt front and waistcoat torn off, and was perfectly enraptured in consequence! And our men were so knocked about that he even gave them five shillings apiece on the spot!!

We moved on to Leeds, where we were again obliged to promise to return, then Halifax, where I read the Carol in the Odd Fellows' Hall. It was too small for us, and, I think, as horrible a place as I ever saw, but I never saw such an audience. They were really worth reading to for nothing – though I didn't do exactly that! Next, in Sheffield, we found the run on tickets was so immense that Arthur was obliged to get great bills out, signifying that no more could be sold. Again, we had to promise to return. My voice was now feeling the strain, and I sent a message back to Georgy to arrange for a fresh supply of "Voice Jujubes" and also of the "Astringent Lozenges" I was using.

Then, on arriving at Manchester, I heard that 700 stalls had been taken at the Free Trade Hall, and when I went there that night, I found 2,500 people had paid, and more were being turned away at every door! The welcome they gave me was astounding, in its affectionate recognition of the late trouble with the printing of the violated letter, and it fairly for once unmanned me. I never saw such a sight or heard such a sound! When they had thoroughly done it, they settled down to enjoy themselves, and did so to the last minute. At the end, I announced that it had been arranged that I should return for two further readings in October – which was met again with loud cheering.

After a short return to London, I read in Darlington at the Central Hall on the 21st September, a mouldy old assembly room without a lamp abutting on the street, so that I passed it a dozen times looking for it when I went down to read. But the place covered itself with glory; all sorts of people came in from outlying places and the town was drunk on the Carol far into the night. The next night I read the Carol again, now in the new Town Hall in Durham, and then walked the 13 miles from Durham to Sunderland, where I read the Carol at the Theatre Royal. It was a very beautiful new theatre and looked a fine house, but it was not fine enough to pay well and we reaped very little profit there.

The next morning I walked the 12 miles to Newcastle, and that night read the Carol and the following day The Poor Traveller, Boots and Mrs. Gamp to large and brilliant audiences in the Town Hall. Mamie and Katey arrived and, though I had arranged for their remaining quiet, they persisted in going to the room to hear the reading. They proposed to go on with me to Scotland and I hoped they would see the coast piece of railway between Berwick and Edinburgh to great advantage, for that kind of pleasure was really almost the only one they were likely to have on their present trip.

On Sunday 26th September we all travelled to Berwick, slept that night there, before travelling on to Edinburgh, where I was to give readings over four days. We turned away hundreds upon hundreds of people; and the last night, for the Carol, in spite of advertisements in the morning that the tickets were gone, the people had to be got in through such a crowd as rendered it a work of the utmost difficulty to keep an alley into the room. They were seated about me on the platform, put into the doorway of the waiting-room, squeezed into every conceivable place; I was completely taken by storm – and my profit in September alone became £900.

Mamie and Katey were infinitely pleased and interested with Edinburgh itself, and also Hawthornden Castle near Roslin where I took them, and we laughed all day. But for me travelling, dining, reading and everything else now just came crowding together into this strange life of mine. We had the strangest journey to Dundee – bits of sea and bits of railroad alternatively, which carried my mind back to travelling in America. Dundee I found an odd place, but the room where I read for two nights was immense, looking like something between the Crystal Palace and Westminster Hall. I could not imagine who wanted it in this place and, as it had never been tried yet for speaking in, I hoped it would succeed. I understood later, however, that some in the back seats left in the interval, being unable to hear.

At Aberdeen we were crammed to the street, twice in one day (4th October). At Perth the next day, where I thought when I arrived there literally could be nobody to come, the gentlefolk came posting in from thirty miles round and the whole town came besides, to hear the Carol and fill the immense room at the City Hall. They were as full of perception, fire and enthusiasm as any people I had seen.

We moved on to Glasgow and there I read three evenings to crowded and very brilliant audiences, and then once at 3 p.m. on Saturday 9th October, where I read Little Dombey. At the end, in the cold light of day, the audience all got up, after a short pause, gentle and simple, and thundered and waved their hats with such astonishing heartiness and fondness that, for the first time in all my public career, they took me completely off my legs, and I saw the whole 1,800 of them reel to one side as if a shock from without had shaken the whole hall.

Mamie and Katey had enjoyed themselves immensely, and their trip with me had been a great success. Notwithstanding which, I must confess to you that I was very anxious to get to the end of my readings, and to be at home again, and able to sit down and think in my own study. But the fatigue, though sometimes very great indeed, hardly told on me at all. And although our people, from Arthur downwards, had given in more or less at times, I had never been in the least unequal to the work, though sometimes sufficiently disinclined for it. As to the effect of it, of course I didn't go on doing the thing so often without carefully observing myself and the people too in every little thing, and without, in consequence, greatly improving it.

But, as to the truth of the readings, I cannot tell you what the demonstrations of personal regard and respect were. How the densest and most uncomfortably packed crowd would be hushed in an instant when I showed my face. How the youth of colleges, and the old men of business in the towns, seemed equally unable to get near enough to me when they cheered me away at night. How common people and gentlefolk would stop me in the street to speak. And if you saw the mothers, and fathers, and sisters, and brothers in mourning, who invariably came to Little Dombey, and if you studied the wonderful expression of comfort and reliance with which they hung about me, as if I had been with them, all kindness and delicacy, at their own little death-bed, you would think of it as one of the strangest things in the world.

CHAPTER XLVIII

Further Readings, Malicious Rumour,
and a Move for the Ternans

I returned to London and, five days later, read in Bradford, before reading again in Liverpool and then Manchester. But upon arrival at Manchester I received an amazing letter from a Mr. MacPhail, an Assistant Inspector of the Poor in Glasgow, whom I had met while in Glasgow. His letter placed me in a very distressing position. He told me that he had been accosted in the street by Mr. Colin Rae Brown, manager of the Glasgow Daily Bulletin – a penny newspaper with the greatest daily circulation in Glasgow – who had expressed, in the presence of another gentleman of the press, that he was newly from London, had heard there all about me and that I was the outcry in London. He further enquired of MacPhail if he knew that my sister-in-law, Georgy, had had three children by me. MacPhail had told him shortly that he knew no such thing, was deeply concerned at the malignant spirit in which this was uttered, and had accordingly written to me to tell me of the events, and to give me the name of Mr. Rae Brown "confidentially."

The Rae Brown lie was too monstrous and intolerable to be borne, and I wrote back to MacPhail immediately that I feared it was impossible that I could, in any decent spirit of respect for myself or any other human being, accept his communication as confidential, for a slander, so infamous and so wanton and inconceivably baseless, had to be positively stopped short. I thanked MacPhail very much for making this thing known to me, but I told him I could not possibly receive it in confidence because I could get no prospect of redress for so unspeakable a wrong, but through bringing this Mr. Rae Brown to answer in a Court of Justice for his abominable words.

I immediately notified Arthur Smith of these events and forthwith dispatched him to London with a draft letter for communication with my solicitors instantly on the subject. They straightway wrote to Rae Brown about this gross and scandalous slander which, if it had the slightest foundation in fact, would render me an outcast from society. I read that night in Manchester under these distressing circumstances, before travelling to London myself to see my solicitors, and then making my way to Birmingham, where I read on three successive nights at the Music Hall. I then received a personal letter from Rae Brown, emphatically denying the slander, followed by a letter from his solicitor saying that he would meet any court action brought against him. I decided to take Counsel's Opinion, now enduring in the thought that Rae Brown or anyone else might be whispering about this monstrous charge with impunity.

Meanwhile I had to continue on with my readings. At Nottingham on the 21st October I read the Carol, on a night that was almost, if not quite, the most amazing we had had, followed in Derby by a room again filled to overflowing. I returned to Manchester on the 23rd, and at the end, such was their enthusiasm, that I was recalled to the platform for further acclamation. But I was now feeling in a very poor condition; I had a bad cold all over me, pains in my back and limbs, and a very sensitive and uncomfortable sore throat.

Counsel's Opinion revealed that a Writ for Slander would not be of any avail in the English Courts in the circumstances I found myself in, and my only remedy might be that I would have to sue in Scotland under Scottish law. I was also cautioned that any trial that resulted might turn on the central question of credibility between MacPhail and Rae Brown. I was so incensed that I still wished to proceed against Rae Brown and instructed Ouvry to find the best Counsel to undertake the matter in Glasgow. I then gave up my second reading in York (planned for the 25th October) and instead returned to London to have a Sunday conference with Ouvry about the whole Rae Brown affair.

Fanny Ternan went to study in Italy, and I strongly advised her mother to move the rest of the family from Park Cottage in Islington as I thought it an unwholesome place. Maria was now playing burlesques at the Strand Theatre and Nelly had returned from Manchester and was playing parts at the Haymarket Theatre, so I assisted them in locating to a better residence at 31, Berners Street, off Oxford Street, and Maria and Nelly moved there together. When in London I would often visit them, but they then told me they had experienced unwarrantable conduct in a policeman. It appeared they had been kept under observation as they made their way to and from their theatres, Maria in particular being a good deal looked after, whereupon a policeman had stopped her and subjected her to questions of the most insulting and derogatory manner. As I had to continue my reading tour with the planned return to Hull, I immediately wrote to Wills – who knew both the young ladies and could answer for them – asking him to call and see them at 31, Berners Street, get the particulars, and once he knew the facts for himself, go to Scotland Yard. Wills later told me of his visit to Scotland Yard, and Maria and Nelly informed me that thereafter the police attention to their lives ceased.

It was also at this time that I heard from T.J. Thompson about my brother Frederick, making mention in his letter of "that astonishing Dorking business." I did not know what he meant, as I was ignorant of the details of the relations between Frederick and his wife Anna. But I now understood that Anna was about to bring a case for judicial separation from Frederick on account of his alleged adultery with a woman at Dorking. Thompson told me of his proposals to Frederick to mediate between the two of them, and I wished to Heaven that Frederick would accept the offer. I later saw Frederick, told him I knew of the Dorking circumstance, and also knew that he had refused to make his wife any allowance. I advised him in the strongest manner, but I had not the faintest reason to suppose that he attached a feather's weight to anything I said.

I gave readings in Hull, Leeds and Sheffield before, after a short rest in London, Leamington, Wolverhampton and Leicester. I then cancelled the next two readings planned for Oxford, as I wished to return to London to confer urgently with Forster and Wills over important issues that had arisen in my mind relating to dealings with Bradbury and Evans, and whether I was able to make a change with Household Words.

CHAPTER XLIX

Household Words, the End of the Reading Tour, and a Portrait

I needed to speak to Forster and Wills about the most important question of all, namely whether I, being the largest proprietor in Household Words, could change the printer and publisher if I chose? On this the whole question of the extent of our power and the manner of its exercise depended. There was no sub-agreement whatever as to printing and publishing, and I asked Wills if he would see Ouvry on this vital question. Then, on seeing Forster and discussing the matter with him, I drafted a notice for Wills to deliver to Bradbury and Evans, requesting them, in compliance with the provisions of the deed of partnership, to convene a special meeting of the partners, to be held within seven days. This was for the consideration of a resolution I proposed that the present partnership be dissolved by discontinuance on the completion of the nineteenth volume scheduled for the following May. I also gave Forster a power of attorney to act for me at that meeting, for it was clear to my mind that, in the light of their contrary actions over my separation from Catherine, no discussion could now take place between me and Bradbury and Evans.

I was relieved that the conclusion of my readings was now so close and that I should soon be at home in my own room again. I was to do two readings in Southampton, two in my native place of Portsmouth and, to finish, three in Brighton. The halls were crowded, with hundreds having to be turned away, and I dined with Wilkie in Brighton to celebrate the ending. I had now every conceivable reason to regard Arthur Smith as one of my most trusty friends, and could not easily imagine myself treading the same road again without him. Not long after, however, I heard that he had been taken severely ill in Paris with diphtheria and scarlet fever and was in an alarming state. I feared that the work of our tour had been a little too hard for him, and immediately wrote to him telling him how grieved I was and sending him my loving word.

Forster (with my power of attorney) and Wills attended the special meeting with Bradbury and Evans on the 15th November and proposed and seconded that, as I wished, the present partnership in Household Words be dissolved. They both voted in favour of this resolution, but Messrs. Bradbury and Evans declined to vote, believing that the resolution was contrary to the condition of partnership and therefore illegal. Shortly thereafter, however, Bradbury and Evans wrote to Forster stating that they had no wish to protract their connection with me, and accordingly were quite prepared to entertain a proposal for the purchase of their share and all works in which they were jointly interested with me, including Household Words. Forster considered the best answer now was to say no more and proceed to carry out the terms of the resolution. I was in agreement and left him to arrange so to do.

Meanwhile, Ouvry persuaded me that the difficulties of pursuing Rae Brown for slander in Scotland were too great, and I agreed now to take the matter no further at law. I had a great need to proceed on with the Household Words Christmas Number, to be done in parts under the collective title of "A House To Let"; Wilkie was writing some of those parts, Mrs. Gaskell and others, as well as myself, the further parts, and I arranged with Wilkie to pass the whole day at the Household Words office on the 29th November to connect up the various portions and get it finally together. We did so, and managed to have it published on the 7th December.

My brother Frederick called on me again at Tavistock House, and said that after consideration, he would now make any reasonable terms with his wife. I wrote a note to Thompson telling him of this but, to my amazement and unspeakable irritation, Frederick then sought to avoid me, communicated to me that he was not prepared to engage in any mediation and, as a result, embarked on lengthy and bitter court proceedings with his wife.

Arthur Smith happily recovered, and was able to return to attend to the readings I gave over the Christmas period in London at St. Martin's Hall – all to overflowing audiences. I also finished a little paper for Household Words entitled "New Year's Day", incorporating in it reminiscences of my own from my childhood. Meanwhile, through Forster, I finally offered Bradbury and Evans the sum of £1,000 for their share in the copyright of Household Words, but they rejected this offer, and Evans proposed to take a case in Chancery against me.

It was at this time that Forster told me that he wished to commission a portrait of myself, to be carried out by that most accomplished of artists, William Powell Frith. Frith notified me that he wished to paint me in my study but, as a preliminary, to have my photograph taken by Herbert Watkins, to which I agreed; shortly after I attended with Frith at Watkins's studio at 34, Parliament Street for the photographs to be taken, with my study table and chair also brought there. Later, in January 1859, I sat for Frith in his studio, and then he came to Tavistock House to a corner of my study to finish the layout design.

CHAPTER L

A House for Nelly, Further Readings, All the Year Round,
and A Tale of Two Cities

I had begun contemplating what I might do with Tavistock House further to the separation and my purchase of Gad's Hill Place. There were thirty-seven more years on the tenancy and I spoke to Wills about placing it in good hands for letting, as well as about the Ternans possibly taking it due to their unsatisfactory experiences at 31, Berners Street. An inventory was drawn up, but Forster heard of the proposal to let the Ternans into occupation and was very strongly against it – as was Wills. I also found that Mamie and Katey were so averse to a long-term letting that I withdrew from that proposal, even if another party should make it, and asked that the agent take the house on his books to let from and after the next June inclusive, for any term not less than 6 months, or more than 12. Meanwhile I searched with the Ternans for alternative accommodation and, after selling £1,500 of a fund held by Coutts Bank in my name, purchased for them an eighty-four year lease at 2, Houghton Place, Ampthill Square, an elegant four-storied terraced house, together with a basement, on the Duke of Bedford's estate, near Mornington Crescent. Fanny and Maria took the lease in their names, whilst I assisted with payments for the ground rent and other expenses, until Nelly became 21 on the 3rd March 1860, when I stipulated that the lease would then be made over to her, and her mother take over the payment of the ground rent – although I would continue to assist them financially thereafter. Mrs. Ternan joined the two girls at the property when she returned from settling Fanny in Florence.

I gave further readings in London to a greater furore than there ever had been, hundreds being turned away unable to get in. I was also approached with a proposal that I should now give a series of public readings in America and discussed this with Arthur, setting out my concerns and the exact nature of the business-inducement I needed to have for so long a voyage, such great fatigue, and such an absence from England. I vowed I would never go, unless a small fortune be first paid down in money on this side of the Atlantic, and having stated the figure of such payment, I expected to hear no more of it, and assuredly resolved to go for no less.

I was anxious now to decide as to how I should proceed with a new publication after the closure of Household Words. I discussed this at great length with Forster, Wills and Wilkie, including proposals for a new name for this venture. I ran through a great many, as to my mind it was the very first thing to settle and I could make no way until I had got a name; and my observation was that the same odd feeling affected everybody else. I considered no less than sixteen names, all of which I rejected, but kept returning to some quote or other from Shakespeare, before suddenly hitting on a quotation and name that in the place where our present Household Words quotation stood, there should instead be:

"The story of our lives, from year to year" – Shakespeare.
ALL THE YEAR ROUND
A weekly journal conducted by Charles Dickens

which was an adaption from Othello that I thought really an admirable one for our purposes. The others readily agreed, and this was adopted.

I searched and found a new office for the new journal – at 26, Wellington Street North, almost facing the Lyceum Theatre, and just a short distance from the Household Words office. I took a lease for twenty-one years at £110 per annum and immediately got the workmen in. The ground floor I turned into the office, and from where we could publish, while above I set out accommodation for myself in five very good rooms for a temporary town tent. I ordered paper and settled with a printer – Charles Whiting of Beaufort Buildings, 95 Strand, who had printed Sketches by Boz and Oliver Twist – before getting an immense system of advertising ready. Ouvry, however, urged caution, and so I delayed the distribution of hand-bills until the end of the month, and declined to advertise the publication in Household Words itself, to avoid any further difficulties with Bradbury and Evans. I went back to Chapman and Hall, and gave them sole agency outside London, allowing them a twelve and a half percent discount on the list price, and credit for six months, but Bradbury and Evans now sought to prevent the progress by issuing proceedings against myself and Wills in the

Rolls Court, seeking to prevent us even issuing a prospectus. In my affidavit to the court, I told the Master of the Rolls that upwards of half a million copies of the advertisement for All the Year Round were now done and nearly the whole was in the trade for distribution. Subject to a minor amendment, the court declined Bradbury and Evans their injunction and so allowed the distribution to go ahead,

I had begun thinking of a new story that I wanted for the start of All the Year Round, and told Forster that I had come upon the name for it that would fit the opening to a 'T' – "A Tale of Two Cities". I also had a rather original and bold idea, namely at the end of each month to publish the monthly part in the green cover, with the two illustrations, at the old shilling, which would give All the Year Round always the interest and precedence of a fresh weekly portion during the month. I also believed it would give me my old standing with my old public and the advantage (very necessary in this story) of having numbers of people who would read it in no portions smaller than a monthly part. I expected a magnificent start to the magazine and my new story, and wrote especially to Thomas Carlyle thanking him most cordially for the friendly trouble he had taken with me, for I had long been a great admirer of his work on the French Revolution and emphasized to him how specially interesting and valuable any help was that came from him. I then set to work on the story in earnest.

I thought that, at this time, I could not be tempted to engage in any other undertaking, however short, but I then received a letter from a Mr. Robert Bonner, the proprietor of the "New York Ledger", offering me £1,000 for a short story for his publication. I could not refuse this, so casting my mind about for a suitable subject, I alighted upon my visit to Newgate more than twenty years before and the encounter with the prisoner Wainewright. I took his story and worked a fictional tale around it entitled "Hunted Down", and sent it to Bonner for publication. He published it in the New York Ledger and a year later he most kindly allowed me to reprint it in All the Year Round, allowing us to now reap the advantage of having it published in Europe.

Once Hunted Down was done, I became hard at work again on A Tale of Two Cities, as well as setting out other items that I felt should be in the first edition of All the Year Round. Bradbury and Evans then renewed their suit at the Rolls Court and I sent Wills along to view the outcome. He reported that he had arrived at half past ten to find that the Master of the Rolls had already disposed of the case in not quite a quarter of an hour, ordering both the dissolution of the partnership and the sale by auction of the copyright and property in Household Words, with either party having leave to bid for it. At once Counsel for Bradbury and Evans offered to buy, but Ouvry declined that civility, begging it to be understood that the ground of the dissolution was purely personal, and not occasioned by any commercial differences. At the auction on the 16th May, Arthur Smith, acting secretly on my behalf, covered himself with glory by affecting to relate anecdotes to those attending and then bid, as it were, accidentally – buying all Household Words and its stock for £3,550. I sold the stock to Chapman and Hall for £2,500 and, as Wills and I owned three-quarters of Household Words, it only required me to pay Bradbury and Evans £262.10 shillings for their share, instead of the £1,000 they had declined from me previously. At the end of May Bradbury and Evans announced that they were seeking to establish a publication of their own entitled "Once a Week", and so to heap over them a vast accumulation of expense; it did not, however, in the least matter to me what they might do, for in the Chancery suit I had carried everything my own way.

I now pressed on with all speed and we were able to publish the first number of All the Year Round, which included the first weekly number of A Tale of Two Cities, on the 30th April. I spent much time thereafter in the office preparing future numbers, and then received the splendid news as to its success. So well had it gone that by the middle of June it was able to repay me, with five percent interest, all the money I had advanced for its establishment (paper, print and all paid, down to the last number), and yet to leave a good £500 balance at the bankers! It was an amazing success and left the circulation of old Household Words in remote distance, my story of the Two Cities taking a great hold, and striking deeper every week.

CHAPTER LI

A Bachelor-State Malady, Entreaties from America,
and A Tale of Two Cities concluded

On the weekend of the 25th June I went to see Frank Beard, who had his medical practice at 44, Welbeck Street, as my bachelor state had engendered a small malady on which I wanted to see him at once. He gave me medicine and I hoped it would cure the problem in short time.

I contacted Ouvry to finalize the Articles of Agreement for All the Year Round business. Wills was appointed sub-editor to me and I delegated the general management to him, but retained overall control. My salary as editor was £504 per annum, and his as sub-editor £420 per annum; with the title and goodwill to be my exclusive property.

I pressed on with A Tale of Two Cities at Gad's Hill, and found it a good place for working. But I was rather disposed to feel my medical problem in my general health and was languid and short of starch. The original complaint was much where it was, with irksome botheration, but I did feel I was round the corner with it. This cause – and the heat – had tended to my doing no more than hold my ground with A Tale of Two Cities in seeking to keep one month ahead of publication, with my old month's advance and the small portions thereof driving me frantic, but the tale took a strong hold and the run upon our monthly parts surprising, selling 35,000 back numbers in the previous month alone. I also received a note from Carlyle that gave me especial pleasure, and furthermore ensured that, as soon as I had the chapters ready, they were sent to Nelly at Houghton Place for her enjoyment in advance of the public reading them.

The American publisher, James Fields from Boston, came to Gad's Hill on the 6th July, urging me with the strongest intensity to go to America to read, but I felt in myself that I should be one of the most unhappy of men if I were to go – and yet I could not help being much stirred and influenced by the golden prospect being held before me. I made further enquiries of Fields, but decided to take the matter no further at that stage.

By the end of July I felt really very little better in health, despite sticking to both branches of the prescription Frank Beard had given me, and so arranged to visit him in London again. I hoped by then to have given the medication a fair trial and that they would show as being more efficacious in throwing the enemy than I had yet found them to be. I continued on with A Tale of Two Cities, having its track now set out before me, and engaged in fine walks from Gad's Hill with my two dogs, Turk and Linda.

I was in conversation with Wills about what should follow A Tale of Two Cities as the serial story in All the Year Round, and found that Wilkie had begun a new story entitled "The Woman in White", which I considered the name of names and very title of titles. Wilkie was at the time in Broadstairs and I wrote to him, wanting very much to go there for a day to see him, but I had to pick up my story and blaze away, with an eye to October to finish it, before going on another reading tour in the country that Arthur had now booked. I had wondered whether a tumble into the sea might do my health problems good....but there was no nitrate of silver in the ocean. However, as time progressed I could not get quite well, and had an instructive feeling that nothing but sea air and sea water would set me right – so I wrote to Wilkie again and asked if he could speak to the noble Ballard at the Albion Hotel and reserve for me a comfortable bedroom and quiet writeable-in sitting room for some five days.

By the end of August, I continued to be unwell, but fought on, still hoping to have the Tale done by the first week in October. I had set myself the task of making a picturesque story, rising in every chapter with characters true to nature, but whom the story itself should express, more than they should express themselves in dialogue; and Carlyle continued to write to me of it with great enthusiasm. Arthur had now arranged that on the 10th October I would go away to read for a fortnight at Ipswich, Norwich, Oxford, Cambridge and a few other places and so I had little spare time now or in prospect. All the Year Round too was a constant exertion, and I wrote to the printer and begged him to send directly to Forster for his appraisal four weeks' proofs that were in type beyond the current number. I felt a wretched sort of creature in my way, but it was a way that got on somehow.

At the beginning of September I moved to the Albion Hotel in Broadstairs, and found that Ballard had added the house at 37, Albion

Street (where we had stayed for three summers from 1840) to the hotel, so I was now able to take our old dining room and sitting room, together with our old drawing room that I used as a bedroom. But I had a cold that was so bad, both in my throat and in my chest, that I could not bathe in the sea, but did get a heavy and cold shower bath every morning at the baths run by Mrs. Crampton along in Albion Street. I did much writing and took walks (one to Ramsgate), before returning to London. There I found a pleasant letter from Mr. William Howitt, who held an interest in ghosts and haunted houses, a subject that was at that time being featured in All the Year Round.

I returned again to Gad's Hill and continued working very hard on the Tale, eventually finishing it at the beginning of October. It had greatly moved and excited me in the doing, and I was very glad that Wilkie liked it so much. After making arrangements with Chapman and Hall for the publication of the completed story in volume form, I made ready to go away to read for the three weeks that Arthur had now booked for me, and thereafter planned to return to the Christmas matters for All the Year Round. Before leaving I had considered the possibility of completing a tunnel from Gad's Hill to the shrubbery across the road, and sought the advice of my brother Alfred, who had been an experienced railway engineer.

I read in Ipswich, Norwich and Bury St. Edmunds, before meeting with Wills at 26, Wellington Street to set up the next number of All the Year Round, and to arrange for Wilkie's "The Woman in White" to follow on as the serial story after mine. I had also been giving thought as to who might contribute a serial story thereafter and was considering Mrs. Lewes (George Eliot), and Charles Lever, the Irish wit and novelist, with whom I had been friendly for more than fifteen years. I gave further readings at Cambridge, Peterborough, Bradford, Oxford, Birmingham and Cheltenham, before returning to Gad's Hill where, to my delight, Forster arrived, bringing with him a message from Carlyle describing A Tale of Two Cities as "wonderful!" This also highly delighted me. I wrote, telling Carlyle that the Tale was to be published some three weeks hence in one volume, and sending him the final proofs to the end so that he could read this before publication. I also told him that I had written the preface to the completed Tale, in which I had said:

"... all the references to the condition of the French people, however slight, are from trustworthy authorities; and that it has been one of my hopes to add something to the popular and picturesque means of understanding that terrible time, though no one can hope to add anything to the philosophy of Mr. Carlyle's wonderful book."

CHAPTER LII

The Uncommercial Traveller, Family Matters and Katey's
Wedding, Relinquishing Tavistock House,
and a Bonfire at Gad's Hill

Forster left Gad's Hill on the 2nd November and I turned my attention to the Christmas Number for All the Year Round. I had been taken by the notions of ghosts and haunted houses put forward by Mr. William Howitt and had received a further note from him on his subject, which I acknowledged, adding to him: "I will only add on the general subject that if you know of any haunted house whatsoever within the limits of the United Kingdom where nobody can live, eat, drink, sit, stand, lie or sleep, without spirit-molestation, I believe I can produce a gentleman who will readily try its effect in his own person." I was greatly irritated when he afterwards published his letter to me in a certain periodical curlpaper called "The Spiritual Telegraph", as well as describing my answer, but he sent me a list of haunted houses, one of which was a public house in Holborn, and I told him my friend (George Moore, a businessman and philanthropist) would begin with that, and that I would try and get the landlord's consent to the house's being exorcised by my friend, as I supposed the restoration of the goodwill to be worth something to him!

On the 10th November I entertained George Lewes and Mary Ann Lewes (George Eliot) to supper at Tavistock House. Then, the following week, against my first impulse and inclination, I thought it best to write to Lewes and go further with him into the question of Mrs. Lewes's writing for All the Year Round. I told him that my story was to finish the following week and Wilkie's then to begin, with his story lasting about 8 months, and asked Lewes directly if I could arrange such a story with Mrs. Lewes thereafter. She had sent me her first novel "Adam Bede" the previous February, which had made such a great impression on me that I could not praise it enough, and I hoped sincerely that she would write a story for our journal. To my disappointment, however, she replied saying that time was an insurmountable obstacle to the proposition as I had put to her. I nevertheless held high hopes that she would become a contributor in some form, as I had become an intense admirer of her and her work.

I then received a letter from Helen Dickens (wife of my brother Alfred) concerning my youngest brother Augustus. Augustus had come to consult with me on some matters some years before when he took a partner into business; but I observed him then to be so stupid in a singular combination of vanity and over-reaching that I felt it would be a positive act of treachery in me to see the partner and imply, however distantly, that I believed it possible for him to succeed with my brother. I then heard that Augustus had deserted his wife and emigrated to America with another woman, and had not been in America three months when he wrote asking me to correspond with some man or other who had done something for him, and would write for a recommendation from me to advance him a sum of money. He did write, and what could I do but hold my peace? I had suffered under injustice in America and did not complain openly of it, but I could not put myself in the way of heaps of not unmerited reproach from the knaves and fools who were always panting to yelp at a public man, by in any way guaranteeing Augustus. I could not deny to myself that the more conspicuous I was, the less right I had to do it, and the more I was bound to stand aloof. Helen told me that Augustus desired some influence over the affairs of an American Railroad Company; Alfred had raised objection to engaging in this, and Alfred's objection applied with ten thousand times greater force to one so notorious as myself. It was a dreadful state of things that Augustus should have fallen into this position, but I did not see how he could be helped in it. He always had been, in a certain insupportable arrogance and presumption of character, so wrong, that, even when he had some prospects before him, I despaired of his ever being right. I had no hope of him. If I had had any suitable employment in my own gift in America, I would have given it to him; but I could not recommend another man to do it, and least of all a stranger, who, doing it at all, would only do it in his confidence in me.

It was then that I heard that my great friend, and near neighbour at Russell House, Frank Stone, had been taken ill. Soon after, I met Stone in a cab in Tavistock Square, and he got out to talk to me. I walked about with him for a little while at a snail's pace, cheering him up; but when I came home, I told them that I thought Stone was much changed and in danger. Two days later, after speaking with Stone's wife Ellen, I sent word to his eldest son Arthur to come and see him, but at two o'clock that afternoon (the 18th November) poor Stone died of a spasm of the heart. The next day I went to Highgate Cemetery and bought a spot of ground for him and appointed his funeral. I also arranged for notices of his death to be put in all the main newspapers and give as much comfort and assistance to the family as I was able, for Stone was not a rich man and, apart from his widow, had left four children – two boys and two girls.

I became particularly fond of one of his boys, Marcus, then 19 years of age, who wished to follow in his father's footsteps to become a fine painter and illustrator. After his father's death, I was not only happy to write introductory letters for Marcus as I knew well by my own knowledge that he was an admirable draughtsman with a most dextrous hand, a charming sense of beauty and a capital power of observation, but I was also delighted to take him under my wing and regard him as one of our family. He would often come to stay with us thereafter at Gad's Hill, usually for a month in the year, and always for a fortnight at Christmas time. I also wrote strongly to Delane at The Times, asking if he would give Stone's eldest son, Arthur, employment should there be a vacancy at the newspaper, and meanwhile set about giving Arthur lessons in shorthand, as proficiency in it (as I had found) was highly desirable above all things in such matters. I considered that, once on that paper and able to hold his own there, he could work his way on in his legal profession without anxiety for present means.

I had a visit from Madame Celeste, who had now taken over the management of the Lyceum Theatre and who told me she wished to have A Tale of Two Cities dramatized for her theatre. I liked my Carton and had a faint idea sometimes that, if I acted him, I could have done something with his life and death, and so I gave her my permission and a copy of the completed book, though I did fear that her company and troupe was a very poor one. I continued hard at work with All the Year Round, encouraging Charlie Collins to continue producing material under the "Eye Witness" title, which I thought a capital name for him, while myself becoming in a state of temporary insanity (an annual event) over the Christmas Number. I had the idea of stories under the title "The Haunted House", but as yet not a story had come to me in the least belonging to the idea. I wanted stories showing that the house was haunted, not simply by strange ghosts, but by memories of the occupants, each of whom occupied a different room – the simplest idea in the world, but every one that turned by a strange fatality in my mind, on a criminal trial! I received half a dozen stories, written for it by regular contributors, but found they were quite impossible to be used, although every year a quantity of material written for the Christmas Number afterwards went instead into the regular numbers. I wrote my own story, and had others that were suitable put together, including those by G.A.Sala and Mrs. Gaskell, and the Christmas Number was then made up. I had also been writing a piece on Leigh Hunt following his death, and was able to include it in tributes gathered by his son, Thornton, for his introduction to a new edition of his father's autobiography. We were able to publish my piece, under the title "Leigh Hunt. A Remonstrance", in our journal on the 24th December after Thornton had seen and approved of it.

In order to provide articles for All the Year Round, I had decided to produce a number of wanderings under the title of "The Uncommercial Traveller", the first arising after I had read in The Times of the wreck of the ship "Royal Charter" off the coast of Anglesey as it returned home, heading for Liverpool, and carrying prospectors who had been gold-digging in Australia. The ship went down with 459 lives lost, amongst them four members of the Hogarth family who were known to Georgy. I now travelled to the scene and made contact with the Reverend Stephen Hughes, Rector of Llanallgo, on Anglesey, where many of the dead had been buried. I learnt that he and his brother, Rector of the adjoining parish of Penrhos, had toiled tirelessly in seeking to identify the dead that had been laid out in the church, and to provide them with a Christian burial, and they now lay undisturbed in the little churchyard, so many being so strangely brought together in such terrible circumstance. The Rector had written over a thousand letters to the bereaved and, in my article, I wrote out of the honest conviction of my heart, as if I had lost the friend of my life in that wreck.

It was then that I heard that Charles Lever had been offered £100 a month for eight months to write a serial story for Bradbury and Evans. I immediately wrote to him, telling him that I would most joyfully take upon myself their proffered terms if he would write such a story for our pages instead and, in due course, he agreed to my proposal. Meanwhile, I had now read Wilkie's book, The Woman in White, and was in no doubt that it was a very great advance on all his former writing, most especially in respect of tenderness. The story also gripped the difficulties of the weekly portion and threw them, in masterly style. I had stopped in every chapter to notice some instance of ingenuity, or some happy turn of writing, and felt no one else could do it half so well. And I now hoped to have a story from Lever to follow on from it – or even from Mrs. Lewes, if I could still persuade her to write for us.

Rehearsals for A Tale of Two Cities were now underway at the Lyceum and I attended, devoting myself for a fortnight, trying to infuse into the conventionalities of the theatre something not usual there in the way of life and truth. It became in very good train, with the crowd (to which I gave particular attention) on the whole good and fierce and not quite conventional. Despite this, however, I felt the whole production needed to be postponed for further rehearsals to be undertaken – and the performance finally opened on the 30th January 1860 to my satisfaction, to be met with loud and continuous applause at its conclusion. After its run in London, this adaptation was taken to New York, where it opened in the middle of April.

In my further wanderings as the Uncommercial Traveller, I made my way to Wapping Workhouse, for I had read in the morning papers that an Eastern police magistrate had said there was no classification there for women, and that the place was a disgrace and a shame, and divers other hard names. I wished to see how the facts really stood and, upon inspection, it agreeably surprised me. I wrote my findings for All the Year Round, and revealed that Eastern police magistrates are not always the wisest men of the East.

Nelly's 21st birthday was celebrated on the 3rd March, when the house at 2, Houghton Place was transferred into her name, and I continued to visit there, often two or three times a week, either alone or taking a friend (including the pianist and composer Francesco Berger), and engaged in the most pleasant of evenings, including discoursing, playing card games and singing duets with Nelly. I turned down public engagements being put to me, as I felt unable to undertake more than I had already made – one undertaking to which I had agreed, however, being to take the chair on the 8th March at the dinner to celebrate the anniversary of the Royal Society of Musicians, where I understand a sensation was caused when I remarked after my speech that I did not believe they should in future expel the fair sex from their banquets.

Greatly engaged with the business of All the Year Round, I spent long days in the office and planning future numbers with Wills, as well as continuing to observe A Tale of Two Cities at the Lyceum. I then began to find I was having a bad pain in my face, particularly after I had received from Chapman and Hall the accounts of A Tale of Two Cities. These showed the heavy cost incurred in printing and distributing the monthly parts, but Chapman and Hall were prepared to drop their percentage on takings which I regarded as very honourable indeed; it gave me real pleasure to have renewed my connection with them when, on their side, they showed such spirit. The story had, of course, had a very great sale in All the Year Round – selling on average 100,000 copies each week – which had forestalled the monthly market to a considerable extent.

I now heard from my son Charley that he was planning to leave Barings and travel to Hong Kong to purchase tea in order to set up as a tea-merchant in London, and wrote to Miss Coutts telling her of the news. I also told her that Gad's Hill was now wonderfully changed and that I wanted to sell Tavistock House. I hoped the time was fast coming on when, for many quiet months at a stretch, Gad's Hill would be my headquarters, with Georgy and Mamie being content to organize and run my household. Georgy, I still felt, would make the best wife in the world, but the children were so dependent on her that I doubted if she would ever marry. I did not know whether to be glad of it or sorry, finding the subject perplexing, for I was not a good judge of marriages. Mamie had not yet started any conveyance on the road to matrimony that I knew of, but I considered it likely enough that she would, as she was very agreeable and intelligent.

Katey meanwhile had, through Wilkie's brother Charlie, met the artist John Millias and I had agreed that she could sit for him as the model for the girl in his painting "The Black Brunswicker". She planned to marry Charlie Collins in the course of the summer; he was bred an artist (the father was one of the most famous painters of English green lanes, and coast pieces), and was attaining considerable distinction, when he turned indifferent to it and fell back upon that worst of cushions, a small independence. He was a writer too, and continued with the "Eye Witness" series in All the Year Round; a gentleman, aged 30 and accomplished, though I did not doubt that Katey might have done much better. However, there was no question that she was very fond of him, and that they came together by strong attraction, so I said no more and took the goods the Gods had provided me.

I had also been giving thoughts to the future for the boys, two of whom were still at school in Boulogne and I had received a letter from the senior master there. Not desiring to unsettle Frank still more, I had not yet intimated to him that I contemplated new arrangements for him, while they were as yet uncompleted. But I hoped to remove him from the school about Easter, for when he was last at home I had thought him in a desultory, unprofitable kind of state; and I had since had it in my mind to find an opportunity of setting him to work. As to Harry, I was very reluctant to withdraw him from the school's care, but I feared I should be obliged to do so at Midsummer. His youngest brother, Plorn, as the only child at home, had become such an article of household furniture that Mamie was unwilling to send him so far as Boulogne. I considered that it was advisable that Harry and Plorn should be educated together; and was inclined initially to think the Rochester Grammer School, near Gad's Hill, would reconcile the difficulties of the case, but then felt later that they should both follow Walter and Alfred to the school they attended in Wimbledon. However, I was pleased to report that the gallant Sydney was now in immense repute in the navy based at Portsmouth, and was shown (I had heard) to visitors as one of the curiosities of the place. When he was in the country with me, he usually lived up a tree or on top of a pole!

But then I also received a note from the lady with whom my mother was living, who was terrified by the responsibility of her charge and utterly relinquished it. Consequently, I had at once to devote myself to the difficult task of finding good hands for her and getting her into them without alarming her. I was at a great loss to settle how this was to be done, and done at once, but was soon relieved to hear that my brother Alfred and his wife Helen had agreed to take her in at their home in Manchester.

I was heartily glad (and not much surprised) to get a letter from Macready telling me that, though aged 67, he planned to marry again, this time to Cecile Spencer, aged 23, who was a good friend of my daughter Katey. Although many had criticized him for so doing, to me it was inexpressibly delightful and interesting to picture him in his new home in Cheltenham, with new life and movement and hope and pleasure about him. This feeling sprung up in me for his sake and for the sake of his children too, for I did not believe that a heart like his was made to hold so large a waste-place as there had been in it since the loss of his wife and the other tragedies in his life that he had suffered. His letter came with the sunshine of a spring morning, and shone into my breast quite as naturally and cheerily, and I was delighted to write to him: "God bless you, and God bless the object of your choice!"

I also received a letter of a different kind from Miss Coutts. This no doubt arose out of her affectionate kindness, and was once again seeking to reconcile me with Catherine – but I had to write back to her again that it was simply impossible that such a thing could be. I told her firmly that in the previous two years I had been stabbed too often and too deep not to have a settled knowledge of the wounded place, and to me that figure was out of my life for evermore (except to darken it) and my desire was never to see it again. Miss Coutts wrote back, fearing that she had failed to express herself to me, but in my further reply I explained that I did not suppose myself blameless; and that when I was very young I made a miserable mistake, and that the wretched consequences which might naturally have been expected from it had resulted from it.

Plans began to be set in train for Katey's wedding at Higham Church on Tuesday 17th July, and I took to inviting old friends to attend and form the congregation. The Reverend Joseph Hindle agreed to perform the marriage service and, I later realized, the villagers began anticipating the event in earnest. Charley by now had gone to Hong Kong, and Walter was still in India, but the naval authorities agreed that Sydney could extend his leave for a day so that he could attend the occasion. Then, on the morning before the wedding, I was exceedingly concerned to receive a note about my brother Alfred from his wife Helen. She spoke of alarming inflammation in the region of his lungs, which I was aware was often a result after having pleurisy, but I trusted they would soon find it yielding.

On the day of the wedding, the railway people arranged to bring down our intimate friends to Higham station at five minutes past 11 in the morning, and I arranged to have them taken straight to the church. I had tried to keep it very quiet, but all the neighbouring country turned out in the most bewildering manner, and I found that the people of the village had strewn flowers in the churchyard and erected triumphal arches. We arranged to be at the church at 20 minutes past 11 for the ceremony, and found it filled with people. The energetic blacksmith of the village had erected a triumphal arch in the lane, and fired guns all night beforehand – to our great amazement: we not having the slightest idea what they meant! However, these were not annoyances to be grave about, so we laughed at them. One very funny thing was the entrance in to the church of the few friends whom I had caused to be brought down by the special train. They didn't know whether they were to look melancholy, beaming or maudlin; and their uncertainty struck me as uncommonly droll.

After the service we all returned to Gad's Hill for the wedding breakfast – with the people of the village coming to look at it, laid out on our table and decorated with none but white flowers – and, as we had so arranged for Katey's departure (for Dover) that she should not have an hour of breakfast, it was rapid with no speechifying, and they were then gone in no time, Forster adding in stentorian voice at the departure:

"Take care of her Charlie, you have got a most precious treasure."

Katey indeed really looked wonderfully pretty, and her appearance and departure produced an immense effect on all beholders. Mamie and all the boys were very much cut up when the parting moment came, but they soon recovered; Mamie in particular commanding herself extremely well. Games were then played on the lawn before a visit to Rochester Castle and on to Chatham, where we heard a military band, before returning to Gad's Hill for some croquet and dinner at 7 p.m. Dinner finished at 9, followed by singing and country dancing, before the guests departed at 11 for their special train waiting for them at Higham station. Once they had all gone however, my feelings took over completely, and I went up to Katey's bedroom and closed the door. On seeing her wedding dress, I fell onto my knees and sobbed into it, before realizing that Mamie had come in. I just managed to express the pain that I felt by struggling to say to Mamie: "But for me, Katey would not have left home" before departing the room.

It was a great relief to hear again from Helen that there had been a change for the better with Alfred, and I trusted he would now hold his ground and advance, however slowly. I also received letters from Frederick, who was now staying with them, and I admired Helen for her patience and solidarity. But then, on the evening of Friday 27th July, I was telegraphed to go to Manchester at once as Alfred had been taken seriously ill. I immediately travelled there, arriving at a quarter past ten, but found that by then poor Alfred had been dead three hours. I stayed in Manchester two days, making all arrangements for his burial at Highgate Cemetery, and brought his poor young widow back with me for the funeral. I found that he had left nothing – worse than nothing. He had two boys, one thirteen (Alfred Charles) and one eleven (Edmund), and three younger daughters (Florence, Katherine and Augusta), and so Helen now had insufficient means with which to cope. I set about doing all I could to help her in her financial plight, including setting up a trust for her, and also wrote to the Earl of Carlisle and others seeking to arrange a pension for her from the Government on account of the good works Alfred had lately done for his country in the course of sanitary improvement.

Wilkie's Woman in White was now drawing to its close in All the Year Round and I corresponded again with Charles Lever in Italy over his follow-on story for us, which he called "A Day's Ride". Lever had written to Wills that he did not wish his story to start in the journal until after his birthday on the 31st August for, as he put it, "the year that proceeds that day has been of almost unbroken ill-luck to me; everything has gone wrong, and myself the most of all!" Wills, however, wrote back pointing out that the early proofs of the journal were always sent to America a month in advance, and that the first number of his story had already been sent there, so that it was now impossible to make the change in the time of beginning.

I also approached Bulwer Lytton, asking him if there was any possibility of him being induced to write a tale for All the Year Round, something that might occupy 6 or 8 months in our journal, and was delighted when my request met with a favourable response. Meanwhile, I had to work against time and tide and everything else to fill up a number being kept open for me as the Uncommercial Traveller, before the plates had to be sent off to America. I managed to complete in time the paper "Living in Chambers", which drew heavily upon my experiences from my time as a boy in legal chambers, particularly those within Gray's Inn.

I continued to have a great deal of anxiety arising out of poor Alfred's death. His affairs were in such a bad state that I knew his widow and children, as well as my mother, must be looked after and cared for. I found Helen as patient, uncomplaining, self-denying and quietly practical in her bearing as it was possible for human nature so circumstanced to be, and I had her, her family and my mother housed for the time being in a farm house near Gad's Hill. Day after day I was scheming and contriving for them, and schemed myself into broken rest and low spirits. My mother, left to me when my father died – I never had anything left to me but relations! – was now in the strangest state of mind from senile decay: and the impossibility of getting her to understand what was the matter, combined with her desire to be got up in sables like a female Hamlet, illumined the dreary scene with a ghastly absurdity that was the chief relief I could find in it. But I knew that it was not new but true to say that life is a fight, and must be fought out without complaint of it.

As I began to have thoughts of a new book in my head, a buyer for Tavistock House came forward, a Jewish solicitor and money lender (and said to be one of the greatest rascals in London), named James Phineas Davis – giving an odd change in the occupation of Tavistock House. I strongly suspected that a good many people about town who had been there now and then during the previous nine years, would present themselves under the new administration in an entirely new capacity! I arranged for Anne Cornelius to show him around, and prepared to negotiate over the fitted and planned furniture. I found he was prepared to proceed with speed, and I consulted with Ouvry over legal matters; the negotiations were soon concluded and the Tavistock House deed signed in the middle of August, with the money (two thousand guineas for the remaining 36-year term) paid. We then had a fortnight to clear out, and I gave directions for this to be done. All the pictures were taken down, including those painted by Stanny, and sent to Chapman and Hall's premises (now at 193 Piccadilly), for them to be put in their warehouse before most were then taken on to Gad's Hill. I also gave detailed directions as to the fitting-out of bookcases and other matters, including transferring my book-jackets to the door of my study at Gad's Hill, for I now proposed to live at Gad's Hill during seven months of the year, whilst taking a small furnished house in town during the other five. I continued to be free to visit Nelly at 2, Houghton Place, and also, of course, always had my five very good rooms above the All the Year Round office for my own use at any time, which after some changes, became as comfortable, cheerful, and private as anything of the kind could possibly be. I decided to keep John Thompson in my employ, and moved him from Tavistock House to a room at the office for his accommodation.

Then, on Monday 3rd September, shocked by the misuse of the private letters of public men which I had constantly observed, and while at Gad's Hill, I decided to burn in the field there the accumulated letters and papers of twenty years. Letters in my mind were but ephemeral and we should not be affected too much either by those which praise us, or by others written in the heat of the moment. Harry and Plorn helped to carry basket after basket of letters and other papers to the fire and, in burning, they sent up a smoke like the genie when he got out of the casket on the sea shore. It was not done without pain, you may believe, but the first reluctance conquered, I was determined henceforth to keep no letters by me, and to consign all such papers to the fire. As it was an exquisite day when I began the burning, and rained very heavily when I finished, I suspected my correspondence of having overcast the face of the Heavens; but nevertheless expressed the wish that, would to God, every letter I had ever written had been on that pile.

CHAPTER LIII

Great Expectations, continuing Bachelor Malady,
and 3 Hanover Terrace

On the morning of 4th September, coming to the office from the station, I met, coming from the execution of "the Walworth Murderer" (William Youngman) outside Horsemonger Lane Jail, such a tide of ruffians as never could have flowed from any point but the gallows. Without any figure of speech, it turned me white and sick to behold them. This was also the day Tavistock House was cleared, and possession delivered up to the house of Israel. I must say on this, that in all things the purchaser, Mr. Davis, behaved thoroughly well, and (despite his reputation) I could not call to mind any occasion when I had money-dealings with a Christian that had been so satisfactory, considerate and trusting. I also found Mrs. Davis to be a very kind and agreeable woman.

I put to work in the All the Year Round office and published – as part of my Uncommercial Traveller series – remembrances from my childhood under the title: "Nurses' Stories", but I now found that with Lever's story of "A Day's Ride", our circulation began to drop rapidly and continuously. I wrote to Lever explaining, as best I could, that his story was not taking hold of readers; I had waited week after week, watching for any sign of encouragement, the least sign being enough, but all the tokens that appeared were in the other direction. I was therefore driven upon the necessity of considering how to act. I knew that if the publication were to go steadily down too long, it would be very, very difficult to raise it again, and so resolved, having called a council of war at the office, that there was but one thing to be done.

A very fine, new, and grotesque idea had opened upon me, and I had begun to wonder if I should reserve this notion for a new book; it so opened out before me that I could see the whole of a serial revolving on it, in a most singular and comic manner. I planned the opening scene of the story Cooling Castle ruins and the desolate church, lying out among the marshes seven miles from Gad's Hill, and took Forster there to show him the very spot. But with Lever's story not taking hold, I resolved that I must abandon now my design for a book and shape the story instead for All the Year Round. The property of All the Year Round was far too valuable in every way to allow it to be much endangered, and felt I must get my story – which in my mind I had entitled "Great Expectations" – into the journal as soon as possible. I planned to begin publishing it on the 1st December – and that, for as long a time as Lever's story continued thereafter, we must go on together.

Meanwhile, as there was the absolute necessity of my giving time to the Christmas Number (which this year I entitled "A Message from the Sea"), I became tied to the grindstone pretty tightly. I told Forster that Great Expectations would be written in the first person throughout, and during the first three weekly numbers (which I had now written) he would find the hero to be a boy-child, like David Copperfield; then I supposed the boy would be an apprentice. Forster had complained of the want of humour in A Tale of Two Cities, but I told him now that he would not have to complain, for I had made the opening (I hoped) in its general effect exceedingly droll. I had put the child (Pip) and a good-natured foolish man (Joe) in relations that seemed to me very funny, but I had also got in the pivot on which the story would turn, the grotesque tragi-comic conception with Magwitch that had first encouraged me. To be quite sure I had fallen into no unconscious repetitions, I read Copperfield again – and indeed was affected by it to a degree you would hardly believe.

I had plans to go to Cornwall with Wilkie to seek out material for the Christmas Number, and ground four weekly numbers of Great Expectations off the wheel, and wished at least another to be turned before leaving. Having done so, on the 1st November I met Wilkie at Paddington Station and we spent the first night at Bideford, in a beastly hotel, before setting off on a two days' posting to Liskeard, where we struck the railway again. By this time we had got everything we wanted, parceled it up to Wills in the office, and got back to London on the 5th November.

I now pressed on with Great Expectations, but by the beginning of December, as Great Expectations began in All the Year Round, I felt that I had rather overworked myself and wanted rest. I decided not to go to the office for the first ten days of the month and remained at Gad's Hill in retreat and occupation there, but was turning over in my mind what might follow my story in All the Year Round after it finished in August of the following year. I received intelligence that Bulwer Lytton was busy writing, and so I contacted him, offering him £1,500 for his story, and he responded favourably. I was delighted, and spent my first Christmas at Gad's Hill, but I was still not quite well, still not rid of the disagreeables that affected me in the hot summer of 1859, and remained being doctored by Frank Beard.

On the 6th January 1861, I became aware that Mr. Lane of the Britannia Theatre (a very respectable man) had announced an unauthorized version of "A Message from the Sea" that was clearly taken from the new Christmas Number by myself and Wilkie. I caused Lane to be served immediately with a notice that he would play the piece at his peril and that, if he did, I would apply to the Court of Chancery. In the light of past events, I was now determined to bring a Chancery action against any manager who dramatized any book of mine without my consent, and wrote a letter to the editor of The Times to this effect, which they duly published. I, however, caused it to be explained to Lane that I had no hostility whatever towards him; eventually Wilkie and I gave our authority for him to perform the adaption for a fee of £50 in place of bringing an action for injunction. It was unfortunate that the first man I had to assert the principle against was a very good man whom I really respected.

I made arrangements, on Mamie's account in particular, to take a furnished house in London until midsummer – at No. 3, Hanover Terrace – a really delightful five-storey house opposite Regent's Park, and in the same terrace where Wilkie had lived (at No.17) when residing with his mother. As this had proved to be the coldest winter in fifty years, I had four tons of coals sent to the property and instructed Thompson about the firewood, as well as making reasonably good preparation in the wine and spirit way. All the Year Round was now doing gloriously, and Great Expectations a great success. I was feeling in better spirits, planning a small dinner at Hanover Terrace for my birthday, and walking about London again.

Katey and Charlie Collins had come home from abroad, but I did not know how long they might remain at Hanover Terrace, nor did they probably know themselves. Katey looked extremely well, and they seemed to get on together admirably. Charlie was at work upon a book describing their journey, with illustrations by himself, though I ardently wished he were painting instead – but of course I did not say so. And there were no "Great Expectations" of prospective Collinses, which I thought a blessed thing – though again I did not say so. Old Mrs. Collins dined with us soon after we moved in, and contradicted everybody upon every subject for five hours and a half and was invariably pig-headed and wrong; I was very glad when she tied her head up in a bundle and took it home – though again I didn't say so. Wilkie was in a potential and popular state, and was beginning to think of a new book, looming some eight or ten months ahead, and had now made his rooms at No.12, Harley Street very handsome and comfortable. We never spoke of the female skeleton in that house (Caroline Graves), and I therefore had not the least idea of the state of his mind on that subject. I hoped it did not run in any matrimonial groove; I could imagine similar cases in which that end was well and wisely put to that difficulty, but I could not imagine any good coming of such an end in this instance.

My son Charley had now just come home from China seeking a mercantile partnership, and, when he found it, I believed he would probably marry the daughter (Bessie) of Evans, the printer – the very last person on earth whom I could desire so to honour me. They had been engaged since they were mere children, so I did not see it as his fault, but it was sure not to answer – if my authority on such a subject could be accepted.

CHAPTER LIV

*Great Expectations concluded, Deaths of Arthur Smith
and Henry Austin, and disgrace of brother Frederick*

By the beginning of May, Chapman and Hall were negotiating with
Bradbury and Evans to buy them out of any rights to copyright arising
from my works, and they also agreed to pay a similar sum to me for
the fourth share I held, so that at the end of the transactions Chapman
and Hall and I would become equally interested in the whole issue of
my books. I had heard that Bradbury and Evans were now in financial
difficulties, including with their rival magazine "Once A Week", and
they finally accepted £3,250 from Chapman and Hall, who then agreed
to pay the same figure to me but, instead of cash, pay me five per cent
interest on the said sum for my lifetime.

I received the revised proofs from Bulwer Lytton of his story and
reading them could not lay them aside. I made some suggestions to
overcome some misgivings Bulwer had expressed, and gave advice as
to how it might be set out for the purposes of weekly publication, but I
was greatly taken by the beauty and power of his writing, as well as its
originality, boldness, and quite extraordinary constructive skill. I also
read the proofs to Nelly, whom I could implicitly trust, and in whom
I had frequently observed, in the case of my own proofs, an intuitive
sense and discretion that I set great store by. Bulwer settled on his title:
"A Strange Story" and it was made ready to place into All the Year
Round after Great Expectations.

By the 11th June, after some pretty close work and a spell by the
sea at Dover, I had finished Great Expectations, and four days later
we gave up 3, Hanover Terrace. Mamie, Georgy and I then travelled
to Knebworth to stay with Bulwer, and I spoke of Great Expectations
to him. I showed him the proofs of the final chapters that were as yet
unpublished, but found that he was so very anxious that I should alter
the end of it – the extreme end, I mean, after Biddy and Joe were done
with – and stated his reasons so well that, upon returning to Gad's Hill,
I resumed the wheel and took another turn at it. My difficulty, however,
was to avoid doing too much. My tendency, when I began to unwind

the thread that I thought I had wound forever, was to labour it and get out of proportion, so I sought to do it in as few words as possible, and upon the whole I thought it was for the better. I had it published in All the Year Round in its altered form, and wrote to Forster explaining the change I had done. I made arrangements for the publication of the volume edition and dedicated it to my old friend and clergyman, Chauncy Hare Townshend, a good, affectionate, gentle creature that I truly loved.

By now I had got a Copperfield reading ready for delivery and then began blazing away with one from Nickleby. I also drew up the tale of the Bastille prisoner from A Tale of Two Cities, and of Mr. Chops the dwarf from our Christmas Number of 1858. Every morning when at Gad's Hill I would "go in" at these for two or three hours, practising these new readings, but at the beginning of September I was concerned to hear that Arthur Smith had not been in good health again. I told him I was at work every day (except Wednesdays, when I went to London) preparing for my next tour, and was anxious to receive better news from him as soon as he could possibly give it.

I began inviting all our contributors to write for the extra Christmas Number of All the Year Round, deciding that this year it might be based upon a hermit I had seen living on the Knebworth estate, with the story weaved into the design under the general title of "Tom Tiddler's Ground". I told them that this time no reference to the Christmas season was in the least necessary; on the contrary such reference was not desired and that their story could be narrated in the first person or the third, time present or time past, and ghostly or otherwise.

I continued to prepare for my readings, but could not stir without referring to poor Arthur's papers. Thomas Headland, his assistant, made two visits to the Wellington Street office to discuss matters and, due to Arthur's serious condition, I felt obliged to engage Headland to act for me. I had by now seen Arthur and my impression of his state was not favourable. I feared his recovery, even to the extent of being able to go with us, to be most unlikely.

I then heard the tragic news that poor Arthur was dead. He died on the 1st October, and I felt I had lost a friend whom I could never replace. He had always gone with me on my readings, and transacted, as no other man ever could, all the business connected with them; without him I now feared they would be dreary and weary to me. I was also greatly at a loss, for I knew very little of the reading arrangements he had presently made for me, only knowing generally that I was bound to go away on the 28th October to read fifty times, but dimly knowing where or when. Arthur was buried on the 5th October, and there was a very touching thing in the chapel. When his body was to be taken up and carried to the grave in Brompton Cemetery, there stepped out, instead of the undertakers' men with their hideous paraphernalia, the men who had always been with him and his brother Albert when they had given their public entertainments at the Egyptian Hall; and they, in their plain, decent own mourning clothes, carried the poor fellow away. Also, standing among the gravestones, dressed in black, I noticed every kind of person who had ever had to do with him – from our own gas man and doorkeepers and billstickers, up to the foremost class of man. His father, brother and he now lie together, and the grave, I suppose, will be no more disturbed. I wrote a little inscription for his stone; in it I tried to tell the truth about him as simply and honestly as possible. He was just 36 years of age when he died.

Then, on the 8th October when I returned to the office in London, I heard that Henry Austin had not been well, and so went to Ealing to see him. He was supposed to have taken a decidedly favourable turn, the doctor (who was to remain all night), dining, and all were as cheerful as might be. I came away and returned to my rooms above the office, but when Thompson came in the next morning at 8 o'clock, he said a messenger had just been to say that Henry was now dead. His disease was inflammation of the windpipe – if I recollect right, he had always a weakness about his chest and throat – and he died very quietly, apparently supposing himself better. Of course, I went out there again, and you can imagine Laetitia under the circumstances, but she certainly came out better than I had expected; I must honestly confess though that I had had a dread of going near her, God forgive me, but I ordered the funeral, paid the bill, and sought to do all I could for her.

After attending Henry's funeral, with what difficulty I sought to get myself back to the readings after all this loss and trouble, or with what unwillingness I worked myself up to the mark of looking my audience in the face, I can hardly say. As for poor Arthur's absence at this time, it was as if my right arm were gone; he had made the reading part of my life as light and pleasant as it could be made, and I held a great regard for him. His death continued to cause me the greatest distress and anxiety, but I knew I must begin in Norwich on the 28th October and then go north in the middle of November. I was now planning to do Copperfield and was curious in particular to test its effect on the Edinburgh people. It had been quite a job so to piece the portions of the long book together as to make something continuous out of it, but I hoped I had got something varied and dramatic.

Before leaving for Norwich, I received a letter from T.J.Thompson on the miserable subject of my brother Frederick. Frederick's court case, subsequent flight, capture, imprisonment and bankruptcy had all now been reported in The Times, and I had no power, or shadow of power, over him, no communication with him and no knowledge whatever of his doings. I found my lack of power over him had been last exemplified, and his deference to me last shown, in his compromising Wills for a large sum of money, and treating him with supreme contempt and defiance, setting him utterly at naught altogether. In which process he was as much restrained by any sense of gratitude to me, or consideration for me of any kind, as the wind that was then blowing. I did not in the least doubt (I wish I did) that he humiliated himself and degraded himself; nor did I affect to have viewed with philosophy, the decay and ruin of so near a relation, for whom I had done more than I could in any reason have hoped to do for each of my own seven boys. But I knew no one could disgrace me but I myself, and that the name I had made was in my keeping, and in no other man's.

CHAPTER LV

Second Reading Tour, Headland's failures,
but my "Blazes of Triumph!"

On the 28th October I set off at the beginning of my reading tour in
Norwich. I read Copperfield that night and I cannot say that we began
well. The hall (a great stone-paved gothic-styled place) was not good and
they were a very lumpish audience indeed. They appeared to be afraid
of me, and of each other, and this did not tend to cheer the strangeness I
felt in being without Arthur. I was not at all myself; everything seemed
forlorn and strange and, with poor dear Arthur gone, the very wind in
the arches (damn them!) seemed to howl about. As a very little thing
would have stirred me, in such a state of mind, to do my best: so a very
little thing stirred me to do my worst – and on the whole I think I did.

The following night, again at Norwich, we now had a large let – I
think 250 stalls – and I was relieved that this time we had a splendid
audience. I read Nickleby and The Trial from Pickwick and it went not
only with roars, but with a general hilarity and pleasure that I had never
seen surpassed. But I continued to miss Arthur dreadfully. We moved
on to Bury St. Edmunds, to the Angel Hotel in Abbeygate Street, where I
had stayed in January 1835 while reporting the Suffolk elections for the
Morning Chronicle and which I had later incorporated into Pickwick.
I read Copperfield to a very fine audience and to great acclaim. On to
Ipswich, where I read Copperfield again and made a great impression.
Then Colchester, where I read Nickleby and the Trial from Pickwick;
there was such a rush that Thompson was nearly swept into space and
the rest were obliged to dive at him, and drag him out of the crowd!

After a short return to Gad's Hill through a snow-storm, I read
at Canterbury, Dover, Hastings, and at Brighton, where I gave three
readings. On leaving Brighton in triumph, I returned to Gad's Hill
before, on the 20th November, travelling to Newcastle to continue the
reading tour. But I now found that, apart from the bills being "lost"
for a week or two, Headland had made an awful mistake in putting up
Little Dombey, which I read here last time, instead of Copperfield! I had
had no more intention of reading Little Dombey than I had of reading

an account of the moon, and it annoyed me beyond expression. The agent could only stand and stare, when people had come to ask what was going to be read and to all this head of misery Headland replied "Johnson's mistake", Johnson being the printer. Then the following morning came a frantic letter from the Edinburgh agent: "I have no bills, no tickets, I lose all the announcement I could have made to hundreds upon hundreds of people tonight, all the most desirable class to be well informed beforehand, I can't announce what Mr. Dickens is going to read, I can answer no question, I have, upon my responsibility, put a dreary advertisement into the papers announcing that he is going to read so many times, and that particulars will shortly be ready, and so I stand bound hand and foot." "Johnson's mistake" said the unlucky Headland, and broke down most awfully.

Of course, I knew that the man who never made a mistake in poor Arthur's time was not likely to be always making mistakes now, but I wrote to Wills asking him to go to Johnson, the printer in St. Martin's Lane, and investigate. Meanwhile I detached Berry from our group and sent him on a train at a few minutes' notice to Edinburgh, and then to Glasgow, where I had no doubt everything was wrong too. Glasgow I felt we might save, though I feared Edinburgh to be irretrievably damaged, but because Headland was so anxious and so good tempered in his nature, I could not be very stormy with him.

Then, on the night of the 22nd, something almost terrible happened in the cram of the Newcastle Music Hall. I had begun reading Nickleby when suddenly, as they were all very still over Smike, my gas batten came down, and it looked as if the room was falling. There were three galleries crammed to the roof, and a high steep flight of stairs, and a panic must have destroyed numbers of people. A lady in the front row of the stalls screamed, and ran out wildly towards me, and for one instant there was a terrible wave in the crowd. I addressed the lady laughing (for I knew she was in sight of everybody there), and called out as if it happened every night: "There's nothing the matter, I assure you; don't be alarmed; pray sit down", and she sat down directly, and there was a thunder of applause. It took some few minutes to mend, and I looked on with my hands in my pockets; for I think if I had turned my back for a moment there might still have been a move. My people were dreadfully alarmed, Boycett in particular who ran the gas equipment, and I suppose had some notion that the whole place might have taken fire. Boycett did me the honour to say afterwards, in addressing the rest: "But there stood the master, as cool as ever I see him a-lounging at a railway station!"

We travelled on to Berwick-upon-Tweed in the freezing cold, the town taking a reading on Arthur's principle that a place in the way paid the expenses of the through journey. Berry joined us, back from Edinburgh and Glasgow, with hopeful accounts. He seemed to have done the business extremely well, and said that it was quite curious and cheering to see how the Glasgow people assembled around the bills the instant they were posted, and evidently with a great interest in them. That evening I read the Carol and the Trial from Pickwick in the Assembly Hall attached to the King's Arms, which was crowded to the door, every available space being crammed, and the audience responding with repeated shouts of laughter and applause.

The next morning we set off for Edinburgh, where I was to give five readings. There I found the crowds frantic and immense, the popularity of the readings quite indescribable. After Nickleby and the Trial from Pickwick, it was reported that both these "contained more general amusement than perhaps has ever been afforded to any other presented in this city." I also wanted to do my very best with Copperfield, and I believe I succeeded, with four great rounds of applause and a burst of cheering at the end, with talk of it ringing through the whole city. The turn-away for all five readings was enormous and, though rather tired, I felt the Blazes of Triumph! Upon request, I had to make a new agreement to return to Edinburgh after my visit to Glasgow, to give a further reading.

Glasgow had already written for "more tickets", and we travelled there on the 3rd December. I began the readings there that night in the large City Hall, filled with people. I read Nickleby and the Trial from Pickwick on the 3rd and 5th, and Copperfield on the 4th and 6th to greatly enthusiastic audiences, and it finished nobly. On the last night it rained sheets of water, coming on at 6 o'clock; yet under these adverse circumstances, even more were crammed into the hall, with that night's receipts alone being enormous. Back in Edinburgh I gave my additional reading to a crowded house and loud cheering, before readings at Carlisle and Lancaster

During my time away I had been in constant contact with Wills over All the Year Round business – I doubt whether any two men could have gone on more happily and smoothly, or with greater trust and confidence in one another – and at our next stop, Preston, and the Victoria Hotel, I heard from him news of the Christmas Number that was indeed glorious, and felt nothing could look brighter or better than the prospects of our illustrious publication. I had also heard of the failure of Bradbury and Evans's venture, which added to my pleasure at the success of All the Year Round.

We travelled to Manchester, and the scene in the Free Trade Hall was really magnificent. I had had the platform carried forward to our "Frozen Deep" point, and my table and screen built with a proscenium and room scenery. When I went in they applauded in the most tremendous manner; and the extent to which they were taken back, and taken by storm, by Copperfield was really a thing to see. It was a most signal and remarkable success, really a grand scene. But then, on arriving at the Adelphi Hotel in Liverpool, I became undecided as to what to do. We had a great let for the following night (the 16th December), but the news had now reached us of the death of Prince Albert. The Mayor recommended closing that following night, but continuing on the 17th and 18th; so did the town clerk and also the agents. But I had a misgiving that they hardly understood what the public general sympathy with the Queen would be. Further, I felt personally that the Queen had always been very considerate and gracious to me, and I would on no account do anything that might seem unfeeling or disrespectful. I contacted Wills by telegram and decided to postpone all my Liverpool readings until after Christmas.

CHAPTER LVI

Tour continued, 16 Hyde Park Gate South, and Readings in London

I celebrated Christmas and caught up with my correspondence, but soon was planning to set off again on the remaining part of my provincial reading tour, before then going to let off Copperfield in London at the St. James's Hall in March. On the 30th December, I travelled to Birmingham for two readings and found Birmingham in a very depressed state on account of the American War. Nevertheless, we did extremely well. Then on to Leamington Spa where, on New Year's Day 1862, I gave two readings, Copperfield at 3 p.m., which absolutely stunned the people, and in the evening Nickleby and the Trial from Pickwick, where they roared and roared until I think they must have shaken all the air in Warwickshire. The next morning I travelled to Cheltenham to read and to spend two days staying with Macready at his home. We had a joyous meeting at the station, but Macready I found decidedly much older and infirmed. However, I don't think I left off talking a minute, from the time of my entering his house to my going to bed, and he was as much amused and interested as ever. Cecile, the new Mrs. Macready, was exceedingly winning; quite perfect in her manner with him and in her ease with his children. I have very rarely seen a more agreeable woman. And Macready's amazement at Copperfield really was something to see. When I got back to his home after the reading he told me, with tears running down his face, how greatly moved he had been by it.

After a day back at Gad's Hill, I read in Plymouth and Torquay, where Headland continued to be a worthy man with the genius for mistakes, which was damned aggravating. I read at Exeter, then immediately travelled back to London and the All the Year Round office, before retiring to Gad's Hill, and on the 16th January read Copperfield for the benefit of the Rochester and Chatham Mechanics' Institute, being always happy to help them. The characters in the reading I found difficult to disassociate from the very stones of Chatham.

As I had postponed some half-dozen readings at Liverpool and nearby on account of Prince Albert's death, I had to go back to work them out. But I became highly irritated by the jack-asses people were presently making of themselves on the subject of the death, and I felt unable to take any part whatever in reference to the memorial to Prince Albert. With a sufficient respect for the deceased gentleman, and all loyalty and attachment towards the Queen, I was so very much shocked by the rampant toadyism that had been given to the four winds on that subject, and by the blatant speeches that had been made respecting it, that the refuge of my soul was silence. The snow and wind came, such that it felt that we were at the North Pole, but I set off for Manchester and read Nickleby and the Trial from Pickwick to an immense audience at the Free Trade Hall on Saturday 25th January, before travelling on to Liverpool for three readings at St. George's Hall, crammed to excess and great numbers turned away. I read in Chester, before travelling through the night back to London in advance of my London readings, which were now due to begin at St. James's Hall on the 13th March, and for three months swapped Gad's Hill for 16, Hyde Park Gate South with Mrs. George Hogge, a friend I had known for some time.

I spent much time in the All the Year Round office, and on the 3rd March Nelly celebrated her 23rd birthday. Shortly after, her sisters Fanny and then Maria went on tour to act, and there were times when her mother was not at home, so allowing me to be alone at Houghton Place with Nelly at this time. On Thursday 13th March, I began the series of readings at St. James's Hall with the condensation of Copperfield; the success on that night was outstanding, and the rush for places for the following readings became quite furious. But I now regarded 16, Hyde Park Gate as an odious little London box, which I thoroughly detested, and could not settle down in it to write. I was trying to plan out a new book, but could not yet get beyond trying. I used to go out regularly after breakfast to the office and elsewhere, but both Mamie and Georgy liked the change from the countryside, and as we were within a few paces of the Ride in the Park and of Kensington Gardens, they both were happy and I had no reason to complain.

I read Copperfield again at St. James's Hall on the 20th and 27th March, the 3rd, 10th and 24th April, again to great acclaim and was finding the general improvement in the audiences to be very remarkable; they were so much more delicate than they had used to be. And the money returns were quite outstanding. The effect of Copperfield exceeded all the expectations which its success in the country had led me to form, and it seemed to take people entirely by surprise.

I attended constantly at the office of All the Year Round and hit upon a title of "Our Mutual Friend" for my new story, but alas! could hit upon nothing else for it. Again and again I tried, but the odious little house in Kensington Gore seemed to have stifled and darkened my invention. I read again in the afternoon of the 7th May, but before my next reading on the evening of the 17th, it became possible that some private business might take me out of town in the course of the following week.

I gave my reading at St. James's Hall on the 17th May, spoke (to much hearty laughter) whilst taking the chair at the Anniversary Festival of the Newsvendors' Benevolent Institution on the 20th May, and then, the following afternoon, read Copperfield again at St. James's Hall. But I was now looking to finish my readings as early in June as I could. I thought Copperfield by far the best reading, but was now planning to read it for the last time in this series on the evening of the 6th June, although I did have two further readings allocated to me – on the 19th and 27th June. But I was relieved to be going back to my own Falstaff House on the 1st June, as I continued to so detest, abominate and abjure the house at Hyde Park Gate South.

CHAPTER LVII

Problems with Georgy, Visits to France, Stay in Paris, and Offers from Australia

I read at St. James's Hall on the 6th June and then remained in London, overwhelmed with business. I read again on the 19th, but had by now arranged to take Georgy – who had become very far from well – away for a week the next morning in the hope of doing her service through a little change. She had some affection of the heart, and I was so anxious and distressed about her that I was altogether dazed.

We stayed in Dover overnight, and spent time in France wandering in the strangest towns, before returning to complete my readings in London on the 27th June. A man from Australia (Felix Spiers) was now in London and said he was ready to pay me £10,000 for eight months of readings in his country, but I was unable to consider this at the moment. I was shut up in my room, in a ferocious and unapproachable condition, with a great accumulation of letters I had to answer. Georgy remained labouring under degeneration of the heart, and though Dr. Elliotson was very hopeful of her, I (who knew her best, I think) saw much in her that filled me with uneasiness. All that alacrity and "cheer of spirit" that used to distinguish her were gone. My present project was to remove to Paris early in the autumn, for a couple of months of complete change, and on the 10th July set off for Paris, returned to Gad's Hill on the 16th, before taking a distant engagement for three days, whilst Georgy continued to alarm me. No man on earth ever had such a friend as I had had – and continued to have – in her, and I also confessed to Wilkie that which was in my secret heart.

What with this anxiety over Georgy, and what with my own load, of which Wilkie now knew something, I became so restless that I could not answer for anything. Sometimes, in a desperate state, I seized a pen, and resolved to precipitate myself upon a story. Then I got up again with a forehead as gnarled as the oak tree outside the window, and found all the lines on my face that ought to have been on the blank paper. Pressed by all manner of business and botheration, on the 23rd July I again left Gad's Hill on a distant engagement, before returning to find Georgy very, very poorly. She grew steadily worse as I travelled to and fro, and I even approached Headland concerning the possibility of some Paris readings – though ordered him to say nothing on the subject yet to anyone. I began thinking of the Christmas Number and, by the middle of September, had done the opening and conclusion of it, entitled "Somebody's Luggage", doing it in the character of a waiter, which I thought exceedingly droll. I had contributors to the journal circulated, inviting them to contribute before the 8th November.

I wrote to Wilkie, speaking of his new book: "No Name", but also telling him I had some rather miserable anxieties which I meant to impart to him one of these days. I told him, however, that I would fight out of them I dare say, being not easily beaten – but that they had gathered and gathered. Georgy was very weak, and I took her to Dover for a week to give her a change, which proved beneficial.

On my return from Dover at the beginning of October, I spent time both in London and at Gad's Hill, where I received a letter from James Fields, asking again if I was thinking of reading in America. I told him I was not, but then received a more serious offer from Australia, to read at an increased fee. I turned matters over in my mind, tempted by this large offer, and consulted with Forster, but felt unable to agree to anything at this time in my distressed state. I had now resolved to go to Paris later in the month for about six weeks, taking Mamie and Georgy with me.

I set off on my own on the morning of Thursday 16th October, directing Mamie and Georgy to follow three days later, when I would meet them at Boulogne. But on the Sunday they were out in a great gale and could not get near Boulogne. I stood five hours, holding on with both hands, on the end of the pier at Boulogne in the height and fury of the storm; it was a wonderful sight, very picturesque and, to my great consolation, only saw one thing I missed in the Copperfield storm. I then received a message that their boat had managed to run in to Calais and they were safe. They had arrived, of course, half drowned, and when I went to Calais, post-haste the next morning expecting to find them half dead, I found them instead elaborately got up to come on to Paris by the next train, the most wonderful thing of all being that they hardly seemed to have been frightened, and looked as if they had passed a mild summer there!

We travelled to Paris and soon put up in an apartment at 27, Rue du Faubourg Saint-Honoré, where I now planned to stay until just before Christmas Day. Once settled, I formalized my business relationship with Chapman and Hall, but also continued to contemplate the renewed possibility of going to Australia for a reading tour. Spiers had brought me letters from the Australian legislature, newspaper editors, and the like, exhorting me to come, saying how much the people talked of me, and dwelling on the kind of reception that would await me there. He had opened the business with me by producing a letter of credit for £10,000 and I took him to be an honourable man. He had by now returned to Australia, but as I sat in Paris, I thought all the probabilities for reading in such a country as Australia were immense; and at home the thing had never missed fire. Moreover, I had got so used to it, and worked so hard at it, that I had got out of it more than I ever thought was in it for that purpose. But the conflict in my own mind was enormous. If I were to go I knew it would be a penance and a misery, and I dreaded that thought more than I can possibly express. The domestic life of the readings was all but intolerable to me when I was away for a few weeks at a time, so what would it be for such a length of time? How painfully unwilling I was to go, and yet how painfully sensible that perhaps I ought to go – with all the hands upon my skirts that I could not fail to feel and see there, whenever I looked around. Of course, one could not possibly count upon the money to be realized by a six month's absence, but £12,000 was supposed to be a low estimate. Being my own master too, I could "work" myself more delicately than if I bound myself for money beforehand, and a great deal of curious experience for after use could be gained over and above the money – the "Uncommercial Traveller Upside Down" I thought could be a part of All the Year Round. I struggled in my mind over and over as to what to do.

CHAPTER LVIII

Paris, Christmas at Gad's Hill, Return to France, Paris Readings, and a "Sick Friend"

I was now being pressed about reading again in London. My decision whether to do this – in February if I was to read at all – was to be mainly guided by my decision on the more difficult and more extensive reading question in Australia. It was also proposed to me to read in Paris, but at this time I did not think I would entertain the idea – I seemed to have enough to think about without it.

The weeks rolled on and I still could not make up my mind what to do about Australia. I spent much of my time in constant occupation considering the contents of All the Year Round in correspondence with Wills and reading every paper for the Christmas Number as soon as it was sent to me. On the 17th November Wills came over to Paris to make the number up with me and, once we had done, All the Year Round stood a restaurant dinner and a box at a play.

Wills returned to London and I continued to be in contact with him over All the Year Round, but before our leaving on the 22nd December, I made two short visits to London, firstly to assist my son Frank, and then to come to the aid of my dear good Dr. Elliotson, who had got into serious dispute with his sisters. I had a weary time in London with Elliotson's miseries, and had quite enough of my own cares to keep me going (or not going) when such affairs failed me.

I reserved a place at the Hotel du Helder for my return to Paris from the middle of January 1863 – there being no likelihood of my going home again until, at the earliest, the middle of February – and sought to arrange a date in January (proposing the 17th) for a reading of Copperfield for charity at the British Embassy. The exact date of the reading I could not be sure of as Lord Cowley, the Ambassador, was away and did not come back until the 27th December. The prices to be charged were to be very high, but as many of the French present would probably not have the faintest notion what the reading was about, I feared it would not be an audience like St. James's Hall; but nevertheless believed it would be a pretty sight, and I would be as good as if they would let me be.

We returned to Gad's Hill, Mamie, Georgy and I coming across the Channel on the 22nd December, directly after a gale and with 150 sick schoolboys on board. However, upon arrival I immediately received the news that the small number of 185,000 copies of "Somebody's Luggage" had now been sold! It was certainly a most single hit, and by Christmas Eve I had the report from the office that it had now sold the rather extraordinary number of more than 191,000 copies!

Gad's Hill for Christmas was pervaded by boys; and every boy had (as usual) an unaccountable and awful power of producing himself in every part of the house at every moment, apparently in fourteen pairs of clashing boots, while I looked on from the cloud-capped pinnacle of my own gloomy antiquity. I planned to leave Gad's Hill in the New Year of 1863, on Tuesday 6th January, and work and sleep at the office in Wellington Street until Saturday the 10th, inviting Wilkie to dine with me whilst I was there, before vanishing into space for a day or two to see a sick friend concerning whom I was anxious, and from whom I would then work my way around to Paris. Meanwhile, over the New Year period, I contemplated over my children.

Charley was now married – though not particularly to my satisfaction – and was in business as an Eastern Merchant in the City. I considered he would do well if he could find continuous energy; otherwise not. Mamie, unmarried, ran the home with Georgy, while Katey went on very happily with her husband Charlie Collins. I now found he was a most excellent husband and an upright good fellow – clever too and making his way. They had no family as yet and, if they would take my word for the fact, were better without one. Walter, with the 42nd Highlanders in India, was spending more than he got, had cost me money and disappointed me. Frank was in my office pending a vacancy in the Foreign Office. Alfred was a good steady fellow but not at all brilliant; he had been educated expensively for engineers or artillery, but for more than a year or so I had had the strongest doubts of his passing the Woolwich examination – and now it seemed unlikely that he would. This made his case a very difficult one for me; I had a horror of him being idle, and felt it would do him good in after-life to be thrown on his self-reliance in some line of life now.

Sydney, a born little sailor, was a Midshipman on H.M.S.Orlando, and I was confident he would make his way anywhere. In reference to

Harry, I thought at that time the Indian civil service the best opening to which his attention could be directed; I spoke to him, and he liked the idea. I told him I would communicate our wish to his Headmaster at his school in Wimbledon and that I believed they would be glad to prepare him for that examination; if he continued to be attentive and industrious, some reliance was placed on his passing through it with credit as he was very bright and clever, and his quickness in learning I had observed to be remarkable, even when he was a mere baby. Plorn was now 10 years of age and he, too, now at the Wimbledon school, but I was not yet decided upon his future.

On Sunday the 11th January I left London to visit my sick friend. I then subsequently arrived at the Hotel du Helder in Paris 4 days later on the 15th January (safe and neuralgic) and found John Thompson already there for me. My little rooms at the hotel were perfectly comfortable and I liked the hotel better than any I had ever put up at in Paris; and John's amazement at, and appreciation of Paris were indescribable – he went about with his mouth open, staring at everything and being tumbled over by everybody!

I attended a state dinner at the Embassy on the 15th, it coming off in the room where I was to read. Then, on the 17th, the reading of Copperfield went ahead and was a most tremendous and brilliant success, the French taking to the reading so astoundingly that they requested me to do it twice more. These further dates were fixed as the 29th and 30th January, but meanwhile I had the neuralgia return and was not able to sleep. Some unstringing of the nerves – coupled with an anxiety not to be mentioned here – held sleep from me. The nights were not long and it didn't much matter, except that I needed to be by myself in the day. I left Paris for a week, returning to the Hotel du Helder on the 28th January. The next morning I went down to the Embassy to the room to rehearse, a thing I had never done in my life before, but I had not read Dombey in the previous twelve months; and I felt as if I could not muster spirits and composure enough to get through the child's death. Reading went horribly against the grain, as the grain was at that moment; though I supposed it would be kinder towards night.

In the event, Paris rushed at my readings and that night (the 29th) I read Little Dombey and the Trial from Pickwick, and the following night the Carol (which was particularly well adapted for the purpose) and the Trial from Pickwick again, all in aid of the British Charitable Fund, and with everything let out. I cannot give you any idea of the success of these readings; no one can imagine the scenes – such audiences and such enthusiasm! I was twice goaded and lifted out of myself into a state that astonished me almost as much as the audience; they ran away with my readings in the most astonishing and rapturous manner. The thing culminated on the night of the 30th in a two hours' storm of excitement and pleasure; they actually recommenced and applauded right away into their carriages and down the street. Never was anything like that last reading – Never. Never. Never! The Parisian sensation on the subject was really indescribable.

The following night I went with Lady Molesworth to hear Faust at the Theatre-Lyrique. It was a splendid work, in which that noble and sad story was most nobly and sadly rendered, but I could hardly bear the thing. It affected me so, and sounded in my ears so like a mournful echo of things that lay in my own heart. I gave in completely.

CHAPTER LIX

In Amiens and Arras, Return to England,
but Sudden Visits to France

I left Paris in the early morning of the 5th February, long before post-time and when all sensible people except myself were in bed, planning not to come back to Paris or near it. I had heard the day before from Wills that the latest half-yearly accounts for All the Year Round, for the 6 months to the end of October 1862, had shown the best income (of £1,889) to date, and was much delighted by this news.

From Amiens, I wrote to Forster sending him a packet and also a note for Georgy at Gad's Hill that I asked him to post on to her in England. I also told Forster: "I walk miles away into the country, and you can scarcely imagine by what deserted ramparts and silent little cathedral closes, or how I pass over rusty drawbridges and stagnant ditches out of and into the decaying town". I had also written to him on my birthday when I had paid a visit to Arras: "You will remember me today, I know. Thanks for it. An odd birthday, but I am as little out of heart as you would have me be – floored now and then, but coming up again at the call of Time…"

I took the boat at Boulogne on the evening of the 16th February, and arrived at my rooms at the office in Wellington Street at about midnight, where Georgy was waiting; I told her all about the circumstances in France. After my success in Paris, I also now arranged to change my reading venue to the Hanover Square Rooms, beginning on the 6th March, principally for the love of the more delicate points in Copperfield. This latter room was quite a wonderful room for sound, and so easy, that the least inflection told everywhere in the place exactly as it left your lips; but I did miss my dear old shilling galleries six or eight hundred strong in St. James's Hall, with a certain roaring sea of response in them.

I read on the 6th, 11th and 13th March at the Hanover Square Room, before I received notice of some rather anxious business I had on hand (not my own) that required me to return immediately to France. I arranged to cross the Channel on the morning of Friday 20th March, and believed the visit would probably detain me four or five days. I eventually returned six days later on the 26th, where I found myself so oppressed with work, that by the late afternoon on that day I had not yet managed to have leisure even to speak to John Thompson. I told Georgy that I would report to her in detail when we met on Monday the 30th. I had become in dull spirits myself just now.

Then, before the weekend had arrived, I received a further hasty summons to attend upon the sick friend at a distance that so threw me out on the Friday and Saturday in obliging me to prepare for a rush across the Channel again that I was not able to visit the Royal Academy to view the pictures of Frederic Leighton, as I had arranged to do. I returned to Gad's Hill on the evening of Monday 30th March, but I had already agreed to take the chair at the Anniversary Festival of the General Theatrical Fund on the Saturday of that week, the 4th April, in place of Wilkie, who was prevented at the last moment from doing so on account of severe illness, so was not able to travel until then. On the 4th I gave a speech, accompanied by much laughter and cheering from the audience, before then hurrying across the Channel – and was only blown back to London on the night of the 8th April.

[EDITOR'S NOTE: *Very many years later, and more than 50 years after Charles Dickens's death, his children Katey and Henry are reported to have both said, independently, that Nelly had a child by their father, a boy, but that it died in infancy. It would appear that Nelly had been housed, probably with her mother, in or around Amiens at this time.*]

I went home to Gad's Hill on the afternoon of the 10th April and stayed five days; on the 13th I was able to say that Georgy was all but quite well now, having no attack of pain or flurry, and being in all respects immensely better. I now felt able to arrange for friends to visit Gad's Hill again in the coming period.

CHAPTER LX

*Hanover Square Readings, Lazy Days at Gad's Hill,
and Uncommercial Travelling in France*

I now had a busy schedule of readings ahead of me in the Hanover
Square Rooms that had been arranged for the 21st, 23rd, 28th and 30th
April, as well as five further readings in May and two in June. As we
had had a place in Paris for some time, I told Mamie that she must
not expect a house in London this season, and so I continued to travel
between Gad's Hill and my rooms above the office.

Before the reading on the 21st April, I went away again for some days,
and then for the next three weeks read twice in each week, which, added
to my ordinary occupations and botherations, rendered it all but hopeless
for me to tie myself to any engagement. There was an immense audience
at the Hanover Square Room on the 21st April, and great numbers were
turned away, but the management of Blockheadland was so mortally
bad, that I was of a mind in all good humour, to get rid of him at the end
of this series. I saw so many doubled fists flourishing into his perspiring
face that night that I trusted his life might be considered in danger.

I noticed a very small drop in the circulation for All the Year Round
at this time and wanted to stop it. Consequently I struck with a new
series of the Uncommercial Traveller, the first being "From Dover to
Calais", an account of my taking the Calais night mail, and the second
"Some Recollections of Mortality", where three scenes of death that I
had witnessed in the past had been brought once again to my mind. In
early May, after my reading on the 8th, I was again absent from England
for some days, before returning to London for a further reading on the
15th. I found also I had to deal with a number of other matters, but
even seeking to deal with these, I felt unable to make appointments of
business, for I could not bear to do anything that I was not reasonably
sure of doing with exactness. I did begin trying, alone by myself, the
Oliver Twist murder as a reading, but got something so horrible out of
it that I was afraid to try it in public.

The readings continued, and on the 29th May I read Copperfield
and Mr. Bob Sawyer's Party from Pickwick. There was on that night

such a tremendous demonstration with Copperfield (now my favourite reading) that I had never seen such an enthusiastic audience; no, not even when I read in Paris! I read again on the 5th June, and with the final reading set for the 12th June the pressure for tickets was so great that it was quite out of my power to send out any, even to relations. Headland told me that the pressure on the stalls was so great that he had been obliged to withhold all but two of the few free admissions that were usually set aside for my own family.

On the 9th June, Maria Ternan married in London, but neither Nelly nor her mother felt able to attend. I wrote a number of articles for All the Year Round, but my head became addled with Uncommercial Travelling and I was happy to be done with it for a time, particularly as I developed a ridiculous swelling in the back of my head which wanted to be something troublesome. I spent many days at Gad's Hill going for fine walks with my two dogs, Turk and Linda, for we had a touch of most beautiful weather, and this country was most beautiful too. I had a favourite spot between Gad's Hill and Maidstone where Georgy, Mamie and I would often take our lunch on a hill-side there, and then I would lie down on the grass with a cigar– a splendid example of laziness.

I received a letter from Mrs. Eliza Davis, wife of the purchaser of Tavistock House, asking for a donation for a convalescent home for poor Jewish people, but at the same time accusing me of encouraging "a vile prejudice" and producing a great wrong (as she put it) for Jewish people by my creation of Fagin in Oliver Twist. My reply was a little tardy, but I wrote back explaining: "Fagin in Oliver Twist is a Jew, because it unfortunately was true of the time to which that story refers, that that class of criminal almost invariably was a Jew. But surely no sensible man or woman of your persuasion can fail to observe – firstly, that all the rest of the wicked dramatis personae are Christians; and secondly, that he is called "The Jew", not because of his religion, but because of his race. If I were to write a story, in which I pursued a Frenchman or a Spaniard as "The Roman Catholic", I should do a very indecent and unjustifiable thing but I make mention of Fagin as the Jew, because he is one of the Jewish people, and because it conveys that kind of idea of him, which I should give my readers of a Chinaman by calling him a Chinese." I enclosed a donation and assured her I had no feeling towards the Jewish people but a friendly one.

By the middle of July I was happy to report myself alright again, and now felt able to engage as an Uncommercial Traveller once more. I paid a visit to a cooking depot for the working classes in Whitechapel and took their meal, which was good, and on the 20th July, went down to Bulwer Lytton's Knebworth to stay for a few days, but thereafter began planning to go away on another "Uncommercial" trip. I was also always thinking of writing again a long book, but was never beginning to do it. I had not been anywhere for ever and ever so long, but I continued to think of evaporating for a fortnight, and although I was planning to travel again to France, I very much feared that France would involve us in general war and uproar. The adventurer on that throne (Napoleon III) had no chance but in the distraction of his people's minds, and in the jingle and glitter of theatrical glory. The deference to him that had been the low policy of the English Government was, to my thinking, as blind as it was base; and I could not express its want of sight more strongly.

On Monday 17th August, I set off by train from Higham Station for a fortnight's Uncommercial Travelling in Northern France. In short I was travelling there, and wanted an excuse for not going away from there, and made it to my satisfaction, and stayed there. But, in the time, I explored the French-Flemish countryside and found it was an area that was neither a bold nor a diversified country, three-quarters Flemish and a quarter French – yet it had its attractions. Though great lines of railway traversed it, the trains left it behind and went puffing off to Paris and the South, to Belgium and Germany, to the Northern Sea-Coast of France and to England, and merely smoking it a little in passing. I did not know it, and there was a good reason for being there; and I could not pronounce half the long queer names I saw inscribed over the shops, and that was another good reason for being there, since I felt I surely ought to have learnt how. On my return at the end of the month, I then had available for publication in All the Year Round, a piece entitled: "In the French – Flemish Country."

CHAPTER LXI

Mrs. Lirriper, Our Mutual Friend, Deaths of My Mother, Thackeray, and Walter, and 57 Gloucester Place

Whilst away in France I had time to think over the Christmas Number which now came round again – it seemed only yesterday that I had done the last – and was full of notions besides for a new story in twenty numbers; when I could clear the Christmas stone out of the road, I told Forster that I thought I could now dash into this on the grander journey. I dined with him on the 3rd September at 46, Montagu Square (his new home), after not having seen him for some time through us both being away.

I drafted a letter for Wills to send out to contributors to All the Year Round so that we could begin the work of getting our Christmas Number together, and telling them it was of great importance that we should get the materials of the number together by the 4th November. This year I decided that the description of the latitude the number admitted of would be a very short one – the tales could be in the first person or in the third, and might relate to any season or period; they could be supposed to be told to an audience, or to the reader, or to be penned by the writer without knowing how they would come to light, for how they came to be told at all did not require to be accounted for. I stated that if they could express some new resolution formed – some departure from an old idea or course that was not quite wholesome – it might be better for the general purpose; but even that was not indispensable. I began the number under the title "Mrs. Lirriper's Lodgings", hoped to make something of her, and thought the title a good one.

I also wrote to Chapman and Hall in reference to a new work in 20 monthly numbers, as of old. I carefully considered past figures and future reasonable possibilities (as no doubt they also did) and proposed to them that they pay me £6,000 for the half copyright throughout and outright, at the times they had already mentioned to me. I told them that for this consideration I was ready to enter into articles of agreement with them, but as I had to be rid of the Christmas Number and of the Uncommercial Traveller before I began work to any great purpose, and as I considered I must be well on before the first number was published, I could not bind myself to time of commencement as yet. But I was really anxious to get into the field before the next spring was out; and I believed our interests could not fail to be alike as to all such points, if we became partners in the story. They agreed, and, with the assistance of Ouvry, an outline of the heads of agreement between us was drafted before the month was out, with the formal terms being finally signed on the 21st November.

Meanwhile, on the 12th September, my poor mother died quite suddenly at last. Her condition was frightful, having been in a fearful state, mental and bodily, for two or three years. She had lived with Helen and her children, and I had contributed to their upkeep, but she had long been in a terrible state of decay and now I had to look after her funeral. I arranged this for the 17th September at Highgate Cemetery, where she was laid to rest beside my father, and I also arranged that 4, Grafton Terrace (where they had been living) now be vacated, Helen and the children proposing to move into Yorkshire.

I was now exceedingly anxious to begin my book, and was bent upon getting to work at it; although I wanted to prepare it for the spring, I was determined not to begin to publish with less than five monthly numbers done. I saw my opening perfectly, with one main line on which the story was to turn, and if I did not now strike while the iron was hot, I was afraid I would drift off again, and have to go through all the uneasiness once more. But I was now continuing to keep my Book of Memoranda to assist me and had my title of "Our Mutual Friend", so I began writing in earnest, passing the forenoon by myself in my own room, no visitors disturbing me or my writing from breakfast to lunch each day.

At the beginning of November I drew together the contributions for the Christmas Number and began putting it together with Wills, but the work caused me to be in some doubt whether I had anything inside my head or no, the number so addling it that I had difficulty recognizing it as mine. I planned to go to France again early on Monday 23rd November, and at that time did not know when I would return. I eventually managed to finish the Christmas Number for press, working late into the night of Saturday 14th November, and then went to Gad's Hill for a week before leaving for France.

I left as planned on the 23rd November, but now proposed to be back in London a week later, and indeed was back in London again at the office on the evening of the 30th before then going to Gad's Hill. The Christmas Number of "Mrs. Lirriper's Lodgings" was published on the 3rd December, and immediately my esteemed friend Mrs. Lirriper made a most extraordinary mark on the public. I doubted if I had ever done anything that had been so affectionately received by such an enormous audience! I could not turn anywhere without encountering some enthusiasm about her, and the Christmas Number became the greatest success so far, shooting ahead of the previous year and selling around 220,000 copies – making the name of Mrs. Lirriper so swiftly and domestically famous as never was. I had a very strong belief in her when I wrote about her, finding that she made a great effect on me, but she certainly went beyond my hopes.

Over Christmas I received news that Thackeray had died on Christmas Eve. It was sudden, and yet not so sudden, for he had long been alarmingly ill. I had met him at the Athenaeum Club on the 16th December and spoken to him for the first time since difficulties had arisen between us at the Garrick Club five years before; we had sat on a settee in the hall and had had a long and cordial talk on familiar topics as in old days. He told me he had been in bed three days, and had had fits of shivering, which, he said, for the time quite took all power of work out of him, but he was very cheerful, looked very bright, and had it in his mind to try a new remedy, which he laughingly described. He was much softened. On the 30th December I went to his burial at Kensal Green, along with a great number of his literary friends and a crowd estimated in the order of 2,000 people, saddened, but pleased I had been able to speak to him. Thereafter I was approached by his magazine, "The Cornhill", to write a memorial to him, and did so. We had had our differences of opinion, and at first I proposed to write merely the few affectionate words that an old friend and brother in arms could say beside a newly-made grave, but in time wrote a couple of pages about him that I would most gladly have excused myself from doing if I felt I could. I tried to avoid the fulsome and injudicious trash that had been written about him in the papers, and delicately to suggest the two points in his character as a literary man that were bad for the literary cause. I thought he too much feigned a want of earnestness, and that he made a pretence of undervaluing his art, which was not good for the art that he held in trust. But when we had fallen upon these topics between ourselves, it was never very grave, and I had a lovely image of him in my mind, twisting both his hands in his hair, and stamping about, laughing, to make an end of the discussion. If, in the reckless vivacity of his youth, his satirical pen had ever gone astray or done amiss, he had caused it to prefer its own petition for forgiveness long before. Other scribes were particularly dwelling on his having been "a gentleman", "a great gentleman" and the like (vile stuff) as if the rest of us were of the tinker tribe; and also on his wonderful gift of putting all people and all companies at their ease, at their perfect repose, enjoyment, and genial ease – which was much as if they should praise me, being dead, for always having lived with my wife.

Of course, the natural result was that everybody else began to disparage the poor fellow, and that people who had beslavered him living began to bespatter him dead. He was only in his fifty-third year when he died; so young a man that the mother who blessed him in his first sleep blessed him in his last. I had seen him first nearly twenty-eight years before his death, when he had proposed to become the illustrator of my earliest book, and the long interval between that time and the time when I saw him last was marked, in my remembrance of him, by many occasions when he was extremely humorous, when he was irresistibly extravagant, when he was softened and serious, and when he was charming with children. But, by none did I recall him more tenderly than by two or three that stand out of the crowd, when he would present himself in my room, announcing that some passage in a certain book "had made him cry yesterday", and how he had come to dinner "because he couldn't help it", and must talk such passage over. No one could ever have seen him more genial, natural, cordial, fresh, and honestly impulsive, than I had seen him at those times. No one could be surer than I of the greatness and the goodness of heart that then disclosed itself. And on that bright wintry day when he was laid in his grave at Kensal Green, the heads of a great concourse of his fellow-workers in the arts were bowed around his tomb.

I considered that I should be very much occupied during the approaching season of 1864, and so deemed it best not to encumber myself with any readings. I became hard at work on my new book, and towards the end of January I had done the first two numbers and was beginning the third. It was a combination of drollery with romance, which required a deal of pains and a perfect throwing away of points that might have been amplified – but I hoped it was very good, and confess, in short, that I thought it was; I felt at first, however, quite dazed in getting back to the large canvas and the big brushes.

Forster and his wife had now moved into a new residence, Palace Gate House in Kensington, which had instantly taken them both by the throat, chest, and nose, and caused them excruciating torments. At present it appeared to be something between a Government office and a hospital – and they looked as if they were put in at six and sixpence a week to take care of it! On another day I told Georgy that I saw Forster flitting about the Athenaeum as I conversed in the hall with all sorts and conditions of men – and pretending not to see me – but I saw in every hair of his whisker that he saw nothing else.

Mamie and Georgy thought of taking a place in town again in February, and remaining until June, so at the end of January I began looking at divers houses, but found nothing. Then I was shown a house at 57, Gloucester Place, Hyde Park Gardens, which was suitable, and my offer of £130 to take it from the 13th February to the 4th June was accepted.

I then heard from India the news that Walter had died on the last day of 1863, at the same time as I had been acting charades with all the children at Gad's Hill. He had been on his way home on sick leave after being very ill but, in Calcutta at the Officer's Hospital, he coughed violently, had a great gush of blood from the mouth, and fell dead, all in a few seconds. It was then found he had extensive and perfectly incurable aneurism of the aorta, which had burst. I kept this from Georgy, as I believed she had the same disorder, and also because I had observed strong traces of it in Sydney. Frank had gone out to Calcutta on the 20th December, counting on seeing his brother after six years, and then heard of his death on touching the shore. I sent an inscription to India for Walter's tombstone.

I continued at work on my new book, though in a rather dull slow way for the moment, planning to have the first number published at the end of April. I had approached Marcus Stone, in place of Browne, to do the illustrations and he had agreed, so I began sending him the numbers as I got them back from the printers. I thought it best for him to read the first two numbers before we took counsel together and then settle, in the first place, what little indication of the story we would have on the cover. The design he produced was excellent, and with some slight alteration that I suggested, it came out to perfection and I gave directions for his name to be put in all future advertisements.

We had by now moved into 57, Gloucester Place and I worked away at Our Mutual Friend, as well as the office proofs with Wills, and took long walks. I found the town beastly at this time, utterly abominable and unwholesome, and wished for the sea. I had wavered and considered, considered and wavered over going to Hastings, but I knew that if I took that sort of holiday, I must have a day or two to spare after it, and at this critical time I had not. I knew that if I were to lose a page of the five numbers I had proposed to myself to be ready by the publication day, I would feel that I had fallen short. I had grown hard to satisfy, and wrote very slowly. And I had so much – not fiction – that was thought of, when I did not want to think of it, that I was forced to take more care than I once took

The publication of the first number of Our Mutual Friend cheered me greatly – 30,000 copies and orders continuing to flow in fast thereafter, to the extent that the print run of that first number rose to 40,000. I then heard of the serious illness of my servant John Thompson. For a time his life hung on a hair and I went out to visit him where he was now staying in Kentish Town, only to hear of the most deplorable circumstances relating to him. His diabolical wife and her sister, being left at night to watch him, got blind drunk together on gin, omitted everything they had undertaken to do, dropped gin and God knows what over his poor dying figure, and pitched into the landlady and attendant gossips when, with natural indignation, they found them in the morning and took their gin away. Thompson was at that stage doubled up, his knees to his head, and sinking out of life, and was so when Frank Beard (who was called for) found him. I wished to take care that he was not left to those amicable mercies any more, and asked Wills to make known these circumstances in their fullest atrocity to everyone at the office, and let everybody be strictly charged never on any pretence to let the women into the house; and let them understand too that I would immediately discharge anyone who, even in mistaken compassion, or for any other mistakenly good reason, disobeyed this injunction. I tumbled the wife out of the sick chamber when I found her there, and it was found that she had been perpetually drunk ever since they had been in Kentish Town. Frank Beard, however, was really a guardian angel to Thompson and, with help, he slowly recovered. Then, at the beginning of June, we gave up 57, Gloucester Place and returned to Gad's Hill.

CHAPTER LXII

Our Mutual Friend, Visits to France, Deaths of Dilke and Leech, and a Swiss Chalet at Gad's Hill

I continued on with Our Mutual Friend at Gad's Hill, and found myself going round and round like a carrier pigeon, before swooping on Number 7 and keeping myself well ahead of the monthly publication dates. I liked exceedingly the sketches Marcus Stone was now doing, and thought them the best we had had, and whilst I made suggestions to him as to the subject matter, I was happy to leave to him what he wished to take. I planned to be in France again on the 30th June for a few day's holiday: I told one correspondent towards the end of June that I was just leaving Gad's Hill "on a ten days or twelve days visit to Belgium", but to Wills on the same day I told him my present "mysterious disappearance" was going to be in the direction of France. It had occurred to me that the next Mrs. Lirriper for the Christmas Number might have a mixing in it of Paris and London – she and the Major, and the boy, all working out the little story in the two places – and I planned to turn this over on French ground with great care.

I managed to leave on Monday 27th June, and returned to the office 10 days later, on the morning of the 7th July, to find further excellent illustrations by Marcus Stone for Our Mutual Friend awaiting me. On then returning to Gad's Hill, I began again inviting, with the promise of a hearty welcome, friends to come and visit, as well as falling to work again on Our Mutual Friend. I was not wanting in industry, but I did find myself wanting in invention, and so began falling back with the book. By the end of July, the next Christmas work began looming large before me, and I could hardly hope to do it without losing a number of Our Mutual Friend; I had very nearly lost one already, and two would take one half of my whole advance of publication. I then became very unwell with a relaxed throat, was out of sorts and, as I knew from two days of slow experience, had a very mountain to climb before I should see the open country of my work.

Nevertheless, I found time to write (as "Well Wisher") a letter to the editors of "The Gad's Hill Gazette" – the newspaper produced for fun by my children to encourage them onward – as well as assisting Wills (who had himself been ill) with All the Year Round. Sala had gone to America, leaving undone the final numbers of his serial story "Quite Alone", and we had to consider what to do. We eventually decided to have the Scottish journalist Andrew Halliday, who was already contributing to All the Year Round, to complete it. I then heard from Forster of the sad news of the death of Charles Dilke. Poor Dilke! I was very sorry that the capital old stout-hearted man was dead, and wrote my sincere condolences to his son. Dilke had played a staunch role in our fight for reform of the Literary Fund, and I told his son in truth that never on this earth should I fight any fight by the side of a more reliable and faithful man, though I were to live as long as he.

I continued to have the strongest faith in Our Mutual Friend doing thoroughly well, believing it to be good, full of variety, and always rising in the working out of the people and the story. I knew I had put into it the making of a dozen books, and the circulation was already larger than that of Copperfield or Chuzzlewit. I began to speak to Chapman and Hall of its publication in volume form, while in the meanwhile pressing on with the story and directing Marcus Stone with his illustrations. In September I was also at work on the Christmas Number, bringing to the fore Mrs. Lirriper once again, including the hunting of a legacy for her in Sens, 120 kilometres by rail South East of Paris. The result was that "Mrs. Lirriper's Legacy" was successfully incorporated into the Christmas Number.

At the beginning of October we had a fire in the All the Year Round office whilst Wills was away ill, but he nevertheless went in and did it all. We had our suspicions as to who had caused this fire, but it was much to be regretted that we could not take the suspect to Bow Street, for in the case of so nefarious an offence there really was a duty to be done to society – though I was almost afraid to use the phrase as it was so horribly abused. I heard from Wilkie that he was planning to go to Paris and wished for me to go with him, but I had such work to deal with and was something the worse for it, that I felt only able to go to Dover and the Lord Warden Hotel with Georgy for a few days change, and so invited Wilkie to join us there instead. I booked a sea-view sitting room and two bedrooms from the 13th October – arriving in the evening – and a third bedroom for Wilkie for two days later when he had agreed to join us; we got the best rooms in the house, and Wilkie found another equally good room reserved for himself when he arrived. He brought with him the proofs of his new novel "Armadale", which struck me greatly when I read them, and I predicted certain success with the story. Georgy read them also and could not sleep until she had finished. Meanwhile I felt myself better able to write by the sea, and gave myself no quarter. I was heartily glad and grateful to be honestly able to believe that Mrs. Lirriper was nothing but a good 'un, but my expectations as to her sale were not so mighty as those held by Wills.

I returned to London, and then Gad's Hill, after the week in Dover and continued on with my writing, as well as Wills and I having the Christmas Number prepared and advertised. I also received the account, with payment from Chapman and Hall, for the sale of the first six numbers of Our Mutual Friend, amounting to just over £2,300. Occasional rallying came off with the family at Gad's Hill, including with Charley, in which another generation began to peep above the table. I once used to think what a horrible thing it would be to be a grandfather, but finding that the calamity fell upon me without my perceiving any other change in myself, I bore it like a man.

On the 29th October I was dining with Marcus Stone at Gad's Hill when a telegram arrived. I opened it and now found that John Leech was dead. The news shocked me terribly, and thereafter I was put out woefully. For the next two days I could do nothing, seeming for a time to have quite lost the power, and was unable to do my number for Our Mutual Friend. It was only by slow degrees thereafter that I began getting back to the track, and Marcus accompanied me to poor Leech's funeral at Kensal Green. I had known Leech since the time I had lived in Furnival's Inn and Cruikshank had sent him to me. He was a wonderful friend and comic artist who became a chief illustrator to my Christmas books, and he was also particularly fond of my sailor son, Sydney. I was deeply saddened by Leech's demise.

I became very run down with a bad cold and could hardly write at all, so decided to go away for a fortnight to France from the 17th November. I told Georgy that she knew how to address me, if need be, and, though did not expect to hear from her, gave her a contact address of the Hotel Imperial du Pavilion in Boulogne. I told her I would not fail to write myself. Then, having crossed to Boulogne, I travelled the 10 kilometres south to the village of Condette and there stayed at a house belonging to my old friend Monsieur Beaucourt-Mutuel that was close to the Chateau de Hardelot. I got rid of any touch of neuralgia there (as I always did in France), on this occasion by the glorious sea-air surroundings.

I found no old friends in my voyages of discovery on that side, such as I had left on this, and returned back to the office at Wellington Street on the evening of the 28th November. The next day I went down to Gad's Hill and, upon arriving at Higham Station, found Georgy and Marsh, my groom, awaiting me in triumph in a beautiful and perfect brougham – a gift from Wills that Mamie had collected while I had been away in France. I found it the lightest and prettiest and best carriage of the class ever made, but I valued it for higher reasons than these. I wrote and told Wills: "It will always be dear to me – far dearer than anything on wheels could ever be for its own sake – as a proof of your ever generous friendship and appreciation, and a memorial of a happy intercourse and a perfect confidence that have never had a break, and that surely never can have any break now after all these years".

I spent Christmas and New Year 1865 at Gad's Hill with the family, including Katey and Charlie Collins, as well as Marcus Stone, Henry Chorley, and fine actor Charles Fechter with his wife Eleonore. I had given assistance to Fechter in the past and he now caused much excitement when he produced a Swiss Chalet for me, which arrived in 94 pieces at Higham Station and which I subsequently had erected in the shrubbery wilderness and amongst the trees on the opposite side of the road to the house. It really was a very pretty thing and I considered that in the summer (supposing it not to be blown away in the spring), the upper room would make a charming study, although as it was being erected it became much higher than I ever supposed.

At the beginning of 1865 Chapman and Hall commenced steps to issue the "People's Edition" of my works at two shillings a volume, which proved extremely popular. It began with Pickwick, and I received a half-share in the profits as they sold. During 1865 over 135,000 volumes were issued and sold, and over 110,000 the following year. I was also pressed (once again) to stand for Parliament but I had by now thoroughly settled it within myself that I was more useful, more congenially occupied, and more free, out of Parliament than I could possibly be in it, and so wrote and told the proposers that I would under no circumstances offer myself to the electors. But I did agree to preside at the second dinner of the Newspaper Press Fund, telling the committee that they could rely on my loyalty to my old calling.

CHAPTER LXIII

Our Mutual Friend, Frost-Bitten Foot, 16 Somers Place,
Visits to France, and an Accident at Staplehurst

On the 1st February I left London for a week's run away, returning to Gad's Hill on the 9th to press on with Our Mutual Friend, as well as entertaining friends over the weekend, including Fechter and Layard, who came down by train. But then we had a fall of deep snow and I wounded my foot with frost-bite from much walking in it. I walked daily in the snow and got wet in the feet. My boots hardened and softened, hardened and softened, my left foot swelled, and I still forced the boot on; sat in it to write, half the day; walked in it through the snow, the other half; forced the boot on again next morning; sat and walked again; and being accustomed to all sorts of changes in my feet, took no heed. At length, going out as usual, I fell lame on the walk, and had to limp home dead lame, through the snow, for the last three miles – to the remarkable terror, by the bye, of the two big dogs. This now caused me considerable tortures and pain, and I became laid up, not able for a time to see any visitors, though I did manage with difficulty to get to the office.

In March I once again took a place in London for the season, this time at 16, Somers Place, Hyde Park West, where we settled in, before I left to go away again for 6 days from the afternoon of the 9th, after settling matters in the office. I had also taken steps to obtain help in disposing of Alfred to Melbourne in Australia in the hope that he might there be able to become self-sufficient in himself. He was now 20 years of age and had been, for two years and more, in a large China House in the City, and his object now was to become employed in some business-house in Australia, and gradually make his way in the world. I made no arrangements for him, beyond providing him with some introductions, as he said he was going out by his own desire to – as the story books say – "seek his fortune." I did however have made up for him before he sailed a quantity of clothing, and told him (as I had in parting from both Sydney and Frank) that if he humbly tried to guide himself by the beautiful New Testament, he would never go wrong, and that I hoped he would never omit under any circumstances to say a prayer by himself night and morning. But I did feel that if the childless Kings and Queens in the stories had only known what they were about, they would never have bothered the fairies to give them families in the first place.

Despite having to spend times on sofas with my frost-bitten foot and feeling like an arctic sailor suffering tortures, I had to proceed on with Our Mutual Friend. But then this confounded foot became as bad as ever again. I consulted Frank Beard after suffering tortures all the night of the 20th March and, where I was never able to close my eyes, it caused me to be at work at the poppy fomentations again. I suppose it was invited by the east wind that was blowing enough to cut one's throat, and it now kept me in bed for two days. All I could see before me until my book was done was work, change of air, training, and work again, before I went back to Kent in June, although I hoped to be able to get away again for some time at the beginning of April.

I did manage to get away, but was back at 16, Somers Place by the 13th April. By this time my frost-bitten foot had begun to conduct itself somewhat more amiably, and by the 22nd I found I could now again walk my 10 miles in the morning without inconvenience, though I was absurdly obliged to sit shoeless all the evening – a very slight penalty, however, as I now detested going out for dinner. I was working like a dragon on my book again and a terror to the household – likewise to all the organs and brass bands in the quarter of Hyde Park where we were located – but I had ordered Gad's Hill to be gorgeously painted so as to have the place pretty and comfortable, and a fitting place to entertain my friends and visitors when we returned on the 1st June.

I went off across the Channel again for a week, thoroughly refreshing myself with its air, and if I had no boys holding on to the skirts of my coat, I think I should have kept a yacht and gone sailing about. I was now crossing the Channel in all weathers. Upon my return, I took the chair and spoke at the dinner held at the Freemasons' Tavern on the 9th May on behalf of the Newsvendors' Benevolent Institution. Wills attended with me and it was a most cheerful evening. I experienced a further hearty evening when I again took the chair at the Freemasons' Tavern on the 20th May, this time as a Vice-President of the Newspaper Press Fund, on the occasion of their second anniversary dinner. On this occasion I was happy in my speech to reminisce on my old times as a newspaper reporter; The Times had shown its opposition to the Fund, but Russell, their War Correspondent, was there and the dinner proved to be a great success.

I worked exceedingly hard to finish my next number of Our Mutual Friend before going to France again, and came to the point where, if I were not going away now, I felt I should break down. No one knew as I did how near to that I became, and believed work and worry, without exercise, would soon make an end of me. I certainly worked myself into a damaged state, but the moment I got away on the 29th May, I began – thank God – to get well again. I hoped to profit by this experience, and to make future dashes from my desk before I wanted them.

However, on the 9th June, after crossing the Channel from France to Folkestone, and travelling back on the Tidal Express train to London, with Nelly and her mother in the carriage, we were in a terrible accident at Staplehurst in Kent. As we travelled over a bridge, suddenly we were off the rail and beating the ground as the car of a half-emptied balloon might. Mrs. Ternan cried out "My God!" and Nelly screamed. I caught hold of them both (Mrs. Ternan sat opposite, and Nelly on my left), and said: "We can't help ourselves, but we can be quiet and composed. Pray don't cry out." Mrs. Ternan immediately answered, "Thank you. Rely upon me. Upon my soul, I will be quiet." Nelly said in a frantic way: "Let us join hands and die friends." We were then all tilted down together in a corner of the carriage, and stopped. I said to them thereupon: "You may be sure nothing worse can happen. Our danger must be over. Will you remain here without stirring, while I get out of the window?" They both answered quite collectedly, "Yes," and I got out without the least notion of what had happened. Fortunately, I got out with great caution and stood upon the step. Looking down, I saw the bridge gone and nothing below me but the line of rail. We were in the first-class carriage that did not go down, but hung in the air over the side of the broken bridge in an inexplicable manner. It had not gone over into the stream, as it was caught on the turn by the broken girders and brickwork of the bridge, just as it was dropping over and seemed impossibly balanced in the act of tilting. The Engine had broken from it before, and the rest of the train broken from it behind, and had gone down into the stream below. Nelly and her mother remained perfectly still in the tilted carriage until I could get them out.

I had a – I don't know what to call it – constitutional (I suppose) presence of mind, and was not in the least fluttered at the time. I then instantly remembered that I had had the manuscript of the next number of Our Mutual Friend (Number 16) with me, and clambered back into the carriage for it. Some people in the two other compartments of our carriage were madly trying to plunge out at the window, and had no idea that there was an open swampy field 15 feet down below them and nothing else! The two guards (one with his face cut) were running up and down on the down side of the bridge (which was not torn up) quite wildly. I called out to them: "Look at me. Do stop an instant and look at me, and tell me whether you don't know me." One of them answered: "We know you very well, Mr. Dickens." "Then," I said, "my good fellow for God's sake give me your key, and send one of those labourers here, and I'll empty this carriage." We did it quite safely, by means of a plank or two and when it was done I saw all the rest of the train, except the two baggage cars, down in the stream.

I got into the carriage again for my brandy flask, took off my travelling hat for a basin, climbed down the brickwork, and filled my hat with water. Suddenly I came upon a staggering man covered with blood (I think he must have been flung clean out of the carriage) with such a frightful cut across the skull that I couldn't bear to look at him. I poured some water over his face, and gave him some to drink, and gave him some brandy, and laid him down on the grass, and he said "I am gone" and died afterwards. Then I stumbled over a lady lying on her back against a little pollard tree, with the blood streaming over her face (which was lead-colour) in a number of distinct little streams from the head. I asked her if she could swallow a little brandy, and she just nodded, and I gave her some and left her for somebody else. The next time I passed her she was dead. Then a man (who evidently had not the least remembrance of what had really passed) came running up to me and implored me to help him find his wife, who was afterwards found dead. No imagination can conceive the ruin of the carriages, or the extraordinary weights under which the people were lying, or the complications into which they were twisted up among iron and wood, and mud and water.

I worked hard for hours among the dying and the dead. No words can describe it; I could not have imagined so appalling a scene. By an extraordinary chance, I had a bottle and a half of brandy with me; I slung the half bottle round my neck, carried my hat full of water in my hands, and called to the others who were helping: "I have brandy here." There was a Mr. Edward Dickenson (aged 17), who had changed places with a Frenchman who didn't like the window down, a few seconds before the accident. The Frenchman was killed, and a labourer and I got Mr. Dickenson out of a most extraordinary heap of dark ruins in which he was jammed upside down. He was bleeding at the eyes, ears, nose, and mouth; but did not seem to know that afterwards, and of course I didn't tell him. In the moment of going over the viaduct, the whole of his pockets were shaken empty! He had no watch, no chain, no money, no pocketbook, no handkerchief, when we got him out; he had been choking a quarter of an hour, when I heard him groaning. If I hadn't had the brandy to give him at the moment, I think he would have been done for. As it was, I later brought him up to London in the carriage with me, and took him to Charing Cross Hotel; I couldn't make him believe that he was hurt, but he was the first person whom the brandy saved. As I had run back to the carriage for the whole full bottle, I saw the first two people I had helped, lying dead – and a bit of shade from the hot sun, into which we had got the unhurt ladies, soon had as many dead in it as living.

After a while special trains were brought to the scene – including in them many medical men – and we were conveyed to London. I spent that night and the following day at the office in Wellington Street, with Wills kindly staying in attendance through that period, he being concerned at my shaking and the full descriptions I gave to him of the scenes I had witnessed. I had also, most unaccountably brought somebody else's voice out of that terrible scene. I was then away directly to Gad's Hill to quieten their minds there. Upon arrival I received many letters of sympathy and concern, including from Miss Coutts and Mrs. Brown, Macready, Maria Winter and Catherine. I had Georgy assist me in replying to them all as I was too much shaken to write many notes. It was the shock of working among the dying and the dead, and not the shock of the stumbling carriage (which was nothing) that affected me somewhat. This two or three hours work afterwards among the dead and dying, surrounded by terrific sights, rendered my hand unsteady – and I also found that my watch, a special chronometer, never went quite correctly thereafter.

I did not want to be examined at the Inquest – first held on the 12th June at the South-Eastern Hotel in London, and then resumed three days later at the Railway Hotel in Staplehurst – and did not want to write about it either. I considered it could do no good either way, and believed I could only seem to speak about myself, which, of course, I would rather not do; I wished to keep very quiet at Gad's Hill for a while. Nelly had told me that in the struggle of being got out of the carriage she had lost a gold watch-chain with a smaller gold watch-chain attached, a bundle of charms, a gold watch-key, and a gold seal engraved "Ellen"; I promised I would make her loss known at headquarters in case these trinkets should be found. I wrote to the Head Station Master at Charing Cross asking him if he would have the kindness to note this application, but nothing further was heard of them. Meanwhile I began to feel curiously weak, weak as if I were recovering from a long illness. I began to feel it more in my head and, though I slept and ate well, I would turn faint and sick if I wrote half a dozen notes.

By the 16th June I felt able to go to London, as I had promised to go and see Miss Coutts and also to go to my doctor (Frank Beard), as well as going on other errands of business. Nelly and her mother had no notion at the time of the accident that there was much the matter with them, as I took them with me in the carriage up to London from the scene of the disaster, but thereafter they had been lying ill ever since. The noise of the wheels of my hansom cab, and the London streets, however, was as much as I could bear, and so I made all speed back to Gad's Hill again – by a slow train though, for I felt I was not up to the express. I was still a little below the mark, and had my work to think of, but was advised by Frank Beard to remain quiet at Gad's Hill and avoid the noise of London until I had recovered.

I returned nevertheless to the office on the 20th June, and remained there for three days as I had anxiety over Nelly and her condition. The medicine Frank Beard had given me had done me good, but my pulse was still feeble and I knew I was unfit for noise and worry and aware that I must have time to get over these little defects. The terrible and affecting incidents of the accident had shaken my nervous system and so I withdrew myself from engagements of all kinds, in order that I might pursue on with Our Mutual Friend, with the comfortable sense of being perfectly free while it was adoing and when it was done.

Returning to Gad's Hill, I continued to think of Nelly at 2 Houghton Place, and on Sunday 25th June sent a message to John Thompson in London for him to take to her the following morning a little basket of fresh fruit, a jar of clotted cream (from Tucker's at 287 Strand) and a chicken, a pair of pigeons, or some nice little bird. I also asked him to go and see her again on the Wednesday and Friday mornings of that week and take her some other things of the same sort, making a little variety each day.

At Gad's Hill, I began to get right, though still low in pulse and very nervous. I ventured to drive into Rochester one day, but felt more shaken than I had since the accident, and still could not bear railway travelling. A perfect conviction, against the senses, came upon me with anything like speed, that the carriage was down on one side – and generally that was on the left, and not the side on which the carriage in the accident really went over – and was inexpressibly distressing. The directors of the South Eastern Railway Company sent me a Resolution of Thanks for "assistance to the unhappy passengers" etc. etc. and for etc. etc. etc. and I heard that they had offered the family of Edward Dickenson (whom I had got out of the carriage just alive), all the expenses and a thousand pounds down. The father declined to accept the offer as it seemed unlikely that the young man, whose destination had been India, would ever be passed for the Army now by the Medical Board, and my indignation became focused on Thomas Milner-Gibson, the President of the Board of Trade and the person in the Government responsible for the railways.

Every day of my life, I thought more and more what an ill-governed country we lived in, and what a pass our political system had got to. Here this enormous "Railway No-System" had grown up without guidance, and now its abuses were so represented in Parliament by directors, contractors, scrip-jobbers, and so forth that no Minister dared touch it. An election was now approaching and if I were a constituent of Milner-Gibson, he would most certainly have heard something from me on his nomination day, not in the least to his advantage.

But then I had another distraction, for in the election week my daughter Mamie was decoyed to Andover in Hampshire – in the Conservative interest! Think of my feelings as a radical parent! The wrong-headed Member for that constituency (William Humphery M.P.) and his wife were friends with whom she hunted, and she was now helping to receive (and deceive) the voters, which was very awful to me. And then, as I began Number 17 of Our Mutual Friend, I found that I had underwritten Number 16 by two and a half pages – a thing I had not done since Pickwick!

CHAPTER LXIV

Our Mutual Friend concluded, Doctor Marigold, Health Concerns, and 6 Southwick Place

By the middle of July, I had no present idea of being away from Gad's Hill for longer than a day or two together until the autumn was out. Croquet was set up on the lawn and I began to invite friends once again to come and visit. Then I had an invitation from Bulwer Lytton to visit Knebworth, and on Saturday 29th July, I joined Forster, Wills and many others (about 30 of us) who were members of the Guild of Literature and Art, and we all travelled together to see the houses that had been erected on his estate for retired artists and authors, which they might be granted free of rent. We inspected the three houses built in the gothic style, and then no less closely investigated a new public house that had sprung up practically opposite, named "Our Mutual Friend"! Thereafter, we drove on to Knebworth, where we were welcomed by our host, and introduced to a large party of the country gentry. Lunch was served in the old hall and as it drew to an end Bulwer climbed onto his chair and addressed us all, recalling how 15 years before "Every Man In His Humour" had been acted out in this very hall, and it was then that the idea began of establishing the Guild of Literature and Art had taken hold. He proposed a toast to the Guild and, to laughter and cheers, I had much pleasure in replying from the same chair. After a delightful day exploring the house and wonderful gardens – and where a band of the Coldstream Guards performed for those wishing to engage in open-air dancing – I left for the station to return home. Some of the guests by now had already made their way to "Our Mutual Friend" and were seated outside on the benches by the road. As I drove by, they all rose and, with uplifted goblets, gave stentorian cheers!

I had been obliged to contact Ouvry as I had discovered that a New Zealand vagabond was now playing the old nefarious game of printing instalments of Our Mutual Friend in breach of copyright. I instructed Ouvry to terrify him (as we had done with the publishers of an Australian journal the year before) and, together with Edward and Frederick Chapman, brought an action for breach of copyright in the

New Zealand Supreme Court, which immediately caused them to cease. Meanwhile the book had me by the throat and I was now constantly working like a dragon in the upper room of the chalet – a most delightful summer atelier and where I had never worked better anywhere. I wrote and told Fechter so, and that I was almost as much attached to it as I was to him! I had put five mirrors in it, and they reflected and refracted, in all kinds of ways, the leaves that were quivering at the windows, and the great fields of waving corn, and the sail-dotted river. My room was up among the branches of the trees; and the birds and butterflies flew in and out, and the green branches shot in at the open windows, and the lights and shadows of the clouds came and went with the rest of the company. The scent of the flowers, and indeed of everything that was growing for miles and miles, was most delicious. But delightful as this was, my life had been caused a great sadness over my poor dogs; Turk had been killed upon the railway, and Linda was almost beyond hope from canker in the ear, the sufferings of the poor creature being very distressing to see.

Into August I continued on very hard at Gad's Hill to finish my book, but by the middle of the month was celebrating the occasion with a little festival of neuralgia in the face. I was thankful that Nelly was much better, though not yet well, and I decided to leave Gad's Hill for three days from the 17th August, but on my return came into the agonies of finishing the book, completing the double Number 19 and 20, with what pains and patience no man knew, except I. Neuralgia flew about as I continued on, continuing to send Marcus Stone the proofs for him to choose the illustrations there from, and with Nelly much the same way as she had been, I hoped I could now finish in the first week of September, when I then planned to meet with Wills in the office before decamping for about a fortnight, although I was already buckling myself up for All the Year Round.

On the 2nd September I was able to send to the printer the whole conclusion of the text of Our Mutual Friend, as well as the preface and now felt the need to go away, perhaps for the rest of September, to France, and so made arrangements to have letters forwarded to me. I managed to get a boot on, made on an extra-large scale but really not very discernible from its ordinary sized companion, before setting off, telling a correspondent I was going immediately to Switzerland, though in fact went to Boulogne and Condette. The heat was excessive however, and on the 7th I got a slight sun-stroke and was obliged to be doctored and put to bed for a day. But I had begun to feel my foot stronger the moment I breathed the sea air, though in the whole time I was away, I was not able to wear a boot after four or five in the afternoon, and had to pass each evening with the foot up and nothing on it. Then, when I could, I walked by the sea perpetually, becoming burnt brown and gradually un-neuralgic. I proposed going to Paris for a single night to make a little purchase for myself and considered I may want more money than I had with me, so wrote and asked Wills if he would send me two £10 notes for the cheque that I enclosed. On the 13th September I stayed in Paris, at the Hotel du Helder, for a night before returning to Boulogne, from where I planned to take the tidal train on the evening of the 16th back to the office.

I returned to London, and thereafter to Gad's Hill, where, just before Harry returned to school in Wimbledon, he spoke to me, telling me that he did not now wish to enter the Indian civil service. My initial response to him was that many of us have many duties to discharge in life which we do not wish to undertake, and that we must do the best we can to earn our respective livings and make our way. I also clearly pointed out to him that I bore as heavy a train as could well be attached to any one working man, and that I could by no means afford to send a son to college who went there for any purpose than to work hard and to gain distinction. We came to the point where I said I would write to his headmaster and beg him between then and Christmas to tell me whether he believed that Harry really would be worth sending to Cambridge, and really had the qualities and habits essential to marked success there – and if he were of that opinion, then Harry would study there accordingly, but, if not, would decidedly go up for the Indian civil service examination. Harry agreed to this, and accordingly I wrote to the headmaster asking him to give me the result of his observation of Harry, and awaited his reply. I did fear that Harry's name was too notorious to help him, unless he could very strongly help himself and that, in competing against others, he would have to justify some higher expectation than would attach to the son of a private gentleman.

Whilst I had been in France, Percy Fitzgerald had sent word that he was getting on with his story ("The Second Mrs. Tillotson") that was to be published in serial form in All the Year Round, but towards the end of September he most kindly sent me an Irish Bloodhound as a gift, that I named "Sultan". I met Sultan for the first time when he came down to the railway to welcome me when I returned to Gad's Hill from the office, and at that first meeting there was a profound absence of interest in my individual opinion of him which captivated me completely. I found him a noble fellow that fell into the ways of our family with a grace and a dignity that denoted a gentleman, and I planned to take him about the country and improve his acquaintance. I also later acquired two young (but large) Newfoundland dogs, one of which was given to me by Frederick Lehman, and I named them "Don" and "Bumble". These Newfoundland dogs I found had the sweetest temper, the utmost spirit of enquiry and the gentlest docility I had ever seen.

I was now thinking of the next Christmas Number for All the Year Round, and began writing of a cheap jack and his adventures in the travelling peddler and auctioneering way under the title "Doctor Marigold's Prescriptions". I was sure that if people at large understood a cheap jack, my part of this Christmas Number would do well, for I thought to make it wonderfully like the real thing, though, of course, a little refined and humoured. I hoped my readers would find something in it that would strike them as being fresh, forcible, and full of spirits for, tired with Our Mutual Friend, and with a depressing notion that I was, for the moment, overworked, I had sat down to cast about for an idea when suddenly one had come to me. It was the little character of Sophie, the adopted deaf and dumb daughter of Doctor Marigold, and all belonging to her came flashing up into my mind in the most cheerful manner, and I had only then to look on and leisurely describe it. When it was finished, Forster was perfectly astonished, and wrote: "Neither good, gooder, nor goodest, but super-excellent. All through there is such a relish of you at your best, as I could not have believed in, after a long story."

After making up the Christmas Number with the printer (always a tough job) incorporating the contributions of Rosa Mulholland and Charlie Collins as well as my own, I spent four days rest and recreation before turning back to business and visits to the theatre. I also heard from Australia about Alfred and how he was being kept out of the fangs of the wolf, idleness; I received another hospitable invitation to visit that land, but I felt now that my prospects of seeing Australia were dim indeed. But I had long held a great desire to read there, and seemed to have done something towards its gratification when I said at home (as I often did): "Who knows! More unlikely things have come to pass."

Having achieved my book and my Christmas Number, and having shaken myself after two years' work, I found time to send my annual greeting to Cerjat in Lausanne. Aside from telling him of my views of the world, I also spoke of the railway accident in which I was preserved. I saw it arising from a muddle of railways in all directions possible and impossible, with no general public scheme, no general public supervision, enormous waste of money, no fixable responsibility and no accountability but under Lord Campbell's Act (the Fatal Accidents Act of 1846, which gave personal representatives new but only limited rights of claiming compensation in the event of death). In my accident, I found that, before the most furious and notable train in the four and twenty hours, the head of a gang of workmen had taken up the rails; that the train changed its time every day as the tide changed; and that the head workman was not provided by the railway company with any clock or watch! Lord Shaftesbury had written to me thereafter to ask me what I thought of an obligation on railway companies to put strong walls to all bridges and viaducts. I told him, of course, that the force of such a shock would carry away anything that any company could set up, and added: "Ask the Minister what he thinks about the votes of the railway interest in the House of Commons, and about his being afraid to lay a finger on it with an eye to his majority."

At Gad's Hill it blew tremendously for a fortnight and on one of those nights (the 29th November) my gardener came suddenly upon a man in the garden, and fired. The man returned the compliment by kicking him dangerously in the groin and causing him great pain. I immediately turned out, and set off in pursuit with Sultan unloosed, but could not find the evil-doer. However, the intelligence of the dog, and the delighted confidence he imparted to me as we stumbled across country in the dark, were quite enchanting. Then two policemen appeared in the distance, making a professional show of stealthiness, and came towards us with professional mystery. But I then had the greatest difficulty in preventing Sultan from tearing them down. They had a narrow escape, for as he was in the air on his way to the throat of one of these eminently respectable constables, I caught him round the neck with both arms and called to the Force to vanish in an inglorious manner. By now Sultan had grown immensely and was a sight, but he was so accursedly fierce, particularly towards other dogs, that I was normally obliged to take him out muzzled. He had also shown an invincible repugnance to soldiers – which, in a military country, was inconvenient – and one day, with his muzzle tight on, such was his spirit that I had witnessed him dashing into the heart of a company in heavy marching order and pulling down an objectionable Private. However, except under such provocation, he was as gentle and docile with me as a dog could possibly be.

On the evening of Tuesday 19th December, I read (as was now my usual custom) to the Rochester and Chatham Mechanics' Institution, on this occasion the Carol and the Trial from Pickwick. It raised almost £70 for the Institution's funds. Fechter at this time was rehearsing at the Lyceum Theatre for his production of "The Master of Ravenswood", a tragedy based on Scott's novel "The Bride of Lammermore." I did not dramatize the piece though I did a good deal towards and about it, having an earnest desire to put Scott – for once – upon the stage in his own gallant manner. As I foresaw, Mrs. Ternan was instantly suggested for the part of old and blind Alice; the weaker the piece, the more store was set by getting her, and Fechter's manager, Humphrey Barnett, went to see her. I let her know he was coming, and she was given the part. On the 20th December, shortly before it opened, I went to observe the rehearsals and, to my horror, found Fechter utterly unacquainted with his part as the lead performer; absolutely ignorant of it and evidently without a fixed purpose as to the way of rendering it. I had never seen anyone in a condition so absurdly unfit for rehearsal as he was. They were all loose in the last degree, except Mrs. Ternan and Carlotta Leclercq (Fechter's leading actress at the Lyceum), who were both what is called "letter perfect." I sat and glowered so gloomily that perhaps I made them worse, but Fechter, even in his stage management, seemed paralyzed.

However, when I attended at the first night with my girls, almost everyone played well, the whole was exceedingly picturesque, and there was scarcely a movement throughout, or a look, that was not indicated by Scott. It was an enormous success, and increased in attraction nightly thereafter. I had never seen the people in all parts of the house so leaning forward, in lines sloping towards the stage, earnestly and intently attentive, as while the story gradually unfolded itself. I found it impossible to see it without crying! – as did my girls and the house in general every night. Carlotta Leclercq (who played Lucy Ashton) astonished me more than the audiences who saw her, for I never suppose her to be capable of such work. The play ran until the 20th April.

When the Christmas Number containing "Doctor Marigold's Prescription" was released with All the Year Round, it sold 250,000 copies in its first week! This delighted me, but I was doubtful whether to read or not in London in the coming season; I was inclined to feel that if I decided to do it at all, I should probably do it on a great scale. Apart from my usual readings, Mrs. Lirriper had also occurred to me, but the difficulty was that, the old lady herself being the narrator, it had to be done with little change of voice, and I was afraid I had accustomed the audience to expect variety in that wise. And also if I did Doctor Marigold, I thought objection would be strengthened by his being in much the same plight. I believed it would be a small objection in a small place, but would expand in objection in proportion to the size of the hall; the greater the room and the larger the audience, the more imperative the necessity for something dramatic. One had to remember the little unchanging figure, seen from afar off, and the very little action that could be got into a bird's-eye view of that table, and my mind was, at that time, divided on the subject of whether or not I should sell myself to a London proposer for five and twenty readings. I did not like the trouble, but the money loomed large.

I passed an enjoyable Christmas at Gad's Hill, but immediately thereafter had to attend to the next number to be made up for All the Year Round, as I had received a poor account of Wills who was, once again, enduring pain and confined to his home. On the 29th December I went into the office to make up the number and then went to his home at 22, Regents Park Terrace to enquire about him. I was truly grieved to know that he was again enduring pain.

Into the New Year of 1866, I spent time both at Gad's Hill and working in the office and then, on the 16th January, attended at the Lord Mayor's Banquet at the Mansion House with Mamie and Georgy. Unfortunately, I had to sit pining under the imbecility of constitutional and corporational idiots, including listening to almost the worst speaker I had ever heard in my life. I was called upon to propose the health of the Lady Mayoress, which I did with characteristic grace, and received some faint consolation for the evening from the company's response.

John Oxenford, the drama critic of The Times, persuaded me to do a single charity reading for works in which he was interested, and so on the night of the 31st January I went up to Islington (of all places in the world) to read for him. There was a large, enthusiastic and attentive audience (as well as crowds turned away) and the effect of Copperfield upon them had me reproached for not going on with such charitable readings. But I had not felt my usual self and asked Frank Beard if he would thoroughly examine me as I had concerns over the weakness of my pulse. He wrote back that with such a pulse as I had described, an examination of the heart was absolutely necessary, and that I had better make an appointment with him alone for the purpose. This I did. His examination showed that there seemed to be degeneration of some functions of the heart; it did not contract as it should, so he gave me a prescription of iron, quinine and digitalis to set it going and send the blood more quickly through my system. I was of the opinion that if it should not seem to succeed, on a reasonable trial, I would then propose a consultation with someone else. Of course, I was not so foolish as to suppose that all my work could have been achieved without some penalty, and had noticed for some time a decided change in my buoyancy and hopefulness so told Wills and Georgy confidentially of these findings, as well as taking another appointment with Beard and keeping in close contact with him.

Despite continuing to feel really unwell, and rest enjoined, nevertheless an occasional reading was rather encouraged than objected to. Towards the end of February (on the 26th) I took another house in London for the season until the middle of June – on this occasion 6,

Southwick Place, Hyde Park West – and wrote to Macready about the possibility of coming again to Cheltenham to read. I was considering engaging with Headland again for the purpose, but then, in early March, Arthur Chappell (of Chappell and Co., Bond Street) approached me with a proposition for 30 public readings in London, the provinces, or elsewhere, as we might agree, for the sum of £1,500 – £500 to be paid on the 5th April before the start, a further £500 when 15 Readings had been given, and a final £500 when the whole of the 30 Readings had been concluded. Chappells agreed to the arrangement that all I had to do was to take in my book and read, at the appointed place and hour, and come out again, with the business of every other kind being done by them. I would have no more to do with any details whatever, and they would transact all the business at their own cost and on their own responsibility. They also agreed to take John Thompson and my gasman, merely for my convenience – and upon these terms I was pleased to agree, for I felt they were disposed to do it in a very good spirit.

As well as seeing Beard, I had also seen Dr. Brinton of Brook Street, who had been called into consultation, and, with tonics already bringing me round, I now felt greatly better, thank God, in both health and spirits – in short, almost myself again. On the 3rd March, I celebrated with Nelly her birthday, an annual engagement which I could not possibly forgo, and so missed on this occasion the meeting of the Association for the Improvement of the Infirmaries of London Workhouses, chaired by the Earl of Carnarvon. I sent them a letter, which I understand was read out at the meeting. But as to my romance, it belonged to my life and I felt it probably would only die out of the same with the proprietor.

CHAPTER LXV

Reading Tour with George Dolby for the Chappells,
and another Request from America

I had now, with immense pains, got up Doctor Marigold as a reading, and proposed to try him in the first two of my readings for Chappells, after giving Forster a notion of what I proposed doing with him. I went into the country for three days, and upon my return found that Chappells had appointed George Dolby as manager of these readings. I hoped he was a man of resources, otherwise he would find considerable pressure put upon him, and the same difficulties would present themselves as Headland faced, which had caused the public readings to have been abandoned for three years. I had decided to read on my own account at Cheltenham on the 23rd and 24th March in the small Assembly Rooms, after Wills had determined to accompany me everywhere, partly so that he might have assurance of their being nothing amiss with me, and partly so that our All the Year Round business might go on as usual without check. It was very good of him, and I did not like altogether to desert him in any place; he was so faithfully attached to me. I wrote and told Macready of my plans to read Little Dombey there, but I found it so difficult, even after all the repetitions, to read it aloud with composure, so I began to go into training again, to harden myself to it. I also invited Forster, Fechter and Charles Kent, together with Wilkie, Browning, Arthur Chappell and Dolby to 6 Southwick Place on the evening of Sunday 18th March to hear me sketch out my reading for Doctor Marigold. Having heard it, they were unanimously favourable towards it.

Wills and I arrived in Cheltenham and I went to see Macready at his home in Wellington Square, but was shocked at what I found. He was greatly aged, and with bronchitis in him, but brightened up wonderfully in the course of a long talk, including talking much about Stanny (who had again not been well), and a little talk about the world of occupation and art did wonders in the way of reviving his old fire. But I could not escape the sad truth that he had aged exceedingly. I read Copperfield and the Trial from Pickwick and, despite the tempestuous weather, a large and appreciative audience turned out. The following day I read Little Dombey, again to another large audience, before bidding Macready farewell. Then, upon my return to London and Gad's Hill, I had to deal with a letter that had appeared in the Athenaeum magazine whilst I was away and signed "R. Seymour" (son of the artist) making once again false assertions (as Seymour's widow had done in July 1849) as to the origin and nature of Pickwick Papers. I made it clear that Mr Seymour the artist never originated, suggested, or in any way had to do with – save as illustrator of what I devised – an incident, a character (except the sporting tastes of Mr. Winkle), a name, a phrase, or a word, to be found in the Pickwick Papers. I also again pointed out that in the preface to the Cheap Edition of The Pickwick Papers I had accurately and in detail described the origin of the work.

Thereafter, I spent time getting myself into training for the 30 readings I had to deliver, and paid a visit overnight 20 miles from town to Slough, where Nelly was now living. I returned to begin at St. James's Hall on the 10th April with the very difficult reading of Doctor Marigold's Prescriptions. The hall was crowded and the audience listened, as The Times reported, from beginning to end with the deepest attention and most manifest delight. Early the following morning I left London for Liverpool, reading in St. George's Hall that night, before travelling the next day to Manchester to read in the Free Trade Hall. The reception there was quite a magnificent sight: the whole of the immense audience standing up and cheering. I thought them a little slow with Marigold, but believed it was only due to the attention necessary in so vast a place. They gave a splendid burst at the end. And after Nickleby, which went to perfection, they set up such a call that I was obliged to go in again. During the evening the unfortunate gasman got a fall off a ladder and sprained his leg. He was put to bed in a public house opposite, and had to be left there as we travelled back to Liverpool for further readings on the 13th and 14th April. I found that the pull of Marigold upon my energy in the Free Trade Hall had been great, but I stuck to my tonic, and felt, all things considered, in good tone. I also found that a dozen oysters and a little champagne between the parts every night constituted the best restorative I had ever yet tried!

The 13th was the first very fine day we had, and I took advantage of it by crossing to Birkenhead and getting some air upon the water;

it was fresh and beautiful. That evening I read in the Small Concert Room in St. George's Hall, and considered it the most perfect hall in the world; my special favourite and extraordinarily easy – almost a rest! Every corner of the place was crammed and I read Copperfield and the Trial from Pickwick. They were a very fine audience and took enthusiastically every point in both readings – including giving a startling outburst of applause at the first mention of Sam Weller – which made the reading a quarter of an hour longer than usual. I heard that one man had advertised in the morning paper that he would give thirty shillings (double) for three stalls, but nobody would sell, and he didn't get in. The police reported officially that three thousand people were turned away that night; I doubt if they were so numerous, but they carried into the outer doors and pitched into Dolby with great vigour.

On the 14th I read Little Dombey, but because again such a large number had to be turned away, Dolby arranged for two extra readings to be given (as part of the 30) a little later in the tour – on the 27th and 28th April. I had experienced difficulty in sleeping, but at two in the afternoon of the 16th April we left Liverpool for Glasgow and Carrick's Royal Hotel, where we arrived at about ten that night. I don't think the journey shook me at all; Dolby provided a superb cold collation and "the best of drinks" and we dined in the carriage. And I made Dolby laugh all the way.

At Glasgow we found the let to be very large. I was to read in the City Hall on the 17th and 19th April, with readings planned for Edinburgh on the 18th (in the Music Hall) and on the 20th and 21st (in the Queen Street Hall). The crowds were enormous, far ahead of all my previous experience. Wills did the genteel at the stalls, while Dolby sought to stem the shilling tide as best he could, but he was pitched into, and one man wrote a sensible letter in one of the local papers, showing to my satisfaction that they really had, through the local agent, some cause of complaint. When I came on the thundering of applause was quite staggering, and my team of people checked off my reception by the minute hand of a watch, and stared at one another, thinking I should never begin. Once I did, they were most brilliant and took "Marigold" with a fine sense and quickness not to be surpassed. I was now keeping quite well, having happily taken to sleeping and felt, all things considered, very little conscious of fatigue.

Taking stock, it was difficult to describe what the readings had grown to be. I was to read again on the 24th April at St. James's Hall, with a let that was now reported as being immense; then to Manchester for a reading in the Free Trade Hall on the 26th, from where they had written: "Send us more tickets instantly, for we are sold out and don't know what to do with the people"; and, for the next reading thereafter in St. James's Hall on the 1st May, the let was already so large that Chappells had written: "That will be the greatest house of the three." Already the whole of my money (£1,500) under the agreement with Chappells had been taken; and the audiences, though so enormous, did nevertheless somehow express a personal affection towards me, which made them very strange and moving to see.

After the reading at the St. James's Hall on the 24th April, I headed north by rail again, but on the way between London and Rugby noticed something very odd in our carriage, not so much in its motion as in its sound. We examined it as well we could, out of both windows, but could make nothing of it. On our arrival at Rugby however, it was found to be on fire! With this slight exception, we came down alright to Manchester where, at the Free Trade Hall on the 26th, I read Boots, Mr. Bob Sawyer's Party and the Trial from Pickwick. There was such a prodigious demonstration that I was obliged (contrary to my principle in such cases) to go back onto the stage after my first departure. The following day I was very tired, for it would be of itself very hard work in that immense place, if there were not to be added eighty miles of railway and late hours to boot.

On the 27th and 28th April I read in St. George's Hall in Liverpool – Doctor Marigold and Nickleby on the 27th and Copperfield and the Trial from Pickwick on the 28th. The local newspaper reported that I was in excellent vein and carried my audience entirely with me – tears, applause and laughter following my varied touches of nature with magic rapidity.

That weekend I returned to Gad's Hill, to find a letter from James Fields in Boston enquiring again (and now that the American Civil War was over) about the possibility of me doing a series of readings in America. I found his letter an excessively difficult one to answer, because at that time I really did not know that any sum of money that could be laid down would induce me to cross the Atlantic to read, nor did I think it likely that any one on his side of the great water could be prepared to understand the state of the case. I told him that I was now just finishing a series of thirty readings, where the crowds attending them had been so astounding, and the relish for them had so far outgone all previous experience, that if I were to set myself the task: "I will make such or such a sum of money by devoting myself to readings for a certain time", I should have to go no further than Bond Street or Regent Street, to have it secured to me in a day. Therefore, I added, if a specific offer – and a very large one indeed – were made to me from America, I should naturally ask myself: "Why go through this wear and tear, merely to pluck fruit that grows on every bough at home?" He had asked me if I could put a price upon fifty readings in America, but I could not, because I did not know that any possible price could pay me for them. And I really could not say to anyone disposed towards the enterprise: "Tempt me", because I had too strong a misgiving that such person could not in the nature of things do it. It was a delightful sensation for me to move new people, but I felt I had only to go to Paris, to find the brightest people in the world quite ready for me.

I told Fields this was the plain truth. I had said this much to him in a sort of desperate endeavour to explain myself to him, but I also told him that if any distinct proposal be submitted to me, I would give it a distinct answer; but as the chances were a round thousand to one that the answer would be "no", I felt bound to make the declaration beforehand.

On the 1st May I read again at St. James's Hall and then on the 2nd at the Crystal Palace Concert Hall, followed by a reading in the Literary Institute Hall in Greenwich on the 4th. By now Chappells were pressing me to give fifty more readings, to begin at Christmas, as the takings on this tour had already reached £4,270, and I discussed the matter with Forster. The Chappells were speculators, though of the worthiest and most honourable kind, and whilst they would make some bad speculations, they had made a very good one in this case, and would set this against those. I had told them when I agreed to these thirty readings to do them at £50 a night, because I know perfectly well beforehand that no one in their business had the least idea of their real worth, but now felt I was bound to look to myself for the future, and so intended to ask £70 a night.

I had been labouring under a bad cold, but nevertheless pressed on with my readings. I travelled to Clifton, before proceeding to Birmingham the following day, but it was now proving very heavy work, getting up at half past 6 each morning after a heavy night, and I became not at all well. I had to travel back to Clifton from Birmingham to read again and felt so severe a pain in the ball of my left eye that it made it hard for me to do anything after 100 miles of shaking on the railway. I had headache and brow neuralgia, my cold was no better, and I had difficulties with my hand. To add to the problems, John Thompson had fallen off a platform about 10 feet high in Birmingham and fainted. He looked all the colours of the rainbow the next day, but fortunately did not seem much hurt beyond being puffed up in one hand, arm and side.

I returned to London for the weekend, made a short visit of a couple of hours to Gad's Hill to pack my portmanteau, and then returned to the office to meet Ouvry to discuss the libel case in New Zealand. That evening I read again at St. James's Hall, before then taking a special carriage on the train to Aberdeen. We arrived at a quarter before 4 in the morning and that night I read, in a somewhat husky voice, to a very large audience in the Music Hall. We then headed south towards Glasgow, halting at Perth where I got a lovely walk, and once in Glasgow took some fresh air aboard a steamer on the Clyde, before reading there, and then travelling to Edinburgh. After reading there at 2 p.m. in the Music Hall, which was filled to overflowing, we left Edinburgh and travelled overnight back to London, arriving at 9.30 on the Sunday morning the 20th May. On Monday the 21st I attended at the Lyceum Theatre to see a production of "The Corsican Brothers" in which both Fechter and Mrs. Ternan appeared, before a reading the next evening at St. James's Hall, followed by travel to Portsmouth (my native place), where I read at St. George's Hall on two nights (the 24th and 25th May) Doctor Marigold and the Trial from Pickwick. Wilkie came down to the room with me.

I now had just 3 more readings before I had completed the agreed 30. These were scheduled for St. James's Hall on the 29th May, the 5th June, with the final reading to take place there on the 12th June. I stayed at 6, Southwick Place, Hyde Park for the majority of this time, but my heavy cold had persisted and I felt very tired and depressed, my distressful position being added to by having allowed Mamie to engage me for every day until we now left town. Having been constantly away and disabled from going out to dine, I had told her before I returned to London that she might do what she would with me between the 28th May and the 18th June; availing herself of this permission, she presented me on my return with a methodically drawn-up set of fetters through which I was now champing!

CHAPTER LXVI

Nelly in Slough, "Disagreeables", Mugby Junction,
and another Reading Tour with Dolby

After the three final readings at St. James's Hall, I was pleased to be able to retire to a private life again and spend more time at Gad's Hill. We gave up 6, Southwick Place and I resumed my life at Gad's Hill, with customary visits to the office in Wellington Street thereafter. I turned down further offers to read, at least until Christmas time, for the truth was that I was tired of reading at that time and had come into the country to rest and hear the birds sing. I was happy to invite friends to visit, including Mary Boyle and Emile de la Rue, and I supervised the weekly publication in All the Year Round of "The Tale of Aunt Margaret's Trouble" by Fanny Ternan, soon to be Mrs. Francis Trollope after planning to marry Thomas Trollope in Paris on the 28th October. When Chapman and Hall thereafter published the little story in book form, it was affectionately dedicated to "E.L.T.", Ellen Lawless Ternan, her sister Nelly.

Nelly was now living with her mother 20 miles from London at Elizabeth Cottage in High Street, Slough, having let out 2, Houghton Place. I agreed to pay the rates for her in Slough, using the names of John Tringham (from January to April 1866) and Charles Tringham (from May 1866 to June 1867) to do so, Tringham being the name of my tobacconist located at 2, Brydges Street, not far from the All the Year Round office. During the summer I spent time visiting Nelly in Slough, as well as walking in the Windsor Park and Eton areas, and also took pleasure in a cricket match in my field at Gad's Hill on the 8th August, being a return match between the villages of Higham and Chalk. Arthur Chappell had again approached me about a further series of readings, to commence after Christmas, and I told him I would consider the matter. Having turned it over in my mind, I told him I was prepared to do so, and agreed a series of 42 readings for £2,500 – on the basis that all expenses would be paid for as before, including my hotel charges, and Dolby acting again as my right-hand man. With that matter settled, I now set my mind to try and discover a Christmas Number for All the

Year Round; and I also began to have thoughts of a possible new story to commence in the journal after the readings.

At the beginning of September I had to deal with my dog Sultan. He was a splendid creature, as big as an average lioness, and the finest dog I ever saw. Between him and me there had grown a perfect understanding but, to adopt the popular phrase, it was so very confidential that "it went no further." He would fly at anybody else with the greatest enthusiasm for destruction; I had seen him, muzzled, not only pound into the heart of a Regiment of the Line, but frequently hold another great dog down with his chest and feet. He had broken loose, muzzled, and come home covered with blood again and again. And yet he never disobeyed me, unless he had first laid hold of a dog. But then he ferociously cast down and bit a village child that he knew and should have respected (the sister of one of the servants). I flogged him, but then knew I had to be disposed of him. At seven the next morning, he went out into the meadow with the greatest cheerfulness, attended by my servant executioner, double-barrelled gun, and wheelbarrow (for conveyance of the body back), as well as supernumeries. Evidently supposing a general lark in contemplation, including a journey to bring back something to eat in the wheelbarrow, he died mistaken.

But I now had concerns over my health. I had been bothered for weeks – months – at intervals with distension and flatulency, and disagreeable pains in the pit of the stomach and chest, without any disarrangement of the bowels worth speaking of. Sometimes I had it all day, sometimes at capricious intervals, sometimes all night after two or so. I had had, in a similar sickly season ten years before at Boulogne, exactly the same uncomfortable symptoms, and Elliotson (who was there at the time) gave me some simple prescription in which the main – if not the only – ingredient was cajeput oil. I now wrote to Frank Beard asking him if, on this diagnosis, he would send me a similar prescription to relieve this distress. Then, in the first week of September, I was also seized in a most distressing manner – apparently in the heart, though I was persuaded it was only in the nervous system. I believed there was some strange influence in the atmosphere and took some time away from Gad's Hill, but was concerned none the less. The prescription Frank Beard gave me at once touched the disagreeables, but it had a tendency to affect the bowels in the way of relaxation, though not moving them oftener than once a day. I wrote to him asking that if it be right, to please return the prescription to the office or, if wrong, to please post me an altered triumph of medical skill!

With the turn into October I began to get into Christmas labour, feeling I was undoubtedly one of the sons of toil, having brought up the largest family ever known with the smallest disposition to do anything for themselves. This Christmas I alighted upon the idea of railway stories, based on Rugby Junction, writing under the title "Mugby Junction". By the middle of the month I had completed a number of contributions and sent them off to the printers, leaving others to produce further such stories for the number. I had read one of the stories "The Boy at Mugby" to Mary Boyle, Mamie, Katey and Georgy at Gad's Hill one evening, and I don't think I ever saw people laugh so much under the prosiest of circumstances. There were such extraordinary peals and tears of laughter that I believed I could foresee a great success. As I had by now written half of this Christmas Number myself, the always difficult work of selecting from an immense heap of contributors was rendered twice as difficult as usual, by the contracted space available. I planned to have it published at the All the Year Round office on the 10th December.

James Fields meanwhile was still pressing from America for me to read there, but I told him I was now going to begin here in the middle of January with my series of readings that would probably occupy me until Easter, and then, early in the summer, I hoped to get to work on another story that I had in mind. Then I heard news from America that my youngest brother Augustus had died there of consumption on the 4th October. Poor fellow, a sad business altogether! And my mind misgave me that this would now bring upon me a host of disagreeables from that country.

On the 2nd November a horrible business occurred at the office of All the Year Round. On the previous afternoon, it was noticed that 8 sovereigns had been stolen from the cashbox. This caused a great disturbance, but then the following morning it was found that they had been replaced. I sent Wills to Scotland Yard for Walker, the head Inspector of the Detective Police, who came with Williamson, the head Superintendent. They examined all the people and places at the office, and came to the irresistible conclusion that the thief was – John Thompson! What was worst of all was that, on a smaller scale, the police found the thing had been often done for a long time and that the wretched Thompson had been impoverished by having to borrow money to make up inexplicable deficiencies in his daily accounts. I gloomily discharged the miserable man from the office, but allowed him to wait as my private servant until he could get some place to put his furniture in and could then move it away. I had implicitly trusted Thompson, and it so shocked me that I had later that day to walk more than usual before I could walk myself into composure again. I replaced the housekeeper for the office by bringing in Mrs. Ellen Hedderley, from Gad's Hill.

I agreed to sit for the photographer Mr. Mason of Bond Street, for him to take pictures of me to be displayed at the forthcoming Exhibition in Paris. He sent me the results, and I thought the camera had let me off more easily than usual, so did not ask that he cancel any of them. He had previously photographed me in 1863, and these had been extremely good, but scarcely a week had passed without my receiving requests from various quarters, to sit for likenesses, to be taken by all the processes ever invented. Apart from my having an invincible objection to the multiplication of my countenance in the shop-windows, I had not – between my avocations and my needful recreation – the time to comply with these proposals.

I began preparing for my new series of readings, first by going with Chappell to St. James's Hall to explain a notion I had for improving the acoustics, and then taking the large back public room at Verrey's Restaurant (at 229, Regent Street) for Dolby to give me any amount of trip-arrangement and detail that he now had available. I had Chapman and Hall make up book-reading copies of "The Boy at Mugby" and "Barbox Brothers" (also from Mugby Junction) so that I might read them as part of the new series. By the 12th December, in two days and a half, we had by then already sold 200,000 of our new Christmas Number, and really did not know what level of sales we might get to. It was already substantially outselling Doctor Marigold by the equivalent dates.

The Annual Gathering at Gad's Hill was now being planned, but all domestic arrangements were subject to Katey, with whom both Georgy and Mamie now were. She had become very ill with nervous fever, but I heard she was now mending steadily, though slowly. She was a bad subject for illness, having long been in an unsatisfactory and declining state. But with Georgy in attendance day and night and Katey keeping better, I went on a visit to Slough for 3 days on the 16th December, before dining in town – and then, with Katey again keeping better, I went back again to Slough for 2 days more before going to Gad's Hill, where my usual Christmas houseful kept me there until Twelfth Night. But I never could imagine myself now as the grandfather of four children (all from Charley), and that objectionable relationship was never permitted to be mentioned in my presence. I made the mites suppose that my lawful name was "Wenerables", which they piously believed.

On Christmas Day we were hard at work all day, building a very pretty course for foot races for the villagers, with the country police predicting an immense crowd for these rustic sports in my field the next day – and so it proved, more than 2,000 people arriving, with the road between Chatham and the house being like a fair all day. Yet not a stake was pulled up, or a rope slackened, or one farthing's worth of damage done. It was surely a fine thing to get such perfect behaviour in the neighbourhood of such a reckless seaport town as Chatham!

As we turned into 1867, Mugby Junction had now the extraordinary circulation of 256,000, odd hundreds, of copies; and, following Twelfth Night, I spent time at Slough before meeting with Dolby. He was not yet able to tell me the full itinerary for the tour but after spending further time at Slough, I conducted the first of the 42 (later increased to 50) readings in St. James's Hall on the 15th January. The audience I found did not have the sensational stages at which to applaud in Barbox but, at the close of it, brought down a perfect storm of accumulated plaudits; The Boy at Mugby however was a shout, with a continuous roar from beginning to end. Dolby had, by now, told me that the next afternoon I was to start for Liverpool, and then on to Chester, Derby, Leicester and Wolverhampton; on the 29th I was to read again in London and then, he said, I could take it "pretty easy for a fortnight", before, on the 16th February reading in Manchester, and then going on to Scotland. I later learnt that he had then filled the "pretty easy fortnight" with no less than nine of the further readings!!

What with Dolby and a skilful valet named Henry Scott, everything was made as easy to me as it possibly could. Dolby would do anything to lighten the work for me, and did everything. Scott also did very well indeed; as a dresser he was perfect. In a quarter of an hour after I went into the retiring-room where all my clothes were airing and everything was set out neatly in its own allotted place, I was ready, and he then went softly out and sat outside the door. In the morning he was equally punctual, quiet and quick. He had his needles and thread, buttons and so forth, always at hand, and in travelling he was very systematic with the luggage. In Liverpool, however, I had quite astonished myself and was taken so faint after the reading that they laid me on a sofa at the hall for half an hour, but I simply attributed it to my distressing inability to sleep at night, and nothing worse.

CHAPTER LXVII

Touring in England, Scotland and Ireland, and Returns to Slough

On my travels I encountered now the worst weather I think I ever saw, with snowstorms and falls of ice – but we had the most tremendous audiences, the people at times being fairly convulsed with laughter. I continued to observe my rule, now long established and in spite of myself, of not going out before or afterwards for dining or entertainment with others, but I was finding the work of these readings, combined with the travelling, so very, very hard. On one train journey from Leicester, the reckless fury of the driving and the violent rocking of the carriages obliged me to leave the express train at Bedford and send an urgent letter to The Times about the situation, for, as I explained, I had been in the Staplehurst accident and in trains under most conceivable conditions, but I had never been so shaken and flung about, and never been in such obvious danger. Dolby and I travelled back to London at a slower pace, and I then spent the weekend at Slough very tired, though could not sleep, having been so severely shaken on that atrocious railway.

I read Barbox Brothers and The Boy at Mugby at St. James's Hall on the evening of the 29th January, before travelling to Leeds and two nights of readings at the Music Hall. I continued to find Leeds a beastly place, one of the nastiest places I knew, and where I read was like a capricious coal cellar, incredibly filthy, though for sound it was perfect. At Manchester we had £190 and boundless enthusiasm, before I travelled back to London. I spent the night at the office before going to Slough for a few days, with visits to the office from there. My next readings were scheduled for the 8th and 9th February in the Assembly Rooms in Bath; they proved to be a remarkably delicate and discriminating audience; very earnest too, and expressing themselves accordingly. I again returned to Slough for the weekend. The next week I busied myself at the office and on the 12th February read Doctor Marigold and the Trial from Pickwick at St. James's Hall. But I was now facing a further period of much reading and travelling, and the truth was that the railways had shaken me greatly since the Staplehurst experience and I felt this very much, including in my handwriting. There was no doubt of the fact that, after Staplehurst, it told more and more on me, instead of (as one might have expected) less and less.

On the 13th February I read the Carol and The Boy from Mugby at the Birmingham Town Hall, before travelling on to Liverpool for two readings at St. George's Hall on the following two nights. On the 14th we had an audience of 1,100 people and an enormous turnaway, and a cram for the following night for Copperfield and The Boy at Mugby, again with great numbers being turned away. Liverpool I regarded as the Copperfield stronghold and the audiences during these two days produced an astonishing effect. I continued to find the room at St. George's Hall charming, and reading there greatly lessened the fatigue of this fatiguing week, for I was able to read with no more exertion than if I had been at Gad's Hill. The weather too was now very fine, and I turned it to wholesome account by walking all the morning of the 15th on the sands at New Brighton, although I was still not quite right within. On the 16th February I read again at the Free Trade Hall in Manchester with, again a splendid spectacle there, and the audience cheered to such an extent after it was over that I was obliged to huddle on my clothes (for I was undressing to prepare for the next journey to Glasgow) and go back out on stage again.

We left for Glasgow on the night train, leaving Manchester at a quarter to two in the morning for the long journey. I had a curious feeling of soreness all around the body, which I supposed to arise from the great exertion of the voice, and the next morning was so unwell with an internal malady, and attended on this occasion with the sudden loss of so much blood, that I wrote an anxious message to Frank Beard asking him for advice. I read Copperfield and the Boy from Mugby that night (the 18th) in Glasgow City Hall, but felt it a little more exertion to read, and afterwards passed a sleepless night. It had originally been planned that I read in Glasgow on the next two nights, but I had already asked Dolby to cancel these so that I could have a rest and increased break, whilst agreeing to read again there on the 21st. So, on the 19th, I travelled to Bridge of Allen, just north of Stirling and famous for its mineral springs, where I stayed at Phillip's Hotel. It was a little inn, a capital house of the best country sort, quiet and, I felt, sure to do me good. The air was excellent and on the 20th I made an interesting walk with Dolby to Stirling to see its sights and (strange to relate) was not bored by them. Indeed they left me so fresh that I knocked at the gate of the prison, presented myself to the Governor, and took Dolby over the jail, to his unspeakable interest. We then walked back again to our excellent country inn.

After the two days at Bridge of Allen I returned to Glasgow to read again. I felt renewed, and in good force and spirits again after the rest, and after the reading, moved on to Edinburgh for my two readings there. Dolby was an excellent manager, an agreeable companion (and a good fellow besides) and with three other men in constant attendance, I continued to find that everything was done for me with the utmost liberality and consideration, every want I could have anticipated, and not the faintest spark of the tradesman spirit ever peeping out.

We took the night train from Edinburgh to Kings Cross and arrived at a quarter before ten in the morning, whereupon I proceeded to Regent Street to get a vapour bath, before going to the office for breakfast. After business there, I headed off to Slough, staying until the 26th, when I returned to the office, and then read again in St. James's Hall in the evening. Whilst in London I had correspondence with the publishers Benjamin Wood of New York, and agreed to write for them, before the 1st August, a new tale of the length of "Hunted Down" and to assign them the copyright of that tale, in consideration of the sum of one thousand pounds.

I conducted further readings in York, Bradford, and Newcastle, although just now I felt as if I was here, there, everywhere, and nowhere all at once. Despite the travelling however, I now felt wonderfully well again, and not tired – and even had triumphantly managed to get a loose back tooth out at Bradford! From Newcastle we travelled to Leeds; there were about 600 in the audience despite it snowing hard, and I read Doctor Marigold and the Trial, cutting short the latter so that I could catch the night train to London and spend a long weekend in Slough.

I read again at St. James's Hall on the 12th March, before now facing up to the prospect of going to Ireland, with Fenian unrest to the fore. I should as soon have thought of going to Ireland at this time out of my head, but Chappell's head thought differently. So profoundly discouraging were the accounts of Ireland at this time that I had several counsels with Chappell about going at all, and had actually drawn up a bill announcing (indefinitely) the postponement of the readings there, and had meant to give him a reading to cover the charges already incurred, but eventually yielded at last to his representations the other way.

We started off by rail from London for Dublin on the night of Wednesday 13th March, and ran through a snow-storm nearly the whole way. We got snowed up among the Welsh Mountains in a tremendous storm of wind, came to a stop at midnight, and they had to dig the engine out! We eventually got to Holyhead at 6 in the morning and went to bed, before getting aboard the mail steamer at two in the afternoon, again in a furious snow-storm. Once in Dublin there was no doubt that great alarm prevailed, with great depression in all kinds of trade and commerce, and our business also shown as very bad, though word from Belfast (where I was next to read) said that there it was enormous. But on the night of the 15th I read Doctor Marrigold and the Trial from Pickwick at the Rotunda and, after all, we did exceedingly well. On the 18th I read again at the Rotunda, on this occasion Copperfield and Mr. Bob Sawyer's Party, to great success and with the Lord Chief Justice of Ireland in the audience. The next day we left for Belfast, and there I read Doctor Marigold and the Trial at the large Ulster Hall on the 20th, where we did wonders. Back to Dublin (with an extremely cold journey), I now found at the Rotunda everything was sold again and again and nearly 4,000 packed in, with people besieging Dolby to put chairs anywhere, in doorways, on my platform, in any sort of hole or corner. Nevertheless, a further 2,000 had to be refused admission due to lack of space, the readings being a perfect rage at a time when everything else was beaten down.

I left Dublin that night after the reading to get to London with all speed and upon arrival went immediately to Slough for four days. During this time Nelly and I went looking at houses in Peckham, and I also read again in St. James's Hall on the 26th, before leaving for Cambridge and Norwich. I was excited moreover by a new request from Ticknor & Fields in Boston to write expressly for their child's magazine. They had already notified me that they intended paying me royalties on their editions of my works that they had bought from Chapman and Hall, and I had written letting them know how high and far beyond the money's worth I esteemed this act of manhood, delicacy and honour. I now agreed to write four little papers for their children's magazine in consideration of the sum of £1,000 – the length of the whole not less than that of the story "Hunted Down" (a copy of which I had sent to them), and to do so by the end of October. I later began the stories for publication under the title "Holiday Romance."

On returning from Norwich I went again to Slough for the weekend; I had not once been at home at Gad's Hill since January and felt I was little likely to get there before the middle of May. I read in Gloucester, Swansea, Cheltenham (where I again saw Macready), and then immediately returned again to Slough. After another reading in St. James's Hall, I set off to Worcester, Hereford, Bristol and back again to Slough. I now had a short period of holiday from my readings and stayed at Slough on the nights of the 13th and 14th April before then going to Gad's Hill for the next three nights. On the 18th I spent the night at Wellington Street, and then on the 19th took Wills to Slough to see Nelly. I had by now rented a second cottage in Slough, in Church Street, and we were able to stay overnight in Slough before catching the morning train to Paddington. I subsequently met with Dolby again and conducted further readings at Preston, Blackburn and Stoke-on-Trent. By now it had been decided that Harry might attend Cambridge University and during this time I had received a letter from Dr. Thompson, the Master of Trinity Hall Cambridge, asking for a declaration from me of the date of Harry's birth, and also a formal certificate of his baptism as proof that he was a member of the Church of England and thus eligible for entry into the University under the Test Act.

By now I was already turning over in my mind the next Christmas Number, and whilst I knew nothing of Wilkie's arrangements at that time, I wrote to him asking if he would like to do it with me, we two alone, each taking half, with our two names appended to the performance – assuming the money question would be satisfactorily disposed of between him and Wills. Wilkie asked Wills for £400 for doing half and this was agreed. The thought that we were to have a bout of working together again filled me with pleasure and interest.

He had written to me, not only speaking about the Christmas Number, but also about proposing to write a serial story for All the Year Round ("The Moonstone"), and I at once said YES. I also told him that, for the Christmas Number, we would have to go to press with it very early in November, and our best way would be to sketch it out under the trees, say in August, and work it out of hand.

On the 2nd May I read in Warrington and then was at Slough again on the 6th and 7th before reading at Croydon on the 8th. I had now only one more reading in this series for Chappells, that being at St. James's Hall on Monday 13th May, which I counted as nothing, and so, on the evening of the 9th I took Nelly to the Lycenum in celebration, but was so tired thereafter that I could hardly undress for bed; I then stayed at Slough until the final reading on the evening of the 13th, where I finished with Little Dombey and Mr. Bob Sawyer's Party.

Upon the conclusion, I wrote to Forster:

"Last Monday I finished the 50 Readings with great success. You have no idea how I worked at them. Finding it necessary, as their reputation widened, that they should be better than at first, I have *learnt them all*, so as to have no mechanical drawback in looking after the words. I have tested all the serious passion in them by everything I know; made the humorous points much more humorous; corrected my utterance of certain words; cultivated a self-possession not to be disturbed; and made myself master of the situation. Finishing with Dombey (which I had not read for a long time) I learnt that, like the rest; and did it to myself, often twice a day, with exactly the same pains as at night, over and over and over again."

CHAPTER LXVIII

More Entreaties from America, Death of Stanny,
Nelly to Peckham, and Dolby to America

Chapman and Hall had begun issuing a new edition of my works which I had revised, added to, and drawn up some new prefaces, but I had found my expenses so enormous that I now began to feel myself drawn towards America though my mind was in a most disturbed state about it. There was no question but that the people there had set themselves on having the readings. Every mail brought me proposals, and the number of Americans at St. James's Hall had been surprising. A New York theatrical impresario, who was highly responsible, had written to me for a second time saying that, if I would give him a word of encouragement, he would come over immediately and arrange on the boldest terms for any number I chose, and would deposit a large sum of money at Coutts Bank. And now James Fields wrote to me on behalf of a committee of private gentlemen at Boston who wished for the credit of getting me out, who desired to hear the readings and did not want profit, and would put down as a guarantee £10,000 – also to be banked here. Every American speculator who came to London repaired straight to Dolby, with similar proposals.

Whilst I was giving thought to the American question, I was deeply saddened to hear of the death of Stanny on the 18th May. I had seen the poor dear fellow (on a hint from his eldest son) at his home in Hampstead in a day's interval between two reading expeditions, and it was clear then that the shadow of the end had fallen on him. What a great loss! I wrote some words in memory of him and had them published in All the Year Round and had three of his paintings taken to Gad's Hill and hung in the hall. I went to his funeral in the Roman Catholic cemetery at Kensal Green on the 27th May, and when I laid my little wreath upon that dear friend's grave, my private loss represented a loss on the part of the whole community. England had lost the great marine painter of whom I was sure she would be boastful ages hence; the national historian of her speciality, the sea; the man famous for his marvellous rendering of the waves that break upon our shores, of her ships and seamen, of her coasts and skies, of her storms and sunshine, of the many marvels of the deep. I believe his grand pictures will proclaim his powers while paint and canvas last. And success never for an instant spoiled him. Dear, Dear Stanny! At his funeral I once again met Mark Lemon, and put aside my differences with him, as Stanny had requested that I did when I had seen him shortly before he died. And in the months that followed, I did all I could to further Stanny's son in his career.

I now had work to do for America which could not wait – writing "George Silverman's Explanation" for Benjamin Wood and "A Holiday Romance" for Ticknor & Fields – which I knew would last me through the summer, together with the Christmas Number with Wilkie, and the clearing off of a vast arrear of business at All the Year Round, all of which filled my mind. And I could hardly believe that I stood at bay at last on the American question, and became in a tempest-tossed condition. The difficulty of determining amid the variety of statements made to me was enormous, and you have no idea how heavily the anxiety of it sat upon my soul. The prize looked so large, but I knew that I would be wretched beyond expression there, in having to leave England's shores for a time. The state of mind in which I knew I should drag on from day to day could not be described, and nothing would induce me to make the experiment if I did not see the most forcible reasons for believing that what I could get by it, added to what I had got, would leave me with a sufficient fortune.

I knew Forster was against my going, and at the beginning of June I received a letter from Wills, setting out his misgivings also. I did not make light of any of these, and every objection Wills made strongly impressed me, and I revolved them in my mind again and again. But I felt the need to present the other side of the question to him and so wrote to him on the 6th June, comparing what happened when I went to America in 1842 and what was proposed now, involving far less travelling than Wills supposed, and that the receipts would be very much larger than his estimate. I also believed that by my going out, an immense impulse could be given to the new edition of my works. Reading profits here would take years to get to £10,000, and to get that sum in a heap so soon was an immense consideration to me – my wife's income to pay – a very expensive position to hold – and my boys with a curse of limpness upon them. Wills did not know what it was to look round the table and see reflected from every seat at it (where they sat) some horrible well remembered expression of inadaptability to anything. I did however acknowledge to him that Nelly was the gigantic difficulty. But you know, as I told Wills, "I don't like to give in before a difficulty, if it can be beaten."

In the next few days I dined with Forster and then Chapman to talk the American matter over, as well as talking to Dolby who was now making some astonishing calculations. On the 13th June I wrote to Fields telling him that I had resolved to send out Dolby to Boston in the first week of August, to go straight to hold solemn council with them before then going to New York, Philadelphia, Hartford, Washington, etc., to see the possible reading rooms for himself and make his estimates. I said he would then telegraph his results to me. I told Fields I had absolute trust in Dolby and a great regard for him, for he went with me everywhere when I read and managed me to perfection. I begged Fields, however, to keep all this STRICTLY SECRET until I finally decided for or against. I chose James Fields at Ticknor & Fields as I considered all the American Publishing Houses, save them, to be raving mad when last heard of.

By the third week in June I had now located with Nelly a substantial detached house for us, with a large garden and stables to one side, named "Windsor Lodge" in Linden Grove, Peckham. It had been built some five years or so before on four floors, and I took it on a lease under the name Charles Tringham, whilst the rates to December were paid in the name of Frances Turnham. The Slough properties were given up and I now began travelling to Peckham to be there with Nelly. Peckham Rye, not far away across the fields, had acquired a railway station two years before, with a link to Waterloo (just across the river by bridge from the office in Wellington Street) and also to Higham on the London, Chatham and Dover line.

At the end of June Wilkie came to stay at Gad's Hill for a couple of days, and brought with him his new story "The Moonstone". He read the first three numbers to me and I then went minutely through the plot of the rest to the last line. It was a series of "narratives", but it was a very curious story – wild, and yet domestic – with excellent character in it, great mystery, and nothing belonging to disguised women (as in "The Woman in White") or the like. I found it prepared with extraordinary care and with every chance of being a hit, and discussed it with Wills as to when we should place it in All the Year Round.

I was now turning my thoughts to the Christmas Number that Wilkie and I were to do together and resolved that it should be forty-eight pages in length, in place of the thirty-two I had originally declared to Wilkie. I had continued with the Holiday Romance story for Ticknor & Fields children's magazine, wanting in the process to combine a child's mind with a grown-up joke, and planned to have Dolby take out the manuscript to them when he sailed for America on the 3rd August. Meanwhile, I had by now heard word that stories about Nelly's history were being told by Nelly's sister Fanny (Mrs. T.T.), which caused me now to feel I did not in the least care for her, and viewed her as infinitely sharper than the serpent's tooth. I knew it would be inexpressibly painful to Nelly to think that someone knew her history, and that it would distress her for the rest of her life if that were so. At that time she had no suspicion of it and I hoped that would remain so, for if she bore that, she would not have the pride and self-reliance which, mingled with the gentlest nature, had born her, alone, through so much.

Dolby sailed on the morning of the 3rd August, in the best spirits possible under the circumstances, looking ruddy and well. He was as airily and neatly lodged as a passenger aboard ship could be, and had a very cheerful and modest gentleman for his travelling companion, but eating and drinking (and being violently shaken by the screw) were said to be the standard amusements of his ship, the Java, and I did tremble to think of his circumference when he landed in the United States!

Thereafter, I immediately returned to town and went back to Peckham. I spoke to Nelly about America and she was very anxious for Dolby's report and said she was ready to commit herself to the Atlantic under his care; to which I always added at this time: "IF I go, my dear, IF I go". I also began writing with Wilkie the Christmas Number under the title: "No Thoroughfare"

In due course I heard from Dolby with a note from Queenstown, then Halifax, and finally Boston. His account of his reception by Ticknor & Fields was delightful, and in not letting them pay for his charges, he did exactly what I would have wished. I also told him that, in reference to the publisher by the name of Wood the money had not been forthcoming, and that if Mr. Wood did not cash up, and Fields liked to have the story on the same terms, by all means let him have it.

I was having trouble with my foot again but was now just able to get a boot on again and walk for an hour. Then it was brought to my attention that a newspaper (the Sunday Gazette) had published a paragraph that had become widely circulated, both in England and abroad, that I was "in a critical state of health" and that "his intended voyage to America is probably prompted more by consideration for his physical wellbeing than anything else." It added: "Eminent surgeons have recommended change of air and scene, and cessation from literary labour for some time to come." This was now bringing many enquiries upon me, overwhelming me with letters and causing me real annoyance. I was also aware it would go around America and lead to all sorts of confusion, and I could not imagine how the paragraph ever got into circulation. Accordingly, I wrote a letter of denial to the editor of the Sunday Gazette and also to the editor of The Times asking if he would allow me to state in his columns that this statement in the Sunday Gazette was wholly destitute of foundation, and that I never was better in my life. I also sent a letter to James Fields dismissing such nonsense.

At last I got a joyous telegram from Dolby telling me that he had now arrived in Southern Ireland at Queenstown. I immediately wrote a telegram to await him at the Adelphi Hotel in Liverpool:

"Welcome back, old boy! Do not trouble about me, but go home to Ross first and see your wife and family, and come and see me at Gad's at your convenience."

The next day I received a further telegram from him that he was now on his way to London where his wife was to meet him, and I replied with a further telegram:

"Come on to Gad's this afternoon with your wife, and take a quiet day or two's rest when we can discuss matters leisurely."

CHAPTER LXIX

The Decision, and Send Off

Dolby and his wife came to Gad's Hill on the 23rd September and I talked the American matters over with him. He told me that there was general enthusiasm and excitement awakened in America (despite some comments in the press to the contrary) and that the people were prepared to give me a great reception. My only concern on this head was that I had an opinion that the Irish element in New York was dangerous and that the Fenians would be glad to damage a conspicuous Englishman. Our original calculations had all been based on me carrying out 100 readings, but Dolby, after careful inquiry on the spot, found that the month of May was generally considered (in the large cities) bad for such a purpose, so we reduced the number of readings upon which to make the calculations to 80. All expenses we calculated on the New York scale, which was the dearest, and 20% deducted for management, including Dolby's commission. Under the most advantageous circumstances possible as to the public reception for 80 readings, it was considered that the net profit to me after the payment of all charges whatever would be £15,500, assuming New York City, the State of New York, Boston and adjacent places, Philadelphia, Washington and Baltimore being good for a very large proportion of the 80 readings. If these places should not be good for so many, then Dolby said it may prove impracticable to get through 80 within the time, by reason of other places that would then come into the list, lying wide asunder, and necessitating long and fatiguing journeys. He allowed in the calculation for the loss consequent on the conversion of paper money into gold, with gold at the present ruling premium counting 7 dollars in the pound.

I wrote out from what he told me "The Case in a Nutshell" and on the 24th September sent this to Wills and to Forster, requesting each of them to give me their opinion on it – to go or not to go? – with no hint of my own tending either way. I also went to Peckham for two days to discuss the matter with Nelly. Thereafter I had a long discussion with Forster and then dined with him and Dolby before finally making up my mind. Forster remained implacably opposed to the idea but, in weighing everything up, I had carefully gone through Dolby's papers, taken no terms from anybody, but made the venture for myself. I doubted the profit being as great as his calculation made it, but the prospect was sufficiently alluring to turn the scale on the American side, and I decided to go. I later told Forster that I was not in very brilliant spirits at the prospect before me, and was deeply sensible for his motive and reasons for the line he had taken, but I was not in the least shaken in the conviction that I could never quite have given up the idea.

The next morning I was up at 5 a.m. and set off for town to send off the decisive telegram to Ticknor & Fields in Boston. Having done so, I then wrote to both Mamie and Georgy at Gad's Hill telling them of my decision, though I was so nervous with travelling and anxiety to decide sensibly, that I could hardly write. That evening I went to Peckham and told Nelly also of my decision, having sought to book my passage on the Cunard Ship "Scotia" from Liverpool on Saturday 2nd November, and wrote a personal letter to James Fields and his wife Annie, thanking them both most heartily for their proffered hospitality but explaining to them that I thought I could not do better than observe the rule on that side of the Atlantic which I observed on this – of never under such circumstances going to a friend's house but always staying at a hotel.

I was notified that the sailing to America on the 2nd November was full, and consequently booked with Cunard for the following week, Saturday 9th November, on their ship "Cuba", which enabled me to have one of the Officers' cabins on deck. I continued on busily at work on the Christmas Number to complete it before I sailed, meeting with Wilkie at the office and staying at both Peckham and Gad's Hill during this period, whilst making preparations for the journey, choosing to have four men with me: Dolby, Scott (my Dresser), Richard Kelly (Ticket Clerk) and George Allison (Gasman).

I arranged for Dolby to leave before me to begin his duties in America, and he sailed from Liverpool on the 12th October on the ship "China". I had spoken to him about Nelly and told him that I had been agonizing over whether or not she could or should accompany me in America; eventually I arranged with Nelly that I would send her a coded instruction from America once I arrived, telling her to note well the details of my message and the meaning of it. If I telegraphed: "all well", it meant she came; if I telegraphed: "safe and well", it meant she did not come. I put these exact details into my pocket diary and told her to expect my message through Wills on either Saturday 23rd or Saturday 30th November. She then left with her mother for the Villa Trollope at Ricorboli, Florence to stay with her sister Fanny, Thomas Trollope and his daughter Bice. I also left the following note with Wills:

"NELLY If she needs any help will come to you, or if she changes her address, you will immediately let me know if she changes. Until then it will be Villa Trollope, a Ricorboli, Firenze, Italy. On the day after my arrival out I will send you a short Telegram at the office. Please copy its exact words, (as they will have special meaning to her), and post them to her as above by the very next post after receiving my telegram. And also let Gad's Hill know – and let Forster know – what the telegram is."

In a further note to Wills, I also told him that Forster knew Nelly as he did, and would do anything for her if he wanted anything done.

I attended a farewell public dinner on the 2nd November, with artists, actors, writers, eminent lawyers, peers, merchants, bankers and press reporters all noted as sitting side by side. The English flag was knit with the Stars and Stripes, and the walls of the room comprised twenty large blank panels with arched tops; boarders of laurel leaves on a deep red ground ran around the panels, and in the arched tops of each the name of one of my works was introduced in gold letters – from Mr. Pickwick to Doctor Marigold. At the conclusion of the dinner Lytton rose to give the toast of the evening and a speech that was repeatedly interrupted by ringing cheers. Then, as soon as I stood to speak, the whole company rose to their feet and cheered again and again; those at the lower tables forced their way up the aisles and I found myself surrounded by a living wall of friends. Others leapt up on chairs, napkins were tossed up, and decanters and half-emptied champagne bottles waved overhead; the ladies fluttered fans and handkerchiefs from the gallery. It was a great demonstration and for the moment it almost struck me dumb, but then on seeking composure I thanked them all for a reception I would never forget, and my speech was greeted by round after round of further loud cheering. After further speeches, including one by the Lord Chief Justice (Sir Alexander Cockburn), the proceedings ended shortly before half past eleven, but I had to shake so many hands and say goodbye to so many friends that it was a long while before I was able to leave. Then, as I appeared outside in Great Queen Street, a crowd that had gathered gave me a last ringing cheer of "Farewell!" The whole evening was, I do suppose, the most brilliant ever seen.

I dined with Forster the next night, having walked to his home in Kensington, and on the following days spent time planning the Christmas Number of "No Thoroughfare" out into a play for Wilkie to manipulate after I had sailed. Every moment of my time had been preoccupied during this period, including having conversation with the Chappells about the time when I got back to England. I told them I would have a series of farewell readings in town and country, and then read no more. They at once offered in writing to pay all expenses whatever, to pay the10% for management, and to pay me for a series of 75, six thousand pounds.

A small group that including Wills, came with me to Liverpool. I gave Wills a detailed memorandum covering everything I could think of and, after spending the night at the Adelphi Hotel, I went aboard the "Cuba" and was established by myself – Scott, Kelly and Allison being located elsewhere on the ship – in the second officer's cabin on deck, where I had an abundance of fresh air, and which was of such vast proportions that it was almost large enough for me to squeeze in – big enough for everything but going to bed in and getting up in!

CHAPTER LXX

Voyage, and Arrival Again in America

The ship was almost full of passengers, many of them American, and I was soon on the best terms with nearly all of them. At table I sat next to the captain (Captain Stone) who, though he was nicknamed "Silent Stone" and reportedly gruff, I found him to be a very good and honest fellow. Because the officers' quarters were close to me, I got to know them all and got reports of the weather and the way we were making when the watch was changed. The weather in the passage to Queenstown was delightful, and we had scarcely any motion beyond that of the screw, which was at its slightest vibration in my particular part of the ship, but at night it was very noisy as the most important working of the ship went on outside my window – open to give me my chief requirement of plenty of air – and also over my head, which made it difficult to sleep.

I spent my time when I could constantly reading, or writing on a writing slab in the cabin which pulled out when wanted, if the motion of the ship would let me. We had some difficult weather, including a heavy gale of wind, but on the forenoon of the 16th November we made Cape Race on the southernmost tip of Newfoundland and begun running towards Halifax at full speed with the land beside us. My foot was now in a very shy condition and rather painful; I hoped the same being from simply walking on the boarded deck. That night at 4 a.m. we got into bad weather again, and the state of things at breakfast-time was utterly miserable. Nearly all the passengers were in their berths as there was no possibility of standing on deck, sickness and groans abounded, and it was impracticable to pass a cup of tea from one pair of hands to another. Later, it slightly moderated and the sun shone, but the rolling of the ship continued to surpass all imagination or description. A pale young curate was in extreme difficulties as he tried to take a church service on board and remain upright! Indeed, one of the most comical spectacles I have ever seen in my life was "church" with a heavy sea on, in the saloon of that Cunard steamer. This officiating minister, an extremely modest young man, was brought in between two stewards exactly as if he were coming up to the scratch in a prize fight. The ship was rolling and pitching so, that the two big stewards had to stop and watch their opportunity of making a dart at the reading desk with their reverend charge, during which pause he held on, now by one steward and now by the other, with the feeblest expression of countenance and no legs whatever. At length they made a dart at the wrong moment, and one steward was immediately beheld alone in the extreme perspective – while the other and the reverend gentleman held on to the mast in the middle of the saloon, which the latter embraced with both arms as if it were his wife! All this time the congregation were breaking up into sects and sliding away – my sect (as in nature) pounding the other sect. And when at last the reverend gentleman had been tumbled into his place, the desk (a loose one, put upon the dining table) deviated from the church bodily and went over to the purser. The scene was so extraordinarily ridiculous, and was made so much more so by the exemplary gravity of all concerned in it, that I was obliged to leave before the service began.

Before Halifax I managed to write some letters with great difficulty, wedged up in a corner, and having my heels on the paper as often as the pen, as well as my desk and I being cast about on the floor. But during the whole voyage I was never sick. Let me tell you that if ever you should be in a position to advise a traveller going on a sea voyage, remember that there is some mysterious service done to the bilious system when it is shaken, by baked apples. Noticing that they were produced on board the Cuba, every day at lunch and dinner, I thought I would make the experiment of always eating them freely. I am confident that they did wonders, not only at the time, but also in stopping the imaginary pitching and rolling after the voyage was over, from which many good amateur sailors also suffer.

After calling at Halifax, we sailed on the thirty-hour journey to Boston, though ours was a very slow passage against head-winds. After the last dinner of the voyage, we had speech-making and singing in the saloon and I think I acquired a higher reputation for drawing out the captain, who sang no end of duets with me and then took a little cruise around the compass in song on his own account. He had never been known to come out before! I made no end of speeches, before finally proposing the ladies in a speech that convulsed the stewards; and we closed with a brilliant success.

As we approached Boston, in the bay we passed the Java, who let off a perfect shower of rockets to welcome us, while Dolby came alongside in a steam tug allowing me to come over the side and into his arms. As the tug took us to Long Wharf, the pilot brought the news on board that the people had stood with the greatest good temper in the freezing street twelve hours, to buy tickets at $2 each from the Ticknor & Fields office for the first four readings here in Boston (the only readings so far announced) and that every ticket for every night was sold. I later found that the gross receipts of those four nights of $14,000 (about £2,000) was £250 beyond our calculation – and that speculators were making a profit of up to $24 a ticket. At the Wharf we met Fields, Ticknor and also Osgood, a partner with the firm, and exchanged hearty greetings, before making our way to an immense place, the Parker House Hotel. I had a suite (No. 338) in a corner high up on the third floor, with hot and cold water laid on in a bath in my bedroom, and other comforts not known in my former experience. Upon entering it I found to my greatest delight that it had been adorned and decorated beautifully with choice flowers by Annie Fields, a delightful woman with a rare relish for humour and a most contagious laugh.

The Bostonians, having been duly informed that I wished to be quiet, really left me as much. This I could not expect to last elsewhere; but it was a most welcome relief here, as I had all the readings to get up; the people were perfectly kind and perfectly agreeable. Every day I took to walking from 7 to 10 miles in peace, and found changes in Boston that exceeded my utmost expectations. What was now the handsomest part of Boston had been a bleak swamp when I saw it 25 years before. The City had increased enormously in size, and had grown more mercantile, but I did not notice any special difference in manners and customs between my old time and this, except there was more of New York in this fine city than there was of yore.

Before the readings began, I engaged in much socializing. Longfellow arrived at the hotel the day after my arrival and I was delighted to see him again. He was now perfectly white in hair and beard, but still a remarkably handsome and notable-looking man. I dined with him the following night, together with a number of his friends, and joined with him again in dining with the "Saturday Club" that met regularly on the last Saturday in each month. I dined also on a number of occasions with James and Annie Fields at their lovely home at 148 Charles Street, looking out over the Charles River, as well as with others, and all the while readying myself for the readings.

I went with Dolby to the hall at the Tremont Temple where I was to read and found it charming and with perfect acoustics when Dolby and I tested it. New York tickets were not yet on sale, but I heard signs of the same excitement there and I could not wait to begin; I began to feel that nothing could possibly be more splendid than our prospects in America. I walked around Boston with Dolby, discussing arrangements in the pleasant air rather than in the hotel room; he was convulsively trying to hold his head up above seas of work. I spent time getting letters ready for England and, on the 22nd November, I sent to Wills at 26 Wellington Street the all-important personal telegram. It read: "Safe & Well   expect good letter   full of Hope". It was my signal for him to tell Nelly that I had decided she should not come to America, and that Wills should also inform Gad's Hill and Forster accordingly.

I wrote a separate letter to Wills thereafter, telling him that, while I was in America, I would address all my private letters to Nelly to his care, for I did not quite know where she would be. I had arranged for her to write to him, and instructed Wills to forward my letters to her, and that in any interval between his receipt of one or more of my letters for her and my Dear Girl so writing to him, he should keep my letters safely by him.

CHAPTER LXXI

Readings in Boston and New York

Dolby went over to New York – where we were now at our wits end how to keep tickets out of the hands of speculators – and returned, reporting that the prospects seemed immense. Tickets for the first four readings in the Steinway Hall (which held 500 more than the hall in Boston) were now put on sale, and they were all sold in a few hours, with enormous queues in two lines each stretching more than three-quarters of a mile for hours. Members of families relieved each other; waiters flew across the streets and squares from the neighbouring restaurant, to serve parties who were taking their breakfast in the open December air; while excited men offered $5 and $10 for the mere permission to exchange places with other persons standing near the head of the line! Speculators went up and down offering "twenty dollars for anybody's place", and receipts were far in excess of our careful estimates made at Gad's Hill.

On Monday 2nd December I carried out my first reading in Boston, where I received the most magnificent reception. Flowers adorned my dressing room and, to my pleasure and amazement, Mary Boyle had now arranged for the usual one from her for my button-hole to be lying on my dressing-table here when I arrived! From the audience, nothing could have been more triumphant, and it was the most single and complete success. People afterwards would hear of nothing else and talk of nothing else, and nothing that was ever done there, they all agreed, evoked any approach to such enthusiasm. I was quite as cool and quick as if I were reading at Greenwich or Chatham, and went at it accordingly. At the conclusion I was perfectly well, and in the best of spirits, and the applause so enthusiastic that I was again forced to break my normal rule and return to the stage to bow in acknowledgement.

It was quite impossible that prospects could now be more brilliant, and I sent a letter to Wills, enclosing one for my dear girl Nelly. After completing the readings in Boston, we moved to New York on the 7th December but continued to be troubled by the speculators. We sold no more than six tickets to any one person for the course of the four readings, but the speculators employed any number of men to buy.

Once in New York, I settled in at the Westminster Hotel, a large hotel on Irving Place and 16th Street, and prepared for my first reading. The hotel was quiet, I was able to go in and out by a side door and little staircase that led straight to my bedroom. New York had grown out of my knowledge from before, and was now enormous; furthermore, everything in it looked as if the orders of nature were reversed, and everything grew newer every day, instead of older. The Steinway Hall, was on the first floor of the building newly erected on 14th Street, with 2,500 seats, and was one of the largest halls in the city, though was about as trying to read in as St. James's Hall in London. I was in capital health and voice – though my spirits would flutter woefully with thoughts of Nelly as that most drearily missed person. I sent Wills another letter for her, to his usual care and exactness, and asked if he could also forward to her some of the New York papers that I had asked Dolby to send to him. Dolby also organized a series of photographs to be taken of me and these were carried out by Jeremiah Gurney and his son Benjamin at their studio at 707 Broadway, the results being distributed to an eager public.

On the 9th December I read the Carol and the Trial from Pickwick in the Steinway Hall, and it was absolutely impossible that we could have made a more brilliant success. The reception was splendid, the audience bright and perceptive, the general delight most enthusiastic, and I believe I never read so well since I began. Then Copperfield and Mr. Bob Sawyer's Party the next night was even a greater success – the audiences far better even than in Boston!

We now began selling, at the Hall, the tickets for the 4 readings for the following week. By nine o'clock in the morning there were 2,000 people in waiting, and they had begun to assemble in the bitter cold as early as two o'clock. All night long Dolby and one of our men had been stamping tickets immediately above my head (by-the-bye, keeping me awake) before going out, and when he returned from the ticket sales, he put such an immense untidy heap of paper money on the table that it looked like a family wash!

I read again on the 12th and 13th December, now with flowers provided that were, I suppose, the finest and costliest basket of flowers ever seen – made of white camellias, yellow roses, pink roses and I don't know what else, a yard and a half round at its smallest part – but Dolby was now being called "pudding-headed Dolby" in the press and elsewhere, the public charging upon him all the annoyances and the difficulties that had attended the purchase of tickets.

My avocations occupied too much of my time to admit to my pursuing the International Copyright question under the existing circumstances and I felt now that I would rather put the subject aside, in friendship towards the American people. At theatres all over the city, comic operas, melodramas, and domestic dramas prevailed, and my own stories played no inconsiderable part in them. But then a winter storm came on, the snow fell, railways closed, and snow became piled up in enormous walls the whole length of the streets. New York became crowded with sleighs, and I turned out in a rather gorgeous one with a quantity of buffalo robes, and made an imposing appearance! Thereafter, my landlord invented for me a drink which he melodiously called a "Rocky Mountain Sneezer" and also introduced me to their favourite drink before getting up, the "Eye Opener".

News of a Fenian explosion in London was telegraphed to New York in a few hours. I did not think there was any sympathy whatever with the Fenians on the part of the American people, though political adventurers might make capital out of a show of it, for I found the local politics in a most depraved condition, if half of what was said to me was true. The Irish element was acquiring such enormous influence in New York city, that when I thought of it, and saw the large Roman Catholic Cathedral of St. Patrick rising there on 5th Avenue, it seemed unfair to stigmatize as "American" other monstrous things that one also saw. I preferred not to talk of these, but at odd intervals looked around for myself.

I was able to notice that great social improvements in respect of manners and forbearance had come to pass since I was here before, and there was generally a much more responsible and respectable tone in newspapers than prevailed formally, however small might be the literary merit among papers pointed out to me as of large circulation. In public life I saw as yet but little change, though there were, undoubtedly, improvements in every direction, and I took my time to make up my mind on things in general.

I read again on the nights of the 16th, 17th, 19th, and 20th December, before seeking to return again to Boston on the 21st for two further readings before Christmas. Apart from Boston, it was Dolby's original plan that I should read in New York every week; all our announced readings there were already crammed, and by the 10th January I calculated that I should have read to 35,000 people in that city alone. But, after very careful consideration, I said "No" to simply reading in New York and Boston, for I knew that would put the readings out of reach of all the people situated behind them. So, I revised Dolby's original plan, proposing on taking Baltimore, Washington, Cincinnati, Pittsburgh, Chicago (!), St. Louis, and a few other places nearer Boston, as well as Cleveland and Buffalo, towards Niagara – taking the best places with the largest halls on the list – and Dolby was now making out a revised tour. I was also by now pledged to Philadelphia for six nights, and considered a scheme could be drawn up that could pretty easily bring us to Boston again twice before the farewells. I wanted, by absence, to get the greatest rush and pressure upon the five farewell readings I proposed in New York in April, and was convinced that this was a sound policy.

By now I had received glorious tidings from Wills of the Christmas Number of "No Thoroughfare", and heard from Ticknor & Fields that they intended to publish the first part of "Holiday Romance" on the 1st January and the remaining 3 parts on the 1st of each following month. They had also taken, for £1,000 (instead of Wood) "George Silverman's Explanation" and arranged to publish it in 3 monthly parts, this too beginning on the 1st January.

I wrote Christmas letters home, including one to Wills and enclosing a letter for Nelly, and set off again for New York, spending our Christmas Day on the railway. At the Westminster Hotel, I plucked up a little and made some hot gin punch to drink a Merry Christmas to all at home in, but it must be confessed that we were all very dull.

I read in the Steinway Hall on the 26th, but it was as much as I could do, and the next day I was so very unwell that I had to send for a doctor. Dr. Fordyce Barker arrived, a very agreeable fellow, but he was in doubt whether I should not have to stop reading for a while. I was diagnosed with a very heavy cold, an irritated condition of the uvula, and a restless low state of the nervous system, but I pointed out to the doctor how we stood committed, and how I must go on if it could be done. He set me on my legs with a tonic and took his leave "professionally", and I found I was then able to carry on with my further readings. I read on the 30th and 31st in the Steinway Hall and turned my thoughts to the readings in January, now proposing to blaze away in Philadelphia, Brooklyn and Baltimore, which places, together with New York and Boston, now set out to occupy my time in the coming month. At Brooklyn I was to read in Mr. Ward Beecher's Church (he being the brother of Mrs. Harriet Beecher Stowe), it being the only building there available for the purpose. It was the Plymouth Church in Orange Street and I went across the water to look at it. Brooklyn was a kind of sleeping-place for New York, and was supposed to be a great place in the money way. I found the Church wonderfully seated for two thousand people and as easy to speak in as if they were two hundred. The people were to be seated in the pews, which we proposed to let pew by pew, but I found myself in a comically incongruous position; I was to stand on a small platform, from which the pulpit was to be removed for the occasion, having emerged from the vestry in canonical form!!

At the close of the year I sent another letter to Wills, enclosing another letter for my darling, although on the last Sunday I lost my old year's pocket book for 1867 with all my entries therein, which did, as Mr. Pepys would add, "trouble me mightily". The New Year brought another fall of snow, succeeded by a heavy thaw, whereupon my intolerable cold returned and steadily refused to stir an inch. It distressed me greatly at times, though it was always good enough to leave me for a needful two hours of a reading. I tried allopathy, homoeopathy, cold things, warm things, sweet things, bitter things, stimulants, narcotics, all with the same result. Nothing would touch it. The work I was engaged in was hard, the climate was hard, the life was hard: but so-far the gain was enormous. Dolby continued to go about with an immense bundle of paper money that looked like the sofa-cushion, but had now risen to the proportion of the sofa itself by the 3rd January, when he left to sell tickets in Philadelphia.

We continued to have difficulties over the speculators and tried to withhold the best front seats from them, but the unaccountable thing was that a great mass of the public bought off them (preferred it), and the rest of the public were injured if we had not got those very seats to sell them. The speculators bought the front seats to sell at a premium (and we also found instances of this being done by merchants in good position!) and the public were perpetually pitching into Dolby for selling them back seats. The result was that they would not have the back seats, and would return their tickets, write and print volumes on the subject, and deter others from coming. Fortunately, this did not prevail to any great extent, as our lowest house was £300, but there was no doubt it did hit us.

But our great labour was now outside the readings. We were obliged to bring our travelling staff up to six (besides a boy or two) by employment of a regular additional clerk, a Bostonian named Marshal P. Wild. It seemed a large number of people, but the business could not be done with fewer. They were now preparing, numbering and stamping 6,000 tickets for Philadelphia and 8,000 for Brooklyn. The moment these were done, another 8,000 tickets were wanted for Baltimore and another 6,000 for Washington – and all this in addition to the correspondence, advertisements, accounts, travelling, and the nightly business of the readings four times a week

The reading in the Steinway Hall on the 3rd January meant I had now read out the first quarter of my list. The following day we travelled back to Boston, where I read again on the 6th and 7th. My schedule then had me rush back to New York, reading again in the Steinway Hall on the 9th and 10th, which meant that my New York readings were then over, except for the farewell nights in April. I had now read to 40,000 people in New York and looked forward to the relief of being out of my hardest hall, for on the night of the 10th, though it was only Nickleby and Boots, I was again dead beat at the end, and was once more laid upon a sofa after being washed and dressed, extremely faint, though the faintness went off after a quarter of an hour when I rallied and came right.

CHAPTER LXXII

Readings in Philadelphia, Brooklyn,
Baltimore, Washington, Hartford and Providence –
and the "American Catarrh"

On the evening of the 12th January I left by rail for Philadelphia for the first of my visits of two nights each, tickets for all being sold. My cold steadily refused to leave me and I was now oppressed with this "American Catarrh" (as they called it), but I otherwise felt as right as one could hope to be under the heavy work, though I found I was losing my hair with great rapidity and what I did not lose was getting very grey. As we travelled along I found the railway car so intolerably hot from the stove that I was often obliged to go and stand on the brake outside, and then the frosty air was biting indeed, and with it snowing and blowing, and the train bumping and the steam flying at me, I would eventually be driven in again. On my first night in Philadelphia (the 13th January), at the Concert Hall, I read the Carol and the Trial from Pickwick to a very impressible and responsive audience, though they were so astounded by my simply walking in and opening my book that I wondered what was the matter. The newspapers were constantly expressing the popular amazement at "Mr. Dickens's extraordinary composure", and they seemed to take it ill that I did not stagger onto the platform overpowered by the spectacle before me, and the national greatness. They were all so accustomed to do public things with a flourish of trumpets, that the notion of my coming in to read without somebody first flying up and delivering an "oration" about me, and flying down again and leading me in, was so very unaccountable to them, that sometimes they had no idea until I opened my lips that I could possibly be Charles Dickens at all!

On returning to New York, I began my four nights in Brooklyn, on the opposite side of the river. Each evening an enormous ferry-boat conveyed me and my state carriage (not to mention half-a-dozen wagons, and any number of people, and a few score of horses) across the river, and then back again at the finish of the evening. The men worked very hard, and always with their hearts cheerfully in the business, so I crammed them into and outside of the carriage, to bring them back from Brooklyn with me. It began to snow hard again, and on the last night there was so much floating ice in the river that we were obliged to leave a pretty wide margin of time for getting over the ferry to read. I read the Carol and the Trial from Pickwick on the 16th, Copperfield and Mr. Bob Sawyer's Party on the 17th, Dr. Marigold and the Trial from Pickwick on the 20th and Nickleby and Boots at the Holly-Tree Inn on the 21st. It was very odd to see the pews crammed full of people, all in a broad roar, but it was a most wonderful place to speak in and it scarcely required an effort. The readings there were an immense success. Mr. Ward Beecher was present in his pew on the last night and I sent to invite him to come round before he left; I found him to be an unostentatious and agreeable fellow, a clever, unparsonic and straightforward bachelor, with a good knowledge of art into the bargain.

At each reading I had now established the custom of taking an egg beaten up in sherry before going in, and another between the parts, which I felt pulled me up; at all events, I had since had no return of faintness, despite my cold sticking to me and scarcely being able to exaggerate what I sometimes underwent from sleeplessness. I would rarely take any breakfast but an egg and a cup of tea, not even toast or bread-and-butter. My dinner I would take at 3 p.m., and then a little quail or some such light thing when I came home at night, being the total of my daily fare.

In New York, before travelling again to Philadelphia, I saw the Cunard steamer "Persia" out in the stream, beautifully smart, her flags flying, all her steam up, and she only waiting for her mails to slip away. She gave me a horrible touch of home-sickness, and I contemplated that when the 1st March arrived, I could then say "next month", and begin to grow brighter. Dolby and Osgood, who did the most ridiculous things to keep me in spirits (I was often very heavy, and rarely slept much) were now determined to have a walking match between themselves at Boston on the last day of February, to celebrate the arrival of that day when I could say "next month!" for home. Beginning this design in joke, they became tremendously in earnest; however neither of them had the least idea what 12 miles (the distance planned) at a pace was. They had the absurdist ideas of what were the tests for walking power, and continuously got up in the maddest manner to see how high they could kick the wall! The wainscot in one place became so scored all over with their pencil marks, and to see them doing this – Dolby a big man, and Osgood a very little one – was ridiculous beyond description.

At Baltimore the Governor showed Dolby and I his new system for putting prisoners to work at their own trades in workshops at the Maryland Penitentiary, a huge hydropathic establishment, but without the privilege of going out for a walk. But upon observation I found the ghost of slavery still haunting this town; the old untidy, incapable, lounging, shambling black served you as a free man – free, of course he ought to be, but the melancholy absurdity of making him a voter, at any rate at present, glared out of every roll of his eye, stretch of his mouth, and bump of his head. One could not help but see that their enfranchisement was a mere party trick to get votes, and I had a strong impression that the race must fade out of the States very fast, for it never could hold its own against a striving, restless, shifty, stronger race of people. In the penitentiary even I had seen the white prisoners dining on one side of the room, the coloured prisoners on the other, and no one having the slightest idea of mixing them. Baltimore, I fancy, still wore a look of sullen remembrance after the war.

I read in the Concordia Opera House on the 27th and 28th January, before travelling back through a snow storm to Philadelphia, where I read again to immense audiences in the Concert Hall, before then travelling to Washington. Here, on Sunday 2nd February, I dined (against my rules) with Charles Sumner, a Massachusetts Senator and old friend, having met him first in 1842 on my earlier visit to the States. With him was Edwin Stanton, the Commander-in-Chief of all the Northern Forces concentrated here during the War and now the War Minister. He was a man of a very remarkable memory, and famous for his acquaintance with the minutest details of my books; give him any passage anywhere, and he would instantly cap it and go on with the context. It was said he never went to sleep at night without first reading something from my books, and which were always with him. I put him through a pretty severe examination, but he was better up than I was! After dinner we fell into a very interesting conversation and Stanton told me about Cabinet Council proceedings that he had attended on the afternoon of the day (14th April, 1865) on which President Lincoln had been shot, where Lincoln had seemed a different man and said he had had a strange dream now three times of drifting in a boat on a great broad rolling river, but without speaking of it further. He was shot that night by Booth at Ford's Theatre, and both Staunton and Sumner told me they had remained with him until he had breathed his last the following morning.

I began my readings here the next night; it was a charming audience, no disaffection whatever at the raised prices, immense enthusiasm with nothing missed or lost, cheers at the end of the Carol – where they gave a great break out, and applauded, I really believe, for 5 minutes – and rounds upon rounds of applause all through. In the audience were the President, President Andrew Johnson, and the chief members of his cabinet; and all the foremost men and their families had taken tickets for the series of four, the President taking a whole row for his family every night.

The President sent to me twice and I arranged to see him on Wednesday 5th February, the day that week I was not reading. But the night before, my amiable cold took it into its head to get into my throat and chest and I lay coughing all night and was obliged to keep close within doors. Accordingly, the President sent to me very courteously asking me to make my own appointment; I did so and went to see him on the morning of my birthday, Friday the 7th. When we met, I was very much surprised by his face and manner. It was, in its way, one of the most remarkable faces I had ever seen; not imaginative, but very powerful in its firmness (or perhaps obstinacy), courage, watchfulness, strength of will, and steadiness of purpose. Each of us spoke looking at the other very hard and each managed the interview (I think) to the satisfaction of the other, but I did feel that I noticed an air of chronic anxiety upon him, though not a crease or a ruffle in his dress. His papers were as composed as himself, and I would have picked him out anywhere as a character of mark, not to be turned or trifled with.

The next week we returned to Baltimore to carry out two finishing nights there at the Concordia Opera House on the 10th and 11th February. The weather continued very severe but the readings continued going on in the same splendid way, and seemed to go better and better every night, though nothing would induce the people to believe that I was really taking "farewells". It was now proposed that I turn my back on the southern part of the country and head northwards, so on Saturday 15th February I returned to the Westminster Hotel in New York for a few days before travelling on again the following week. Upon arrival at the hotel I picked up the most interesting book on Mr. Lincoln ("The Inner Life of Abraham Lincoln" by Francis B. Carpenter) and sat down quietly to read some pages of it. But I found that it interested me so exceedingly that the book did not leave my hand till I had read it through to the last word, whereupon I wrote to the author thanking him cordially for it.

Then, with my "true American" still sticking to me, I left New York at seven o'clock on the morning of Tuesday 18th February to read that night in the Allyn Hall in Hartford, Connecticut. The hall, seating 1,400 people, was full and the audience highly enthusiastic. From there I travelled on to Providence, Rhode Island where, although there had been some problems over ticket sales, I read in the City Hall where the spacious hall produced in the outcome a brilliant audience. The Americans had laughed so unrestrainedly at the Trial from Pickwick, that I had now lengthened it and it had grown to be about half as long again as it used to be, and they left, retiring with faces beaming with satisfaction.

I was doing enormous business, but it was a wearing life, away from all that I loved. I had had another letter from Wills and replied to him, adding that he had seen (I hoped) my dear Nelly, and in doing so would have achieved what I would joyfully have given a thousand guineas to achieve myself at that present moment. But generally, the people here had been very good audiences indeed, and among the many changes I continued to find was the comfortable change that the people were in general extremely considerate, and very observant of my privacy. Even in a place such as Providence, I was really almost as much my own master as if I were in an English country town. But, nevertheless, I hoped that the time would soon begin to spin away for my journey home.

CHAPTER LXXIII

Boston and the "Great International Walking Match",
Syracuse, Rochester, Buffalo, and Niagara

The next week I returned to Boston to read a further four times at the Tremont Temple, my catarrh no better, but no worse; the weather intensely cold, Annie Fields more delightful than ever, Fields himself even more hospitable, and my room at the Parker House Hotel always radiant with brilliant flowers of their sending. The Boston audiences, I do believe, had come to regard the readings and the reader as their particular property; and you would have been at once amused and pleased if you could have seen the curious way in which they seemed to plume themselves on both. They had taken to applauding too, whenever they laughed or cried, and the results on the 24th and 25th February were very inspiring. On Wednesday the 26th I had a day free from the readings, and Fields and I took the opportunity to go over the ground of the walking match that was planned for the Saturday, to measure out the miles. We went at a tremendous pace. The condition of the ground was something indescribable, from half-melted snow, sheets and blocks of ice and running water, and I was sure the two performers, Dolby and Osgood, did not have the faintest notion of the weight of the task they had undertaken. I planned a dinner for 18 at my hotel after the event, selected the wines, and settled the bill of fare for the occasion.

The next night there was a fine house for the Carol and Boots at the Holly-Tree Inn and such an enthusiastic one. They took the Carol so tremendously that I was stopped every five minutes; but as I had got to know the reading so well, I couldn't then remember it and occasionally went dodging about in the wildest manner to pick up lost pieces; while one poor young girl in mourning burst into a passion of grief about Tiny Tim, and was taken out.

That night it snowed all night and turned the City into a miserable condition. The "true American" took a fresh start on me, as if it were quite a novelty, and became, on the whole, rather worse than ever. Nevertheless, the following day after resting, I read Nickleby and the Trial from Pickwick in the evening to another enthusiastic audience and was determined that the next day, Saturday 29th February, I would supervise our famous walking match.

The "Great International Walking Match" – Dolby representing England as the "Man of Ross" and Osgood for America as the "Boston Bantam" – came off as a great success, and everybody delighted. The course was now 13 miles, along the Mill Dam Road, from Boston to Newton Centre and back, with Fields ("Massachusetts Jemmy") and I ("the Gad's Hill Gasper" on account of my "American") accompanying them the whole way. It was over tremendously difficult ground, against a biting wind and through deep snow-wreaths; the two were close together at the Newton Centre turning point, but then Osgood went ahead at a splitting pace and with extraordinary endurance. He won by half a mile, but Dolby did very well indeed and begged not to be despised. In the evening I gave a very splendid dinner in the Crystal Room at the Parker House Hotel, with eighteen covers, most magnificent flowers, and such table decoration as was never seen in these parts.

During this time in Boston I wrote twice again to Wills and, on each occasion, enclosed a letter for him to pass on to Nelly. I had heard that Wilkie had been ill, as well as his mother, and that the mad woman he had been living with (Caroline Graves) was now causing him grave difficulties. I asked Wills to give him my love and to tell him that I earnestly hoped he was now much better.

Meanwhile, America had now been struck by much political excitement for, on the 24th February, it had been decided in the House of Representatives that President Johnson should be impeached for "high crimes and misdemeanours" after he had dismissed Edwin Stanton from his position as Secretary of State for War, in defiance of the Tenure of Office Act and without the consent of the Senate. It had been proposed initially that in the following week I should make four further readings in Boston, but by good fortune they had not yet been publicly announced, and I considered it would be wise now to suppress these and watch the course of events. It would also give the political uproar and excitement that much time to take a distinct direction and be intelligible to a foreigner.

We left Boston for Syracuse on the 6th March, travelling most comfortably in a "drawing-room car", of which (Rule Britannia!) we bought exclusive possession. This carriage was, literally, a series of little private drawing-rooms, with sofas and a table in each, opening out of a little corridor. In each too was a large plate-glass window, with which you could do as you liked. As you paid extra for this luxury, it might be regarded as the first move towards two classes of passengers on express trains. We stayed overnight at Albany and next day travelled on to Syracuse, with a thaw placing the whole country under water. Wieting Hall, where I was to read, was a marvel of dirt. It was a most out of the way and unintelligible-looking place with apparently no people in it, and yet we had taken considerably over £300 there when, on the Monday night (the 9th) I read the Carol and the Trial from Pickwick. We moved on to read the same the next night in the Corinthian Hall at Rochester, but found Rochester in a very curious state. The Great Falls of the Genessee River (really very fine, even so near Niagara) were at this place and, in the height of a sudden thaw, an immense bank of ice above the rapids refused to yield, so that the town was threatened (for the second time in four years) with submersion. Boats were ready in the streets, all the people were up all night, and none but the children slept. In the dead of night, a thundering noise was heard, the ice gave way, the swollen river came raging and roaring down the Falls, but the town was safe. Very picturesque! but "not very good for business", as Dolby said – especially as the hall stood in the centre of danger, and had 10 feet of water in it on the last occasion of the flood. But I think we had above £200 English on that night.

From there we went on to Buffalo, again for the same reading, in their St. James's Hall, with Dr. Marigold and Mr. Bob Sawyer's Party on the second night, before having two brilliant sunny days thereafter in Niagara and seeing that wonderful place again under the finest of circumstances. I took all the men as a treat, and once there we went everywhere at the Falls, and saw them in every aspect, the scene splendid beyond description. I shall never forget the last aspect in which we saw Niagara on our second day, Sunday 15th March. We had been everywhere, when I thought of struggling in an open carriage up some very difficult ground for a good distance, and getting where we could stand above the river and see it coming for miles and miles as it rushed forward to its tremendous leap. I chartered a separate carriage for our men, so they might see all in their own way, and at their own time. We went up to the rapids above the Horseshoe – 2 miles from it – and stood with our backs to the bright sun, looking at, and through, the great cloud of spray. All away to the horizon on our right was a wonderful confusion of bright green and white water. As we stood watching it with our faces to the top of the Falls, our backs continuing towards the sun, the majestic valley below the Falls, so seen through the vast cloud of spray, was made of rainbow; the high banks, the riven rocks, the forests, the bridge, the buildings, the air, the sky, were all made of rainbow. Nothing in Turner's finest water-colour drawings, done in his greatest day, was so ethereal, so imaginative, so gorgeous in colour, so celestial, as what I then beheld. I seemed to be lifted from the earth and to be looking into Heaven. What I once felt, as I had witnessed the scene five and twenty years before, all came back at this most affecting and sublime sight. Dolby and I said to one another: "Let it forever remain so" and shut our eyes, before then coming away.

CHAPTER LXXIV

Rochester again, Albany, Springfield, Worcester,
New Haven, Hartford, New Bedford, Portland,
and Farewells in Boston

We got back to Rochester, where I read again on Monday 16th March at the Corinthian Hall, to a larger audience, far ahead of the first. There was now a great thaw over the country, which seemed to have done my catarrh good, but we heard of a great deal of water out between Rochester and New York which made travelling very uncertain. We had come back from our furthest point west and were to steadily work towards home and, in the midst of my home-sickness, I wrote again to Wills, enclosing another letter for Nelly. But I now felt depressed all the time (except when reading), beginning to be tired and had lost my appetite. My next two readings were scheduled in Albany on the 18th and 19th March, and so on the morning of the 17th we rose at 6 to face an eleven hours railway journey to that place.

After creeping through water for miles upon miles, our train finally gave it up as a bad job, stranding us at a place called Utica in the early afternoon. In the flood we had seen villages deserted, bridges broken, fences drifting away, nothing but tearing water, floating ice, and absolute wreck and ruin. The telegraph posts were beaten down by the water and the floating ice, so even that communication was damaged. Let loose in Utica for the night, the greater part of which was under water, some of the wretched passengers passed the night in the train, while others stormed a hotel. I was fortunate enough to get a bedroom in these queer quarters, but with nothing particular to eat, though the people were so very anxious to please that what they did provide was better than the best cuisine. I garnished my room with an enormous jug of gin-punch (using the bedroom pitcher) and Dolby and I played double-dummy rubber and drank our love to James and Annie Fields – Dolby having more than his share, under the pretence of devoted enthusiasm!

The next morning, as I was due at Albany that evening (with all tickets sold), a very active superintendent of works did all he could to "get Mr. Dickens along", and eventually we resumed our journey through the water, but only at four or five miles an hour, with a hundred men in seven league boots pushing the ice from before us with long poles. How we got to Albany, I can't say. We had to take the passengers out of two trains that we came upon that had had their fires put out by the water four-and-twenty hours before, and the passengers composedly sitting all night until relief should arrive; and we also had to unpack and release into the open country a great train of cattle and sheep that had been in the water I don't know how long. We got to Albany at last and arrived in time to find the Albanians in a state of great excitement, and for me to read the Carol and the Trial triumphantly in the Tweddle Hall. My people (I had 5 of the staff with me that night) turned to at their work with a will, and did a day's labour in a couple of hours. The next night I read Dr. Marigold and Mr. Bob Sawyer's Party in the same hall, before being able the following day to travel on to Springfield. My catarrh was at last much better, but my foot had become again rather troublesome. It had been constantly wet from walking in melted snow, which I supposed to be the occasion of its swelling in the old way.

In Springfield we stayed at the Massasoit House Hotel, which Ticknor had reported to us as being excellent, and I read the Carol and the Trial from Pickwick at the Music Hall, but then lo and behold! that night it began to snow again with a strong wind – and in the morning a snow drift covered Springfield with all the desolation once more. I never was so tired of the sight of snow. But during this pause in Springfield I began calculating my likely profit for this American tour. While the expenses were very great, nevertheless, unless the Impeachment excitement would at all interfere with the Boston and New York farewell readings I had planned, I hoped to turn £20,000 of clear profit, after having all charges, including Dolby's 10% on the receipts and the conversion of greenbacks into gold at a considerable premium. Not so bad I thought! By now I had also arranged with Chappells that, on my return home, I would take my leave of the readings for good and all in 100 autumnal and winter farewells. I knew Wills was against this as he had told me so, but I thought the £8,000 that Chappells had offered me for them was quite as much as they could reasonably bear, and I was aware of the accounts that Dolby had kept for the last series.

I read at the Mechanics Hall in Worcester on the 23rd March and then at New Haven the following night without problems. From there we travelled to Hartford where, on the 25th, I read at the Allyn Hall, before returning exhausted to Boston again. On Friday 27th I ought to have left Boston for New Bedford (55 miles) before 11 in the morning, but I had taken some laudanum at night and it was the only thing that did me good, though it made me sick in the morning. I was so exhausted that I could not be got up, and Fields was very grave about me going on. But I did, got to New Bedford by the evening train just in time, and read at the Liberty Hall with my utmost force and vigour. I was now, however, having to lie down on the sofa in my dressing room at the close of the reading for twenty minutes to half an hour in a state of the greatest exhaustion, and taking a wine-glassful of champagne to give action to my heart. The life in this climate I did find so very hard.

The next morning, well or ill, I had to turn out at 7 a.m. to get back to Boston, on my way north to Portland, but with the return of snow, the "true American" (which had lulled) came back as bad as ever. I coughed from two or three in the morning to five or six and was absolutely sleepless. I had no appetite besides and no taste, but it was impossible to make the people about me understand, however zealous and devoted, that the power of coming up to the mark every night, with spirits and spirit, might coexist with the nearest approach to sinking under it; it was impossible even to make Dolby understand until the pinch came. Back at Boston, I dined at three, but then at five had to go on to Portland (130 miles or so) as there was no Sunday train. Once in Portland I wrote to Dolby (who was now in New York) to call on Dr. Fordyce Barker and get from him a further prescription for laudanum or other composing medicine as a sleeping draught, in as much as without sleep I felt I could not get through.

At Portland I was able to have a fine walk by the sea and then, without any artificial aid, I was pleased to say I got a splendid night's rest. As a consequence, the next morning I felt very much freshened up, and was able to take another good walk, this time on the heights overlooking the town. I found that three parts of the town had been burnt down in a tremendous fire three years before, and the people had lived in tents while their city was rebuilding. The charred trunks of the trees with which the streets of the old city were planted, yet stood here and there in the new thoroughfares like black spectres, and the rebuilding was still in progress everywhere. On the night of Monday 30th March I read the Carol and the Trial from Pickwick in triumphant fashion, taking £360 English (where a costly Italian troupe, using the same hall the following night, did not book more than £14!), but I was once again exhausted at the end of it, and then got no sleep again in the night.

With this sleeplessness besetting me, I felt nearly used up and now the climate, distance, catarrh, travelling and hard work began to tell heavily upon me. But I did arrive safely back in Boston feeling better, as I considered now that my work was virtually over. Six farewell readings were planned for Boston and, after a five-day break, five more farewells in New York, before I took the now confirmed Cunard Mail Steamer "Russia" for home on the 22nd April. I had been given the Chief Steward's cabin on deck, it being on the sunny side of the ship.

James and Annie Fields had become the most devoted of friends, never in the way and never out of it, and my room at the Parker House Hotel continued to be well decorated with flowers, but I was concerned about the continuing political crisis. It was the same all over the country, and I considered the worst was yet to come. Everything was becoming absorbed in the Presidential impeachment, helped by the next Presidential election, and I now feared that it may damage the farewells by about one half. I had news that the New York press were proposing to give me a public dinner on Saturday 18th April in the midst of my farewell readings there, but then heard some worrying news that Wills had had a bad fall whilst out hunting and was, or had been, laid up. I had not heard this from Wills directly, so waited to hear about it from him.

I began my Boston farewells at the Tremont Temple on Wednesday 1st April, and we took £300 English. Dr. Fordyce Barker had prescribed for me promptly and to see me at my little table, you would have thought me the freshest of the fresh. The reading was the crowning marvel of Fields's life and Longfellow too was present again, easily seen with his perfectly white flowing beard and long white hair. Dolby had turned to being as tender as a woman and as watchful as a doctor over me. He now never left me during the reading, and would sit at the side of the platform and keep his eyes on me all the time. Ditto George the gasman, the steadiest and most reliable man I ever employed. I felt tremendously "beat" and could not eat to anything like the ordinary extent; I did not eat more than half a pound of solid food in a whole four-and-twenty hour period, if so much.

I read again on the 2nd April, feeling somewhat better, and not forgetting that it was Forster's birthday, or that it was another anniversary (that of my wedding); but by Friday 3rd April my catarrh was worse than ever, and by 4 o'clock in the afternoon I did not know whether I could read that night or have to stop. My spirits and my spirit so deserted me that I lost the confidence in myself with which experience had inspired me, and I was on the verge of stopping, with Longfellow and all the Cambridge men urging me to give in, but I physicked myself until I hated myself, and went on, and read as I never did before. It astonished the audience quite as much as myself; you never saw or heard such a scene of excitement.

I knew over the weekend I must give up going out on both days and must "go in" for rest and training with a view to avoiding such a risk again. I did it with the most ungracious grace in the world, but I knew it must be done. Flowers continued to arrive, including from Mrs. Ticknor, who sent them by the hands of her good husband. I did go out for a ride with Dolby instead of my usual walk, but otherwise remained in my room making myself ready for the 4th farewell reading on Monday the 6th, and fancied that I had turned my worst time.

Another snowstorm blew up, but I went ahead with the reading, of Copperfield and Mr. Bob Sawyer's Party. By a quarter of an hour this was the longest of my readings but I felt far fresher afterwards than I had been in the previous three weeks, and so much stronger, both in body and hopes, that I was much encouraged. I could not tell whether the catarrh may have done me any lasting injury in the lungs or other breathing organs until I rested and got home, but I hoped and believed not.

Yet another snowstorm blew up, and on the 7th April Boston was blotted out in a ceaseless whirl of snow and wind. I had Dombey to do that night and so went through it carefully before the reading. I seemed quite naturally and placidly to have regained my old condition, and with it the quiet consciousness that I could bear the little that remained of this long strain. I read that night and found the personal affection of the people of Boston charming to the last. My final farewell reading there was on the 8th April when I read Dr. Marigold and Mrs. Gamp to an audience that was larger than ever, the receipts being the greatest of any of my American readings. Flowers abounded all around my reading table and the enthusiasm of the audience put me in the finest form. At the close the prolonged and enthusiastic applause was so great that it drew me back as I was leaving the platform. I thanked them for my gracious and generous welcome in America that had begun here in Boston, and which could never be obliterated from my remembrance. I told them that I had not, until that moment, really felt that I was going away, and added:

"In this brief life of ours it is sad to do almost anything for the last time, and I cannot conceal from you, although my face will soon be turned towards my native land, and to all that makes it dear, that it is a sad consideration with me that in a very few moments from this time, this brilliant hall and all that it contains, will fade from my view for evermore. But it is my consolation that the spirit of the bright faces, the quick perception, the ready response, the generous and cheering sounds that have made this place delightful to me, will remain; and you may rely upon it that that spirit will abide with me as long as I have sense and sentiment."

After saying a few more words that bid my farewell, I left the stage to three cheers and overwhelming applause.

CHAPTER LXXV

Farewells in New York, Home to England, and to Nelly

I now made my preparations to leave Boston on Good Friday (10th April) for my final five farewell readings in New York. I returned to the Westminster Hotel and prepared to begin in the Steinway Hall on Monday 13th April, the faithful Fields's coming to New York with us. I read that Monday night, and the next night continued with another large audience, but I returned to my hotel room very, very tired. The next was a day of rest, allowing me to recover for the further readings I did on the 16th and 17th; meanwhile, Dolby and I had a surprise visit from a collector of taxes and a colleague of his, threatening to arrest Dolby, as my manager, for not having made an income tax return relating to my income in America. Dolby dealt with this and successfully resisted the claim.

I heard from Wills, his letter giving me hope that I might find him quite restored from the hunting accident I had heard about; I wrote to him again, enclosing one last letter for Nelly. By now I was in great pain as my right foot had swollen and I could not wear my boot upon it. Dolby called in Dr. Fordyce Barker once more and he attended at the hotel on Saturday 18th, as over 200 members of the American press – said to be the largest and most influential assemblage of newspaper men ever seen in America – were assembling at Delmonico's for a dinner in my honour. The doctor treated and bandaged my leg and Dolby was eventually able to borrow a gout-stocking (from an Englishman) to put over the bandages for me to attend, but I was still in great pain and attended over an hour late. I was met by the committee at the door and taken upstairs to the dinner by Horace Greely, editor of the New York Tribune, and introduced to tremendous cheers. After the dinner I replied to their toasts to me by telling them how astounded I had been of the amazing changes I had seen around me on every side in America since my previous visit. I chided them in a light way for some of the material they had written about me, but stressed that I was not so arrogant to suppose that in five-and-twenty years there had been no changes in me and that I had nothing to learn and no extreme impressions to correct from when I was here first; and promised to republish, as an appendix to later editions of American Notes and Chuzzlewit, my testimony to these changes, for I did hold a genuine affection for America in how I now found it. I ended by saying:

> "Finally gentlemen, and I say this subject to your correction, I do believe that from the great majority of honest minds on both sides, there cannot be absent the conviction that it would be better for this globe to be riven by an earthquake, fired by a comet, overrun by an iceberg, and abandoned to the arctic fox and bear, than that it should present the spectacle of these two great nations, each of which has, in its own way and hour, striven so hard and so successfully for freedom, ever again being arrayed the one against the other."

This was met with tumultuous applause, with the whole company rising and cheering.

The next day I told Dolby, to his astonishment: "I am too far gone, and too worn out to realize anything but my own exhaustion. Believe me, if I had to read but twice more, instead of once, I could not do it." I knew it was the travelling that I had felt throughout but, on the evening of Monday 20th April, I gave that final reading (of the Carol and the Trial from Pickwick) to over 2,000 people crammed into the Steinway Hall. The takings on that last night were almost as large as those at my last reading in Boston, but before I entered the hall, a certificate from Dr. Barker was distributed, stating that I was suffering from a neuralgic affection of the right foot, but that I should be able to read without much pain or inconvenience, "his mind being set on not disappointing the audience." I believe I did not disappoint them. At the end of the reading I said a few words, entreating them to believe that in passing from my sight, they would not be passing from my memory, and added:

> "I shall often, often recall you as I see you now, equally by my winter fire and in the green English summer weather. I shall never recall you as a mere public audience, but rather as a host of personal friends, and ever with the greatest gratitude, tenderness, and consideration.

Ladies and gentlemen, I beg to bid you farewell – and pray God bless you, and God bless the land in which I leave you."

I finally left the platform to great cheering, shouting, applause and waving of handkerchiefs, exhausted but relieved that the tour was now over.

On the 22nd April I took my departure from America. A small group of friends, including Fields and Osgood, Palmer (the proprietor of the Westminster Hotel) and Will Morgan (son of my great friend Captain Morgan) accompanied me on Will Morgan's private boat out to the S.S. Russia. After emotional farewells locked in each other's arms, I boarded the Cunard steamer and then found my small cabin, which was laden with flowers.

The Russia was a magnificent ship, and we were soon dashing along bravely. Once under way I began to feel greatly better, and soon was able to get my right boot on again. Within three days on the passage I become myself again; the "true American" seemed to be turning faithless at last and my appetite began returning, starting with a "Gad's Hill breakfast". I began a lengthy note to Fields, proposing to post it at Queenstown for the return steamer; I had talked about him and his dear, dear wife Annie continually since being on board and could not stop thinking of them. I told him he would never know how I loved them both, or what they had been to me in America, and would always be to me everywhere; or how fervently I thanked them.

While on board, Dolby and I settled together to calculate our finances, but we had great difficulty in getting the American accounts squared to the point of ascertaining what Dolby's commission amounted to in English money. We were obliged to call in the aid of a money-changer to determine what he should pay as his share of the average loss of conversion into gold. With this deduction made, I think his commission (I have not the figures at hand) was £2,888; Ticknor & Fields had a commission of £1,000, besides 5% on all Boston receipts. The expenses in America to the day of our sailing were $38,948 – roughly £13,000. The preliminary expenses were £614. The average price of gold was nearly 40%, and yet my profit was within a hundred or so of £20,000. I wrote to Forster in confidence that, supposing me to have got through the present engagement in good health, I will have made IN TWO YEARS by the readings £33,000: that is to say £13,000 from the Chappells and £20,000 from America. What I had made by the readings before the Chappells I could only ascertain by a long examination of Coutts's books, but I believed it was certainly not less than £10,000: for I remembered that I made half that money in the first town and country campaign with poor Arthur Smith. I asked Forster if he did not think these figures rather remarkable.

The Russia arrived in Liverpool on the 1st May. Dolby and I came ashore, dined and slept at the Adelphi Hotel that night, and the next morning travelled together to London, where I parted from him at Euston Station at 3 o'clock in the afternoon. Nelly had by now returned to Peckham from Florence and I was eager to see her again, so I hurried to Windsor Lodge with all speed and spent the next week there with her.

CHAPTER LXXVI

Business without Wills, Gad's Hill, Capital Punishment,
Charley's Financial Woes, and Plorn's Departure

During my first week of return I paid visits to the All the Year Round office and found that Wills's accident was more serious than I had supposed, he having received concussion of the brain from his accident in the hunting field. I visited him at his home before he was banished into Sussex for perfect rest; having seen him, I did not think it likely we would have better news of him for months to come and at this time he was strictly prohibited from even writing a note. As a result of this misfortune, I was soon wallowing in half a year's arrears of papers at the office and, consequent upon his absence, all the business and money details of the journal devolved on me and I had to get them up too, having never had experience of this in the past.

I was most anxious to see the theatrical performance of "No Thoroughfare" now at the Adelphi Theatre, and on the night of the 4th May took a box there to see Fechter and Adeline Billington perform it. I never thought I would have cried or shed a tear at my own work as I was made to do by Mrs. Billington's performance. Fechter however, I learnt from speaking to him, was now in serious dispute with his acting manager, Humphrey Barnett, over monies said to be owed by Fechter; I told him to seek professional advice from Ouvry, and that if Ouvry told him he had no defence to the action, he should make no further resistance. This proved to be the case, and because I had that regard and trust in Fechter, I agreed to lend him the money (£1,700) to pay the claim. I told Ouvry I would not take interest on it, but wished Ouvry to arrange that I was repaid by Christmas. Fechter duly repaid me the money, as arranged.

I returned to Gad's Hill on Saturday 9th May. Mamie and Georgy had got wind of a conspiracy among the villagers of Higham to take the horse out, if I had come to our own station, and draw me to Gad's Hill. When I was warned of this, we arranged that I should come to Gravesend, 5 miles off, and be met with the usual carriage (the basket phaeton) and the usual driver (Marsh). My two Newfoundland dogs (both young) came also to meet me and behaved exactly in their usual manner, coming behind the basket phaeton as we trotted along, and lifting their heads to have their ears pulled – a special attention which they received from no one else. When I drove into the stable yard, Linda the St. Bernard was greatly excited; weeping profusely, and throwing herself on her back that she might caress my foot with her great fore-paws. Mamie's little dog too, Mrs. Bouncer, barked in the greatest agitation on being called down and asked by Mamie: "Who is this?" and tore round and round me like the dog in the Faust outlines. All the farmers had turned out on the road in their market-chaises to say: "Welcome home, sir!" and all the houses along the road dressed with flags; and our servants, to cut out the rest, had dressed Gad's Hill so that every brick of it was hidden. They had asked Mamie's permission to "ring the alarm bell" (!) when Master drove up, but Mamie, having some slight idea that that compliment might awaken my sense of the ludicrous, had recommended bell abstinence. But the next day, the Sunday, the village choir (which included the bell ringers) made amends. After some unusually brief pious reflections in the crowns of their hats at the end of the sermon, the ringers bolted out, and rang like mad until I had got home from church! Everything at Gad's Hill looked beautiful, and I found it really a pretty place; it was lovely and in perfect order, with divers birds singing there all day, and the nightingales at night. And the scent of the flowers, and indeed of everything that was growing for miles and miles, was most delicious. I felt in good spirits again, brown beyond belief, and causing the greatest disappointment in all quarters by looking so well. It was really wonderful what those fine days at sea had done for me.

Back in London, and without Wills, I had much to do in running the All the Year Round office. One of the subjects that took my interest at this time was the Married Woman's Property Bill presently before Parliament, for enabling a married woman to possess her own earnings. I wrote to one of our regular contributors, Joseph Parkinson, a clerk at the Inland Revenue, asking if he would take it and write an article upon the Bill, for I felt I should much like to champion the sex reasonably, and to dwell upon the hardship inflicted by the present law on a woman who found herself bound to a drunken, profligate, and spendthrift husband – who was willing to support him – did so – but then had her little savings continually bullied out of her. Parkinson agreed to take it on, and I published his article "Slaves of the Ring" in the journal.

But at the end of June, into my perfect whirlpool of occupation, there then additionally tumbled onto my shoulders an unspeakable world of vexation and worry over my son Charley. His connection with a Paper Mill Company (the Kennet Paper-Making Co.) – against which, and his previous associates (including Frederick Evans, son of the partner in Bradbury and Evans), I had written him a letter of warning when it first loomed in the Evans atmosphere – was now coming to irretrievable bankruptcy, smash and ruin. The company's affairs became, on inquiry, far more hopeless than at first appeared, and even as to Charley personally, he owed a thousand pounds! I consulted with Ouvry who recommended doing nothing at that present time, except to give Charley some supply for current expenses. I sent him £50 to enable him to break up his establishment and pay his way as he went on; but I was at my wits end to know what to do, as he staggered back, now with a family of five children, onto the parental shoulder.

With all the distractions in my head and all the work I had to do on All the Year Round, I felt completely unable to devise a Christmas Number for the journal this year; I seem to have left my invention in America and, for the soul of me, could not (hammer and think of it as I did) raise the ghost of an idea for it that was in the least satisfactory to me. I had invented so many of these Christmas Numbers, and felt they had become so profoundly unsatisfactory after all, with the introduced stories and their want of cohesion or originality, that I feared I was sick of the whole thing.

Although Wills was not able to work, I did correspond with him about All the Year Round matters. He expressed concern to me about our main serial story that had been running since January – Wilkie's "The Moonstone" – and I quite agreed with him. I now found the construction wearisome beyond endurance, and there was a vein of obstinate conceit in it that made enemies of readers. I also told Wills that, on reflection, I was still very unwilling to abandon the Christmas Number, though even in the case of my little Christmas books (which had been immensely profitable) I had let the idea go in the past when

I thought it was wearing out. But I was now determined not to give up until August was out, though I knew I had become weary of having my own writing swamped out by that of other people.

On the 13th August it was reported that the first execution had now taken place inside Maidstone Prison, as required by the Capital Punishment Within Prisons Act, 1868, rather than in public as before, and such news revived my previously expressed feelings on the subject. I had seen articles in newspapers concerning this first private execution and strongly disapproved of the tone and terms of these articles, and thought that kind of writing discreditable to the press – with the notable exception of The Times, who had set a good example in the reticence it had observed in its reporting. I regarded that evidence of a disposition to assist the altered law, and to veil the horrible details, as being right and wholesome. That there was a curiosity to know them I did not question, but I believed it was a morbid curiosity that should not be gratified.

At the end of August the great subject in England had become the horrible accident to the Irish mail train that had left Euston heading for Holyhead. Near Rhyl in North Wales it had collided with goods trucks loaded with barrels of petroleum, and 33 people were burnt to death. I was now haunted by this dreadful accident, for my escape in the great Staplehurst accident of three years before was not to be obliterated from my nervous system. I used to make nothing of driving a pair of horses habitually through the most crowded parts of London, but I could not now drive, with comfort to myself, even on the country roads around Gad's Hill – and I doubted if I could ride at all in the saddle. I continued to have sudden vague rushes of terror, even when riding in a hansom cab, which were perfectly unreasonable, but quite insurmountable, and Dolby knew so well when one of these odd seizures came upon me in a railway carriage, for he would instantly produce a dram of brandy, which rallied the blood to my heart and generally prevailed. But this Irish catastrophe had naturally revived in me all the dreadful things I had seen on that day at Staplehurst.

Arrangements were now under way for Plorn to join Alfred in Australia. I paid the London Armoury Company for him to have a rifle and a small armoury of other items to take with him, and arranged his passage aboard ship (the S.S. Sussex) that was due to leave Plymouth at the end of September, bound for Melbourne. I was also fitting Harry out for Trinity Hall, Cambridge but, as I had no personal experience in this wise, I cast about in my mind for an advisor and wrote to Joe Chitty, a barrister who had come out of college life so brilliantly, having taken a First in Greats at Balliol College, Oxford. Forster was a good friend of Chitty, having undertaken pupillage in Chitty's father's Chambers, and I asked Chitty what allowance I should now give Harry and whether there was any express precaution I could take or enjoin upon him. I had already told Harry that he was going to College to work and achieve distinction and that if he failed to set to in earnest, I would take him away, and was confident Harry fully understood this. In due course I received a patient and considerate letter from Joe Chitty, which I showed to Harry and used to guide myself strictly in accordance with this advice.

I then received letters from Charley's bankruptcy solicitor and two letters from creditors of his firm. One was from a man who had lent it £2,500 and represented it as "a private debt" of my son's and another from an angry firm at Nottingham (creditors for £400) saying they meant to apply to the Lord Mayor for summonses, warrants, or what not, against the whole concern as having got credit without meaning to pay. On top of this I now heard that Sydney at sea was running up bills that he could not pay. I just could not get my hat on in consequence of the extent to which my hair stood on end at the costs and charges of these boys. Why was I ever a father! Why was my father ever a father!

Dolby and I now began making in earnest the arrangements for my forthcoming reading tour. I decided to strike "The boy from Mugby Junction" out of my selected readings as, having looked at him again, I had taken a dislike to him, having too much Boy about me altogether. The level of work at the All the Year Round office continued to be a great strain and would give me an addled head at the close of a day's work there in the absence of Wills. He was getting on very slowly, doing well enough as long as he did nothing. He had a violent bumping and banging in his ears and, as soon as he tried any occupation, he became uneasy and confused, and the distress of noise beset him in an aggravated degree.

As the time arrived for Plorn to depart, I wrote him a note as I wanted him to have a few parting words from me to think of now and then at quiet times. In it I said:

"I need not tell you that I love you dearly, and am very, very sorry in my heart to part with you. But this life is made up of partings, and these pains must be born. It is my comfort and my sincere conviction that you are going to try the life for which you are best fitted. I think its freedom and wildness more suited to you than any experiment in a study or office would ever have been; and without that training, you could have followed no other suitable occupation."

I put a New Testament among his books, because I believed it was the best book that ever was or will be known in the world, and because it taught the best lessons by which any human creature who tried to be truthful and faithful to duty could possibly be guided.

When the day came, he travelled from Higham station most completely fitted out (including with an immense dog calculated, I should think, to be an unspeakable comfort to the sheep) to London with Harry. Harry told me, when they reached London, that Plorn had broken down in the railway carriage after leaving Higham station; but only for a short time. Meeting them in London, I saw that Plorn was pale and obviously had been crying, but he went away from Paddington Station on the afternoon of the 26th September, poor dear fellow, as well as could possibly be expected. Just before the train started he cried a good deal, but not painfully, and these are hard, hard things – but they might have to be done without means or influence, and then they would be far harder. Harry went with him to Plymouth, but for me it was a hard parting at the last. He had seemed to become once more my youngest and favourite little child as the time drew near, and I did not think I could have been so shaken. When you come (if you ever do) to send your youngest child thousands of miles away for an indefinite time, and have a rush into your soul of all the many fascinations of the last little child you can ever dearly love, you will have a hard experience of this wrenching life.

It did not now seem to me very likely that Wills could ever wholly resume his old work, and I had to decide how the All the Year Round office should run in the future. As well, I had to turn Charley's education to the best account I could, and considered he might be put into Henry Morley's place in the office, at least until I could hit upon some other start in life. Charley had pressed me to give him the opportunity of turning a liberal education to account at the office, and as he had always been a good fellow and had, of course, a strong and near claim upon me, I wished to do that much for him if he would do the rest for himself. I hoped Morley would not think it unfriendly or unreasonable in me if, in the circumstances, I was thus to try my eldest son in the affairs of All the Year Round. I told Morley that I earnestly hoped he would not write the less for the journal or give it a wider birth in any way because of my making this experiment.

CHAPTER LXXVII

Farewell Reading Tour in England and Scotland,
Nancy's Murder, Harry to Cambridge, and Death
of My Brother Frederick

The time was approaching when I should now begin my "final farewell" reading tour in the United Kingdom. While in America I had agreed with Chappells to undertake these 100 Readings for the sum of £8,000, Chappells to pay all expenses, and with Dolby as my manager for the entire period. Once again, all the business arrangements would rest with Messrs. Chappell and Co. and Dolby, including the prices of admission; I merely stipulated that there should always be good one shilling places in every room where I read. I looked forward to the approaching campaign with pleasure and took great interest in all the details, which to an extent took my mind away from the sorrow of Plorn's departure, for I found myself constantly thinking of him. Before the titles of the readings had even been announced, there was a run on the ticket department of Messrs. Chappell's establishment to secure the best seats, but I became more convinced of the necessity for a powerful novelty in the form of a new reading in order to keep up the receipts – and my mind became drawn to the "Sikes and Nancy" murder in Oliver Twist, and wondered if I should seek to incorporate this into my reading list.

I began the readings with Dr. Marigold and the Trial from Pickwick on the 6th October at St. James's Hall, with a crowd and enthusiasm beyond all former experience. The galleries could have been filled three or four times over and, at a reasonable calculation, we turned a thousand people away. It was reported that Dr. Marigold held the entire audience spell-bound and, for the Trial, the laughter was simply inextinguishable. Then, on the 9th, I left to face my heavy spell of work, to begin with the Manchester Free Trade Hall on the 10th, and thereafter at St. George's Hall in Liverpool on the 12th, 13th, and 14th, staying in the Adelphi Hotel all week. Frank Beard had made up a prescription for me and I had been in wonderful voice since I had begun to try it, but something in it went against my stomach. I tried it twice, and each time felt sick and loose after it; I found now I was so easily nauseated after these nightly exertions.

Harry had now arrived at Trinity Hall, Cambridge and from the Adelphi Hotel I wrote to him enclosing funds and insisted to him that we must have no shadow of debt and that he must square up everything whatsoever that it had been necessary to buy, emphasizing to him: "Let not a farthing be outstanding on any account, when we begin together with your allowance; be particular in the minutest detail." I also told him I would treat him with perfect confidence, and added: "Whatever you do, above all other things keep out of debt, and confide in me. If you ever find yourself on the verge of any perplexity or difficulty, come to me. You will never find me hard with you while you are manly and truthful."

It was now that I revealed to Forster that I had made a short reading of the murder in Oliver Twist, but that I could not make up my mind whether to do it or not. I had no doubt that I could perfectly petrify an audience by carrying out the notion I had of the way of rendering it, but whether the impression would not be so horrible as to keep them away another time, was what I could not satisfy myself upon. I had adapted and cut about the text with great care, and it was very powerful. I asked Forster what he thought, and also referred the book and the question to the Chappells as they were so largely interested.

On the 17th October I read Copperfield and Mr. Bob Sawyer's Party to between four and five thousand people at the Manchester Free Trade Hall, before journeying back to London and preparation for a reading in Brighton, at the Grand Concert Hall, on the 19th. I spent time in the All the Year Round office, before catching the train for Brighton, read there, and then returned to London to read Copperfield (I had come to like Copperfield the best of all the readings) and Mrs. Gamp the following day (the 20th) at St. James's Hall. That night we had £410 (an advance from our previous £360) in take, with, it was reported, hundreds of baffled candidates for admission crowding the entrances and the contiguous corridors. As I left the platform at the end, I received round after round of applause.

The next evening I had to start for Brighton again, for a further reading on the 22nd October, only to find once I got there a letter sent from my son Charley, enclosing a note from a doctor informing me that my unfortunate younger brother Frederick had died in Darlington,

Yorkshire and that the funeral was to take place on the 23rd. I was obliged to send Charley off to look after the funeral for me, Charley informing me that Frederick's death had been attended with little or no suffering at the home of an innkeeper. I also asked Dolby to attend on my behalf. Although there had come to be estrangement between Frederick and me, I was glad to remember that it never involved, on my side, a feeling of anger. He had lost opportunities that I had put in his way, but there were unhappy circumstances in his life which demanded great allowance. He was my favourite when he was a child, and I was his tutor when he was a boy. His was a wasted life, but God forbid that one should be hard upon it, or upon anything in this world that is not deliberately and coldly wrong.

In relation to the Oliver Twist murder, the Chappells suggested to me that a trial might be run at St. James's Hall on the 18th November, when everything in use for the previous day's reading there could be made available for a private reading before a dozen or so people to see what effect it made. Although I had not been well, and had been heavily tired, I had little to complain of and agreed to this suggestion. I wrote to Forster giving him the earliest notice of it and hoped it might suit him to attend. Meanwhile I pressed on "working off" my series, travelling again to Liverpool and Manchester, London and Brighton, with the success of these farewells proving something overwhelming.

Because of the level of electioneering now happening in the country, Dolby and the Chappells decided to stop the readings for the remainder of November, save the one booked for the 17th November at St. James's Hall. By now I had decided to move my private trial of Nancy's murder to the previous Saturday (14th November) and so sent out invitations to a handful of private friends to attend. I told them it would not occupy more than an hour, and that my purpose in doing this was because I could still not make up my mind whether to read the murder to the public or no. Forster agreed to attend, but Wills felt unable to do so, on account of his illness.

I had read the murder to Dolby beforehand, and he had sought to dissuade me from continuing with it (on account of my health, he said), but my reason for pressing on with this idea was that I wanted, if I could, to leave behind me the recollection of something very passionate and dramatic; done with simple means, if the art would justify the theme, and to find out the truth about it if we could. I had also tried it, merely sitting over the fire in a chair, with both Georgy and Nelly separately. They had each said to me in so many words: "O good Gracious, if you are going to do that, it ought to be seen; but it's awful." Then, as the day approached, it was considered advisable that, instead of the invitations being restricted to a limited circle of close and intimate friends, this circle should be extended by inviting persons whose judgement could be relied upon, and, amongst these, leading members of the press. This extended the audience to between 100 and 150 persons, composed of all classes representing art, with arrangements now made to liken it to a public reading, with everything done as if it had been one of these. However, I changed my stage. Beside the back-screen, I had two large screens of the same colour, set off, one on either side, like the "wings" at a theatre. And besides those, I had a quantity of curtains of the same colour, with which to close in any width of room from wall to wall. Consequently, my figure was now completely isolated, and the slightest action became much more important.

On Saturday the 14th I went through the reading, and, once concluded, descended into the body of the hall to discuss the merits or demerits of it. Meanwhile the reading table and screens I arranged to be swiftly removed, and in their place on the platform a long table drawn up, arranged for an oyster supper, with a large staff of men in readiness to open oysters and set champagne corks flying. This reveal disclosed one of the prettiest banquets you could imagine; and when all the people came up, and the gay dresses of the ladies were lighted up by those powerful lights of mine, the scene was exquisitely pretty.

It was a matter of no surprise to me, however, to find considerable hesitation on the part of my friends and special guests in expressing an opinion with regard to the reading. All the company were, before the wine went round, unmistakably pale, and had horror-stricken faces. One guest, the Reverend William Harness, a celebrated critic, expressed an opinion as to the danger of giving it before a mixed audience, as he said he had had an irresistible desire to scream. A celebrated physician, Dr. William Priestley, concurring in this, declared that "if only one woman cries out when you murder the girl, there will be a contagion of hysteria all over the place." Some of the ladies described it as "awful"; whilst one, the celebrated actress Mrs. Mary Keeley (and a good judge of what was likely to be successful), on being asked by me whether it should be done in public or not, said: "Why, of course do it! Having got at such an effect as that, it must be done." Then, rolling her large black eyes very slowly, and speaking very distinctly, she added: "The public have been looking out for a sensation these last fifty years or so – and by Heaven they have got it!" With which words, and a long breath and a long stare, she became speechless.

These and similar opinions caused me still to waver in my determination; Forster was against it, but I felt we might have to differ about it very well. I had a vague sense of being "wanted" as I walked about the streets turning the matter over in my mind, but I felt it was now certainly worth a trial with the public, particularly as I had now been at pains of getting it up, and Messrs. Chappell were not indisposed towards it. The press gave favourable reviews, and accordingly it was decided to arrange that the first public reading should take place at the commencement of the New Year in London on the 5th January 1869 at St. James's Hall, and simultaneously decided that it should also be tried shortly thereafter in Dublin, these two readings to settle the fate of it forever. I took the view that it was impossible to soften it without spoiling it, and became rather anxious to discover how it would go on the 5th January.

I continued to attend to All the Year Round matters in the absence of Wills, the work in the office being burdensome without him. I began work on another Uncommercial and read again on the 1st December at St. James's Hall, before setting off for Scotland in the early morning of the 5th December. I made a calculation on the way that the railway travelling over such a distance involved something more than 30,000 shocks to the nerves; Dolby did not like it at all. The signals for a gale were up at Berwick, and it came on just as we arrived at Edinburgh and then blew tremendously hard all night. We could not sleep for the noise, but we were very comfortably quartered in the hotel, and the next morning went up Arthur's Seat, which was a pull for our fat friend. When I stepped onto the stage that night they gave me a most magnificent welcome-back from America. The next day Dolby went off to Glasgow, while I spent time on my new reading from Oliver Twist. Wilkie had suggested how it should conclude and I had got this together in a very short space and began trying it daily with the object of rising from that blank state of horror into a fierce and passionate rush for the end. As yet I could not make a certain effect of it, but felt that when I had gone over it as many score of times as over the rest of the reading, perhaps I may then strike one out. I sat at a side window in the hotel, looking up the length of Prince's Street, very dark and very wet, watching the mist change over the castle and murdering Nancy by turns. Thereafter I conducted a number of readings in both Edinburgh and Glasgow before, on the 19th December, I started southward by the mail train that night, having ordered for Gad's a number of Scottish specialities for Christmas. The manager of the railway had been at one of my previous readings, and had written to me the next morning saying that a large saloon should be prepared for my journey to London, if I would let him know when I proposed to make that journey. On my accepting the offer he wrote again, saying that he had inspected "our northern saloons" and, not finding them so convenient for sleeping in as the best English, had sent to Kings Cross for the best of the latter: which would I please consider my own carriage, as long as I wanted it. The affectionate regard of the people in Scotland I found exceeded all bounds, and had been shown to me in every way.

CHAPTER LXXVIII

Further Readings and Reactions to Nancy's Murder,
Charley at the Office, and My Foot Inflamed Again

On arrival back in London, I carried out a final reading before Christmas on the 22nd December at St. James's Hall, where Carol captured the spirit for this time of year, and shortly after the reading, made my way to Gad's Hill for the Christmas gathering. Harry came from Cambridge, Charley and his wife and a child or two from wheresoever they were, with Katey and Charlie Collins joining us from London on Christmas Eve. Also present were Austen Layard (from Gladstone's New Government as Chief Commissioner of Public Works), and Marcus Stone. Dolby had sent a turkey and mistletoe for our Christmas festivities; both had arrived in blooming order, and were received with acclamations. On Boxing Day I began rehearsing my reading of Oliver and the murder of Nancy, but I so terrified Layard – sitting in the front spare room with an official red morocco box of papers – that he came plunging out on the staircase to ascertain what had happened! I planned to polish the murder minutely every day for the following week; I had had a few occasional reminders of my "true American Catarrh", though my doctor was of the opinion that the disorder originated in vegetable poison and directed that I attack it with strong and sudden doses of quinine in hot brandy and water. This was remarkably effectual and, although I exerted my voice very much, it had not yet been once touched thereafter.

On the 5th January 1869, at St. James's Hall, I presented Boots at the Holly-Tree Inn, Mrs. Gamp, and the Murder of Nancy. The hall was packed for the occasion, and as I built to the climax with the murder the people were frozen while it went on, but came to life when it was over and rose to boiling point; it was reported that I "brought down the house." Once the reading was done it put me in a highly edifying state, having murdered Nancy in a highly successful and bloodthirsty manner, but I had little time to rest, for the next night I set off for Ireland. I went first to Belfast, where on the 8th January I read the Carol and the Trial from Pickwick at the Ulster Hall, before travelling on to Dublin to read for 3 nights at the Rotunda.

Enormous houses filled the Rotund, the crowds being so great that on the second and third nights strong bodies of police – mounted and on foot – were required in an effort to bring a form of control, and nearly 200 extra chairs were produced for the final evening, when I was to do the murder, such was the overwhelming interest. The emotions of the audience during the murder were reported as being held literally spell-bound from the beginning to the end, with emotions not always under control, but at the close pent-up feelings found full vent in enthusiastic cheers given with a zest and a sincerity seldom witnessed. It was said to be "a masterpiece of reading, quite unparalleled in its way", and I had by now decided that I should incorporate further readings of the murder into my farewell schedule, the next being in London on the 19th January.

Meanwhile, I travelled back to Belfast to read again in the Ulster Hall before, the next day, leaving by the limited mail train in order to catch the mail boat from Kingstown, Dublin the same evening. The train consisted of just two carriages for passengers, with the necessary travelling post-office carriages and guards' vans. As we only wished to have our own party of five persons for our society, Dolby had secured a coupé for our special use on this journey, the carriage being composed almost entirely of plate glass. Then suddenly, whilst running along at a rapid speed about forty miles south of Belfast, we received a severe jolt which threw us all forward in the carriage. Looking out, I observed an enormous piece of iron flying along a side line, tearing up the ground and carrying some telegraph posts along with it. The brakes were suddenly applied, a lumbering sound heard on the roof of the carriage, and the plate glass windows were bespattered with stones, gravel and mud. I threw myself to the bottom of the carriage and all the others followed my example, it bringing immediately to my mind the incident at Staplehurst. Mercifully the train was speedily brought to a stand-still, and on dismounting and taking a view of the situation, we found that the great iron tyre of the driving-wheel had broken, and that the piece of iron seen travelling with such destructive force and carrying the telegraph posts with it was a portion of the tyre, and that the noise on the roof had been caused by another enormous piece of iron falling on it. We all realized that had this piece of iron struck the glass, instead of the framework of the carriage, it would have been impossible for us to escape, and in all probability there could have been a repetition of the Staplehurst catastrophe, but the promptitude with which the driver brought the train to a stand prevented the engine leaving the metals. We waited for an hour at this lonely spot for the arrival of another engine to take us on to Dublin, but we were all grateful to think that no one personally was the worse for the circumstance, and that the only damage was done to the engine, into the machinery of which huge pieces of metal had been driven, mixed with ballast. It was with great relief when we later found ourselves safe on the Holyhead boat, making our way once more for home.

I read again at St. James's Hall on Tuesday 19th January and decided not only to do the murder, but also The Chimes. I had not read The Chimes for ten years and, although it was a little dismal, I had shortened and brightened it as much as possible, reducing its length to about one third of the original text. The next day I started for the West of England and firstly travelled to Clifton, reading in the Victoria Rooms that night. There was a tremendous house cramming the room, and I read Boots, the Murder, and Mr. Bob Sawyer's Party. It was decidedly by far the best murder yet done and, though the place was not hot, during the murder there was a contagion of fainting. I should think that we had from a dozen to twenty ladies borne out, stiff and rigid, at various times. It became quite ridiculous. The following day I travelled to Newport in South Wales, and there read the Carol and the Trial from Pickwick to a vast number of people from every walk of life, in the Victoria Assembly Rooms, a queer out-of-the-way place. From there I moved on to Cheltenham to do the Murder especially for Macready. We put him in the front row, where he sat grimly staring at me; when I saw him afterwards he looked well in the face, but I continued to feel that "age with his stealing steps" had overtaken him too soon. He said he was of the opinion that the murder was "two Macbeths" and declared he had heard every word of the reading – but I doubted it.

I spent that weekend with Dolby at his home (Wilton House, Bridstow, near Ross in Herefordshire), the coldest house I ever in my life set foot in. He had it prettily furnished, like the best sort of railway hotel, but it was wanting in cheap contrivances that would have made it seem larger and be much more commodious. I could have done wonders with it, and not spend more than £20. On the Sunday there were awful foreshadowings of some female relative coming to dinner, considered detestable by Dolby, and a doctor also darkly hinted at, as coming to dinner likewise. As it was a fine frosty day, I decided to take myself off on a ten-mile walk to Monmouth.

I read at Torquay and Bath before returning to London, conducting business in the All the Year Round office before reading again at St. James's Hall on the evening of Tuesday 2nd February. That night we had an enormous house, but I was now finding the work so very hard, with every little scrap of rest and silence that I could pick up as precious. But even those morsels were so flavoured with "All the Year Round" that they were not quite the genuine article, and I felt I must somehow and somewhere do an Uncommercial in the next week, as well as manfully training for I had a great deal of murdering before me yet, and felt obliged to reject any social pleasures that were offered.

Before continuing on my farewell tour, I spoke to Wills about the possibility of now taking son Charley on the ship's books at All the Year Round at 6 guineas per week. Wills agreed, Wills himself still being unable to work, and I then set off again, on this occasion to read in Nottingham and Leicester. I went to Gad's Hill for the weekend of my birthday and had the Forsters and Wilkie to keep it, but this was the only time since Christmas that I had been to Gad's. Back in London I became as restless as if I were behind bars in the zoological gardens, and earnestly wished to continue on with my readings. I was due to read again in London on the 16th February and to set off for Scotland again the following day. and had hoped to have finished all my farewell readings in May. But Dolby had now found I could not clear the country off in sufficient time and so the last night of all was scheduled for Friday 11th June.

I was then joyful to hear from James and Annie Fields with a most welcome announcement of their probable visit to England and hoped they would arrive before the farewells were over. I told them that we were doing most amazingly, and that in the country the people usually collapsed with the murder, and did not fully revive in time for the final piece; while in London, where they were much quicker, they were equal to both. I had found it very hard work, but had never for a moment lost voice or been unwell – except that my foot occasionally gave me a twinge.

But then my foot did become highly inflamed. Beard and Dolby called in Sir Henry Thompson (Professor of Clinical Surgery at University College Hospital) to look at me. Thompson thought it to be a bad case of gout and would not let me read that night nor would he let me go to Scotland the next day. He and Beard signed the following certificate:

"We the undersigned hereby certify that Mr. Charles Dickens is suffering from inflammation of the foot (caused by over-exertion), and that we have forbidden his appearance on the platform this evening, as he must keep his room for a day or two."

I sent up to the Great Western Hotel for apartments for our team and moved there that evening. It threw us all back, and I calculated that the cancellations would cost me some five hundred pounds.

I stayed four nights at the Great Western Hotel and in that time gradually got better – much better. I began to sleep better and both Arthur and Tom Chappell came to see me to discuss matters. On Thursday the 18th I took an airing in an open carriage, and the next day a medical decision was set to be made, with Arthur Chappell in close attendance. My foot felt immensely better and free from pain, but I could still not stand upon it. And in the mornings I had become so very faint while dressing that I was within an ace of gone. I feared I could not go upon a platform to read without the possibility of becoming faint there also, and that a journey to Scotland and the effort it would entail might spoil me for the next London murder – by far (as it seemed to me) the most important night of all. I told Dolby I recognized it was an immensely difficult question; and that with every desire to be right, I did not know at that stage how to be right. I was also troubled that Dolby had wrongly advertised that I was to read "The Poor Traveller" in Scotland; I could not have been more amazed when I saw it announced than if I had seen myself announced to read Jack the Giant Killer! I told Dolby in the strongest manner that it was absurd to have to get it up for only one night and that it was particularly onerous to have to get anything up under the present circumstances.

CHAPTER LXXIX

More Readings, Death of Tennent,
and a Banquet in Liverpool

Frank Beard examined me thoroughly on Friday 19th February to decide whether I could start for Scotland the next morning. I recognized that the weakness of the case was that I might start and get there, and still be unable to read. After the examination, we decided in favour of the journey, but Arthur Chappell kindly volunteered to go with me and take care of me, and we postponed the Edinburgh Readings to the 24th and 26th February, cancelling the one that had been planned earlier. Accordingly, on Saturday the 20th I set off for Edinburgh, with a sofa provided in the railway carriage for me. I came down lazily upon it, and hardly changed my position the whole way. The railway authorities did all sorts of things, and I was more comfortable than on the sofa at the hotel. The foot gave me no uneasiness and was then quiet and steady all night; I had ordered a bootmaker in London to make me another boot and asked Georgy to send it to me in Edinburgh when it was done. In Edinburgh I consulted James Syme, Professor of Clinical Surgery at Edinburgh University, who warned me against over-fatigue in the readings, gave me some slight remedies, and reported that I was in "joost pairfactly splendid condition". He declared the disorder to be an affection of the delicate nerves and muscles originating in cold after walking in the snow and, with care, he thought the pain might be got rid of.

I read the Murder twice in both Edinburgh and Glasgow, and received a new boot from Georgy. The foot bore the fatigue wonderfully well, only a little fatigued by the standing at night (and doing four Murders in one week), but not overmuch. It merely ached at night – and so did the other, sympathetically, I suppose – but really occasioned me no inconvenience beyond the necessity of wearing this new boot I had now received, a big work of art. The Murder took some 40 minutes and drove all the breath out of my body, but during the readings I had now completely left off drinking champagne, I think with good results, and only took a very little weak iced brandy and water. Business was enormous, and Dolby jubilant.

After these readings I sat alone with Dolby for supper and sought to fix the readings for the remainder of the tour, thinking I should do, out of four readings a week, three Murders. Dolby, on account of my health and to save me unnecessary fatigue, suggested I should reserve the Murder for certain of the large towns only, which highly annoyed me and caused me to rise from the table and throw my knife and fork on the plate, smashing it in the process. I protested that his infernal caution would be his ruin of me one of these days, but he replied that he was exercising it in my interest, and stepped away from the table. I then realized he had only my best interests at heart in saying what he did and, with sobs and tears in my eyes, I went to him and embraced him affectionately, saying: "Forgive me Dolby! I really did not mean it; and I know you are right. We will talk the matter over calmly in the morning." When we did so, I realized that perhaps there was too much "Murder" in the future arrangements and that it would be better in certain places to moderate my instincts in that respect.

I now had 50 more readings to do and, for Tuesday 2nd March, St. James's Hall was sold out, filled in every part for another Murder, which was even more successful than before. I celebrated with Nelly her 30th birthday on the 3rd March and then, on the way to Manchester, stopped in Wolverhampton to read. In Manchester, without much greater expenditure of voice than usual, I read the Murder there for the first time in the immense Free Trade Hall, which produced a night of excitement for Cottonopolis. The following day was an enjoyable and quiet Sunday, and, as it did not rain, Dolby and I drove to Alderley Edge, causing me to feel wonderfully revived by the fresh air. Both feet were still sympathetically sensitive, but I was now able to wear my regular boots again, had no other inconveniences, and was able to walk for an hour at a time, pretty comfortably.

Next to Hull where, before reading I walked about the town. In Whitefriargate I came upon Dixon's, the Silk Mercer shop and, on entering, there spoke with the assistant (Edward Simpson-Long) asking if I could see some ladies' silk stockings. He obliged and I struck up a conversation with him. It was clear he did not recognize me at that stage, so I asked him what he did with himself in an evening. He replied: "Well, I sometimes go to the theatre, if there is a good Shakespearean play on, or dramatic readings, same as tonight. But it is by subscription, so I shall not be able to go." I then asked him if he had read Dickens's books and he said he had read most of them, and added that he could find many characters to fit them. After some further conversation, I asked him if he would like to go to the Dickens reading that evening and, on hearing that he would, I took out one of my personal cards and wrote on the reverse "Please Admit Bearer" and handed it to him. He was exceedingly surprised when he turned the card over and saw the name thereon! I purchased six of their black silk ladies' stockings, and later made arrangements for his seating to be on the platform, not far from my reading desk. I read Boots, the Murder, and Mrs. Gamp in the Assembly Rooms that night (10th March), and was able to see the assistant as I read.

I had by now heard that an old friend, Sir James Emerson Tennent, had died and his funeral was to take place at Kensal Green cemetery on Friday of that week (the 12th) and, much as I hated the dismal pomp and ceremony of funerals, I knew I must go. I had a reading arranged in the Festival Concert Hall in York for the night of the 11th and I attended for it, but I had to make special arrangements as the train for London left York at 9.45 p.m. that night and my readings were not normally over before 10 o'clock; with half an hour for a change of dress usually undertaken thereafter, while it needed a further 10 minutes to drive to the station. As a means of meeting the case, I arranged to take 20 minutes out of the time allotted to the readings, this time to be gained by sacrificing the rest I normally took after the Murder, and to press on with the reading in the meanwhile. Dolby arranged with the courteous manager of the Great Northern Railway at York to let me have a saloon carriage with comfortable sofas and, if necessary, to keep the train for me three or four minutes, and sent Scott to the station in advance with a change of clothes. After the reading, Scott gave me his usual rub down, and Dolby and I were able to arrive together at the railway station, two minutes before the advertised starting time of the train. Punctually at 9.45 p.m. the train steamed out of the station and Dolby and I proceeded to divest ourselves of our evening dress, and assume that of the traveller of the period. Our saloon carriage presented a mixed appearance of a miniature dressing and dining room, and after our supper had been disposed of with infinite relish and a cigar smoked, we settled down for the night. I thereafter slept the whole way to London, not awaking until we were close to Kings Cross, and then feeling much refreshed.

I attended at the burial and thereafter at Tennent's house, where I made an ass of myself and did the wrong thing, as I invariably did at a funeral. I arrived at the house and was met in the hall by an elderly gentleman, who extended his hand. I presumed this was a friend of Tennent whom I had met somewhere but forgotten, and shook his hand, saying "We meet on a sad occasion". "Yes, indeed" came the reply, adding "Poor dear Sir James", and followed by a long-drawn sigh. I passed on to the dining room where several other of Tennent's friends were congregated, and for a time forgot the friend in the hall – until he entered with a trayful of hats adorned with long mourning bands, piled so high it almost hid him from view. I then realized he was the undertaker's man and had held his hand out for my hat for the purpose of funeral decoration! The seriousness of the occasion notwithstanding, I could not help but be amused at the mistake I had made.

On the 16th March I read again at St. James's Hall, then readings at Ipswich and Cambridge (where I met with Harry) before travelling to Manchester for two further readings and then returning to London in good spirits, to spend time in the All the Year Round office. On Easter Saturday, I spent some 5 hours on Wilkie's play "Black and White", finalizing matters for him before its opening at the Adelphi on Easter Monday. I attended, and the play went brilliantly and was extremely well played throughout. I had rarely seen Fechter to greater advantage and it was more like a fiftieth night than a first.

On 30th March I read Dombey at St. James's Hall before, the following morning, setting off for Sheffield, Birmingham and Liverpool. At Liverpool, due to overwhelming demand, Dolby had found that the St. George's Hall was not now large enough for our purposes, and so had hired the Theatre Royal instead for these readings. This theatre, which had fallen into disuse for some time, had been in a distressingly dirty state, but Dolby had organized a fortnight's rubbing, scrubbing and sweeping, with a liberal allowance of red baize and carpets in the passage-ways and in the stalls, and so converted it into a perfect reading-house. I was delighted, for I preferred a theatre to any other class of building and, when I saw it, it looked remarkably well and bright; and I heard from Dolby that the lets were already large. These readings were to be followed by the Civic Banquet for me, arranged by the Mayor and Corporation, on Saturday (10th April), with 600 people to attend. The St. George's Hall was the only one in the town capable of dining 600 persons together, and for this reason it was selected, though a more unsuitable place for such a purpose could not well have been chosen. The proposed arrangement of the tables I knew would prevent a word of the speeches being heard and I suggested a plan whereby the difficulty might be got over, but it was found that the organizing committee, for some inscrutable reasons of their own, could not submit to any alteration of their plan such as I had proposed, to the possible detriment of the whole affair. With the acoustics of that hall and the positioning of the tables (both as bad as bad could be) my only consolation was, that if anybody could be heard, I probably could be.

Both my feet were now very tender and often felt as though they were in hot water. I had a cold too, but I did feel nevertheless wonderfully well and strong and in good voice. In the town there appeared a great curiosity to hear the Murder and on the 5th April I read Boots, the Murder, and Mr. Bob Sawyer's Party; on the 6th Dr. Marigold and the Trial from Pickwick; on the 8th the Murder and Mrs. Gamp; and on the 9th the Murder and the Carol. The Liverpool Mercury wondered whether I had ever before received a more numerous, sympathetic and appreciative audience, and the total receipts of the four readings exceeded £1,000. At one time Dolby and I were afraid that the excitement in connection with the public banquet would detract from the success of the readings, by drawing the money in another direction, but that proved not to be the case.

For the banquet, St. George's Hall was bedecked with beautiful decorations, and in order to attempt correction of the acoustic defects, the honorary secretary of the committee had sent to the guard ship (the "Donegal") lying in the River Mersey, for the loan of a number of the ship's flags for the purpose. The captain, with a ready courtesy, not only granted this request, but sent a boats' crew to hang and drape the flags, and I personally superintended the whole matter as to their assignment, with some hope of stopping echoes. The seamen were all hanging on aloft upside down, holding to the gigantically high roof by nothing, and carrying out their tasks in the most wonderfully cheerful manner. By now it had been arranged that over 650 guests were to sit down to dine, with as many more to be allowed as spectators in the gallery and orchestra, matters being organized on a grand scale. The principal tables were laden with flowers and plants, sparkling with rich silver candelabra, and specimens of fine art work. A silver-gilt fountain, which dispensed refreshing streams of rose water, was placed in front of the chairman's seat, and the band of the police force placed in the vestibule to play during the arrival of the guests. At half past five I led the way with the Mayor and took our places, with the whole audience rising and cheering vociferously.

The Mayor was nominally the chairman of the evening, but being in ill health and not a great speaker, after the meal he handed the toast over to Lord Dufferin, Chancellor of the Duchy of Lancaster. I spoke to much hearty laughter and cheering, with many others making their contributions. It made my farewell visit to the town a pleasant memory, and the next day, as I walked to the station, the good feeling of the people of Liverpool showed itself heartily in the street, for during my progress to the station I was repeatedly stopped by persons of the working classes wanting to shake hands with me, and all eager to thank me for the pleasure my books had afforded them. A good number of those from the banquet came to the station to see me off, and on the journey to London we were rather a large party – and a very jolly one – for many London friends who had attended the banquet returned with us in our saloon carriage.

CHAPTER LXXX

Further Readings, Great Indisposition, and My Will

I spent further time in the All the Year Round office and, though my foot was growling again, I felt I could reasonably expect nothing less from the work and a sudden heat in the weather. I had also, in the dark in the Theatre Royal in Liverpool, tripped over an extra "stay" of strong galvanized wire used for my batten and cut the shin of my left leg rather smartly. I had managed to bring myself up without being pitched into the pit, but had to bathe and bind the cut surgically, it being a bad place to heal. I additionally had a return of effusion of blood from piles and asked Frank Beard if he would kindly send me a receipt for the medicine that did me so much good before. Nevertheless, I pressed on, reading again on Tuesday 13th April at St. James's Hall before setting off the next afternoon for readings in Bradford and Leeds, but my foot had become bad again, bad all the way from London, and was exceedingly inflamed and swollen, and remained so. This naturally made us very anxious, but I never saw any man like my assistant, Scott – he had everything with him that the foot could require if it were to get worse. I was so afraid of it that I thought it prudent to send him out for poppy heads, but it appeared he had a plentiful supply with him, and the necessary flannels and everything else, "for action in a moment" as he said.

We had a large let in the St. George's Hall in Bradford and I read Boots, The Murder and Mr. Bob Sawyer's Party. The next night I repeated these readings in the Mechanics' Institute in Leeds, having noticed that our five-shilling tickets were now being advertised in the newspapers at a guinea each. I wonder who got the money – I know I didn't! Being in Leeds at this time and having two vacant days before going to the Lancashire manufacturing towns of Blackburn, Bolton and Preston the following week, Dolby and I decided to escape from the smoke and gloom in which we had been living, and as Chester, with its old walls and picturesque streets, promised a pleasant change, we went there for the Saturday and Sunday.

At Chester on the Saturday night, after unusual irritability, I felt extremely giddy, with a tendency to go backwards, and to turn around. Afterwards, desiring to put something on a small table, I pushed it and the table forwards undesignedly, and felt extremely uncertain of my footing, especially on the left side. I also had a strangeness in my left hand and arm, missed the spot on which I wished to lay that hand unless I carefully looked at it, and felt an unreadiness to lift my hands towards my head (especially my left hand) when, for instance, I was brushing my hair. These symptoms made me very uncomfortable; I had a very bad night, and my great uneasiness continued into the Sunday. It was the subject of my conversations with Dolby at breakfast and, as the weather was beautifully fine and warm for the season, he suggested a drive into the country and as far as Mold, a small and picturesque Welsh market town about fourteen miles from Chester. I agreed, a carriage was turned out immediately after breakfast, and we started out for this place. I felt greatly revived by the invigorating air and the sight of the spring blossoms as we travelled through the country, but I could not get over the miserable night I had had and the depressing thoughts about the possible future of the tour that this had engendered. I was concerned as to the interests of Messrs. Chappell, whose losses would be very great if we relinquished any more readings in order that I might have a rest – though Dolby said he felt sure the Chappells would do all and everything in their power to adapt their arrangements to the altered condition of my health. He also suggested that we should go to London that evening to consult Frank Beard on the situation, and further said that, as he had gone before to Glasgow to return money there, so he might now hasten back to the Lancashire towns and do the same thing in the places arranged for the following week.

But Dolby and I then found that it was now impossible to get back to Chester in time to catch the only train there was to London that Sunday afternoon, so this plan had to be given up. After further talk on the subject, I determined to write a letter to Frank Beard the moment we should get back to the hotel in Chester, detailing my symptoms, and await the result of his reply while, at the same time, carefully watching the effects on me of the next two readings. I told Dolby not to communicate to the Chappells what had happened in Chester before I had received a reply from Frank Beard and, upon receiving his assurance that he would not do so, I fell asleep in the carriage in the balmy air and awoke again at the hotel.

There I took some rest, and the next day (Monday 19th April) we travelled to Blackburn for my reading that night at the Exchange Assembly Rooms, before I then wrote to Frank Beard from the hotel there, setting out the symptoms in detail that I had now been experiencing. I wondered if the cause had been anything in the medicine he had given me, and told him I had taken it twice a day only, and had taken barely a bottle in all. I awaited his reply, having asked him, if he could, to send one word in answer by return, to the Imperial Hotel, Blackpool, where Dolby and I now proposed a short stay. I then dismissed the matter from my mind, though still feeling dull in myself.

That night I read the Carol and Mr. Bob Sawyer's Party in my usual manner at the Blackburn Exchange Assembly Rooms, though I now felt half dead with travelling every day and reading afterwards, the tremendously severe nature of this work shaking me a little. I realized I had not seen my own house since Christmas and did not anticipate seeing it again until midsummer; I had been almost incessantly reading since October, in all parts of the compass, and was becoming confused as to where I was, seemingly being in a different place every day. When I went to London I was only there for a short period, and immediately after reading there, I was away again as fast as an express could carry me; and the only thing upholding me through such work was the prospect of soon working it out.

I read Dr. Marigold and the Trial from Pickwick at the Temperance Hall in Bolton on the night of the 20th April (abridging the Trial somewhat) and then went for a two-day rest at the Imperial Hotel in Blackpool. Dolby had arranged for some most comfortable apartments, and the fresh breeze blowing from the sea I found invigorating and beneficial. There I found a kind note from Frank Beard and immediately replied to him by telegraph, giving him my next addresses as he evidently thought my symptoms worthy of immediate attention. He said he wished to take me in hand without any loss of time and that it was quite impossible that these symptoms came from my simple medicine. He said he recognized the exact description I had given him, being indisputable evidence of over-work, which he wished to treat immediately.

The symptoms had greatly moderated since the Sunday in Chester, though they were still there, and all on the left side. I told Frank Beard that six weeks would carry me through the readings, if he could fortify me a little bit, and then please God I could do as I liked, so he should "go in and win". I had a delicious walk by the sea, slept soundly and had picked up amazingly in appetite. My foot was greatly better too, and I now wore my own boot again. I was to read at Preston on the 22nd April, and the following night at Warrington, and then I calculated I would have but 25 more nights to work through. I felt that if Frank Beard could coach me up for them, I did not doubt that I would get it all right again – as I had when I became free in America. The foot was now giving me very little trouble, yet it was remarkable that it was the left foot too, and I had an inward conviction that whatever it was, it was not gout. I had told Frank Beard, a year after the Staplehurst accident, that I was certain that my heart had been fluttered, and wanted a little helping. This the stethoscope had confirmed; and considering the immense exertions I was undergoing, and the constant jarring of express trains, the case seemed to me quite intelligible. I said little in the Gad's Hill direction about my being a little out of sorts, but did tell James Fields that when I had become ill in my reading only Nelly observed that I staggered and my eyes failed, and only she dared to tell me.

After two good nights' sleep in Blackpool, and an invigorating walk with Dolby to the railway station in a gale of wind, I went with him to Preston at about midday on the 22nd April, in the full conviction that the Chester attack (whatever it might have been) had passed away. Upon our arrival at the Bull Hotel in Preston, Dolby met with the local ticket agent and, while he spoke with him, I went to our quarters. Dolby soon joined me in our sitting room to tell me that every ticket for the reading that evening in the Guildhall had been disposed of and the proceedings amounting to nearly £200, but I then showed him a telegram that I had just received from Frank Beard telling me that my communication from Blackpool had decided on him coming to Preston at once; that he was now on his way, and would arrive in Preston at about half past three that afternoon.

Dolby and I passed the time until then in superintending the erection of the reading screen and, having done that, went to the station to meet Beard's train which, in the perversity of things, was an hour late. Notwithstanding it was now considerably past our dinner hour, I insisted we wait for Beard's arrival. When at length he came, we walked to the Bull Hotel, calling in by the way at the Guildhall to show him the platform with the "fit up" as arranged for the evening's reading. Once at the hotel however, Beard began an immediate examination of me that lasted over half an hour. Dolby then joined us, and Beard said:

"All I have to say is this: if you insist on Dickens taking the platform tonight, I will not guarantee but that he goes through life dragging a foot after him."

I felt deeply upset and, with tears rolling down my face, I crossed the room to Dolby where, throwing myself on his neck, could only say:

"My poor boy! I am so sorry for all the trouble I am giving you! With all the tickets sold, and so late in the day too! How will you manage with these people?"

I then turned to Beard and said:

"Let me try it tonight. It will save so much trouble."

Beard said:

"As you like, but I have told Dolby what I think. If you insist on reading tonight I shall have only to stand by and watch the results."

I asked Dolby how he would get through if I did not read, and his response was:

"Never mind me, I'll get through somehow." He also suggested that Beard and I leave town at once. "Go anywhere you like" he said, "to the Adelphi at Liverpool, for instance – and I will join you sometime tonight."

Before leaving shortly after 5 p.m., Beard drew up a notice about me for Dolby's use which stated:

"I have found it necessary – in consequence of Mr. Dickens's Heart and Voice, superinduced solely by excessive travelling and fatigue – to prescribe some remedies, which render it imperative on me to forbid his appearing in public tonight. If he did, I am satisfied he could not get through his reading.....I recommend his immediately going to London with me."

Beard signed and dated this. We then both left Dolby to sort out matters for that night in Preston, and the following night in Warrington, and caught the 6.15 p.m. train for London.

I understand that Dolby, with the assistance of the landlord of the Bull Hotel, the Mayor and the Chief Constable, managed to arrange matters in Preston before getting to the Adelphi Hotel himself at about midnight, and the next day going to Warrington to deal with matters there. Meanwhile, after a night's rest in London, I then had a consultation with Frank Beard and Sir Thomas Watson (Fellow of the Royal Society and Physician Extraordinary to the Queen), where I told them the full history of my symptoms and how they had affected me. The doctors stated that the attack at Chester was, in their opinion, evidence of a disposition to paralysis, that the readings must be instantly stopped, and that I was to be prescribed months of rest. "It must be done" they said, "or you will be severely ill. No half measures will do."

Upon that I gave in, and they drew up a further certificate, which they both signed, and which read:

"The undersigned certify that Mr. Charles Dickens has been seriously unwell, through great exhaustion and fatigue of body and mind, consequent upon his public readings and long and frequent railway journeys. In our judgement, Mr. Dickens will not be able with safety to himself to resume his readings for several months to come."

I wrote to Forster, telling him that I was well enough, but tired; in perfectly good spirits and not at all uneasy, but in my own mind I now knew the readings had to be stopped and that I had had symptoms that must not be disregarded. I also wrote to Messrs. Chappell and Co. expressing my grief at the turn matters had taken. I subsequently received a note from Thomas Chappell, the senior partner, to the effect that they felt that my overwork had been "indirectly caused by them, and by my great and kind exertion to make their venture successful to the extreme." There was something so delicate and fine in this, that I felt it deeply, to say nothing of their noble and munificent manner of sweeping away into space all the charges incurred uselessly, and all the immense inconvenience and profitless work thrown upon their establishment. I do believe that such people as the Chappells are very rarely to be found in human affairs, and I replied to him that I was really touched by his letter; I most truthfully assured him that their part in the inconvenience of this mishap had given me much more concern than my own – and that if I did not hope to have our London farewells yet, I should be in a very gloomy condition on their account. I also told him not to suppose that they were to blame for my having done a little too much, and that the simple fact was that the rapid railway travelling had been stretched a hair's breadth too far, and that I ought to have foreseen it.

I felt as well as any man could be under such circumstances; I ate and drank well, slept well and was in good spirits. The novel prospect of comparative idleness rather astonished me, and I was deeply disappointed that I could not have my remaining readings in London. But I put the disappointment – and the money loss too – aside, and contacted Ouvry to draw up a new draft of my Will, in as short a manner as possible, and indeed wished to write the whole Will myself in its final form.

I sent him a note of my instructions. I wished to continue to give the legacies that were in my existing Will. These were:

£1,000 (free of legacy duty) to Miss Ellen Lawless Ternan, late of Houghton Place, Ampthill Square (though not disclosing that she was now living at Windsor Lodge, Linden Grove, Peckham);
£19.19 shillings to my faithful servant Mrs. Anne Cornelius;
£19.19 shillings to Anne Cornelius's daughter;
£19.19 shillings to each and every domestic servant, male or female, in my employ at the time of my death, so long as they had been in such employment for at least a year;
 £1,000 (free of legacy duty) to my daughter Mamie; and a further annuity of £300 per annum for her life so long as she continued unmarried; if she should marry, she should share with my other children in the provision that I made for them;
£8,000 (free of legacy duty) to Georgy, as well as all my personal jewellery, all the little familiar objects from my writing table, and all my private papers. I regarded Georgy as the best and truest friend man ever had.

To my eldest son Charley, I now gave my library of printed books, my engravings and prints, the silver salver presented to me at Birmingham and the silver cup presented at Edinburgh, as well as my shirt studs, shirt pins, and sleeve buttons;

I bequeathed to Charley and Harry £8,000 upon trust to invest to pay the annual income (of £600) to my wife Catherine during her life, and then after her death the money for my children;

To my dear and trusty friend John Forster I gave my gold repeater watch presented to me at Coventry (together with the chains, seals and appendages), and any manuscripts of my published works in my possession at the time of my death.

I appointed Forster and Georgy executor and executrix, and ordered that any house or land property that I possessed on my death to be sold as soon as may be, and converted into money towards my purposes; that my copyrights be sold (or not) as Forster and Georgy deemed best, and my children to benefit by them, share and share alike; that the whole residue of my estate to be divided among my children, share and share alike – except unmarried Mamie, as being otherwise provided for. I intended that Forster and Georgy should feel as unshackled as possible in carrying out all my intentions.

Having set out my wishes to Ouvry, I went to Gad's Hill for a couple of days. I felt alright (I thought) except for a rather dazed sensation of being greatly fatigued and that I must be slow and quiet yet awhile. Above all things I could not bear to be hurried or flurried and I knew I should be almost ashamed of myself if I did not know the unconditional knocking off for a time, from all reading wear and tear, to be a precautionary rather than a curative measure. After these days at Gad's Hill I returned to London, and met with Ouvry at the All the Year Round office to correct and finalize the matters I required in my Will, as the draft he had sent me was not quite as I had meant. Thereafter I dined with Forster, his wife, and Georgy at the office and explained to them my intentions over the Will.

I was now delighted to hear that James and Annie Fields were, with friends, actually on their way from Boston to visit England, and began planning what I might show them. I knew Fields had a passion to be taken to see Canterbury, in an open carriage with the old scarlet jackets, and as the old road between Gad's Hill and Canterbury was charming in the summer weather, I decided to fix a time in June that would also suit Ouvry as I wished him to join us. By now the sharp precautionary remedy of stopping the readings instantly was allowing me to recover with great rapidity and, just as three days repose on the Atlantic steamer had made me, in my altered appearance, the amazement of the captain, so this last week had now set me up again, thank God, in the most wonderful manner. The sense of exhaustion seemed a dream already and I felt that if I trained myself carefully all through the summer and autumn, being as idle as I could and only oscillating between London and Gad's Hill, in the spring I trusted I should then be able to report to the Chappells that I would be ready to take my farewells in London.

CHAPTER LXXXI

Continuing Onward, the Fields Visit,
and Thoughts of a New Story

I continued with All the Year Round business, now being helped by Charley, and I wrote to Wills telling him that I was really all right, particularly as I was not now being shaken by constant express travelling. Indeed, I felt that the rest and a little care had immediately unshaken the railway shaking and I was soon feeling my normal self again. I wrote a letter to James and Annie Fields, hoping it would be put into their hands on board their ship (the Russia) when they arrived at Queenstown, assuring them that I was myself again and was good for all country pleasures with them, and looking forward to showing them Gad's Hill, Rochester Castle, Cobham Park, red jackets and Canterbury. I also told them that when they came to London, we would probably be staying in a hotel; and I subsequently took rooms for myself, Mamie and Georgy in the St. James's Hotel at 77 Piccadilly.

Meanwhile I had heard word from Australia that Plorn (now 17) was having difficulties in adapting himself to the necessities of a bush life and, from obtaining a place at a sheep station, he had within 10 days given it up and returned to Melbourne. I was quite prepared for his not settling down without a lurch or two for, though I thought he had more, au fond, than his brothers, he had always been a queer wayward fellow with an unformed character, and yet with the makings of a character restlessly within him. I still hoped he might take to a colonial life, wanted to give him a reasonable trial, and to try him fully.

I had also heard from Sydney on board his ship, HMS Zealous, under the date "Vancouver Island, Friday March 19th", in which he informed me that he had fallen heavily into debt and "drawn very heavily" upon others. He wrote:

"You can't understand how ashamed I am to appeal to you again. You know what American people are, you know their habits of drinking – and that has run me into debt. It is with shame and regret I inscribe myself your son....The result of your refusal (to help me) you can imagine is not exaggerated – utter ruination."

I ended up paying off these debts.

Once the Fields and their friends arrived, I began making arrangements to show them aspects of our English way of life. I had made a close study of their police system in New York when I had been there and now wished to show them how our system operated. I arranged a night-time East End sight-seeing tour based at Leman Street Police Station in Goodman's Fields, and going out with the great detective, Inspector Field. This proved to be of such interest that we went out with the police at night on a second occasion, this time with Dolby and a couple of Inspectors of lodging-houses, when we visited properties, including an opium den, in the neighbourhood of Radcliffe Highway, Shadwell. We finished up in a place of resort for sailors of every nationality, known as "Tiger Bay".

I also determined to show them our General Post Office and to take them on a stroll through some of the stonyhearted streets of London. From the All the Year Round office, I took them on a walk among the cheap theatres and lodging-houses for the poor; I also showed them Furnival's Inn where I had begun Pickwick, followed by a walk through the thieves' quarter that I had highlighted in Oliver Twist. We dined at the All the Year Round office, where Nelly was invited, and I also invited Frederick Chapman to meet the Fields with me over dinner one evening at the Star and Garter in Richmond, after I had taken them on a visit to both Windsor and Richmond. They took a three-day excursion to see Tennyson on the Isle of Wight and I also invited them thereafter to the theatre and to Gad's Hill. I invited Dolby to join us at Gad's, and as the house would now be full, I arranged for him to join the party and be lodged with others comfortably at the Falstaff across the road.

I felt my health now quite restored, thank God – indeed I now felt ashamed of myself as a sort of imposter in having rested at all! – and welcomed them all at Gad's Hill at the beginning of June. By now those in the party comprised:

James and Annie Fields;

Miss Mabel Lowell, daughter of the American Ambassador – a charming little thing, very retiring in manner and expression, and whom I christened "snowdrop";

Mr. Childs, a newspaper proprietor from Philadelphia, and his wife, both of whom I had met in America;

Mr. Sol Etynge, the American artist, who was engaged in illustrating a new edition of Pickwick that was about to be published by Messrs. Fields and Osgood in America;

Dr. Fordyce Barker, my medical man in New York;

Frederic Ouvry, my solicitor, and George Dolby.

I also invited officers from Chatham and a number of my neighbours to meet with the party at Gad's.

The country was looking its very best, the trees and hedgerows resplendent with blossom, and the fields a mass of colours. The nightingales, too, were in full song, which astonished and delighted the Americans. I also invited them to play croquet and bowls, two games comparatively unknown in America, and they took to both with enthusiasm. I took them on many rambles in the area, including to Cobham Park, Rochester (where Mr. Elynge made some original sketches for the edition of Pickwick on which he was engaged), as well as misty walks to the marshes at Cooling, that they might get a realistic notion of the dreariness and loneliness of the scenes in Great Expectations that I had made famous through Pip and the convict.

One of the most delightful days was occupied by the drive I had promised to Canterbury. Canterbury was a journey of some twenty-nine miles from Gad's Hill along the old Dover Road, through Rochester, Chatham, Sittingbourne and Faversham. I arranged for two post-carriages to be turned out with postilions, fully dressed in the red jackets of the old Dover Road, together with buckskin breeches and top boots. I also organized the filling of hampers and wine baskets for my guests, which blocked the steps of the house before they were packed into the carriages. We made an early start sharp on time on a beautiful sunny day, so as to give plenty of time for luncheon in a spot on the way I had chosen and to allow for a ramble afterwards.

Everyone was in the best of spirits, the weather continued to be all that could be desired, and the ladies did honour to it by the brightness of their costumes. We travelled merrily over the road, with hop gardens on either side, until we reached Rochester, our horses making such a clatter in the slumberous old city that all the shopkeepers in the main street turned out to see us pass. I was in the foremost carriage and ordered the pull-up at a shop and went inside. I noticed a small crowd collect around the carriages and, on coming out, saw a man in the crowd point at Fields and cry out: "That's Dickens!" – whereupon I handed up the parcel I had to him and said: "Here you are, Dickens, take charge of this for me!!"

We travelled on through Rochester, skirted Chatham, and on to Sittingbourne, where a relay of fresh horses awaited us. After the short rest and the change in that brick-making town, we continued on to the lunch place, a wood that I had selected. The baskets were carried into the wood, everybody doing something, and the cloth speedily laid. I allowed an hour for luncheon, the postilions getting their meal when we had finished, and I was insistent that every vestige of our visit to the wood – in the shape of lobster shells and other debris – be cleaned up before we started again. We drove into Canterbury in the early afternoon just as the bells of the Cathedral were ringing for afternoon service. Entering the quiet city under the old gate at the end of the High Street, it seemed as though its inhabitants were indulging in an afternoon's nap after a midday dinner, but our entry and the clatter of our horses' hoofs roused them as it had done the people of Rochester, and they came running to their windows and out into the streets to learn what so much noise might mean. We turned into the bye-street of the Fountain Hotel, where the carriages and horses were put up while I showed the visitors the city.

I took them first to the Cathedral, where a service was just commencing. We joined a very small congregation, but I was greatly disappointed at the careless, half-hearted manner in which the service was performed, and the indifference of the officiating clergy jarred most acutely with me. I could not conceive how any person, accepting an office or a trust so important as the proper rendering of a beautiful cathedral service, could go through their duties in such a mechanical and slip-shod fashion. My only consolation was to hear Ouvry, a man who believed in nothing in heaven or hell, joining in with all the responses louder than any of us! After the service, I showed my friends the many objects of interest in the Cathedral, and had to get rid of a tedious verger who wanted to lead the way instead.

We rambled the streets of Canterbury and the Americans asked if they could be shown the very house where David Copperfield went to school at Dr. Strong's. I laughed at this, and merely told them "there are several that would do!" We took tea at the hotel and at six o'clock started on our homeward journey, the people of Canterbury hearty in their salutations as we left the town. We sped along at a rattling pace and, while the journey to Canterbury (including luncheon) had taken nearly five hours, we made home to Gad's Hill in less than three.

The next day I had the red-jacketed postilions out again to take my friends to see Chatham, the place where I had spent so much of my time in my youth. I now had many friends among the naval and military officers and their families, and the General commanding the district was now General Freeman Murray, whom I knew well. He organized a reception for us at his house, Government House in Chatham Barracks, with a military band in the grounds, and then conducted us through other parts of the barracks, before arranging a lively and terrifying drive home through Cobham Park in the Drag, his private stage-coach. I held a grand dinner-party at Gad's that evening, with a reception afterwards, and invited many friends in the neighbourhood to join us. I had the furniture removed from the drawing-room during the dinner to allow for dancing, and it was not until the morning light peeped in at the windows that the guests separated. It was the most cheerful of occasions.

For ten days I was perpetually journeying and sightseeing with my American friends, and during that time found that Fields had developed a collector's mania for bric-a-brac and old furniture. I spent whole afternoons with him (and often Dolby also) in Wardour Street, Hanway Street and New Oxford Street looking at old chairs and old furniture displayed at fabulous prices. I had to frequently intervene or Fields would have bought enough to fill the hold of an Atlantic steamer and, once he had gone on his travels, I could not resist writing to him, after Dolby and I had seen a chair in a shop in Great Queen Street:

"There is a chair (without a bottom) at a shop near the office, which I think would suit you. It cannot stand of itself, but will almost seat somebody, if you put it in a corner, and prop one leg up with two wedges and cut another leg off. The proprietor asks £20, but says he admires Literature and would take £18. He is of Republican principles, and I think would take £17. 19s. 6d. from a cousin. It is very ugly and wormy. Shall I secure this prize? It is related – but without proof – that on one occasion Washington declined to sit down on it. Please telegraph without delay!"

The Americans left for a visit to Scotland, taking up my pet rooms in Edinburgh at Kennedy's Hotel, 8 Princes Street, as well as thereafter going to the Continent, allowing me then to catch up with business and letters. I asked my publishers to send a complete set of the Charles Dickens Edition of my works to General Freeman Murray at Chatham Barracks as a thanks for his generous hospitality, and was pleased to receive better news of one of my boys. In a year that had brought trouble with them, it now brought comfort too, for I heard that Harry had won the second scholarship at Trinity Hall, Cambridge, which gave him £50 a year for as long as he stayed there; and I now began to hope that he would get a fellowship, though I had learnt to be moderate in such expectations. It was a timely gleam in my boy-outlook.

Wills, in consequence of his broken health, had now bought a country place in Hertfordshire, at Sherrards, by Welwyn, to retire in a gentleman-like manner, having given up any thoughts of continuing as sub-editor of All the Year Round – indeed he had also stood down as Secretary of the Guild of Literature and Art (a post now taken up by Charley) – and I was now faced with a rush of All the Year Round business. However, I was finding that, despite making a terrible mess of his paper-making business, Charley was a very good man of office business, and he also evinced considerable aptitude in sub-editing work; it was most fortunate that this post fell in just as he was stranded, and I began to put him to work too in writing articles for All the Year Round.

I now felt happy enough to report myself not only perfectly well but flourishing and, with Dolby, prepared to announce the resumption and conclusion of the broken series of farewell readings, in a London course of twelve, beginning early in the New Year. I was taking it as easy as I could through the summer – though this was not very easy with a weekly publication always clutching at my sleeve. I spent my time between Gad's Hill, London and the office, working and corresponding, as well as meeting and dining with friends. The public houses I liked best were The Cock and The Cheshire Cheese in Fleet Street, the Blue Posts at 13 Cork Street, Clunns Hotel in Covent Garden Market and the Albion opposite Drury Lane Theatre. After dinner I would often attend at a theatre but, if there was no special attraction, I would call in at the Princess Theatre where Fechter was playing his farewell engagement. I was often with Dolby and would invite him to the office for a glass of my celebrated gin punch and a cigar before separating for the night, though not without making an appointment for a future time. On Sunday 1st August General Freeman Murray appeared at Gad's Hill with his Drag and took us all (including Austen Layard and his young wife) for a ride. But we all went through appalling dangers, and Arthur Helps (assistant to the Queen), who was also with us, was so terrified riding on the top that he got inside. I stayed behind the box-lady, and as we went into the park of Cobham, we took some curly variations on the turf, in which I thought my left cheek would brush the dew off the grass!

My mind had continued thinking of a new story and I wrote again to Forster, telling him I had now laid aside a fancy I had told him of, and had a very curious and new idea in my head. It involved the murder of a nephew by his uncle, the originality of which would consist in the review of the murderer's career by himself at the close, where its temptations would be dwelt upon as if, not he the culprit but some other man, were the tempted. The last chapters would be written in the condemned cell, to which his wickedness – all elaborately elicited from him as if told to another – had brought him. I told Forster that I felt the idea to be a strong one, though difficult to work, and not otherwise communicable or the interest of the book would be gone.

I had this story forming in my mind sufficient to write to Frederick Chapman asking him to consider, at his convenience and without hurry, what he would give in ready money for half the copyright if I were to decide on doing my new story in 12 one-shilling monthly numbers. I did not yet have a title for this new tale and was sorely puzzled for a long while to find one, but at length alighted upon "The Mystery of Edwin Drood" and held a small dinner party to celebrate the christening of it. After considerable negotiations with Chapman and his new business partner, Henry Trollope, we came to an agreement that was eventually signed on the 1st February 1870. This provided that Chapman and Hall should pay £7,500 for the first 25,000 copies of each monthly issue (to be printed at their own cost and for their own benefit), and that thereafter we share the profits equally. It was proposed that the work should be completed in 12 monthly parts, the first to be published in March 1870, when £3,750 of the sum should be paid to me, followed by £1,875 on the publication of the sixth monthly part, and the further £1,875 on the publication of the last. As well as clauses as to costs and expenses (including those relating to advertising), commission and rights of translation into foreign languages, the agreement also made provision (following my Chester illness) that if I died during the composition of the work or otherwise became incapable of completing the 12 monthly numbers, then Forster (or, in default Her Majesty's Attorney General for the time being) should determine the amount to be repaid to Chapman and Trollope by way of compensation. The sum of £7,500 was the largest given for any work of mine, or indeed to any other author, and in addition it was arranged that I was to receive a further £1,000 for the advance sheets sent to America; and Baron Tauchnitz agreed to pay liberally (as he always did) for his Leipzig reprint translated into German.

CHAPTER LXXXII

Final Farewell Readings, The Mystery of Edwin Drood,
5 Hyde Park Place, and An Audience with The Queen

I had to begin the preparation that was necessary for my 12 final farewell readings in London, and had also promised to deliver an Inaugural Address as President of the Birmingham and Midland Institute to their meeting in Birmingham on the 27th September. In early January I had been informed that I had been unanimously elected as their President for the ensuing year and I wrote to them accepting this distinction thus conferred upon me, with great satisfaction, and was proud of it. I had long been a resolute supporter of the Institute and in 1853 had given Christmas readings on their behalf which, I later discovered, resulted in the largest contribution it had ever received – and they could still obtain no help whatsoever from the Government. I had also to continue pressing on with All the Year Round business, ensuring that the journal was published in four and twenty pages to my satisfaction each week, as well as responding to my extensive private correspondence, and so it became necessary for me to decline all other hospitable invitations – save that I was pleased to speak at the banquet held in the Crystal Palace on the 30th August, after the long-awaited rowing match between Oxford and Harvard that had taken place between Putney and Mortlake three days before. Following a titanic battle, Oxford had come home the winners by just three-quarters of a length and, to loud cheers and laughter, I was happy to praise both crews and the spirit that existed between our countrymen and those from the United States. The Harvard crew were a very good set of fellows and very modest – at least on this side of the Atlantic!

On the 27th September, at the Town Hall in Birmingham, it was so crammed that the committee of the Institute felt they had no alternative but to give up a portion of the platform to the audience. This was an arrangement to which I always had strong objection, for I always hated talking to people who sat behind me, and I asked Dolby to rearrange this, but the committee proved unalterable and I had to proceed in this manner. I spoke upon the subject: "Education for the People" to a highly enthusiastic audience, and in the course of my speech told them a little truth which held equally good in my own life, and the life of every eminent man I had ever known – namely: "The one serviceable, safe, certain, remunerative, attainable quality in every study and in every pursuit is the quality of attention." I was able to add: "My own invention or imagination, such as it is, I can most truthfully assure you, would never have served me as it has, but for the habit of commonplace, humble, patient, daily, toiling, drudging attention." At the conclusion I promised to return at Christmas, at the end of my year as President, to distribute the prizes.

I had come to Birmingham with Dolby to dine and sleep in the hotel, and had told Dolby I had a notion, if it suited him, of supplementing the speechmaking with a small excursion the next day with Nelly on her own to Stratford or Kenilworth, or both, or somewhere else, in a jovial way. While in Birmingham, I went with Dolby to the Elkington Factory in New Hall Street – silversmiths, electroplaters and gilders – to make some purchases before leaving there. On being escorted over the factory, my eye detected some dilapidated tea urns, which seemed of familiar appearance. Upon inquiry, I learnt they were old friends, from one of the refreshment rooms (Stafford) on the London and North Western Railway that had been sent to the factory for repairing and, on looking at the insides, saw the shockingly bad state for myself, which instantly put me in mind of what I had written of such urns in The Boy at Mugby, where they had been "for Heaven knows how many years the cause of poisoning the passengers with a beverage produced under the active agency of hot water, and a mixture of decomposed lead, copper, and a few other deadly poisons."

Through September I had been thinking over the contents of my new serial story, dwelling on the opium dens I had seen in association with our American visitors, and finding that Charlie Collins wished to try his hand at illustrating the story. I wanted him to try the cover first and asked Chapman to send down to him at Gad's Hill any of our old green covers that Chapman might have. At Gad's I had changed the house and surrounds greatly since my purchase of it, much to the surprise of the many visitors who came there, but I now wished to have a conservatory built, opening off both the drawing-room and the dining-room, and sought an estimate for the purpose.

At the beginning of October, Fields had returned from his travels and I invited him and Annie to Gad's Hill once more. They arrived for the weekend on the 9th October, and the day after received them into my small library and there read and acted out the first number of Edwin Drood that I had now written, the opium smoking that I described being exactly as I had seen with them (penny ink-bottle and all) down in Shadwell. Fields thought it as powerful as anything I had ever written.

Much fortified by this, I continued on writing through October, as well as going regularly to the All the Year Round office (though not to sleep or stay), and authorizing the start of the building of the conservatory at Gad's Hill. Meanwhile, Forster had been ill with a very troublesome return of his bronchitis, and his wife had been very much troubled by him, but he then took a turn greatly for the better and I dined with them alone that month. I found him looking far stronger than I had expected, with his cough quite mild, but he lived in one perpetual terror of taking cold. I told him I had heard from Macready, and we fell into a long talk about the dear old days and, later in the month, read to him what I had now written of Edwin Drood.

I now pressed on very hard with the story, seeking to get as much as I could done before the time of my readings in the New Year. Dolby visited me at Gad's Hill, and was also in correspondence with Nelly, and my health remained invariably good, although the return to hard work, and the confinement consequent on it, brought back the trouble to my foot, and towards the end of the year I was frustrated in being quite unable to take any real walking exercise. Then I discovered that Charlie Collins had found that the sitting down to draw brought back all the worst symptoms of his old illness that occasioned him to leave his old pursuit of painting – and here I was without an illustrator! I wrote immediately to Frederick Chapman telling him of this and that we could use Collins's cover that he had now completed, but that he had given in altogether as to further subjects. There was no time to be lost and I arranged to come to town to meet with Chapman at the All the Year Round office so that we might immediately consider what was to be done. Then I also found to my horror that when the first two numbers of Edwin Drood were printed up, each of them was found to be 6 printed pages too short! Consequently, I had to transpose a chapter from Number 2 to Number 1 and remodel Number 2 altogether. This was the more unlucky, as it came upon me at the time when I was being obliged to leave the book in order to get up my readings, which I found had quite gone out of my mind since I had left them off, but I stuck to the story and got it done, with both numbers then put into type. Forster now thought Number 2 "a clincher."

In early December I proposed, particularly on Mamie's account, to take a house again in London and agreed to rent 5, Hyde Park Place, a charming house opposite Marble Arch belonging to Thomas Milner Gibson, someone I had known since my Devonshire Terrace days, taking it from the beginning of January to the end of May 1870. At the same time, I saw some illustrations in a new magazine called "The Graphic" done by the illustrator (Samuel) Luke Fildes that impressed me greatly. Accordingly, I sent Fildes a note asking if he would send me some specimens of his art, and in due course he sent some highly meritorious and interesting ones that I examined with the greatest pleasure before returning them to him. He also told me he had done a drawing from David Copperfield and I was naturally curious to see it so that I could compare it with my own idea. He produced the Copperfield design, in which there were many points of merit, but I felt it wanting in a sense of beauty and, as in the new book I had two beautiful and young women, strikingly contrasted in appearance and both to be very prominent in the story, I had some concerns. But from what I had seen in a great number of his drawings I did entertain the greatest admiration for his remarkable power, supposed he would be up to the requirement, and hearing also the very earnest representations about him from John Millais, Chapman and I were happy to take him on as the illustrator for Edwin Drood. He redesigned Collins's drawing for the cover and produced 12 of his own drawings for the story, the first number of which was now due to be published on the 30th March.

Dolby would report to me weekly on the take-up for tickets for my 12 farewell readings and the news that he brought always cheered me, there being an extraordinary demand for tickets, long in advance of the dates now fixed for their delivery. I was most anxious to have the new book as far forward as possible before I took again to the platform and, as the readings approached, I felt the pressure of them, particularly for the commencement when there were to be two readings a week. I went to Gad's Hill for Christmas, but the turkey Dolby promised did not arrive. It subsequently transpired that he did bargain to supply a particularly fine bird from Ross-on-Wye, but it was transferred (together with other hampers he sent) by the railway to a horse-box at Gloucester, which then caught fire en-route and was destroyed into charred remains by the time it reached Reading. This misfortune must have proved a blessing to the poor inhabitants of Reading, who were enabled to purchase the charred remains of this and other turkeys and joints of beef at sixpence a-piece, the price at which the railway company sold off the contents of the horse-box!

With the coming of Christmas Day I had been so put about by conflicting engagements – readings, writings, editing, Birmingham correspondence, and other botherations – that I felt this Christmas to be one of great pain and misery; I was confined to bed the whole day and was only able to get up in the evening to join the family party in the drawing-room after dinner, where we drank the health of old friends, and played a memory game. As I lay on the sofa and the game proceeded for some time, with the words to memorize growing to a great length, it came again to my turn. After successfully repeating a string of words, I had to add my own contribution and, after a moment's thought, did so with the words "Warren's Blacking, 30 Strand". Although this held a special meaning for me, the family remained unaware of it and I said no more.

On New Year's Eve I went up from Gad's Hill to Forster's house and read the fresh number of Edwin Drood I had just written. But my pains in somewhat modified form had returned in both my left hand and my left foot a few days earlier and were still troubling me. Then, on the 6th January 1870, though I had developed an invincible dislike of railway travel, I nevertheless travelled to Birmingham as I had promised in September, and on that evening in the Town Hall distributed the prizes and certificates to members of the Institute. There was a very large assembly gathered in the hall and my speech was greeted with loud applause and laughter, but I had to decline the offer of the council of the Institute to dine with them the following day, for the work I had now before me during the next three months caused me to sacrifice every tempting engagement to it, as in my case there was no happy medium between many festivities and none.

I felt a little shaken by my railway journey to Birmingham and consulted with Frank Beard, but then we moved into 5, Hyde Park Place, where I had a large room, with three fine windows overlooking the park, that was unsurpassable for airiness and cheerfulness – though when I put my papers away for the day, I would get up and fly. I was in good heart, notwithstanding (as I told Forster) Gladstone's new Chancellor of the Exchequer, Robert Lowe, and his worrying scheme, for collecting a year's taxes in a lump at the beginning of the year, which I was told was damaging books, pictures, music and theatres beyond precedent. Nevertheless, our let at St. James's Hall was, as Dolby confirmed to me, enormous, and as I left Gad's Hill the new conservatory was taking shape in glass and iron, a brilliant success but expensive, with foundations as of an ancient Roman work of horrible solidarity.

I gave the first of my twelve farewell readings at St. James's Hall on the evening of Tuesday 11th January, with the greatest brilliancy. It was agreed that Frank Beard should be in attendance at each of these readings, to monitor my pulse rate and oversee my general welfare, and he did so. It was subsequently found that the ordinary state of my pulse was 72; Copperfield brought it up to 96; Dr. Marigold 99; Nickleby took it to 112; and Dombey to 114. On the first night of the Murder it was 112, and the second 118; on one occasion it rose to 124. Leaving the platform on the termination of a Murder, I had to be supported to my retiring-room and laid on a sofa for a full 10 minutes before I was able to speak a rational or consecutive sentence. But at the end of the interval I would rearrange myself, swallow a wine-glassful of weak brandy and water, and hurry on to the platform for the final reading of the evening. I always made this reading a light one for, not only did this assist me, but more particularly I considered it necessary for the audience as a form of antidote to what had gone before.

I agreed to give two afternoon readings, beginning at 3 p.m. (a beastly proceeding which I particularly hated) on behalf of the theatrical profession, and carried out the first of these on Friday 14th January, when I read the Carol. I read again on the night of Tuesday the 18th, while the next afternoon reading took place on Friday, the 21st, when I read Boots and the Murder. It was a very curious scene; the actors and actresses (most of the latter looking very pretty) mustered in extraordinary force, and were a fine audience. I set myself to carrying out of themselves and their observation those who were bent on watching how the effects were got – and I believe I succeeded. But it was these afternoon readings that particularly disturbed me at my book-work, though I hoped nevertheless to lose no way on their account, for by now I had a curious interest steadily working up to Number 5 of Edwin Drood which required a great deal of art and self-denial. I believed also, apart from character and picturesqueness, that I had placed the young people in the story in a very novel situation – or so I hoped – and at Numbers 5 and 6 I planned that the story would turn upon an interest suspended until the end.

I could hardly believe it, but the 16th January had been Harry's 21st birthday. I gave a small dinner-party at Hyde Park Place to celebrate the event and entered him at the Inner Temple of lawyers for admission to practice as a Barrister upon the completion of his studies at Cambridge. Despite Charlie Collins's collapse, Katey seemed to be always improving, and had made some more capital portraits. The conservatory at Gad's Hill was completed and I then received an invitation to dine with the Prime Minister, Mr. Gladstone, on Wednesday 26th January. I wrote saying it would afford me great pleasure to do so, but on the day appointed I had to write most unwillingly after consulting with my doctor, that I was unable to attend due to a substantial injury to my right thumb, which I had increased by using it unbandaged the previous night. The following week, however, I was well enough to dine (together with Mamie) with Arthur Stanley, the Dean of Westminster.

In February I received a letter from Arthur Helps, enclosing some royal photographs from the Queen herself, and making reference to The Frozen Deep. This reference emboldened me to ask Helps to explain what I thought and hoped (but could not be sure) had been explained to her at the time when she did me the honour of sending for me on that memorable evening – namely that I was already dressed for the farce in a ridiculous wig and dressing gown and felt, not being a professional actor, that there would be something incongruous in my so presenting myself before the Queen and the late Prince Consort. I sent Helps some photographs of battlefields in the American Civil War that I had been given on my visit to America, to pass on to the Queen in return, in the hope that she might find them interesting.

I read at St. James's Hall on each Tuesday through February (the 1st, 8th, 15th and 22nd) to immense audiences, but between my readings, Edwin Drood (upon which I was getting on very well) and dealings with All the Year Round, I was really hard put to it occasionally. However, the 3rd March was Nelly's thirty-first birthday and so I organized a small dinner for her, together with Wills and Dolby, at Blanchard's, the famed wine merchants, at 169 Regent Street. I also planned to give a dinner on the 12th March to Thomas and Arthur Chappell and Dolby, to thank them for the business-conduct of my readings, which were now drawing to a close, the final three being set down for the Tuesdays 1st, 8th and 15th March.

I heard again from Helps, with talk of a Baronetcy (to which I told him in jest that we would have "of Gad's Hill Place" attached to it, for if my authority was worth anything, believe on it that I was going to be nothing but what I was), together with a gracious message from the Queen thanking me for the photographs, and a wish to thank me in person as she said she "wished to make my acquaintance." Accordingly, I replied to Phelps:

"Will you kindly present my duty and thanks to the Queen and the assurance that I shall be proud and happy to wait on Her Majesty whenever it may suit her pleasure."

A meeting was then arranged for the 9th March, and on that afternoon at 5 o'clock I attended at Buckingham Palace and for half an hour had an Audience and very interesting conversation with the Queen. She received me most graciously and, because Court etiquette required that no one, in an ordinary interview with the Sovereign, should be seated, she remained the whole time leaning over the head of a sofa. She expressed her deep regret at not having heard one of my readings, but expressed the pleasure she had derived in witnessing my acting in The Frozen Deep in 1857. She showed much interest and curiosity with regard to my recent American experiences, and made reference to a supposed discourtesy that had been shown to Prince Arthur on one occasion in

America. I assured her that no true-hearted American was in sympathy with the Fenian body in that country (that lay behind that incident), and that nowhere in the world was there a warmer feeling towards her, the English Queen, than existed throughout the whole of the United States – a sentiment she was pleased to hear from someone whom she regarded as so observant an authority. She also asked my opinion on the "servant question" and whether I could account for the fact that, as she said, "we have no good servants in England as in the olden times". I regretted that I could not account for this fact, except perhaps on the hypothesis that the English system of education was a wrong one. I told her I had my own ideas on the subject of National Education, but saw no likelihood of them being carried into effect. We talked of other things, including the price of provisions (particularly the cost of butcher's meat and bread) and the plight of the poor, and I told her that I felt sure that a better feeling and a much greater union of classes would take place in time.

Before I left the interview, Her Majesty begged my acceptance of a copy of her "Journal in the Highlands", in which she had placed an autograph inscription and her own sign manual. On handing it to me she remarked that she felt considerable hesitation in presenting so humble a literary effort to one of the foremost writers of the age. She asked me to look kindly on any literary faults of her book and expressed a desire to be the possessor of a complete set of my works, if possible that afternoon. I was pleased to gratify this wish, but begged to be allowed to defer sending the books until I had had a set especially bound for her acceptance. This was agreed, and after the interview I contacted Chapman to put in hand at once a best copy of all my books to be bound by Hayday (now run by William Mansell at 31, Little Queen Street, Lincoln's Inn Fields) in red morocco and gold with gilt edges and to be done with as little delay as was consistent with the best workmanship. I subsequently asked Chapman to request to the binder that when he sent the books to 5, Hyde Park Place he should pack volume 1 separately, so that I might write an inscription in it without disturbing all the rest. In the meanwhile, I sent Helps, for Her Majesty, the first number of Edwin Drood, five days before its official publishing date.

Immediately after the interview, I arranged to meet Dolby in the Burlington Arcade and then dine together at the Blue Posts in Cork

Street. I took my brougham to the Piccadilly end of the Arcade and, on alighting and greeting Dolby, I instructed my servant to drive straight to 5, Hyde Park Place and deliver the Queen's book to Mamie. I then slipped my arm into Dolby's and we passed through the Arcade and on to our dining-place, where Dolby had cause for my favourite corner to be kept. After settling down to dinner, I told him of my conversations with the Queen and how I had been received, telling him that her kindness on the occasion had impressed me greatly.

Tuesday 15th March was my final farewell reading at St. James's Hall. The day before my throat was queer, and I was obliged to gargle and poultice. At 1 p.m. on the day of the reading I went with Dolby (as I did now on all these occasions) to the hall to ensure all was in order. This final farewell reading was one of the hardest I had to face and Dolby told me that long before the doors were opened, an immense crowd had assembled at the Regent Street and Piccadilly entrances to the hall, and it was but the work of a few moments to sell sufficient tickets to fill the shilling seats. The numbers turned away were, he said, far greater than those that were able to be admitted and had the hall been twice or three times the size we should have filled it easily. As it was, Chappell's staff had contrived to pack over two thousand persons into the Hall, and the receipts that night alone amounted to nearly £425.

The whole of the platform was, as usual, screened off by my "fit-up", consisting of the back screens and curtains, with the ends of the balconies partitioned off in conformity with the reading-screens and curtains, and as I took to the stage with my book, punctual to the moment at 8 o'clock, attired in my evening dress and with the gas-light streaming down upon me, the whole audience rose and cheered me to the echo for several minutes. I began this final reading with the Carol and, after the interval, concluded with the Trial from Pickwick. I felt a sadness inside me at this being my last reading, but nevertheless read with the greatest spirit and energy that I could muster – and it was said that I never read better in my life than on this last evening. I left the stage, but was obliged to respond several times to the calls for my reappearance and then, at last, returned to my little table to finally speak to the audience. They listened in silence as I addressed them:

"Ladies and Gentlemen. It would be worse than idle – for it would be hypocritical and unfeeling – if I were to disguise that I close this episode in my life with feelings of very considerable pain. For some 15 years, in this hall and many kindred places, I have had the honour of presenting my own cherished ideas before you for your recognition; and, in closely observing your reception of them, have enjoyed an amount of artistic delight and instruction which, perhaps, is given to few men to know. In this task, and in every other which I have ever undertaken, as a faithful servant of the public, always imbued with a sense of duty to them, and always striving to do his best, I have been uniformly cheered by the readiest response, the most generous sympathy, and the most stimulating support. Nevertheless, I have thought it well, at the full flood-tide of your favour, to retire upon those older associations between us, which date from much further back than these, and henceforth to devote myself exclusively to that art which first brought us together."

After the applause had subsided, I then added:

"Ladies and Gentlemen. In but two short weeks from this time I hope that you may enter, in your own homes, on a new series of readings, at which my assistance will be indispensable; but from these garish lights I vanish now for evermore, with a heartfelt, grateful, respectful, and affectionate farewell."

As I left the stage, thunderous applause erupted, and I proceeded to my retiring room with tears rolling down my cheeks. But the audience still would not allow me to depart, and for the final time I returned to the stage to be met with a more surprising outburst than before, together with a dazzling array of waved handkerchiefs. I respectfully kissed my hand to them and retired for the last time, recalling to Dolby thereafter what I had felt and said at my farewell in Boston, that in this brief life of ours it is sad to do almost anything for the last time.

CHAPTER LXXXIII

Edwin Drood, the Future of All the Year Round,
Deaths of Maclise and Lemon, Neuralgia in the Foot,
and Back to Gad's Hill

With the conclusion of my farewell readings, I was now able, at 5 Hyde Park Place, to focus my attention further on Edwin Drood and also to consider the future of All the Year Round. It was now proposed that at the end of April, Wills would formally retire from the journal, and Charley take his place, so I wrote to Ouvry asking him to consider what endorsement the agreement for the establishment of the journal would require, or what other deed might be necessary, to record the new arrangement. On Wills's formal retirement from management, he was to fall back on the eighth share, to which his wife would be entitled in the event of his death, and for an eighth share to go to Charley when he took up the role at the end of April. I was to have my six-eighths and the supreme authority over the whole concern, literary and otherwise. Draft Articles of Agreement were drawn up by Ouvry that came into effect on the 2nd May, and he also drew up a Codicil to my Will leaving all my interest in the journal, stereotypes, stock, etc. to Charley, and this I eventually signed on the 2nd June.

I began to notice again, as I had during the previous summer, that as I walked along the London streets I was not able to read more than the right-hand half of the names over the shops, but I put this down to the effect of the medicine I had been taking rather than any grave cause, and that my other troubles were exclusively local. Then, at the end of March, my uneasiness and haemorrhage, after having left me as I supposed, came back with an aggravated irritability that it had not yet displayed; I had a sudden violent rush of it one day (the 29th March) that put me in a dreadful state, and yet it did not appear to have the slightest effect on my general health that I knew of. These disagreeable effects passed and I was able to be free for Forster's birthday on the 2nd April, and to take the chair as President of the Newsvendors' Benevolent and Provident Institution at their Annual Dinner at the Freemasons' Tavern on the 5th. They had wished to congratulate me on my successful tour in, and my safe return from, America and had invited me to preside at their Anniversary Dinner the year before, but I had been taken ill shortly before the event and had been unable to attend. I was now keen to return the compliment, particularly as they had informed me that they considered I had done more to cement the friendship between our two countries than ages of diplomacy could effect. At the dinner I led the toasts and addressed them to much laughter and cheers, before making a call for funds and proposing a toast to the prosperity of the Institution.

I had also by now, after my audience with the Queen, received an invitation to attend at the next Royal Levee, due to be undertaken on the Queen's behalf by the Prince of Wales at Buckingham Palace at 2 p.m. on the 6th April. She also invited Mamie to be presented at the Drawing Room immediately following the Levee, and to both of these invitations we consented, though I knew as a consequence I should have to wear a fancy-dress costume to which I was quite unaccustomed. On the day, as I was dressing for the event, Dolby and others dropped in at Hyde Park Place just to see how I looked in my cocked hat and sword. Much merriment ensued, particularly over the cocked hat, for I did not know what on earth I should do with it! It was suggested that I should wear it "fore and aft" or "th'wart ships", while others said it was not intended to be worn at all and was a mere appendage any way, and should be carried under the arm! This latter suited my purpose, so tucking it under my arm, I turned to Dolby and said: "Come along Dolby, drive down to Buckingham Palace with me, and leave me in good society, where at least I shall be free of these ignorant people!"

At the Levee, the Prince of Wales and the King of the Belgians accepted an invitation to dine on a future date with Lord Houghton (a patron of literature and recently elected Fellow of the Royal Society) and, at the special desire of the Prince, I was also invited to join the party. I was pleased to accept. A couple of days later Mrs. Watson kindly invited me (and Mamie) to a family party at Rockingham on the 2nd May and I accepted with the greatest pleasure, the dear old Rockingham days always being fresh in my heart.

By now, as I told Frank Beard, I was "getting better nicely" (as is the nurse's phrase) and was working hard again on Edwin Drood – including working hard out of town on the 8th – 11th April, though I was obliged to avoid writing after dinner or by candlelight. I was still however directing from London that improvements be carried out at Gad's Hill, and an idea received from my new gardener, George Brunt, of partitioning the vinery and so getting our hot house, caused me to sought out an estimate for the cost of the work, and telling Brunt at the same time that I wanted to avoid any unnecessary expense, and that what we wanted was merely to have efficient means of preparing plants for the conservatory.

I had now heard from Chapman that we had been doing wonders with the first number of Edwin Drood. It had very, very far outstripped every one of its predecessors, opening with 50,000 copies printed, as against 38,000 for Little Dorrit and 40,000 for Our Mutual Friend. I continued hard at work upon it at 5, Hyde Park Place, and turned down additional social engagements (as I found them difficult of reconcilement with my work) and stuck to it like a Spartan, whilst keeping to my custom of complimenting the work with long country walks.

I continued to speak with Fildes over the illustrations for the story, and to have great hopes for him – particularly after Frith had pleased me with what he had said to me about him. But towards the end of April I began to find things particularly difficult, being most perseveringly and ding-dong-doggedly at work but making only slow headway. Spring always had a restless influence over me, and I wearied beyond expression, indeed at any season, of this London dining out, and yearned for the country again. Then, on the 29th April on returning from a visit to Gad's Hill, I had the greatest shock of reading in the newspaper at Higham Railway Station of the death, through the contraction of pneumonia, of my old dear friend and companion Daniel Maclise. It was only after great difficulty, and after hardening and steeling myself to the subject by at once thinking of it and avoiding it in a strange way, that I was able to get any command over it or over myself. Maclise had fallen into a wayward life, and become something of a recluse in the previous five years in his home at 4, Cheyne Walk in Chelsea, when I saw little of him; but Forster had introduced me to him in 1838 and for many years I was one of his two most intimate friends and companions. He was a genius in his chosen art and no artist, of whatever denomination, ever went to his rest leaving a more golden memory pure from dross, or having devoted himself with a truer chivalry to the art-goddess whom he worshipped.

The next day I was due to dine and speak at the annual dinner of the Royal Academy, and I told Forster that, if I felt at that time I could be sure of the necessary composure, I would make a little reference to Maclise's death in my speech. When the time came I was able to do so, and my reference to him was met with loud and continued cheering, but I also told them that since I had first entered the public lists as a very young man it had been my constant fortune to number amongst my nearest and dearest friends members of the Royal Academy who had been its grace and pride, but that they had now so dropped from my side one by one that I had already begun to feel like the story told of a Spanish monk, who had grown to believe that the only realities around him were the pictures which he loved, and that all the moving life he saw, or ever had seen, was a shadow and a dream.

I had to decline my proposed visit to Rockingham on the 2nd May as I had to be in attendance on a sick friend, and also declined that week an invitation to breakfast from Mr. Gladstone. I found I could not go out in the morning, and afterwards do anything that day, and got into a horrible state of complicated and constant engagements for that month that were crowding in before we gave up Hyde Park Place, and my life was positively made wretched. This always happened in the last month of any term of stay that we made in London, but this year it was worse than ever; I felt I could do nothing that I wanted to do, and could go nowhere to please myself.

I continued on with Edwin Drood and attending at the All the Year Round office, and then received an invitation to the Queen's Ball to be held at Buckingham Palace on the 17th May. I was also engaged to be present and to speak at the 25th anniversary dinner of the General Theatrical Fund at St. James's Hall on the 16th May with the Prince of Wales in the Chair – but then on the evening of the 10th May the violent neuralgic affection of my foot set in, which would yield to nothing but days of fomentation and horizontal rest, and I wrote to the General Theatrical Fund, setting the matter out with clarity:

"For a few years past, I have been liable, at wholly uncertain and incalculable times, to a severe attack of neuralgia in the foot, about once in the course of a year. It began in an injury to the finer muscles or nerves, occasioned by over-walking in deep snow. When it comes on, I cannot stand and can bear no covering whatever on the sensitive place. One of these seizures is upon me now. Until it leaves me, I could no more walk into St. James's Hall than I could fly in."

I set aside attendance at all functions and was now, constantly, in very great pain, only able to get a night's rest under the influence of laudanum. The neuralgia hung about me very heavily; I had the poultices constantly changed, hot and hot, day and night which, due to these very hot applications, caused little risings and then blisters on the foot, which became much enlarged. At such times the foot, until gradually scalded back into form and usefulness, was a mere bag of pain which refused to be carried about. Although I did manage to make my way to the All the Year Round office, my mobility and way of life was greatly curtailed, and I cancelled everything in the way of private dining, including with Forster, as a precaution after this horrible pain and the remedies I had been taking. I also declined to be involved in starting a memorial for Maclise, but had to take swift action with Ouvry when I learnt that Messrs. Fields, Osgood and Co. were proposing to publish parts of Edwin Drood in America before they were published in England, which would have caused the loss of my copyright in England for those parts so published. Accordingly, I had positively to prohibit such anticipation with them, knowing also that there were people enough in England, always on the watch, who would instantly avail themselves of my making so fatal a mistake, although I assured Messrs. Fields, Osgood and Co. that I wanted to do the utmost for them that I could, without the least reference to any extra gain, consistent with the safety of my property.

I heard of, and then from, Alfred in Australia that he was doing well, which did not surprise me, for I had unbounded faith in him. But I was doubtful if Plorn was taking to that country, and asked Alfred if he would find out Plorn's real mind. I noticed that Plorn always wrote as if his present life was the be-all and the end-all of his emigration, and as if I had no idea of Alfred and Plorn becoming proprietors, and aspiring to the first position in the Colony, without casting off the old connection. Plorn had always been the most difficult of boys to deal with away from home, though there was not the least harm in him, and he was far more reflective than any of his brothers. But he seemed to have been born without a groove, which could not be helped, but I felt that if he could not or would not find one, I must try again, and die trying. What was most curious to me was that he was very sensible, and yet did not seem to understand that he had qualified himself for no public examination in England, and could not possibly hold his own against any competition for anything to which I could get him nominated, though I did agree to buy him a sheep "run" on the River Darling.

Despite the pain and acute sensitivity in my foot continuing, I was pressed hard to attend the dinner with Lord and Lady Houghton and where the Prince of Wales and the King of the Belgians were to be guests. This dinner had now been fixed for the evening of the 24th May, and I was trying every means of qualifying myself to keep faith in the engagement. I still could not walk at all, or stand upon the foot two minutes, and up to the last moment it was a matter of doubt whether I would be able to go, but I did go and, though I was unable to go upstairs to meet the company in the drawing-room, I was able to proceed, with assistance, straight to the dining-room, where I participated in an enjoyable evening, particularly with the Prince of Wales. At the close of the dining I was again unable to go upstairs, but left, with the Prince of Wales expressing a hearty wish for a speedy and complete recovery.

At this time I was much shocked to hear of the death of Mark Lemon at his home (Vine Cottage, Crawley in Sussex) and wrote my condolences to his second son Harry, on behalf of the whole of their family in their great bereavement, their sadness now being added to, for I believe Lemon's heart had been nearly broken by the rascality of his eldest son. I told Harry that circumstances had divided me from his father for some years, but that there was never any serious estrangement between us, and I was glad to remember now that we had embraced affectionately when we had met at Stanfield's grave. I could not go to Lemon's funeral, but Charley went, and I instructed him to try and find out in what circumstances the family were left, for if he found them to be poor, I resolved to go to Mr. Gladstone and try him to get for Mrs. Lemon a small pension.

Our tenancy at 5, Hyde Park Place was now drawing to a close and, while Mamie and Georgy were intent on organizing a series of entertainments – including a concert with Charles Hallé and others – I wished to now be away to the quiet countryside of Gad's Hill, to get myself into my usual gymnastic condition. Being deprived of my normal walks was a very serious matter to me, for I could not work unless I had my constant exercise; without it I felt helpless and moody. The need to be intensely virtuous and press on with Edwin Drood hung over me, and on the 26th May I fled to Gad's Hill to take refuge, leaving Mamie and Georgy to complete their London season to the end of the month.

I had, at Gad's Hill, turned the whole garden topsy-turvy at great expense, and now with Brunt had a regular professed gardener in all the branches of the art. I had been glad to get rid of Russell, his predecessor, for he was not a good gardener; he had a general shakiness in money matters, as well as a general vague beeriness, and would have been quite unequal to the conservatory. We now had a forcing house for forcing every sort of flower, and melon frames, cucumber frames, and mushroom beds to produce in every week in the year. One hundred loads of gravel had been put on the paths to raise them; a model stable constructed with zinc fittings and water laid on for every horse, drainage so ingeniously complicated that I expected it would never act, and the devil knows what else to swell the items of the bill, all astonishing mankind in place of the old simplicities. All the dogs had got so fat during our stay in London that they were a tight fit in the stable yard and nothing could get by them. In the house, a new staircase reared its modest form (gilded and brightly painted) in the old place, all the upper landing was inlaid in a banquet of precious woods – and I found that the nice parlour maid was going to be married in a fortnight at Higham Church!

As I had now left Hyde Park Place, I told William Day of Clowes and Sons (the printers of Edwin Drood) to send proofs in future for correction either to Gad's Hill or to the All the Year Round office (where I was now every Thursday), and I set to again at Gad's on the story. My method was that no story should be planned out too elaborately in detail beforehand or the characters would become mere puppets and would not act for themselves when the occasion arose, but I did by now have a general idea of the journey I intended to take towards the conclusion. I told Forster that my foot was no worse, but no better, and pressed on, also inviting him to Gad's to speak with him about the Guild of Literature and Art and the possibility of funding, through them, a scholarship for the study of English Literature, a matter that I had already discussed with Ouvry.

On Thursday 2nd June I was again in the All the Year Round office, greatly absorbed in business matters, though I was still having difficulties with the pain. Dolby arrived for luncheon and over it we talked of many plans for the future, including for him to make an early visit to Gad's Hill to inspect the new conservatory and the several other improvements I had done to the place. We shook hands heartily across the office-table and on parting I said to him "next week then" as I rose from the table and, with some difficulty, followed him to the door. He had gone a little earlier than normal as I had told him I was to be very busy that afternoon; my business in the office included signing the Codicil to my Will, witnessed by George Holsworth and Henry Walker, who had both earlier, on the 12th May, also witnessed me signing my Will.

Later that day I returned to Gad's Hill. Mamie and Georgy were now there, having finished their London season at Hyde Park Place. I ordered four boxes of my usual cigars from Mr. Carlin of 189 Regent Street and also a voltaic band ("the magic band") for my right foot from Messrs. Pulvermacher and Co. of 200 Regent Street, that had been recommended to me by Mrs. Bancroft, the actress, and wife of the actor Squire Bancroft. I was by now prepared to try any remedy that was recommended to me, and Mrs. Bancroft assured me she had derived great relief from a similar complaint by the use of one of these bands. I was prepared to give it the fairest trial, and a few days later it arrived and I enclosed to Messrs. Pulvermacher and Co. a postal order for the band safely received, but I found it had been obtained by mistake for a shilling or two more than the right amount and I told Messrs. Pulvermacher that they could, if they pleased, return the balance in postage stamps.

Meanwhile I continued working on Edwin Drood in the chalet, and on the evening of Saturday 4th June Katey joined us. The next day Katey asked to talk to me about going on the stage as a means of earning a little extra money. She had been offered an engagement by Alfred Wigan, who had seen her act in The Frozen Deep, and she sought my advice.

I told her we could talk about it later when the others had gone to bed. That evening, after a lively dinner with the meal accompanied by merry laughter, I smoked my customary cigar and strolled once again into the conservatory, having told them all laughingly that this was to be positively the last improvement I was going to do at Gad's Hill! Katey then remained as the others said their goodnights and, once they had gone, I asked Katey to tell me all about it. She told me of the offer Wigan had made to her, but with great earnestness I sought to dissuade her from going on the stage. I told her she was pretty and I had no doubt she would do well, but I also told her she had too sensitive a nature to bear the brunt of much that she would encounter. I knew there were nice people on the stage, but I also knew there were some who would make your hair stand on end – and she was clever enough to do something else. We talked at length and I finally dismissed the subject by saying that I would make it up to her for the disappointment she felt about it. I also spoke of other subjects to her, the regrets I had and the wish that I had been a better father and a better man, but it had so happened that I had fallen in love with this girl, Nelly Ternan. We talked on into the night and did not part for bed until 3 o'clock in the morning.

That weekend I wrote to George Holsworth at the All the Year Round office instructing him to purchase for me a mahogany slope, such as I had upon my table in my business room in the office, in order to assist me in my writing at Gad's Hill. Then, on the Monday morning (6th June), Katey came to the chalet where I was again working on Edwin Drood, to say goodbye; she and Mamie were going to her tiny home at 10 Thurloe Place, South Kensington in London. She came in and I kissed her very affectionately. She left, but soon after came back again and tapped on the door, which was behind me, and after I called out: "Come in", I turned and saw her again. I held out my arms and she ran into them; we embraced and again I kissed her very affectionately before she left. Thereafter I continued on with Edwin Drood and in the afternoon walked with my dogs into Rochester and posted some letters before returning home. Georgy and I were now the only ones remaining at Gad's Hill.

On Tuesday 7th June I continued on with Edwin Drood in the chalet and wrote to Fildes inviting him to travel down to Gad's Hill over the weekend; I told him I would be there (probably alone with Georgy) from Saturday to Tuesday or Wednesday and asked if he could come down on Saturday or Sunday, telling him a bedroom would be ready for him and that I would send for him to Higham Station at any time he appointed. I wished to discuss further with him the illustrations I required for the story and proposed taking him around the vicinity, in which some of the scenes I was describing in Edwin Drood were laid.

On Wednesday 8th June, in the morning, I again went into the chalet in the shrubbery and pressed on with Edwin Drood. I was now working on the sixth number of the story and planned to make my weekly Thursday visit to the All the Year Round office the following day. I wrote to Charles Kent, the dearest of friends and editor of The Sun (based at their office in the Strand), who wished to meet with me when I came to the office:

"Tomorrow is a very bad day for me to make a call, as in addition to my usual office business, I have a mass of accounts to settle with Wills. But I hope I may be ready for you at 3 o'clock. If I can't be – why, then I shan't be."

EDITOR'S NOTE

Charles Dickens never arrived at the All the Year Round office at 26, Wellington Street in London on Thursday 9th June 1870, nor to a meeting with Charles Kent on the same day, but the evidence of what happened to him and where he was diverges. For the following 120 years it was believed, based on the sole evidence of Georgina Hogarth, that Dickens spent the whole of Wednesday 8th June writing *The Mystery of Edwin Drood* in his chalet in the shrubbery at Gad's Hill. After speaking with Georgina Hogarth, John Forster (in his publication "The Life of Charles Dickens") claimed that Dickens came over to the house for luncheon; "and, much against his usual custom, returned to his desk." Thereafter, he says, "he was late in leaving the chalet" and that he then took his dinner at 6 o'clock with Georgina Hogarth, where "Miss Hogarth saw, with alarm, a singular expression of trouble and pain in his face." Forster then adds that for an hour Dickens spoke with Georgina Hogarth before collapsing; and, in his 3-volume life story of Dickens, he makes no mention of Nelly Ternan, except when setting out Dickens's Will without comment in his Appendix.

Evidence has now come to light over the years which fundamentally calls into question this version of Dickens's life and death. The evidence now available, and included in this volume, shows that in fact Nelly became a central part of Dickens's life following their meeting in 1857 and that thereafter she remained so until his death. Furthermore there is evidence that, contrary to Forster's version of events (as supported by Georgina Hogarth), Dickens did not return to his desk in the chalet after luncheon on Wednesday 8th June, but instead went to The Sir John Falstaff Inn and obtained some money from the landlord by cashing a cheque, before then making his way to Peckham to see Nelly, and with the intention of staying there (as he had done many times before) before travelling on to the All the Year Round office in the morning. However, it was there in Peckham that afternoon that he had his seizure and Nelly then arranged for him to be transported back to Gad's Hill, where he died the following day, five years to the day after the Staplehurst rail crash.

Dickens in his Will had specifically stated:

"I emphatically direct that I be buried in an inexpensive, unostentatious, and strictly private manner; that no public announcement be made of the time or place of my burial; that at the utmost not more than three plain mourning coaches be employed; and that those who attend my funeral wear no scarf, cloak, black bow, long hat band, or other such revolting absurdity. I DIRECT that my name be inscribed in plain English letters on my tomb, without the addition of "Mr." or "Esquire." I conjure my friends on no account to make me the subject of any monument, memorial, or testimonial whatever. I rest my claims to the remembrance of my country upon my published works, and to the remembrance of my friends upon their experience of me in addition thereto. I commit my sole to the mercy of God through our Lord and Saviour Jesus Christ, and I exhort my dear children humbly to try to guide themselves by the teaching of the New Testament in its broad spirit, and to put no faith in any man's narrow construction of its letter here or there."

Discussion then arose as to where he should be buried. During his lifetime, Dickens had suggested a place in a small graveyard under Rochester Castle wall, or in either of the churchyards of Shorne or Cobham parish churches not far from Gad's Hill, but none of these proved suitable and so a grave was prepared in St. Mary's Chapel within Rochester Cathedral. However, as the news of his death spread, the feeling of the nation (particularly encouraged by Forster and The Times newspaper) overwhelmingly decreed that he should be buried in Westminster Abbey and, with Dean Stanley's willing consent, his plain oak coffin was taken there on the morning of the 14th June in the manner as he had directed in his Will. After a short private burial service, internment took place five feet below ground in the Poet's Corner area of the Abbey, but because of the huge public desire to pay their last respects to him, the Dean consented that the grave be left open for a further two days to allow people to visit. Thousands upon thousands did so and his grave and the area surrounding it became filled to overflowing with flowers and personal notes. At midnight on the 16th June the grave was closed and, as was his wish, a simply inscribed marble gravestone placed over it that reads:

CHARLES DICKENS
BORN 7TH FEBRUARY 1812
DIED 9TH JUNE 1870

Dickens had a particular love of bright flowers, none more so than the scarlet geranium, and badges depicting his favourite flower are now worn by devotees in the Dickens Fellowship around the world in memory of this most remarkable man.

Lightning Source UK Ltd.
Milton Keynes UK
UKHW010744021220
374498UK00003B/507